Brewer's Curious Titles

Brewer's Curious Titles

Compiled by Ian Crofton

CASSELL

First published in the UK 2002 by

Cassell
Wellington House, 125 Strand, London WC2R 0BB

Reprinted 2003

British Library Cataloguing-in-Publication Data
A catalogue record for this book is available from the British Library

ISBN 0–304–36130–5

Printed and bound in Great Britain by Mackays of Chatham, Kent

Contents

Preface

'Curiouser and curiouser!' cried Alice.

LEWIS CARROLL: *Alice in Wonderland* (1865), chapter 1

Curiosity is an infinitely subjective emotion, and thus what brings about a distending of the nostrils and a sharpening of the eyes in one person may well induce an indifferent shrug, or even a drooping eyelid, in another. So it is with curious titles. In selecting titles for inclusion, I have concentrated on those that are either curious in themselves, or that have a curious story behind them. Thus many canonic works – from *Hamlet* to *Middlemarch* to *Women in Love* – are omitted, as this book is not intended as a comprehensive cultural companion, but as an exploration of byways, oddities and serendipities (where else would *Woodcarving with a Chainsaw* appear on the same page as 'Ode to a Nightingale'?). I have spread my net widely, but have deliberately omitted TV programmes and popular music, each of which would require a volume in themselves.

One of the commonest categories of curious title is the quotation – *Alien Corn*, *All for Love*, *All Passion Spent*, *All This and Heaven Too*, *Anglo-Saxon Attitudes*, and so on. One of the indexes at the end of the book lists sources of titles by author, from which it will be seen that – to no one's surprise – the Bible and Shakespeare come out top, with Milton trailing somewhere behind.

A related category is that of allusions – examples include *Aaron's Rod*, *The Admirable Crichton*, *Adonais* and *The American Dream*. Generally speaking, I have omitted titles that are the names of well-known historical characters (for example, *Richard III*), or well-known biblical figures (*Adam and Eve*), or stories from classical mythology (*The Judgement of Paris*), or incidents from the lives of the saints (*The Martyrdom of St Sebastian*). I have – naturally – broken these guidelines at will, and make no apology for including entries or features on the likes of *Young Adolf*, *Salome*, *Prometheus* and *St Cecilia*.

Another category of curious title is the odd or bizarre or otherwise intriguing title. Over the last decade it has become almost obligatory to give offbeat titles to new works of fiction. A trawl of just a few pages of a recent copy of *The Bookseller* yields *A Big Boy Did it and Ran Away*, *Triggerfish Twist*, *White Meat and Traffic Lights*, *Choke*, *The Hundred and Ninety Nine Steps* and many more. Because such titles are now so commonplace (and in most cases ephemeral), I have generally eschewed them, however catchy or ingenious. However, works with such titles that have more firmly established themselves have been included. Examples include *The Sleep of Reason Brings Forth Monsters* (Goya), *The History and Adventures of an Atom* (Smollett), *The Deformed Transformed* (Byron), *The Shaving of Shagpat* (Meredith), *At Swim-Two-Birds* (Flann O'Brien), *The Bald Prima Donna* (Ionesco), and many more.

A final (overlapping) category of curiosity comprises explanations of why titles – or nicknames – have come to be. Thus I have included many nicknames of musical works, notably the symphonies and string quartets of Haydn and Mozart – why 'Bear', 'Hen', 'Clock', 'Jupiter', etc.? There are also many works where the final title has emerged after some debate: *Catch-22* was at one time to have been *Catch-18*, *The Mill on the Floss* superseded *Sister Maggie*, and *Jaws* might have been *Leviathan Rising* or even *What's That Noshin' on My Laig?*

I have also included a number of features. Some of these consist of figures or motifs that have generated a wealth of titles, for example, Faust, Death and the Maiden, Don Juan, Endymion, the Dance of Death; while others, more playfully, list titles that include days of the week, or scatological terminology, or US states, or places in London, or meals, or months, and so on. Readers might care to while away their idle hours by adding titles to my existing themes, or creating their own. I originally had many more items in my lists, and many more themes.

Indeed, my original text was about twice the current length – and could easily have been four times as long – but publishing practicalities dictated the need for a limit. So if you were to say, 'Why hasn't he included such-and-such?' the answer may well be that at one time he did, or considered doing so. Having said that, I would be delighted to hear of any curiosities that you would care to suggest, in the great Brewer's tradition of a continuing and fruitful dialogue between readers and compilers.

I would like to express my gratitude to the following: Richard Milbank, my publisher at Cassell, for the idea, for innumerable suggestions, and for drafting a number of entries; Neil Wenborn for copy-editing the text, suggesting various useful points, and for drafting some additional entries; Rebecca Skipwith of Cassell for guiding the book through its pre-press stages; Adrian Room, David Pickering and Antony Kamm, some of whose articles on 20th-century plays, poems, films, musicals and novels in *Brewer's Dictionary of Modern Phrase and Fable* I have borrowed (and often adapted); Ben Dupré for advice concerning matters Greek and Latin; and finally my parents John and Eileen, my wife Sally and my children Claire and Archie for many suggestions for the thematic lists – fun for all the family …

Ian Crofton
JULY 2002
ian@crofton1.demon.co.uk

The Dictionary

A

Aaron's Rod. A novel (1922) by D.H. Lawrence (1885–1930). The story concerns Aaron Sisson, who abandons his wife and his colliery job to pursue a wandering career playing his flute. The title comes from the Old Testament high priest and brother of Moses:

> And the Lord spake unto Moses, saying,
> Speak unto the children of Israel, and take of every one of them a rod according to the house of their fathers …
> And it shall come to pass, that the man's rod, whom I shall choose, shall blossom …
> And it came to pass, that on the morrow Moses went into the tabernacle of witness; and, behold, the rod of Aaron for the house of Levi was budded, and brought forth buds, and bloomed blossoms, and yielded almonds.
>
> Numbers: 17:1–2, 4–5, 8

The unfinished opera *Moses und Aron* by Arnold Schoenberg (1874–1951), first performed in 1957, follows the story in Exodus, in which Aaron erects the golden calf.

À Bout de Souffle. *See* BREATHLESS.

Absalom! Absalom! A novel (1936) by William Faulkner (1897–1962), recounting the ultimately doomed efforts of Thomas Sutpen to become accepted in Mississippi society and found a dynasty. Sutpen refuses to acknowledge his first, part-black son, Charles Bon. Sutpen's second son,

Henry, ends up killing Bon, and is forced into hiding. Thus Sutpen loses two sons. The title recalls the lament of David for Absalom:

> O my son Absalom, my son, my son Absalom! would God I had died for thee, O Absalom, my son, my son!
>
> 2 Samuel 18:33

Absalom and Achitophel. A satirical mock-epic (1681) by John Dryden (1631–1700), in which he uses the biblical story as an allegory of contemporary events. Absalom was the third son of King David, remarkable for his good looks. Aided by Achitophel, he rose in rebellion against his father. In his flight after defeat Absalom was trapped in the branches of a tree and slain by Joab, the king's general. David is subsequently filled with sorrow (2 Samuel 18).

In Dryden's poem Absalom represents the Protestant duke of Monmouth (1649–85), bastard son of King Charles II (David), while Achitophel is Anthony Ashley Cooper, 1st earl of Shaftesbury (1621–83), who led the unsuccessful movement to exclude Charles's Catholic brother, the duke of York, from the succession. In 1681 Shaftesbury was charged with treason, and fled to the Netherlands. In some ways Dryden's poem is prophetic: after the duke of York succeeded to the throne as James II in 1685, Monmouth rose in rebellion, but was captured and beheaded.

Abschiedsymphonie. *See* 'FAREWELL' SYMPHONY.

Absinthe Drinker, The. A painting (1859) by Edouard Manet (1832–83) of an unshaven young man in an alley with a glass of absinthe and a discarded bottle. Absinthe was a very popular liquor in 19th-century France. It has a high alcohol content – typically 68% – and is based on a strong spirit such as brandy, flavoured with a number of ingredients, principally wormwood (*Artemesia absinthium*), which gives the bitter taste. Absinthe was banned in many countries (in France in 1915) because the chemical thujone found in wormwood had come to be associated with deleterious effects on health, such as mental deterioration, convulsions, hallucinations and psychoses.

> There is only one absinthe drinker, and that's the man who painted this idiotic picture.
>
> THOMAS COUTURE: comment in c.1859

Manet's fellow impressionist Edgar Degas (1834–1917) painted a young woman sitting in a bar with a *Glass of Absinthe* (1876), dull-eyed with the effects of her drink.

Accidental Death of an Anarchist (Italian title: *Morte accidentale di un anarchico*). A play, by the Italian playwright and actor Dario Fo (b.1926). First performed in 1970, the play concerns the inquiry following the death of a political activist after he falls from the window of Milan police station while being interrogated about terrorist bomb explosions. The play was based on real events, the original anarchist being Giuseppe Pinelli, a railway worker and political extremist who died in the same manner while being questioned about a terrorist bomb attack on a Milan bank in 1969. The play had to be altered on a nightly basis during its first run as more facts about the Pinelli case leaked out.

Accompaniment to a Film Scene. An orchestral piece, opus 34, by Arnold Schoenberg (1874–1951), first performed in 1930. The work was not actually intended to accompany any particular film, but the titles of the three movements – 'Danger threatens', 'Angst' and 'Catastrophe' – suggest the kind of stark silent melodrama popular at that period.

> My music is not modern, it is only badly played.
>
> ARNOLD SCHOENBERG: quoted in Rosen, *Schoenberg* (1976)

***Adieux* Sonata.** See *LEBEWOHL, DAS*.

Admirable Crichton, The. A play (1902) by J.M. Barrie (1860–1937) about a resourceful manservant who proves the salvation of his social superiors when they are all cast away on a desert island. It was filmed (1957) under the same title, with Kenneth More in the title role, and earlier provided the basis for the Hollywood musical *We're Not Dressing* (1934), with Bing Crosby and Carole Lombard. The original of Barrie's character was the Scots adventurer, scholar, linguist and poet James 'The Admirable' Crichton (1560–82), whose brief but eventful life, culminating in his death in a brawl in Mantua, was the subject of Sir Thomas Urquhart's *Ekskubalauron* or *The Discoverie of an Exquisite Jewel* (1651) and of the Harrison Ainsworth novel *Crichton* (1837). The idea of a social inferior proving the better man on a desert island may have been originally suggested to Barrie by Sir Arthur Conan Doyle.

Adonais. An elegy on the death of John Keats (1795–1821) by Percy Bysshe Shelley (1792–1822). Keats died in Rome on 23 February 1821, and Shelley wrote his elegy in Pisa during the early days of June of that year. Adonais, or Adonis, was a beautiful youth who was killed by a wild boar, and so in the poem he represents Keats, who died aged only 25.

In the ancient world Adonis became the subject of a cult celebrating the vegetative cycle. The cult originated in western Asia before spreading to Greece and Rome: the Phoenician *adōni*, meaning 'my lord', was a title of the god Tammuz, and is related to the Hebrew Adonai, a name for God.

Shelley is said to have based his poem on the *Lament for Adonis* (2nd century BC) by the Greek pastoral poet Bion.

> From the contagion of the world's slow stain
> He is secure, and now can never mourn
> A heart grown cold, a head grown grey in vain.
>
> SHELLEY: *Adonais*, stanza 40

Adoration of Captain Shit and the Legend of the Black Star Part Two, The. A painting (incorporating some elephant dung) by the black British artist Chris Ofili (b.1968). Given that it was not an installation or a video, it was something of a surprise when this relatively conventional work won the Turner Prize in 1998.

See also SCATOLOGY (panel, p.407).

Adventures in a Perambulator. An orchestral suite (1915) by John Alden Carpenter (1876–1951), American businessman and composer. The music presents a baby's perspective on a little outing, the four movements being entitled 'The Policeman', 'The Hurdy-Gurdy', 'The Lake' and 'The Dogs'.

Aeneid. *See* ILIAD.

African Queen, The. A novel (1935) by C.S. Forester (1899–1966), adapted as a film (1951) by James Agee. Set in Africa during the First World War, it depicts the changing relationship between hard-living Charlie Allnut (played in the film by Humphrey Bogart), skipper of the tramp steamer *African Queen*, and domineering missionary spinster Rose Sayer (played by Katharine Hepburn) as they try to escape – and then attack – the Germans on the River Ulonga-Bora in 1915. Director John Huston's autocratic attitude to his actors and his preoccupation with shooting an elephant instead of getting on with the film (allegedly his reason for insisting upon filming on location in the Congo) was chronicled in the film *White Hunter, Black Heart* (1990), directed by and starring Clint Eastwood, based on a book by Peter Viertel (who worked on the screenplay of Huston's film). Katharine Hepburn's account of the making of the film was published as *The Making* *of the African Queen, or How I Went to Africa with Bogart, Bacall and Huston and Almost Lost My Mind* (1987).

Ai No Corrida. *See* EMPIRE OF THE SENSES.

'Air on the G String'. An arrangement for solo violin and piano of the second movement of the suite no 3 in D major for orchestra by J.S. Bach (1685–1750). The arrangement was made in 1871 by the German violinist and teacher August Wilhelmj (1845–1908). In it the first violin part is transposed down so that it is played on the G string, the lowest string on the violin. The piece was popularized to the point of cliché by its use in a series of television commercials for Hamlet cigars.

Alabama. A poster-like painting (1965) by the US Pop artist Robert Indiana (b.1928), consisting of two concentric circles within which is enclosed a map of the US state, with the town of Selma marked. In 1965 Civil Rights groups began a voter-registration drive among African-Americans in Selma, and on 7 March the local police attacked 600 Civil Rights demonstrators there at the beginning of a planned march on the state capital Montgomery. Indiana inscribed in the concentric circles of his painting the following biblical-sounding words:

> Just as in the anatomy of man every nation must have its hind part.

Indiana leaves us in no doubt that this applies to Alabama – the word is written right across the foot of the painting.

À la recherche du temps perdu. *See* REMEMBRANCE OF THINGS PAST.

Alastor, or The Spirit of Solitude. A long poem by Percy Bysshe Shelley (1792–1822), written in the summer of 1815, when the poet rented a house on Bishopgate Heath, on the borders of Windsor Forest. It was published in 1816. Alastor is the Greek name for the Avenging Deity, literally 'he who does not forget' (Greek *a-*, 'not', and *lanthanomai*, 'I forget'). In Shelley's poem the poet seeks a transcendent vision, away from the company of men, but in the end this costs him his life. As Shelley wrote in his preface to the poem:

> The Poet's self-centred seclusion was avenged by the furies of an irresistible passion pursuing him to speedy ruin.

Alien Corn. A play (1933) by the US playwright Sidney Howard (1891–1939) about a music teacher who falls in love with the married college head and abandons her ambition of a career as a concert pianist.

The title comes from Keats's 'ODE TO A NIGHTINGALE':

> The voice I hear this passing night was heard
> In ancient days by emperor and clown:
> Perhaps the self-same song that found a path
> Through the sad heart of Ruth, when, sick for home,
> She stood in tears amid the alien corn.

The reference is to the biblical Book of Ruth 2:2–3.

All for Love. A tragedy (1678) by John Dryden (1631–1700), subtitled *The World Well Lost*. The play was inspired by Shakespeare's *Antony and Cleopatra* (*c.*1607), but Dryden's rigorously classical version focuses on the hours leading up to the lovers' deaths. The title comes from Spenser:

> And all for love, and nothing for reward.
>
> EDMUND SPENSER: *The Faerie Queene* (1596), Book 2, Canto 3

All Passion Spent. A novel (1931) by Vita Sackville-West (1892–1962). It is a study of ageing and of independence in old age. The title comes from *Samson Agonistes* (1671) by John Milton:

> His servants he, with new acquist
> Of true experience from this great event,
> With peace and consolation hath dismissed,
> And calm of mind, all passion spent.

All Quiet on the Western Front (German title: *Im Westen nichts neues*). A novel (1929) of the First World War by the German writer Erich Maria Remarque (1898–1970). Brutally realistic and written in the first person, it is prefaced with a statement:

> This book is to be neither an accusation nor a confession, and least of all an adventure, for death is not an adventure to those who stand face to face with it. It will try simply to tell of a generation of men who, even though they may have escaped its shells, were destroyed by the war.

In 1933 the book was publicly burned by the Nazis as being 'defeatist', and Remarque was deprived of his citizenship. The title is ironic. It refers to the fact that a whole generation of his countrymen was destroyed while newspapers reported that there was 'no news in the west'. The film version (1930), directed by Lewis Milestone, was a landmark of American cinema.

The title, together with that of Agatha Christie's *Murder on the Orient Express* (1934), is played on in *All Quiet on the Orient Express*, a novel (1999) by Magnus Mills (b.1954) about a man who doesn't take a train to India.

All's Well that Ends Well. One of the 'dark' comedies (*c.*1604) of William Shakespeare (1564–1616). The plot is based on a traditional folk tale, found in Boccaccio's *The* DECAMERON. Helena, enamoured of Bertram, count of Rousillon, is given to him in marriage by the king of France, whose life she has saved. However, Bertram spurns her ('A poor physician's daughter my wife?') and leaves for the Italian Wars. From there he writes to her:

> When thou canst get the ring upon my finger, which never shall come off, and show me a child begotten of thy body that I am father to, then call me husband; but in such a 'then' I write a 'never'.
>
> III.ii

However, in disguise, Helena follows him to Italy, where she finds he is in love with a Florentine maid, whose place she takes in the dark, gets the ring and conceives his child. In the end she wins his love, after he has believed her dead.

The title *All's Well that Ends Well* is from an old English proverb, known from the mid-13th century. It is somewhat ironic given the dark mood of the play, although it also has a suggestion of ends justifying means. At the end of the play the king, after all has been resolved, says:

> All yet seems well; and if it end so meet,
> The bitter past, more welcome is the sweet.
>
> V.iii

He then adopts the role of Epilogue, and, in accordance with theatrical convention, begs the audience's indulgence for the play:

> The King's a beggar, now the play is done.
> All is well ended if this suit be won,
> That you express content; which we will pay
> With strife to please you, day exceeding day.
> Ours be your patience then, and yours our parts;
> Your gentle hands lend us, and take our hearts.
>
> V.iii, Epilogue

All the President's Men. A film (1976) directed by Alan J. Pakula about the uncovering of the Watergate scandal, based on a book (1974) of the same title by the *Washington Post* journalists Bob Woodward and Carl Bernstein (played respectively by Robert Redford and Dustin Hoffman). The president of the title is Richard M. Nixon, and the title refers to the attempts of the president and others in the White House to cover up the scandal. The title plays on a line from the nursery rhyme:

> Humpty Dumpty sat on a wall.
> Humpty Dumpty had a great fall.
> All the king's horses and all the king's men
> Couldn't put Humpty together again.

All This and Heaven Too. A romantic film melodrama (1940) starring Charles Boyer and Bette Davis, based on the bestselling novel (1938) by the US writer Rachel Field (1894–1942) about a French aristocrat who falls in love with the governess and murders his wife. The title phrase originates with the otherwise obscure English clergyman Philip Henry (1631–96), whose words 'All this, and heaven too!' were quoted in Matthew Henry's *Life of Mr Philip Henry* (1698). The title is played on in a film collage (1977) of the Second World War, *All This and World War Two*, directed by Susan Winslow.

Alpine Symphony (German title: *Eine Alpensinfonie*). An unnumbered symphony or tone poem, opus 64, by Richard Strauss (1864–1949), first performed in 1915. The work is intended to convey a day in the Bavarian Alps, and there are evocations of a thunderstorm, a waterfall and the view from a summit. The work requires a large orchestra of some 150 players, and wind and thunder machines.

> [Of the *Alpine Symphony*] That's a real piece of hocus-pocus ... better to hang oneself than ever to write music like that.
>
> PAUL HINDEMITH: letter to Emmy Ronnefeldt, 1917

Also sprach Zarathustra (German, *Thus Spake Zarathustra*). A work by the German philosopher Friedrich Nietzsche (1844–1900), published in four volumes between 1883 and 1885. The work, which introduces Nietzsche's idea of the 'superman', is in the form of a biblical narrative. Zarathustra (Zoroaster; *c*.628–*c*.551 BC) was the Iranian prophet who founded Zoroastrianism. The work inspired the tone poem of the same name (opus 30, 1896) by Richard Strauss ((1864–1949), some of which is used in the film of 2001: A SPACE ODYSSEY. *A Mass of Life* (1908–9) by Frederick Delius (1862–1934) includes settings of Nietzsche's words.

Ambassadors, The. The title of two works of art: a double portrait (1533) by Hans Holbein (1497/8–1543), and a novel (1903) by Henry James (1843–1916).

In Holbein's painting only one of the men, Jean de Dinteville, a nobleman, was in fact an ambassador, representing the French king in London. He is the flamboyantly dressed man on the left, standing confidently with legs apart. The more diffident and sombrely dressed man on his right is the classical scholar and bishop of Lavaur, Georges de Selve, who was visiting his friend Dinteville in London. Smeared across the floor is a bizarre shape, which, when viewed from the side of the painting, resolves itself into the image of a human skull.

In Henry James's novel *The Ambassadors*, one of his last works, the 'ambassadors' are not diplomats in the conventional sense; they are intended to represent New England values and interests in Europe. The first 'ambassador' is Lambert Strether, the elderly suitor of the wealthy and upright Mrs Newsome, who sends him to Paris to disentangle her son Chadwick (Chad) from the charming Comtesse de Vionnet and to persuade him to return to Woolett, Massachusetts. However, Strether becomes converted to European ways and cosmopolitan values, and when a second 'ambassador', Chad's sister Sarah Pocock, arrives, he urges Chad to stay in Paris, remarking 'Live all you can; it's a mistake not to.'

American Buffalo. A play (1975) by David Mamet (b.1947) about the bungled attempts of three small-time crooks to steal a coin collection. The title of the play, which effectively lampoons modern capitalism, refers to an old US buffalo-head nickel that one of them produces in the second act, a symbol of their preoccupation with financial gains. Mamet wrote the screenplay for the film version (1996), which starred Dustin Hoffman, Dennis Franz and Sean Nelson.

American Dream, The. A blackly satirical one-act play (1959) by Edward Albee (b.1928). The similarly titled *An American Dream* is a novel (1965) by Norman Mailer (b.1923) about a man who murders his wife. The phrase was originally coined, unironically, by James T. Adams in *The Epic of America* (1931), to suggest that the US social, political and economic system makes success possible for every American.

See also GREAT AMERICAN NUDE.

American Gothic. A painting (1930), perhaps the most reproduced (and most parodied) American work of art of the 20th century, by Grant

Wood (1891–1942). It purports to be a portrait of a stern, rather sinister farmer-preacher and his daughter, the former holding a pitchfork, while behind is their house, with a simple Gothic window set in the gable end. Actually, Wood used his sister, Nan, and his dentist, B.H. McKeeby, as models for the painting. The title has been taken as satirical, although Wood's avowed intention was to reflect the values of provincial American life. The hard, cold style reflects the influence of north European Renaissance painting that Wood absorbed during a visit to Munich in 1928.

American Gothic is also the title of a 1988 horror movie starring Rod Steiger.

American in Paris, An. A classic musical film (1951) that ranks among the most popular MGM productions of the golden age of the American musical. Directed by Vincente Minnelli, it stars Gene Kelly as a frustrated artist (thereby providing an excuse for lots of backdrops based on famous French paintings) and Leslie Caron. The film was based on the tone poem 'An American in Paris' (1928) by George Gershwin (1898–1937), and Ira Gershwin allowed the piece's title to be used for the film provided that his brother provided all the music for the movie.

The title echoes the long-established adage 'Good Americans, when they die, go to Paris', credited by Oliver Wendell Holmes to Thomas Appleton (1812–84). It was this saying that prompted Oscar Wilde in *A Woman of No Importance* (1893) to suggest that if good Americans went to Paris when they died, then bad Americans undoubtedly went to America. Ironically, the film was shot in the United States against specially built sets.

American Pie. A hilarious and sometimes serious rites-of-passage film (1999) directed by Paul Weitz and with a screenplay by Adam Herz, in which four teenage boys attempt to lose their virginity before they graduate. Like the famous song 'American Pie' (1971) by Don McLean, an allusive threnody for '60s American youth in the form of a tribute to Buddy Holly, the title refers to the saying 'As American as mom's apple pie'. In the film, mom's apple pie finds a novel role as a masturbatory aid for the frustrated Jim. His concerned father – who dispenses facts-of-life advice with the aid of pornographic magazines – catches Jim and the pie *in flagrante delicto*, and points out the unsatisfactory nature of such a relationship.

'American' Quartet. Nickname given to the string quartet in F, opus 96 (1893), by Antonín Dvořák (1841–1904). Like his 'NEW WORLD' SYMPHONY, the work was written while the composer was in America, staying at the Czech colony of Spillville, in Iowa. The quartet is said to contain elements of black American music of the period (hence its former unfortunate alternative nickname, 'Nigger Quartet').

> I should be glad if something occurred to me as a main idea that occurs to Dvořák only by the way.
>
> JOHANNES BRAHMS: quoted in Šourek (ed.), *Antonín Dvořák: Letters and Reminiscences* (1954)

Amityville Horror, The. An enormously successful horror film (1979), based on a lurid bestselling book of the same title (1977) by Jay Anson concerning a sensational case of alleged diabolical presence in a house at Amityville, Long Island, New York. The Lutz family of five moved into a large Dutch colonial house in Amityville on 18 December 1975, undisturbed by the report that it had been the scene of a mass murder the previous year. They were soon subjected to a series of ghostly apparitions and other evil manifestations, forcing them to flee on 14 January 1976. It eventually emerged that the Lutzes had fabricated the whole ghoulish scenario with a view to having a book published and reaping the reward of the ensuing publicity. The case resulted in a string of lawsuits. Despite this, *The Amityville Horror* was followed by a host of similar stories and movies based on the theme of a possessed house.

Amoretti. A sonnet sequence by Edmund Spenser (?1552–99), published in 1595 along with the poet's *EPITHALAMIUM*. The work reflects Spenser's passionate wooing of his wife, Elizabeth Boyle, in the previous year. An *amoretto* is a representation of Cupid in the form of a small, chubby, naked boy; the term entered the English language in the 16th century. In Italian, the word has been used to mean 'flirtation' (literally 'little love'), and is also applied to a type of almond biscuit.

Anatomy Lesson of Dr Tulp, The. A painting (1632) by the Dutch painter Rembrandt van Rijn (1606–69). The innovative composition of this group portrait established Rembrandt as a portraitist in Amsterdam. Dr Nicolaes Tulp was the praelector (chief surgeon) of the city's guild of surgeons, and it was among his duties to give an annual anatomy demonstration. An earlier painting of this annual event was made by

Thomas de Keyser (1565–1621), and is entitled *The Anatomy Lesson of Dr Sebastian Egbertsz* (1619). *The Anatomy Lesson* (1983) is also the title of a semi-autobiographical novel (1983) by the US writer Philip Roth (b.1933).

Ancient Mariner, The Rime of the. A long poem by Samuel Taylor Coleridge (1772–1834), published in *Lyrical Ballads* (1798), his joint collection with William Wordsworth. The poem opens with the Ancient Mariner buttonholing a guest at a wedding to tell him his tale. Having shot an albatross (traditionally bad luck at sea), the Ancient Mariner and his shipmates were subjected to fearful penalties. On repentance he was forgiven, and on reaching land told his story to a hermit. At times, however, distress of mind drives him from land to land, and wherever he stays he tells his tale of woe, to warn against cruelty and to persuade men to love God's creatures.

The story is partly based on a dream told by Coleridge's friend George Cruikshank, and partly gathered from his reading. Wordsworth told him the story of the privateer George Shelvocke, who shot an albatross while rounding Cape Horn in 1720, and was dogged by bad weather thereafter. Other suggested sources are Thomas James's *Strange and Dangerous Voyage* (1683) and the *Letter of St Paulinus to Macarius, In Which He Relates Astounding Wonders Concerning the Shipwreck of an Old Man* (1618). A full examination of the possible sources is to be found in *The Road to* XANADU (1927) by J.L. Lowes.

> *The Ancient Mariner* would not have taken so well if it had been called *The Old Sailor*.
>
> SAMUEL BUTLER: *Notebooks* (1912)

And Quiet Flows the Don. The English title (1934) of a two-part translation of the four-volume work, *Tikhy Don* ('The Quiet Don', 1928–40), by the Russian author Mikhail Sholokhov (1905–84). The second part was *The Don Flows Home to the Sea* (1940), published in the United States as *Seeds of Tomorrow* (1935) and *Harvest on the Don* (1960). The River Don flows through central Russia into the Black Sea. The complete work covers the years 1912–22 and reflects with objectivity the effect of the Russian Revolution during peace and war on the Cossack communities in the region. Sholokhov received the Nobel prize for literature in 1965, despite charges of plagiarism levelled by, among others, Alexander Solzhenitsyn.

Sholokhov's work inspired the opera *Quiet Flows the Don* by the Soviet composer Ivan Dzerjinsky (1909–78), who also wrote the libretto. It was first performed in 1935, and was praised by Stalin.

Androcles and the Lion. A play by George Bernard Shaw (1856–1950), published and first performed in 1913. The play is based on a story that has many variants, the oldest going back to Aesop (6th century BC). The tale as told by Aulus Gellius (*c.*130–180) tells how Androcles, a runaway slave, takes refuge in a cavern. A lion enters and, instead of tearing him to pieces, lifts up its forepaw in a plea for Androcles to remove a thorn from it. Androcles is later recaptured and sentenced to fight with a lion in the Roman arena. By chance the same lion is led out against him, and, recognizing his benefactor, shows him every demonstration of love and gratitude. A Christian version of the story is told in the Apocryphal Acts of Paul (*c.*160–180).

And When Did You Last See Your Father? A painting (1878) by W.F. Yeames (1835–1918) that for many years was held up mockingly as the archetype of the Victorian 'story' picture, in which aesthetic form is subsumed to narrative content. The painting, set during the English Civil War of the mid-17th century, depicts a young Cavalier boy standing in what appears to be his family mansion, while he is interrogated by a stern Roundhead officer.

The title was borrowed by the poet and critic Blake Morrison (b.1950) for a moving memoir (1993) of his relationship with his father. It had earlier been adapted by Christopher Hampton (b.1946) for the title of his first play, *When Did You Last See My Mother?* (1966).

Angel in the House, The. A sequence of poems (1854–61) in praise of married love by Coventry Patmore (1823–96). The title subsequently became a mainly ironic term for a woman who is completely devoted to her husband. In this context it was introduced by Virginia Woolf in the 1930s:

> You who come of a younger and happier generation may not have heard of her – you may not know what I mean by the Angel in the House. I will describe her as shortly as I can. She was intensely sympathetic. She was immensely charming. She was utterly unselfish. She excelled in the difficult arts of family life. She sacrificed herself daily. If there was a chicken, she took the leg; if there was a draught she sat in it – in short she was so constituted that she never had

a mind or a wish of her own, but preferred to sympathize always with the minds and wishes of others.

VIRGINIA WOOLF (1931) in Michèle Barrett: *Virginia Woolf: Women and Writing* (1979)

Angel of the North. A huge sculpture of an angel with outstretched wings by Antony Gormley (b.1950). It was erected on a hillside next to the A1 near Gateshead in the northeast of England in 1998. The angel is 20m high, and its wingspan is 54m. The structure – erected with the help of major engineering firms – celebrates the region's industrial past (the wings are those of an early aeroplane) and also marks the boundary of different countries, the lands of the Venerable Bede (*c.*673–735) and St Columba (*c.*521–597). Gormley has said of his work:

> The hilltop site is important and has the feeling of being a megalithic mound. When you think of the mining that was done underneath the site, there is a poetic resonance. Men worked beneath the surface in the dark. Now in the light, there is a celebration of this industry.

Gateshead Council's only Conservative member commented:

> I think it is ruining a piece of nice countryside.

Anglo-Saxon Attitudes. A novel (1956) by Angus Wilson (1913–91), whose central theme is an archaeological fraud. It is also a partly satirical, partly realistic dissection of attitudes that the author sees as prevalent among a particular group within middle-class English society. The title comes from a remark made by the King to Alice in Lewis Carroll's *Through the Looking-Glass* (1872) as the Messenger approaches 'skipping up and down, and wriggling like an eel, with his great hands spread out like fans on each side':

> He's an Anglo-Saxon Messenger – and those are Anglo-Saxon attitudes.

Animal Crackers. A film (1930), based on the Marx Brothers' stage show of the same title, in which the brothers have fun at the expense of American high society. The film, which features Groucho as Captain Spaulding the explorer, includes some classic insults aimed at the perpetually nonplussed Margaret Dumont:

> You're the most beautiful woman I've ever seen, which doesn't say much for you.

Animal crackers are small, semi-sweet biscuits in the shape of animals,

ANGELS

The ANGEL IN THE HOUSE, poems (1864–51) by Coventry Patmore

Ayala's Angel, a novel (1881) by Anthony Trollope

The BLUE ANGEL, a film (1930) starring Marlene Dietrich (who also starred in the 1937 Ernst Lubitsch romantic comedy *Angel*)

Angels with Dirty Faces, a film (1938) in which the street urchins of the title admire a New York gangster (played by James Cagney)

The Exterminating Angel, a film (1962) by Luis Buñuel

An Angel at My Table, a volume of autobiography (1984) by the New Zealand writer, Janet Frame, turned into a film (1990) by Jane Campion

The Angelic Conversation, a Derek Jarman film (1985) in which young men pose while Judi Dench reads Shakespeare's sonnets

Angels and Insects, two novellas (1992) by A.S. Byatt (film version 1995)

ANGEL OF THE NORTH, a statue (1998) by Antony Gormley

Miss Garnet's Angel, a novel (2000) by Salley Vickers

popular among American children. The confection was popularized outside the United States by Ray Henderson and Ted Koehler's song 'Animal Crackers in my Soup', sung with saccharine sentiment by seven-year-old Shirley Temple in the film *Curly Top* (1935).

Animal Farm. A satire in fable form by George Orwell (1903–50), published in 1945 and depicting a totalitarian regime like that of the Soviet Union under Stalin. The story describes how the animals, accompanied by the slogan 'Four legs good, two legs bad', overthrow their human oppressors. However, the pigs, by cunning, treachery and ruthlessness, come to dominate the more honest, gullible and hard-working animals.

Their ultimate slogan is: 'All animals are equal, but some animals are more equal than others.' The leader of the pigs is Napoleon, representing Stalin, and at the end the pigs are in cahoots with the humans, even beginning to totter around on two legs. An animated film of the novel appeared in 1955.

ANIMALS

A BRIEF TAXONOMIC TOUR

Kingdom Animalia:

'Animals as Criminals', an article (1896) in *Pearson's Magazine* by J. Brand

ANIMAL CRACKERS, a Marx Brothers film (1930)

MY FAMILY AND OTHER ANIMALS, a memoir (1956) by Gerald Durrell

Flattened Fauna, a 'field guide to common animals of roads, streets and highways' (1987) by Roger M. Knutson. This work edged out the earlier market-leader, James Simmons's *Feathers and Fur on the Turnpike* (1938)

Class Mammalia, Order Primates:

Monkey Business, a Marx brothers film (1931)

A Monkey in Winter, a French comedy film (1962)

The Monkey King, a novel (1978) by Timothy Mo

Spanking the Monkey, a film (1995) in which a young man explores his sexuality

The NAKED APE, a popular study of human behaviour (1967) by Desmond Morris

Order Proboscidea:

The ELEPHANT MAN, a film (1980) by David Lynch

When Elephants Last in the Doorway Bloomed, a collection of poetry (1973) by the US writer Ray Bradbury (*see* 'WHEN LILACS LAST IN THE DOORYARD BLOOMED')

EXHUMATION OF THE MASTODON, a painting (1806) by Charles Wilson Peale

Order Perissodactyla (odd-toed ungulates):

Equus, a play (1973) by Peter Shaffer

Horse Feathers, a Marx brothers film (1932)

The Horse Whisperer, a romantic film (1998) based on Nicholas Evans's novel

THEY SHOOT HORSES, DON'T THEY?, a film (1969) set in the US Depression

BRING ON THE EMPTY HORSES, a volume of memoirs (1975) by the film actor David Niven

All the Pretty Horses, a lyrical Western novel (1992) by Cormac McCarthy

The GOLDEN ASS, a prose romance (2nd century AD) by Lucius Apuleius

The Devil is an Ass, a play (1616) by Ben Jonson

'The Donkey', an alternative nickname for Haydn's 'FIFTHS' QUARTET

TRAVELS WITH A DONKEY, a travel book (1879) by Robert Louis Stevenson

RHINOCEROS, a play (1959) by Eugène Ionesco

EXHIBITION OF A RHINOCEROS AT VENICE, a painting (1751) by Pietro Longhi

Order Artiodactyla (even-toed ungulates):

Live Like Pigs, a play (1958) set on a deprived housing estate by John Arden

The Hippopotamus, a comic novel (1994) by Stephen Fry

'OX MINUET', a minuet once attributed to Haydn

Raging Bull, a boxing film (1980)

AMERICAN BUFFALO, a play (1975) by David Mamet

SOME TAME GAZELLE, a novel (1950) by Barbara Pym

The Deer Hunter, Michael Cimino's gruelling film (1978) about blue-collar Americans in their native Pennsylvania (where the deer hunt takes place) and in Vietnam

The HIND AND THE PANTHER, a religious allegory (1687) by John Dryden

The MONARCH OF THE GLEN, a portrait of a red deer stag (1850) by Sir Edwin Landseer

Shag the Caribou, a children's book (1949) by C. Bernard Rutley

The SCAPEGOAT, a painting (1855) by William Holman Hunt

The Flying Goat, a novel (1939) by H.E. Bates

SHEEP MAY SAFELY GRAZE, an aria (1713) by J.S. Bach

Do Androids Dream of Electric Sheep?, a short story (1968) by Philip K. Dick (*see* BLADE RUNNER)

The SILENCE OF THE LAMBS, a horror novel (1989) by Thomas Harris

Order Lagomorpha:

HOW TO EXPLAIN PICTURES TO A DEAD HARE, a piece of performance art (1965) by Josef Beuys

Who Framed Roger Rabbit?, a comedy film (1988) using both animated and live action

What Do Bunnies Do All Day?, a children's book (1988) by Judy Mastrangelo

Order Rodentia:

OF MICE AND MEN, a novella (1937) by John Steinbeck

The Guinea Pig, a film (1948) in which a working-class boy is the first to win a scholarship to an English public school

The Porcupine, a novella (1992) by Julian Barnes

GROUNDHOG DAY, a film comedy (1993)

Order Insectivora:

The TAMING OF THE SHREW, a comedy (*c.*1592) by William Shakespeare

Order Carnivora (*see also* DOGS AND THEIR RELATIVES, panel, pp.118–19; CATS AND THEIR RELATIVES, panel, pp.72–3):

Tarka the Otter, a novel (1927) by Henry Williamson

The Bear, a story (1942) by William Faulkner; also the title of a one-act Chekhov play, and the nickname of a Haydn symphony (*see* 'BEAR, THE').

Order Cetacea:

MOBY-DICK, a novel (1851) by Herman Melville

Inside the Whale, essays (1940) by George Orwell

LEVIATHAN, a treatise (1651) on political theory by Thomas Hobbes

Class Aves. *See* BIRDS (panel, pp.40–2).

Class Reptilia:

LANDSCAPE WITH A MAN KILLED BY A SNAKE, a painting (*c*.1648) by Nicolas Poussin

The PLUMED SERPENT, a novel (1926) by D.H. Lawrence

The Night of the Iguana, a play (1962) by Tennessee Williams

The Tortoise Droning Selected Pitches from the Holy Numbers for the Two Black Tigers, the Green Tiger and the Hermit, a musical work (1964) by LaMonte Young

Crocodile Dundee, an Australian comedy film (1986) written by and starring Paul Hogan

Class Amphibia:

The Frogs, a play (405 BC) by Aristophanes

'The Frog Prince', a traditional fairy story

'FROG' QUARTET, the nickname of a Haydn quartet

Toad of Toad Hall, A.A. Milne's dramatization (1929) of Kenneth Grahame's *The WIND IN THE WILLOWS*

Classes Agnatha, Chondrichthyes and Osteichthyes. *See* FISH (panel, p.161).

A few miscellaneous invertebrates, actual or mythical (*see also* INSECTS AND ARACHNIDS, panel, pp.224–5):

The SHRIMP AND THE ANEMONE, a novel (1944) by L.P. Hartley

Sh! The Octopus, a horror film (1937)

The KRAKEN WAKES, a science-fiction novel (1953) by John Wyndham

The Supernatural History of Worms, a work (1931) by Marion C. Fox

And finally to the **Kingdoms Protista and Monera:**

The Psychic Life of Micro-Organisms, a monograph (1889) by Alfred Binet

Is God Amoeboid?, a controversial work (1966) by John W. Doherty

---

Anna of the Five Towns. A regional novel (1902) by Arnold Bennett (1867–1931), set within the five towns of the Staffordshire Potteries where he was born. Anna is the epitome of altruism, to the extent that she even allows herself to be married to a man she does not love. The 'five towns' themselves are Bursley (representing real-life Burslem), where Anna lives; Turnhill (Tunstall); Hanbridge (Hanley, where Bennett himself was born); Knype (Stoke-on-Trent); and Longshaw (Longton).

Anne of Green Gables. A novel (1908) by the Canadian children's author L.M. Montgomery (1874–1942). Anne – Anne Shirley in full – is the young red-haired heroine who is taken on by an elderly couple, making herself useful on their farm, Green Gables. She is somewhat precocious and outspoken, but she is winning and winsome and was described by Mark Twain as 'the dearest and most loveable child in fiction since the immortal Alice'. Her adventures have been adapted for stage, film and television, and the US child film actress Dawn Paris (1918–93) legally adopted her name after playing her in *Anne of Green Gables* (1934). The unfortunately titled sequel, with the same star, was called *Anne of Windy Poplars* (1940).

Annie Get Your Gun. A musical comedy (1946) with a score by Irving Berlin (1888–1989) about the sharpshooter Annie Oakley (1860–1926), one of the stars of Buffalo Bill's Wild West Show. The show contains many memorable numbers, including 'There's no Business like Show Business' and 'The Girl that I Marry', but although Oakley was a real person, the plot of the musical is largely fictional. In US theatrical slang an 'Annie Oakley' became a nickname for a complimentary ticket, the punched appearance of these being reminiscent of the playing cards that the sharpshooter used to pepper with bullet holes during her act.

Annus Mirabilis. A long poem (1667) by John Dryden (1631–1700). The *annus mirabilis* ('wonderful year') was 1666, the year of the Fire of London and of continuing war with the Dutch. Queen Elizabeth II alluded to the phrase in a speech at the Guildhall, London, when she referred to 1992 as an '*annus horribilis*' (a coinage that had been suggested to her by a 'sympathetic correspondent'); this was the year when fire caused extensive damage to the royal residence at Windsor Castle, Princess Anne was divorced, and the Duke of York separated from the Duchess of York, topless photographs of whom appeared in the tabloids.

Antic Hay. A novel by Aldous Huxley (1894–1963), published in 1923. The book is a satire on intellectual posturing in London's bohemia in the years after the First World War. The title comes from Christopher Marlowe (1564–93):

> My men, like satyrs grazing on the lawns,
> Shall with their goat feet dance an antic hay.
>
> *Edward II* (1593), I.i

'Antic' is an archaic word for 'fantastical' or 'grotesque', while a 'hay' was an old country dance in which the dancers weave in and out of a circle. Thus the title sums up what Huxley thought of the goings-on of his contemporaries.

> There are few who would not rather be taken in adultery than in provincialism.
>
> ALDOUS HUXLEY: *Antic Hay*, chapter 10

'Anvil Chorus, The'. A chorus sung by the gypsies in act 2 of Verdi's opera *Il TROVATORE* (1853), in which an anvil is played – in this instance a real one rather than an orchestral anvil, which is an instrument made of steel bars struck with a wooden or metal beater. The piece became enormously popular. In 1869 the US bandmaster Patrick Gilmore organized a concert of 10,000 performers to celebrate the National Peace Jubilee, and his rendition of 'The Anvil Chorus' involved 100 firemen beating anvils.

Anyone for Denis? A stage comedy (1981) by John Wells based on the 'Dear Bill' column in the satirical magazine *Private Eye*; this purported to comprise letters from Denis Thatcher, husband of prime minister Margaret, to W.F. (Bill) Deedes, former editor of the *Daily Telegraph* (*see also*

SCOOP). The title is based on the phrase 'Anyone for tennis?', commonly thought of as a typical line in a 1920s drawing-room comedy and uttered by a well-dressed young man entering the room carrying a tennis racket. The precise provenance of the phrase is uncertain, although it has a clear pre-echo in G.B. Shaw's play *Misalliance* (1910) in which one of the characters, Johnny Tarleton, a young businessman, rises from a swinging chair and asks the assembled company, 'Anybody on for a game of tennis?' The phrase was adopted as the title of a 1968 television play by J.B. Priestley.

Anything for a Quiet Life. Although sounding like a 1970s TV sitcom, this is actually the title of a play by Thomas Middleton (1580–1627), possibly in collaboration with John Webster (*c.*1578–*c.*1626), written *c.*1621. The title has become a common cliché or catchphrase. It was adopted by Charles Dickens for Sam Weller:

> Anythin' for a quiet life, as the man said wen he took the sitivation at the lighthouse.
>
> *Pickwick Papers* (1837), chapter 43

Apocalypse Now. A film (1979) directed by Francis Ford Coppola, loosely based on the story *HEART OF DARKNESS* (1902) by Joseph Conrad (1857–1924). The title refers to the Revelation of St John the Divine, also called the Apocalypse; 'apocalypse' (Greek *apokalupsis*) literally means an uncovering, but is popularly taken to mean the violent end of the world as we know it, as described by St John. The 'Now' in the title refers to the fact that the film is set during the Vietnam War (which had come to an end four years before the film's release). The film stars Martin Sheen as a US Army captain detailed to assassinate the renegade Colonel Kurtz, played by Marlon Brando, and includes such epic set-pieces as a helicopter assault conducted to the accompaniment of Wagner's 'The Ride of the Valkyries'. The massive cost of the film, which was shot in the Philippines and complicated when Martin Sheen suffered a heart attack, was compounded by the extent to which it went over schedule. In the film business it became known by the alternative titles *Apocalypse When?* or *Apocalypse Later*. During filming Coppola referred to the film as his 'Idiodyssey'. He later said:

> We made *Apocalypse* the way Americans made war in Vietnam. There were too many of us, too much money and equipment – and little by little we went insane.

In 2001 Coppola released his own cut, *Apocalypse Now Redux* (*redux* is Latin for 'brought back', 'restored'), which included the fabled 'French plantation sequence', the existence of which had been rumoured among fans for years.

Apollo Belvedere. An ancient Roman copy of an even more ancient Greek sculpture, credited to Leochares (*fl.* mid-4th century BC), although some think it commemorates the repulse of an attack by Gauls on Apollo's shrine at Delphi in 279 BC. The Roman copy was found at Anzio in 1485, and is now in the Belvedere Gallery at the Vatican, hence its name. It depicts the god in his beardless youth, with his cloak thrown back to display his 'naked perfection'.

> The Apollo Belvedere ... the ultimate beauty beyond which there was nothing to desire or hope for.
>
> GOETHE: *Italian Journey* (1786–8)

The work was highly influential on later artists. For example, the pose of *Commodore Keppel* (1753) by Sir Joshua Reynolds (1723–92) is based on that of the Apollo Belvedere.

Appassionata. The title, meaning 'impassioned', given by his publisher to the piano sonata no 23 in F minor, opus 57 (1804–5), by Beethoven (1770–1827).

Après-midi d'un faune, L' (French, 'the afternoon of a faun'). A dramatic poem by the French symbolist, Stéphane Mallarmé (1842–98), begun in 1865 and published in 1876. The poem can be read as an evocation of the sexual frustrations and fantasies of a faun (the Roman equivalent of a satyr), but the language is sensuously dense and complex, and meanings multiply and shimmer like mirages. The tone poem *Prélude à l'Après-midi d'un faune* (1894) by Debussy (1862–1918) is intended as an 'impression' of Mallarmé's poem. The poet approved, writing on a copy of the score:

> *Sylvain d'haleine première,*
> *Si ta flûte a réussi*
> *Ouïs toute lumière*
> *Qu'y soufflera Debussy.*

– which might be literally translated as 'Sylvan creature of the first breath, if your flute has succeeded, hearken to all light which Debussy will breathe into it'. Not everybody was so enthusiastic:

Je deviendrais vite aphone,
Si j'allais en étourdi
M'égosiller comme un faune
Fêtant son après-midi.

('I would soon lose my voice if I went round roaring vacuously like a faun celebrating its afternoon.')

CAMILLE SAINT-SAËNS: *Rimes familières*

As well as the *Prélude*, Debussy had intended to write an *Interlude* and a *Paraphrase finale*, but these never materialized. Debussy's music was used in a ballet of the same title (1912), choreographed by Nijinsky for Diaghilev's Ballets Russes, in which Nijinsky, taking the title role, caused something of a scandal by simulating orgasm.

Arabian Nights Entertainment or ***The Thousand and One Nights.*** A collection of ancient tales from India, Persia and Arabia. They were first introduced into western Europe in a French translation by Antoine Galland (12 volumes, 1704–17), derived from an Egyptian text, probably dating from the 14th or 15th century. English translations based on Galland were made by R. Heron (1792) and W. Beloe (1795). The later translations by Henry Torrens (1838), E.W. Lane (1839–41) and John Payne (1882–4) and Sir Richard Burton's unexpurgated edition published at Benares (Varanesi; 16 volumes, 1885–8) are based on a late 18th-century Egyptian text. The standard French translation (1899–1904) by J.C. Mardrus has been severely criticized.

The framework of the tales is the story of Scheherazade, daughter of the grand vizier of the Indies. The Sultan Schahriah, having discovered the infidelity of his sultana, has resolved to have a fresh wife every night and to have her strangled at daybreak. Scheherazade entreats to become his wife, and so amuses him with tales for a thousand and one nights that he revokes his cruel decree, bestows his affection on her and calls her 'the liberator of the sex'. Her stories include the tales of Aladdin, Sinbad the Sailor and Ali Baba.

The film *Arabian Nights* (1942) is an Oriental adventure involving the caliph of Baghdad, but has no stronger link to the original tales. Much more in the spirit of the original is *The Arabian Nights* (1974), a visually beautiful film by Pier Paulo Pasolini (1922–75) that also encompasses some of the original's complex narrative structure (tales within tales, and so on). *The Thief of Baghdad* (1940), a wonderful fantasy film directed by Michael Powell and others, features elements of the tales in a story about an urchin imprisoned for theft who is joined in his cell by the deposed prince, whom he helps to regain his throne. The first film with this title (1924) was written by and starred Douglas Fairbanks, and there were remakes in 1960 and 1978.

Several pieces of music have been inspired by the *Arabian Nights*. The best known is *Sheherazade*, a symphonic suite (1888) by Rimsky-Korsakov (1844–1908), which Fokine turned into a ballet (1910). *Shéhérazade* (1903) is a set of three songs by Maurice Ravel (1875–1937), setting poems by Tristan Klingsor. Scheherazade also makes an interesting appearance in one of the novellas in *Chimera* (1972) by the US writer John Barth (b.1930).

'Archduke' Trio. The nickname given to the piano trio in B flat, opus 97 (1811), by Beethoven (1770–1827). It was dedicated to the Archduke Rudolf of Austria, who was one of Beethoven's piano and composition pupils.

Areopagitica. 'A Speech of Mr John Milton for the Liberty of Unlicensed Printing, to the Parliament of England', a classic defence of free speech by John Milton (1608–74). It was published in 1644, and directed against the bill for the licensing of printing that had been passed by Parliament in the previous year. The title deliberately mimics the *Areopagiticus* of the Greek orator Isocrates (436–338 BC), so named because it was addressed to the Areopagus, the oldest, aristocratic council of ancient Athens. The council in turn took its name from the place where it sat, the Areopagus – the 'hill of Ares' (the Greek god of war) – situated northwest of the Acropolis.

Arms and the Man. A comedy by George Bernard Shaw (1856–1950), first performed in 1894 and published in 1898. Set in the Balkans, the play pokes fun both at false patriotism and at delusions of romantic love. The ironic title comes from the opening words of Virgil's *Aeneid*: '*Arma virumque cano*' (translated by John Dryden as 'Arms, and the man I sing'). The undeluded heroine calls the deluded hero her 'chocolate soldier', which supplied the title for the 1908 operetta by Oscar Straus (1870–1954), based on the play.

Arnolfini Marriage, The. A painting (1434) by the Flemish painter Jan van Eyck (d.1441), also known as *Double Portrait of Giovanni di Arrigo Arnolfini and his wife, Giovanna*. Arnolfini was a wealthy Italian merchant living in Bruges, and both he and his wife (née Cenami) came originally from the town of Lucca in Tuscany. However, the only basis for identifying these two as the subject of the portrait is a reference to a similar painting in a document of 1516. It is also not certain that a wedding is being portrayed, although there are a number of visual symbols associated with matrimony: the mirror on the back wall (the purity of virginity), the fruit on the windowsill (reminding us of the marriage of Adam and Eve before the Fall), the dog (fidelity), the bed with its carving of St Margaret (patron saint of childbirth). One might assume that the woman, with her apparently full, rounded stomach, is pregnant, but experts point out that this look was fashionable at the period, and that the impression of pregnancy is largely due to the fact that she holds folds of her rich green dress in front of her. The man holding her hand raises his other hand as if making a vow, and some authorities point out that it was possible at that time to make a legally binding marriage without a priest by swearing the appropriate oaths in front of two witnesses; reinforcing this theory is the fact that in the mirror on the back wall – a celebrated *tour de force* of representational painting – can be seen not only the painter but another figure. Furthermore, on the wall above the mirror is written (in a legal style of script) '*Johannes de eyck fuit hic*' (Latin, 'Jan van Eyck was here'), perhaps turning the painting itself into a witnessed marriage certificate.

Around Ireland with a Fridge. A travel book (1998) by the English humorist Tony Hawks. The expedition recounted arose from a drunken night when a friend wagered £100 that he wouldn't travel round Ireland accompanied by a refrigerator. His subsequent book, *Playing the Moldovans at Tennis* (2000), was also the result of a bet, and involved Hawks attempting to defeat each of the members of the Moldovan national football team.

Arsenic and Old Lace. A film comedy (1941, but released in 1944) based on a play (1941) by Joseph Kesselring (1902–67), which was a huge success on Broadway. The plot revolves around two kindly but deranged old ladies (hence the 'old lace') who poison (hence the 'arsenic') elderly gentlemen who visit their home, wishing to relieve them of their loneliness. They bury the bodies in their cellar. The film, which was directed by Frank Capra, starred Cary Grant as the ladies' hapless and appalled nephew, Mortimer Brewster. The title of Kesselring's play was suggested by that of Myrtle Reed's novel *Lavender and Old Lace* (1902), criticized by reviewers of the day for its saccharine sentimentality. The phrase 'lavender and old lace' subsequently came to denote old-fashioned gentility.

During the Second World War the irascible parliamentary duo of Emanuel Shinwell (Labour) and Cecil, Viscount Tournour (Conservative) became known as 'Arsenic and Old Face'.

Artist of the Floating World, An. A novel (1986) by the Japanese-born British novelist Kazuo Ishiguro (b.1954), about a Japanese artist looking back on his life after the Second World War. 'The floating world' is a Japanese euphemism for the entertainment districts of Japanese cities, scenes from which were depicted in the genre called *ukiyo-e* ('pictures of the floating world'), a type of painting particularly popular during the Tokugawa period (1603–1867) in Japan. Subjects included courtesans, actors, scenes from plays and erotica. A well-known work of fiction from the period is *Ukiyo monogatari* (*c.*1661; 'tales of the floating world') by the Samurai turned novelist Asai Ryoi.

Ascent of F6, The. A play (1937) by the British poets and playwrights W.H. Auden (1907–73) and Christopher Isherwood (1904–86) about an ill-fated British mountaineering expedition to a fictional peak identified simply as F6, on the frontier between the equally fictional British Sudoland and Ostnian Sudoland. The expedition leader, Michael Ransom, was based on the real-life soldier and writer T.E. Lawrence (1888–1935); *see also The* SEVEN PILLARS OF WISDOM.

The name F6 echoes the style used by the 19th-century Survey of India, in cases where native names or English names had not been established for remote mountains in the Himalaya. Today, K2 (the world's second-highest mountain) is the only major peak to retain its 'temporary' designation, which indicated that it was the second mountain in the Karakoram range to be measured (in 1856). Its alternative name, Mount Godwin Austen (after the mountain's first surveyor, Colonel H.H. Godwin Austen), has not survived.

As I Walked out One Midsummer Morning. An autobiographical account (1969) of his youth by the poet Laurie Lee (1914–97). The work is a sequel to *CIDER WITH ROSIE*, and describes how the young Lee leaves his Gloucestershire village with little more than a fiddle. He first travels to London, and then to Spain on the eve of civil war. A third volume of memoirs, *A Moment of War*, was published in 1991. 'As I Walked out One Midsummer Morning' is a traditional English folk song, in which the singer meets a maid.

> Old men in the pubs sang, 'As I Walked Out', then walked out and never came back ...
>
> LAURIE LEE: *Cider with Rosie* (1959), 'Last Days'

As I Was Going Down Sackville Street. The first volume of memoirs (1937) of the Irish poet and surgeon Oliver St John Gogarty (1878–1957). Sackville Street (previously Drogheda Street) in central Dublin is now called O'Connell Street, in honour of 'the great liberator', Daniel O'Connell (1775–1847), who did much to achieve Catholic Emancipation in the Westminster Parliament. O'Connell Street is the location of the General Post Office, which was the rebel headquarters during the 1916 Easter Rising, and one of the few buildings to survive the fighting then and during the Troubles in 1922. For many years Nelson's Pillar stood opposite, but was blown up in 1966, presumably by nationalists who regarded it as an affront.

Gogarty himself was associated with leading figures of the Irish literary renaissance, such as W.B. Yeats (who included 17 of his poems in his 1936 *Oxford Book of Modern Verse*), George Moore and George Russell (Æ), but resented the appearance of his student self as 'stately plump Buck Mulligan' in James Joyce's *ULYSSES*. He published two other volumes of memoirs, *Tumbling in the Hay* (1939), and *It Isn't This Time of Year at All* (1954). The title of the latter comes from the following exchange recorded in the book:

> I said, 'It is most extraordinary weather for this time of year.' He replied, 'Ah, it isn't this time of year at all.'

Asphalt Jungle, The. A film noir (1950) based on the novel (1949) of the same name by W.R. Burnett (1899–1982). Directed by John Huston and starring Sterling Hayden and Louis Calhern, it depicts the disintegration of a gang of thieves following a daring robbery attempt. The title of the film conveys appropriate overtones of savagery in a bleak urban setting, where the paving is asphalt and the 'law of the jungle' prevails. The title may also have inspired the phrase 'concrete jungle', which arose in the 1960s to denote the harshness of the modern urban environment.

See also BLACKBOARD JUNGLE, THE.

As You Like It. A comedy (*c.*1600) by William Shakespeare (1564–1616). The story is based on *Rosalynde: Euphues' Golden Legacy* (1590), a romance by Thomas Lodge (1557–1625), although the clown Touchstone and the gloomy philosopher Jaques are purely Shakespeare's inventions. Orlando is forced to flee the court of the usurping Duke Frederick. He takes refuge in the Forest of Arden, where the usurped Duke and his followers are now living. Rosalind, the daughter of the usurped Duke, is also obliged to flee, having previously fallen in love with Orlando (and he with her). Disguised as the youth Ganymede she befriends Orlando, and encourages him to practise his wooing of Rosalind on 'him' (i.e. Ganymede). There are certain complications, involving various other sets of lovers. In the end all is revealed, four pairs of lovers marry and Frederick the usurper surrenders the dukedom to its rightful ruler.

The title indicates the playwright's desire to please with his offering. At the very end, Rosalind addresses the audience directly:

> I charge you, O women, for the love you bear to men, to like as much of this play as please you; and I charge you, O men, for the love you bear to women – as I perceive by your simp'ring none of you hates them – that between you and the women the play may please.
>
> V.iv, Epilogue

'What You Will', the subtitle of *TWELFTH NIGHT*, has an equivalent implication. Similar epilogues, asking the audience for their approbation and indulgence, were something of a theatrical convention at the time; for example, at the end of *The TEMPEST* Prospero speaks the Epilogue, ending:

> As you from crimes would pardon'd be,
> Let your indulgence set me free.
>
> V.i, Epilogue

There is another example at the end of *ALL'S WELL THAT ENDS WELL*.

There have been two film versions of *As You Like It*. The 1936 version includes Laurence Olivier in the cast, and J.M. Barrie co-wrote the screenplay. The 1992 version turns the Forest of Arden into a London 'cardboard city' for the homeless.

At Five in the Afternoon. A stark abstract painting (1949) by Robert Motherwell (1915–91). The work dates from the same year that the artist began his series of *ELEGIES TO THE SPANISH REPUBLIC*. The title is a translation of '*A las cinco de la tarde*', the dirge-like refrain of Federico García Lorca's great elegy, *Llanto por Ignacio Sánchez Mejías* ('Lament for Ignacio

Sánchez Mejías'), in memory of a bullfighter who had been gored to death in 1934. The poem was published in 1935, and the following year Lorca himself was assassinated by nationalists shortly after the outbreak of the Spanish Civil War.

Atmospheric Skull Sodomizing a Grand Piano. A calm painting of a small Spanish village by Salvador Dalí (1904–89), the peace disturbed only by the event described in the title, in which a piano has been rendered almost airborne by the force of the skull's phallically extended jawbone. It is to paintings such as these that James Thurber was no doubt referring when he wrote:

> The naked truth about me is to the naked truth about Salvador Dali as an old ukulele in the attic is to a piano in a tree, and I mean a piano with breasts.
>
> JAMES THURBER: *The Thurber Merry-Go-Round* (1945)

Atom, The History and Adventures of an. An anonymous satire on leading contemporary politicians published in 1769. It was almost certainly written by the novelist Tobias Smollett (1721–71). The atom in question has been incarnated several times, most recently in the body of somebody in Japan. Smollett's Japan is clearly England, and the various Japanese characters would have been easily identified by contemporary readers as figures such as the former prime ministers William Pitt the Elder and the duke of Newcastle. It was the ancient Greek philosopher Democritus who first suggested that all matter was made up of tiny, indivisible particles, which he called atoms (meaning 'that which cannot be cut'). Atomic theory advanced no further than this until the work of John Dalton (1766–1844) in the early 19th century, after Smollett's time. However, Smollett was not unscientific in suggesting that the same atom could be incarnated in a succession of living creatures.

At Swim-Two-Birds. A modernist novel (1939) by Flann O'Brien (one of several pseudonyms of Brian O'Nolan; 1911–66). It hovers between burlesque and parody of popular fiction, and of Irish legend, such as had been promoted in the Irish Literary Revival. Snáimh-dá-en ('Swim-two-birds') was one of the resting-places of Mad Sweeney, hero of the Early Irish legend, *Buile Shuibne* ('The Frenzy of Suibne'); it is to be identified with Devenish Island, between Clonmacnois and Shannonbridge, near where O'Brien spent part of his childhood. Jamie O'Neill's novel, *At Swim, Two Boys* (2001), plays on the title.

At the Boar's Head. A one-act opera by Gustav Holst (1874–1934), first performed in 1925. Much of the music is based on English folk songs. For the text the composer used passages involving Falstaff in Shakespeare's *Henry IV, Part 1* and *Part 2*, the Boar's Head Tavern being one of Falstaff's favourite resorts. The real inn was in Eastcheap, London, where today there is a statue of William IV. The original tavern was destroyed in the Great Fire of London in 1666, and two years later it was replaced by a brick building, which had figures of Falstaff carved round the door. This was demolished in 1831. 'Reverie in the Boar's Head Tavern of Eastcheap' is the title of an essay (1760) by Oliver Goldsmith (1730–74).

August is a Wicked Month. *See* WASTE LAND, THE.

'Auld Lang Syne'. A song, particularly associated with the arrival of the New Year, often attributed to Robert Burns (1759–96), but actually much older. The title means 'old long since', i.e. times past. Burns's version was published in volume 5 (1796) of James Johnson's *Scots Musical Museum* (1787–1803). In James Watson's *Choice Collection of Comic and Serious Scots Poems* (1706–11) it is attributed to Francis Sempill (d.1682); it has also been attributed to Sir Robert Aytoun (1570–1638). Burns wrote in a letter to George Thomson (1793): 'It is the old song of the olden times, which has never been in print ... I took it down from an old man's singing.' And in another letter: 'Light be on the turf of the heaven-inspired poet who composed this glorious fragment.'

> Should auld acquaintance be forgot,
>   And never brought to min'?
> Should auld acquaintance be forgot,
>   And auld lang syne.
>
> CHORUS
> *For auld lang syne, my jo,*
>   *For auld lang syne,*
> *We'll tak a cup o' kindness yet,*
>   *For auld lang syne.*
>
> ROBERT BURNS: 'Auld Lang Syne' (1796)

Aureng-Zebe. A tragedy (1675) by John Dryden (1631–1700). The real Aurangzeb (1618–1707) was still alive when Dryden wrote. He was the Mogul emperor of India, who fought his brother for the succession and deposed his father, Shah Jehan, in 1658. These events occur in Dryden's play, but while Dryden's Aureng-Zebe is a figure of upstanding virtue, the real Aurangzeb was a ruthless ruler whose fierce Islamic orthodoxy alienated his Hindu subjects, and led to the weakening of the Mogul empire.

> If Dryden's plays had been as good as his prefaces he would have been a dramatist indeed.
>
> HARLEY GRANVILLE-BARKER: *On Dramatic Method* (1931)

Autobiography of Alice B. Toklas, The. Actually the autobiography of the US modernist writer Gertrude Stein (1874–1946), written as if the autobiography of her shy and retiring companion, Alice B. Toklas (1877–1967). Stein claimed she wrote the book 'as simply as Defoe did the autobiography of Robinson Crusoe', and referred to it by the alternative titles *My Life with the Great* and *My Twenty-Five Years with Gertrude Stein*. Toklas herself was the author of *The Alice B. Toklas Cook Book* (1954), with its famous recipe for hashish brownies, and penned her own short memoir, *What Is Remembered* (1963).

Awkward Age, The. A novel by Henry James (1843–1916), published in 1899. The 'awkward age' is a common phrase denoting adolescence, the difficult period when one is no longer a child but not yet fully an adult. The term dates from the end of the 19th century and may have been borrowed from French *l'âge ingrat*. James's novel concerns a young woman's emergence into an understanding of the world, and the milieu is said to be modelled on the Asquith circle. In 1918 Ezra Pound described the novel's opening as:

> a cheese soufflé of the leprous crust of society done to a turn …

B

Back to Methuselah. A play (1921) by the Irish playwright George Bernard Shaw (1856–1950) consisting of five loosely linked plays on a variety of philosophical themes, including that of old age. Methuselah is the oldest man mentioned in the Bible, in which he is said to have lived to the age of 969. Shaw himself lived to the age of 94. He once ascribed his long life to the location of his home in the village of Ayot St Lawrence, Hertfordshire, explaining that he had decided 'this is the place for me' after spotting a gravestone with the legend: 'Jane Eversley. Born 1825. Died 1895. Her time was short.'

Bacon, Lettuce and Tomato. *See* *HAMBURGER WITH PICKLE AND TOMATO ATTACHED.*

Bald Prima Donna, The (French title: *La Cantatrice chauve*). A one-act play by the Romanian-born French playwright Eugène Ionesco (1912–94), which was first performed in Paris in 1950 to an audience of three. Described by the author as an 'anti-play', it is an apparently nonsensical entertainment in which the words exchanged by the characters seem to have no relation to each other, and it owed its genesis to the author's fascination with examples of bizarre English phrases in language books. The 'bald prima donna' herself is the subject of just one obscure reference in the text, which actually came about in rehearsal when the Fire-chief garbled the words Ionesco had originally written:

> *Fire-chief*: By the way, what about the Bald Prima Donna?
> *Mr Smith*: Ssh!

> *Mrs Smith*: She always wears her hair the same way!

La Cantatrice chauve holds the record for the longest-running play in the French theatre.

Ballo in maschera, Un. *See* MASKED BALL, A.

Barber of Seville, The (Italian title: *Il Barbiere di Siviglia*). An opera by Gioacchino Rossini (1792–1868), with a libretto by Cesare Sterbini after the play *Le Barbier de Séville* (1775) by Pierre-Augustin Caron de Beaumarchais (1732–99). The first performance was in 1816, and Rossini had originally titled his work *Almaviva, ossia L'inutile precauzione* ('Almaviva, or the fruitless precaution'). The 'barber' (actually a barber-surgeon) is Figaro, who helps Count Almaviva woo and win Rosina, the ward of Dr Bartolo. An earlier operatic adaptation, first performed in 1782, had been made by Giuseppe Petrosonelli with music by Giovanni Paisiello (1740–1816), and supporters of this version gave Rossini's opera a stormy reception at its first performance (which was also marred by Almaviva's out-of-tune guitar, an unintended pratfall and resultant nosebleed from Bartolo, and a stage-struck cat going crazy during the finale). Mozart's *The* MARRIAGE OF FIGARO (1786), in which Figaro has become the Count's valet, is based on Beaumarchais's sequel, *Le Mariage de Figaro* (1784).

> Rossini, in music, is the genius of sheer animal spirits. It is a species as inferior to that of Mozart, as the cleverness of a smart boy is to that of a man of sentiment; but it is genius nevertheless.
>
> LEIGH HUNT: 'Going to the Play Again' (1828)

barcarolle. A French word for a boating song, from the Italian *barcarola* (itself from *barca*, 'a boat'). Originally a *barcarola* was a song of a Venetian gondolier, but came to be applied to any piece with a similar rhythm. Examples include that by Chopin for piano (opus 60) and the one featured in Offenbach's *Tales of Hoffmann* (1881).

Barefoot in the Park. A play (1963) by the US playwright Neil Simon (b.1927) about a newly married couple who experience their first fallings-out as they move into their first home, a tiny flat at the top of five flights of stairs. The title relates to the wife's complaint that her lawyer-husband is too strait-laced when he turns down an invitation to walk barefoot in the park in the freezing weather (he subsequently does so, despite a raging cold). Simon also wrote the screenplay for the film (1967), which starred Jane Fonda and Robert Redford as Corle and Paul Bratter and Ethel Banks as Corle's mother, Mildred.

Bartholomew Fair. A 'citizen' comedy – i.e. one dealing with contemporary London – by Ben Jonson (1572–1637), first performed in 1614. The play follows the fortunes of a number of characters at Bartholomew Fair, the annual fair held at Smithfield in London on St Bartholomew's Day (24 August) and the two days following.

Bartholomew Fair was established by Rahere, King Henry I's jester, who also founded the Hospice of St Bartholomew in 1133. Originally a cloth fair, by Jonson's time it had become more concerned with general entertainment, featuring players, tumblers, fire-eaters, wrestlers and so on. The fair survived the Puritans and the Commonwealth period, but was eventually shut down by the City of London authorities in 1855.

Battle of the Books, The. A prose satire by Jonathan Swift (1667–1745), written in 1697 and published in 1704. The complete title, *A Full and True Account of the Battle Fought Last Friday, between the Ancient and Modern Books in St James's Library*, more or less explains the gist of the piece. Swift was disinterestedly mocking the contemporary debate as to the relative merits of the ancient and modern authors. In Swift's fantasy, Plato, Homer, Euclid, Virgil and Homer are ranged against moderns such as Dryden, Hobbes, Milton and Descartes. The work ends while the outcome is still uncertain.

> Satire is a sort of glass, wherein beholders do generally discover everybody's face but their own.
>
> JONATHAN SWIFT: *The Battle of the Books*, preface

Battleship Potemkin, The. A film (1925) commissioned by the Soviet regime to commemorate the 20th anniversary of the unsuccessful 1905 Revolution. Director Sergei Eisenstein focused on a single crucial episode of the 1905 Revolution, namely the mutiny of sailors on board the battleship *Potemkin* in the Crimean seaport of Odessa. The ruthless crushing of the rebellion by tsarist troops was encapsulated in the most famous scene of Eisenstein's film, that of the massacre of civilians on the Odessa Steps (one of the most famous, and most parodied, images in 20th-century cinema). In fact, this and many other scenes in the film diverged sharply from historical fact, and there is little real evidence of any such massacre taking place.

The battleship itself was named after Grigory Aleksandrovich

Potemkin (1739–91), the distinguished Russian field marshal and statesman who became the favourite (and for two years the lover) of Catherine the Great.

Battle Symphony or ***Battle of Victoria*** or ***Battle of Vitoria.*** *See* WELLINGTON'S VICTORY.

'Bear, The' (French name: '*L'Ours*'). The nickname given to the symphony no 82 in C (1786) by Haydn (1732–1809), one of his 'PARIS' SYMPHONIES (hence the French form of the nickname). The last movement is thought to sound like a bear dancing to the bagpipes, while others claim to have detected a growling in the bass line in this movement. *The Bear* is also a short play by Anton Chekhov (1860–1904) dating from the 1890s (the title refers to a big bumbling character), and a short story (1942) by William Faulkner (1897–1962) about a hunting expedition.

Beata Beatrix (Latin, 'the blessed Beatrix'). A painting (1863) by Dante Gabriel Rossetti (1828–82), in which he depicts his dead wife Elizabeth Siddal as Beatrice, the idealized love of the poet Dante (*see The* DIVINE COMEDY). Prior to her marriage to Rossetti in 1860, Siddal had been his mistress and model. In 1862 she died from an overdose of laudanum (an opiate), and in his grief Rossetti buried with her the only complete manuscript of his poems. Seven years later he changed his mind, and persuaded a supposed friend, Charles Augustus Howell, to retrieve the manuscript from the coffin. This Howell did, and used the incident to blackmail Rossetti. There is a degree of mystery about Howell's death in 1890; it has been suggested that he was found in a gutter with his throat cut and a sovereign symbolically stuck in his mouth.

Beautiful Game, The. A musical (2000) by the composer Andrew Lloyd Webber and the comedian Ben Elton. The setting is Belfast in 1969, just as the Troubles are returning, and the story follows a group of teenagers who are members of a local soccer team. The phrase 'the beautiful game', denoting football, has been attributed to the Brazilian footballer Pelé (b.1940), whose autobiography was entitled *My Life and the Beautiful Game* (1977).

Beckus the Dandipratt. A concert overture, opus 5 (1948), by the English composer Malcolm Arnold (b.1921). Dandipratt or dandiprat is an archaic term dating from the 16th century for a dwarf, a pageboy or a conceited little fellow; the classical scholar Richard Stanyhurst calls Cupid a 'dandiprat' in his translation of Virgil's *Aeneid* (1582). A dandiprat was also a small coin issued in the 16th century, with a value of three halfpence. The idea for the character of Beckus seems to have come to Arnold when he was accosted by an urchin on the beach at Padstow, Cornwall, in 1943.

bed, Tracey Emin's. *See* EVERYONE I'VE EVER SLEPT WITH.

Beggar's Opera, The. A popular comic (or ballad) opera by John Gay (1685–1732), first performed in 1728. The setting is London, the hero is the highwayman Macheath, and the beggar of the title has only a speaking role. The music was made up of traditional ballads and popular tunes of the day (including pieces by Purcell and Handel) arranged by the German composer Johann Pepusch (1667–1752). The opera was full of topical satire, and was enormously successful. The producer was John Rich, and the opera was said to have made Gay rich and Rich gay. It also brought about a change in popular taste in London, forcing Handel to abandon writing serious Italian-style operas:

> Ballad opera pelted Italian opera off the stage with Lumps of Pudding [a tune in *The Beggar's Opera*].
>
> GEORGE FRIDERIC HANDEL: quoted in Lee, *Music of the People* (1970)

> [Of *The Beggar's Opera*] There is in it such a labefaction of all principles as may be injurious to morality
>
> SAMUEL JOHNSON: quoted in Boswell, *Life of Johnson* (1791)

Brecht and Weill's *The* THREEPENNY OPERA is an updated version of *The Beggar's Opera*. The French composer Darius Milhaud (1892–1974) also made an arrangement with the title in French: *L'Opéra des gueux* (1937). Numerous English versions of the opera include one (1948) by Benjamin Britten (1913–76).

'Belle Dame sans Merci, La'. A short ballad by John Keats (1795–1821), written in 1819 and published in 1820. The title means 'the beautiful lady without mercy' (not, as Michael Flanders, of Flanders and Swann, once suggested, 'the beautiful lady who never says thank you'). The poem famously begins:

> O, what can ail thee, knight-at-arms,
> Alone and palely loitering?

The trouble, it transpires, is that the knight fell in love with the lady, 'a faery's child', who took him back to her 'elfin grot' and lulled him asleep, and when he awoke he was alone on 'the cold hill side'. The lady also fleetingly appears in Keats's 'The EVE OF ST AGNES':

> He played an ancient ditty, long since mute,
> In Provence called, 'La belle dame sans mercy'.

This is presumably a reference to the medieval poem (1424) by the French writer Alain Chartier (*c.*1385–*c.*1433), with an English translation by Sir Richard Ros (once attributed to Chaucer), from which Keats apparently derived his title.

There is a musical setting of Keats's ballad by the US composer Wallingford Riegger (1885–1961), scored for four solo voices and chamber orchestra (1924).

Belle Jardinière, La (French, 'the beautiful gardener'). The name given to a Madonna (*c.*1507) by Raphael (1483–1520) that now hangs in the Louvre. *La Belle Jardinière* subsequently became the name of a fashionable Paris store. The German surrealist Max Ernst (1891–1976) borrowed the title for his painting *The Creation of Eve or The Fair Gardener* (1923), which depicts two overlapping naked female forms. One is executed in the manner of a line drawing, in which parts of the figure are draped in fruit (somewhat in the manner of the Italian Renaissance painter Arcimboldo). The other is more modelled, and at the woman's open womb a dove attends, suggesting the Annunciation. In 1937 the painting was seized by the Nazis, shown in their touring exhibition of 'Degenerate Art', and subsequently disappeared. Ernst particularly felt the loss of this picture, and in 1967 painted a new version, entitled *The Return of the Fair Gardener*. The Fair Gardener also appears in Ernst's 1929 collage *Hornebom and The Fair Gardener*, in which a woman in Victorian bathing costume carries through a hothouse a giant pigeon which obscures her head. The collage is part of Ernst's graphic novel *La FEMME 100 TÊTES*.

Bells and Pomegranates. A series of collections of poems and plays by Robert Browning (1812–89), published in eight volumes between 1841 and 1846. The series included *PIPPA PASSES* and *A BLOT IN THE 'SCUTCHEON*. When Browning eventually conceded (in the last volume) an explanation of his title, he said that it suggested 'an alternation, or mixture, of music with discoursing, sound with sense, poetry with thought'. The phrase comes from the Old Testament, in a description of the robe of the high priest Aaron:

> And beneath upon the hem of it thou shalt make pomegranates of blue, and of purple, and of scarlet, round about the hem thereof; and bells of gold between them round about:
> A golden bell and a pomegranate, a golden bell and a pomegranate, upon the hem of the robe round about.
>
> Exodus 28:33–34

Belshazzar's Feast. A dramatic oratorio by William Walton (1902–83), setting words from the Bible selected by Sacheverell Sitwell (1897–1988), first performed in 1931. Belshazzar, the last king of Babylon, was the son of Nebuchadnezzar. At the king's feast an unseen hand writes the words 'Mene, mene, Tekel, Upharsin' on the wall, which the prophet Daniel claims is a divine warning of the destruction of Babylon and Belshazzar's own death (Daniel 5:25).

bergomask (French *bergamasque*; Italian *bergamasco*). A rustic dance, so called from Bergamo, a Venetian province in northern Italy. The dance was popular in the 16th and early 17th centuries, and came to be associated with one particular tune, which provided the basis of variations by several composers, including Girolamo Frescobaldi. In Shakespeare's *A MIDSUMMER NIGHT'S DREAM* (V.i), after the rude mechanicals have finished their performance, Bottom asks:

> Will it please you to see the Epilogue, or to hear a Bergomask dance between two of our company?

The inhabitants of Bergamo were apparently noted for their clownishness, to which Shakespeare is possibly making allusion, and the word 'bergomask' has also been used for a clown. This is picked up in the *Suite Bergamasque* (1890) for piano by Debussy (1862–1918), which has no musical connection with the old dance tune. However, one of the movements is called '*Clair de lune*', from Verlaine's poem (1866), which begins:

> *Votre âme est un paysage choisi,*
> *Que vont charmant masques et bergamasques*
> *Jouant du luth et dansant …*
>
> ('Your soul is a chosen country, whence come charming masques and bergomasks, lute playing and dancing …')

BIRDS

The Birds, a play (414 BC) by Aristophanes; an orchestral suite (1927) by Respighi; a sinister film (1963) by Alfred Hitchcock, based on a story by Daphne du Maurier, in which birds attack humans

'BIRD' QUARTET, (1781) by Haydn

Sweet Bird of Youth, a play (1959) by Tennessee Williams

The PARLIAMENT OF FOWLS, a poem (late 14th century) by Geoffrey Chaucer

Oiseaux exotiques (1955–6) for orchestra, and *Catalogue d'oiseaux* (1956–8) for piano by Olivier Messiaen

Great Northern?, a novel for children (1947) by Arthur Ransome (the title refers to the great northern diver)

The Herne's Egg, a play (1938) by W.B. Yeats (a herne is a heron)

Wild Swans, a memoir of revolutionary China (1991) by Jung Chang

Swan Lake, a ballet (1877) by Tchaikovsky

Duck Soup, a Marx brothers film (1933)

GOLDENEYE, a James Bond film (1995)

The WILD GEESE, an adventure film (1978)

The Wild Goose Chase, a comedy (1621) by John Fletcher

MOTHER GOOSE, the subject of many collections of fairy stories and nursery rhymes

The Eagle of the Ninth, a children's historical novel (1954) by Rosemary Sutcliff, describing the search north of Hadrian's Wall by a retired Roman centurion, Marcus, for a lost legion (the Ninth) and its standard (a silver eagle)

The MALTESE FALCON, a thriller (1930) by Dashiell Hammett

A Kestrel for a Knave, a novel (1968) by Barry Hines

'HEN' SYMPHONY, an orchestral work (1786) by Haydn

The Art of Faking Exhibition Poultry, a treatise (1934) by George Ryley Scott, author of *The Truth About Poultry* (1927)

The LIVER IS THE COCK'S COMB, a painting (1944) by Arshile Gorky

The Golden Cockerel, an opera (1909) by Rimsky-Korsakov

Turkey Time, a Christmas farce (1931) by Ben Travers

JUNO AND THE PAYCOCK, a play (1924) by Sean O'Casey

Coot Club, a novel for children (1934) by Arthur Ransome

Curlew River, a musical church parable (1964) by Benjamin Britten

Penguin Island, a satire (1908) by Anatole France

Les Pélicans, a play (1921) by the French writer Raymond Radiguet, with music by Georges Auric

The SEAGULL, a play (1896) by Chekhov

The Dove, a short film spoof (1968) of Ingmar Bergman, in which the bird in question defecates on the narrator's windscreen, bringing back a flood of memories

The VOICE OF THE TURTLE, a play (1943) by John Van Druten

Les deux pigeons, a ballet (1886) by André Messager

The Pigeon that Took Rome, a film (1962) about US agents in German-occupied Rome during the Second World War

FLAUBERT'S PARROT, a novel (1984) by Julian Barnes

The Cockatoos, a story and collection title (1974) by the Australian Nobel laureate Patrick White

On Hearing the First Cuckoo in Spring, an orchestral piece (1913) by Frederick Delius

The Owl and the Nightingale, an anonymous medieval poem (early 13th century)

'The Owl and the Pussycat', a poem (1871) by Edward Lear

NIGHTHAWKS, a painting (1942) by Edward Hopper

The Lark Ascending, a piece for violin and orchestra (1914) by Ralph Vaughan Williams

'LARK' QUARTET, a string quartet (1789) by Haydn

'To a Skylark', a poem (1819) by P.B. Shelley (*see also* *BLITHE SPIRIT*)

SWALLOWS AND AMAZONS, a novel for children (1930) by Arthur Ransome

'ODE TO A NIGHTINGALE', a poem (1819) by John Keats

The Djinn in the Nightingale's Eye, short stories (1994) by A.S. Byatt

'Thirteen Ways of Looking at a Blackbird', a poem (1923) by Wallace Stevens

TO KILL A MOCKINGBIRD, a novel (1960) by Harper Lee

The CAT AND THE CANARY, a stage thriller (1922) by John Willard, subsequently filmed

'The Jackdaw of Rheims', a poem (1840) by J.H. Barham (*see THIEVING MAGPIE, THE*)

The THIEVING MAGPIE, an opera (1817) by Gioacchino Rossini

Crow, a poetry collection (1970) by Ted Hughes

Bigger Splash, A. The best known of the many swimming-pool pictures by David Hockney (b.1937), painted in 1967. It was the third of a series, which explains the title, as Hockney himself recalls:

> *The Little Splash*, which is a tiny painting ... was the first of three paintings ... from a photograph I found in a book about how to build swimming pools I found on a news stand in Hollywood. It was a nice little subject, a splash ... And I thought, it's worth making this bigger, doing it a little differently, and so I did a slightly bigger one, *The Splash*, and I took a bit more care with it. But then I thought the background was perhaps slightly fussy, the buildings were a little too complicated, not quite right. So I decided I'd do a third version, a big one using a very simple building and strong light.
>
> *David Hockney by David Hockney* (1976)

Big Sleep, The. The first crime novel (1939) by the US writer Raymond Chandler (1888–1959). It is set in Los Angeles and introduces the detective Philip Marlowe, a man of sentiment, wit and morality, as well as toughness. Chandler's aim was to present criminals as they really are, not as the writers of detective novels then represented them. The title refers to a passage at the end of the book:

> What did it matter where you lay once you were dead? ... You were dead, you were sleeping the big sleep.

A complex but pacey film version (1946), with Humphrey Bogart as Marlowe, was directed by Howard Hawks.

'Bird' Quartet (German *Vogelquartett*). The nickname for the string quartet in C, opus 33 no 3 (1781), by Haydn (1732–1809), one of the 'RUSSIAN' QUARTETS. The name derives from the avian character of the themes in the first movement.

Birthday Boys, The. A historical novel (1991) by Beryl Bainbridge (b.1934). The inspiration for this recreation of the doomed Antarctic expedition of Captain Robert Falcon Scott (1868–1912) was the letter written by Scott to the dramatist and novelist James Barrie (1860–1937) as Scott and his companions waited for death: 'We are very near the end, but have not and will not lose our good cheer.' The title refers to the birthday party for Petty Officer Edgar ('Taff') Evans just before the attempt on the Pole and to the fact that Captain Oates walks out of the tent to his death on his birthday.

> I am just going outside and may be some time.
>
> CAPTAIN L.E.G. OATES: last words

See also *YOUNG ADOLF*.

Birth of a Nation, The. An early film epic (1915), directed by D.W. Griffith and based on a racist novel, *The Clansman* (1905), by the southern Baptist minister Thomas Dixon (1864–1946). The film follows the fortunes of two families during and after the American Civil War (1861–5). It was the most ambitious motion picture produced up to that time, and has been praised by cinéastes for its formal innovations. However, in political terms it is probably the most controversial film ever released in the United States, as it justifies and celebrates the white South's 'Redemption' from Reconstruction – the Northern liberal reorganization of the Southern states (1865–77) that followed the Northern victory in the Civil War. In the end Reconstruction failed: Southern blacks were disenfranchised and rigid racial discrimination and segregation returned to the states of the old Confederacy. The nation 'born' in the title is thus a white-dominated society that has turned its back on the fratricidal folly of the Civil War and the supposed black despotism of Reconstruction. The film portrays the Ku Klux Klan as triumphant defenders of white America, and blacks as an inferior race.

> It is like writing history with lightning and my only regret is that it is all so terribly true.
>
> PRESIDENT WOODROW WILSON: remark, 18 February 1915

Blackboard Jungle, The. The first novel (1954) of the US writer Evan Hunter (b.1926), based on his personal experience. It is a somewhat sensationalized account of an American urban high school where the boys are rough, the headmaster a bully, and the teachers overworked and additionally plagued by personal problems. As a result of the book, the expression 'blackboard jungle' became a popular idiom for any undisciplined school of this type. The phrase itself is a variant on *The ASPHALT JUNGLE.* A film version (1955), directed by Richard Brooks, is now chiefly remembered for its soundtrack, featuring 'Rock Around the Clock' by Bill Haley and the Comets.

Blade Runner. A bleak science fiction film (1982) directed by Ridley Scott, starring Harrison Ford and Rutger Hauer, and set in Los Angeles in the year 2019. Ford plays a detective who is hunting down rogue androids or 'replicants'. The special police squads to which Ford belongs are called Blade Runner Units, whose job it is to 'retire' (i.e. execute) replicants. This is explained in the opening scrolling text, but no further explanation of the title is proffered.

'The Bladerunner' was originally the title of a very different science fiction story by Alan E. Nourse, where smugglers called 'blade runners' supply an impoverished society with medical supplies. William S. Burroughs wrote 'Bladerunner (A Movie)' (1979) after reading Nourse's book, though the name is the principal similarity between the stories. Hampton Fancher, the screenwriter for Ridley Scott's movie, found Burroughs' book and Scott liked it enough to adopt the title for the screenplay, buying the rights for the use of the name.

The story of the film is based on a short story by Philip K. Dick (1928–82) entitled *Do Androids Dream of Electric Sheep?* (1968), which won that year's Nebula Award.

Blam. *See WHAAM!*

Bleak House. A novel (1852–3) by Charles Dickens (1812–70). Bleak House is the name of the house of kind John Jarndyce, and it also becomes the home of his two young relatives, Richard Carstone and Ada Clare, the two alternative heirs in the interminable case of Jarndyce vs. Jarndyce, which has been dragging through the Court of Chancery for generations.

> The one great principle of the English law is, to make business for itself.
>
> chapter 39

Richard and Ada fall in love and secretly marry, but by the time the Court eventually rules in his favour, Richard has died, and all the money in the estate has been used up in legal costs. Ada lives on at Bleak House with their son.

This satire on the Court of Chancery is perhaps less interesting than the other main plot line, which involves the efforts of Lady Dedlock to conceal the evidence of a long-past affair, and the mystery as to what happened to her illegitimate daughter. This plot in turn is a means by which Dickens provides a savage and gloomy picture of the England of his time, itself a 'Bleak House', wracked by social ills and inhabited by miserable individuals.

Blessed Virgin Chastises the Infant Jesus before Three Witnesses: A.B., P.E. and the Artist, The. A painting (1926) by the German surrealist Max Ernst (1891–1976), in which the bare-bottomed boy Jesus is spanked on the lap of the Madonna. His halo has fallen on the floor, while hers remains in position. The work was deliberately conceived as a piece of anti-clerical agitprop, probably by André Breton (A.B.), who, with Ernst and Paul Éluard (P.E.), observes the scene through a window. The poets Breton (1896–1966) and Éluard (1895–1952) were leading figures in the Surrealist movement. Ernst was inspired in his composition by the famous *MADONNA OF THE LONG NECK* (*c.*1535) by Parmigianino.

Blind Leading the Blind, The. A painting (1568) by Pieter Bruegel the Elder (*c.*1525–69) of one blind beggar leading two others as they tumble into a ditch. It was one of Bruegel's paintings illustrating proverbs, this one suggesting that those who are unfit to do so should not give advice to or attempt to lead others. The origin is in the Bible:

> Let them alone: they be blind leaders of the blind. And if the blind lead the blind, both shall fall into the ditch.
>
> Matthew 15:14

See also 'COUNTRY OF THE BLIND, THE'.

Blithe Spirit. A stage comedy (1941) by Noel Coward (1899–1973), involving a somewhat caddish writer being bothered by the mischievous ghost (the 'blithe spirit') of his first wife. In the film version (1945), Rex Harrison is the writer and Margaret Rutherford the medium. The title comes from Percy Bysshe Shelley's 'To a Skylark' (1819):

> Hail to thee, blithe Spirit!
> Bird thou never wert,
> That from Heaven, or near it,
> Pourest thy full heart
> In profuse strains of unpremeditated art.

Blood Wedding (Spanish title: *Bodas de sangre*). A play by the Spanish poet and dramatist Federico García Lorca (1898–1936), first performed in 1933. Bloodshed and tragedy follow after a bride elopes with a former lover on the day fixed for her marriage to another man. Lorca based his story on a real incident reported in the newspapers of Almería in 1928, in which a bride and her lover were hunted down by the family of the thwarted bridegroom. The play was first staged in New York in 1935 under the title *Bitter Oleander* and subsequently in London as *The Marriage of Blood.*

Blot in the 'Scutcheon, A. A play by Robert Browning (1812–89), unsuccessfully produced in 1843, and published the same year as the fifth volume of *BELLS AND POMEGRANATES*. The work, set in the 18th century, concerns the love affair of an aristocratic lady and the murder of her lover by her brother. A 'blot on one's escutcheon' is a stain on one's character or reputation, an escutcheon being a shield bearing a coat of arms, and the phrase was already long current:

> The banishment of Ovid was a blot in his escutcheon.
>
> JOHN DRYDEN: *Virgil*, ii, Dedication (1697)

Blue Angel, The (German title: *Der blaue Engel*). A film (1930) adapted by Carl Zuckmayer from the novel *Professor Unrat* (1905) by Heinrich Mann (1871–1950), the brother of Thomas Mann. Shot simultaneously in German and English, the film made an international star of Marlene Dietrich. Dietrich plays the nightclub singer Lola, who leads a 'respectable' man to destruction; the title, which is the name of the nightclub, suggests a sexual ('blue') variation on the angel of death. Dietrich herself was subsequently sometimes referred to as 'the Blue Angel'. Today the film is best remembered for Dietrich's rendition of 'Falling in Love Again'.

BLUE

The BLUE BOY, a portrait (*c.*1770) by Thomas Gainsborough

RHAPSODY IN BLUE, a work for piano and orchestra (1924) by George Gerswhin

The BLUE ANGEL, a film (1930) starring Marlene Dietrich

The Man with the Blue Guitar, the title poem of a collection (1937) by the US poet Wallace Stevens

I Am Curious – Blue, a Swedish film (1968) by Vilgot Sjöman (*see* I AM CURIOUS – YELLOW)

Porterhouse Blue, a satirical novel (1974) by Tom Sharpe

BLUE REMEMBERED HILLS, a memoir (1983) by Rosemary Sutcliff

Three Colours: Blue, a Polish film (1993) (*see* NUMBERS, panel, pp.328–9)

Blue Boy, The. The popular name for a full-length portrait (*c.*1770) of a boy on the verge of youth by Thomas Gainsborough (1727–88). The boy is dressed in a blue silk suit and white stockings, and his Cavalier-like dash, and Gainsborough's execution, is influenced by Anthony Van Dyck. The sitter (or, more correctly, stander) is thought to have been Jonathan Buttall (d.1805), the son of a friend of Gainsborough who owned an ironmongery in Soho, London.

Blue Remembered Hills. A memoir (1983) by the English children's novelist Rosemary Sutcliff (b.1920). The title comes from *A* SHROPSHIRE LAD:

Into my heart an air that kills
  From yon far country blows:
What are those blue remembered hills,
  What spires, what farms are those?

A.E. HOUSMAN: *A Shropshire Lad* (1896), XL

Blue Remembered Hills is also the title of a television play (1979) by Dennis Potter (1935–94).

BODY PARTS

BRING ME THE HEAD OF ALFREDO GARCIA, a Western film (1974)

A SEVERED HEAD, a novel (1961) by Iris Murdoch

Hair, a 'rock opera' (1968), in which the cast let their long hair down and strip off in protest against the Vietnam War

The RAPE OF THE LOCK, a mock-heroic epic (1712) by Alexander Pope

The Dog Beneath the Skin, a play (1935) by W.H. Auden and Christopher Isherwood

The Valley of Bones, a novel (1964) in Anthony Powell's sequence *A DANCE TO THE MUSIC OF TIME*

The SKULL BENEATH THE SKIN, a detective novel (1982) by P.D. James

The Brain Eaters, a horror film (1958)

Eyes Wide Shut, a film (1999) by Stanley Kubrick, consisting of a dreamlike journey through a sinister erotic underworld in New York

The Ear, a Czech film (1970), in which a government minister's apartment is bugged

SCARFACE, a gangster film (1932)

The Nose, an opera (1930) by Shostakovich, based on a story by Nikolai Gogol

The Poor Mouth, a novel (1941) by Flann O'Brien

JAWS, a film (1975) about a man-eating shark

Dentologia, a 'poem on the diseases of teeth and their proper remedies' (1840) by the US dentist Solyman Brown

The SKIN OF OUR TEETH, a play (1942) by Thornton Wilder

DEEP THROAT, a notorious pornographic film (1972)

The Hand that Rocks the Cradle, a suspense film (1991) about a murderous nanny. The title refers to the saying 'The hand that rocks the cradle rules the world.'

A FISTFUL OF DOLLARS, a Western film (1964)

A HANDFUL OF DUST, a novel (1934) by Evelyn Waugh

The MOVING FINGER, a detective story (1942) by Agatha Christie

CLAIRE'S KNEE, a film (1970) by the French director Eric Rohmer

My Left Foot, a biopic (1989) starring Daniel Day-Lewis as the disabled Irish painter and poet Christy Brown

The HEART IS A LONELY HUNTER, a novel (1940) by Carson McCullers

The LIVER IS THE COCK'S COMB, a painting (1944) by Arshile Gorky

The Breast, a novella (1972) by the US writer Philip Roth in which a male literature professor metamorphoses into a gigantic mammary gland

Les MAMELLES DE TIRÉSIAS, an *opéra burlesque* (1947) by Francis Poulenc

RUM, BUM, AND CONCERTINA, the autobiography (1977) of George Melly

The War of Don Emmanuel's Nether Parts, a novel (1990) by Louis de Bernières

DELTA OF VENUS, a collection of erotic fiction (1977) by Anaïs Nin

A Maidenhead Well Lost, a play (1634) by Thomas Heywood

The VAGINA MONOLOGUES, a stage show (1998) by Eve Ensler

Here Lies Johnny Penis, a parody (1931) of Verlaine which landed its author, Geoffrey, Count Montalk, in Wormwood Scrubs for six months

PUPPETRY OF THE PENIS, a cabaret show (1998) conceived by Simon Morley and David Friend

Boar's Head. *See* AT THE BOAR'S HEAD.

Bohème, La (French, 'the bohemian girl'). An opera by Giacomo Puccini (1858–1924), to a libretto by Giuseppe Giacosa and Luigi Illica, first performed in 1896. The story is based on the novel *Scènes de la vie bohème* (1847–9) by Henri Murger (1822–61). The setting is the bohemian Latin quarter of Paris, and the bohemian girl is Mimi, whose 'tiny hand is frozen' (according to the famous aria sung by her lover, the penniless poet Rodolfo). In the end she dies of tuberculosis. There is also an opera of the same name by Ruggiero Leoncavallo (1857–1919), first performed in 1897.

Boléro. A long, slow and sexy orchestral crescendo by Maurice Ravel (1875–1937), unremittingly utilizing the rhythm of the traditional Spanish dance of the same name. Originally the music was for a ballet (1928), but it immediately became a very popular concert piece. *Boléro* featured on the soundtrack of the romantic film comedy *10* (1979), in which Dudley Moore lusts after Bo Derek, and was also famously used by the British ice-dancers Jayne Torvill and Christopher Dean in their performance at the 1984 Winter Olympics, for which they won the gold medal.

Bonfire of the Vanities, The. A novel (1987) by the US writer Tom Wolfe (b.1931), providing an acerbic and panoramic picture of 1980s New York society, intermixing a variety of metropolitan tribes, from Manhattan yuppies to the ghetto-dwellers of the Bronx.

The title refers to the two occasions in the 1490s when, at the urging of the reformer Girolamo Savonarola (1452–98), the citizens of Florence made a huge 'bonfire of vanities' on which they immolated their worldly goods. One supposes that Wolfe intended his novel to serve the same purpose for 1980s New York yuppie values.

A misguided attempt at a film version (1990) was directed by Brian de Palma.

See also VANITY FAIR.

Bonjour Tristesse. A novel (1954; English translation, 1955) by Françoise Sagan (pen-name of Françoise Quoirez; b.1935). The title literally translates as 'Good morning, sadness', although the English translation uses the French title. The book, written in ten weeks in a deserted family apartment after a tiff with her mother, is about the self-discovery of a precocious 17-year-old girl, Cécile, who is obsessed with life and love. The title quotes from a poem by Paul Éluard:

> *Adieu tristesse*
> *Bonjour tristesse*
> *Tu es inscrite dans les lignes du plafond*
> *Tu es inscrite dans les yeux que j'aime*
> *Tu n'es pas tout à fait la misère*
> *Car les lèvres les plus pauvres te dénoncent*
> *Par un sourire*
> *Bonjour tristesse.*
>
> ('Farewell sadness/Good morning sadness/You are written in the lines of the ceiling/You are written in the eyes that I love/You are not entirely misery/For your weakest lips betray you/By a smile/Good morning sadness.')
>
> PAUL ÉLUARD: *La vie immédiate* (1932)

Book of the Duchess, The. A long elegiac 'dream' poem by Geoffrey Chaucer (*c.*1343–1400), written *c.*1369–70. The 'Duchess' in question is assumed to be Blanche, duchess of Lancaster, the first wife of John of Gaunt. She died of the plague in September 1369. The reason for this identification is that in part of the poem a 'man in blak' remembers his love for his wife 'White' (Blanche) and laments her death.

Box and Cox. A farce by John Maddison Morton (1811–91), first performed in 1847. The story, derived from two French vaudevilles, concerns the deceitful Mrs Bouncer, a lodging-house landlady, who lets the same room to two men, Box and Cox. Unknown to each other they occupy the room alternately, one being out at work all day, the other all night. Arthur Sullivan turned the farce into a short opera, *Cox and Box*, with a libretto by Francis Cowley Burnand, which was first performed in 1867. Subsequently the phrase 'Box and Cox' has come to mean 'by turns', 'turn and turn about' or 'alternately'.

Boys from Brazil, The. A film (1978) based on a novel of the same name (1976) by Ira Levin (b.1929). Although the title suggests a light-hearted musical about samba players, the 'boys from Brazil' are clones of Adolf Hitler prepared by Dr Josef Mengele (played by Gregory Peck), a real-life Nazi doctor known as the 'Angel of Death' because of his hideous experiments on concentration-camp inmates. Mengele (1911–?78) escaped to

South America after the Second World War, and his body was found in Brazil in 1986. In the film he is pursued by Ezra Lieberman (played by Laurence Olivier), a character reminiscent of the real-life Nazi hunter Simon Wiesenthal.

Boy's Own Story, A. The first (1982) in a trilogy of semi-autobiographical novels by the US novelist Edmund White (b.1940). It charts a boy's growing awareness of his homosexuality. The others are *The Beautiful Room is Empty* (1988) and *FAREWELL SYMPHONY* (1997).

The title is an ironic echo of *The Boy's Own Paper* (often referred to as 'the BOP'), a boys' magazine published from 1879 to 1967, initially by the Religious Tract Society. The last issue of the BOP featured on its cover the 21-year-old Manchester United footballer George Best, described as a role model who 'doesn't smoke, drinks only occasionally and restricts his card-playing to sessions which ease the boredom of travelling'.

Brandy of the Damned. A collection of essays on classical music (1964) by Colin Wilson (b.1931). The title comes from a line of Don Juan in Shaw's play *MAN AND SUPERMAN* (1903):

> Hell is full of musical amateurs. Music is the brandy of the damned.
>
> GEORGE BERNARD SHAW: *Man and Superman*, III

Brave New World. A dystopian novel (1932) by Aldous Huxley (1894–1963). Its portrayal of an imagined future world state in which men and women are processed into standardized batches by genetic engineering and lifelong conditioning was originally conceived as a challenge to the claims of H.G. Wells (1866–1946) for the desirability of eugenics. The title derives from Miranda's exclamation in Shakespeare's *The TEMPEST* (1611):

> O brave new world,
> That has such people in't!
>
> V.i

Breakfast at Tiffany's. A novella (1958) by the US writer Truman Capote (1924–84) about the uninhibited exploits in New York of 18-year-old Holly Golightly. She has a homespun cure for the 'reds', worse than the mere 'blues', the latter being 'because you're getting fat or maybe it's been raining too long':

> Reds are horrible. You're afraid and you sweat like hell ... something bad is going to happen and you don't know what.

The remedy is 'to get into a taxi and go to Tiffany's', the upmarket jewellery store. A bland, asexual film version (1961), directed by Blake Edwards, starred Audrey Hepburn as Holly.

Breath. The sparest play (1970) of the increasingly minimalist playwright Samuel Beckett (1906–89). Life, the universe and everything is pared down to a 30-second drama in which the lights go up on a stage covered with rubbish; nothing moves, but the sound of a breath is heard, and then a cry. In the same year Beckett refused to go to Stockholm to receive his Nobel Prize in person because he did not wish to make a speech.

Breathless (French title: *À Bout de Souffle*). An influential film (1959) by the French Nouvelle Vague ('New Wave') director, Jean-Luc Godard (b.1930), based on a story suggested by François Truffaut (1932–84). It starred Jean-Paul Belmondo and Jean Seberg in a largely improvised plot about small-time gangsterism and helped to establish a new genre in European cinema. Both narrative and editing are jumpy and frenetic – indeed 'breathless'. A limp 1983 remake with the same English title, directed by James McBride, starred Richard Gere and transferred the action to Los Angeles.

Bride of Lammermoor, The. A novel by Sir Walter Scott (1771–1832), published in 1819. The 'bride' is Lucy Ashton, who kills her husband and goes mad, and 'Lammermoor' refers to the wild but gently rolling Lammermuir Hills of East Lothian. The novel is perhaps not as well known as the operatic version by Gaetano Donizetti (1797–1848), *Lucia di Lammermoor* (1835; libretto by Salvatore Cammarano), with its famous 'mad scene'.

Brideshead Revisited. A novel (1945) by Evelyn Waugh (1903–66) about the aristocracy and the Catholic faith in the years 1923–39, subtitled *The Sacred and Profane Memories of Captain Charles Ryder*. Brideshead Castle is the seat of the Marchmain family, and the story is told in retrospect by Charles Ryder, whose army unit in the Second World War is billeted at Brideshead. When he was a student at Oxford, Charles was romantically involved with Sebastian Flyte, the charming but dissolute younger Marchmain son, owner of a teddy bear called Aloysius, and his sister Julia. In his letters, Waugh referred to the evolving novel as his 'M.O.'

(Magnum Opus) and 'G.E.N.' (Great English Novel; compare *The* GREAT AMERICAN NOVEL). The lavish and highly acclaimed television series (1981) was scripted by John Mortimer; Brideshead itself was played by Castle Howard, in Yorkshire.

The 'revisited' formulation in titles – as in Samuel Butler's EREWHON *Revisited* – probably goes back to Wordsworth's poem 'Yarrow Revisited' (1831), which followed his 'Yarrow Visited' (1814), itself so titled because during his 1803 tour of Scotland the poet ran out of time to visit the valley of the River Yarrow, in the Borders, and wrote a poem called 'Yarrow Unvisited'.

Bride stripped bare by her Bachelors, even, The. A painting on two large panels of glass by the Dadaist Marcel Duchamp (1887–1968); it is also called *The Large Glass* (to distinguish it from the same artist's *Little Glass*). The work consists of meticulously painted but indecipherable fragments of machinery (although a coffee grinder is apparent). Duchamp worked on the piece between 1915 and 1923, in search of an ideal of 'painting of precision and beauty of indifference'. The painting is said by some to mock the frustrations of physical love, and by others to satirize the cult of the machine.

Bridge, The. A long poem (1930) by the US poet Hart Crane (1899–1932). The work is a Whitmanesque celebration of America, its culture and history, and the image of Brooklyn Bridge acts as a link between past and present, a symbol of imagination and striving:

> O Sleepless as the river under thee,
> Vaulting the sea, the prairies' dreaming sod,
> Unto us lowliest sometime sweep, descend
> And of the curveship lend a myth to God.
>
> HART CRANE: *The Bridge*, proem 'To Brooklyn Bridge'

Brooklyn Bridge is a suspension bridge in New York City, spanning the East River and so linking Brooklyn and Manhattan Island. It was built in 1869–83, and incorporates a number of impressive technical innovations. With its tough, angular, futuristic structure, it became something of an icon for American modernists, being the subject of semi-abstract paintings by, for example, John Marin (1910 and 1932) and Joseph Stella (1917–18). More recently, David and Victoria ('Posh Spice') Beckham chose to call their son Brooklyn, allegedly because he was conceived while they crossed the bridge.

Bridge of San Luis Rey, The. A novel (1927) by the US writer Thornton Wilder (1897–1975), which won the Pulitzer Prize for fiction.

> On Friday noon, July the twentieth, 1714, the finest bridge in all Peru broke and precipitated five travellers into the gulf below.

Brother Juniper, a witness to the accident, works for six years, 'knocking at all the doors in Lima, asking thousands of questions', to investigate why God should have chosen those five to die. In the end his book is burned and he goes to the stake for heresy. The conclusion of the abbess, who as a nun brought up one of the victims, is that:

> There is a land of the living and a land of the dead, and the bridge is love, the only survival, the only meaning.

A film version (1944) was directed by Rowland V. Lee.

'Bridge of Sighs, The'. A poem (1844) by Thomas Hood (1799–1845) about the repentance and suicide of a 'fallen woman'. The original 'Bridge of Sighs' is in Venice, a short covered passageway at first-storey level. It traverses the canal between the Doge's Palace and the neighbouring building, the former state prison of the Venetian Republic – hence the name. It was designed in 1589 by Antonio da Ponte (1512–*c.*1595), and features in Byron's *CHILDE HAROLD'S PILGRIMAGE*. The name has also been given to the similar bridge built in 1827–31 across the River Cam at St John's College, Cambridge, and to one across a lane in Oxford (1913) linking two parts of Hertford College.

> The bleak wind of March
> Made her tremble and shiver;
> But not the dark arch,
> Or the black flowing river.
>
> THOMAS HOOD: 'The Bridge of Sighs'

Bridge on the River Kwai, The. A film (1957) adapted by Carl Foreman and Michael Wilson from the novel *The Bridge over the River Kwai* (1952) by Pierre Boulle (1912–94). Directed by David Lean, it starred Alec Guinness as Colonel Nicholson, the commanding officer of British prisoners of war forced by the Japanese to build a railway bridge over the River Kwai in Burma during the Second World War. Nicholson was based on the real Lieutenant-Colonel Philip Toosey, who was the senior officer in a Japanese prisoner-of-war camp at Tamarkan. Unlike the film character, Toosey actively assisted those who tried to escape and sanctioned various attempts to sabotage the two bridges his men were obliged to build. The two bridges, one wood and one metal, were disabled by Allied bombers but never totally destroyed as they are in the film.

The film famously included the mass-whistling of 'Colonel Bogey', a bracing march tune composed in 1914 by the military bandmaster Kenneth Alford, whose real name was Frederick Ricketts (1881–1945), and which was enthusiastically adapted in the Second World War for an anonymous bawdy quatrain about the Nazi leadership:

> Hitler has only got one ball,
> Goering has two but very small,
> Himmler has something similar,
> But poor old Goebbels has no balls at all.

Bridges of Madison County, The. A romantic novel (1993) by the US writer Robert James Waller (b.1939). The story, a novel within a novel, concerns Francesca, a housewife whose life is suddenly transformed while her family is away by Robert Kincaid, a man who asks for directions. He has come to Madison County, Iowa, to photograph the seven local covered bridges, a noted architectural feature of the area. They have a fleeting affair. A film version (1995) proved more acceptable to the critics; it was directed by Clint Eastwood, who also took the role of Kincaid, playing opposite Meryl Streep. Blaise Aguirre's *The Fridges of Madison County* (1997) is a parody.

Bridge Too Far, A. A memorable and star-studded film (1977) based on a book by Cornelius Ryan (1920–76) about the 1944 Allied airborne landings in the Netherlands. The landings were intended to capture eleven bridges needed for the Allied invasion of Germany, but the enterprise failed grievously at Arnhem. In advance of the operation General Frederick Browning is said to have protested to Field Marshal Montgomery, who was in overall command: 'But, sir, we may be going a bridge too far.' The phrase 'a bridge too far' has since become a journalistic cliché.

Brief History of Time, A. A book (1988), subtitled 'From the Big Bang to Black Holes', by the British theoretical physicist Stephen Hawking (b.1942), which attempts to explain to a lay audience his ideas about the beginning of the universe, the nature of space-time and black holes, and the possible synthesis of quantum mechanics with the theory of relativity. In it the author asks such questions as 'Why does the universe go to all the bother of existing?' The book was a surprise

BRIDGES

'The BRIDGE OF SIGHS', a poem (1843) by Thomas Hood

'The Tay Bridge Disaster', a masterpiece of poetic bathos (1880) by William McGonagall:

> Beautiful Railway Bridge of the Silv'ry Tay!
> Alas, I am very sorry to say
> That ninety lives have been taken away
> On the last Sabbath day of 1879,
> Which will be remember'd for a very long time.

The BRIDGE OF SAN LUIS REY, a novel (1927) by Thornton Wilder

The BRIDGE, a long poem (1930) by Hart Crane

Waterloo Bridge, two films (1931, 1940), featuring a tragic wartime romance in London

Comedy on the Bridge, an opera (1937) by Bohuslav Martinů

A View from the Bridge, a play (1955) by Arthur Miller involving a longshoreman and illegal immigrants

The BRIDGE ON THE RIVER KWAI, a film (1957) set in the Second World War

The Bridge at Remagen, a film (1968) about the Second World War battle to cross the Rhine

A BRIDGE TOO FAR, a Second World War film (1974)

The BRIDGES OF MADISON COUNTY, a novel (1993) by Robert James Waller, later a film

---

success, remaining on the UK bestseller list for more than three years, though it was axiomatically more bought than read.

Brighton Rock. An 'entertainment' (1938) by Graham Greene (1904–91), centring on crime and corruption in the seaside resort of Brighton, Sussex, with Pinkie, a young scarfaced hoodlum, as the anti-hero. 'Rock' here is the confection in the form of a cylindrical stick of hard peppermint-flavoured sugar, often pink on the outside, sold at holiday resorts, with the name of the place worked round the inside all the way down the stick. A film version (1947), to whose script Greene contributed, was directed by John Boulting, with Richard Attenborough in the role of Pinkie.

Bring Me the Head of Alfredo Garcia. A Western (1974) directed by Samuel Peckinpah. The head in question belongs to the man who seduced the daughter of the rich Mexican who issued the edict of the title. Gene Shalit was not alone in his criticism when he wrote, 'Bring me the head of the studio that released this one.' A 2001 remake, more ploddingly entitled *The Mexican*, met with more muted critical acclaim.

Bring on the Empty Horses. A second volume of memoirs (1975) by the film actor David Niven (1909–83), following a first volume entitled *The Moon's a Balloon* (1972). The explanation of the title given by Niven is that during the filming of *The Charge of the Light Brigade* (1936), the Hungarian-born director Michael Curtiz shouted 'Bring on the empty horses!' – meaning that he wished for the entrance of a hundred horses without riders.

Broadway Boogie-Woogie. A painting (1942–3) by the Dutch painter Piet Mondrian (1872–1944). For decades Mondrian had been painting 'neo-plasticist' abstracts consisting of no more than a few rectangles and lines with titles such as *Composition in Yellow and Blue* (1929); latterly colour itself had begun to absent itself from his works. Then, when the Second World War forced him to New York in 1940, the shock of being separated from his native polders seems to have given him a much-needed shot in the arm. *Broadway Boogie-Woogie* not only brings back primary colours, but includes more lines and rectangles than you could count in one glance. It is regarded as one of his finest works. Mondrian was to become even less inhibited in his *Victory Boogie-Woogie*, in which the geometrical shapes are much more loosely painted; this work was unfinished at the time of Mondrian's death.

Bronze Horseman, The (Russian title: *Medny vsadnik*). A long poem by Aleksandr Pushkin (1799–1837), written in 1833. It is a 'story of St Petersburg', in which Yevgeny, who has lost his beloved in the floods of 1824, wanders the city until he comes across the statue of Peter the Great, popularly known as the 'Bronze Horseman'. It was Peter who had built the city in 1703, reclaiming land from the marshes of the delta of the River Neva, and Yevgeny angrily blames him for his loss. The statue then comes alive, and, like the elemental force of the flooding river, pursues him in a nightmare through the streets. The statue of the 'Bronze Horseman', created by Étienne Falconet in 1782, can still be seen in Decembrists' Square (formerly Senate Square) in St Petersburg. There is a ballet (1949) of the same title, with music by the Russian composer Reinhold Glière (1875–1956).

Browning Version, The. A play (1949) by the British playwright Terence Rattigan (1911–77) about an ailing public school teacher who is humiliated both by his failure in his career and by his wife's infidelity. The title refers to a copy of Browning's translation of Aeschylus' *Agamemnon* that is presented to the teacher, Andrew Crocker-Harris, by one of his few admiring pupils. The character of Crocker-Harris was based on one of Rattigan's teachers at Harrow School, Coke Norris, who was similarly presented with a copy of the 'Browning version'. The role of Crocker-Harris was played by Michael Redgrave in the 1951 film version and by Albert Finney in the 1994 remake.

Brownout on Breadfruit Boulevard. A satirical novel (1995), set in Southeast Asia, on international political and academic organizations, by the Hong Kong-born novelist Timothy Mo (b.1950). Breadfruit Boulevard is a highway in Manila. A brownout is a reduction in electrical power causing a partial blackout, such as occurs in her hotel room just before one of the participants decides to introduce a computer virus into the records of a conference. The word also reflects the character Professor Pfeidwengeler's particular perversion, coprophilia.

Buddha of Suburbia, The. A novel (1990) by Hanif Kureishi (b.1954). The Buddha of the title is the narrator's Indian father, who precipitates a round of sexual musical chairs by leaving his English wife and setting up home with another Englishwoman, becoming regarded as a guru at her parties in the suburbs of south London. A television adaptation (1993) caused controversy for its alleged sexual explicitness.

Bulldog Drummond. An adventure thriller (1920), the first in a series, by Sapper (pen name – from his war service in the Royal Engineers, known as Sappers – of Lieutenant-Colonel H.C. McNeile; 1888–1937). Subtitled *The Adventures of a Demobilized Officer Who Found Peace Dull*, it features a hard-drinking, athletic, ex-army, amateur anti-crime agent of the

Robin Hood school, who always somehow manages to keep on the right side of the law, although his actions and attitudes are hopelessly racist, protofascist and anti-Semitic.

The nickname Bulldog (his real name is Hugh), denoting tenacity, comes from 'We are the boys of the bulldog breed', in a jingoistic music-hall song of the times by Ian Colquhon and Arthur Reece, 'Sons of the Sea, All British Born' (1897).

Drummond was based on the soldier and writer Gerard Fairlie (*c.*1900–83), but his character also displays traits of Sapper himself. Apparently Sapper urged young army officers 'of spunk' to follow his hero's example, and it was reported that a group of them had rounded up 'dope pedlars and other degenerates' from London's West End, taken them to a garage off the Great West Road and flogged them with dog whips.

A silent film version (1922), with Carlyle Blackwell in the title role, was followed by a lengthy series of British and US Bulldog Drummond films of varying quality. The last was *Some Girls Do* (1970), a feeble sequel to *Deadlier than the Male* (1967), with Richard Johnson as Drummond played *à la* James Bond, for whom he was undoubtedly an inspiration.

Bubbles. A painting (1886) by the former Pre-Raphaelite Sir John Millais (1829–96), depicting a young, curly-haired boy, clad in velvet, with pipe and bowl, blowing bubbles. The work became widely familiar when used as an advertisement for Pears' Soap. The boy concerned became Admiral Sir William James (1881–1973), affectionately known in the Royal Navy as 'Bubbles James'.

Burial of Count Orgaz, The. A painting (1586–8) by El Greco (Domenikos Theotokopoulos; 1541–1614), the Cretan-born painter active in Spain. The picture is generally regarded as one of his masterpieces, and is painted in his unique and feverish style. Orgaz is a town in central Spain, near Toledo, where, in the church of S. Tomé, the painting still hangs. According to the legend that is the subject of El Greco's picture, the Count of Orgaz had been so generous to the church that Saint Augustine and Saint Stephen appeared in person to place the noble benefactor in his tomb.

The British artist John Latham (b.1921) gave the title *The Burial of Count Orgaz* to one of his earliest 'book sculptures' (1958). Latham's bookish interests manifested themselves in the 1960s in a number of 'happenings', such as *The Skoob Tower Ceremonies*, involving the destruction of towers of books. At the end of the decade he attempted to eat a copy of the book *Art and Culture* by Clement Greenberg, the US art critic, formalist and champion of abstract expressionism.

Burning Fiery Furnace, The. A 'church parable' by Benjamin Britten (1913–77), with a libretto by William Plomer based on the Old Testament. The first performance was in Orford Church, Aldeburgh, Suffolk, in 1966.

> And whoso falleth not down and worshippeth shall the same hour be cast into the midst of a burning fiery furnace.
>
> Daniel 3:4–6

'Burnt Norton'. *See* FOUR QUARTETS.

Bury My Heart at Wounded Knee. A historical study (1971) by Dee Brown (b.1908) of the conquest of the American West and the destruction of the Native American tribes. The title comes from the last verse of a poem, 'American Names' (1927), by Stephen Vincent Benét (1898–1943):

> I shall not rest quiet in Montparnasse.
> I shall not lie easy in Winchelsea.
> You may bury my body in Sussex grass,
> You may bury my tongue at Champmedy.
> I shall not be there. I shall rise and pass.
> Bury my heart at Wounded Knee.

Wounded Knee, in South Dakota, was the site of a massacre of Teton-Sioux by US forces on 29 December 1890, in which at least 150 Native Americans, and 25 US soldiers, were killed. It marked the final suppression of Native American resistance. In the Wounded Knee protest of 1973, two years after the publication of Brown's book, some 200 armed members of the American Indian Movement occupied the symbolic site. The occupation ended after a 70-day siege, but helped to focus international attention on the US government's treatment of Native Americans.

... but all shall be well. A short orchestral work (1993) by the British composer Thomas Adès (b.1971). The title is from:

> Sin is behovely, but all shall be well and all shall be well and all manner of thing shall be well.
>
> JULIAN (or JULIANA) OF NORWICH (1342–after 1416): *Revelations of Divine Love*, chapter 27, revelation 13

These words are also quoted at the end of T.S. Eliot's 'Little Gidding' (*see FOUR QUARTETS*):

> And all shall be well and
> All manner of thing shall be well
> When the tongues of flame are in-folded
> Into the crowned knot of fire
> And the fire and the rose are one.
>
> T.S. ELIOT: *Four Quartets*, 'Little Gidding' (1942), part 5

By Grand Central Station I Sat Down and Wept. A novel (1945), in the form of a prose poem, by the Canadian novelist Elizabeth Smart (1913–86). It reflects some of the circumstances of her long-term affair with the British poet, George Barker (1913–91), with whom she had four children while Barker was married to another woman. The title plays on the first verse of Psalm 137:

> By the rivers of Babylon, there we sat down, yea, we wept, when we remembered Zion.

It refers to the narrator's reaction at Grand Central Station in New York when a meeting is missed and the affair appears to be over. There are further biblical references, drawn from the Song of Solomon, in an exchange between the police and the narrator, who has been arrested, with her lover, on a charge of crossing a state boundary for an immoral purpose.

By the Pricking of My Thumbs. A detective story (1968) by Agatha Christie (1890–1976). The title comes from the words with which the Second Witch greets the return of Macbeth, now a murderer, in Shakespeare's play:

> By the pricking of my thumbs,
> Something wicked this way comes.
>
> SHAKESPEARE: *Macbeth* (1606), IV.i

See also SOMETHING WICKED THIS WAY COMES.

C

Cabbages and Kings. The first volume of stories (1904) by O. Henry (pen name of William Sydney Porter; 1862–1910). They are set in Latin America, where Porter took refuge from justice after having been accused of embezzling funds from the chaotically organized bank for which he worked. He returned home because of his wife's illness and gave himself up to the authorities in 1897 when she died. Found guilty on a technicality, he served three years in prison, where he began writing stories to support his young daughter. The title of the first collection is from 'The Walrus and the Carpenter' by Lewis Carroll (1832–98) in *Through the Looking-Glass and What Alice Found There* (1871):

> 'The time has come,' the Walrus said,
> 'To talk of many things:
> Of shoes – and ships – and sealing wax –
> Of cabbages – and kings.'

Cakes and Ale. A novel (1930) by W. Somerset Maugham (1874–1965), in which the author satirizes the British literary establishment. Of the three novelists portrayed, Edward Driffield was said to be based on Thomas Hardy (1840–1928), Grand Old Man of Literature, and Alroy Kear on Hugh Walpole (1884–1941), while Willie Ashenden is in some respects Maugham's *alter ego*. The title comes from a remark by Sir Toby Belch to Malvolio in Shakespeare's *TWELFTH NIGHT*:

> Dost thou think, because thou art virtuous, there shall be no more cakes and ale?
>
> II.iii

Cakes and Ale is also the title of a collection of short stories (1842) by Douglas Jerrold (1803–57).

Calamity Jane. A soft-hearted Western musical (1953) starring Doris Day and Howard Keel. The original Calamity Jane was Martha Jane Burke, *née* Cannary (*c.*1852–1903), an American frontierswoman famed for her skill at riding and shooting, particularly during the Gold Rush days in the Black Hills of Dakota. It is claimed that she threatened 'calamity' to any man who tried to woo her, although she did in fact marry. In the film, she hooks up with Wild Bill Hickok.

'Caliban upon Setebos'. A dramatic monologue by Robert Browning (1812–89), published in *Dramatis Personae* (1864). Caliban is the 'savage and deformed slave' in Shakespeare's *The* TEMPEST (1611) and Setebos is his god. In Browning's poem, Caliban, speaking of himself in the third person,

> ...talks to his own self, howe'er he please,
> Touching that other, whom his dam called God.

Camille. *See* DAME AUX CAMÉLIAS, LA.

Campbell's Soup. The well-known brand of comestible was multiply immortalized by Andy Warhol (1928–87) in his 1962 stencilled picture *100 Cans of Campbell's Soup* and again in *Four Campbell's Soup Cans* (1965). Warhol's idea was not original: in 1960 Jasper Johns (b.1930) had made a sculpture of two cans of Ballantine Ale entitled *Painted Bronze*. But then, as Warhol predicted in 1963:

> Some day everybody will be thinking alike.

Canterbury Tales, The. A poem of some 17,000 lines by Geoffrey Chaucer (*c.*1343–1400). It was probably begun around 1387 and worked on into the 1390s, but apparently not completed. It was one of the first pieces of literature to be printed in England, in 1477 by William Caxton. The tales do not come from Canterbury, but are, within the fictional framework of the work, told by various pilgrims en route to the shrine of St Thomas à Becket at Canterbury – one of the most popular pilgrimage destinations in the Middle Ages. There is some uncertainty as to what order Chaucer intended the stories to be in, but the following is how they appear in the authoritative *Riverside* edition, following the Ellesmere manuscript:

General Prologue

The Knight's Tale

The Miller's Tale

The Reeve's Tale (a reeve was a manorial steward)

The Cook's Tale

The Man of Law's Tale

The Wife of Bath's Tale

The Friar's Tale

The Summoner's Tale (a summoner summoned delinquents to appear before an ecclesiastical court)

The Clerk's Tale (a clerk was an ecclesiastical student)

The Merchant's Tale

The Squire's Tale

The Franklin's Tale (a franklin was a landowner of free but not noble birth, probably ranking below the gentry)

The Physician's Tale

The Pardoner's Tale (pardoners sold papal indulgences, a much abused practice)

The Shipman's Tale (a shipman was a ship's master)

The Prioress's Tale

Chaucer's Tale of Sir Thopas

Chaucer's Tale of Melibeus

The Monk's Tale

The Nun's Priest's Tale

The Second Nun's Tale

The Canon's Yeoman's Tale

The Manciple's Tale (a manciple was a servant who bought provisions for a college or inn of court)

The Parson's Tale

Chaucer's Retraction

It seems that Chaucer's original idea was to have many more stories, since in the General Prologue the host proposes that each of the 30 or so pilgrims tells four tales each.

A film version (1971) by Pier Paolo Pasolini (1922–75), focusing on the bawdier tales, was not well received.

Cantos, The. The long poem-in-progress of Ezra Pound (1885–1972), begun in 1915 or earlier, on which Pound worked for the rest of his life. A *canto* (Italian, literally 'song') is a subdivision of a long poem; the term was used by Dante, Ariosto and others, introduced into England by Edmund Spenser, and subsequently used by Byron. As early as 1912, in an early draft of a Canto, Pound explained the work's *raison d'être*:

> ... the modern world
> Needs such a rag-bag to stuff all its thought in.

The work as it unfolded is indeed a rag-bag, formidably allusive (in places Chinese ideograms are deployed), at times dazzlingly lyrical, at others ploddingly prosaic and propagandist. As Cyril Connolly wrote:

> One enters them like a sunlit church with a service going on in a dark corner and suddenly the music pierces ... A moment later all is muttering and mumbling.

The work was published in stages. The first three Cantos were published in *Poetry* in 1917, then there followed: *A Draft of XXX Cantos* (1930), *Eleven New Cantos* (1934), *The Fifth Decad of Cantos* (1937), *Cantos LII–LXXI* (1940), *The* PISAN CANTOS (1948), *Section: Rock-Drill* (1955), *Thrones* (1959), and *Drafts and Fragments of Cantos CX to CXVII* (1970).

Capriol Suite. A suite of six dances for string orchestra by the English composer Peter Warlock (Philip Heseltine; 1894–1930). Capriol was a character in *Orchésographie* (1589), a book on dance by the French priest Thoinot Arbeau (Jehan Tabouret; 1519–95), which included tunes that form the basis of Warlock's suite.

Captain Corelli's Mandolin. A novel (1994) by Louis de Bernières (b.1954), set on the Greek island of Cephalonia. The major part of the action takes place during the Second World War and concerns the romance between the local doctor's daughter and Captain Antonio Corelli, a member of the Italian occupying forces, who is a skilled performer on the mandolin. A survey in 2000 revealed that the book was one of the ten sources most used for readings at weddings. A highly simplified film version was released in 2001, with Nicolas Cage as Corelli.

Caravan Passes, The. *See* DOGS BARK, THE.

Carmina Burana. A highly rhythmic and lyrical 'scenic oratorio' by Carl Orff (1895–1982), first performed in 1937. The title means 'Songs of Beuron', and the subtitle *cantiones profanae* means 'profane songs'. The text consists of poems in Old French, Old German and Latin about love, drink and other pleasures; they come from a 13th-century manuscript found in the Benedictine monastery of Beuron in Bavaria. In Britain the work is usually given in a concert version, but in Germany it is often staged.

Carnaval: Scènes mignonnes sur quatre notes. A set of 20 pieces for piano (opus 9, 1835) by Robert Schumann (1810–56). The French subtitle translates as 'dainty scenes on four notes', which are derived from Asch, the home town of Ernestine von Fricken, with whom Schumann was then in love. ASCH are also the only letters in the composer's name that yield notes: *As* is the German for A flat (or 'AS' can be A natural plus *Es*, German for E flat); C; and B natural (written as *H* in Germany). The music portrays a carnival ball at which Schumann (in his contrasting personae of Florestan and Eusebius), Chopin, Paganini and Clara Wieck (Schumann's future wife) are all present. Schumann's *Carnival Jest from Vienna* (German *Faschingsschwank aus Wien*), a set of five piano pieces (opus 26, 1839), is also based on the notes ASCH, and may at one time have been destined to become part of *Carnaval.*

Carpetbaggers, The. A novel (1961) by Harold Robbins (born Francis Kane, when he was adopted in 1927 taking the name Harold Rubin, which he later changed to Robbins; 1916–97). Robbins explains the origin of his title:

> And behind the Northern Armies came another body of men. They came by the hundreds, yet each travelled alone … And on their back, or across their saddle, or on top of their wagon was the inevitable faded multicoloured bag made of worn and ragged remnants of carpet into which they had crammed all their worldly possessions. It was from these bags that they got their name. The Carpetbaggers.

Originally a 'carpetbagger', as Robbins indicates, was a Northerner who moved into the South at the end of the American Civil War (1861–5) to participate in Reconstruction (the political and social reform of the ex-slave states). Southern whites thought of these incomers – some of whom stood for political office where they had no local connections – as entirely motivated by self-interest and resented them deeply. The word subsequently came to be used generally of an unscrupulous opportunist, especially in politics or the financial markets.

Robbins's novel is about big business and sex and is based on the career of the US industrialist, film producer and aviator Howard Hughes (1905–76). The action, set between 1925 and 1945, with flashbacks, mainly concerns Jonas Cord, whose outward interests are 'airplanes, explosives and money and, when the spirit moves him, occasionally [making] a motion picture'. A melodramatic film version (1964) was directed by Edward Dmytryk.

***Carry On* films.** A long-running series of British film comedies that began with *Carry On Sergeant* in 1958. The order 'Carry on, sergeant' is commonly given by an officer after the latter has been addressing his men; while 'to carry on' is to cause a fuss or commotion, and/or to indulge in morally dubious behaviour. The humour of the films was mostly unsubtle, broadly camp or even 'blue', but the series won a loyal following and still has its devotees, despite (or because of) the complete lack of political correctness. There were 31 in the sequence, all with titles beginning *Carry On*, such as *Carry On Doctor* (1960) and *Carry On up the Khyber* (1968), and regular members of the cast included Kenneth Williams, Charles Hawtrey, Sid James, Joan Sims, Barbara Windsor and Hattie Jacques. The series proper ended in 1978, although the formula was temporarily revived for *Carry on Columbus* (1992), into which Julian Clary injected his own brand of camp.

Carve Her Name with Pride. A film (1958) based on a book by R.J. Minney about the heroic wartime career and ultimate death of Violette Szabo, who was executed in 1945 by the Germans as an Allied spy following her capture on active service in France during the Second World War. The film starred Virginia McKenna as Szabo, and the title refers to the carving of Violette Szabo's name on a memorial after the war. Szabo, who was awarded a posthumous George Cross, was the daughter of a London taxi driver and a French woman. She was recruited into the Special Operations Executive (SOE) and was only 23 years old when she was executed. SOE's code and cypher expert, Leo Marks, wrote a poem that was used by agents in France as the basis for encrypting radio messages to be sent back to Britain. Previously agents had used well-known poems, but this made it too easy for the Germans to crack the codes. Marks's poem is quoted in the film:

The life that I have
Is all that I have
And the life that I have
Is yours.
The love that I have
Of the life that I have
Is yours and yours and yours …
Is yours and yours and yours …

Casablanca. A classic romantic film melodrama (1942), based on a script by Julius and Philip Epstein, largely set in a bar in wartime Casablanca, in Vichy-held Morocco. Starring Humphrey Bogart as bar-owner Rick and Ingrid Bergman as his old flame, the film defied all expectations for its success. Originally intended as a vehicle for star George Raft, it was demoted to a B-picture when he was unavailable, and the parts were passed to Bogart and Bergman only after being first offered to Ronald Reagan and Ann Sheridan. The performers rather then the plot were the key to the film's success. A remake in 1983, starring David Soul, was greeted with derision, as was another version in 1990, Sydney Pollack's *Havana*, set in Cuba and starring Robert Redford. The highly crafted and extensively quoted script has given rise to other movie titles, such as *PLAY IT AGAIN SAM* and *The USUAL SUSPECTS*.

See also NIGHT IN CASABLANCA, A.

Castle Rackrent. A lively novel (1800) with an Irish setting by Maria Edgeworth (1768–1849). The story concerns the decline in the fortunes of three generations of Rackrents, members of the Protestant Ascendancy, and is narrated by their steward, Thady Quirk. Legally speaking, 'rack-rent' is the annual rent that can reasonably be charged for a property, but colloquially 'rack-rent' is any rent that is 'racked' (i.e. stretched) to an excessively high amount.

Castration: An Abbreviated History of Western Manhood. An academic study (2001) by Gary Taylor, described in the catalogue of publisher Routledge as 'cutting-edge' (from the *Bookseller*, 24 August 2001).

Cat and the Canary, The. A stage thriller (1922) by John Willard (1885–1942) that has inspired a host of film adaptations and imitations. As mourners gather for the reading of a will in an old, dark house, several of them fall victim to the maniac who haunts its spooky corridors, preying on them as a cat might tease and kill a canary. Most film adaptations played the story for laughs, including the best known 1939 version, which did much to establish comedian Bob Hope as a major star.

Catcher in the Rye, The. The first novel (1951) by J.D. Salinger (b.1919), about a mixed-up teenager called Holden Caulfield. The character first appeared in a story published in the *New Yorker* in 1946, in which year Salinger withdrew an earlier version of the book. The title of this cult novel is alluded to in chapter 22, when Holden's younger sister goads him into naming 'something you'd like to be'. It transpires that he has misread the lines

> Gin a body meet a body
> Comin' thro' the rye …

in the song 'COMIN' THRO' THE RYE' by Robert Burns (1759–96), as 'catch a body':

> 'I keep picturing all these little kids playing some game in this big field of rye … And I'm standing on the edge of some crazy cliff … I have to catch everybody if they start to go over the cliff … I'd just be the catcher in the rye. I know it's crazy.'

Catch-22. A novel (1961) by Joseph Heller (1923–99) about the experiences of Captain Yossarian of the 256th United States (Army) bombing squadron in Italy during the Second World War. Yossarian's main aim is to avoid getting killed. 'Catch-22' has become part of everyday speech to indicate a 'no-win' situation. Heller originally defined Catch-22 in chapter 5 of the novel:

> There was only one catch and that was Catch-22, which specified that a concern for one's own safety in the face of dangers that were real and immediate was the process of a rational mind. Orr was crazy and could be grounded. All he had to do was to ask; and as soon as he did, he would no longer be crazy and have to fly more missions. Orr would be crazy to fly more missions and sane if he didn't, but if he was sane he had to fly them. If he flew them he was crazy and didn't have to; but if he didn't want to he was sane and had to.

Heller's original title had been *Catch-18*, but his editor Robert Gottlieb pointed out that they were publishing Leon Uris's *Mila 18* in the same season. Heller later recalled:

> I thought of *Catch-Eleven*, because it's the only other number to start with an open vowel sound. I guess we doubled that.

A film version (1970) with Alan Arkin as Yossarian was directed by Mike Nichols. Heller's novel *Closing Time* (1994) features some of the same characters in later life.

'Cathédrale engloutie, La' (French, 'the engulfed cathedral'). A piano piece by Debussy (1862–1918), written in 1909 and included as no 10 in the first book of *Préludes*. The cathedral is that of the legendary drowned city of Ys, said to lie beneath the waters of the bay of Douarnenez in Brittany, and whose bells are said to be audible from time to time. Debussy's piece inspired a number of paintings with the same title by the Welsh artist Ceri Richards (1903–71). The legend of Ys gave rise to the opera *Le Roi d'Ys* (1888) by Edouard Lalo (1823–92), with a libretto by Edouard Blau, in which the city is saved from drowning by its patron saint.

Cathleen ni Houlihan. A play by W.B. Yeats (1865–1939), first performed in 1902. The title role was played by the ardent nationalist Maud Gonne (1865–1953), with whom Yeats was passionately in love. However, she rejected his several proposals of marriage, and instead married Major John MacBride, who was to be executed for his part in the Easter Rising of 1916. Cathleen (or Kathleen) ni Houlihan (or Hoolihan) is a personification of Ireland as a woman, as the Marianne is of France. She originated with the Irish Jacobite poets of the 18th century. In Yeats's play she is the mysterious wandering 'Old Woman':

> Some call me the Poor Old Woman, and there are some that call me Cathleen, the daughter of Houlihan.

She inspires Michael, who is about to be married, to join the uprising of the United Irishmen in 1798. When last seen, according to one of the other characters, she has transmogrified into 'a young girl, and she had the walk of a queen.'

> If you want to interest him [an Irishman] in Ireland, you've got to call the unfortunate island Kathleen ni Hoolihan and pretend she's a little old woman.
>
> GEORGE BERNARD SHAW: *John Bull's Other Island* (1904)

> Did that play of mine send out
> Certain men the English shot?
>
> W.B. YEATS: 'The Man and the Echo', in *Last Poems* (1939)

Cat on a Hot Tin Roof. A play (1955) by Tennessee Williams (1911–83) that was subsequently turned into a successful film (1958) starring Elizabeth Taylor, Paul Newman and Burl Ives. The title echoes the old English saying 'like a cat on hot bricks', which dates back to at least the 17th century, and this link is interestingly furthered by the fact that one of the main characters in Williams's story is named Brick. The play began life as a short story entitled 'Three Players of a Summer Game', but Williams changed it when he developed the tale for the stage, during the course of which he first introduced Brick's wife Maggie ('Maggie the Cat'). The author later explained that his own father had coined the phrase, habitually complaining to his wife that she made him 'nervous as a cat on a hot tin roof'.

> What is the victory of a cat on a hot tin roof? – I wish I knew … Just staying on it, I guess, as long as she can.
>
> *Cat on a Hot Tin Roof*, I

Cats. A musical comedy (1981) with a score by Andrew Lloyd Webber (b.1948) in which all the main characters are cats. It is based on poems from *Old Possum's Book of Practical Cats* (1939) by T.S. Eliot (1888–1965), and royalties from its long West End run transformed the fortunes of Eliot's original publisher, Faber and Faber.

CATS AND THEIR RELATIVES

'Cat's Fugue', a piece for harpsichord by Domenico Scarlatti

'CAT' WALTZ, a piano piece by Chopin

'The Black Cat', a story (1845) by Edgar Allan Poe, also made into a couple of films

'The Owl and the Pussycat', a poem (1871) by Edward Lear

The CAT AND THE CANARY, a stage thriller (1922) by John Willard

CAT ON A HOT TIN ROOF, a play (1955) by Tennessee Williams

Fritz the Cat, an adult cartoon film (1971) by Robert Crumb

TOUCH NOT THE CAT, a romantic thriller (1976) by Mary Stewart

CATS, a musical comedy (1981) with a score by Andrew Lloyd Webber, based on *Old Possum's Book of Practical Cats* by T.S. Eliot

Pussy, King of the Pirates, a novel (1995) by Kathy Acker, also recorded on CD with the punk band the Mekons

ANDROCLES AND THE LION, a play (1913) by George Bernard Shaw

The LION, THE WITCH AND THE WARDROBE, a children's fantasy (1950) by C.S. Lewis

The LION IN WINTER, a film (1968) about Henry II

The Lion King, a Disney animated film (1994)

'The Tyger', a poem (1794) by William Blake

Save the Tiger, a film (1973) starring Jack Lemmon as a middle-aged businessman

MOON TIGER, a novel (1987) by Penelope Lively

Crouching Tiger, Hidden Dragon, an Oscar-winning martial arts romance (2001) directed by Ang Lee

The HIND AND THE PANTHER, a religious allegory (1687) by John Dryden

'The Panther', a poem (1907) by the German poet Rainer Maria Rilke

The LEOPARD, a novel (1958) by Giuseppe di Lampedusa

'Cat' Waltz. A nickname of the piano waltz, opus 34 no 3, by Chopin (1810–49), a passage of which is supposed to have been inspired by a cat running up and down the composer's keyboard. A similar story lies behind the so-called 'Cat's Fugue' for harpsichord by Domenico Scarlatti (1685–1757). *See also* 'MINUTE' WALTZ (the alternative nickname for the 'Dog' Waltz).

Caucasian Chalk Circle, The (German title: *Der kaukasische Kreidekreis*). A play (1948) by the German playwright Bertolt Brecht (1898–1956) set in Caucasia in the aftermath of the Second World War, in which the competing claims of a child's biological mother and its foster mother are decided by a bogus judge (actually a thief and poacher). The judge, Azdak, orders that the matter be settled by the two women having a tug of war with the child within a chalk circle. The foster mother lets go first, fearing the child will be hurt, thus demonstrating her greater love, and is granted custody of the child. The story has clear similarities to the biblical judgment of Solomon (1 Kings 3:16–28), but Brecht's play was based on an earlier play, *Der Kreidekreis* (1924) by the German writer Klabund (pseudonym of Alfred Henschke, 1890–1928), which was itself an adaptation of a Chinese play from the Yunan dynasty (1206–1368).

Cavalleria rusticana. *See* PAGLIACCI, I.

'Cav and Pag'. *See* PAGLIACCI, I.

Cecilia, St. *See* ST CECILIA (panel, pp.397–8).

Celtic Twilight, The. A collection of stories (1893) by W.B. Yeats (1865–1939) based on Irish folk tales. 'Celtic twilight' has subsequently come to be used somewhat disparagingly for Irish folklore in general, particularly as romantically revivified by Yeats, Lady Augusta Gregory and others in the 1890s. The anonymous obituary of Yeats in the *Daily Express* (30 January 1939) said the poet 'scoffed at fairies, but they made his living'.

Cement Garden, The. A novella (1978) by Ian McEwan (b.1948). The teenage narrator lives with his family, but the death of his father, and then of his mother, leaves him, his two sisters and their small brother alone in the house. Rather than tell anyone, with the risk that they will be taken into care and separated, they conceal their mother's body in the cellar in a tin trunk, filled with cement ('the cement garden'). A gamut of sexual deviation propels the action to its dark denouement. A disturbing film version (1993) was directed by Andrew Birkin.

Cenci, The. A tragedy in verse by Percy Bysshe Shelley (1792–1822), published in 1819 but not performed until 1891. In his preface Shelley outlines the origin of his title and his story:

> A manuscript was communicated to me during my travels in Italy, which was copied form the archives of the Cenci Palace at Rome, and contains a detailed account of the horrors which ended in the extinction of one of the noblest and richest families of that city during the Pontificate of Clement VIII, in the year 1599. The story is, that an old man having spent his life in debauchery and wickedness, conceived at

> length an implacable hatred towards his children; which showed itself towards one daughter under the form of an incestuous passion, aggravated by every circumstance of cruelty and violence.

The daughter, Beatrice Cenci, with the aid of her brother and mother-in-law, proceeded to plot and carry out the murder of the old man, Count Francesco Cenci, for which they were put to death.

The English composer Patrick Hadley (1899–1973) wrote a *Scene from Shelley's The Cenci* (1951) for soprano and orchestra.

Chandos Anthems. Twelve anthems by Handel (1685–1759), written between 1716 and 1720 when Handel was director of music for James Brydges, earl of Carnarvon (1673–1744), who was to become the duke of Chandos. The anthems were intended for performance at the earl's chapel at Cannons, his palace near Edgware, Middlesex.

Changeling, The. A tragedy by Thomas Middleton (1580–1627), in collaboration with William Rowley (?1585–1626), written in 1622 (published 1653). The title comes from the sub-plot, set in a madhouse, in which Antonio, enamoured of Isabella, the wife of the keeper, pretends to be a 'changeling' in order to be near her. Traditionally, a changeling is a child swapped by the fairies for the parents' real child; such a story explained a sickly, backward or mad person. In Middleton and Rowley's play, the more symbolic 'changeling' is the anti-heroine of the main plot, Beatrice-Joanna, who, from innocent beginnings, becomes immersed in a downward spiral of lust and murder.

Chariots of Fire. A film (1981) about the rivalry between two British runners – Harold Abrahams and Eric Liddell – competing in the 1924 Olympics. Written by Colin Welland (b. 1934) and starring Ben Cross and Ian Charleson, it features a memorable (though now rather hackneyed) soundtrack by Vangelis, which quickly became a signature tune for sporting enthusiasts everywhere. The title came from William Blake's poem 'Jerusalem', the preface to his epic *MILTON* (1804–8). Today 'Jerusalem', in its 1916 musical setting by Hubert Parry (1848–1918) is best known as an anthemic hymn with strong patriotic overtones:

> Bring me my bow of burning gold!
> Bring me my arrows of desire!
> Bring me my spear! O clouds, unfold!
> Bring me my chariot of fire!
>
> WILLIAM BLAKE: 'JERUSALEM'

The rugby league and union wing Martin Offiah (b.1966) is nicknamed Chariots Offiah because of his speed and strength as a runner.

Charlie and the Chocolate Factory. A fantasy novel (1964) by Roald Dahl (1916–90), in which Charlie Buckett wins a ticket that allows him to visit a chocolate factory owned by Mr Willy Wonka and manned by tiny men called Oompa-Loompas. It was filmed as *Willy Wonka and the Chocolate Factory* (1971), with Gene Wilder as Willy Wonka. Dahl's sequel, *Charlie and the Great Glass Elevator*, was published in 1973.

'Chasse, La' (French, 'the hunt'). A nickname given to the symphony no 73 in D (1781) by Haydn (1732–1809), which includes themes akin to hunting calls, and to Haydn's string quartet in B flat, opus 1, no 1 (*c*.1755). The string quartet no 17 in B flat, K458 (1784), by Mozart (1756–91) is also nicknamed '*La Chasse*' or the '*Jagd*' or 'Hunt' Quartet, because of the nature of the first subject of the first movement. *See also* 'HORN SIGNAL' SYMPHONY.

Cheap Imitation. A piano piece by John Cage (1912–92), composed in 1969 as an 'impression' of the music of Erik Satie. Cage made an orchestral version in 1972. *See also 4'33"*.

Cheminée du roi René, La (French, 'King René's chimney). A wind quartet (1939) by the French composer Darius Milhaud (1892–1974). Like a number of Milhaud's works (such as *Suite Provençale* and *Carnaval d'Aix*) it reflects his boyhood in the south of France: La Cheminée du roi René is the name of an old street in Aix-en-Provence, named after René I or René d'Anjou (1409–80). René – who died in Aix – was duke of Anjou, duke of Bar, count of Provence and Piedmont, and for seven years (1435–42) king of Naples.

CHESS

A GAME AT CHESS, a play (1624) by Thomas Middleton

Checkmate, a mystery novel (1871) by the Irish writer J.S. LeFanu

Chess Fever, a silent Soviet film comedy (1925), written and directed by Nikolai Shpikovsky

Checkmate, a ballet (1937) with music by Sir Arthur Bliss and choreography by Ninette de Valois

The Passionate Game: Lessons in Chess and Love, an instructional book (1937) by Gustav Schenk

Knight's Gambit, a novel (1949) by the US writer William Faulkner

ENDGAME, a play (1957) by Samuel Beckett

Red Queen, White Queen, a novel (1958) by Henry Treece

A number of historical novels by Dorothy Dunnett: *Game of Kings* (1962), *Queens' Play* (1964), *The Disorderly Knights* (1966), *Pawn in Frankincense* (1969), *The Ringed Castle* (1972) and *Checkmate* (1975)

The Chess Players, a film (1977) written and directed by Satyajit Ray about two Indian noblemen engrossed in their games of chess while the British take over their land

Knight Moves, a thriller film (1992) about a chess player suspected of murder

The Knight's Move: The Relational Logic of the Spirit in Theology and Science (1992), by James E. Loder

Pawn to Queen Four: a novel (1995) by Lars Eighner

Soft Pawn, an instructional book (1995) by William Hartston, author of *How to Cheat at Chess*

The Red Queen: Sex and the Evolution of Human Nature (1995), by Matt Ridley

The Bourbaki Gambit, a novel (1996) by Carl Djerassi

Checkmate in the Carpathians, a novel for children (2001) by Mary Reeves Bell

There have also been innumerable mass-market titles – in genres such as detective mystery, romance, erotica, science fiction and fantasy – that borrow their titles from chess. Examples include: *Checkmate* (numerous), *Archangel Checkmate*, *White Rook*, *The Red Queen*, *White Queen*, *Gambit*, *Devil's Gambit*, *Falklands Gambit*, *Bishop's Pawn*, *Bishop as Pawn*, *Chevalier's Pawn*, *The Devil's Pawn*, *King's Pawn*, *Magic's Pawn*, *Passion's Pawn*, *Pawn of Chaos*, *Pawn of Prophecy*, *Yesterday's Pawn* and *A Pawn for the Queen*.

Chicken Soup with Barley. A play (1958) by Arnold Wesker (b.1932) about the life of the Jewish Kahn family in East London in the 1930s. It is the first part of a trilogy, completed by ROOTS (1959) and *I'm Talking about Jerusalem* (1960), in which the central theme is that of caring. The play owed its title to the chicken soup young Ada Kahn is brought by a kind neighbour when she is ill.

Chicken soup is traditional Jewish comfort food, as in the bestselling American collection of spiritually uplifting stories, *Chicken Soup for the Soul* (1993), by Jack Canfield and Mark Victor Hansen. This has spawned numerous sequels and 'Chicken Soup' is now a registered trademark.

Chien Andalou, Un (French, 'an Andalusian dog'). A classic surrealist film (1928), the result of a collaboration between two Spaniards, the painter Salvador Dalí (1904–89) and the film-maker Luis Buñuel (1900–83). The film comprises a series of scenes connected only by the bizarre logic of a dream. Images include a hand being eaten by ants, dead donkeys on pianos and a close-up of an eyeball being sliced by a razor; however, dogs (Andalusian or otherwise) are notable by their absence.

Childe Harold's Pilgrimage. A long poem by Lord Byron (1788–1824), published in 1812 (Cantos I and II), 1816 (Canto III) and 1818 (Canto IV). 'Childe' is a medieval word for a young man of noble birth; and Harold is not a pilgrim in the conventional religious sense, but rather a world-weary youth who roams, like his creator, from place to place to escape from himself. His travels take him to Portugal, Spain, Turkey, Belgium, Switzerland, Venice, Rome and Florence. After the publication and runaway success of Cantos I and II, Byron wrote 'I woke and found myself famous.'

Childe Harold was as popular in mainland Europe – particularly in France. In 1825 the French Romantic poet Alphonse de Lamartine (1790–1869) published a long poem entitled *Le Dernier Chant du pèlerinage d'Harold* ('the last song, or canto, of Harold's pilgrimage'). However, *Harold in Italy* (opus 16, 1834), a symphony with viola *obbligato* (solo) by Berlioz (1803–69), is only loosely connected to Byron's poem. Berlioz said that the viola represented 'a sort of poetic dreamer of a similar type to Byron's Childe Harold', and the settings in the Abruzzi mountains of Italy are derived from Berlioz's own wanderings. The piece had been commissioned by the virtuoso violinist Niccolò Paganini.

However, when the music was delivered Paganini declined to play it as the viola part did not give him the opportunity to display his extraordinary technical abilities.

'Childe Roland to the Dark Tower Came'. A poem by Robert Browning (1812–89), published in *Men and Women* (1855). 'Childe' is a medieval word for a young man of noble birth. The dreamlike poem relates a knight's quest across a desolate landscape in search of the Dark Tower. When at last he reaches it –

> Dauntless the slug-horn to my lips I set,
> And blew. '*Childe Roland to the Dark Tower came.*'

Thus the poem mysteriously ends. This last line and the poem's title come from a fragment spoken by Edgar in *King Lear*, when he is feigning madness:

> Child Rowland to the dark tower came;
> His word was still 'Fie, foh, and fum,
> I smell the blood of a British man.'
>
> SHAKESPEARE: *King Lear* (1605), III.iv

The figure of Childe Roland comes from an old Scottish ballad, in which he is the youngest brother of the 'fair burd Helen'. Guided by the wizard Merlin, he successfully undertakes to bring his sister from Elfland, where the fairies had taken her. The only connection between the old ballad and Browning's poem is in the latter's title.

Child of Our Time, A. A wartime oratorio by Michael Tippett (1905–98) with a libretto by the composer. The work was written in 1939–41 and first performed in 1944. The 'child' of the title is Herschel Grynspan, a Polish-Jewish student whose assassination in Paris of the German diplomat Ernst vom Rath on 7 November 1938 led to the infamous *Kristallnacht*, a night of violence against Jews and their property in Germany on 9–10 November. Escalating official persecution followed. Tippett uses Negro spirituals at important points in the score, as Bach had used chorales in his Passions. The title, stressing the universality of the story, was suggested by that of a novel (1938) by the German-Hungarian writer and diplomat Ödon von Horváth (1901–38), *Ein Kind unserer Zeit*.

Children of a Lesser God. A play (1979) by the US dramatist Mark Medoff (b.1940) about the efforts of a hearing therapist to develop a relationship with a profoundly deaf young woman who refuses all offers of help. Written especially for the deaf actress Phyllis Frelich, it was filmed with Marlee Matlin, also deaf, in 1986. The title refers to the tendency of people with good hearing to dismiss the hearing-impaired as inferior beings.

Children's Corner. A set of six charming piano pieces by Claude Debussy (1862–1918), dedicated to his daughter and written in 1906–8. The titles of the pieces are in English, presumably influenced by the family's English governess. The first piece is 'Doctor Gradus ad Parnassum', a parody of a series of studies by Clementi from 1817 (*see* GRADUS AD PARNASSUM); the other pieces are 'Jimbo's Lullaby' (thought to be an error for 'Jumbo', given that Jimbo is a toy elephant), 'Serenade of the Doll', 'The Snow is Dancing', 'The Little Shepherd' and 'Golliwog's Cakewalk'. A cakewalk was a kind of black American competitive dance with complex steps, for which a cake was awarded as a prize, and the 'Golliwog's Cakewalk' includes a satirical musical quotation from Wagner's love-and-death music drama, *Tristan und Isolde* (1865).

Children's Hour, The. A play (1934) by US playwright Lillian Hellman (1905–84) about the scandal that erupts after a teacher is accused of lesbianism by a vengeful pupil. Filmed in 1936, the play was based on a real case that was reported in Scotland in the 19th century and pointed out to the author by her close friend, the crime novelist Dashiell Hammett. The title itself comes from the first verse of a poem by Longfellow:

> Between the dark and the daylight,
>   When the night is beginning to lower,
> Comes a pause in the day's occupations,
>   That is known as the Children's Hour.
>
> H.W. LONGFELLOW: *Birds of Passage*, Flight the Second, 'The Children's Hour' (1860)

Chips with Everything. A play (1962) by Arnold Wesker (b.1932), which examines what happens when young men from different classes are thrown together during National Service. 'Chips with everything' was a common description of the cuisine on offer in the British armed forces.

Chitty-Chitty-Bang-Bang. A series of children's stories (1964) about a magical car by the thriller writer Ian Fleming (1908–64), creator of James Bond. Chitty-Chitty-Bang-Bang is a 'supercharged Paragon Panther' boasting twelve cylinders. It is owned by the inventor Commander Caractacus Potts, and is capable of flying and other exciting stunts. A successful film adaptation, with a screenplay by Roald Dahl, was released in 1967. A stage musical was produced in 2002.

Christina's World. One of the best known and most popular works of the US artist Andrew Wyeth (b.1917). Painted in 1948, it depicts an eerily lit, sharply delineated but featureless farm landscape, with two farm buildings on the high horizon, while in the foreground is the mysterious figure of Christina, a thin-limbed girl propping herself up on the grass. Christina, whose view of the landscape we share, was a crippled neighbour of Wyeth's in the Brandywine Valley, Pennsylvania.

Chrononhotonthologos, The Tragedy of. 'The Most Tragical Tragedy that was ever Tragedized by any company of Tragedians', a burlesque (1734) of contemporary tragedies by Henry Carey (1687–1743). Chrononhotonthologos is the king of Queerumania, and the other characters include Bombardinion, Aldiborontiphoscophornia and Rigdum-Funnidos. The parody of 'high style' is indicated by the following bombastic lines:

> Go call a coach, and let a coach be called;
> And let the man who calls it be the caller;
> And in his calling, let him nothing call,
> But coach! coach! coach! Oh! for a coach, ye gods!

Cider with Rosie. An autobiographical account (1959) of his early years by the poet Laurie Lee (1914–97), evoking the landscape and innocent rural life of the Slad valley near Stroud in Gloucestershire where he was born and brought up. He and Rosie Burdock

> sat very close, breathing the same hot air. We kissed only once, so shy and dry, it was like two leaves colliding in the air ... Rosie, having baptized me with her cidrous kisses, married a soldier, and I lost her for ever.

Whether or not Rosie actually existed, Lee would never reveal. A TV dramatization was scripted by John Mortimer. Lee followed up *Cider with Rosie* with *AS I WALKED OUT ONE MIDSUMMER MORNING*.

'City of Dreadful Night, The'. A poem by the insomniac alcoholic James Thomson (1834–82), published in 1874. It is an evocative exercise in anguished pessimism:

The City is of Night, but not of Sleep;
There sweet sleep is not for the weary brain;
The pitiless hours like years and ages creep,
A night seems termless hell.

The city itself is an imaginary, desolate 'Venice of the Black Sea', whose main waterway is the 'River of Suicides'.

Thomson's poem was later to inspire the name 'City of Dreadful Knights' for the Welsh capital Cardiff. This arose from the post-First World War scandal in which Prime Minister Lloyd George was alleged to have sold honours for cash; three people connected with prominent South Wales newspapers were among the recipients of these honours.

Claire's Knee (French title: *Le Genou de Claire*). A French film (1970), one of the director Eric Rohmer's six 'moral tales'. The film concerns the attraction experienced by a mature man for two adolescent girls, to one of whom the eponymous knee belongs. To touch or not to touch, that is the question.

'Clock' Symphony. The nickname given to the symphony no 101 in D (1794) by Haydn (1732–1809), one of the 'SALOMON' SYMPHONIES. The accompaniment to the first theme in the second, slow movement sounds like a clock ticking.

Clockwork Orange, A. A futuristic, dystopian novel (1962) by Anthony Burgess (pen-name of John Anthony Burgess Wilson; 1917–93). It describes an attempt to turn its adolescent anti-hero Alex – a member of a teenage gang that indulges in extreme violence, including rape – into a 'mechanical man' by means of therapy and brainwashing.

The story is told in the first person in a jargon called Nadsat, in which the words are based on Russian, as is *nadsat* itself, representing the equivalent of '-teen'; examples of this youth slang include *droog*, 'friend', *horrorshow*, 'good' and *gloopy*, 'stupid'. Burgess often adds the English equivalent in the narrative, but even where he does not the sense is usually perceptible.

The title derives from the Cockney expression 'queer as a clockwork orange', meaning 'homosexual'. The relevance of this to the novel or any of its characters is uncertain, although in the narrative itself it is the title of a book being typed up by a writer whose house Alex and his mates burst into:

Then I looked at its top sheet, and there was the name – A CLOCK-

> WORK ORANGE – and I said: 'That's a fair gloopy [silly] title. Who ever heard of a clockwork orange?' Then I read a malenky [little] bit out loud in a sort of very high type preaching golos [voice]: ' – The attempt to impose upon man, a creature of growth and capable of sweetness, to ooze juicily at the last round the bearded lips of God, to attempt to impose, I say, laws and conditions appropriate to a mechanical creation, against this I raise my sword-pen –'
>
> chapter 2

A film version (1971) of the novel was directed by Stanley Kubrick (1928–99). Burgess had reservations about changes made in the film adaptation of his novel and suggested that the film should be retitled *Clockwork Marmalade*. Kubrik also had reservations about his film, after several rapes and killings appeared to have been inspired by it. A gang chanting 'Singin' in the Rain', a tune accompanying a vicious mugging in the film, was said to have raped a girl in Lancashire, and a judge condemned the film after a teenage boy wearing the 'droog' uniform of white overalls, false nose and black bowler beat up a younger child. Kubrik withdrew the film in 1973, and it was not re-released until after his death, in 2000.

Close Encounters of the Third Kind. A science-fiction film (1977) directed by Steven Spielberg (b.1947), in which apparently benevolent aliens land on Earth. The title draws on the categories proposed in J. Allen Hynek's *The UFO Experience: A Scientific Enquiry* (1972). A 'close encounter of the first kind' is simply a sighting of a UFO, while a 'close encounter of the second kind' is evidence of an alien landing. A 'close encounter of the third kind' involves contact with aliens, while a 'close encounter of the fourth kind' is an abduction by aliens. Oddly enough, close encounters of the fourth kind – usually involving a period in the Great White Space, being prodded and poked in the interests of intergalactic science – appear to be experienced almost exclusively by citizens of the United States of America.

Clouds of Witness. A detective novel by Dorothy L. Sayers (1893–1957), published in 1926. The title comes from the New Testament:

> Wherefore seeing we also are compassed about with so great a cloud of witnesses, let us lay aside every weight, and the sin which doth so easily beset us, and let us run with patience the race that is set before us.
>
> Epistle of St Paul to the Hebrews 12:1

Cockaigne. A boisterous concert overture by Edward Elgar (1857–1934), subtitled 'In London Town'. It was first performed in 1901 and was intended to be an evocation of Edwardian London. 'Cockaigne' or 'Cockayne' (from which the word 'Cockney' is allegedly derived) refers to a land of idleness and luxury that features in medieval European folklore, and which is the subject of a painting by the Flemish painter Pieter Bruegel the Elder (*c.*1525–69), entitled *Land of Cockayne.* Bruegel's painting was inspired by a Flemish proverb, 'The greatest fool is an idle glutton', and depicts three recumbent and satiated men, a peasant, a soldier and a cleric, surrounded by such items as a self-carving pig and a hedge full of sausages. The word itself derives from Middle Low German *kokenje*, a small cake, from which the houses in this idyllic land were supposed to be made (the hut in Bruegel's painting has a roof covered in cakes). The idea is a persistent one: in the Great Depression of the 1930s in the United States, hobo lore evoked the land of the 'Big Rock Candy Mountain'. Despite expectations, the word 'Cockaigne' bears no etymological relationship to 'cocaine'; the latter derives from the South American Quechuan word *kúka* (coca).

'Coffee' Cantata. The nickname given to J.S. Bach's secular cantata *Schweigt stille, plaudert nicht* (1732; 'be quiet, don't chatter'). The text, by Picander, refers to the craze for the then novel beverage.

Cold Comfort Farm. A novel (1932) by Stella Gibbons (1902–89), parodying the humourless and loamy rural novels of D.H. Lawrence (1885–1930) and Mary Webb (1881–1927), and in particular the latter's *PRECIOUS BANE* (1924). The title was suggested to the author by the writer Elizabeth Coxhead, who took the name from a real farm near her home at Hinckley, Leicestershire. Farms of the name still exist today, and 'cold comfort' as a phrase for little cheer goes back to medieval times.

> I do not ask you much:
> I beg cold comfort.
>
> WILLIAM SHAKESPEARE: *King John* (1591–8), V.vii

A TV film version (1995), written by Malcolm Bradbury and directed by John Schlesinger, never quite captured the spirit of the original.

> Something nasty in the woodshed.
>
> chapter 10

Colin Clouts Come Home Again. A pastoral by Edmund Spenser (?1552–99), published in 1595. The work was written a few years earlier, and includes an allegorical account of Spenser's visit to London with Sir Walter Raleigh to present Queen Elizabeth I ('Cynthia') with the first three books of *The* FAERIE QUEENE. Spenser himself is 'Colin Clout', the rural innocent awed by the splendour of the court. Colin Clout had earlier appeared as a voice for the poet in *The Shepheardes Calender* (1579). His first appearance, however, is in *Collyn Clout* (1522) by John Skelton (?1460–1529), in which Clout is a vagabond, a persona that enables the poet to attack the corruption of the clergy in robust verse:

> For though my rhyme be ragged,
> Tattered and jagged,
> Rudely rain-beaten,
> Rusty and moth-eaten,
> If ye take well therewith,
> It hath in it some pith.

'Colonel Bogey'. *See* BRIDGE ON THE RIVER KWAI, THE.

Colour Symphony, A. An orchestral work by Arthur Bliss (1891–1975), first performed in 1922. The work is based on the heraldic symbolism of colours, and the titles of the movements are 'Purple', 'Red', 'Blue' and 'Green'.

> There is only a little of the spider about me, spinning his own web from his inner being. I am more of a magpie type. I need what Henry James calls a 'trouvaille' or a 'donnée'.
>
> ARTHUR BLISS: *As I Remember* (1970)

Come Unto These Yellow Sands. A painting (1842) of strange, partially clad figures dancing on a seashore by Richard Dadd (1819–97), who shortly afterwards was confined in a lunatic asylum (*see The* FAIRY-FELLER'S MASTER STROKE). The title comes from one of Ariel's haunting spirit songs in Shakespeare's *The* TEMPEST:

> Come unto these yellow sands,
> And then take hands.
> Curtsied when you have and kissed,
> The wild waves whist,
> Foot it featly here and there;
> And, sweet sprites, the burden bear.
> Hark, hark!
>
> *The Tempest*, I.ii

The painting was very well received when exhibited at the Royal Academy, one critic saying it came nearer to the essence of poetry than anything he had ever seen. *See also* THIS MUSIC CREPT BY ME UPON THE WATERS; FULL FATHOM FIVE.

'Comin' thro' the Rye'. An old song, adapted by Robert Burns (1759–96), and published in volume 5 (1796) of James Johnson's *Scots Musical Museum* (1787–1803). The commonly received version goes:

> Gin a body meet a body
>   Comin' thro' the rye;
> Gin a body kiss a body,
>   Need a body cry?

However, the version (from *The Merry Muses of Caledonia*, published 1800) preferred by Tom Scott, the editor of *The Penguin Book of Scottish Verse* (1970), goes:

> Gin a body meet a body
>   Comin' thro' the rye;
> Gin a body fuck a body,
>   Need a body cry?

In the 1891 Kilmarnock edition, the editor, William Scott Douglas – oblivious of such textual disparities – appends the following note:

> In the *Glasgow Herald* of 20th July, 1867, an article appeared – 'New Readings of an Old Poet' – in which it is insinuated that the 'comin' through the rye' refers to the 'Rye *Water*,' at Dalry. This we controverted in a following No. of the *Herald*, saying that it was an opinion endorsed by the entire common-sense of mankind, that Burns had no other idea in writing the song than that of a lass going through a dewy field of rye.

Scott's preferred version, proving Douglas's point, continues:

> Comin' throu the rye, my jo,
>   An' comin' throu the rye;
> She fand a staun o staunin graith
>   Comin' throu the rye.

A misreading of the poem by the novel's leading character provides the title of J.D. Salinger's *The* CATCHER IN THE RYE.

COMPASS POINTS

Eastward Hoe, a comedy (1605) by George Chapman, Ben Jonson and John Marston (*see* WESTWARD HO!)

The East Wind of Love, a novel (1937) by Compton Mackenzie

East Coker, a poem (1940) by T.S. Eliot (*see* FOUR QUARTETS)

EAST OF EDEN, a novel (1952) by John Steinbeck

East, a play (1975) by Steven Berkoff treating London's East End in Homeric style

East, West, a collection of short stories (1994) by Salman Rushdie

East into Upper East, a collection of short stories (1998) by Ruth Prawer Jhabvala

EAST IS EAST, a comedy film (1999)

Westward Hoe, a comedy (1607) by John Webster and Thomas Dekker (*see* WESTWARD HO!)

WESTWARD HO! a tub-thumping historical novel (1855) by Charles Kingsley

The GIRL OF THE GOLDEN WEST, an opera (1910) by Puccini

GO WEST, YOUNG MAN, a film (1937) starring Mae West

The West Wind of Love, a novel (1940) by Compton Mackenzie

Westward Ha! a miscellaneous collection (1948) by the US humorist S.J. Perelman

WEST SIDE STORY, a musical (1957) by Leonard Bernstein

Northward Hoe, a comedy (1607) by John Webster and Thomas Dekker (*see* WESTWARD HO!)

The Narrow Road to the Deep North, an account (1694) of a journey to the north of Japan by the poet Basho

NORTH AND SOUTH, a novel (1854–5) by Mrs Gaskell; also a verse collection (1946) by the US poet Elizabeth Bishop

The North Wind of Love, a novel in two books (1944–5) by Compton Mackenzie

The North Ship, an early poetry collection (1945) by Philip Larkin

NORTH BY NORTHWEST, a film thriller (1959) directed by Alfred Hitchcock

North of Thursday, a novel (1960) by the Australian writer Jon Cleary

North, a collection of poems (1975) by the Irish Nobel laureate Seamus Heaney

North of South, an account (1978) of an African journey by the Trinidadian writer Shiva Naipaul

South Moon Under, a novel (1933) by the US writer Marjorie Rawlings

SOUTH RIDING, a novel (1936) by Winifred Holtby

The South Wind of Love, a novel (1937) by Compton Mackenzie

South of No North, a collection of short stories (1973) by the US writer Charles Bukowksi

---

Concerning the Eccentricities of Cardinal Pirelli. A novel (1926) by Ronald Firbank (1886–1926), written while he was dying of tuberculosis. It has just two pieces of action, both of which take place in a cathedral. In the first, Pirelli ceremonially baptizes a young dog. In the second, he chases Chicklet, a young boy of dubious morality, around the cathedral before falling dead beneath a sacred painting, naked but for his mitre. The whole is presented in Firbank's distinctive style, which he suggested 'calls to mind a frieze with figures of varying heights all trotting the same way'.

Concord Sonata. A work for piano, with solos for viola and flute, by the US composer Charles Ives (1874–1954). It was composed between 1909 and 1915. The title refers not to the harmoniousness of the piece, which is highly experimental and features note-clusters, but to Concord, Massachusetts, home of the New England Transcendentalists. The full title of the work is *Sonata No. 2 (Concord, Mass., 1840–1860)*, and the four movements are named after the leading Transcendentalists: 'Emerson', 'Hawthorne', 'The Alcotts' and 'Thoreau'.

Confederacy of Dunces, A. A satirical novel (1980) by the US novelist John Kennedy Toole (1937–1969). Thanks to the efforts of his mother it was published more than ten years after he committed suicide, and went on to win the Pulitzer Prize for fiction. It is set in New Orleans, and the central character, Ignatius Reilly, is an overweight, argumentative layabout, who interrelates with a cast of equally eccentric and accident-prone characters. The title comes from Jonathan Swift:

> When a true genius appears in the world, you may know him by this sign, that the dunces are all in confederacy against him.
>
> SWIFT: *Thoughts on Various Subjects, Moral and Diverting* (1711)

Confessions of a Justified Sinner, The Private Memoirs and. A novel by James Hogg (1770–1835), the 'Ettrick Shepherd', published in 1824. The 'justified sinner' is an extreme Scottish Calvinist, Colwan, who believes God's grace has made him one of the elect, predestined for salvation ('justified') whatever evil acts he performs. The first part of the book is a conventional third-person narrative, while the second part comprises Colwan's 'private memoirs and confessions', from a manuscript supposedly found in his grave.

Hogg was also the author of *The Shepherd's Guide: being a Practical Treatise on the Diseases of Sheep* (1807), which, in order for it to fit on the spine of the book, the Edinburgh publisher Archibald Constable abbreviated to *Hogg on Sheep*.

Connecticut Yankee in King Arthur's Court, A. A satirical novel (1889) by the US humorist Mark Twain (Samuel Langhorne Clemens, 1835–1910), in which a down-to-earth, practical New Englander finds himself transplanted to the world of medieval chivalry. His common-sense, progressive, technological approach is contrasted with the superstition and reaction of his European ancestors, who oppose his attempt to improve social conditions. There have been two film versions (1931 and 1949), with Will Rogers and Bing Crosby respectively in the title role.

Consider Phlebas. A science-fiction novel (1987) by the Scottish writer Iain M. Banks (b.1954). Set during a massive galactic war of the future, the story concerns the attempts by the rival civilizations, the Idirians and the Culture, to find a lost Mind, and ends with nearly everybody dead. At one point there is a slow drowning in sewage, which perhaps links to the origin of the title, in the short part IV, entitled 'Death by Water', of T.S. Eliot's *The Waste Land* (1922), the subject of which is the drowning at sea of Phlebas the Phoenician:

> Gentile or Jew
> O you who turn the wheel and look to windward,
> Consider Phlebas, who was once handsome and tall as you.

Consider the Lilies. *See* LILIES OF THE FIELD.

'Convergence of the Twain, The'. A poem (1914) by the British poet and novelist Thomas Hardy (1840–1928) about the sinking of the *Titanic* in 1912. The 'twain' of the title are the ship and the iceberg with which it collided, an event that to Hardy was dictated by the mysterious force of Fate that governs the universe:

> Well: while was fashioning
> This creature of cleaving wing,
> The immanent Will that stirs and urges everything
> Prepared a sinister mate
> For her – so gaily great –
> A Shape of Ice, for the time far and dissociate.

The British poet Simon Armitage (b.1963) used the same title for a poem he wrote and broadcast in response to the terrorist attacks on the twin towers of the World Trade Center in New York on 11 September 2001.

Corridors of Power. A novel (1963) by C.P. Snow, later Baron Snow (1905–80), the antepenultimate volume in his *Strangers and Brothers* sequence. Snow first used the phrase in an earlier volume, *Homecomings* (1956):

> The official world, the corridors of power.
> chapter 22

Although Snow may not have coined the phrase, he helped to popularize it, and it quickly entered common usage to denote the ministries in Whitehall and their top-ranking civil servants.

> Boffins at daggers drawn in corridors of power.
> *The Times* (headline) (8 April 1965)

CREATION

The biblical creation of the world, as recounted in Genesis, has inspired a number of composers and writers.

The oratorio *The Creation* (German title: *Die Schöpfung*) by Haydn (1732–1809), first performed in 1798, has a text by Baron van Swieten consisting of translations from Genesis and Milton's *Paradise Lost*.

> I was never so devout as when I was at work on *The Creation*.
>
> JOSEPH HAYDN: quoted in Hughes, *Haydn* (1970)

The name 'Creation' Mass has also been given to Haydn's Mass in B flat (1801), owing to the fact that the 'Gloria' quotes from the duet for Adam and Eve in Haydn's *Creation* oratorio.

The ballet *La Création du monde*, with music by Darius Milhaud (1892–1974) and choreography by Jean Börlin was first performed in 1923. Alternative choreographies were subsequently created by Ninette de Valois and Kenneth MacMillan.

Creation: A Philosophical Poem (1712) by Sir Richard Blackmore (1654–1729) was admired by Dr Johnson but by few others. *The Creation* (1720) by Aaron Hill (1685–1750) is another forgotten verse epic. The novel *Creation* (1981) by Gore Vidal (b.1925) is set in the 5th century BC, and features the Persian emperors Darius and Xerxes, and the Chinese philosopher Confucius.

Così fan tutte. An opera by Mozart (1756–91) with a libretto by Lorenzo da Ponte (Emmanuele Conegliano; 1749–1838), first performed in 1790. The full Italian title, never successfully translated, is *Così fan tutte, ossia la scuola degli amanti*, literally 'Thus do all women, or the school for lovers'. The story turns on a wager as to whether the loved ones of two young officers will remain faithful to them while they are away. The opera was regarded as indecent in the 19th century; Beethoven, for one, was shocked by the libretto, which was often changed wholesale. Today, however, it is regarded as one of the greatest of human comedies.

> In *Così fan tutte* the dying eighteenth century casts a backward glance over a period outstanding in European life for grace and charm and, averting its eyes from a new age suckled on a creed of iconoclasm, sings its swan-song in praise of a civilization that has passed away for ever.
>
> THOMAS BEECHAM: *A Mingled Chime* (1944)

'Country of the Blind, The'. Short story (1904) by H.G. Wells (1866–1946) about a man who finds himself in a remote Andean valley where all the people are blind. The title (and the hero, frequently) alludes to the traditional saying 'In the country of the blind the one-eyed man is king', of which there are versions in several languages, for example '*In regione caecorum rex est luscus*' quoted in Erasmus's *Adagia* (1500). An early English version is John Skelton's 'An one eyed man is Well syghted when he is amonge blunde men' (1522).

Cox and Box. *See* BOX AND COX.

Cranford. A novel of provincial village life by Mrs Gaskell (1810–65), published in 1853 in Dickens's *Household Words*. Mrs Gaskell's fictional village, Cranford, is based on Knutsford in Cheshire, where the author was raised by a maternal aunt in an atmosphere of quiet gentility and fine social distinctions. The village of Hollingford in *Wives and Daughters* (1866) is also modelled on Knutsford.

Cricket on the Hearth, The. The third of Charles Dickens's Christmas books, published in 1845. The title comes from Milton's poem 'Il penseroso' (1645):

> Where glowing embers through the room
> Teach light to counterfeit a gloom,
> Far from all resort of mirth,
> Save the cricket on the hearth.

In Dickens's tale, John Peerybingle suspects his much younger wife Dot of dallying with another. However, the Cricket on the Hearth succeeds in banishing gloom, in particular using its magical powers to make John forgive Dot, although it turns out she was innocent all along.

Crucible, The. A historical drama (1953) by the US playwright Arthur Miller (b.1915) about the witchcraft hysteria that swept through Salem,

Massachusetts, in 1692. As well as suggesting the cauldrons and other utensils indispensable to traditional magic-making, the title also suggests the hot-house atmosphere and pressing material conditions that prevailed at the time (fear of war with France, a bad winter, a smallpox epidemic, raids by pirates and the like) and the unconscious desire to find scapegoats to blame for such ills. There is also an inevitable echo of:

> America is God's Crucible, the great Melting-Pot where all the races of Europe are melting and re-forming!
>
> ISRAEL ZANGWILL: *The Melting Pot* (1908), act I

Treated by Miller as a parallel for the McCarthyite investigations of the 1950s, the original witchcraft trials created a furore at the time and several of the jurors involved went so far as to publish a public 'Confession of Error'.

Cunning Little Vixen, The (Czech title: *Příhody Lišky Bystroušky*). An opera by Leoš Janáček (1854–1928), with a libretto by the composer, first performed in 1924. The text was based on the verse captions by Rudolf Těsnohlídek for a strip-cartoon drawn by Stanislav Lolek, which had been serialized in the Brno newspaper *Lidové noviny* in 1920. The dramatis personae comprise a mixture of animals and humans, and the vixen herself is called Bystrouška (or Sharpears in English versions). She is not particularly cunning (although she manages to trick a badger out of his set), and is shot by a poacher.

D

Dame aux camélias, La (French, 'the lady of the camellias'; English title: *Camille*). A novel by Alexandre Dumas *fils* (1824–95), published in 1848. It was a great success, and even more successful when Dumas adapted it for the stage in 1852. The story concerns the love of the courtesan Marguerite Gautier for the respectable Armand Duval. She agrees to abandon the demimonde to live with him in the country, but his father, unknown to Armand, persuades her to leave him, as their liaison is blocking the marital prospects of Armand's sister. Marguerite obliges, out of love for Armand, and gives the impression of going back to her old ways. Armand is devastated, pursues her back to Paris and in a jealous rage insults her in public. Armand eventually discovers the truth about her enduring love for him, but by this time she is fatally ill with consumption, and dies in his arms. There is an autobiographical element to this story, for at the age of 20 Dumas had himself fallen in love with the beautiful courtesan Marie Duplessis (also called Alphonsine Plessis), who died of tuberculosis in 1847 – the year before Dumas published his novel.

Marguerite is called 'the lady of the camellias' (or 'Camille') because she finds that strong-scented flowers make her cough, so constantly holds a bouquet of camellias, which are virtually unscented. It is difficult to swallow the alternative explanation offered by one commentator:

> The title refers to her habit of wearing a red camellia on those days of the month when she was 'not available'.
>
> ROBERT THICKNESSE: *The Times Opera Notes* (2001)

Dumas' sympathetic portrayal of a 'fallen woman' struck a chord with some elements of the French play-going public, but outraged others. More likely to appeal to the latter group was *Le Mariage d'Olympe* (1855; 'the marriage of Olympia'), one of the most popular plays of the conservative French dramatist Émile Augier (1820–89). *Le Mariage* rejects Dumas' belief that a prostitute can be saved through love, and indeed appears to suggest that the best way of dealing with a fallen woman should she work her way into the bosom of a respectable family is to shoot her.

Verdi's opera *La Traviata* (Italian, variously translated as 'the woman who was led astray', 'the woman gone astray', 'the fallen woman', 'the wayward one'), with a libretto by Francesco Maria Piave, is closely modelled on *La Dame aux camélias*, although Marguerite becomes Violetta and Armand becomes Alfredo. It was first performed in Venice in 1853, with the 130kg (20st 7lb) Fanny Salvini-Donatelli playing the fading consumptive heroine.

> The music of *La Traviata* is trashy; the young Italian lady [Piccolomini] cannot do justice to the music, such as it is. Hence it follows that the opera and the lady can only establish themselves in proportion as Londoners rejoice in a prurient story prettily acted.
>
> *The Atheneum*, reviewing the first London production, 1856

At least two ballets have been based on Dumas' play: *La dama delle camelie* (1945) with music by the Romanian composer Roman Vlad (b. 1919), and *La Dame aux camélias* (1957) with music by the French composer Henri Sauguet (1901–89). The play has also inspired several films, starting with a 1927 silent version with Norma Talmadge and Gilbert Roland. The most famous version is George Cukor's *Camille* (US, 1937), starring Greta Garbo and Robert Taylor. Garbo dies stunningly, uttering such lines as:

> It's my heart. It's not used to being happy ... Perhaps it's better if I live in your heart, where the world can't see me.
>
> ZOË AKINS, FRANCES MARION and JAMES HILTON: screenplay for *Camille* (1937)

The 1981 *Dame aux camélias*, directed by Mauro Bolognini and starring Isabelle Huppert, shows Dumas rehearsing his play and remembering his dead love. The exuberantly tongue-in-cheek musical, *Moulin Rouge*

(2001), shifts the action to fin-de-siècle Paris, where Nicole Kidman is a cabaret artiste at the eponymous night club and Ewan McGregor her innocent suitor, a would-be writer. He wins her over by apparently creating and singing hits by Elton John and other popsters, but all the songs in Tin Pan Alley cannot prevent her final, terminal exit.

See also OUR LADY OF THE FLOWERS.

Damned Serious Business, A. The memoirs (1990) of the actor Rex Harrison (1908–90), recalling the advice of the 18th-century English actor-manager David Garrick:

> Any fool can play tragedy, but comedy, sir, is a damned serious business.

The original version of Garrick's advice, to the actor Charles Bannister who wanted to concentrate on comic roles, was probably:

> No, no! You may humbug the town some time longer as a tragedian, but comedy is a serious thing.
>
> Quoted in MRS CLEMENT PARSONS, *Garrick and His Circle* (1906).

DANCE OF DEATH

The dance of death (French *danse macabre*; German *Totentanz*) is an allegorical representation of Death (usually depicted as one or more dancing skeletons or corpses) leading people to the grave in order of social precedence. It is first found in the 14th century, the time of the Black Death and the Hundred Years War between England and France (1337–1453). The French word *macabre* used in this context may derive from *macabé*, 'relating to the Maccabees', who were associated with death (see the Apocryphal II Maccabees 12:43–46).

One of the earliest visual representations of the dance of death was a series of paintings (1424–5) in the Cimetière des Innocents in Paris, but these were destroyed in 1699. Similarly, in the 15th century there was a dance of death, called *The Dance of St Paul's*, painted in the cloister of the old St Paul's Cathedral in London (destroyed in the Great Fire of

1666); the paintings were accompanied by translations of French verses by John Lydgate (*c.*1370–1451). French poems on the theme also influenced the anonymous Spanish masterpiece *Danza de la muerte* (early 15th century), a long poem in which Death interrogates his victims.

There is a series of woodcuts on the subject by Hans Holbein the Younger (1497–1543), and the Swiss artist Niklaus Manuel (*c.*1484–1530) painted a *Dance of Death* in 1516–19, which was destroyed in 1660. The theme was a favourite subject of the German painter Hans Baldung Grien (1484/5–1545), who also made several versions of DEATH AND THE MAIDEN (*see* panel, p.105). Another pictorial representation is found in Lucerne, Switzerland, where the roofed bridge called the Spreuerbrücke contains over 50 paintings on the theme, dating from the early 17th century. There is also a series of prints (1649) by the Swiss illustrator Matthäus Merian (1593–1650).

The idea of the dance of death was revived in the Romantic era. Musical settings include the *Totentanz* for piano and orchestra (1849) by Franz Liszt (1811–86), comprising variations on the *DIES IRAE*; the *Danse Macabre* (1874) for orchestra by Camille Saint-Saëns (1835–1921), which also quotes the *Dies Irae*, and represents Death playing the violin; and *Songs and Dances of Death* (1875–7) by Modest Mussorgsky (1839–81), setting words by the poet Arseny Golenishchev Kutuzov.

The subject lends itself to satire, and this is the tone of *The English Dance of Death* (1815), a series of prints by Thomas Rowlandson (1756–1827), with verses by William Combe (1741–1823). The *Dance of Death* woodcut series (1848) of the German artist Alfred Rethel (1816–59) was conceived in reaction to the Revolutions of 1848; one woodcut shows a mounted skeleton leading the revolutionaries.

Literary manifestations in the 20th century include:

- Strindberg's play *Dance of Death* (1901), a grotesque depiction of marital warfare, burlesquing conventional tragedy; there is also a film version (UK, 1968) starring Laurence Olivier and Geraldine McEwan

- *The Dance of Death*, a musical play (1933) by W.H. Auden
- *Totentanz und Gedichte zur Zeit* ('dance of death and poems of the times') (1947) by the German poet Marie Luise Kaschnitz
- *Totentanz*, a novel (1948) by the German writer Bernhard Kellermann (1879–51)
- A verse satire *The Dance of Death at London, Ontario* (1963) by the Canadian poet James Crerar Reaney
- *Danse Macabre*, a horror novel (1981) by Stephen King

There is a notable cinematic dance of death at the end of Ingmar Bergman's film, *The SEVENTH SEAL* (1975).

Dances with Wolves. An elegiac Western film (1990) of epic length, directed by and starring Kevin Costner, based on a novel by Michael Blake. Costner plays a cavalry officer who, at the end of the Civil War, is sent out alone into the prairies. There he befriends a lone wolf and the Sioux Indians, who give him the name 'Dances with Wolves'. The film didn't appeal to the more cynical critics: Pauline Kael said 'Costner has feathers in his hair and feathers in his head.'

While the movie was still in production many people in the film business doubted that it would enjoy the success it eventually did, and it was commonly referred to as *Kevin's Gate*, drawing parallels with the disastrous *HEAVEN'S GATE* (1980).

Dance to the Music of Time, A. A *roman fleuve* (1951–75) by Anthony Powell (1905–2000), comprising twelve novels:

A Question of Upbringing (1951)

A Buyer's Market (1952)

The Acceptance World (1955)

At Lady Molly's (1957)

Casanova's Chinese Restaurant (1960)

The Kindly Ones (1962; *see* EUMENIDES)

The Valley of Bones (1964)

The hand of the Lord was upon me, and carried me out in the spirit of the Lord, and set me down in the midst of the valley which was full of bones.

Ezekiel 37:1

The Soldier's Art (1966)

The Military Philosophers (1968)

Books Do Furnish a Room (1971)

Temporary Kings (1973)

Hearing Secret Harmonies (1975)

The title of the overall sequence is borrowed from that of a painting by Nicolas Poussin (1594–1665). At the start of the first novel, *A Question of Upbringing*, the narrator, Nicholas Jenkins, sees in the attitude of some workmen gathered around a bucket of coke a suggestion of

> Poussin's scene in which the Seasons, hand in hand, facing outward, tread in rhythm to the notes of the lyre that the winged and naked greybeard plays.

The books have a chronological framework corresponding to Powell's own experience and times, and tread a line between the tragic and the comic.

Poussin's painting was given its title – *Le quattro stagioni che ballano al suono del tempo* ('The four seasons that danced to the music of time') – by the Italian art theorist and collector Giovanni Pietro Bellori (1615–96). Powell has described how the painting inspired him:

> I found myself in the Wallace Collection, standing in front of Nicolas Poussin's picture there given the title *A Dance to the Music of Time*. An almost hypnotic spell seems cast by this masterpiece on the beholder. I knew at once that Poussin had expressed at least one important aspect of what the novel must be.
>
> ANTHONY POWELL: *To Keep the Ball Rolling* (1976–82)

Darkening Ecliptic, The. A collection of poems published in May 1944 by the avant-garde Australian journal *Angry Penguins*. The poems purported to be by a dead mechanic, Ern Malley, and the painting for the cover was supplied by Sidney Nolan. In June 1944 it was announced that the poems were a hoax perpetrated by the poets Harold Stewart and James McAuley, who wished to show up the gullibility of the audience for experimental verse.

Here the peacock blinks the eyes
Of his multipennate tail …
I said to my love (who is living)
Dear we shall never be that bird
Perched on the sole Arabian tree

'ERN MALLEY': *The Darkening Ecliptic*, 'Petit Testament'

The bird mentioned is the Phoenix, who in 'The PHOENIX AND THE TURTLE' (attributed to Shakespeare) sits 'On the sole Arabian tree'.

In astronomy, the ecliptic is the great circle on the celestial sphere marking the annual passage of the sun relative to the other stars; such a geometrical construct cannot darken. As an adjective, ecliptic describes anything relating to an eclipse; but an adjective cannot darken either.

Dark Materials, His. *See HIS DARK MATERIALS.*

Darkness at Noon. A novel (1940) by Arthur Koestler (1905–83), originally written in German and translated by Daphne Hardy. It draws on Koestler's experience as a member of the Communist Party from 1931 to 1938, during which time he was commissioned by the Communist International to write a book on the first five-year plan in Russia. The novel follows an earlier one, *The Gladiators* (1939), in which Spartacus is doomed because he did not apply the 'law of detours', whereby leaders should be 'pitiless for the sake of pity' and execute dissidents. In *Darkness at Noon* an elderly Bolshevik follows the 'law' and sends people to their execution without compunction, until he himself is deemed expendable and is forced to sign a confession that consigns him to his death.

The title echoes words from Milton's *SAMSON AGONISTES* (1671) relating to the blindness of Samson:

O dark, dark, dark, amid the blaze of noon,
Irrecoverably dark, total eclipse
Without all hope of day!

It is possible that Koestler was also aware of an anonymous booklet published in Boston in 1806 and entitled *Darkness at Noon, or the Great Solar Eclipse of the 16th June 1806*.

Darling Buds of May, The. A comic novel (1958) by H.E. Bates (1905–74), the first of several about the carefree Larkin family in rural England. The title comes from Shakespeare:

Rough winds do shake the darling buds of May,
And summer's lease hath all too short a date.

Sonnet 18

Other titles featuring the Larkin family are:

A Breath of French Air (1959)
Hark, Hark, the Lark (1960), from

Hark, hark, the lark at heaven's gate sings,
And Phoebus 'gins arise ...

SHAKESPEARE: *Cymbeline* (1609–10), II.iii

Oh! To be in England (1963), from

Oh, to be in England
Now that April's there ...

ROBERT BROWNING: 'Home-Thoughts, from Abroad' (1845)

A Little of What You Fancy (1970), from

A little of what you fancy does you good.

MARIE LLOYD: title of music-hall song

In 1991–3 the books became the basis of a popular television series starring David Jason as Pop Larkin.

See also SUMMER'S LEASE.

Davidsbündlertänze (German, 'dances of the members of the League of David'). A set of 18 piano pieces, opus 6 (1837), by Robert Schumann (1810–56), each one signed either 'F' or 'E', standing for Florestan and Eusebius, the composer's two contrasting personae. Schumann had created the imaginary *Davidsbund* (League of David) – which was opposed to the Philistines, as was the biblical King David – in his magazine *Neue Zeitschrift für Musik*. He also included a '*Marche des Davidsbündler contre les Philistins*' in his CARNAVAL.

Day in the Death of Joe Egg, A. A play (1967) by Peter Nichols (b.1927) about the struggles of a man and woman to cope with a severely disabled daughter. Based largely upon Nichols's own experiences as the father of a similarly handicapped child, the play took its title from a children's rhyme:

Joe Egg's a fool,
He tied his stocking to a stool.

DAYS OF THE WEEK

Monday Stories (French title: *Contes du lundi*), a collection of tales (1873) by the French writer Alphonse Daudet

Black Tuesday, a film (1954) with Edward G. Robinson as an escaped convict taking hostages

IF IT'S TUESDAY, THIS MUST BE BELGIUM, a comedy film (1969)

'Ash Wednesday', a poem (1930) by T.S. Eliot

I Loved You Wednesday, a romantic comedy film (1933)

The MAN WHO WAS THURSDAY, a novel (1908) by G.K. Chesterton

Thursday's Child, a film (1942) about a successful but big-headed child actress, based on a novel by Donald Macardle. The title refers to the nursery rhyme, in which 'Thursday's child has far to go'

Black Friday, a film (1940) in which a gangster's brain is transplanted into the head of a college professor

The LONG GOOD FRIDAY, a film (1980) in which London gangsters square up against the IRA

Saturday Night Fever, a disco-dance film (1978)

Saturday Night and Sunday Morning, a novel (1958) by Alan Sillitoe (film version 1960)

Saturday, Sunday, Monday, a play (1959) by Eduardo De Filippo

'Mr Eliot's Sunday Morning Service', a poem (1920) by T.S. Eliot (*see SAMSON AGONISTES*)

SUNDAY AFTERNOON ON THE ISLAND OF THE GRANDE JATTE, a painting (1884–5) by Georges Seurat

SUNDAY, BLOODY SUNDAY, a film (1971), directed by John Schlesinger and with a screenplay by Penelope Gilliatt

Sunday in the Park with George, a musical (1984) by the US composer and lyricist Stephen Sondheim

Day of the .... A popular formula for a novel title, especially when indicating some sinister person or force. Examples are Nathanael West's *The* DAY OF THE LOCUST (1939), John Wyndham's *The* DAY OF THE TRIFFIDS (1951), Paul Scott's *The Day of the Scorpion* (1968; *see The* RAJ QUARTET) and Frederick Forsyth's *The* DAY OF THE JACKAL (1971).

Day of the Jackal, The. The first novel (1971) by Frederick Forsyth (b.1938). This thriller established his basic formula, an international crisis and a mixture of fictional and historical characters. The narrative follows the progress of an international plot to kill the French president, General de Gaulle (1890–1970), at the hands of a professional killer known as the Jackal. A suspenseful film version (1973) was directed by Fred Zinnemann; a less exciting remake, *The Jackal*, appeared in 1997.

Inspired by Forsyth's title, the press applied the nickname 'The Jackal' to the Venezuelan-born assassin Illich Ramirez Sanchez (b.1949), who himself used the nom de guerre Carlos. Sanchez worked with various terrorist gangs in different countries. In the 1970s he was involved in various acts of international terrorism in the cause of Palestinian liberation, including the 1972 massacre at Tel Aviv airport and the 1975 kidnapping of oil ministers at the OPEC meeting in Vienna. He was arrested and sentenced to life imprisonment in 1997.

Day of the Locust, The. A dark novel (1939) by the US writer Nathanael West (1903–40). The work explores the seamy underside of Hollywood (where West had himself worked as a scriptwriter), and shows how it eats away at people's better selves. At the end Homer, a harmless but unexciting accountant, knocks down a boy who attacks him, and is in turn overwhelmed by a crowd of people (like a swarm of locusts) who are waiting for the arrival of stars at a premiere.

> I will restore to you the years that the locust hath eaten, the cankerworm, and the caterpillar, and the palmerworm, my great army which I sent among you.
>
> Joel 2:25

John Schlesinger's 1975 film of West's book, with Donald Sutherland and Karen Black, was highly regarded.

Day of the Scorpion, The. *See* RAJ QUARTET, THE.

Day of the Triffids, The. A science-fiction novel (1951) by John Wyndham (1903–69). An agricultural experiment has produced giant, man-eating, perambulating plants, which threaten a civilization already hit by blindness after a stellar explosion. Wyndham himself invented the word 'triffid' for the plants, apparently basing it on 'trifid', meaning 'divided into three parts', since he describes the plants as being supported on 'three bluntly-tapered projections extending from the lower part [of their bodies]'. An unsubtle film version (1962) was directed by Steve Sekely.

Days of Wine and Roses. A Blake Edwards film (1962), starring Tony Curtis and Lee Remick as a pair of alcoholics. The title comes from Ernest Dowson's fin-de-siècle poem, 'Vitae Summa Brevis' (1896):

> They are not long, the weeping and the laughter,
> Love and desire and hate.
> ...
> They are not long, the days of wine and roses.

Another Dowson poem supplied the title for GONE WITH THE WIND.

Dead Poets Society. A film (1989) written by Tom Schulman and directed by Peter Weir about the disturbing events that unfold after an unconventional English teacher (played by Robin Williams) arrives at a conservative Vermont prep school in 1959. Inspired by their teacher to develop an interest in literature, the pupils assemble their own anarchic 'Dead Poets Society', so called for its dedication to the values of canonic writers, and especially to Horace's dictum '*carpe diem*' ('seize the day'), which becomes a focus of their rebellion against the educational establishment.

death, dance of. *See* DANCE OF DEATH (panel, pp.96–7).

Death in Venice (German title: *Der Tod in Venedig*). A novella (1912; English translation 1928) by the German novelist Thomas Mann (1875–1955). It is a study, overlaid with symbolism, of the fatal attraction of an ailing and ageing writer, Gustave von Aschenbach, for a beautiful 13-year-old boy, Tadzio. He remains in Venice, watching Tadzio play on the beach, even in the face of a cholera epidemic, in which he dies.

In the film version (1971), written and directed by Luchino Visconti, Aschenbach is re-imagined as a composer, transparently based on Mahler, and the moving Adagietto from Mahler's symphony no 5 (1901) – which Mahler had written as a love song to his wife Alma, and intended to be played at a much faster tempo than in the film – accompanies the slow

DEATH AND THE MAIDEN

The motif of death and the maiden – combining the macabre and the erotic – comes up again and again in Western (especially northern European) culture. It is thought to have originated in the medieval fondness for reminders of mortality, particularly at the time of the Black Death in the 14th century. It became a favourite subject of Hans Baldung Grien (1484/5–1545), one of the leading German painters of the early 16th century; examples include *The Knight, Death and the Maiden*, (1503–5, Louvre), and *Death and the Maiden* (1517, Basel). The motif also features in other German works of the period.

The poem '*Der Tod und das Mädchen*' by Matthias Claudius (1740–1815) provided the words of a song (D531) by Schubert (1791–1828), composed in February 1817. Schubert used the theme of the piano introduction to the song as the basis for the variations in the second movement of his string quartet no 14 in D minor (D810), which has subsequently been nicknamed the 'Death and the Maiden' Quartet.

At the end of the 19th century, the Norwegian painter Edvard Munch (1863–1944) became fascinated by the pairing, giving the title to a painting (1893) and a drypoint print (1894). The motif also occurs in various works by the German and Austrian expressionists of the early 20th century.

Death and the Maiden is also the title of a play by the Chilean writer Ariel Dorfman, in which a woman confronts the man who tortured and raped her when she was a political prisoner. The film version (1994) was directed by Roman Polanski, and starred Sigourney Weaver and Ben Kingsley.

evolution of the story. It is known that Mann himself had this piece of music in mind when he wrote the novella, the name Tadzio bearing some resemblance to 'adagio'. Cynics dubbed the film 'Death in a Deckchair'.

Another notable version is the opera by Benjamin Britten (1913–76), with a libretto by Myfanwy Piper, first performed in 1973.

Death of a Salesman. A Pulitzer Prize-winning play (1949) by the US playwright Arthur Miller (b.1915). It concerns the tortured relationships between failed salesman Willy Loman and his two sons. The play, which culminates in Loman's suicide, was originally titled *The Inside of His Head*, a reference to the salesman's delusions about himself and his family.

> A salesman is got to dream, boy. It comes with the territory.
>
> ARTHUR MILLER: *Death of a Salesman*, 'Requiem'

Death of Klinghofer, The. A controversial opera by the US composer John Adams (b.1947), with a libretto by Alice Goodman, first performed in 1991. The story concerns the Palestinian hijacking in October 1985 of the Italian cruise ship *Achille Lauro*, and the murder of a disabled Jewish passenger, Leon Klinghofer.

Death of Marat, The. A painting (1793) by the French neoclassical artist Jacques-Louis David (1748–1825), depicting a dead man holding a pen in a bath. Jean-Paul Marat (1743–93) was the leader of the radical Montagnard faction during the French Revolution, opposed by the conservative Girondin faction. Marat suffered from a skin disease that obliged him to spend much time in medicinal baths, and it was thus that the young Girondiste Charlotte Corday (1768–93) found him on 13 July 1793, and stabbed him to death. She had entered his rooms on the pretext of seeking his protection, and he had been jotting down the names she had given him of opponents to be executed when she drew the knife from her dress. She was immediately arrested, tried and guillotined. Marat himself was promptly apotheosized into a revolutionary martyr, and his name was given to more than twenty French towns. Many years later the Soviet Union called one of its first battleships the *Marat*. David painted two other revolutionary martyrdoms, those of the now forgotten Bara and Lepeletier de Saint-Fargeau.

> The school of David can only paint bodies; it is decidedly inept at painting souls.
>
> STENDHAL: in *Le Journal de Paris*, 1824

Decameron, The. A collection of 100 tales by the Italian writer Giovanni Boccaccio (1313–75), completed in *c.*1353. Many of the tales were already old at this time, and many later writers – including Chaucer and Shakespeare – borrowed stories from the collection. In the framework story, seven ladies and three gentlemen escape from Florence when the Black Death arrives in 1348, and spend their time each telling one tale per day for ten days (*Decameron* comes from Greek *deka*, 'ten', and *hēmera*, 'day'). (There is a comparable framework story in *The CANTERBURY TALES*.) A film version (1971) by Pier Paolo Pasolini (1922–75) concentrates on some of the earthier tales. A similar collection to Boccaccio's entitled *The Heptameron* (1558) was ascribed to Margaret of Angoulême (1492–1549), queen of Navarre. The tales are said to have been related in seven days (Greek *hepta*, 'seven').

Decline and Fall. The first novel (1928) by Evelyn Waugh (1903–66). A comic reprise of some of the author's own experiences at Oxford University and as a teacher at a private school, it nevertheless deals with quite serious matters.

> I expect you'll be becoming a schoolmaster, sir. That's what most of the gentlemen does, sir, that gets sent down for indecent behaviour.

The degeneracy is halted when the protagonist, a man who has innocently been caught up in the activities of his circle, enters the church. The title echoes that of *The Decline and Fall of the Roman Empire* by Edward Gibbon (1737–94). A film version (1968), with Robin Phillips as Paul Pennyfeather, was directed by John Krish.

Deep Throat. A notorious pornographic film (1972), in which US star Linda Lovelace takes fellation to new depths. Subsequently 'Deep Throat' became the code name for the anonymous source in the White House during the presidency of Richard M. Nixon who supplied *Washington Post* journalists Carl Bernstein and Bob Woodward with information that aided them in their Watergate investigations of 1972–4. The rumour that 'Deep Throat' did not in fact exist was hotly denied by Woodward.

Douglas Adams adapted the name for the most powerful computer in the universe, Deep Thought, in the radio and TV series, and related books, *The HITCH-HIKER'S GUIDE TO THE GALAXY*.

See also ALL THE PRESIDENT'S MEN.

Deformed Transformed, The. An incomplete drama by Lord Byron (1788–1824) – who himself was born with a club foot – published in 1824. This variation on the Faust legend (*see* FAUST OR FAUSTUS, panel, pp.152–6) features the hunchback Arnold ('Of seven sons / The sole abortion'), who at the beginning is about to use a knife to sever

> This withered slip of nature's nightshade – my
> Vile form – from the creation, as it hath
> The green bough from the forest.

Just then a stranger appears and offers him the opportunity to adopt the form of the Greek hero Achilles. Arnold goes on to become 'Count Arnold', a great solder who leads an attack on Rome.

Déjeuner sur l'herbe, Le (French, 'lunch on the grass', 'the picnic'). A painting by Édouard Manet (1832–83) exhibited in Paris in 1863 at the Salon des Refusés. The picture shows the influence of the Renaissance masters – specifically Giorgione's *Concert champêtre* and Raphael's *Judgment of Paris* – but the combination of men in modern dress and naked women, together with the relative harshness of the treatment, caused a scandal.

> Is this drawing? Is this painting? … I see boneless fingers and heads without skulls. I see sidewhiskers made of two strips of black cloth that could have been glued to the cheeks.
>
> JULES CASTAGNARY: in *Salons*, 1863

> Giorgione had conceived the happy idea of a *fête champêtre* in which although the gentlemen were dressed, the ladies were not. Now some wretched Frenchman has translated this into modern French realism, on a much larger scale, and with the horrible modern French costume instead of the graceful old Venetian one.
>
> PHILIP GILBERT HAMERTON: in *Fine Arts Quarterly Review*, 1863

> Unfortunately the nude hasn't a decent figure and one can't think of anything uglier than the man stretched out next to her, who hasn't even thought of taking off, out of doors, his horrid padded cap. It is the contrast of a creature so inappropriate in a pastoral scene with this undraped bather that is so shocking.
>
> THÉOPHILE THORÉ: in *L'Indépendence belge*, 1863

> There is [a nude] in Manet's *Déjeuner sur l'herbe* who will be in a hurry

> to get herself dressed after her tedious ordeal on the chilly grass in the company of those men without ideals ... What are they talking about? Nothing innocent, I would guess.
>
> ODILON REDON: Journal, 1888

Manet's painting has since achieved iconic status, and various artists have made their *homages*. An example is *Le Petit-Déjeuner sur l'herbe* ('the breakfast on the grass'; 1935–6) by the German surrealist Max Ernst (1891–1976), in which a variety of anthropoid creatures with the heads of birds tangle painfully with each other. Ernst revisited Manet's title in 1944 with *le déjeuner sur l'herbre*; the painting features a fearsome-looking spotted flatfish about to devour a feather.

Le Déjeuner sur l'herbe is also the title of a film (1959) by Jean Renoir, son of Manet's fellow impressionist Pierre Auguste Renoir. In the film a renowned scientist has an affair with a housemaid in the countryside.

Delta of Venus. A collection of erotic stories (published posthumously in 1977) by the French-born author Anaïs Nin (1903–77), one-time mistress and lifelong friend of Henry Miller. She had written them on commission when down on her luck in the early 1940s. The title none too subtly suggests the triangular shape of the female pubic region. Compare *FANNY HILL*.

Demoiselles d'Avignon, Les. A revolutionary canvas with which Pablo Picasso (1881–1973) heralded the arrival of cubism. The austere simplicity of the work, painted in 1907, incorporates Picasso's discovery of African and ancient Iberian art: it features five nudes, four of whom are standing, and three of whom have mask-like faces. Surprisingly, given that the painting has become such an icon of modernism, the work was not reproduced until 1925 and not exhibited in public until 1937. The title was jokingly given to the work by the critic André Salmon, who suggested that the young ladies in the painting might be *demoiselles* ('young ladies') in a brothel in the Carré d'Avinyo (Avignon Street) in Barcelona. In homage, Patrick Caulfield (b.1936) made a screenprint depicting *Les Demoiselles d'Avignon, Vues de Derriere* ('seen from behind').

Density 21.5. A piece for solo flute by the avant-garde French-born US composer Edgard Varèse (1883–1965), composed in 1936. The title refers to the density of platinum (relative to the density of water), the piece having been written for a platinum flute. Compare *FAHRENHEIT 451*.

Desperate Remedies. The first novel of Thomas Hardy (1840–1928), published in 1871. It is a tale of thwarted love, albeit with a happy conclusion. The title comes from the proverb, known from the mid-16th century, 'Desperate diseases must have desperate remedies.'

> Diseases desperate grown,
> By desperate appliances are relieved,
> Or not at all.
>
> SHAKESPEARE: *Hamlet* (1601), IV.ii

> A desperate disease requires a dangerous remedy
>
> GUY FAWKES: on 6 November 1605

Dettingen Te Deum. A choral work by Handel (1685–1759), written in 1743 to celebrate the victory at Dettingen on the River Main in Germany on 27 June of that year, during the War of the Austrian Succession. At the battle, the 'Pragmatic Army' of Britain and its allies – commanded by George II – defeated the French. It was the last time a British monarch was to lead his troops on a battlefield. Regarding Handel's composition, it is widely accepted that some of the music was borrowed from a *Te Deum* by Francesco Antonio Urio, (?1631–?1719).

Deutsches Requiem, Ein. *See A* GERMAN REQUIEM.

Deutschland über Alles (German, 'Germany above all' or 'before' or 'beyond everything'). The German national anthem since 1922, also called the *Deutschlandslied* ('Germany song'). It uses words written by Hoffmann von Fallersleben in 1841, and the music Haydn wrote as the Austrian national anthem (*see* 'EMPEROR'S HYMN') in 1797. The original words were a call for German unification, but after the Second World War the first verse, speaking of a 'greater Germany' and with the ambiguous phrase '*über Alles*', was dropped.

'Devil and Daniel Webster, The'. *See* FAUST OR FAUSTUS (panel, pp.152–6).

Devil's Dictionary, The. A glossary of aphorisms (1911), first published as *The Cynic's Word Book* (1906) by Ambrose Bierce (1842–?1914). Typical entries are:

> APOLOGIZE: To lay the foundation for a future offence.
>
> INSURANCE: An ingenious modern game of chance in which the player is permitted to enjoy the comfortable conviction that he is beating the man who keeps the table.

> MARRIAGE: The state or condition of a community consisting of a master, a mistress and two slaves, making two in all.

Bierce is believed to have died in battle at the age of 71, having been caught in Ojinaga, on the Rio Grande, when it was besieged and taken by Mexican rebels.

'Devil's Trill, The' (Italian name: *Trillo del Diavolo* or *Sonata del Diavolo*). The nickname of a violin sonata in G minor by Giuseppe Tartini (1692–1770), published posthumously in 1798. The story is that the composer dreamt that he sold his soul to the Devil, who then gave a virtuoso performance on the violin. On awaking, Tartini tried to write down the music of his dream, but always said the result was not as good as the original. The trill in question occurs in the last movement. The story formed the basis of a ballet, *Le Violon du diable*, with music by Pugni, first performed in 1849. The association of the Devil with spectacular feats on the fiddle is not uncommon; for example, the great violin virtuoso Niccolò Paganini (1782–1840) was believed by many to be in league with the Devil, such was his remarkable technical mastery of the instrument.

> The demonic is that which cannot be explained in a cerebral and a rational manner ... Paganini is imbued with it to a remarkable degree and it is through this that he produces such a great effect.
>
> GOETHE: *Conversations with Eckermann* (1827)

***Diabelli Variations*.** A set of piano pieces, opus 120, by Beethoven (1770–1827) written in 1819–23. Anton Diabelli (1781–1858) was a music publisher and composer, who commissioned 51 composers – including Czerny, Hummel, Moscheles, Schubert and the twelve-year-old Liszt, as well as Beethoven – to write one variation each on a waltz tune of his own composition. Beethoven got carried away and delivered 33 variations, which were published as volume 1 of Diabelli's two volumes of variations, entitled *Vaterländischer Künstlerverein* (1824).

Diagram Prize. *See* ODDEST TITLE OF THE YEAR AWARD.

'Diamond as Big as the Ritz, The'. A short story in *Tales of the Jazz Age* (1922) by F. Scott Fitzgerald (1896–1940). The bizarre tale concerns a holiday visit of a boy to a schoolfriend's home in Montana, where his family own land that includes a diamond mine and a mountain consisting of a single diamond with a volume of one cubic mile. This eventually collapses.

Diamonds Are Forever. The eighth film (1971) in the James Bond series, starring Sean Connery as Bond and based on a book of the same title (1956) by Ian Fleming (1908–64). The title (which was reinforced by a theme tune sung by Shirley Bassey) was inspired by a slogan devised in 1939 by US advertising writer B.J. Kidd on behalf of De Beers Consolidated Mines in South Africa as part of a campaign to promote diamond engagement rings. The slogan may in turn have been inspired by the cynical Anita Loos (1888–1981):

> So I really think that American gentlemen are the best after all, because kissing your hand may make you feel very very good but a diamond and safire bracelet lasts forever.
>
> ANITA LOOS: *Gentlemen Prefer Blondes* (1925)

In the 1949 film of *Gentlemen Prefer Blondes* Leo Robin provided the following song lyric:

> A kiss on the hand may be quite continental,
> But diamonds are a girl's best friend.

Diary of a Drug Fiend, The. A confessional (1932) by would-be wizard and Satanist, Aleister Crowley (1875–1947), who liked to be known as 'the Great Beast'. The drugs concerned were opiates, just one of the many vices enthusiastically indulged in by 'the wickedest man alive'.

> Do what thou wilt shall be the whole of the Law.
>
> ALEISTER CROWLEY: *Book of the Law* (1909)

Diary of a Nobody, The. The 'diary' (1892) of the fictional Charles Pooter, by George (1847–1912) and Weedon (1852–1919) Grossmith. Pooter, who lives with his wife Carrie and son Lupin in Holloway, north London, suffers from the social anxieties of the not quite established suburban lower middle classes. The opportunities of humiliation for such a person are frequent:

> I left the room with silent dignity, but caught my foot in the mat.
>
> chapter 12

> I am a poor man, but I would gladly give ten shillings to find out who sent me the insulting Christmas card I received this morning.
>
> chapter 13

The book is notable for the wealth of prosaic details of such an unexceptional life, and many regard it as a comic classic. It has given rise to the adjective 'Pooterish'.

Diary of One Who Disappeared. A song cycle by Leoš Janáček (1854–1928), using the texts of a series of anonymous poems the composer read in the Brno newspaper *Lidové noviny* – which also provided the source of Janáček's opera *The* CUNNING LITTLE VIXEN. The work, which was composed in 1917–19 and first performed in 1921, arose out of Janáček's unreciprocated passion for Kamila Stösslová, a much younger woman whom he met after his separation from his wife in 1917. There are 22 songs in the cycle, mostly for tenor and piano, describing a young man who falls for the Gypsy girl Zefka and abandons his family. Three of the songs (9–11) also involve a mezzosoprano (representing Zefka) and/or a women's chorus, while no 13 is an '*intermezzo erotico*' just for piano (the tenor and mezzo being otherwise engaged).

Janáček's fierce obsession with the cool Kamila continued until his death, and he wrote some 700 love letters to her. In one of these he declared that 'While writing the *Diary* I thought only of you. You were Zefka!' Janáček's last work, his second string quartet, is subtitled *Intimate Letters*, and refers to his relationship with Kamila: 'This piece was written in fire,' he said. Shortly afterwards he was dead.

Dies Irae (Latin, 'day of wrath'). A hymn on the Last Judgment attributed to Thomas of Celano (d.1260), Celano being in the Abruzzi mountains of Italy. The hymn begins:

> *Dies irae, dies illa,*
> *Solvet saeclum in favilla,*
> *Teste David cum Sybilla.*
>
> ('That day, the day of wrath, will turn the universe to ashes, as David and also the Sybil foretell.')

The words are derived from the Vulgate version of Zephaniah 1:15, which in the Authorized Version appear as:

> That day is a day of wrath, a day of trouble and distress, a day of wasteness and desolation, a day of darkness and gloominess, a day of clouds and thick darkness.

In the 13th century the words became associated with a particular plainsong sequence (a repetition of the same tune at a different pitch). The words became part of the Requiem Mass, and in many Renaissance settings the composers kept the original plainsong melody, although later composers, such as Mozart and Verdi, provided their own dramatically fearsome settings. The plainsong melody also appears in a number of works of the Romantic era, including Berlioz's SYMPHONIE FANTASTIQUE (1830) and Liszt's *Totentanz* (*see* DANCE OF DEATH, panel, pp.96–8).

Disasters of War, The. A series of grim, powerful etchings (1810–14) by Francisco de Goya (1746–1828) depicting the horrors of the occupation of Spain by Napoleon's French forces. Goya was influenced by *Les Grandes Misères de la guerre* ('the great miseries of war', 1633) by the French engraver Jacques Callot (1592/3–1635), inspired by the horrors of the Thirty Years War (1618–48). In Goya's own time, the Peninsular War (1808–14) saw action by the original *guerrillas*, and the French took heavy reprisals. Appalling brutalities were committed by both sides. As a boy Victor Hugo – whose father was a French military governor in Spain – saw

> a cross to which were nailed limbs of a young man who had been hacked to pieces. Someone had had the horrible intention of rearranging the pieces and reconstructing a corpse out of the remains.

Goya recorded many such scenes of horror – a man being garrotted, a corpse being beaten by peasants, an armless, naked cadaver impaled on a tree stump – with a mixture of acute realism and surreal fantasy. His titles for the etchings include 'The Carnivorous Vulture', 'Bury Them and Be Silent', 'They Will Not Arrive in Time', 'With Reason or Without', 'This Is Worse', 'One Cannot Look at This' and 'Why?' The series constitutes perhaps the most powerful visual indictment of war ever created.

> Of all the great Spaniards who were subtle and savage, Goya is the most subtle, the most savage.
>
> ELIE FAURE: quoted in Chabrun, *Goya* (1965)

'Dissonance' Quartet (German *Dissonanzen Quartett*; French *Les Dissonances*). The nickname given to the string quartet in C, K465 (1785), by Mozart (1756–91). There are some notable dissonances in the introduction to the first movement.

'Distratto, Il' (Italian, 'the absent-minded man' or 'the distracted man'). The nickname given to the symphony no 60 in C (1774–5) by Haydn (1732–1809), most of which is derived from the composer's incidental music for a comedy by J.F. Regnard (1655–1709) entitled *Le Distrait* (German *Der Zerstreute*).

Divine Comedy, The. An epic poem by Dante Alighieri (1265–1321), who completed it in 1321, just before his death. The original title was simply *Commedia* (Italian, 'play'), and it was not until after the 16th century that it became known as the *Divina Commedia*. There are three parts, *Inferno* (Hell), *Purgatorio* and *Paradiso*.

The poet starts his journey through these regions on Good Friday, 1300, guided by the Roman poet Virgil (70–19 BC). Virgil takes him through Hell, which consists of nine levels or circles spiralling down into the earth. The first circle is Limbo, the region for those who cannot go to heaven simply because they have not been baptized, or were born before Jesus Christ. The subsequent circles, from second to ninth, are for the perpetrators of successively more heinous sins. Carnal sinners such as FRANCESCA DA RIMINI (*see* panel, pp.175–6) are on the second circle, and many other historical characters (including several popes) are encountered during the course of Dante's descent. Our vision of Dante's Inferno has largely been shaped by the series of engravings (1861) by the French illustrator Gustave Doré (1832–83).

Subsequently, on Easter morning, Virgil guides Dante up the peak of Purgatory. At the summit Virgil must leave him, as, being a pagan, the ancient Roman cannot take him further upward. That role is left to Beatrice. Beatrice Portinari had become Dante's idealized love when she was just a girl; however, she married another, Simone de Bardi, in 1287, and died in 1290, not yet 24. In *The Divine Comedy* she represents the wisdom of faith, and she leads him through Paradise to God.

The film *Dante's Inferno* (1935) has little to do with *The Divine Comedy* apart from a ten-minute sequence in which an unpleasant carnival owner (Spencer Tracy) is forced to experience a vision of Hell. Other titles inspired by Dante and/or *The Divine Comedy* include:

Dante Sonata, a piano piece (1837–9) by Liszt, originally entitled *Après une lecture du Dante* (French, 'after a reading of Dante').

Dante Symphony (German title: *Eine Symphonie zu Dantes Divina Commedia*), an orchestral piece by Liszt, first performed in 1857, with movements entitled *Inferno* and *Purgatorio*, and ending in a Magnificat.

The System of Dante's Hell (1965), a novel by the African-American writer LeRoi Jones (b.1934) set in the slums of Newark.

The First Circle (1969), a novel by the dissident Soviet writer Alexander

Solzhenitsyn (b.1918), where contemporary Russia is seen as Dante's Limbo.

Hope Abandoned (1974), a memoir by Nadezhda Mandelstam (d.1980) of her husband, the poet Osip Mandelstam (1891–?1938), who was arrested in one of Stalin's purges and died somewhere in the GULAG ARCHIPELAGO. The title of the memoir, a sequel to *Hope Against Hope* (1971), comes from the inscription above the entrance to Dante's Inferno: 'Abandon hope, all ye who enter here' (Canto 3).

Dante's Drum-Kit (1993), a verse collection by the Scottish poet Douglas Dunn (b.1942).

Numerous operas have also been inspired by Dante, few of them memorable.

Division of the Spoils, A. *See* *RAJ QUARTET, THE.*

Do Androids Dream of Electric Sheep? *See* *BLADE RUNNER.*

Doctor Faustus. *See* FAUST OR FAUSTUS (panel, pp.152–6).

Dr Jekyll and Mr Hyde, The Strange Case of. A short novel by Robert Louis Stevenson (1850–94), published in 1886. Dr Jekyll is a physician who is conscious of the duality, the mixture of good and evil, in his own person, and he becomes fascinated by the possibility of what would happen if the two sides could be embodied in different personalities. He succeeds by means of a drug, and is taken over by the evil personality of Mr Hyde. The result for both is disaster. The phrase 'Jekyll and Hyde' has come to denote two contrasting or opposing aspects of one person: Jekyll is the 'good man', Hyde 'the evil that is present'.

Stevenson's tale has been a favourite with film-makers. The earliest, silent version (1921) starred John Barrymore in the title roles, although the version starring Fredric March (1931) is regarded as the classic interpretation. Spencer Tracy essayed the parts a decade later (1941), prompting the *New York Times* to comment, 'Not so much evil incarnate as ham rampant'. There have been several other versions and variations on the theme, including *Dr Jekyll and Sister Hyde* (1971).

Dr Strangelove: or, How I Learned to Stop Worrying and Love the Bomb. A film (1963) based on the novel *Red Alert* by Peter George about the threat of global nuclear destruction. The film was directed by Stanley Kubrick and starred Peter Sellers in three roles, including that of

Dr Strangelove himself (a crippled ex-Nazi scientist) and that of the US president who finds himself helpless to stop events spiralling out of control.

Gentlemen, you can't fight in here. This is the War Room!

Such was the success of the film that in subsequent years any hawkish Cold War warrior was liable to be labelled as a 'Dr Strangelove'.

Doctor Zhivago. A novel (1957) by the Russian writer Boris Pasternak (1890–1960). Set against the background of the Russian Revolution and the ensuing civil war, it tells the story of poet and physician Yuri Zhivago, whose love for the beautiful Lara causes pain for all involved. In Russian, *zhivago* means 'the living', and the word has strong religious connotations: the Russian version of 'Why do you seek the living among the dead?' (the question the angels ask the women who come to see Christ's tomb in the Gospel of St Luke) is '*Chto vy ischyote zhivago mezhdu myortvykh?*' In addition, Yuri is the Russian version of George – the dragon-slaying saint.

The book brought Pasternak himself little happiness. Following his award of the Nobel Prize for Literature, he was pilloried by literary rivals, who accused him of plagiarizing other works, and his companion Olga Ivinskaya, on whom Lara was based, was thrown into prison by the Soviets. The first Russian publication of the novel did not take place until 1987.

David Lean's epic film version (1965) lasts over 190 minutes, and stars Omar Sharif as Zhivago and Julie Christie as Lara. Maurice Jarre's haunting 'Lara's Theme', played on the balalaika, has become a favourite in all places where muzak is played.

Dog Day Afternoon. A film (1975) written by Frank Pierson and directed by Sidney Lumet about a bisexual man (played by Al Pacino) who stages a bank robbery in order to fund a sex-change operation for his transvestite lover (played by Chris Sarandon). The plot was based on a magazine article about a real incident. The 'dog days' have been identified since Roman times as the hottest days of the summer, between early July and mid-August, when Sirius, the Dog Star, is reputed to add its heat to that of the sun.

DOGS AND THEIR RELATIVES

'Dog' Waltz, an alternative name for Chopin's 'MINUTE' WALTZ (1847)

The Hound of the Baskervilles, a Sherlock Holmes novel (1902) by Arthur Conan Doyle

DYNAMISM OF A DOG ON A LEASH, a painting (1912) by Giacomo Balla

BULLDOG DRUMMOND, an adventure thriller (1920) by Sapper

The Rubaiyat of a Scotch Terrier, a work (1926) by Sewell Collins

Un CHIEN ANDALOU, a classic surrealist film (1928)

The Dog Beneath the Skin, a play (1935) by W.H. Auden and Christopher Isherwood

Who's Who in Cocker Spaniels, a reference work (1944) by Marion Frances Robinson Mangrum

The Hundred and One Dalmatians, a fantasy (1956) for children by 'Dodie' Smith

Straw Dogs, a notoriously violent film (1971) directed by Sam Peckinpah and starring Dustin Hoffman

The DOGS BARK, a collection of essays and profiles (1973) by Truman Capote

The DOGS OF WAR, a thriller (1974) by Frederick Forsyth

DOG DAY AFTERNOON, a film (1975) about a bank robbery

Plague Dogs, a novel (1977) by Richard Adams

VOLPONE, OR THE FOX, a play (1605–6) by Ben Jonson

The CUNNING LITTLE VIXEN, an opera (1924) by Leoš Janáček

The LITTLE FOXES, a play (1939) by Lillian Hellman

Fox, a typically gloomy film (1975) by the German director Rainer Werner Fassbinder

The DAY OF THE JACKAL, a thriller (1971) by Frederick Forsyth

The Lone Wolf, a novel (1914) by Louis Joseph Vance, featuring a gentleman thief

Homo Homini Lupus Est (Latin, 'man is a wolf to man'), a painting (1944–8) of a corpse on a gibbet by the French artist Georges Rouault

Peter and the Wolf, a charming musical tale for children (1936) by Sergei Prokofiev

The Wolf Man, a classic Lon Chaney horror film (1941)

I Was a Teenage Werewolf, a fantasy-horror film (1957)

An American Werewolf in London, a semi-spoof but nevertheless scary horror movie (1981)

DANCES WITH WOLVES, an elegiac Western film (1990)

Dogs Bark, The. A collection of essays and profiles (1973) by Truman Capote. The title alludes to the proverb (possibly either Turkish or Arab) 'The dogs bark but the caravan passes.' The saying also appears in the title of George Tabori's book *The Caravan Passes* (1951).

Dogs of War, The. A thriller (1974) by Frederick Forsyth (b.1938). The theme is the attempt by a band of mercenaries to overthrow an African dictator. The title comes from Shakespeare:

> Caesar's spirit, ranging for revenge,
> With Ate by his side, come hot from hell,
> Shall in these confines, with a monarch's voice
> Cry, 'Havoc!' and let slip the dogs of war.
>
> SHAKESPEARE: *Julius Caesar* (1599), III.i

A film version (1980), directed by John Irvin, lacked the tension of the original.

'Dog' Waltz. *See* 'MINUTE' WALTZ.

Dolce Vita, La. A long and episodic film (1960), co-written and directed by Federico Fellini about the meaninglessness of an Italian gossip writer's life (played by Marcel Mastroianni) among the rich, glamorous bored young of Rome. The title, meaning 'the soft life' or 'the sweet life', is an ironical reference to the apparent ease and comfort of life among the jet set. One of the characters, a celebrity snapper called Paparazzo (played by Walter Santesso), gave his name to the paparazzi, the collective name for opportunistic celebrity photographers.

DON JUAN

Don Juan, the archetypal philanderer, has featured in numerous plays, poems, stories and operas. The figure is possibly based on one Don Juan Tenorio, the son of a notable family in 14th-century Seville. The story is that he killed the commandant of Ulloa after seducing his daughter. He then invited the statue of the murdered man (erected in the Franciscan convent) to a feast, at the end of which the sculptured figure despatched him to hell.

Don Juan first appears in literature in the play *El Burlador de Sevilla y convidado de piedra* (1630; 'the seducer (or trickster) of Seville and the stone guest') by the Spanish dramatist Tirso de Molina (1584–1648). In this play Don Juan is a lively and humorous figure, defying his eventual fate. He subsequently made appearances, with different aspects of his personality stressed, in works by Molière (1622–73), Mozart (1756–91) and Byron (1788–1824), among many others.

Molière's *Don Juan, ou le festin de pierre* (1665; '...or the stone feast') provided the basis for the dramatic ballet of the same title (1761) by Christoph Willibald von Gluck (1714–87) with scenario by Ranieri Calzabigi (1714–95) and choreography by Gasparo Angiolini (1731–1803).

The full title of Mozart's opera is *Il dissoluto punito, ossia Il Don Giovanni*. His librettist, Lorenzo da Ponte, used as a particular source Giovanni Bertati's play *Don Giovanni, ossia Il Convitato di Pietra* (1775). This had also given rise to an opera by Giuseppe Gazzaniga, first performed earlier in the same year (1787) as Mozart's work.

Byron's long, unfinished poem *Don Juan* (1819–24) departs radically from the traditional story. Byron's Don Juan is an innocent young man seduced by women who will not leave him alone; he would be honourable if only a depraved, 'civilized' society offered any honourable options. The work is satirical in intent, and the voice of the poet urbane and ironic.

Many other works (including dozens of long-forgotten operas) have been inspired by the legend, including:

- *The Libertine*, a play (1676) by Thomas Shadwell (Dryden's *MAC FLECKNOE*)
- *Don Juan und Faust*, a tragedy (1829) blending Mozart's *Don Giovanni* with Goethe (*see* FAUST OR FAUSTUS, panel, pp.152–6) by Christian Grabbe (1801– 36); this became the basis of the opera by Hermann Reutter, *Don Juan und Faust* (1950)
- 'Les Âmes du Purgatoire' ('the souls of Purgatory'), a short story (1834) by Prosper Mérimée (1803–70), based on a real character, Miguel de Mañara (d.1697), and in which the hero ultimately repents
- *Don Juan de Mañara*, a play (1836) based on the above by Alexandre Dumas *père* (1802–70)
- *The Stone Guest*, a play (1839) by Aleksandr Pushkin (1799–1837), which inspired the opera of the same title (first performed 1872) by Aleksandr Sergeyevich Dargomyzhsky (1813–69), completed after his death by Cui and Rimsky-Korsakov
- *Don Juan Tenorio* (1844) by José Zorrilla y Moral (1817–93), one of the most popular plays in 19th-century Spain, in which the hero repents and which is traditionally performed every Halloween
- *Don Juan*, a posthumously published epic (1851) by the Austrian poet Nikolaus Lenau (1802–50); the basis of Richard Strauss's symphonic poem, opus 20 (1889)
- *Fifine at the Fair*, a long poem (1872) by Robert Browning, in which Don Juan is the speaker
- *A morte de D. João* (1874; 'the death of Don Juan'), a realist, anti-Romantic version of the character by the Portuguese poet Abílio Manuel Guerra Junqueiro (1850–1923)
- *Le Don Juan suisse*, an opera (1880) by Léo Delibes (1836–91)
- 'Don Juan in Hell', the dreamlike third act of Shaw's *MAN AND SUPERMAN* (1905), sometimes performed as a separate piece
- *Fräulein Don Juan*, an opera (1915) by Ralph Benatzky (1844–1957)
- *Don Juan*, a Warner Brothers film (US, 1926) notable for having

a synchronized musical soundtrack (synchronized dialogue was introduced in the following year with *The Jazz Singer*)

- *Juan in America*, a humorous tale (1931) of an innocent abroad, by the Scottish novelist Eric Linklater (1899–1974)
- *The Private Life of Don Juan*, a film (1934) directed by Alexander Korda and starring Douglas Fairbanks Snr and Merle Oberon
- *Don Juan*, a ballet (1936) created by Michel Fokine (1880–1942)
- *Don Juan de Mañara*, an opera (1937) by Eugene Goossens (1893–1962), the English conductor and composer
- *Don Juan*, a poetic drama (1953) by Ronald Duncan (1914–82), British playwright
- *Don Juan, or The Love of Geometry* (1953), a reinterpretation of the story by the German–Swiss dramatist Max Frisch (1911–91)
- *Don Zhuan*, a puppet play (1976) by Sergey Obraztsov (1901–92), Russian puppeteer
- *Don Juan de Marco*, a film (1995) in which Johnny Depp, in modern California, believes himself to be the great romancer. Marlon Brando plays his psychiatrist

---

Domestic Symphony. *See* SYMPHONIA DOMESTICA.

Don Giovanni. *See* DON JUAN (panel, pp.120–2).

Double Indemnity. A classic film noir (1944), adapted by Raymond Chandler and Billy Wilder (who also directed) from a novel of the same title by James M. Cain (1892–1977). It starred Fred MacMurray as the insurance salesman who becomes the lover of the scheming Barbara Stanwyck. She persuades him to help her murder her husband for the insurance money she will receive, but does not allow for the interference of insurance investigator Edward G. Robinson. The title refers to the clause in the insurance policy that promises payment of a double benefit in the case of accidental death. The plot was based on an actual murder case, the notorious Snyder Gray affair of 1927. Lawrence Kasdan's film *Body Heat* (1981) made steamy use of the same basic story.

DRINK

'COFFEE' CANTATA, a secular cantata (1732) by J.S. Bach

The ABSINTHE DRINKER, a painting (1859) by Edouard Manet

CAKES AND ALE, a novel (1930) by W. Somerset Maugham

WHISKY GALORE, a novel (1947) by Compton Mackenzie (film version 1948)

TEA AND SYMPATHY, a play (1953) by Robert Anderson

CIDER WITH ROSIE, an autobiographical account (1959) of his early years by Laurie Lee

DAYS OF WINE AND ROSES, a film (1962) about alcoholics

BRANDY OF THE DAMNED, a collection of essays on classical music (1964) by Colin Wilson

RUM, BUM, AND CONCERTINA, the autobiography (1977) of George Melly

MAKING COCOA FOR KINGSLEY AMIS, a poetry collection (1986) by Wendy Cope

Like Water for Hot Chocolate, a novel (1990) by the Mexican writer Laura Esquivel, filmed as *Like Water for Chocolate* in 1991. The book and film combine passion, magic realism and some excellent recipes.

Down and Out in Paris and London. An autobiographical study (1933) by George Orwell (1903–50), the author's first published book. It is an account of working with the poor in London's East End, and performing menial jobs in a working-class district of Paris, while trying to get his writing published. A useful piece of advice in the book is to stick to the cheaper restaurants in Paris, as in the more glamorous establishments the waiters are likely to spit in the soup.

Dream of Gerontius, The. A choral piece (the composer rejected the label 'oratorio') by Edward Elgar (1857–1934), using a text taken from a long mystical poem by Cardinal Newman (1801–90). The work was first performed in 1900 at the Birmingham Festival. Newman's poem, published in 1866, concerns the agonizing death of Gerontius (from Greek *gerōn, geront-*, 'old man') and his experiences in the afterlife. A copy of the poem was found near the body of Gordon of Khartoum, covered in Gordon's jottings, and it was a copy of this annotated text that inspired Elgar. Newman's poem includes such infelicitous lines as:

> They sing of thy approaching agony,
> Which thou so eagerly didst question of

which Elgar nevertheless managed to set to music.

George Moore described Elgar's piece as 'Holy water in a German beer barrel', while Charles Villiers Stanford complained that it was 'stinking of incense'. Frederick Delius opined that '*Gerontius* is a nauseating work', although Pope Pius XIII believed it to be 'a sublime masterpiece'.

Dreigroschenoper, Der. *See* THREEPENNY OPERA, THE.

'Drum' Mass. *See* 'KETTLEDRUM' MASS.

'Drum Roll' Symphony (German '*Symphonie mit dem Paukenwirbel*'). The nickname for the symphony no 103 in E flat (1795) by Haydn (1732–1809), one of the 'SALOMON' SYMPHONIES. It opens with a roll on the kettledrums, which is repeated later in the first movement.

Drunk Man Looks at the Thistle, A. A 2500-line poem (1926) by the Scottish poet Hugh MacDiarmid (C.M. Grieve, 1892–1978), written in a variety of the Scots language synthesized from his own upbringing in the Scottish Borders and from Jamieson's *Etymological Dictionary of the Scottish Language* (1808). The framework story of the poem – reminiscent of Burns's phantasmagoric 'TAM-O'-SHANTER' – is that a Scots drunk has stumbled into a ditch in the dark on the way back from the pub to his wife Jean, and there sees a thistle in the moonlight. However, MacDiarmid's aim was to create a work as modernist as T.S. Eliot's *The* WASTE LAND, and at the same time to return Scots literature from a parochial 'kailyard' (cabbage patch) to the international stage it had occupied during the Renaissance – hence his slogan 'Not Burns – Dunbar!' (*see* 'LAMENT FOR THE MAKARIS').

> A Scottish poet maun assume
> The burden o' his people's doom,
> And dee to brak' their livin' tomb.

So the poem combines more traditional Scots lyrics with dramatic monologues and complex metaphysical meditations, full of allusions to the culture and thought of many nations, via which MacDiarmid struggles to redefine Scotland, the Scots and the role of the individual poet:

> I'll ha'e nae hauf-way hoose, but aye be whaur
> Extremes meet – it's the only way I ken
> To dodge the curst conceit o' bein richt
> That damns the vast majority o' men.

The title was suggested to MacDiarmid by his friend and former teacher, the composer F.G. Scott, and the use of the indefinite and definite articles is important. '*A* drunk man' is any man, Everyman:

> The wee reliefs we ha'e in booze,
> Or wun at times in carnal states,
> May hide frae us but canna cheenge
> The silly horrors o' oor fates.

'*The* thistle' is a protean symbol, transmogrifying in the moonlight (and with the aid of whisky) from – among many other things – skeleton to pickled foetus to crucifix to bagpipes to tormenting labyrinth to the sail on Ahab's *Pequod* in pursuit of 'the muckle white whale' (*MOBY-DICK*):

> And this deid thing, whale-white obscenity,
> This horror that I writhe in – is my soul!

But the thistle is above all, and throughout all these painful convolutions, a symbol of Scotland – and had been for centuries.

The origin of the thistle as the symbol of Scotland goes back to early medieval times, when, according to legend, the Scots were alerted to the presence of a Viking raiding party when one of them trod on a thistle in the dark. The thistle was later adopted as the heraldic emblem of Scotland, probably by James III (ruled 1460–88), and it later became associated with the motto '*Nemo me impune lacessit*' (Latin, 'nobody touches, or provokes, me with impunity', or, in Scots, 'Whaur daur meddle wi' me?'), which first appeared on coinage during the reign of James VI (1567–1625).

MacDiarmid returned to the thistle in the title of a 1947 collection, *A Kist of Thistles*. This plays on the Scots term for a church organ, a *kist* ('chest') *of whistles*.

'Dry Salvages, The'. *See FOUR QUARTETS.*

Dry White Season, A. A novel (1979) by the South African writer André Brink (b.1935), originally written and published in Afrikaans as *'n Droë wit seisoen*, and translated by himself. It is one of six novels he wrote between 1958 and 1967, using modern narrative techniques, as a counterblast to those Afrikaans novels that he described as a 'literature of drought and poor whites'. The message of this one, in which a white teacher, believing himself to be apolitical, embarks on a quest for justice after the death in custody of a black colleague, is that in the prevailing situation in South Africa it was impossible for anyone to remain politically uncommitted. A film version (1989) was directed by Euzhan Palcy.

'Dulce et Decorum Est'. A poem (1918) by the war poet Wilfred Owen (1893–1918) in which he describes the horrors of a gas attack in the trenches of the First World War. The poem was informed by Owen's personal experiences of the trenches and made doubly poignant by his own death in the last week of the war, when he was killed in action on the Sambre Canal. The title, with which the poem also ends, is a quotation from Horace's *Odes*:

> *Dulce et decorum est pro patria mori.*
>
> HORACE: *Odes*, III.ii

This is usually translated as: 'It is sweet and becoming to die for one's country.'

> If you could hear, at every jolt, the blood
> Come gargling from the froth-corrupted lungs,
> Obscene as cancer,
> Bitter as the cud
> Of vile, incurable sores on innocent tongues, –
> My friend, you would not tell with such high zest
> To children ardent for some desperate glory,
> The old Lie: Dulce et decorum est
> Pro patria mori.
>
> WILFRED OWEN: 'Dulce et Decorum Est' (1918)

Dumbarton Oaks. A 'little concerto in the style of the Brandenburg Concertos' by Igor Stravinsky (1882–1971). It was commissioned in 1938 by Mr and Mrs R.W. Bliss, who lived in the mansion of Dumbarton Oaks in Georgetown, near Washington DC. Between 21 August and 7 October 1944 the same mansion played host to a conference of Allied powers (China, the Soviet Union, the United States and the United Kingdom) that laid the foundations of what was to become the United Nations.

'Dumky' Trio. The nickname given to the piano trio, opus 90 (1891), by Dvořák. Each of its six movements is a *dumka* (plural *dumky*), originally a Slavonic word for a sentimental or sad folk ballad, but which Dvořák came to use for a piece that alternates between melancholy and exuberance; there are examples of such *dumky* in his string sextet and piano quintet. There is also a set of piano pieces by Tchaikovsky entitled *Dumka* (1886).

dump. A 16th-century English term for a mournful song, elegy or lament, found in the titles of musical pieces of the period such as the anonymous harpsichord piece from the 1540s, 'My Lady Carey's Dompe'. Such titles usually contain the name of a person, usually memorializing them, for example 'A Dump upon the death of the most noble Henry Earl of Pembroke'. The word is related to the phrase 'down in the dumps':

> Why, how now, Katherine! in your dumps?
>
> SHAKESPEARE: *The Taming of the Shrew* (1593), II.i

Dunciad, The. A mock-heroic epic by Alexander Pope (1688–1744), of which the first three books were published in 1728, *The Dunciad Variorum* added in 1729, and a fourth book, *The New Dunciad*, in 1742. Pope acknowledged authorship of the previously anonymous work in 1735, and a revised edition of the whole work appeared in 1743. The hero of Pope's epic is the Shakespearian scholar and poet Lewis Theobald (1688–1744), who had criticized Pope's edition of Shakespeare for its intrusive emendations. In *The Dunciad*, Theobald becomes the favourite son of the Goddess of Dulness, although in the complete edition he is replaced by Colley Cibber (1671–1757), the poet laureate and actor-manager, who had annoyed Pope (and many other people). The work concerns the failings of many contemporary writers, which Pope sees leading to the triumph of Dulness and the consequent expiration of religion and morality. The poem ends in a dystopian vision:

> Lo! thy dread Empire, Chaos! is restor'd;
> Light dies before thy uncreating world;
> Thy hand, great Anarch! lets the curtain fall,
> And universal Darkness buries All.

Pope's title is, of course, modelled on those of genuine epics – the *ILIAD* of Homer (which Pope had translated) and the *Aeneid* of Virgil. A similar device was used by the anonymous author of an 1808 parody of Wordsworth, entitled *The Simpliciad.*

Dynamism of a Dog on a Leash. A painting (1912) by the Italian Futurist Giacomo Balla (1871–1958). The work (which is now in the Museum of Modern Art, New York) depicts the dog in motion using a technique similar to time-lapse photography. The concept is similar to that realized in Marcel Duchamp's *NUDE DESCENDING A STAIRCASE*, painted in the same year.

E

Eagle Has Landed, The. A film (1976) adapted by Tom Mankiewicz from a bestselling novel by Jack Higgins (1975) about a fictional Nazi plot to kill Winston Churchill during the Second World War. The film starred Donald Sutherland as the hitman detailed to execute the assassination. In the original novel Heinrich Himmler receives the message that 'the eagle has landed' and thereby knows that his agent is safely on British soil. Higgins himself claimed that at least half of his story was based on truth, but left it to the reader to decide what was true and what was fiction.

Higgins cannot have been unaware that in 1969 the phrase became the first words spoken by a human being on the surface of the moon, when it was used by US astronaut Neil Armstrong to report the safe touchdown of the lunar module *Eagle*:

> Tranquillity Base here – the Eagle has landed.
>
> NEIL ARMSTRONG: radio transmission (1969)

'East Coker'. *See* *FOUR QUARTETS*.

East is East. A comedy film (1999) set in the north of England about the family of an English mother and a strict Pakistani father. The title comes from Kipling:

> Oh, East is East, and West is West, and never the twain shall meet,
> Till Earth and Sky stand presently at God's great Judgement Seat;
> But there is neither East nor West, Border, nor Breed, nor Birth,

When two strong men stand face to face, tho' they come from the ends of earth!

RUDYARD KIPLING: 'The Ballad of East and West' (1892)

East of Eden. A novel (1952) by John Steinbeck (1902–68). The story covers two families in the Salinas Valley through three generations of discord. It centres on Adam Trask, his murderous wife Kathy, who abandons her family and becomes the madam of a brothel, and their twin sons, Aron and Caleb, whose rivalry recalls the biblical story of Cain and Abel (also sons of an Adam). The title is drawn from that account:

And Cain went out from the presence of the Lord, and dwelt in the land of Nod, on the east of Eden.

Genesis 4:16

A film version (1955), starring James Dean, was directed by Elia Kazan.

Eastward Hoe. *See* *WESTWARD HO!*

Eating People is Wrong. A satirical campus novel (1959) by Malcolm Bradbury (1932–2000), set in a provincial redbrick university. The hero is Professor Treece, a no-longer-young liberal humanist. The title phrase comes from Michael Flanders's song 'The Reluctant Cannibal' (music by Donald Swann), which featured in their review *At the Drop of a Hat* (1957). The eponymous hero of the song – the son of the Chief Assistant to the Assistant Chief – maintains 'I won't let another person pass my lips'. His father, infuriated at his son's wilful ways, eventually wins the argument by saying, 'Don't Eat People? You might as well say Don't Kill People' – which they both agree is *ridiculous*.

Ebony Concerto. A clarinet concerto by Igor Stravinsky (1882–1971), written for the American jazz clarinetist Woody Herman, and first performed by him and his band at Carnegie Hall in 1946. 'Ebony stick' was US jazz slang for a clarinet.

1812 Overture. The popular name for *The Year 1812*, a concert overture, opus 49 (1880), by Tchaikovsky (1840–93). The work celebrates Napoleon's retreat from Moscow in 1812, and both 'La MARSEILLAISE' and the tsarist Russian national anthem can be heard. There are optional parts in the score for cannon and a military band, and the work has become particularly popular as an accompaniment to firework displays.

Eight Songs for a Mad King. A piece of music theatre for male voice and chamber orchestra by Peter Maxwell Davies (b.1934), first performed in 1969. The 'Mad King' is George III, who suffered from intermittent episodes of insanity (perhaps caused by the rare hereditary disease porphyria) for some decades before becoming permanently incapacitated in 1810. The text by Randolph Stow includes quotations from George III.

See also The MADNESS OF GEORGE III.

84 Charing Cross Road. A correspondence between the spirited US writer Helen Hanff (1916–97) and the rather reserved Frank Doel of Messrs Marks and Co, sellers of rare and secondhand books at 84 Charing Cross Road, London. The 20-year correspondence began in 1949, when Hanff saw an advertisement for Marks and Co's mail-order service, and warmed into a kind of bibliophiles' love affair, although the two never met. A stage version was the basis of the 1987 film, starring Anne Bancroft and Anthony Hopkins.

Eikon Basilike (Greek, 'royal image'). *Eikon Basilike: The Portraicture of His Sacred Majestie in His Solitudes and Sufferings* appeared in 1649, very soon after the execution of Charles I. It purported to be his own account of his reflections and feelings during, and before, his imprisonment. It greatly strengthened royalist sentiment and led to the less influential *Eikonoklastes* ('image breakers'; 1649), commissioned as a riposte by Parliament from John Milton (1608–74). Dr John Gauden (1605–62) later claimed authorship of *Eikon Basilike* at the time of his election to the bishopric of Worcester. It appears that he had edited the king's papers, and his version received the royal approval. His claim is discussed at length in F.F. Madan's *A New Bibliography of the Eikon Basilike.*

Electric Kool-Aid Acid Test, The. An account (1968) by the US journalist Tom Wolfe (b.1931) of a tour across America with the hippie writer Ken Kesey and his companions, the Merry Pranksters, in the first-ever psychedelic bus. The hyper-hip title includes a reference to LSD ('acid'). The book provoked surprisingly unstaid responses from America's more respectable newspapers:

> Vibrating dazzle!
>
> *New York Times*

> A Day-Glo book, illuminating, merry, surreal!
>
> *Washington Post*

> Electrifying!
>
> *San Francisco Chronicle*

Electrification of the Soviet Union, The. An opera by Nigel Osborne (b.1948) with a libretto by Craig Raine (b.1944), based on the novel *The Last Summer* and the poem *Spectorsky* by Boris Pasternak (1890–1960). It was first performed in 1987 at Glyndebourne. The story concerns a young poet's loves and his response to society, and the title comes from Lenin's famous practical definition of communism, from his report to the 8th party congress of 1920:

> Communism is Soviet power plus the electrification of the whole country.

Elegies to the Spanish Republic. The title of a series of paintings by the great abstract expressionist Robert Motherwell (1915–91), characterized by vertical bands and ovals in black, white and subdued colours. Motherwell began the series in 1949, on the tenth anniversary of the final defeat of the Spanish Republic by Franco's nationalists. Over the next three decades he painted almost 150 of these *Elegies*.

See also AT FIVE IN THE AFTERNOON.

Elegy for Young Lovers. An opera by Hans Werner Henze (b.1926), with a libretto by W.H. Auden (1907–73) and Chester Kallman (1921–75), first performed in 1961. The story, set in the Austrian Alps, concerns a selfish and egotistical poet, Gregor Mittenhofer, who uses the people around him for his inspiration. The young lovers of the title are Elisabeth and the poet's stepson Toni, sent out by Mittenhofer to gather edelweiss on the Hammerhorn, where they die. This gives Mittenhofer the inspiration for his finest poem, 'Elegy for Young Lovers'.

Elegy Written in a Country Church-Yard. *See* GRAY'S ELEGY.

Elephant Man, The. A film (1980), shot in black and white and directed by David Lynch, about a man whose grossly distorted ('elephantine') features (resulting from disease) sentences him to a life as a carnival-show freak until he attracts the attention of a sympathetic member of the medical establishment. The film, starring John Hurt, was based upon the life story of the real John Merrick, who was thus disfigured and became the subject of medical curiosity in Victorian England.

Elia, Essays of. A series of essays by Charles Lamb (1775–1834), published in the *London Magazine* between 1820 and 1823 under the *nom de plume* 'Elia'. The first essay was a description of the South Sea House, where Lamb had briefly worked, and where there had been an Italian employee called Elia, a 'gay light-hearted foreigner', and where his brother worked as a clerk. Lamb apparently adopted a pseudonym to spare his brother's embarrassment, but Elia also developed into a persona for the essayist. A second series, *The Last Essays of Elia*, was published in 1833.

Embarkation for Cythera, The (French title: *L'Embarquement pour l'île de Cythère*). The title of three paintings (the best known and finest one dating from 1717) by the French artist Jean-Antoine Watteau (1684–1721). The painting belongs to the genre of *fêtes galantes* – courtly entertainments taking place in parkland, with the participants sometimes dressed in rustic costumes. In this case, the landscape where the courtiers prepare for their departure to the island of love is empty and somewhat melancholy. Traditionally, in French and Italian culture, the journey to Cythera is a difficult quest, while with Watteau the island itself seems evanescent, an impossible dream.

The real Greek island of Cythera (Kíthira) lies between the Peloponnese and Crete, and was originally a Minoan colony. It became associated with love because it was one of the earliest and most important centres of the cult of Aphrodite, the Greek goddess of love – who was also known as Cythereia. According to Hesiod, Aphrodite sprang from the sea foam resulting from the severing of the genitals of Uranus, and according to one version she came ashore at Cythera (another version says Cyprus).

Quelle est cette île triste et noir? C'est Cythère,
Nous dit-on, un pays fameux dans les chansons,
Eldorado banal de tous les vieux garçons.
Regardez, après tout, c'est un pauvre terre.

('What is that sad black island? It's Cythera, they tell us, a land celebrated in song, the banal Eldorado of all the old boys. Look, after all, it's a poor land.')

CHARLES BAUDELAIRE: *Les Fleurs du mal* (1857), 'Un Voyage à Cythère'

Emin's tent and bed, Tracey. *See* EVERYONE I'VE EVER SLEPT WITH.

'Emperor' Concerto. The nickname given in English-speaking countries to the piano concerto no 5, opus 73 (1808) by Beethoven (1770–1827). The origin of the name is unknown, although it suits the majesty of the work.

'Emperor' Quartet (German, *Kaiserquartett*). The nickname given to the quartet in C, opus 76 no 3 (*c.*1799), by Haydn (1732–1809). The slow movement consists of variations on Haydn's tune for the 'EMPEROR'S HYMN'.

'Emperor's Hymn' (German, *Kaiserlied*). A patriotic hymn by Haydn, composed in 1797 to words by Leopold Haschka (1749–1827), beginning '*Gott erhalte Franz den Kaiser*' ('God preserve the emperor Francis'). This immediately became the Austrian national anthem, and remained as such until the establishment of the Austrian republic in 1918, when, although Haydn's tune was retained, new words by Ottokar Kernstock were adopted, beginning '*Sei gesegnet ohne Ende*' ('thine be never-ending blessings'). Both tune and words were abandoned in 1946, the former being replaced by a piece of Mozart (K483) and the latter by a text beginning '*Land der Berge, Land am Strome*' ('land of mountains, land on the river'). Haydn re-used his tune, which he derived from a Croatian folk melody, in his 'EMPEROR' QUARTET, and it was later borrowed for *DEUTSCHLAND ÜBER ALLES*. It also appears in English hymn books under the name 'Austria', to which the hymn 'Glorious things of thee are spoken' is sung, the words being by John Newton (1725–1807).

Empire of the Senses (Japanese title: *Ai No Corrida*; also called *Empire of the Passions* and *In the Realm of the Senses*). A notorious Japanese film (1976) written and directed by Nagisa Oshima (b.1932). The graphic sex – the story concerns the passionate affair between a servant girl and her master, and ends in the former killing and mutilating the latter – ensured that the film did not receive a certificate for public exhibition in Britain until 1991. Oshima was inspired by an incident in 1936 in which a woman was found wandering around Tokyo with her lover's severed penis.

One of the English titles was parodied by self-styled 'Post-Modern Literature's Girl Wonder', US writer Kathy Acker (1948–97), in her experimental novel *Empire of the Senseless* (1988). This is set in a Paris of the near future, and features the terrorists and occasional lovers Thivai, a pirate, and Abhor, a semi-human robot.

Enchanted Castle, The. The popular name for a painting (1664), more properly called *Psyche outside the Palace of Cupid*, by Claude Gellée (Le Lorrain; 1600–82). The popular name was first bestowed by the engraver William Woollett in his print of the painting in 1782, and was picked up by the poet John Keats (1795–1821):

> You know the Enchanted Castle it doth stand
> Upon a rock on the border of a lake
> Nested in trees, which all do seem to shake
> From some old magic like Urganda's sword.
>
> Letter to John Hamilton Reynolds, 25 March 1818

The figure in the foreground of the desolate scene is actually Psyche, who fell in love with the god Cupid (as related in Apuleius' *The* GOLDEN ASS). Cupid took her to his palace (the dark 'enchanted castle' that stands on the shore of a lake in Claude's painting), but forbade her to ever see him, visiting her only at night. Psyche disobeyed his injunction, and looked at him by the light of a lamp while he slept. But Cupid woke up, and left her heartbroken. In Claude's painting there is an open casement in the side of the castle, showing the way he has flown. Keats homed in on this open casement in his 'ODE TO A NIGHTINGALE' (1819):

> The voice I hear this passing night was heard
> In ancient days by emperor and clown:
> Perhaps the self-same song …
>
> …
>
> Charm'd magic casements, opening on the foam
> Of perilous seas, in faery lands forlorn.

Endgame. A play by the Irish writer Samuel Beckett (1906–89), first performed in French, in London in 1957, with the French title *Fin de partie.* The English version, with the title *Endgame*, was published the following year. In the play four enigmatic characters, blind Hamm, Clov his helper, and Nagg and Nell, their 'accursed progenitors' (who are encased in dustbins), inhabit a bare room with just two small curtained windows. The play was said to be the author's favourite among his own works. The title refers to chess, in which the endgame is the final series of moves in which only a few pieces are left on the board, and one player completes his victory over the other.

> *Clov:* Do you believe in the life to come?
> *Hamm:* Mine was always that.

ENDYMION

The story of Endymion has inspired a number of works of literature. In Greek mythology Endymion was the handsome king (or shepherd king) of Elis (a region in the northwest corner of the Peloponnese). Selene, the moon goddess, falls in love with him and bears him 50 children; in Romanized versions she is replaced by Cynthia, a name for Diana (Artemis) used to denote the moon. Later Zeus gives Endymion the chance to choose his own fate, and Endymion chooses to sleep for ever on Mount Latmus, never growing old. In later reworkings, it is Selene who puts Endymion to sleep, so that she may enjoy him. In another version Endymion is taken up to heaven, falls in love with Hera, and is cast down into Hades for his presumption.

Endimion, the Man in the Moon is a prose drama by John Lyly (?1554–1606). It was first performed by a children's company in 1588, and published in 1591. Endimion leaves Tellus (the earth) for Cynthia (the moon); Tellus and the witch Dipsas send Endimion to sleep for 40 years, but Cynthia wakes him with a kiss.

Endimion and Phoebe is a long poem by Michael Drayton (1563–1631), modelled on Ovid and published in 1595. In Greek myth, Phoebe was a Titaness, the daughter of Uranus and Gaea, who became identified with Artemis (Diana), the moon goddess. In poetic contexts the name is used to denote the moon. Drayton's poem was one of the sources used by Keats for his *Endymion*.

Endymion is a long poem by John Keats (1795–1821), published in 1818. It was dedicated to the young poet and literary forger Thomas Chatterton, who had taken his life in 1770 and subsequently became an icon of the Romantic movement. In Keats's poem Endymion pursues his ideal and transcendent love, Cynthia (the moon), and in the end finds her embodied in an earthly maiden, Phoebe (a name that in other contexts frequently denotes the moon). The poem had a notoriously rough ride with the critics:

> It is a better and a wiser thing to be a starved apothecary than a starved poet; so back to the shop Mr John, back to 'plasters, pills, and ointment boxes'.
>
> JOHN GIBSON LOCKHART: in *Blackwood's Edinburgh Magazine*, August 1818. Keats had trained as an apothecary, before abandoning that profession for poetry

Endymion is also the title of a novel by Benjamin Disraeli (1804–81), published in 1880. Here the title refers to one of the central characters, who shares little with the Endymion of myth, although he is a quiet and pleasant boy. The novel's setting is the British political world earlier in the 19th century, and by the end of the book Endymion has become prime minister.

One of the more notable appearances of Endymion in painting is in the proto-Romantic *The Sleep of Endymion* (1792) by Anne-Louis Girodet-Trioson (1767–1824). The painting is in the Louvre, Paris. Finally, in botany, the bluebells comprise the genus *Endymion*.

> The moon sleeps with Endymion,
> And would not be awak'd.
>
> SHAKESPEARE: *The Merchant of Venice* (1596), V.i

English Bards and Scotch Reviewers. A verse riposte by Lord Byron (1788–1824) to a hostile review of his *Hours of Idleness* in the *Edinburgh Review*. In the poem, published in 1809, Byron declares:

> Fools are my theme, let satire be my song.

Among these 'fools' are to be found the editor of the *Edinburgh Review*, Francis Jeffrey ('Self-constituted judge of poesy'); the 'ballad-monger' Robert Southey (whose 'epics cram the creaking shelves'); Walter Scott ('And think'st thou, Scott! by vain conceit perchance, / On public taste to foist thy stale romance ...?'); S.T. Coleridge (he of the 'turgid ode and tumid stanza'); and William Wordsworth ('Who, both by precept and example, shows, / That prose is verse, and verse is merely prose').

Byron later had cause to return to the subject of 'Scotch reviewers', when John Gibson Lockhart mounted a series of vicious attacks on the young poet John Keats in *Blackwood's* magazine, and was joined in this by the *Quarterly Review* (both journals being published in Edinburgh). This hostile criticism was taken by many to have hastened the death of the young poet:

> 'Tis strange the mind, that very fiery particle,
> Should let itself be snuff'd out by an article.
>
> BYRON: *Don Juan*, XI

> Who killed John Keats?
> 'I,' says the Quarterly,
> So savage and Tartarly;
> ''Twas one of my feats.'
>
> BYRON: 'John Keats' (1821)

English Patient, The. A novel (1992) by Michael Ondaatje (b.1943), which was joint winner of the Booker Prize for fiction with *Sacred Hunger* by Barry Unsworth (b.1930). It is set in a battered Tuscan villa surrounded by unexploded mines, as the Second World War draws to a close in 1945. Four characters inhabit the villa: Kip, an Indian bomb-disposal expert; Caravaggio, a Canadian spy and thief; Hana, a young nurse; and her charge, the 'English patient', who has been appallingly burnt in a plane crash in North Africa. Little by little we come to find out more about this character's history. He is in fact a Hungarian, Count Almasy, and Ondaatje based him on the real Count Laszlo Almasy, the noted explorer of the Libyan Desert who did indeed make the discoveries featured in the novel. During the war (Hungary being allied to Nazi Germany) he helped the Afrika Korps, and his knowledge of the desert helped him to deliver two German agents behind British lines, the pair later establishing themselves in Cairo. His obituarist in the journal of the Royal Geographical Society concluded:

> On his desert record and on his war record, the judgment can safely be passed: 'a Nazi but a sportsman'.
>
> *Geographical Journal*, vol. 107 (2), June 1951

Ondaatje's characters Geoffrey and Katherine Clifton are loosely based on Sir Robert and Lady Clayton East Clayton. Sir Robert died in 1932, at the age of 24, shortly after returning from an expedition with Almasy. The following year Lady Clayton East Clayton (née Dorothy Mary Durrant), who was also a great adventurer, 'met with her death at Brooklands when engaged in aviation' (*The Times*, 16 September 1933).

A visually glossy Oscar-winning film version of *The English Patient* (1996) was directed by Anthony Minghella. Starring Ralph Fiennes as Almasy, Juliette Binoche as Hana, and Kristin Scott Thomas and Colin Firth as Katharine and Geoffrey Clifton, the film largely eschewed the narrative obliquities and moral ambivalences of the original in favour of old-fashioned but wholehearted romance.

Enigma Variations. An orchestral work by Edward Elgar (1857–1934), opus 36, first performed in 1899. The words on the title page of the score are 'Variations on an original theme', the word 'Enigma' only appearing on the first page of the music. The work is 'Dedicated to my friends pictured within'. Each of these friends, identified cryptically, has a variation. They are:

1 C.A.E. – Elgar's wife, Caroline Alice Elgar

2 H.D.S-P. – Hew David Steuart-Powell, an amateur pianist

3 R.B.T. – Richard Baxter Townshend, a writer whose impersonation of an old man in an amateur theatrical production is evoked in the variation

4 W.M.B. – William Meath Baker, 'country squire, gentleman and scholar'

5 R.P.A. – Richard Arnold, son of the poet Matthew Arnold

6 Ysobel – Isabel Fitton, an amateur viola player

7 Troyte – Arthur Troyte Griffith, a friend whose limitations as a pianist the variation depicts

8 W.N. – Winifred Norbury, a woman associated with the Worcestershire Philharmonic Society

9 Nimrod – A.J. Jaeger, a close friend of Elgar (*Jaeger* is German for 'hunter', and Nimrod was the great hunter mentioned in Genesis 10:8–9)

10 Dorabella – Dora Penney, a friend

11 G.R.S. – George Sinclair, organist at Hereford Cathedral, although the variation is said by some to depict Sinclair's dog

12 B.G.N. – Basil Nevinson, an amateur cellist

13 *** – some say this was Lady Mary Lygon, who had recently sailed for Australia, while others have suggested the asterisks stand for

Helen Weaver, Elgar's former fiancée, who had earlier emigrated to Australia; the variation appositely quotes from Mendelssohn's *Calm Sea and Prosperous Voyage*

14 E.D.U. – the composer himself, whose wife called him 'Edoo'.

The identity of the various personalities is only the beginning of the puzzle. In the programme notes to the first performance, Elgar is quoted as follows:

> The Enigma I will not explain – its 'dark saying' must be left unguessed, and I warn you that the apparent connexion between the Variations and the Theme is often of the slightest texture; further, through and over the whole set another and larger theme 'goes', but is not played.

It is the identity of this 'larger theme' that has exercised musical detectives for more than a century. Many ingenious suggestions have been made, ranging from 'AULD LANG SYNE' to 'RULE, BRITANNIA', together with many passages from Mozart. Others again have suggested that the whole thing was a mischievous joke on Elgar's part, and that no such 'larger theme' exists. Whatever the truth of it, Elgar died without revealing his secret.

Entry of Christ into Brussels, The. A huge, bizarre, proto-expressionist painting (1888) by the Belgian artist James Ensor (1860–1949). The canvas, painted in a wild, loose, garish style, is filled with an array of grotesque figures, masks, skeletons, and so on, as if the good burghers of Brussels mock and jeer the imperfectly painted Christ (the title refers to Christ's entry into Jerusalem prior to his Passion and Crucifixion). The work provoked Ensor's expulsion from Les Vingt ('the twenty'), a group of Belgian symbolist painters. After this Ensor withdrew into increasingly misanthropic isolation, pursuing his unique vision. His fascination with masks probably originated in his mother's curiosity shop, and his other paintings include *Scandalized Masks*, *Masks (Intrigues)* and *Portrait of the Artist Surrounded by Masks*. When *The Entry of Christ into Brussels* was exhibited again in 1929, Albert, King of the Belgians, made Ensor a baron.

> Reason is the enemy of art.
>
> JAMES ENSOR: speech, 1923

Epicene, or The Silent Woman. A comedy by Ben Jonson (1572–1637), first performed in 1609 or 1610, and published in 1616. A grumpy old bachelor, Morose, decides he will marry in order to disinherit his nephew, so long as his wife is the 'silent woman' of the sub-title. Such a wife, called Epicene, is duly found, but after the wedding turns out to be anything but quiet. The adjective 'epicene' means having characteristics of both sexes, and, in the end, Epicene is revealed for what she is – a boy in disguise.

The play inspired the opera *Die Schweigsame Frau* ('the silent woman') by Richard Strauss (1864–1949) with a libretto by Stefan Zweig (1881–1942), first performed in Dresden in 1935. However, it was withdrawn after a few performances as the Nazis did not like the fact that the libretto was written by a Jew.

Epipsychidion. A long poem by Percy Bysshe Shelley (1792–1822), published in 1821. The work is addressed to Emilia Viviani, the poet's ideal love, and the title is Greek for 'this soul out of my soul' (although it may also play on 'epithalamium'; *see EPITHALAMION*). The poem concerns the poet's quest for Beauty in a succession of wives and mistresses:

> I never was attached to that great sect,
> Whose doctrine is that each one should select
> Out of a crowd a mistress or a friend,
> And all the rest, though fair and wise, commend
> To cold oblivion.

Epithalamion. A poem by Edmund Spenser (?1552–99), written in 1594 and regarded as his greatest lyric. An *epithalamion* or *epithalamium* is a generic term for a poem or song celebrating a marriage. The form originated in ancient Greece (Greek *thalamos* means 'bridal chamber'), the oldest surviving example being a fragment from Sappho's seventh book (*c*.600 BC). Early Latin examples include those by Catullus from the 1st century BC. The epithalamium was revived in the Renaissance, and there are examples by the Italian poet Torquato Tasso, the French poet Pierre de Ronsard, and, in English, by Sir Philip Sydney, John Donne (his was for Lady Frances Howard, who later poisoned her husband) and Richard Crashaw, as well as the well-known piece by Spenser.

Spenser wrote his *Epithalamion* to celebrate his own marriage to Elizabeth Boyle. It was printed with his *AMORETTI* in 1595. Spenser went on to coin the word *Prothalamion*, which he used as the title for his 'Spousall Verse' (1596) in honour of the double marriage of Lady Elizabeth and Lady Katherine Somerset, daughters of the Earl of

Worcester, to Henry Gilford and William Peter, Esquires. 'Prothalamion' has since more generally been used for a song sung in honour of the bride and bridegroom before the wedding.

> Thee gentle Spenser fondly led;
> But me he mostly sent to bed.
>
> WALTER SAVAGE LANDOR: 'To Wordsworth ...' (1846)

Equivalent VIII. *See* TATE BRICKS, THE.

Erewhon. A satirical novel (1872) by Samuel Butler (1835–1902) that is at once utopian and dystopian. 'Erewhon' is an anagram of 'nowhere', and some of the inhabitants of Butler's imagined country also have anagrammatical names, for example, Yram (Mary) and Mr Nosnibor (Robinson). The narrator comes across Erewhon after traversing a range of mountains based on the Rangitoto Mountains of New Zealand (a country in which Butler spent several years); the landscape and people of Erewhon itself somewhat resemble those of northern Italy. The Erewhonians value physical beauty and strength, regard illness as a crime, and have banished machines as evolutionary competitors. Butler's book has its seed in his earlier essay, 'Darwin among the Machines' (1863), and he published a sequel, *Erewhon Revisited*, in 1901. *Erewhon* was about the only one of his many books from which Butler made any significant profit: £62 3s 6d.

Eroica. The popular name for the symphony no 3 in E flat, opus 55 (1804) by Beethoven (1770–1827). The full title given to it by the composer was *Sinfonia eroica, composta per festeggiare il sovvenire d'un grand' uomo* ('heroic symphony, composed to celebrate the memory of a great man'). Beethoven had originally, in a republican fervour, called the work *Sinfonia grande Napoleon Bonaparte*, but when he heard that Napoleon had made himself emperor he fiercely scratched this out. The symphony was conceived on an unprecedentedly grand scale.

> The symphony would be all the better – it lasts a whole hour – if Beethoven could reconcile himself to making some cuts in it and to bringing to the score more light, clarity and unity.
>
> *Allgemeine Musikalische Zeitung*: review of the first performance

The name *Eroica Variations* is also given to Beethoven's variations and fugue for piano, opus 35 (1802), as they are based on the same theme as the last movement of the symphony. This theme first appeared in the seventh of Beethoven's *Contretänze* for piano (*c.*1800), and Beethoven had also used it in *The Creatures of Prometheus*, opus 43 (1801) (*see* PROMETHEUS, panel, pp.364–5); as a result the *Eroica Variations* are sometimes called the *Prometheus Variations*.

Et in Arcadia Ego (Latin, 'and I too in Arcadia'). A painting (1638) by the French classical painter Nicolas Poussin (1593/4–1665), in which three young shepherds and a shepherdess make out the inscription 'Et in Arcadia Ego' on a tomb, and discuss its meaning. Arcadia was a district of the Peloponnese in southern Greece which according to Virgil was the home of pastoral simplicity and happiness; and it is generally taken that the 'I' is death. The inscription (of unknown authorship) is found in other depictions of tombs in works of Poussin's time, for example in a painting by Guercino (1591–1666). The title was revived by the Scottish artist and concrete poet, Iain Hamilton Finlay (b.1925), for various works in which items of modern military technology, such as tanks and submarines, are located in Arcadian settings.

Euclidian Abyss, The. A painting (1946–7) by the US abstract expressionist Barnet Newman (1905–70), one of the first in which his trademark 'zipper' cuts down the canvas from top to bottom. Newman's title (and the work itself) suggests his attempt to move away from the dryness of geometrical abstraction. Newman later explained in an exhibition catalogue (1966):

> Instead of using outlines, instead of making shapes or setting off spaces, my drawings declare the space. Instead of working with the remnants of space, I work with the whole space.

As for the famous zipper, he remarked in a documentary entitled *Painters Painting* (1972):

> I do not feel my zip divides the painting, in fact it does the opposite, it unites the thing … the beginning and end are there at the same time.

Eulenspiegel, Till. *See* TILL EULENSPIEGEL (panel, p.460).

Eumenides. The last play in Aeschylus's dramatic trilogy, *The Oresteia*, first performed in 458 BC. In fact, it is thought to be the last thing Aeschylus wrote before he was killed by a tortoise that was dropped on his bald head by an eagle. In the play Orestes is pursued by the Erinyes (the Furies, literally 'the moving ones') for killing his mother Clytemnestra in revenge for her role in the death of his father Agamemnon. The Erinyes were known by the Greeks as the Eumenides ('the kindly ones'), as it would have been unpropitious to call them by their real name. *The Kindly Ones* is also the title of the sixth volume (1962) in Anthony Powell's *DANCE TO THE MUSIC OF TIME*.

'Eve of St Agnes, The'. A narrative poem by John Keats (1795–1821), written in 1819 and published in 1820. The poem relates how on St Agnes' Eve (20 January):

> Young virgins might have visions of delight,
> And soft adorings from their loves receive
> Upon the honey'd middle of the night,
> If ceremonies due they did aright;
> As, supperless to bed they must retire,
> And couch supine their beauties, lily white.

The heroine of Keats's poem, Madeline, loves Porphyro, but her family does not approve. He sneaks into the house and her room as she dreams of him, and then she wakes –

> And they are gone – ay, ages long ago
> These lovers fled away into the storm.

The belief that young women could dream of their future husbands on St Agnes' Eve appears to be an old tradition. John Aubrey in his *Miscellanies* (1696) tells how on St Agnes' night you take a row of pins and pull out each one, one at a time; you then say a paternoster, stick a pin in your sleeve and you will dream of the one you will marry.

St Agnes herself, the patron saint of girls, was a Roman martyr of the early 4th century. As a young maiden she refused all bridegrooms but Christ, and as punishment for her Christian beliefs she was forced into a brothel. However, such was her presence that she came to no harm. She is subsequently said to have died at the age of 13 in the persecution instigated by the Emperor Diocletian in *c*.304.

Every Good Boy Deserves Favour. A play (1977) by the Czech-born British dramatist Tom Stoppard (b.1937), with music by the US conductor André Previn. The play is about a dissident confined in a Soviet psychiatric hospital, and the ironic title refers to the mnemonic used in music teaching for the notes on the lines of the treble stave: E, G, B, D, F.

Every Man in His Humour. A comedy by Ben Jonson (1572–1637), first performed in 1598, and published in 1601. The concept of the 'humours' originated with the ancient Greeks, and was taken up in medieval and Renaissance medicine. There were held to be four principal humours in the body: phlegm, blood, choler (or yellow bile) and melancholy (or black bile). If any of these predominated it determined the temper of the mind and body, hence the terms phlegmatic, sanguine, choleric and melancholic. A just balance made a good humour, and a preponderance of any one of the four an ill or bad humour. In Jonson's comedy, each of the four main characters embodies one of the humours.

Jonson followed up his success with *Every Man out of His Humour*, first performed in 1599 and published in 1600. In it he wished his audience to

> see the time's deformity
> Anatomized in every nerve, and sinew.

These plays earned Jonson the title of 'the Humorous Poet' from his rival Thomas Dekker (*see The* POETASTER).

Everyone I've Ever Slept With. A tent constructed by Britart *enfant terrible* Tracey Emin (b.1963), embroidered with the names of everyone she had ever shared a bed with. She followed this up with *My Bed*, an unmade bed featuring soiled sheets, empty vodka bottles and used condoms, which surprisingly failed to win the 1999 Turner Prize.

Everything You Always Wanted to Know About Sex but Were Afraid to Ask. This formulaic phrase, as the title of a book of 1970 by David Reuben, spawned a host of similar titles, among them:

Everything That Linguists Have Always Wanted to Know About Logic but Were Ashamed to Ask

Everything You Always Wanted to Know About Drinking Problems and Then a Few Things You Didn't Want to Know

Everything You Always Wanted to Know About Mergers, Acquisitions and Divestitures but Didn't Know Whom to Ask

Everything You Wanted to Know About the Catholic Church but Were Too Pious to Ask

Woody Allen's 1972 film, *Everything You Always Wanted to Know About Sex (but Were Afraid to Ask)*, comprised a sequence of seven sketches, one involving a sheep.

Evil Cradling, An. An account (1992) of his years of imprisonment as a hostage of fundamentalist Muslims in Lebanon by Brian Keenan (b.1950). The title is from sura 5 of the Koran:

> Say to the unbelievers: 'You shall be overthrown, and mustered into Gehenna – an evil cradling!'

Excursion, The. A long, somewhat tendentious poem by William Wordsworth (1770–1850), published in 1814 (revised edition 1827). The banal (to modern ears) title reflects the framework of the poem, in which a poet travels with a pedlar, the thoughtful Wanderer. The poem was originally intended to form part of a larger work (*see The* PRELUDE).

> This will never do.
>
> FRANCIS, LORD JEFFREY: review of *The Excursion* in the *Edinburgh Review*, November 1814

> A drowsy frowzy poem, called the 'Excursion',
> Writ in a manner which is my aversion.
>
> BYRON: *Don Juan* (1819–24)

In *La Soeur de la reine*, a privately circulated fantasy by the poet Algernon Charles Swinburne (1837–1909), Queen Victoria – whose imaginary twin sister works as a prostitute in London's Haymarket – suffers an 'unfortunate lapse from virtue' when Wordsworth's reading of *The Excursion* so inflames her that she allows herself to be ravished by the old poet.

Execution of the Emperor Maximilian, The. A painting (1867) by Édouard Manet (1832–83). In 1864 the Emperor Napoleon III of France had offered the crown of Mexico to Archduke Maximilian (1832–67), brother of Franz Josef, emperor of Austria. However, faced with Mexican and US hostility, French troops were withdrawn from Mexico in March 1867, and in May Maximilian was captured by rebel forces. Despite pleas from Victor Hugo, Giuseppe Garibaldi and many others, the following month Maximilian was executed by firing squad on a hill outside Querétaro. Manet's painting shows some influence from Goya's *The THIRD OF MAY 1808*.

Exhibition of a Rhinoceros at Venice. A painting (1751) by Pietro Longhi (1702–85), depicting a number of masked Carnival revellers viewing a rhinoceros. This particular rhinoceros was exhibited as part of the Carnival festivities in Venice in 1751, having arrived in Nuremburg from Africa ten years earlier. Its horns have been removed.

Exhumation of the Mastodon. A painting (1806) by the US artist and patriot Charles Wilson Peale (1741–1827), who had earlier fought as a colonel during the American Revolution, and in 1786 established the country's first museum, principally of natural history. In 1801 Peale was with the expedition that dug up the skeleton of a mastodon – an extinct relative of the elephant that died out around 8000 years ago – on a farm in New York state. The skeleton became one of Peale's prize exhibits.

Experiment with the Air Pump. A painting (1768) by Wright of Derby (Joseph Wright; 1734–97). Executed in his trademark candlelit manner, the painting depicts a group of men, women and children watching an experiment to show the effect of a vacuum on living creatures – in this case a dove in a glass bowl from which the air has been pumped.

Eyeless in Gaza. A novel (1936) by Aldous Huxley (1894–1963), in which some of the circumstances reflect those of the author; the work heralded Huxley's final, philosophical phase, in which pacifism and mysticism are predominant. The novel's theme is that freedom without values is a form of blindness. It follows the journey of an able man, who is incapable of forming personal relationships, to self-discovery in the unlikely environment of a revolution in Mexico. The title is from *SAMSON AGONISTES* (1671) by John Milton:

> Ask for this great deliverer now, and find him
> Eyeless in Gaza at the mill with slaves.

F

Faerie Queene, The. A long allegorical poem by Edmund Spenser (?1552–99), written in what became known as Spenserian stanzas. The first three books were published in 1590, and the second three in 1596. The original orthography of the title is traditionally preserved. The queen of the land of Faerie is GLORIANA – a personification of Glory, and more particularly a representation of Queen Elizabeth I, to whom Spenser dedicated the work. Queen Elizabeth also appears in several other guises in the poem. Each of the six books tells an adventure of one of Gloriana's knights.

> ... the *dullest thing out*. *Blast* it.
>
> PHILIP LARKIN: handwritten comment on a copy of Spenser in St John's College, quoted in Kingsley Amis, *Memoirs* (1992)

Fahrenheit 451. A fantasy of the near future (1953) by Ray Bradbury (b.1920), the author's first published novel. The theme is the triumph of the imagination under the threat of obliteration, and in particular the destruction by fire of all books. The title signifies the temperature at which book paper is said to ignite and burn. Dissidents respond by memorizing the texts. A suitably futuristic film version (1966) was directed by François Truffaut. Compare *DENSITY 21.5.*

Fairy-Feller's Master Stroke, The. An enormously detailed fairy painting (1855–64), typical of the work of Richard Dadd (1819–97), who was confined for the rest of his life to a variety of institutions (including Bedlam and Broadmoor) after he had murdered his father in 1843 (possibly under instructions from the Egyptian god Osiris). Among the numerous bizarre characters depicted in Dadd's painting are, in addition to the Fairy-Feller himself (who wields a golden axe, presumably in readiness for felling some fairies): Monk Ploughman, Waggoner Will, a clodhopper with a satyr's head, a politician, a fairy dandy, a nymph, two elves, a crouching pedagogue, an arch-magician, two dwarf conjurors, QUEEN MAB, Spanish dancers, Oberon, Titania, a harridan, Tatterdemalion, a 'junketer', a dragonfly trumpeter, and the group from the children's counting rhyme, namely tinker, tailor, soldier, sailor, ploughboy, apothecary and thief. The painting inspired a 1970s song by the rock group Queen.

Fame is the Spur. A novel (1940) by the Welsh journalist and novelist Howard Spring (1889–1965) about the rise of a Labour politician. The title comes from Milton:

> Fame is the spur that the clear spirit doth raise
> (That last infirmity of noble mind)
> To scorn delights, and live laborious days.
>
> JOHN MILTON: 'Lycidas' (1638)

Famous Five, the. The four children and their dog who have unlikely adventures at various holiday locations around Britain in the novels of Enid Blyton (1897–1968). They are the two brothers Julian and Dick, their sister, Anne, and their tomboy cousin Georgina, known as 'George', together with the mongrel dog Timmy. They first appeared in *Five on a Treasure Island* (1942) and continued their exploits in a further 20 volumes, all with a title beginning *Five*. The tales were the inspiration for television farces in the *Comic Strip Presents* ... series of the 1980s, the first being *Five Go Mad in Dorset* (1982).

Fanatic Heart, A. A short story collection (1984) by Edna O'Brien (b. 1932). The title comes from the poem 'Remorse for Intemperate Speech' (28 August 1931) by W.B. Yeats (1865–1939) in *The Winding Stair and Other Poems* (1933):

> Out of Ireland have we come.
> Great hatred, little room,
> Maimed us at the start.
> I carry from my mother's womb
> A fanatic heart.

Fanny Hill. The popular name for *Memoirs of a Woman of Pleasure* (1748–9), a classic of English pornography by John Cleland (1710–89), one-time British consul in Smyrna, who, down on his uppers, agreed to write the book for a fee of 20 guineas. Its publication led to Cleland's arrest and appearance before the Privy Council, who, however, sympathized with his predicament and awarded him a pension. The book was last seized by the police in 1963. The heroine and narrator, Fanny Hill, is thought to have been based on the famous London courtesan, Sarah Pridden (1692–1723). The name Fanny (short for Frances) is also British slang for the female pudendum or vagina (although this usage is possibly no older than the mid-19th century); and joined with the surname Hill the whole evokes the *mons veneris* (Latin, 'mound of Venus'), the fleshy pad that in women covers the junction of the pubic bones. Compare *DELTA OF VENUS*.

'Farewell' Sonata. See *LEBEWOHL, DAS*.

'Farewell' Symphony (German name: *Abschiedsymphonie*). The nickname given to the symphony no 45 (1772) by Haydn (1732–1809). Since 1761 Haydn had been composer to Prince Nicolaus Esterházy, who insisted that Haydn and his musicians spend longer and longer with him at his remote castle at Esterház. This led to dissatisfaction, as the musicians missed their families back in Vienna. With typical benevolence and diplomacy, 'Papa' Haydn (as Mozart called him) came up with an idea. This manifested itself in the last movement, the adagio, of his new symphony, in which all the instruments stopped playing one by one, and the players blew out the candles on their music stands and left the stage, until only two violins were left playing – Tomasini and Haydn himself. Thus nudged, Prince Nicolaus ordered that the court pack up and return to Vienna the following day. The novel *Farewell Symphony* (1997) by Edmund White (b.1940), is named after the Haydn work, and concerns a gay man who survives many of his friends.

Far from the Madding Crowd. A novel (1874) by Thomas Hardy (1840–1928), concerning the love of three men for the spirited and beautiful farm-owner, Bathsheba Everdene. The novel has an uncharacteristically (for Hardy) happy ending, in so far as the good and devoted shepherd Gabriel Oak gets his girl. There is, however, a good dose of tragedy along the way, with one suitor, Sergeant Troy, shot dead by another, Farmer Boldwood, who is declared insane. The title is from Thomas Gray's 'Elegy Written in a Country Church-Yard' (1751) (*See* GRAY'S ELEGY):

> Far from the madding crowd's ignoble strife,
> Their sober wishes never learned to stray;
> Along the cool sequestered vale of life
> They kept the noiseless tenor of their way.

John Schlesinger's film version (1967) boasted a screenplay by Frederic Raphael, photography by Nicolas Roeg and music by Richard Rodney Bennett and starred Julie Christie, Alan Bates, Terence Stamp and Peter Finch.

Fast and Loose. The title of three films: an undistinguished melodrama (US, 1930); a comedy thriller in *The* THIN MAN vein (US, 1939), starring Robert Montgomery and Rosalind Russell and involving a missing Shakespearean manuscript; and a romantic comedy (UK, 1954). The expression 'playing fast and loose' denotes running with the hare and hunting with the hound, blowing both hot and cold, saying one thing and doing another. The origin of the phrase is thought to lie in an old cheating game once practised at fairs. A belt or strap was doubled and rolled up with the loop in the centre and placed on edge on a table. The player then had to catch the loop with a skewer while the belt was unrolled, but this was done in such a way by the trickster as to make the feat impossible. Shakespeare alludes to the game in *LOVE'S LABOUR'S LOST*, III.i:

> To sell a bargain well is as cunning as fast and loose.

Fastes de la Grande et Ancienne Mxnxstrxndxsx, Les (French, 'annals of the great and ancient order of mxnstrxlsx'). A harpsichord suite by François 'Le Grand' Couperin (1688–1733), published in 1717. *Mxnxstrxndxsx* stands for *Ménestrandise* (minstrelsy), and the whole suite is a grotesque satire on the quarrel between the organists of Paris and the corporation of minstrels that had erupted earlier in the century. The last movement depicts the disruption of the procession of minstrels by drunkards, dancing bears and monkeys.

FAUST or FAUSTUS

The legend of a man who sells his soul to the devil in exchange for knowledge and power was current in medieval Germany, and indeed the idea of making a pact with the devil for worldly reasons is ultimately of Jewish origin. The basis of the Faust story is that he sells his soul to the Devil in return for 24 years of further life, during which he is to have every pleasure and all knowledge at his command. The climax comes when the Devil claims him for his own.

In the 16th century the German legend became attached to a real, if shady, historical character. Dr Johann Faust or Faustus (*c.*1480–*c.*1540) was a magician and astrologer born in Württemberg, about whom many stories soon began to circulate, crediting him with supernatural gifts and evil living. He first appears in print in the anonymous *History of Dr Faustus, the Notorious Magician and Master of the Black Art*, published by Johann Spies at Frankfurt in 1587, and commonly referred to as the *Faustbuch*. In this work Faust becomes the protagonist of many older stories about earlier magicians such as Roger Bacon and Albertus Magnus. However, the devilish tempter Mephistopheles is a creation of the *Faustbuch*'s author.

The English translation of the *Faustbuch*, *The History of the Damnable Life, and Deserved Death of Doctor John Faustus* (1592), was the main source for Christopher Marlowe's play *The Tragical History of Dr Faustus*. Marlowe's tragedy was first performed in 1594 or earlier, and survives in two very different editions, one of 1604 and one of 1616. Marlowe's Faustus is infinitely ambitious at first, although he uses his new powers for increasingly banal tricks of a knockabout nature (of the sort found in the *Faustbuch*). Nevertheless, as his eternal fate approaches, Faustus attains the anguished dignity of a tragic hero:

> *O lente, lente, currite noctis equi.*
> The stars move still, time runs, the clock will strike,
> The devil will come, and Faustus must be damned.
> O I'll leap up to my God: who pulls me down?

> See, see, where Christ's blood streams in the firmament.
> One drop would save my soul, half a drop. Ah, my Christ!

Marlowe's play gave rise to various German versions, and Faust dramas and puppet plays subsequently became popular in Germany. In addition, handbooks of magic often used the name 'Faust' in their titles.

With the coming of the Enlightenment, new perspectives on the Faust legend began to appear. G.E. Lessing (1729–81) wrote an unfinished Faust play (1784), in which the hero's quest for knowledge is seen as noble, despite the pact with the Devil, and is justified to God. Johann Wolfgang von Goethe (1749–1832) picked up this approach in his *Faust* (Part I 1808, Part II 1832), in which the hero personifies the struggle between man's higher and lower natures: 'Man will err while yet he strives' (Part I, prologue). Faust is tempted to seduce Gretchen (Margaret), who dies as a result. He fails to attain absolute knowledge, but is rescued from despair by a life of useful service to humanity, and after he dies his soul is carried away by angels.

Goethe's *Faust* inspired numerous musical works. One of the best known is the opera *Faust* (1859) by Charles François Gounod (1818–93). The libretto, by Jules Barbier and Michel Carré, is based on Goethe's Part I, but ends with Faust heading for damnation, and the work as a whole tends towards the sanctimonious and the sentimental. Wagner described it as 'music for sluts'. Because *Faust* was so much more successful than Gounod's other operas, one contemporary critic suggested that Gounod could not have written it – but withdrew this accusation after the composer challenged him to a duel. After Gounod's death there re-emerged rumours about the opera's authorship, some suggesting that Gounod had stolen the score from a mad but brilliant composer locked up in a mental institution. Such stories have a suitably sulphurous tang.

Other operas based on Goethe include:

- Two entitled *Faust et Marguerite* (Lutz 1855 and Barbier 1869)
- An unfinished Faust tetralogy by Brüggemann (1910 and after)
- *Faust* (1964) by N.V. Bentzon
- *Votre Faust* (1961–7) by Henri Pousseur (b.1929) with a libretto

by the composer and Michel Butor, in which the audience is asked to choose between alternative endings

- The operetta *Le Petit Faust* by Hervé (Florimond Roger; 1825–92) parodies both Goethe and Gounod.

Goethe himself said, in *Conversations with Eckermann* (1827), 'Mozart should have composed Faust'.

There are a number of non-operatic musical works inspired by Goethe:

- *A Faust Overture* (1839–40) by Wagner (1813–83), which was not intended to accompany an opera
- *Scenes from Goethe's Faust* (1844–53) for chorus and orchestra by Schumann (1810–56)
- *The Damnation of Faust* (1846) by Berlioz (1803–69), a dramatic cantata incorporating the composer's earlier *Huit Scènes de Faust* (1828)
- *A Faust Symphony* (1857) by Franz Liszt (1811–86), who dedicated the work to Berlioz
- Liszt's four *Mephisto Waltzes* (1862–85) for the piano, the first of which was adapted from the second of his own orchestral *Episodes from Lenau's Faust* (1862; for Lenau's version of the legend, *see below*).

> Mephistopheles disguised as an abbé.
>
> AN ANONYMOUS CONTEMPORARY describes Liszt, quoted in Beckett, *Liszt* (1963)

The second part of the 8th Symphony (1906–7) of Gustav Mahler (1860–1911) – the so-called 'SYMPHONY OF A THOUSAND' – is entitled 'Concluding scene from Faust'.

Several other operas have been based on the older Faust legend, rather than on Goethe. Among these are:

- Hanke's *La Ceinture* ['belt' or 'girdle'] *du Docteur Faust* (*c.*1796)
- I. Walter's *Dr Faust* (1797)
- *Faust* (1816, revised 1852) by Ludwig Spohr (1784–1859)
- *Dr Fausts Mantel* ('coat') (1817) by Wenzel Müller (1767–1835)

- Saint-Lubin's *Le Cousin du Docteur Faust* (1829)
- The uncompleted *Doktor Faust* (1925) by Ferruccio Busoni (1866–1924)
- Hermann Reutter's *Dr Johannes Faust* (1936, revised 1955) and *Don Juan und Faust* (1950), the latter based on Grabbe's 1829 tragedy (*see below*)
- Engelmann's *Dr Fausts Höllenfahrt* ('journey to hell') (1951)
- J. Berg's *Dr Johannes Faust* (1967).

Since the early 19th century, there have been a number of literary reworkings of the Faust legend. These include:

- *Faust, Ein Versuch* ('an experiment', 'an attempt') (1804) by Adelbert von Chamisso (1781–1838), who also wrote a fairy tale reminiscent of the Faust legend, *Peter Schlemihls wundersame Geschichte* (1814; 'Peter Schlemihl's remarkable story')
- Byron's *The* DEFORMED TRANSFORMED (1824)
- *Don Juan und Faust*, a tragedy (1829) blending Mozart's *Don Giovanni* (*see* DON JUAN, panel, pp.120–2) with Goethe by Christian Grabbe (1801–36)
- *Faust: Ein Gedicht* ('a poem') (1836, revised 1840) by Nikolaus Lenau (1802–50), which finds Faust facing an absurd universe (the work inspired Liszt's *Episodes from Lenau's Faust*; *see above*)
- *Josephus Faust* (1847) by Woldemar Nürnberger
- The mock-epic *Doktor Faust: Ein Tanzpoem* (1851) by Heinrich Heine (1797–1856)
- *Mon Faust* (1946) by Paul Valéry (1871–1945)
- *A Faust Book* (1978), a collection of poems on the legend by D.J. Enright (b.1920).

There were several silent Faust films, the most notable of which (1926) was directed by F.W. Murnau and starred Emil Jannings. *All That Money Can Buy* (US, 1941) is based on the short story 'The Devil and Daniel Webster' (1937) by Stephen Vincent Benét (1898–1943), in which the Faust figure is a hard-up farmer who gives in to the Devil's temptations but who is saved by the intervention of the noted orator Daniel Webster

(1782–1852). The film version of Marlowe's *Dr Faustus* (UK, 1967) starred Richard Burton as Faustus, with Elizabeth Taylor appearing wordlessly as Helen of Troy, 'the face that launched a thousand ships'. (One critic quipped 'It turns out to be the story of a man who sold his soul for Elizabeth Taylor'.) Istvan Szabo's film *Mephisto* (Hungary, 1981) is an updating of the legend to the Germany of the 1920s and 1930s. The Faust figure is an actor (played by Klaus Maria Brandauer) who becomes a puppet of the Nazis for the sake of his career.

The most important reworking of the legend since Goethe is the great novel *Doktor Faustus* (1947) by the German Nobel laureate Thomas Mann (1875–1955). The Faust of this complex and densely wrought work, which includes passages from the original 1587 *Faustbuch*, is Adrian Leverkühn, a composer who rejects tonality, expressiveness and the struggle of the artist to create. Instead he embraces an abstract, emotion-free system of composition – in fact based on the twelve-note system devised by Arnold Schoenberg. At one point Leverkühn writes:

> Take Beethoven's notebooks. There is no thematic conception there as God gave it. He remoulds it and adds 'Meilleur' [better]. Scant confidence in God's prompting, scant respect for it is expressed in that 'Meilleur' – itself not very enthusiastic either. A genuine inspiration, immediate, absolute, unquestioned, ravishing, where there is no choice, no tinkering, no possible improvement; where all is as a sacred mandate, a visitation received by the possessed one with faltering and stumbling step, with shudders of awe from head to foot, with tears of joy blinding his eyes: no, that is not possible with God, who leaves the understanding too much to do. It comes but from the divel [sic], the true master and giver of such rapture.

Leverkühn's story parallels that of Germany, which gave up its soul, and the whole of the Western humanist tradition, in favour of unquestioning acceptance of the nihilistic 'rapture' offered by the Nazis, only to pay the price of destruction in the Second World War. The price that Leverkühn himself pays is isolation and, ultimately, madness and death.

See also PICTURE OF DORIAN GREY, THE.

Father and Son. An autobiography (1907) of his early years, subtitled *A Study of Two Temperaments*, by the literary critic Edmund Gosse (1849–1928). Gosse was the only son of Philip Gosse (1810–88), the fundamentalist writer on zoology, with whom, after his mother's death in 1857, Gosse went to live in Devon. The book explores the conflict between generations incurred by a restricted upbringing.

Fathers and Sons (1862), a novel by the Russian writer Ivan Turgenev (1818–83), also involves generational conflict. Turgenev coined the term 'nihilist' to describe his revolutionary hero, Bazarov.

Fattypuffs and Thinifers. The English title of *Patapoufs et Filifers* (1930) by the French writer André Maurois (1885–1967). It tells of two brothers, one fat, one thin, who discover two contrasting nations beneath the surface of the earth. The suitably obese Fattypuffs do little but eat and sleep, while the slender and fastidious Thinifers work six days a week and do without lunch. An invasion of the land of the Fattypuffs by the Thinifers sets in train a reconciliation between the two peoples, who eventually agree to unite.

Fauvel, Roman de. *See* ROMAN DE FAUVEL.

Fear and Loathing in Las Vegas. An offbeat account (1972) by the 'gonzo journalist' Hunter S. Thompson (b.1939) of an assignment to cover the 'Mint 400', an off-road motorbike race outside Las Vegas. The work is subtitled *A Savage Journey to the Heart of the American Dream* (*see* AMERICAN DREAM, THE). Accompanied by Dr Gonzo, his lawyer, Thompson (using the alias Raoul Duke) – himself much of the time under the influence of a range of recreational drugs, and therefore achieving little or nothing in the way of sporting reportage – confronts casino operators, bartenders, tourists, police officers and other members of the community. The opening gives some feel of the drug- and reality-fuelled fear and loathing that is to follow:

> We were somewhere around Barstow on the edge of the desert when the drugs began to take hold. I remember saying something like 'I feel a bit lightheaded; maybe you should drive ...' And suddenly there was a terrible roar all around us and the sky was full of what looked like huge bats, all swooping and screeching and diving around the car, which was going about a hundred miles an hour with the top down to Las Vegas. And a voice was screaming: 'Holy Jesus! What are these goddamn animals?'

A film version (1998), directed by Terry Gilliam, was appropriately off the wall, but inevitably lacked Thompson's mastery of what has subsequently been dubbed 'gonzo' prose.

Thompson followed up *Fear and Loathing in Las Vegas* with a number of sequels, including:

Fear and Loathing on the Campaign Trail, '72 (1972)

'Fear and Loathing at the Superbowl' (in *Rolling Stone*, 15 February 1973)

'Jacket Copy for Fear and Loathing in Las Vegas' (in *The Great White Shark Hunt*, 1979)

Femme 100 têtes, La (French, 'the woman 100 heads'). A graphic novel (1929) by the German surrealist Max Ernst (1891–1976). The novel consists of 147 collages (mostly made up from 19th-century engravings). There is no particularly clear unifying theme, although many of the pictures are anticlerical in intent, in the manner of his earlier *The* BLESSED *VIRGIN CHASTISES THE INFANT JESUS BEFORE THREE WITNESSES: A.B., P.E. AND THE ARTIST*. The titles or captions of the collages in *La Femme 100 têtes* include:

In the Paris Basin the head bird Hornebom brings night-time nourishment to the lanterns

Accompanied by immaculate parasites the Great Nicholas [a bishop, presumably St Nicholas] *is steered from afar by means of lateral appendages*

Let us give thanks unto Satan and rejoice in the goodwill he has shown us

At each bloody riot she blossoms forth filled with grace and truth

And now I show you the uncle whose beard we loved to tickle on a Sunday afternoon

Hornebom and the Fair Gardener (*see* BELLE *JARDINIÈRE, LA*)

Feuersymphonie. *See* 'FIRE' SYMPHONY.

Fever Pitch. An autobiographical work (1992) by Nick Hornby (b.1957), subtitled *A Story of Football and Obsession*. It charts the author's personal relationship with the game as a fan (from the age of ten) of Arsenal Football Club. The book, which soon became a bestseller, gave an insight into the thinking and attitude of the typical 'New Lad'. The title has obvious punning connotations. A film version (1996), directed by Michael Carlin, presented the original as a romantic comedy.

Fiddler on the Roof. A stage musical (1964) and film (1971), with a book by Joseph Stein, score by Jerry Bock and lyrics by Sheldon Harnick. Set in pre-revolutionary Russia, and culminating in a pogrom, it relates the story of Tevye, a Jewish father (memorably played by Topol in the film), and his disapproval of the matrimonial choices made by his daughters. The musical is based on the Yiddish short story collection *Tevye and His Daughters* by the Russian-born US writer Sholom Aleichem (1859–1916). The significance of the title is obscure: it may be based on a proverbial expression meaning to 'eat, drink and be merry', but it may be taken generally to signify a person who cheerfully makes the best of things, whatever the circumstances.

Fidelio. *See* LÉONORE.

'Fifths' Quartet (German *Quintenquartett*). The nickname for the string quartet in D minor, opus 76 no 2 (1797–8), by Haydn (1732–1809). The first movement opens with a sequence of two falling fifths (A–D, E–A) from the first violin. Some have heard the tolling of a bell or the braying of a donkey in this sequence, hence the less familiar alternative nicknames 'The Bell' and 'The Donkey'. The minuet of the quartet is sometimes nicknamed the '*Hexenmenuett*' ('Witch Minuet').

Fighting 'Temeraire', The. One of the best-known paintings of J.M.W. Turner (1775–1851), first exhibited at the Royal Academy, London, in 1839 and now in the National Gallery, London. The full title is *The Fighting 'Temeraire', tugged to her Last Berth to be Broken up, 1838.* At its first showing it was accompanied by these lines:

> The flag which braved the battle and the breeze,
> No longer owns her.
>
> Adapted from THOMAS CAMPBELL, 'Ye Mariners of England'

The *Temeraire*, a 98-gun warship of the second rate launched in 1798, was named after the French ship *Le Téméraire* (*téméraire* means 'reckless', 'bold'), captured at Lagos Bay in 1759. By the 1830s the *Temeraire* was one of the few surviving ships that had fought at the battle of Trafalgar in 1805, where it had followed Nelson's *Victory* in breaking the French line. The melancholy scene painted by Turner shows the old warship being towed up the Thames on 5–6 September 1838, on its way to the breaker's yard at Rotherhithe.

> There is something in the contemplation of such a scene which affects us almost as deeply as the decay of a noble human being.
>
> The *Morning Chronicle*, 7 May 1838

Filth. A novel (1998) by the Scottish writer Irvine Welsh (b.1957) about a corrupt Edinburgh policeman, one of whose faeces narrates part of the story – possibly a first in the rhetoric of fiction. 'The filth' is also a disrespectful slang term for the police. In the same year Welsh's play *You'll Have Had Your Hole* was premiered at the West Yorkshire Playhouse.

Fingal's Cave Overture. *See* HEBRIDES, THE.

Finnegans Wake. A radically experimental modernist novel (1939) by James Joyce (1882–1941). He began work on it in 1922, but was too superstitious to reveal the title; sections were published (1927–30) in New York as 'Work in Progress'. *Finnegans Wake* is a record of a night, in which the mind of the sleeping H.C. Earwicker is interpreted with great virtuosity and invention of language, with meaning piled upon meaning. Joyce illustrated his literary method by saying that he was tunnelling through a mountain from two sides. The structure largely follows the Italian philosopher Giovanni Battista Vico (1668–1744), who divided human history into three ages, divine, heroic and human, to which Joyce added a fourth, return, emphasizing Vico's theory of evolutionary cycles in civilizations. The circularity of Joyce's work is emphasized by the fact that the last sentence merges into the first:

> riverrun, past Eve and Adam's, from swerve of shore to bend of bay, brings us by a commodius vicus of recirculation back to Howth Castle and Environs.

The punning title derives from an Irish-American ballad about Tim Finnegan, a drunken hod-carrier who falls from his ladder and is killed. A splash of whiskey at his wake awakes him, and he exclaims, 'Do ye think I'm dead then?' The title also suggests the return (awakening) of Fionn mac Cumhaill, mythical hero of the Ossianic cycle of stories.

Among the many coinages in *Finnegans Wake*, one in particular has come into wider usage. It was from Joyce's phrase 'Three quarks for Muster Mark' that the US physicist Murray Gell-Mann (b.1929) took the word 'quark', which he applied to what were then hypothetical elementary particles making up the protons and neutrons in the nucleus of an atom. Intriguingly, quarks have such properties as charm, colour and strangeness.

FISH

'TROUT' QUINTET, a Schubert piano quintet (1819)

Salar the Salmon, a novel (1935) by Henry Williamson

A SURFEIT OF LAMPREYS, a detective novel (1941) by Ngaio Marsh

The SILVER DARLINGS (as herring are called), a novel (1941) by Neil Gunn

'A Perfect Day for Bananafish', a short story by the US writer J.D. Salinger, published in *Nine Stories* (1953)

The Fish Can Sing, a novel (1957) by Icelandic Nobel laureate Halldór Laxness

JAWS, a film (1975) about a man-eating shark

The Flounder, a novel (1977) by the German Nobel laureate Günter Grass

The Fish that Saved Pittsburgh, a film (1979) in which a baseball team recruits players with the star sign Pisces

A FISH CALLED WANDA, a film comedy (1988) written by and starring John Cleese

Passion Fish, a film (1992) about a disabled actress and her nurse

Piranha to Scurfy, the title story in a collection of horror and mystery stories (2001) by Ruth Rendell (the title refers to a volume of an encyclopedia)

'Fire' Symphony (German *Feuersymphonie*). The nickname given to the symphony no 59 in A by Haydn (1732–1809). The name may result from the fact that while Haydn was at Esterház a play called *Die Feuerbrunst* ('the conflagration') was performed there, and Haydn's music may have been used as the overture.

Fireworks Music. The popular name for the *Music for the Royal Fireworks*, a suite for wind band by Handel (1685–1759), first performed in Green Park, London, in 1749. It was a somewhat belated celebration of the treaty of Aix-la-Chapelle that had ended the War of the Austrian Succession the year before. Handel later added string parts to the score.

Fish Called Wanda, A. A film comedy (1988) written by and starring John Cleese (b.1939) and based on a story by Cleese and Charles Crichton about a repressed English barrister who becomes chaotically involved in a jewel robbery. Wanda is the sexually alluring thief Wanda Gershwitz (played by Jamie Lee Curtis) for whom Cleese develops a passion (although a pet fish of the same name plays a significant role in the convoluted plot).

Fistful of Dollars, A. A Western film (1964), written and directed by Sergio Leone (1921–89), about a nameless and taciturn gunfighter – 'the Man with No Name' – (played by a cheroot-smoking, poncho-wearing Clint Eastwood) who becomes involved in the struggle for power between two rival families. The title refers to the gunfighter's mercenary status, hired first by one family and then by the other. The basic plot is derived from Akira Kurosawa's *Yojimbo* (1961), in which the mysterious stranger is a samurai warrior.

The success of the film helped to establish the genre of the Spaghetti Western (the disparaging name for Italian imitations of American Western films) and spawned the sequels *For a Few Dollars More* (1965) and *The* GOOD, THE BAD AND THE UGLY (1967).

The title also inspired a couple of imitations: Sergio Leone's own *A Fistful of Dynamite* (1971; also called *Duck, You Sucker*), and writer-director Edgar Wright's *A Fistful of Fingers* (1995), 'the greatest Western ever made … in Somerset', in which No-Name pursues the villainous Squint on a pantomime horse with the aid of Running Sore, a Native American brave. The genre was parodied in *A Fistful of Travellers Cheques* in the TV series *Comic Strip Presents …*

Five Little Pigs. A detective story (1942) by Agatha Christie (1890–1976). The title comes from the child's toe or finger rhyme:

> This little pig went to market,
> This little pig stayed at home,
> This little pig had roast beef,
> This little pig had none,
> And this little pig cried, Wee-wee-wee-wee-wee,
> I can't find my way home.

The rhyme goes back at least to the early 18th century. The US title of the book is *Murder in Retrospect*.

Flag. A painting (1954) of the US flag by Jasper Johns (b.1930), regarded by some as marking the beginning of the Pop Art movement. Although clearly depicting the Stars and Stripes, the work's richly textured encaustic surface begs the question as to whether it is a painting or a flag. Johns later recalled (in a 1972 documentary):

> One night I dreamt I painted a large American flag, and the next morning I went out and bought the materials to begin it.

Flaubert's Parrot. A novel (1984) by Julian Barnes (b.1946), in which the life and literary pursuits of the French novelist Gustave Flaubert (1821–80) are investigated by Geoffrey Braithwaite, a retired English doctor, as a means of coming to terms with the suicide of his wife. Parallels are drawn between Flaubert's eight-year affair with the poet Louise Colet (1810–76) and the unfaithfulness of Braithwaite's wife. The title refers to a stuffed parrot that Flaubert borrowed from a museum and set on his desk while writing the story 'Un Cœur Simple', in which a parrot, alive and then stuffed, is an object of reverence to the heroine.

> Books say: she did this because. Life says: she did this. Books are where things are explained to you; life is where things aren't.
>
> *Flaubert's Parrot*, chapter 13

Flesh and Blood. A phrase forming the titles of three films: *Flesh and Blood* (UK, 1951), a Scottish period piece; *The Flesh and Blood Show* (UK, 1972), in which a group of actors are murdered one after the other; and *Flesh & Blood* (US, 1985), a piece of quasi-medieval sexploitation. The phrase comes from St Paul's Epistle to the Ephesians, 6:12:

> For we wrestle not against flesh and blood, but against principalities, against powers, against the rulers of the darkness of this world, against spiritual wickedness in high places.

Flesh and the Devil. A steamy silent film (1926) starring Greta Garbo and John Gilbert, who were conducting an affair off-screen at the time. The title comes from the Litany in the Book of Common Prayer:

> From all the deceits of the world, the flesh, and the devil,
> Good Lord, deliver us.

The World, the Flesh and the Devil is the title of a fantasy film (1959) set in the wake of a nuclear apocalypse.

Fleurs du mal, Les (French, 'the flowers of evil'). A collection of verse (1857) by the French poet Charles Baudelaire (1821–67). The title – reflecting the poet's pursuit of beauty in the grotesque, the morbid and the deformed – was suggested to him by the critic Hippolyte Babou. On publication Baudelaire and his publisher and printers were prosecuted for obscenity and blasphemy, found guilty and fined. Six of the poems were banned from publication in France until 1949. The association of beauty and evil is found in a later French work, Jean Genet's *OUR LADY OF THE FLOWERS*.

Flight of the Bumble Bee, The. An orchestral interlude in the opera *The Legend of Tsar Saltan* (1900) by Rimsky-Korsakov (1844–1908) The rapidly paced music represents a prince who turns into a bee and stings his annoying relations. There are many arrangements for virtuoso instrumental solos.

FLOWERS

See also FOOD (panel, pp.168–70, for fruit and vegetables); GARDENS (panel, p.181)

Roman de la Rose, a medieval allegorical romance

'A Red Red Rose', a poem (1796) by Robert Burns

La DAME AUX CAMÉLIAS, a novel (1848) by Alexandre Dumas *fils*

Le SPECTRE DE LA ROSE, a poem by Théophile Gautier (1811–72)

'WHEN LILACS LAST IN THE DOORYARD BLOOMED', a poem (1865–6) by Walt Whitman

Lavender and Old Lace, a novel (1902) by Myrtle Reed (*see ARSENIC AND OLD LACE*)

The SCARLET PIMPERNEL, a novel (1905) by Baroness Orczy

A DRUNK MAN LOOKS AT THE THISTLE, a long poem (1926) by Hugh MacDiarmid

Passion Flower, a romantic film (1930)

'The force that through the green fuse drives the flower', a poem (1934) by Dylan Thomas

Black Narcissus, a novel (1939) by Rumer Goden, filmed by Michael Powell in 1946

Peonies and Ponies (1941), a novel by Sir Harold Acton set in Beijing

GOD IS A LILY OF THE VALLEY, a painting (1961) by Robert Indiana

An UNOFFICIAL ROSE, a novel (1962) by Iris Murdoch

LILIES OF THE FIELD, a film (1963) starring Sidney Poitier

Consider the Lilies, two novels both published in 1968, by Iain Crichton Smith and Auberon Waugh

Daisies, a Czech film (1966) about two girls revolting against conformity

The Effect of Gamma Rays on Man-in-the-Moon Marigolds, a film (1972) directed by Paul Newman and starring Joanne Woodward

The NAME OF THE ROSE, a novel (1980) by Umberto Eco

STEEL MAGNOLIAS, a play (1987) by Robert Harling (film version 1989)

Fly Away Home. A children's film (1996), based on a true story about a girl who looks after a flock of goslings and helps them to make their southward winter migration. The title comes from the nursery rhyme:

> Ladybird, ladybird,
> Fly away home,
> Your house is on fire
> And your children all gone.

In their *Oxford Dictionary of Nursery Rhymes* (1951, 1997), Iona and Peter Opie explain:

> Traditionally the insect is set on a finger before being [thus] addressed … When the warning has been recited (and the ladybird blown upon once), it nearly always happens that the seemingly earthbound little beetle produces wings and flies away.

Flying Dutchman, The (German title: *Der Fliegende Holländer*). An opera by Richard Wagner (1813–83), first performed in 1843. The libretto, by the composer, was based on Heinrich Heine's *Memoiren des Herrn von Schnabelewopski*.

> A musical horror, a mixture concocted of bad taste and brutality in equal doses.
>
> *Deutsche Musikzeitung*

The story was already well established in maritime legend. In some accounts *The Flying Dutchman* was a spectral ship that haunted the seas around the Cape of Good Hope and lured other vessels to their destruction or caused them other misfortunes. According to Auguste Jal's *Scènes de la vie maritime*, the Flying Dutchman was a Dutch captain who persisted in trying to round the Cape, in spite of the violence of the storm and the protests of the passengers and crew. Eventually a form, said to be the Almighty, appeared on deck, but the captain did not even touch his cap, instead firing his gun at the apparition and cursing and blaspheming. For punishment, the Dutchman was condemned to sail and to be a torment to sailors until the Day of Judgment.

In Wagner's opera it is the Devil who condemns the Dutchman to sail the seas for ever, unless he can be redeemed by the love of a good woman. Other appearances include the skeleton ship in Coleridge's *Rime of the* ANCIENT MARINER (1798), and 'the Flying Dutchman of the Tappan Sea' in Washington Irving's *Chronicles of Wolfert's Roost* (1839–40). Captain Marryat's novel *The Phantom Ship* (1839) tells of Philip Vanderdecken's successful but disastrous search for his father, the captain of *The Flying Dutchman*. Similar legends are found in many other countries.

> The Demon Frigate braves the gale;
> And well the doom'd spectators know
> The harbinger of wreck and woe.
>
> SIR WALTER SCOTT: *Rokeby* (1813), II, xi

Flying Shit. A mural-sized work composed of dyed photographic prints (1994) by Gilbert and George (Gilbert Proesch, b.1943; George Pasmore, b.1942). The work includes a number of portraits of the artists, including photographs of them standing naked on comet-like turds zipping earthwards across the sky.

folía (Portuguese, 'folly'). A Portuguese dance dating from the Middle Ages, so called because it was wild and abandoned (and possibly linked to fertility rites). There were several melodies associated with this dance, but one in particular has had a remarkably enduring fascination for composers over the centuries. This was the inspiration of innumerable variations, known collectively in French as *les folies d'Espagne*. Although in many manifestations the tune has taken on a stately air, there is no doubt that the tune has an obsessional quality that prevents composers from leaving it alone. One of the most famous sets of variations is *La Follía*, the violin sonata no 12 (from opus 5, 1700) by Arcangelo Corelli (1653–1713). Other composers who have succumbed to *les folies* include Frescobaldi, Marais, Pasquini, Vivaldi, Alessandro Scarlatti, Domenico Scarlatti, J.S. Bach (in his 'PEASANT' CANTATA), C.P.E. Bach, Cherubini, Liszt (in his *Spanish Rhapsody*) and Rachmaninov (in his *Variations on a Theme by Corelli*). The tune was formerly known in Britain as 'Farinel's Ground', from a version by the French composer Michel Farinel (b.1649).

Folly to be Wise. A film comedy (1952) starring Alastair Sim about a 'Brains Trust' in the army. The title comes from Thomas Gray's *Ode on a Distant Prospect of Eton College* (1747):

> Thought would destroy their paradise.
> No more; where ignorance is bliss,
> 'Tis folly to be wise.

By the end of the 18th century 'Where ignorance is bliss, 'tis folly to be wise' had become proverbial.

F-111. A 10ft-high by 86ft-long painting (1965), designed to cover all four walls of a room, by the US billboard painter turned Pop artist James Rosenquist (b.1933). The General Dynamics F-111 fighter-bomber was the first operational 'swing-wing' aircraft, and in Rosenquist's mural it extends right across the panels that make up the painting, although some of the panels carry other images, such as tinned spaghetti, a child in a hairdryer shaped like the aeroplane's nose cone, and a nuclear explosion covered by an umbrella. After Rosenquist painted it, the F-111 went on to play an important role in the US bombing of North Vietnam.

> Painting is probably more exciting than advertising – so why shouldn't it be done with that power and gusto, that impact?
>
> JAMES ROSENQUIST: interview in *Art News*, 1963–4

FOOD

See also MEALS (panel, p.289)

Of the Irritability of Vegetables, a treatise (1809) by Robert Lyall

How to Cook Husbands, a guide (1899) by Elizabeth Strong Worthington, also author of *The Gentle Art of Cooking Wives*

Trois Morceaux en forme de poire ('three pieces in the shape of a pear' – although there are actually six pieces), a piano work (1903) for four hands by Erik Satie

Pernicious Pork; or, Astounding Revelations of the Evil Effects of Eating Swine Flesh, a discourse (1903) by William T. Hallett

LOVE FOR THREE ORANGES, a comic opera (1921) by Sergei Prokofiev

SCHLAGOBERS, a ballet (1924) with music by Richard Strauss

The Cocoanuts, a Marx Brothers film (1929)

CAKES AND ALE, a novel (1930) by W. Somerset Maugham

Duck Soup, a Marx brothers film (1933)

HURRAH, THE BUTTER IS FINISHED!, a photomontage (1935) by John Heartfield

Soft Construction with Boiled Beans, the alternative title for *PREMONITION OF CIVIL WAR* (1936), a painting by Salvador Dalí

The GRAPES OF WRATH, a novel (1939) by John Steinbeck

The Chocolate Soldier, a film musical (1941)

SALAD DAYS, a musical comedy (1954)

Wild Strawberries, a film (1957) by the Swedish director Ingmar Bergman

Bitter Lemons, a book (1957) about Cyprus by Lawrence Durrell

CHICKEN SOUP WITH BARLEY, a play (1958) by Arnold Wesker

A TASTE OF HONEY, a play (1958) by Shelagh Delaney

Greengage Summer, a novel (1958) by Rumer Goden (film version 1961)

A Raisin in the Sun, a film (1961) based on a play by Lorraine Hansberry about a black family in Chicago

CHIPS WITH EVERYTHING, a play (1962) by Arnold Wesker

A CLOCKWORK ORANGE, a novel (1962) by Anthony Burgess (film version 1971)

100 Cans of CAMPBELL'S SOUP, a picture (1962) by Andy Warhol

HAMBURGER WITH PICKLE AND TOMATO ATTACHED, a large sculpture (1963) by Claes Oldenburg

Bacon, Lettuce and Tomato, the title of two large Pop art sculptures, one by Claes Oldenburg (1963) and the other by Robert Watts (1965)

Hot Dogs, a sculpture (1964) by the US Pop artist Robert Watts

The Wonderful Ice Cream Suit, a play (1965) by Ray Bradbury

A Melon for Ecstasy, a comic novel (1971) by John Fortune and John Wells

NOURISHMENT: SLOW AND DIFFICULT ABSORPTION OF 600 GRAMMES OF MINCED MEAT WHICH DISTURB THE USUAL DIGESTIVE OPERATIONS, a piece of body art (1971) by Gina Pane

Bananas, a Woody Allen comedy film (1971)

The Onion Field, a US police film (1979) based on a novel by Joseph Wambaugh

An Ice-Cream War, a novel (1982) by William Boyd

Real Men Don't Eat Quiche, a humorous book (1982) on the do's and don'ts of machismo by Bruce Feirstein and Lee Lorenz

Sour Sweet, a novel (1982) by Timothy Mo about a Chinese family who set up a restaurant in outer London (film version 1988)

Can She Bake a Cherry Pie?, a romantic comedy film (1983)

ORANGES ARE NOT THE ONLY FRUIT, a novel (1985) by Jeanette Winterson

Dim Sum, a film (1985) set in San Francisco's China Town

Gargling with Jelly, a children's book (1985) by Brian Patten

How to Cook Roadkill, a 'gourmet cooking' book (1987) by Richard Marcou

The Thermodynamics of Pizza, a work of science (1991) by Harold J. Morowitz

FRIED GREEN TOMATOES AT THE WHISTLE STOP CAFÉ, a film (1991) set in the American South

BROWNOUT ON BREADFRUIT BOULEVARD, a novel (1995) by Timothy Mo

Canadian Bacon, a film (1995) in which Alan Alda, as a US president, decides Canada poses a global threat

AMERICAN PIE, a comedy film (1999)

Chocolat, a film (2000) in which Juliette Binoche plays a chocolatière who brings joy and romance to a repressed French village

Bread and Roses, a film (2001) by Ken Loach

---

for colored girls who have considered suicide when the rainbow is enuf. A play (1974) by the US writer Ntozake Shange (b.1948) consisting of 20 'choreopoems' about the experiences of African-American women in modern Western society. One of the longest running shows in Broadway history, the play's extraordinary title, with its unconventional spellings and rejection of accepted grammatical rules, was intended by the author to represent the independence of African-American culture from Western influence. The mutilation of words throughout the title and text are reportedly meant to remind the reader of the mutilation of African slaves through branding and other punishments.

For Men Only, MM and BB Starring. A painting (1961) by the British Pop artist Peter Phillips. *Men Only* is a top-shelf men's magazine, while the initials stand for the sex goddesses Marilyn Monroe and Brigitte Bardot, small portraits of whom appear, along with (punningly) two five-pointed stars, a hare and scenes from a striptease act. The composition has been compared to a cross between a games board and a Sienese altarpiece.

'Forty-eight, The'. *See* WELL-TEMPERED CLAVIER, THE.

42nd Street. A classic film musical (1933) featuring choreography by Busby Berkeley (1895–1976). The setting is backstage in New York's theatreland, in which, at all costs, the show must go on. At that time

42nd Street, near Broadway, was suffering in the Great Depression, and many of its theatres were being turned into burlesque houses, and later cinemas. Theatres survive there, however. *Vanya on 42nd Street* (1994) is Louis Malle's stunning production of the Chekhov play *Uncle Vanya* (adapted by David Mamet), filmed as a rehearsal in a New York theatre.

For Whom the Bell Tolls. A novel (1940) by Ernest Hemingway (1899–1961) about an American, Robert Jordan, who fights on the Republican side in the Spanish Civil War (1936–9). Hemingway himself had covered the war in Spain as a journalist in 1937, accompanied by fellow war correspondent Martha Gellhorn (1908–98), to whom he dedicated the book and whom he married in 1940. The novel is a tale of passion, courage and cowardice, centred round an attack on a bridge. At the end, the wounded Jordan thinks:

> I have fought for what I believed in for a year now. If we win here we will win everywhere …

The title is a quotation from John Donne:

> No man is an Island, entire of itself; every man is a piece of the Continent … Any man's death diminishes me, because I am involved in Mankind; And therefore never send to know for whom the bell tolls; it tolls for thee.
>
> *Devotions upon Emergent Occasions* (1624), Meditation XVII

A stolid, depoliticized film version (1943), directed by Sam Wood, starred Gary Cooper and Ingrid Bergman.

Foucault's Pendulum (Italian title: *Il Pendolo di Foucault*). The second novel (1988; English translation 1989) by Umberto Eco (b.1932), which he wrote 'because one novel could have been an accident' (his first novel had been *The* NAME OF THE ROSE). Experimental in form, it features computer science and Rosicrucianism. The pendulum devised by Léon Foucault (1819–68) to demonstrate the rotation of the Earth is the motif with which the novel opens:

> The sphere, hanging from a long wire set into the ceiling of the choir, swayed back and forth with isochronal majesty.

Foul Play. An indifferent thriller film (1978) starring Goldie Hawn and Chevy Chase. By this time 'foul play' was so well entrenched in everyday cliché that it is possible the film's makers were unaware of its origin in Shakespeare's *Hamlet*, I.ii:

My father's spirit in arms! All is not well.
I doubt some foul play.

Fountain. The title given by the Dada artist Marcel Duchamp (1887–1968) to one of his 'ready-mades' – a urinal placed on its side (1915). It was signed 'R. Mutt', the name of a firm of sanitary engineers. As a member of the jury of the first New York *Salon des Indépendents*, Duchamp submitted this work to his fellow jurors for consideration. Predictably enough, they rejected it with indignation, and Duchamp resigned. However, its shock value wore off in time: at a Dada exhibition in the 1950s it hung over the main entrance, filled with geraniums. The American Morton Schamberg (1882–1918) picked up Duchamp's baton in his assemblage involving an S-bend, to which he gave the title *God* (*c.*1918). Continuing the lavatorial tradition is a drawing of what might be some rather imaginative architectural plumbing entitled *That Makes Me Piss* (1919) by Max Ernst (1891–1976).

Four Feathers, The. A novel (1902) by A.E.W. Mason (1865–1948). The four white feathers, symbols of cowardice, are given to Harry Feversham by three fellow officers and by his fiancée when, fearful that he cannot measure up to his father's standards of bravery, he resigns his commission after his regiment is ordered to Egypt on active service. Harry follows after the regiment and in disguise performs two acts of incredible heroism, as a result of which the feathers are taken back, and he gets his girl after all. The story has been filmed several times, notably in 1939 under the direction of Zoltan Korda. This included the notable screen title:

THE KHALIFA'S ARMY OF DERVISHES AND FUZZY-WUZZIES MASSES ON THE NILE.

The 1956 version was titled *Storm over the Nile*, while an effective television version (1977) starred Beau Bridges, Robert Powell, Simon Ward, Richard Johnson and Jane Seymour.

400 Blows, The. *See* QUATRE CENT COUPS, LES.

4′ 33′′. A controversial and certainly unusual work by the US composer John Cage (1912–92), scored for any instrument or any combination of instruments. The piece consists of 4 minutes and 33 seconds of silence. It was first performed in 1952. Ten years later Cage went one better with *0′ 00′′*, designed 'to be performed in any way to anyone'. In his book entitled *Silence* (1961), Cage observed:

nothing is accomplished by writing a piece of music
nothing is accomplished by hearing a piece of music
nothing is accomplished by playing a piece of music

Four Quartets. A group of four poems by T.S. Eliot (1888–1965), published successively, and then all in one volume in 1943. The four poems, with their dates of first publication, are: 'Burnt Norton' (1935), 'East Coker' (1940), 'The Dry Salvages' (1941) and 'Little Gidding' (1942). In the overall title, Eliot intended an analogy to a set of string quartets; each poem has five 'movements', and a carefully considered structure of themes and images. Each poem represents a different season, and one of the four elements of earth, air, water and fire. As a whole, the poems form a meditation on time and eternity.

Time present and time past
Are both perhaps present in time future
And time future contained in time past.

'Burnt Norton', I, opening lines

'Burnt Norton' evokes a garden in the Cotswolds:

Footfalls echo in the memory
Down the passage which we did not take
Towards the door we never opened
Into the rose-garden.

'Burnt Norton', I

East Coker is a village in Somerset, the home of Eliot's ancestor who left for the New World in 1669 – and also, incidentally, the birthplace of William Dampier (1651–1715), the explorer of the coasts of Australia. Eliot himself provided a note on 'The Dry Salvages':

The Dry Salvages – presumably *les trois sauvages* – is a small group of rocks, with a beacon, off the N.E. coast of Cape Ann, Massachusetts. *Salvages* is pronounced to rhyme with *assuages.*

The poem deploys striking images drawn from the sea. 'Little Gidding' derives its title from the religious community established in 1625 at the hamlet of Little Gidding in Cambridgeshire by Nicholas Ferrar (1592–1637). The community was broken up by the Puritans in 1646.

You are here to kneel
Where prayer has been valid.

'Little Gidding'

Four Saints in Three Acts. The teasingly misleading title of an opera by Virgil Thomson (1896–1989) to a libretto by Gertrude Stein (1874–1946). The opera, which is set in Spain, actually has four acts, and more than four saints (among whom are St Theresa and St Ignatius). Its first performance in 1934 was given by an all-black cast dressed in cellophane.

Four Seasons, The. *See THE SEASONS* AND *THE FOUR SEASONS* (panel, pp.412–13).

Four Temperaments, The. The subtitle of two pieces of music. The first is the symphony no 2 (1902) by the Danish composer Carl Nielsen (1865–1931), and the second is the *Theme and Variations* for piano and strings (1940) by the German composer Paul Hindemith (1895–1963). In both cases, the 'temperaments' are the medieval 'humours', namely phlegm, blood, choler and melancholy, each of which is associated with an aspect of personality (for a more detailed account of the humours, *see EVERY MAN IN HIS HUMOUR*). In Nielsen's symphony, each of the four movements is allocated to a different temperament; similarly, each of Hindemith's four variations represents a temperament. Note that 'temperament' here is not used in its musical sense, i.e. a method of tuning (*see WELL-TEMPERED CLAVIER, THE*).

Four Weddings and a Funeral. An astonishingly successful British film comedy (1994), written by Richard Curtis and directed by Mike Newell, about a reserved young Englishman's abiding love for an American called Carrie, which survives the four weddings and a funeral of the title before its consummation. Hugh Grant plays the young Englishman in his trademark 'charmingly diffident' manner. The film begins, famously, with the repetition by Grant of the word 'fuck', and it includes a moving reading of W.H. Auden's 'Funeral Blues', which briefly took a collection of the poet's verse into the bestseller lists, just as the film of *The ENGLISH PATIENT* engendered a short-lived interest in Herodotus.

Fraffly Well Spoken. A didactic work (1968) by Professor Afferbeck Lauder (Alistair Morrison) on how to speak the brand of English heard in the upmarket environs of London's West End. A follow-up book (1969) was entitled *Fraffly Suite*. Both volumes present comic dialogues in which upper-class English speech is spelled out phonetically to demonstrate its drawling absurdities. Thus 'York air scissors good as mine' translates as 'Your guess is as good as mine', 'Egg-wetter gree' as 'I quite agree', and 'Rilleh quettex trod nerreh!' as 'Really quite extraordinary!' *See also LET'S TALK STRINE*.

FRANCESCA DA RIMINI

The life of Francesca da Rimini (d. *c.*1283), with its story of doomed love, has inspired many writers, composers and artists. Her original name was Francesca da Polenta, and she was the daughter of Guido da Polenta, lord of Ravenna. She was married to Gianciotto Malatesta for reasons of state, the Malatestas being an important family in Rimini. However, Francesca fell in love and committed adultery with Malatesta's younger brother Paolo. When Malatesta discovered their affair, he put them both to death. In Canto V of Dante's *Inferno* (*c.*1309–20; *see* DIVINE COMEDY, THE), the poet encounters the lovers in the second circle of hell, and it is this encounter that has ensured their immortality.

Today, Francesca's most familiar incarnation is in the symphonic fantasy, opus 32 (1876), by Tchaikovsky (1840–93), which was inspired by Gustave Doré's illustration (1861) of the episode in the *Inferno*. There is also a symphonic poem (1905) by Henry Hadley. Francesca has appeared in many operas, the most notable being that by Sergei Rachmaninov (1875–1943), first performed in 1906. Literary and dramatic works on the subject include:

- *Francesca da Rimini*, a tragedy (1815) by Silvio Pellico
- *The Story of Rimini*, a poem (1816) by Leigh Hunt
- *Paolo and Francesca*, a verse tragedy (1898) by Stephen Phillips
- *Francesca da Rimini*, a tragedy (1902) by Gabriele D'Annunzio
- *Francesca da Rimini*, a tragedy (1902) written for Sarah Bernhardt by F.M. Crawford

Finally, Rodin's celebrated (and at first scandalous) sculpture *The Kiss* (*Le Baiser*, 1886), depicting a seated naked couple in a passionate embrace, was originally conceived as a depiction of Paolo and Francesca for *The Gates of Hell* (*La Porte de l'Enfer*). This was meant to be a bronze door for the Musée des Arts Décoratifs; it was commissioned in 1880, but was still unfinished at the time of Rodin's death in 1917. Rodin's equally famous and equally naked sculpture, *The Thinker* (*Le Penseur*, 1880) – now a much parodied icon of philosophical contemplation – was also originally intended for the door, as a portrait of Dante.

Frankenstein. *See* PROMETHEUS (panel, pp.364–5).

French Connection, The. A film (1971) adapted by Ernest Tidyman from a book of the same title by Robin Moore about a detective's efforts to combat the illegal drug trade in New York. Starring Gene Hackman as Detective 'Popeye' Doyle and Roy Scheider as his partner, both characters were based on actual drug squad officers. The film contains one of the most memorable chase scenes ever filmed. The title refers to the link between drug dealers in Marseilles and New York that the two detectives uncover, the word 'connection' being doubly significant in that it is also slang for a drug dealer or pusher.

The name was adopted by the chain of fashion retailers whose UK arm notoriously operates under the acronym 'fcuk'.

French Lieutenant's Woman, The. A ludic historical novel (1969) by John Fowles (b.1926). It opens in Lyme Regis in the 1860s, at a spot overlooked by the 18th-century house in which Fowles has lived since 1965. The author post-modernistically offers alternative endings. The 'woman' is Sarah Woodruff, believed to have been deserted by a French lieutenant, and therefore regarded as not 'respectable'. She is unsuccessfully pursued by a young palaeontologist, Charles Smithson, at the cost of his own engagement. A film version (1981) was directed by Karel Reisz from a screenplay by Harold Pinter.

Fried Green Tomatoes at the Whistle Stop Café. A film (1991) directed by Jon Avnet and with a screenplay by Fannie Flag, adapted from her own novel. Evelyn Couch, a middle-aged housewife, finds inspiration in the story told her by Ninny Threadgoode, an octogenarian lady in an old folk's home. Her story from her youth concerns a relative, Idgie Threadgoode, an early feminist, who many years before had run the café in Whistle Stop, Alabama. Idgie rescues her friend Ruth from an abusive marriage, and Ruth joins her at the café, cooking such Southern delights as fried green tomatoes.

'Frog' Quartet (German *Froschquartett*). The nickname given to the string quartet in D, opus 50 no 6, by Haydn (1732–1809). Some have heard croaking in the last movement.

From Here to Eternity. The first novel (1951) by James Jones (1921–77), who was serving in the US infantry in Hawaii when the Japanese bombed Pearl Harbor in 1941. Twice promoted and twice reduced to private, he fought at Guadalcanal and was wounded in the head by a mortar fragment. The novel, which won a National Book Award, draws on his own experiences in Hawaii and caused a sensation for its exposé of army brutality and its outspokenness about sex and military mores. The film (1952) was a slick, sexually oblique version directed by Fred Zinnemann. The title comes from the poem 'The Gentlemen-Rankers' (1889) by Rudyard Kipling (1865–1936), about oppressed junior ranks:

> Gentlemen-rankers out on the spree,
> Damned from here to Eternity,
> God ha' mercy on such as we.

From My Life (Czech title: *Z mého zivota*). The title of the string quartet no 1 in E minor (1876) by Bedřich Smetana (1824–84).

> My quartet, *From My Life*, does not consist merely of a formal game of tones and motifs, by means of which the composer exhibits his skill. On the contrary, my aim was to present the listener with scenes from my life.
>
> BEDŘICH SMETANA: quoted in Morgenstern, *Composers on Music* (1958)

On another occasion Smetana described the quartet as a private musical conversation 'about the things which so deeply trouble me'. One of his greatest troubles at this time was the onset of deafness, represented in the quartet by the sustained high E on the first violin in the final movement. The year before writing the quartet, Smetana had confided in his diary:

> If my illness is incurable, then I should prefer to be delivered from this miserable existence.

From Russia with Love. A spy novel (1957) by Ian Fleming (1908–64). It became the second James Bond film in 1963, and has proved to be one of the best in the long-running series. It stars Sean Connery as Bond, Robert Shaw as the villain Red Grant, and the great prewar cabaret singer Lotte Lenya as a ruthless East German intelligence officer. The title was inspired by a standard formula on British holiday postcards, here given a chilling Cold War edge.

From the House of the Dead (Czech title: *Z Mrtvého Domu*). A surprisingly uplifting opera by Leoš Janáček (1854–1928), with a text by the composer based on the prison reminiscences *Memoirs from the House of the Dead* (1862) by Fyodor Dostoyevsky (1821–81). The 'House of the Dead' in question is a Siberian prison camp at Omsk, where Dostoyevsky was confined from 1850 to 1854 because of his interest in French socialist theory. Nothing much happens in the opera, although the Dostoyevsky figure (called Alexander Goryanchikov in the opera) arrives at the beginning and departs at the end. At the head of the score Janáček wrote: 'In every human being there is a divine spark.' He left the work unfinished at the time of his death; it was completed by Bretislav Bakala and O. Zitek and first performed in 1930.

From the New World. The subtitle of the symphony no 9 in E minor, opus 95, by Antonín Dvořák (1841–1904), more usually known as the 'New World' symphony. Dvořák wrote the symphony in 1893 during his stay in the USA, and it was first performed in New York at the end of that year. In places Dvořák incorporates the spirit of – rather than quotations from – black American music into the symphony; conversely, one of Dvořák themes in the symphony became the tune for the Negro spiritual 'Goin' Home'. But much of the music is strongly Bohemian, rather than American, in character; indeed, it was homesickness that provoked Dvořák to leave America for his native Bohemia in 1895. The first subject of the slow movement was famously appropriated by the Hovis bread company for a series of sentimental television commercials.

Full Fathom Five. A wild action painting (1947) by Jackson Pollock (1912–56). Most of Pollock's subsequent works had titles such as *Number One*, *Number Thirty Two*, or, marginally more excitingly, *Black and White Number Five*. However, this one is a quotation from Shakespeare:

> Full fathom five thy father lies;
> Of his bones are coral made;
> Those are pearls that were his eyes …
>
> *The Tempest* (1611), I.ii

These are the words that Ariel sings to Ferdinand, who believes his father has drowned in the storm. While he was still in his teens, Pollock had lost his own father; as he himself said, 'Every good painter paints what he is'. *See also* COME UNTO THESE YELLOW SANDS; THIS MUSIC CREPT BY ME UPON THE WATERS.

Full Metal Jacket. A film (1987) directed by Stanley Kubrick (1928–99) about the training of a squad of US Marines and their subsequent experiences in Vietnam. It was based on the novel *The Short Timers* by Gustav Hasford and was filmed entirely in the UK (a gasworks in the East End of London serving for Vietnam, complete with imported palm trees). The title is army slang for full combat gear. The reality of the film was heightened by the fact that Gunnery Sergeant Hartman was played by R. Lee Ermey, a former army drill instructor who was hired initially just to advise, but who persuaded Kubrick to let him play the part himself.

Full Monty, The. A comedy film (1997), directed by Peter Cattaneo and starring Robert Carlyle, about a group of unemployed male steel workers in Sheffield, England, who raise money by staging a strip act at a local club. 'The full monty' means everything – 'the works'– and is used of anything done to the utmost or fullest degree. In the case of the film, this means stripping down completely, thongs and all.

> Ladies and gents, and you buggers at the back – we may not be young, we may not be pretty and we may not be reet good, but for one night and one night only, we are here, we're live and we're going no less than the Full Monty.

The origin of the expression is uncertain. It may derive from 'the full amount' or the Spanish card game *monte* (literally 'mountain', i.e. heap of cards), or allude to a full three-piece suit from the men's outfitters Montague Burton. One explanation traces the term to Field Marshal Bernard Montgomery, nicknamed 'Monty' (1887–1976), said to have begun every day with a full English breakfast when campaigning in the African desert in the Second World War. Yet another derives it from the city of Montevideo, Uruguay, on the grounds that fleece-packers shipping sheepskins from there graded them as 'full Monte'.

Funny Thing Happened on the Way to the Forum, A. A film musical (1966) based on a stage show of the same title (1962), with music by Stephen Sondheim and book by Burt Shevelove and Larry Gelbart, about a Roman slave's farcical attempts to gain his freedom. Starring Zero Mostel, Phil Silvers and an ageing Buster Keaton, the film was, like the stage show, ultimately derived from the comic writings of the Roman dramatist Plautus (*c*.254–184 BC).

G

G. *See* LETTERS, SYMBOLS AND INITIALS (panel, pp.255–6).

Game at Chess, A. A comedy by Thomas Middleton (1580–1627), first performed in 1624. However, the play's satirical content restricted its first, otherwise hugely successful, run to nine performances. In the all too obvious allegory, the Black King and his men represent the king of Spain and the Jesuits, who are checkmated by the White Knight – Prince Charles, the future Charles I. At this time, England and Spain were meant to be on good terms. The Spanish ambassador was outraged, King James I closed down the play, and Middleton and the actors were summoned to appear before the Privy Council.

Garden of Earthly Delights, The. An extraordinarily fantastical triptych by the Netherlandish painter Hieronymus Bosch (*c.*1450–1516). A continuous landscape links the three panels. The left-hand panel depicts the Garden of Eden and the right-hand panel Hell, while the larger central panel gives the work its overall title. The Garden of Eden is populated by an array of real and surreal animals, while the complex torments in the dark, nightmare Hell include a man being eaten head-first by a bird-headed demon while blackbirds fly out of his smoking bottom. The dreamlike Garden of Earthly Delights itself is peopled by hundreds of ecstatic, naked lovers, giant birds, flying fish, big pink spiky things and all kinds of odd goings-on. Art historians and psychoanalysts have spent long and happy hours trying to interpret the work, although it seems likely that the central panel draws on the medieval literary convention

GARDENS

See also FLOWERS (panel, pp.164–5).

The GARDEN OF EARTHLY DELIGHTS, a triptych by Hieronymus Bosch; *A Garden of Earthly Delights* is also the title of a novel (1967) by Joyce Carol Oates

The Garden of Cyrus, a disquisition (1658) on the quincunx and the number five by Sir Thomas Browne

The Secret Garden, a children's novel (1911) by Frances Hodgson Burnett

The Walk to the Paradise Garden, an orchestral interlude (1910) by Frederick Delius

The Chalk Garden, a play (1955) by Enid Bagnold (film version 1964)

Tom's Midnight Garden, a novel (1958) for children by Philippa Pearce

The Garden of the Finzi-Contini, a novel (1962) by Giorgio Bassani (film version 1970, directed by Vittorio de Sica)

High Tide in the Garden, a poetry collection (1971) by Fleur Adcock

The KNOT GARDEN, an opera (1974) by Michael Tippett

I Never Promised You a Rose Garden, a film (1977) about a teenage girl with psychiatric problems

The CEMENT GARDEN, a novella (1978) by Ian McEwan

In the Garden of the North American Martyrs, the US title of Tobias Wolff's short story collection, *HUNTERS IN THE SNOW* (1981)

Midnight in the Garden of Good and Evil, a portrait (1994) by John Berendt of Savannah, Georgia, focusing on a society murder; Clint Eastwood directed a film version (1997) starring Kevin Spacey of the Garden of Love, as found, for example, in *The Romance of the Rose*, and there are also alchemical references scattered throughout the work (some of Bosch's wife's family were apothecaries). It is thought that the work would have been interpreted in fairly conventional (albeit apocalyptic) theological terms by Bosch's contemporaries.

The work was probably commissioned by Henry III, Count of Nassau, and passed on to his son, William the Silent, one of the leaders of the Dutch Revolt against Spanish rule that broke out in 1568. During the Revolt the Duke of Alba, the ruthless Spanish commander, seized the work from William's palace in Brussels. It passed via Alba's natural son to the Escorial Palace near Madrid in 1593, and is now in the Prado, Madrid.

Gaudy Night. A detective novel (1935) by Dorothy L. Sayers (1893–1957). The story takes place at an Oxford college during its 'gaudy' – a gaudy (from Latin *gaudium*, 'joy') being the name given at that university to commemorative feasts, often held for the benefit of former members of a college. The word has also been used more generally for a holiday or feast day:

> Let's have one other gaudy night. Call to me
> All my sad captains; fill our bowls once more;
> Let's mock the midnight bell.
>
> SHAKESPEARE: *Antony and Cleopatra* (1606–7), III.xiii

The same passage gave rise to *My Sad Captains, and Other Poems* (1976) by the British poet Thom Gunn (b.1929). *The Gaudy* is the title of a novel by J.I.M. Stewart (1906–94), the Oxford don who also wrote detective novels under the pseudonym of Michael Innes.

Gazza ladra, La. *See* THIEVING MAGPIE, THE.

'General William Booth Enters Heaven'. A poem by the US poet Vachel Lindsay (1879–1931), first published in 1913 in *Poetry* magazine. The poem established Lindsay's reputation. He had some years previously made his way by lecturing for the YMCA and the Anti-Saloon League (a temperance organization), before travelling the country reciting his poems in exchange for board and lodging. In this poem Lindsay celebrates the apotheosis of William Booth (1829–12), the British founder of the Salvation Army (another temperance organization), who is followed into heaven by a host of criminals and slum dwellers:

Christ came gently with a robe and crown
For Booth the soldier, while the throng knelt down.

The rhythm mimics the drumbeats of a Salvation Army band, and the poem was intended to be sung to the tune of 'Washed in the Blood of the Lamb'.

Booth died blind and still by faith he trod,
Eyes still dazzled by the ways of God.

German Requiem, A (German title: *Ein Deutsches Requiem*). A choral work, opus 45 by Johannes Brahms (1833–97). The work was written between 1857 and 1868, and the first complete performance was in 1869. The title derives from the fact that the text is not that of the Roman Catholic Mass for the Dead (*Missa pro defunctis*), but is rather drawn from Luther's translation of the Bible. The work was composed in memory of Brahms's mother.

His Requiem is patiently borne only by the corpse.

GEORGE BERNARD SHAW: in *The Star*, 1892

A German Requiem is also the title of a verse collection (1981) by the British poet James Fenton (b.1949).

'Ghost' Trio (German *Geister Trio*). The nickname given to the piano trio in D, opus 70 no 1 (1808), by Beethoven (1770–1827). The name was inspired by the mysteriously elusive motifs of the slow movement, in which there is a theme that at one point Beethoven considered using in a planned (but never realized) opera on *Macbeth*, or for incidental music to the play.

'Giant' Fugue. The nickname for the prelude for organ (from the *Clavierübung*, part III) by J.S. Bach (1685–1750), based on his chorale '*Wir glauben all' an einen Gott*' ('we all believe in one God'). The piece is thus intended to embody the firmness of faith. The nickname was given to the piece by the English organist George Cooper (1820–76), because of the giant-like figure on the pedals, which, in particular, reminded him of the bass aria 'O ruddier than the cherry' sung by the giant Polyphemus in Handel's masque *Acis and Galatea* (1718).

Gioconda, La. *See* MONA LISA.

Girl of the Golden West, The (Italian title: *La Fanciulla del West*). An opera by Giacomo Puccini (1858–1924), to a libretto by Guelfo Civinini and Carlo Zangarini, first performed in 1910, in New York. The 'girl' is

Minnie, the heroine who stands by (and saves) her man, and the 'Golden West' is California during the 1849 gold rush. The opera was based on the play of the same title (1905) by the American producer and playwright David Belasco (1853–1931), known as the 'bishop of Broadway' because of his austere dress and demeanour. Belasco's play *MADAME BUTTERFLY* (1900) also gave Puccini a plot.

Glagolitic Mass. A setting of the Ordinary of the Mass for solo voices, chorus, organ and orchestra by Leoš Janáček (1854–1928). The title is a misnomer: the composer thought 'Glagolitic' referred to the Old Slavonic language of the 9th century, the time of St Methodius and St Cyril; however, the term only refers to the Old Slavonic alphabet, supposedly invented by St Cyril. Of the work, which was first performed in 1927, Janáček wrote:

> I wanted to portray the faith in the certainty of the nation, not on a religious basis but on a basis of moral strength which takes God for witness.

Glengarry Glen Ross. A film (1992), directed by James Foley, based on a play (1984) by David Mamet (b.1947), who also wrote the screenplay. It is about the pressures sales staff at a real-estate office find themselves under when they learn that the two least successful among them will be sacked. Glengarry Glen Ross is the name of the useless areas of land that are to be sold.

> Put that coffee down. Coffee's for closers only.
>
> DAVID MAMET: *Glengarry Glen Ross*

Glittering Prizes, The. A six-part TV series and novel (1976) by Frederic Raphael (b.1931) that follows the progress of a group of clever and often self-satisfied Cambridge arts graduates through the 1950s and 1960s to 1972. Cambridge is itself described as the 'City of perspiring dreams' – in contrast to the traditional description of Oxford as a place of 'dreaming spires'. The title comes from the address that F.E. Smith (Lord Birkenhead), the Conservative politician and witty lawyer, gave on 7 November 1923 in his capacity as rector of Glasgow University:

> The world continues to offer glittering prizes to those who have stout hearts and sharp swords.

Gloriana. An opera by Benjamin Britten (1913–76) with a libretto by William Plomer (1903–73). It was commissioned by Covent Garden to celebrate the coronation of Elizabeth II and was first performed in the queen's presence in 1953. Gloriana was one of the names that Edmund Spenser (*c.*1552–99) gave to Queen Elizabeth I in *The FAERIE QUEENE*, and Britten's opera concerns the relationship between Elizabeth I and Essex. Some members of the public objected that the opera's portrayal of an ageing and all too human monarch was unsuitable for the dawn of the young Elizabeth II's reign.

Glories of Our Blood and State, The. A choral ode by Hubert Parry (1848–1918), first performed in 1883. The title comes from the playwright James Shirley (1596–1666):

> The glories of our blood and state
> Are shadows, not substantial things;
> There is no armour against fate;
> Death lays his icy hand on kings:
> Sceptre and crown
> Must tumble down,
> And in the dust be equal made
> With the poor crooked scythe and spade.
>
> JAMES SHIRLEY: *The Contention of Ajax and Ulysses* (1559), I.iii

God. *See FOUNTAIN.*

Godfather, The. A film (1972) adapted from a novel (1969) by Mario Puzo (1902–99) about an Italian Mafia family in New York. Directed by Francis Ford Coppola and starring Marlon Brando as the head (or 'Godfather') of the powerful Corleone clan, it inspired one equally acclaimed sequel (1974) and one that was less well received (1990). The film firmly established the use of 'the Godfather' to describe any person at the head of an organization, particularly one suspected of employing dubious, underhand or plain illegal methods. In business circles a takeover bid for a company that is so generous no one can afford to turn it down is commonly referred to as a 'godfather offer', with reference to the tradition of Mafia gangsters making 'an offer you can't refuse'. The football manager Don Revie (1928–89) was called 'the Godfather' because of his autocratic style of management.

God is a Lily of the Valley. A poster-like painting (1961) by the US Pop artist Robert Indiana (b.1928) in which the words of a Negro spiritual are enclosed in circles:

God is a Lily of the Valley,
He is a Tiger,
He is a Star,
He is a Ruby,
He is a King,
He can do Everything but Fail.

Lily of the valley (*Convallaria majalis*) is a beautifully scented woodland plant with clusters of nodding white bell-shaped flowers. It is native to parts of Europe, Asia and eastern North America.

'God Save the King'. The British national anthem ('Queen' being substituted as appropriate). The tune has been attributed to Dr John Bull (*c.*1562–1628), organist at Antwerp Cathedral (1617–28), and the words to a number of 18th-century writers, including Henry Carey (*c.*1690–1743). The following, by Mme de Brion, was sung before Louis XIV in 1686:

Grand Dieu sauvez le roi,
Grand Dieu vengez le roi,
Vive le roi!
Qu'à jamais glorieux,
Louis victorieux,
Voie ses ennemis toujours soumis,
Vive le roi!

('Great God, save the king,
Great God, avenge the king,
Long live the king!
May ever glorious
Louis victorious
See his foes always beaten,
Long live the king!')

The Authorized Version of the Bible has:

And all the people shouted, and said, God save the king.
1 Samuel 10:24

The song became popular at the time of the 1745–6 Jacobite Rebellion as a demonstration of loyalty to George II and opposition to the Jacobites, to whom the following lines are thought to refer:

Confound their politics,
Frustrate their knavish tricks.

An arrangement for four voices was made in 1745 by Thomas Arne (1710–78) for the Drury Lane Theatre, and in the following year Handel incorporated it into his *Occasional Oratorio* (1746). A number of composers – including Beethoven, Liszt and Paganini – have written variations on the theme. The tune has also been quoted by composers wishing to make a British reference – for example, Beethoven in his occasional piece *WELLINGTON'S VICTORY*. In America the tune is used for the patriotic 'My Country, 'Tis of Thee'. During his London tours Haydn was so impressed by the enthusiasm of Britons for 'God Save the King' that he was inspired to compose his own 'EMPEROR'S HYMN'.

Goldberg Variations. 'An aria with different variations for harpsichord with two manuals, designed for the refreshment of music lovers' – as J.S. Bach (1685–1750) described his 30 variations on an original theme, comprising the fourth and final part (1742) of his *Clavierübung* ('keyboard practice'). Johann Goldberg (1727–56) was a pupil of Bach's, and Bach is thought to have written the variations for him to play to the insomniac Count Keyserling or Kaiserling, formerly the Russian ambassador to the court of Saxony.

Golden Apples of the Sun, The. A collection of science-fiction short stories (1953) by the US writer Ray Bradbury (b.1920). The title comes from Yeats:

> And pluck till time and times are done
> The silver apples of the moon,
> The golden apples of the sun.
>
> W.B. YEATS: 'Song of Wandering Aengus' (1899)

Golden Apples (1935) is a novel by the US writer Marjorie Kinnan Rawlings (1896–1953), author of *The Yearling*, while *The Golden Apples* (1949) is a short story collection by the US writer Eudora Welty (b.1909).

Golden Ass, The. The title usually given to a satirical prose romance by the Roman writer Lucius Apuleius (2nd century AD), who himself used the title *Metamorphoses*. It relates the adventures of Lucian, a young man who, being accidentally metamorphosed into a donkey while sojourning in Thessaly, falls into the hands of robbers, eunuchs, magistrates and so on, and is ill-treated by all. Ultimately, however, he recovers his human form. The work includes the story of Cupid and Psyche (*see ENCHANTED*

CASTLE, THE). The adjective 'golden' in the title apparently refers to the excellence of the work.

Golden Bough, The. A massive work on anthropology and myth (1890–1915) by Sir James Frazer (1854–1941). He himself characterized the work as a description of 'the long evolution by which the thoughts and efforts of man have passed through the successive stages of magic, religion, and science'. Frazer's title comes from book 6 of William Pitt's 1743 translation of Virgil's *Aeneid*: 'A mighty tree, that bears a golden bough.' T.S. Eliot drew extensively on *The Golden Bough* in his poem *The WASTE LAND* (1922).

Golden Bowl, The. The last completed novel of Henry James (1843–1916), published in 1904. The story, of great subtlety and complexity, centres on an American heiress, Maggie, and deals with infidelity, duplicity and the end of innocence. The golden bowl – the image is derived from Ecclesiastes – flits symbolically in and out of the story. It is actually gilt-covered crystal, not gold, and has a hidden flaw. The flaw is eventually revealed and the bowl deliberately broken, symbolizing the shattering of Maggie's innocent view of the world.

> Or ever the silver cord be loosed, or the golden bowl be broken, or the pitcher be broken at the fountain, or the wheel broken at the cistern.
> Then shall the dust return to the earth as it was: and the spirit shall return unto God who gave it.
> Vanity of vanities, saith the preacher; all is vanity.
>
> Ecclesiastes 12:6–8

Goldeneye. A James Bond film (1995), with Pierce Brosnan as the suave secret agent, who goes to Russia to foil the fiendish plots of a criminal mastermind. In temper with the changing times, M is played by Judi Dench (just as, in the 1990s, MI5 was headed by a woman, Stella Rimington). Unlike earlier Bond films, it was not based on any of the Bond novels by Ian Fleming (1908–64), but adapted from a story by Michael France. Goldeneye was the name of Fleming's house in Jamaica, which he had named after one his Second World War operations, when he worked as a senior officer in naval intelligence. Originally, goldeneye is a handsome species of duck (*Bucephala clangula*) with striking black and white plumage. It summers in northern Russia and Scandinavia, and is a winter visitor to British shores.

Golden Notebook, The. A novel (1962) by Doris Lessing (b.1919). The work is experimental in form and ambitious in scope. The writer Anna Wulf keeps four notebooks – coloured black, red, yellow and blue – in which she records different aspects of her experience: her time in Africa during the Second World War, her membership of the Communist Party of Great Britain, a fictionalized version of her love life, and an introspective record of her psychoanalysis. Eventually Anna manages to free herself from this fragmentation and to unite her experiences in a golden notebook. The novel was important in the revival of the women's movement in the 1960s.

> There's only one real sin, and that is to persuade oneself that the second-best is anything but the second-best.
>
> *The Golden Notebook*

Goldfinger. A thriller (1959) by Ian Fleming (1908–64), featuring his secret-service agent James Bond. Bond's adversary has gained the sobriquet Goldfinger, not just because he has a passion for the metal but because he has a habit of painting his girlfriends all over with it. The plot includes a classic golf match. A lively film version (1964), directed by Guy Hamilton, has Sean Connery as Bond and Honor Blackman as the outrageously named Pussy Galore.

Golliwog's Cakewalk. *See* CHILDREN'S CORNER.

Gone With the Wind. A highly acclaimed film (1939) based on a romantic historical novel (1936) of the same title by Margaret Mitchell (1900–49). The film, which depicts the experiences of thrice-married Southern belle, Scarlett O'Hara, during the US Civil War, starred Vivien Leigh as Scarlett and Clark Gable as her lover, Rhett Butler, and has long been the stuff of Hollywood legend. The title comes from a line in Ernest Dowson's poem 'Non sum qualis eram' (1896):

> I have forgot much, Cynara! Gone with the wind,
> Flung roses, roses riotously with the throng,
> Dancing, to put thy pale, lost lilies out of mind;
> But I was desolate and sick of an old passion,
>   Yea, all the time, because the dance was long:
> I have been faithful to thee, Cynara! in my fashion.

Dowson's title was itself based on the refrain in one of Horace's *Odes* (IV.i):

Non sum qualis eram bonae
Sub regno Cynarae

('I am not as I was when good Cynara was my queen.')

To Dowson, Cynara represented a twelve-year-old Polish girl, Adelaide Foltinowicz ('Missie'), with whom he fell in love after seeing her serving in her parents' restaurant in Sherwood Street, London.

While still working on the novel, Mitchell used the working title 'Pansy', the original name of her heroine. Other titles she considered included 'Tote the Weary Land', 'Tomorrow Is Another Day' and even 'Ba! Ba! Black Sheep'.

> There was a land of Cavaliers and Cotton Fields called the Old South. Here in this patrician world the Age of Chivalry took its last bows. Here was the last ever seen of the Knights and their Ladies fair, of Master and Slave. Look for it only in books, for it is no more than a dream remembered, a Civilization gone with the wind.
>
> *Gone with the Wind* (Prologue) (1939)

Goodbye to Berlin. A novel (1939) by Christopher Isherwood (1904–86), who as himself is the observer and narrator:

> I am a camera with its shutter open, quite passive, recording, not thinking.

The book begins and ends with extracts from 'A Berlin Diary', respectively for Autumn 1930 and Winter 1932–3, the period that Isherwood was teaching English in Berlin. The four linked sketches in between reflect the situations of various characters and their reactions to the brittle political situation. Elements concerning the promiscuous cabaret performer, Sally Bowles, were made into a play, *I Am a Camera* (1951) by John van Druten (1901–57); this was filmed under the same title in 1955, inspiring the variously attributed critical notice, 'Me no Leica'. Van Druten's play was in turn the basis of a musical, *Cabaret* (1966), the film version of which (1972) starred Liza Minnelli as Sally Bowles.

Good Morning, Darling. *See* WHAAM!

Goodness Had Nothing To Do With It. The autobiography (1959) of the feisty American actress and writer Mae West (1892–1980). The title comes from a line West spoke in the character of Mandie Triplett in the film *Night After Night* (1932), written by Vincent Laurence but 'with additional dialogue' by West. Another character exclaims on seeing her, 'Goodness! What beautiful diamonds!', to which West responds: 'Goodness had nothing to do with it, dearie.'

Good, the Bad and the Ugly, The. The last film (1966) in Sergio Leone's 'Man With No Name' trilogy of spaghetti Westerns (*see* FISTFUL OF DOLLARS, A). Set during the American Civil War, it stars Clint Eastwood as Joe ('the Good'), Lee Van Cleef as Setenza ('the Bad') and Eli Wallach as Tuco ('the Ugly'), all of whom are after a fortune buried in an unmarked grave. The title has become a common journalistic catchphrase, much played on by headline writers.

Go Tell It on the Mountain. The first novel (1953) of the black US writer, James Baldwin (1924–87). The book has autobiographical undertones, and the climax is the religious conversion of a 14-year-old Harlem boy. At the centre of the book are the boy's troubled relations with his stepfather, a preacher of the storefront Temple of the Fire Baptized. Aspects of the slave era and of life in a dysfunctional family are recounted in flashbacks. The phrase 'Go Tell It on the Mountain' appears in the refrain of an African-American spiritual:

> Go, tell it on the mountain,
> Over the hills and everywhere
> Go, tell it on the mountain,
> That Jesus Christ is born.

Götterdämmerung (German, 'twilight of the gods'). An opera by Richard Wagner (1813–83), with libretto by the composer, first performed in 1876. The opera is the last of four comprising *The* RING, and features the death of the hero Siegfried – the opera was originally entitled *Siegfrieds Tod* ('Siegfried's death') – and the destruction by fire of Valhalla, the home of the gods. *Götterdämmerung* is the German equivalent of the Scandinavian Ragnarök (Old Norse, also meaning 'the twilight of the gods'), the day of doom on which the old world and all its inhabitants are destroyed.

> We've been rehearsing for two hours – and we're still playing the same bloody tune.
>
> SIR THOMAS BEECHAM: remark while rehearsing *Götterdämmerung*, quoted in Reid, *Thomas Beecham* (1961)

> Is Wagner a human being at all? Is he not rather a disease? He contaminates everything he touches – he has made music sick …
> Wagner's art is diseased.
>
> FRIEDRICH NIETZSCHE: *Der Fall Wagner* (1888)

Nietzsche – initially, but not by this stage, a fan of Wagner – wrote a summary of his own thought in a book entitled *Die Götzen-Dämmerung* (1889; *Twilight of the Idols*) – the title reflecting his own dictum that 'God is dead'.

In Germany *Götterdämmerung* is also used as the title of Visconti's operatic film *La Caduta degli dei* (1969; 'the fall of the gods'). Known in English as *The Damned*, the film depicts the decline of a family of German industrialists as the Nazis rise to power.

The English musicologist Wilfrid Mellers (b.1914) gave the title *Twilight of the Gods* to his 1973 study of the Beatles, who had split up in 1970.
See also *FLYING DUTCHMAN, THE*; *MEISTERSINGER VON NÜRNBERG, DIE*; *RIENZI*.

Go West, Young Man. A film (1937) whose title contains a reference to its star Mae West (1892–1980) while punning on a well-known exhortation to new arrivals in the United States in the mid-19th century, when the western territories of the country were being opened up to settlers. The slogan is usually attributed to the newspaperman Horace Greeley (1811–72), who ran unsuccessfully for the presidency, but it was, in fact, coined by John Babsone Lane Soule, writing in the Terre Haute (Indiana) *Express* in 1851:

> Go west, young man, and grow up with the country.

Gradus ad Parnassum (Latin, 'steps to Parnassus'). The fanciful title of a once popular dictionary of Latin prosody used in schools for the teaching of Latin verse. It was also the title of a well-known treatise on musical counterpoint written in Latin by Johann Joseph Fux (1660–1741) and published in Vienna in 1725, which was for long a standard work on the subject. Muzio Clementi (1752–1832) gave the same title to his collection of piano studies (1817). The first piece in Debussy's suite *CHILDREN'S CORNER* (1906–8) is a parody of Clementi's studies and is entitled 'Dr Gradus ad Parnassum'.

Parnassus itself is a mountain near Delphi, Greece, with two summits, one of which was consecrated to Apollo and the Muses, the other to Bacchus. It is supposedly named after Parnassus, a son of Neptune.

Because of its connection with the Muses, it came to be regarded as the seat of poetry and music; hence 'climbing Parnassus' is an old expression for writing poetry.

Grande Bouffe, La. A film (1973) written and directed by Marco Ferreri about four successful men who eat and fornicate themselves to death. The French word *bouffe* can mean 'grub' or 'nosh', and also 'belly'. The English title of the film is *Blow-Out*, although aficionados prefer the onomatopoeic French version.

Grande Jatte, La. *See* SUNDAY AFTERNOON ON THE ISLAND OF THE GRANDE JATTE.

Grapes of Wrath, The. A novel (1939) by John Steinbeck (1902–68), which won the Pulitzer Prize for fiction. It charts the vicissitudes of a farming family, who migrate from the dustbowls of Oklahoma in search of a better future in California during the Great Depression. The title comes from 'The Battle Hymn of the Republic' by Julia Ward Howe (1819–1900):

> Mine eyes have seen the glory of the coming of the Lord,
> He is trampling out the vintage where the grapes of wrath are stored.

Steinbeck's widow was once offered in a Japanese bookshop a translation of her husband's work under the title *Angry Raisins*.

A highly regarded film version of the book (1940) was directed by John Ford.

Gravity's Rainbow. A novel (1973) by Thomas Pynchon (b.1937), set in Europe towards the end of the Second World War and immediately after. The phantasmagorical world that Pynchon conjures up seems to involve mysterious and powerful conspiracies. At its simplest, the complex plot concerns a US soldier who has erections in places in London that are due to be hit by V-2 missiles. The progeny of these missiles will in turn become the method of delivering the nuclear armaments that were being developed in the United States at the same time. 'Gravity's Rainbow' refers both to the arc of the missile and to the metaphorical trajectory of civilization as it moves towards its own destruction.

> War was never political at all, the politics was all theatre, all just to keep the people distracted … secretly, it was being dictated instead by the needs of technology.

The novel shared the National Book Award. It was selected for the Pulitzer Prize only to be thrown out by the advisory board as 'obscene' and 'unreadable', but won the Howells Medal, which the author refused.

Gray's Elegy. The popular name for 'Elegy Written in a Country Church-Yard' (1751) by Thomas Gray (1716–71), published in 1751 but many years in the making. The common name led to the trick quick-fire question formerly aimed at unsuspecting schoolchildren: 'Who wrote Gray's Elegy?' The graveyard concerned is thought to be that at Stoke Poges, Buckinghamshire, where Gray himself was subsequently buried.

> [General James Wolfe, on the eve of capturing Quebec in 1759,] repeated nearly the whole of Gray's Elegy ... adding, as he concluded, that he would prefer being the author of that poem to the glory of beating the French to-morrow.
>
> J. PLAYFAIR: *Biographical Account of J. Robinson* (1815)

Grease. A film musical (1978) based on a stage show (1972) with music by Jim Jacobs and Warren Casey about a group of lively teenagers during the rock 'n' roll era of the 1950s. Starring John Travolta and Olivia Newton-John, the film was a massive international success, spawning several major pop hits. The title, referring to the grease most young men put in their hair at that time, was changed to *Glease* when the film was released in Japan, to *Vaselino* when released in Mexico, and to *Brilliantine* when shown in France. A sequel, *Grease 2* (1982), was entirely unmemorable.

Great American Dream, the. *See* AMERICAN DREAM, THE.

Great American Novel, The. The title of two novels, borrowing a phrase first coined in 1868 by the US novelist John William DeForest (1826–1906). The first (1938), by Clyde Davis (1894–1962), is about a journalist who dreams vainly of writing such a novel, while his own life in fact encapsulates the American experience. The second (1973), by Philip Roth (b.1933), uses the decline of a once great baseball team as an allegory of contemporary developments in American politics and society. Achieving 'The Great American Novel' has long been the Holy Grail of American writers, and the accolade has been bestowed on works as different as *MOBY-DICK* and *The GREAT GATSBY*. The US poet William Carlos Williams (1883–1963) published a collection of essays in 1923 entitled *The Great American Novel*.

Great American Nude. A series of paintings and mixed-media works by the US Pop artist Tom Wesselmann (b.1931), including *Great American Nude No. 10* (1961) and *Great American Nude No. 54* (1964). In some of the works the flatly painted nude contrasts with the actual room fittings in the assemblage, such as a radiator, a telephone that rings, a window and curtains. The title is a 'Swinging Sixties' dig at the 'Great AMERICAN DREAM' and the 'GREAT AMERICAN NOVEL'. Simon Mason's tragicomic novel *The Great English Nude* (1990) plays on the title.

Greatest Story Ever Told, The. A biblical film epic (1965) that attempted to make great cinema of the life of Christ, the 'greatest story' of the title. Starring Max von Sydow as Christ and filmed largely in Utah rather than Palestine, it was generally considered a failure, chiefly because of the distracting appearance of well-known Hollywood stars in bit parts. One such was John Wayne as a Roman centurion, whose drawling delivery of the line 'Truly, this man was the Son of God' provoked hilarity.

Great Expectations. A novel by Charles Dickens (1812–70), published in 1860–1. The 'expectations' are those of the central character, Pip, who starts as a simple country boy. As he grows older he receives money and hints that he may expect much more; he sets himself up as a gentleman and disowns his humble beginnings. He believes the elderly Miss Havisham is his benefactor, but it turns out to be Magwitch, the convict he helped to escape as a child. He is spoilt by his expectations, but when penury strikes he returns to a life of honest toil.

Great Gatsby, The. A novel (1925) by F. Scott Fitzgerald (1896–1940), set on Long Island, New York. The story is told by the somewhat passive participant, Nick Carraway. His neighbour is the glamorous but mysterious Jay Gatsby, who holds lavish parties at his mansion in fictional West Egg on Long Island. When younger and poor, Gatsby had fallen in love with Nick's cousin Daisy, who married instead the rich, dim and violent Tom. It transpires that Gatsby has made himself wealthy through crime, and he succeeds in making Daisy his mistress. Tom takes as his lover Myrtle Wilson, whose husband works in a garage. Daisy, driving Gatsby's car, accidentally kills Myrtle and does not stop. Tom tells Myrtle's husband that it was Gatsby who was driving. Wilson shoots Gatsby and then turns the gun on himself. Regarded by many as a leading candidate for the title of the 'GREAT AMERICAN NOVEL', the book is also a disillusioned meditation on the 'Great AMERICAN DREAM'.

> I thought of Gatsby's wonder when he first picked out the green light at the end of Daisy's dock ... his dream must have seemed so close that he could hardly fail to grasp it. He did not know that it was already behind him, somewhere back in that vast obscurity beyond the city, where the dark fields of the republic rolled on under the night.

Several alternative titles were considered prior to the book's publication, including *Trimalchio in West Egg*, an allusion to the ostentatious dinner-party host, Trimalchio, in Petronius' *Satyricon* (1st century AD).

Great Masturbator, The. A probably self-referential painting (1929) by Salvador Dalí (1904–89). Dalí was himself a lifelong devotee of onanism, an enthusiasm happily tolerated by his wife Gala. Among the more identifiable features of the painting is the head of an attractive young woman sniffing with apparent pleasure at the scantily covered genitalia of an adolescent boy.

GREEN

Gawain and the Green Knight, a long, anonymous medieval poem (14th century)

'GREENSLEEVES', an Elizabethan ballad

The HOUSE WITH THE GREEN SHUTTERS, a novel (1901) by George Douglas

ANNE OF GREEN GABLES, a children's classic (1908) by L.M. Montgomery

Greenmantle, a thriller (1916) by John Buchan

The Corn is Green, a play (1938) by Emlyn Williams

After Every Green Thing, the first volume of poems (1948) by Dannie Abse

The Green Man, a novel (1969) by Kingsley Amis

The GREEN KNIGHT, a novel (1993) by Irish Murdoch

How Green Was My Valley, a novel (1939) by Richard Llewellyn

Green Knight, The. A novel by Iris Murdoch (1919–99), published in 1993. The key characters are two brothers, Lucas and Clement. When the former tries to kill the latter a stranger intervenes and is attacked by Lucas. Thereafter the stranger demands compensation for the assault, and the novel explores themes of guilt and atonement. The title and other aspects of this dense novel come from the anonymous medieval English poem *Sir Gawain and the Green Knight* (*c.*1385), which begins when the monstrous Green Knight appears at King Arthur's court and challenges the knights to cut off his head, on condition that they agree to have their own heads cut off in a year's time. Sir Gawain accepts and cuts off the Green Knight's head. The Green Knight picks up his head and rides off. A year later, Sir Gawain's honour is put to the test.

'Greensleeves'. A popular ballad in the time of Elizabeth I, published in 1581. 'Greensleeves' is the sobriquet of an otherwise unnamed woman, who has stolen the singer's heart.

> Greensleeves was all my joy,
> Greensleeves was my delight,
> Greensleeves was my heart of gold,
> And who but Lady Greensleeves?

The ballad was included in Clement Robinson's *Handefull of Pleasant Delites* (1584) under the title 'A new Courtly Sonnet of the Lady Greensleeves, to the new tune of "Greensleeves"'. It is also mentioned in Shakespeare:

> ... they do no more adhere and keep place together than the Hundredth Psalm and the tune of Greensleeves.
>
> WILLIAM SHAKESPEARE: *The Merry Wives of Windsor* (1597), II.i

> Let the sky rain potatoes; let it thunder to the tune of Greensleeves ...
>
> WILLIAM SHAKESPEARE: *The Merry Wives of Windsor* (1597), V.v

The tune in question is of the same period. It was used for many ballads, and during the English Civil Wars (1642–51) it became the party tune of the Royalists. Samuel Pepys mentions it in his diary (23 April 1660) under the title of 'The Blacksmith'. More recently, Vaughan Williams (1872–1958) used the tune in his opera *Sir John in Love* (1929; based on *The Merry Wives of Windsor*) and combined it with that of 'Lovely Joan' in his *Fantasia on Greensleeves* (1934). It also appears in Gustav Holst's *SAINT PAUL'S SUITE* (1913) for string orchestra.

Groundhog Day. A film comedy (1993) adapted by Danny Rubin and Harold Ramis from a story by Rubin about an obnoxious television weather presenter (Bill Murray) who finds himself reliving the same day over and over again until he becomes a better person. In the United States Groundhog Day is Candlemas Day (2 February), the name deriving from the saying that the groundhog first appears from hibernation on that day. If he sees his shadow, he goes back to his burrow for another six weeks, indicating six more weeks of winter weather. The general idea is that a sunny day (when he sees his shadow) means a late spring, whereas a cloudy day (when he does not see it) means an early spring. The groundhog, or woodchuck, *Marmota monax*, is a North American marmot, with reddish-brown fur.

Guernica. A painting (1937), perhaps the most famous of the 20th century, painted by Pablo Picasso (1881–1973) in 1937 in horrified protest at a notorious atrocity in the Spanish Civil War. On 27 April 1937, bombers of the German Kondor Legion, in support of Franco's nationalists, destroyed the ancient Basque capital of Guernica, causing many civilian casualties. Picasso's stark monochromatic painting has become a symbol of the barbarity of modern warfare. There is a (probably apocryphal) story that while Picasso was living in Paris in the Second World War, a Gestapo officer visited his studio. Looking at the canvas of *Guernica*, the Nazi asked 'Did you do that?' 'No,' Picasso replied, 'You did.'

Gulag Archipelago, The (Russian title: *Arkhipelag Gulag*). A three-volume history (1973–6; English translation 1974–78) by the Russian novelist Alexander Solzhenitsyn (b.1918) of the Gulag, the Soviet administrative department responsible for maintaining prisons and forced labour camps. 'Gulag' is the abbreviation of Russian *Glavnoye upravleniye ispravitel'no-trudovykh lagerey*, 'Chief Administration for Corrective Labour Camps'. Such camps – scattered across Siberia like an archipelago of islands – were a notorious feature of the Soviet Union from 1930 to 1955 and resulted in the deaths of millions. Having been awarded the Nobel Prize for Literature (1970), Solzhenitsyn was in 1974 deported after the publication in Paris of the first two volumes and the suicide of his former assistant who, after five days of interrogation by the KGB, had revealed where she had hidden a copy of the complete work.

Gulf Stream, The. A marine painting (1899) by the US artist Winslow Homer (1836–1910). A black man lies in a small sailing boat, which has lost its sails, mast and rudder in a storm. Sharks circle, and a water spout approaches, while in the distance, unseen by the sailor, a ship passes by, unaware of the man's predicament. The Gulf Stream is the great warm ocean current that emerges from the Gulf of Mexico into the northern Atlantic, and the title emphasizes the puniness of man in the context of vast elemental forces. Homer's painting may have been inspired by 'The Open Boat' (1898), a short story by the US poet, novelist and journalist Stephen Crane (1871–1900), which was based on Crane's own experience when the ship that was taking him to Cuba sank in 1897.

> Never put more than two waves in a picture: it's fussy.
>
> WINSLOW HOMER: quoted in Goodrich, *Winslow Homer* (1945)

Gurrelieder. An early Wagnerian-style extravaganza by Arnold Schoenberg (1874–1951). It was completed in 1911 and is scored for five solo singers, three male choruses, one mixed chorus, a narrator and a vast orchestra, which includes a set of iron chains. The title means 'Songs of Gurra', and the text is a German translation of poems by the Danish poet J.P. Jacobsen (1847–85). Gurra itself is a 14th-century castle, in which lives the heroine Tove, who is loved by the Danish king, Waldemar IV. In his 1981 book *The Tongs and the Bones* Lord Harewood wrote of the piece:

> A proof if you want it – and I often do – that Schoenberg could, as they used to say about Picasso, draw when he wanted to.

Guys and Dolls. A collection of stories (1931) by the US writer Damon Runyon (1884–1946), comprising amusing tales of gangster life, told in Runyon's colourful version of New York underworld patois. This first collection was followed by several others, and the stories feature characters such as Joe the Joker, Nicely-Nicely, Apple Annie, and Regret the Horseplayer. The musical comedy entitled *Guys and Dolls* (1950), based on Runyon's stories and with music and lyrics by Frank Loesser (1910–69) and book by Jo Swerling and Abe Burrows, focuses on the romance that develops between a Salvation Army worker (representing the 'dolls') and gambler Sky Masterson (representing the 'guys'). It was filmed in 1955 starring Frank Sinatra, Marlon Brando and Jean Simmons.

Gymnopédies, Trois. Three piano pieces by Erik Satie (1866–1925), written in 1888 and introducing some new harmonies to Western music.

Two of the pieces were later orchestrated by Debussy. The title apparently refers to a festival in ancient Sparta in honour of Apollo; Satie himself explained that a '*gymnopédie*' was an ancient Greek dance performed by naked children (Greek *gymno-*, 'naked', *pais, paid-*, 'child'). Although this title yields to rational explanation, many of Satie's other titles do not: examples include *Trois Morceaux en forme de poire* ('three pieces in the shape of a pear'; there are actually six pieces); *Choses vues à droite et à gauche (sans lunettes)* ('things seen to right and left, without spectacles'); and *Embryons desséchés* ('desiccated embryos'). His scores contain instructions to the player such as 'light as an egg' and 'with much sickness'. The title of his ballet *RELÂCHE* involves a typical prank. Jean Cocteau suggested that

> Satie gave comic titles to his music in order to protect his works from persons obsessed with the sublime.

'Haffner' Serenade. The nickname of the suite in D, K250, by Mozart (1756–91), written for the wedding of Elizabeth Haffner in Salzburg, 22 June 1776. Mozart's symphony no 35 in D, K385 (1782), is also called the 'Haffner' Symphony, as it re-used the music of another serenade (not K250) he had written in the same year for the Haffner family.

Half a Sixpence. A musical comedy (1963) with music and lyrics by David Heneker (b.1906) about a poor young man who wins a fortune, loses it and is finally redeemed by his love for his wife. Based on the novel *Kipps* (1905) by H.G. Wells (1866–1946), the title refers to the sixpence that the two lovers split in two, each keeping half to remind them of the other.

'Hallelujah Chorus'. *See* MESSIAH.

Hallelujah, I'm a Bum. A whimsical film (1933), featuring Al Jolson as a 'bum' (US slang for 'tramp') in New York's Central Park. The title comes from a song (1928) of the same name by Harry Kirby McClintock, famously sung by Burl Ives. In the UK the film's title was coyly changed to *Hallelujah, I'm a Tramp*. The film was also shown under the title *Lazy Bones*.

Hamburger with Pickle and Tomato Attached. A large (6ft × 6ft × 6ft) sculpture created in 1963 by the US Pop artist Claes Oldenburg (b.1929). This piece is made from plaster, cloth, metal and enamel, but more typical of the Oldenburg oeuvre are his giant 'soft' sculptures of everyday items made from vinyl stuffed with kapok, for example *Bacon, Lettuce and Tomato* (1963).

> I have a very high idea of art. I'm still romantic about that, but this process of humbling it is just to test it, to reduce everything to the same level and *then* see what you get.
>
> CLAES OLDENBURG: interview in *Art News*, 1963–4

Another US Pop artist, Robert Watts, also created a *Bacon, Lettuce and Tomato* (1965), in which a transparent sandwich is filled with a colour photograph of the ingredients. Watts also made a piece called *Hot Dogs* (1964), comprising two frankfurters on a plate, all made of chrome-plated lead.

'Hammerklavier' Sonata. The name usually given to the piano sonata in B flat, opus 106, by Beethoven (1770–1827). *Hammerklavier* (literally 'hammer keyboard') is the late 18th- and early 19th-century German word for piano (to distinguish it from the harpsichord, for which keyboard – German *Klavier* – sonatas were typically composed before that time). Beethoven actually used the word *Hammerklavier* in the manuscripts of four of his piano sonatas – opus 101, opus 109 and opus 110, as well as opus 106. This has led some musicologists to get very exercised about the restriction of the term in popular usage to opus 106 alone.

'Handel's Largo'. The name given to a number of pious arrangements of the aria *Ombra mai fù* from the comic opera *Serse* (Xerxes; 1738) by Handel (1685–1759). The aria, in fact marked *larghetto* (a little faster than *largo*), is actually addressed to a tree, and praises its shade.

Handful of Dust, A. A blackly comic novel (1934) by Evelyn Waugh (1903–66), in which everything ends up more or less badly, with Tony Last, the decent, cuckolded husband (a common character in Waugh) held against his will somewhere in Amazonia, forced to read Dickens aloud to mad Mr Todd. Waugh himself included the epigraph from T.S. Eliot's *The WASTE LAND*:

> I will show you fear in a handful of dust.

This is in itself an echo of Joseph Conrad's *Youth* (1902):

> I remember my youth and the feeling that will never come back any more ... the triumphant conviction of strength, the heat of life in the handful of dust, the glow in the heart that with every year grows dim ...

Hangover Square. A thriller (1941) by Patrick Hamilton (1904–62), subtitled *A Story of Darkest Earl's Court*, an area in west London. A schizophrenic haunts the streets and public houses in an almost perpetual hangover, obsessed, in his lost periods, with murdering the woman he loves. The title puns on London's Hanover Square.

Happiness is a Warm Puppy. A cartoon book (1962) by Charles M. Schulz featuring Snoopy the dog. The phrase – itself evolving from a caption to a panel in an earlier strip showing a small child hugging the dog – spawned a raft of advertising slogans, since 'happiness' is the goal of all manufacturers and service providers. Among them were 'Happiness is egg-shaped' (British eggs), 'Happiness is a quick-starting car' (Esso petrol), 'Happiness is a cigar called Hamlet' (first in 1964) and 'Happiness can be the color of her hair' (Miss Clairol). The words equally suggested themselves to motorists as suitable bumper-sticker fodder, as 'Happiness is being single', 'Happiness is seeing Lubbock, Texas, in the rear view mirror' (a line from a Country and Western song), 'Happiness is Slough in my rear-view mirror', 'Happiness is a Warm Gun' (title of a song of 1968 by John Lennon, from 'Happiness is a warm gun in your hand', a slogan used by the US National Rifle Association), and dozens more along the same lines.

Harmonie der Welt, Die (German, 'the harmony of the world'). An opera by the German composer Paul Hindemith (1895–1963), with a libretto by the composer, first performed in 1957. The work is based on the life of the great post-Copernican astronomer Johannes Kepler (1571–1630), who established the three famous laws of planetary motion. The last of these is to be found in Kepler's quasi-mystical work *De Harmonices Mundi* (Latin, 'on the harmonics of the world'), in which he demonstrates that the velocities of the orbiting planets are related to their distances from the sun. The idea of the 'harmony of the spheres' – that the planets in motion must make a sound, each in harmony with the others – goes back to Pythagoras.

Harmoniemesse (German, 'wind ensemble Mass'). The nickname given to the Mass in B flat (1802) by Haydn (1732–1809), owing to the prominence of wind instruments in the music (*Harmonie* is the German term for an ensemble of wind instruments).

'Harmonious Blacksmith, The'. The nickname given to a harpsichord piece by Handel (1685–1759), namely the air and variations in the fifth suite of his first book of harpsichord suites (1720). An ingenious but baseless fabrication – probably originating in Richard Clark's *Reminiscences of Handel* (1836) – ascribed the origin of the name to the hammering at his forge of a blacksmith, William Powell (*c.*1702–80), said to have inspired Handel to compose this air. Powell's grave at Little Stanmore, near Edgware, Middlesex, was originally surrounded by a wooden rail on one side of which was painted: 'Sacred to the memory of William Powell, the HARMONIOUS BLACKSMITH, died Feb. 27, 1780, aged about 78', and on the other: 'He was Parish Clerk at this Church many years, and during the Time the Immortal Handel resided much at Cannons [palace] with the Duke of Chandos'. In 1868 this was replaced by a stone bearing, in a sunken medallion, a hammer, anvil, laurel leaf and a bar of music, with the following inscription: 'He was parish clerk during the time the immortal Handel was organist of this church.'

An alternative explanation of the title suggests that the blacksmith in question was a certain Lintern, who sold music in Bath; he had been brought up as a blacksmith before changing career, and was often asked to play this particular piece, and published it separately. However, no documentary evidence for this anecdotal story exists.

Harold in Italy. *See* *CHILDE HAROLD'S PILGRIMAGE.*

'Harp' Quartet. The nickname of the string quartet in E flat, opus 74 (1809), by Beethoven (1770–1827). The name derives from the *pizzicato* (plucked, as on a harp) arpeggios in the first movement.

'Haydn' Quartets. The nickname given to a set of string quartets (nos 14–19, written 1782–5) by Mozart (1756–91), including the 'DISSONANCE' QUARTET and the 'Hunt' Quartet (*see* CHASSE, LA). Mozart dedicated each of them to the older composer, whom he affectionately referred to as 'Papa Haydn'. In early performances *chez* Mozart, Haydn played the first violin, while Mozart played viola. Haydn reciprocated Mozart's respect and affection:

> I tell you before God, as an honest man, that your son is the greatest composer I know, either personally or by repute.
>
> JOSEPH HAYDN: to Leopold Mozart, quoted in letter from Leopold Mozart, 1785

Haydn Variations. *See* *ST ANTHONY VARIATIONS.*

Hay Wain, The. A painting (1821) by John Constable (1776–1837), perhaps his most famous landscape. The scene must have been one of the most familiar to the artist, as it is the view from Flatford Mill in Suffolk, of which Constable's family had the tenancy. The hay wain (i.e. wagon) itself is fording the River Stour, heading towards Willy Lott's cottage. Although Constable made studies of the scene *en plein air*, he executed the actual painting in his London studio. When he first exhibited it at the Royal Academy in London, the painting had the title *Landscape, Noon*. Constable, with his watery meadows and cloud-filled skies, was mocked by some for his 'dampness', the artist Henry Fuseli remarking to the porter at the Royal Academy:

> Bring me my umbrella – I am going to see Mr Constable's pictures.

The Hay Wain is also the title of a very different painting by the Netherlandish painter Hieronymus Bosch (*c.*1450–1516). Here the hay wain appears to be a symbol of carnal pleasures. Many are crushed under its wheels, while many others clamour to get on board, and even popes and emperors are shown in pursuit of this alluring but deadly juggernaut.

Heart is a Lonely Hunter, The. A novel (1940) by Carson McCullers (1917–67) of the 'Southern grotesque' school. It features a deaf-mute, to whom the other main characters wrongly attribute the faculty of inner serenity that they lack. The title is from the poem 'The Lonely Hunter' (1896) by Fiona Macleod (pen-name of William Sharp; 1855–1905):

> My heart is a lonely hunter that hunts on a lonely hill.

A rather pale film version (1968) was directed by Robert Ellis Miller.

Heart of Darkness. A tale or short novel by Joseph Conrad (1857–1924), published in 1902. The story is told by Marlow, who captains a river boat in the Congo and slowly sails upriver into the 'heart of darkness', which is both Africa, the 'dark continent', and the heart of evil. Marlow's mission is to reach Kurtz, the most successful of the company's agents. He finds that the charismatic Kurtz, once a man of culture and civilization, has turned himself into an omnipotent ruler by the use of unimaginable cruelty, hinted at by the row of heads impaled beside his compound. Kurtz's dying words are 'The horror! The horror!' The story ends:

> The offing was barred by a black bank of clouds, and the tranquil waterway leading to the uttermost ends of the earth flowed sombre under an overcast sky – seemed to lead into the heart of an immense darkness.

When he was a child in Poland, Conrad had jabbed his finger at the centre of a map of Africa and declared that one day he would go there. In 1890 he did, when he took command of a river boat in the Congo Free State. The Congo was then the private fiefdom of the Belgian king, Leopold II, and was exploited with the utmost barbarity. Eventually, in 1908, international outrage led the Belgian government to take over the colony.

Heart of Darkness inspired Francis Ford Coppola's film *APOCALYPSE NOW*, and the words 'Mistah Kurtz – he dead' follow the title of T.S. Eliot's 'The HOLLOW MEN'.

Heart of Midlothian, The. A novel (1818), now perhaps his most highly regarded, by Sir Walter Scott (1771–1832). The 'Heart of Midlothian' was the nickname of the old Edinburgh Tolbooth, the city's prison (Midlothian being the county in which Edinburgh is situated). This is explained in the first chapter:

> 'Then the tolbooth of Edinburgh is called the Heart of Midlothian?' said I. 'So termed and reputed, I assure you.'

The significance of the Tolbooth in Scott's novel is twofold. A highlight of the early part of the novel is a vivid description of the true events of the Porteous Riots (1736), which broke out in the wake of the hanging of a popular smuggler. After the execution there was some disturbance from the crowd and John Porteous, captain of the city guard, ordered his men to fire, resulting in several deaths. Porteous was convicted of murder and sentenced to death, but was reprieved for six weeks by Queen Caroline. A furious crowd assembled, dragged Porteous from the Tolbooth where he was being held, and lynched him.

The second role of the prison in the novel is as the place of incarceration of Effie Deans, who is accused of murdering her child. Her sister, Jeanie Deans, determines to walk to London, where she eventually succeeds in obtaining a pardon for her sister. Many readers have interpreted the title of the novel as referring to Jeanie, who is a figure of simple virtue and kindness. This story is again modelled on a real case, involving one Isobel Walker and her sister Helen. The Scottish composer Hamish MacCunn (1868–1916) wrote an opera called *Jeanie Deans* (1894).

The Tolbooth was demolished in 1817, and today the place – near the High Kirk of St Giles on Edinburgh's Royal Mile – is marked by red paving stones in the shape of a heart. The name is also memorialized in the full name of Hearts, one of Edinburgh's football teams: Heart of Midlothian FC.

'Heart of Oak'. A nautical song and naval march, originally from the pantomime *Harlequin's Invasion* by David Garrick (1717–79) with music by William Boyce (1711–79). It was written in 1759, 'the year of victories' against the French in the Seven Years War (Quiberon Bay, Quebec, Minden), hence the allusion to 'this wonderful year' in the opening lines. 'Heart of Oak' refers to the timber from which the ships of the Royal Navy were built.

> Heart of oak are our ships,
> Heart of oak are our men:
> We always are ready;
> Steady, boys, steady;
> We'll fight and we'll conquer again and again.

Heaven's Gate. A Western film (1980), written and directed by Michael Cimino (b.1940). It is set against the 1892 Johnson County wars in Wyoming. Starring Kris Kristofferson, the film cost somewhere between $35 million and $50 million and lost more than any other film ever made. It was slated by critics and public alike but the doomed extravagance of the project entered movie legend. Within the film, 'Heaven's Gate' is the name of a local roller-skating rink popular with settlers in Wyoming in the early 1890s. The title phrase can be traced to a number of sources:

> This is none other but the house of God, and this is the gate of heaven.
>
> Genesis 28:17

> Haply I think on thee, and then my state,
> Like to the lark at break of day arising
> From sullen earth, sings hymns at heaven's gate.
>
> SHAKESPEARE: Sonnet 29

> Hark! Hark! the lark at heaven's gate sings.
>
> SHAKESPEARE: *Cymbeline* (1609–10), II.iii

> I give you the end of a golden string;
> Only wind it into a ball:
> It will lead you in at Heaven's gate,
> Built in Jerusalem's wall.
>
> WILLIAM BLAKE: *Jerusalem*, 1815, plate 77, 'To the Christians'

Hebrides, The. A concert overture (effectively a tone poem), opus 26 (1832), by Felix Mendelssohn (1809–47). The full title is *The Hebrides (Fingal's Cave)*, and the piece was inspired by the composer's visit to Scotland in the summer of 1829. The spectacular Fingal's Cave on the small island of Staffa, near the Isle of Mull, is constructed of basaltic columns of a similar type to those of the Giant's Causeway in County Antrim, Northern Ireland. The cave, into which the Atlantic swell washes, gets its name from the legendary Gaelic hero Fingal, one of whose homes it is said to have been. Although Mendelssohn did visit Staffa, he had already noted down the opening 'breaking sea' theme prior to his visit. He called the first version (1830) *The Lonely Island*, and when the work was first performed in 1832 it was under the title *The Isles of Fingal*.

Henderson the Rain King. A novel (1959) by the US Nobel laureate Saul Bellow (b.1915). Henderson, a disillusioned millionaire, journeys to Africa on an impulse, yearning for new forms of satisfaction. He causes a disastrous mishap in one village when trying to cleanse its water supply. He then reaches another village where he befriends the local chief and is declared to be 'Sungo', the official rainmaker, after apparently causing a deluge by moving the goddess out of the clouds. He becomes the chief himself on the incumbent's death. Fearing for his safety, Henderson escapes from the village and returns home a somewhat wiser man.

> Of course, in an age of madness, to expect to be untouched by madness is a form of madness. But the pursuit of sanity can be a form of madness too.
>
> *Henderson the Rain King*

'Hen' Symphony. The nickname given to the symphony no 83 in G minor (1786) by Haydn (1732–1809), often referred to by the French name *La Poule*. It is one of Haydn's 'PARIS' SYMPHONIES. The name may come from the fancied 'clucks' of the oboe in the first movement. Others have pointed out a vague similarity between the slow movement and Rameau's piece *La Poule*, no 46 in his harpsichord suites.

Herland. A feminist Utopian novel (published serially in 1915) by the US writer Charlotte Perkins Gilman (1860–1935). Gilman was the great-niece of Harriet Beecher Stowe, the author of *Uncle Tom's Cabin* (1852). Herland is an imaginary country populated solely by women. Its inhabitants are strong and athletic, while the older women have an ageless quality of power and beauty. All wear their hair short, and their clothes are comfortable and practical, in the form of close-fitting tunics worn over knee-breeches. The culture of Herland revolves around motherhood and the raising of children, and the language is simple and rational.

Hickory, Dickory, Dock. A detective story (1955) by Agatha Christie (1890–1976). The title comes from the nursery rhyme:

> Hickory, dickory, dock,
> The mouse ran up the clock.
> The clock struck one,
> The mouse ran down,
> Hickory, dickory, dock.

The rhyme was formerly used by children to decide who should begin a game, or who would be 'out'. The US title of the book is *Hickory, Dickory, Death.*

High Wind in Jamaica, A (US title: *The Innocent Voyage*). The first novel (1929) by Richard Hughes (1900–76). It was inspired by a real event in 1822, recounted in a manuscript that was passed on to his mother. Seven amoral children, whose parents think they will be safer in England after a high wind and storm have ravaged their Jamaican home, are unintentionally hijacked by a band of incompetent pirates. The film version (1965) was directed by Alexander Mackendrick.

Hind and the Panther, The. A religious allegory (1687) by John Dryden (1631–1700). Written after Dryden had converted to Catholicism, the poem is a defence of the Roman Catholic Church (the Hind) against the Church of England (the Panther) and various other sects represented by wild beasts.

Hipocondrie a 7 (French, 'hypochondria in seven parts'). An unusual baroque orchestral piece in A major by the Bohemian composer and double bass player Jan Dismas Zelenka (1679–1745), scored for two oboes, two violins, viola, bassoon, and basso continuo. *Hipocondrie* exhibits a febrile inventiveness entirely appropriate to its curious title. Formally it bears some similarity to a French overture, and abounds in rich harmonic textures, unpredictable progressions, strange modulations and dissonances, and highly complex counterpoint (for which Zelenka was celebrated in his lifetime). The individuality of Zelenka's music, allied to the enigma that attaches to his life and career – no extant portrait of him exists, and he and his works languished in obscurity for more than 200 years after his death – has endowed him with a particular fascination for posterity.

Hiroshima mon amour. The first feature film (1959) by the French New Wave director Alain Resnais, with a screenplay by Marguerite Duras. While a French actress is making a film in Hiroshima – the Japanese city destroyed by an atom bomb at the end of the Second World War – she embarks on an affair with a Japanese man. This brings back memories of her wartime affair in occupied France with a German soldier, who is killed. The film was much admired for its formal innovations, and for its sensitive explorations of a variety of themes. The title (literally 'Hiroshima my love') is open to a variety of interpretations relating to love and death.

His Dark Materials. A highly praised trilogy of fantasy novels for children by Philip Pullman (b.1946), consisting of *Northern Lights* (1995; US title *The Golden Compass*), *The Subtle Knife* (1997) and *The Amber Spyglass* (2000). The 'northern lights' in the title of the first volume are the aurora borealis. The trilogy's title comes from John Milton's *Paradise Lost* (1667), of which it is in part a reworking:

> … Unless the almighty maker them ordain
> His dark materials to create more worlds …

The novels themselves move between different universes: one 'which is like ours but different in many ways; the universe we know; and a third universe, which differs from ours in other ways again.' In 2002 *The Amber Spyglass* became the first children's book to win the Whitbread Book of the Year award.

History of the World in 10½ Chapters, A. A novel (1989) by Julian Barnes (b.1946) consisting of ten linked pieces and a 'half-chapter' entitled 'Parenthesis' inserted two-thirds of the way through, in which the author expounds his theories on the nature of love, fiction, history, and so on. The biblical, historical and imaginative incidents that make up the book are linked thematically, especially by sea voyages and shipwrecks – for example, the story of Noah's ark is told by a woodworm.

> Does history repeat itself, the first time as tragedy, the second time as farce? No, that's too grand, too considered a process. History just burps, and we taste again that raw-onion sandwich it swallowed centuries ago.
>
> *A History of the World in 10½ Chapters*, 'Parenthesis'

Hitch-Hiker's Guide to the Galaxy, The. A cult radio serial by Douglas Adams (1952–2001), broadcast in 1978 and 1979. The story begins with the imminent destruction of Earth to make way for a hyperspace express route, and the escape of Earthling Arthur Dent and his extraterrestrial friend Ford Prefect by hitching a ride on a Vogon spacecraft. The programme combined the comic with the surreal and introduced a host of eccentric characters. In 1981 the serial was adapted for television. The fictional book mentioned in the title gives handy tips to space travellers, and is frequently quoted; its verdict on the Earth is 'Mostly harmless'. It transpires that the Earth was originally constructed to solve the question of Life, the Universe and Everything, to which the answer turns out to be 42.

Adams went on to adapt and extend the idea in book form, characteristically producing a 'trilogy in five parts': *A Hitchhiker's Guide to the Galaxy* (1979), *The Restaurant at the End of the Universe* (1980), *Life, the Universe and Everything* (1982), *So Long, and Thanks for All the Fish* (1984) and *Mostly Harmless* (1992).

Hobbit, The. A children's fantasy novel (1937) by J.R.R. Tolkien (1892–1973). The hobbit in question is called Bilbo Baggins, hobbits being an imaginary race of benevolent, half-size, hairy-footed people. In their own language, 'hobbit' apparently means 'hole-dweller', which renders the first sentence of the novel somewhat tautologous:

> In a hole in the ground there lived a hobbit.

The story concerns the home-loving Bilbo's reluctant participation in a quest, accompanied by the wizard Gandalf and a dozen dwarves, to slay a dragon and recover a lost treasure. Bilbo and his kind reappear in *The* LORD OF THE RINGS.

Hobson's Choice. A play (1916) by the British playwright Harold Brighouse (1882–1958) about a tyrannical shoe-shop owner who is eventually obliged to succumb to the wishes of his equally strong-willed daughter after she takes up with his gormless apprentice, Willie Mossop. The title refers to the proverbial 'Hobson's choice' available to those who have no choice at all. The original Hobson was the Cambridge liveryman Thomas Hobson (*c.*1544–1631) who always offered his customers the horse nearest the door of the stable, and no other.

'Hollow Men, The'. A poem by T.S. Eliot (1888–1965), published in 1925. After the title Eliot quotes the words 'Mistah Kurtz – he dead' from Conrad's HEART OF DARKNESS. The 'Hollow Men' are the speakers of this piece; they are Guys or scarecrows, 'Headpiece filled with straw'. They evoke a spiritual emptiness in 'death's twilight kingdom', but also a stumbling yearning for faith, echoing Eliot's own experience prior to his conversion to Anglo-Catholicism.

> This is the way the world ends
> Not with a bang but a whimper.
>
> 'The Hollow Men', final lines

Homage to New York. A giant (27ft-high) self-destructing sculpture (1960) by the Swiss artist Jean Tinguely (1925–91), comprising various bits and pieces such as a piano, a pram, a meteorological balloon, plus numerous wheels and motors. These latter failed to operate as intended and after it caught fire it had to be destroyed by firemen with axes rather than by itself. The remains are in the Museum of Modern Art, New York. Tinguely ensured the successful consummation of subsequent self-destroying sculptures by employing large amounts of explosives.

Homage to QWERTYUIOP. A collection of reviews (1987) by the novelist Anthony Burgess (1917–94). The letters QWERTYUIOP comprise the top row (below the numbers) on a typewriter keyboard; this conventional layout is often referred to simply as QWERTY. The layout, still found even on modern computer keyboards, was originally designed to slow down typing and so prevent jamming of the keys on the early manual machines. The idea was to keep alternating between opposite sides of the keyboard to prevent adjacent keys tangling. It so happens that all the letters needed to type the word 'typewriter' are in the top line of the layout, but the theory that this was intended to help non-skilled sales staff demonstrate the machine is an old secretaries' tale.

'Homme armé, L' (French, 'the armed man'). The title of a French chanson dating from the 15th century. The tune became the *cantus firmus* ('fixed song'), i.e. thematic basis, of very many polyphonic settings of the Mass between the 15th and 17th centuries. Composers who wrote *Homme armé* masses include Dufay, Tinctoris, Obrecht, Josquin, Palestrina and Carissimi. In the 20th century the British composer Peter Maxwell Davies (b.1934) used it in his *Missa super l'homme armé* (1968) for speaker and ensemble.

Hope Abandoned. *See* DIVINE COMEDY, THE.

'Horn Signal' Symphony (German '*mit dem Hornsignal*'). The nickname given to the symphony no 31 in D (1765) by Haydn (1732–1809). The work features major parts for four horns (two horns were standard in works at this time), and includes hunting fanfares. It is also sometimes known as *Auf dem Anstand* (German, 'at the hunting station'). *See also* 'CHASSE, LA'.

'Horseman' Quartet (German *Rittquartett* or *Reiterquartett*). The nickname given to the string quartet in G minor, opus 74 no 3 (1793), by Haydn (1732–1809). Riding rhythms have been detected in the first and last movements. It is also called the 'Rider' Quartet.

Horst Wessel Song (German title: *Die Fahne Hoch*, 'Raise the flag'). The party anthem of the Nazis. The words were written by a student, Horst Wessel (1907–30), killed in the communist quarter of Berlin where he lived as commander of an SA (Brownshirt) section. The tune was a music-hall song popular at the German Front in 1914.

House of Mirth, The. A novel by Edith Wharton (1862–1937), published in 1905. Set in fashionable New York at the turn of the century, the novel follows the story of Lily Bart, an orphan in search of a rich husband, who is in the end destroyed when she is accused of being a rich man's mistress. As Wharton herself wrote:

> A frivolous society can acquire dramatic significance only through what its frivolity destroys.

The title comes from the Old Testament:

> The heart of the wise is in the house of mourning; but the heart of fools is in the house of mirth.
>
> Ecclesiates 7:4

House of the Dead, The. *See* FROM THE HOUSE OF THE DEAD.

House of the Seven Gables, The. A novel (1851) by the US writer Nathaniel Hawthorne (1804–64). The grandiose house in question is built in the late 17th century by the cruel and mean Colonel Pyncheon, on land he has swindled from Matthew Maule by accusing him of witchcraft. Before he is executed, Maule pronounces a curse on Pyncheon's family, which reverberates down the generations to the mid-19th century, when most of the story takes place. The curse is eventually broken after descendants of both Maule and Pyncheon fall in love. Hawthorne wondered whether the relative decline in his own family's fortunes might have been some kind of retribution for the role played by his ancestor John Hathorne as a judge in the Salem witch trials of 1692.

House with the Green Shutters, The. A grimly realistic novel (1901) by the Scottish writer George Douglas (George Douglas Brown, 1869–1902). It tells the story of the rise and fall of an unpleasant village businessman, whose pride and joy is the house of the title.

Howards End. A novel (1910) by E.M. Forster (1879–1970). Howards End is a country house, based on Forster's early home in Hertfordshire. The question of who will inherit it underlies the basic conflict, which is between culture and commerce. The germ of the idea seems to have occurred to Forster in 1906, as a result of visiting a newlywed couple who lived in rural isolation. The wife was pretty, pleasant, clever and cultured; the husband boorish and philistine.

> Only connect! ... Only connect the prose and the passion, and both will be exalted, and human love will be seen at its height.
>
> *Howards End*, chapter 22

A noted film (1991) was made of the novel, produced by Ismail Merchant, directed by James Ivory and with a screenplay by Ruth Prawer Jhabvala.

'How do you do?' Quartet. *See* 'RUSSIAN' QUARTETS.

'How They Brought the Good News from Ghent to Aix'. A poem by Robert Browning (1812–89), published in *BELLS AND POMEGRANATES*, volume vii, *Dramatic Romances* (1845). Although the title suggests it, and under the title is written '[16—]', the poem is not based on any historical event. Ghent (Flemish name: Gent; French name: Gand) is a medieval city in Belgium, while Aix-la-Chapelle (nowadays known by its German name, Aachen), is a spa city in northwest Germany, and was once the capital of Charlemagne's empire. The news is carried by three galloping riders, but two of the horses die of exhaustion on the way, and the third (called Roland, and ridden by the narrator) is only saved on arrival by a draught of wine. We never learn the nature of the news, apart from the fact that the 'good news' from Ghent 'alone could save Aix from her fate'.

How to Explain Pictures to a Dead Hare. A piece of performance art, or 'Action', carried out in 1965 by the German artist Joseph Beuys (1921–86). The work involved Beuys smearing his face with honey and gold leaf, wearing one shoe made of felt and one shoe made of iron, and wandering through an art gallery for a couple of hours explaining the art on display to a dead hare he held in his arms. Felt and iron both had a particular significance for Beuys, along with fat and copper. During the Second World War he was a Luftwaffe pilot, and after being shot down over the Crimea in 1943 he was looked after by the local Tartars, who kept him warm using fat and felt.

How to Win Friends and Influence People. The title of a self-help book published in 1936 by Dale Carnegie (1888–1955), a US lecturer and writer who specialized in teaching public speaking. The book, which sought to show how anybody could make a success of their lives, became an immense bestseller, and its title a hardy perennial of catchphrases and clichés.

HPSCHD. A chamber music piece by John Cage (1912–92), written between 1967 and 1969. The piece is for seven harpsichords and 51 tape machines, and may also involve performers in costume, a light show and slide projections.

Huis Clos (British title: *In Camera*; US title: *No Exit*). A play by the French existential philosopher Jean-Paul Sartre (1905–80), involving three people shut together in a room for eternity. The French term *huis clos*, like the English 'in camera', is used to describe a trial or judicial hearing from which the public are barred. The play includes a line that has become almost proverbial:

> *Vous vous rappelez: le souffre, le bûcher, le gril ... Ah! quelle plaisanterie. Pas besoin de gril, l'enfer, c'est les autres.*
>
> ('Do you remember, brimstone, the stake, the gridiron? ... What a joke! No need of a gridiron, Hell is other people.')
>
> scene 5

Hunters in the Snow. One of the best known paintings (1565) by Pieter Bruegel the Elder (*c.*1525–69), a bold depiction of a stark winter landscape, cut by a white diagonal and some vertical black trees. The painting was part of a series called *The Months* (of which five survive), commissioned by the banker Nicolaes Jonghelinck.

The painting inspired John Berryman's poem 'Winter Landscape' (1948):

> The three men coming down the winter hill ...
> Are not aware that in the sandy time

To come, the evil waste of history
Outstretched, they will be seen upon the brow
Of that same hill: when all their company
Will have been irrecoverably lost ...

In Tobias Wolff's short-story collection *Hunters in the Snow* (1982), the title story is about three hunters, one of whom, Kenny, shoots a dog, and is shot in turn by Tub.

'Hunt' Quartet. *See* 'CHASSE, LA'.

Hurrah, the Butter is Finished! A typically satirical photomontage (1935) by the left-wing German artist John Heartfield (1891–1968), who had changed his name from Helmut Herzfelde during the First World War in protest against German militarism. In this picture, in a room decorated with swastika wallpaper, a family is shown eating all kinds of metallic objects – principally bits of bicycles, although the baby is chewing on the sharp end of an axe. At the foot of the picture are the words:

> Hurrah, the butter is finished! As [the leading Nazi Hermann] Goering said in his Hamburg address: 'Iron ore has made the Reich strong. Butter and dripping have at most made the people fat.'

Joseph Goebbels said much the same thing in a speech in 1936 in Berlin.

Hydriotaphia, Urn Burial, or, A Discourse of the Sepulchral Urns lately found in Norfolk. A prose work (1658) by Sir Thomas Browne (1605–82), which is at the same time an archaeological treatise, a survey of funeral rites at different times and different places, and a meditation on death and the transitory nature of fame. The burial urns referred to dated from Roman times, and *hydriotaphia* is simply Greek for 'urn burial'.

> Man is a noble animal, splendid in ashes, and pompous in the grave.
>
> chapter 5

Hyperion. An incomplete epic poem by John Keats (1795–1821). It exists in two fragmentary versions: *Hyperion: A Fragment* and *The Fall of Hyperion*. Keats worked on them in 1818–19, abandoning the first version to start the second; the former was published in 1820, and the latter in 1856. In Greek myth, Hyperion was one of the Titans, the father of Eos (the dawn), Helios (the sun) and Selene (the moon). Hyperion (Greek *huper*, 'over', and *eimi*, 'to go') was himself a personification of the sun – which 'goes over' – and was sometimes identified with his son Helios (often called Helios Hyperion in Homer). *Hyperion: A Fragment* begins:

> Deep in the shady sadness of a vale
> Far sunken from the healthy breath of morn,
> Far from the fiery noon, and eve's one star,
> Sat grey-haired Saturn, quiet as a stone.

Saturn and the other fallen Titans hope that the still unfallen Hyperion, the sun god, will help them regain Saturn's kingdom, from which he has been ejected by Jove. There is not enough of either version to know how Keats planned to complete the work.

Hyperion is also the title of an unfinished novel by the German Romantic poet Friedrich Hölderlin (1770–1843), some of which was published by Schiller in 1793. The work is in epistolary form and concerns a disillusioned participant in the contemporary fight for Greek independence.

In 1848 the seventh moon of the planet Saturn was discovered, and named Hyperion.

I

I Am a Camera. *See* GOODBYE TO BERLIN.

I Am Curious – Yellow. A film (1967) by the Swedish novelist and director Vilgot Sjöman (b.1924), who had already made a number of films exploring taboos such as incest (*My Sister, My Love*, 1966) and bestiality (*491*, 1964). The curiosity of the title is evinced by the protagonist, a drama student (Lena Nyman) who plays the role of a sociologist. While questioning her fellow Swedes about their attitudes to a range of political and social issues, she also indulges in some frankly depicted sexual experimentation. There are also appearances by, among others, Olaf Palme, Yevgeni Yevtushenko and Martin Luther King. The film was seized by US Customs, but its clearance by the courts opened the way for more explicit sex in US cinema. There is a companion piece entitled *I Am Curious – Blue* (1968), using footage not employed in the Yellow edition.

> *Over a close-up of Lena, the title:*
> I AM CURIOUS
> *Over a close-up of Vilgot:*
> I AM CURIOUS
> *Elderly Lady (answering the titles):* But I'm not. You stick to your films!
>
> *I Am Curious –Yellow*, transcript

Shortly after this opening, the question of the colours is explained. Over a trade-union building flies the Swedish flag, a yellow cross on a blue background. While this shot is held, we hear voices:

Male voice: Buy our film. Buy it! Buy it! The only film that's shown in two editions: One yellow and one blue!
Female voice: Buy the yellow! Buy the blue! Buy our film because it's two!

Icarus, Landscape with the Fall of. *See* LANDSCAPE WITH THE FALL OF ICARUS.

Ice Cold in Alex. A classic adventure film (1958) set in North Africa in 1942, during the Second World War. The commander of an ambulance (John Mills) tries to get his passengers across the desert and back to safety in Alexandria (Alex), where they are promised ice-cold beers on arrival. The promise is duly kept. The beer-sipping scene was wittily appropriated for a memorable TV beer commercial.

Iceman Cometh, The. A play (1946) by the US playwright Eugene O'Neill (1888–1953) in which a disparate group of characters gather in Harry Hole's saloon to lament the death of their collective illusions. The play was inspired by the down-at-heel characters O'Neill encountered in the bars of lower Manhattan during his own early years of disillusion and depression. The mysterious 'iceman' of the title (the man bringing ice to the saloon) is referred to several times in the script and comes to represent death. The choice of the word 'cometh' suggests biblical overtones, and Hickey the cheery salesman is commonly interpreted as a Christ figure.

The title is often quoted and adapted, for example in 'The Gasman Cometh', a song about the ineptitude of British tradesmen by Michael Flanders and Donald Swann.

'If –'. A famous moralistic poem by Rudyard Kipling (1865–1936), which originally appeared in *Rewards and Fairies* (1910). It enumerates twelve conditions, the successful fulfilment of which will bring the doer

> the Earth and everything that's in it,
> And – which is more – you'll be a Man, my son!

The poem gave the ironic title of the highly praised film IF .... The poem was voted Britain's favourite in a recent poll.

If .... An allegorical film (1968), written by David Sherwin and John Howlett, about the violent rebellion of pupils at an English public school against the authority of their masters. Directed by Lindsay Anderson and starring Malcolm McDowell, the script was originally titled *The*

Crusaders but acquired its final title in ironic reference to the values of Rudyard Kipling's celebrated poem 'IF – '. *If* … is also the name of a satirical cartoon strip by the illustrator Steve Bell, which first appeared in the *Guardian* newspaper in the 1980s.

If It's Tuesday, This Must Be Belgium. A comedy film (1969) concerning the adventures of a group of Americans on a whistlestop tour of Europe. The title refers to the sort of words frequently put into the mouths of American tourists to suggest their response to the cultural treasures of Europe.

If on a Winter's Night a Traveller (Italian title: *Se una notte d'inverno un viaggiatore*). An avant-garde novel (1979; English translation 1981) by Italo Calvino (1923–85). It concerns the narrator's quest, which begins in a railway station, for the elusive Ludmilla. The quest chapters are interspersed with episodes in which Calvino plays games with the reader. At one point sections of *If on a Winter's Night a Traveller* are said to have been bound up with those from another novel, *Outside the Town of Malbork*. This particular exercise continues through the book, with consecutive chapter headings making finally a complete sentence, beginning, 'If on a winter's night a traveller, outside the town of Malbork …'.

I Know Why the Caged Bird Sings. A volume of memoirs (1970) by the African-American writer, singer and actress Maya Angelou (b.1928). Angelou borrowed her title – a metaphor for the African-American experience – from the US writer Paul Lawrence Dunbar (1872–1906):

> I know why the caged bird sings, ah me,
> When his wing is bruised and his bosom sore, –
> When he beats his bars and he would be free;
> It is not a carol of joy or glee,
> But a prayer that he sends from his heart's deep core,
> But a plea, that upward to Heaven he flings –
> I know why the caged bird sings!
>
> PAUL LAWRENCE DUNBAR: 'Sympathy', in *The Complete Poems* (1895)

Dunbar may have been inspired by an earlier line:

> We think caged birds sing, when indeed they cry.
>
> JOHN WEBSTER: *The White Devil* (1612), V.iv

Iliad. An epic poem in 24 books attributed to the ancient Greek poet Homer (8th century BC), recounting the siege of Troy in Asia Minor.

This had been prompted by Paris, son of King Priam of Troy, who, while staying as a guest with Menelaus, king of Sparta, had run away with Helen, his host's beautiful wife. Menelaus persuaded the other Greek leaders to set sail for Troy to avenge the perfidy. The *Iliad* begins in the tenth year of the siege, with a quarrel between Agamemnon, the Greek commander in chief, and Achilles, the hero who had retired from the Greek army in ill temper. The Trojans now prevail, and Achilles sends his friend Patroclus to oppose them, but Patroclus is slain. Enraged, Achilles rushes into battle and slays Hector, the commander of the Trojan army. The poem ends with the funeral rites of Hector.

The Greek title *Iliados* means 'of Ilium', Ilium being another name for Troy. It was used by Roman authors such as Virgil, and also appears in English literature, for example when Doctor Faustus conjures up Helen:

> Was this the face that launched a thousand ships,
> And burnt the topless towers of Ilium?
>
> CHRISTOPHER MARLOWE: *Doctor Faustus* (*c.*1594), II.i

The title of the *Aeneid*, the epic poem of the Roman poet Virgil (70–19 BC), is formed on the same model. It tells the story of Aeneas, a Trojan prince, who escapes from the Greek destruction of his city. After a time dallying with Dido in Carthage, he lands in Italy, beats the locals and becomes the ancestor of Octavian Caesar (the Emperor Augustus). Alexander Pope's mock epic, *The DUNCIAD*, is another example of this title formation, as is *Hérodiade*, Massenet's opera about Herodias, the mother of SALOME (*see* panel, pp.399–402).

Illywhacker. A novel (1985) by the Australian novelist Peter Carey (b.1943), purporting to be the epic autobiography of a 109-year-old boaster, aviator and conman. 'Illywhacker' is an Australian slang word of 1940s provenance for a confidence trickster, especially one who follows fairs around the country.

'Il Penseroso'. *See* 'L'ALLEGRO'.

I'm All Right Jack. A film (1959) adapted by John Boulting and Frank Harvey from Alan Hackney's novel *Private Life* about the comical clashes between a communist trade unionist and factory management during a strike. Starring Peter Sellers as the shop steward in question and Ian Carmichael as a management representative caught in the middle of the dispute, the film was re-titled in reference to the traditional English saying 'I'm all right, Jack', denoting the selfishness of a man who does not care what happens to those around him as long as his own interests have been taken care of. A nautical equivalent of the phrase is 'Pull up the ladder, Jack, I'm inboard.'

I Married a .... *See* *I WAS A* ... AND *I MARRIED A*... (panel, p.229).

Importance of Being Earnest, The. 'A Trivial Comedy for Serious People' by Oscar Wilde (1854–1900), first performed in 1895. The title puns on the fact that Jack – who is known as Ernest in town – pretends to his ward Cecily that Ernest is his wicked brother. As it turns out, his real name *is* Ernest, which is just as well, as Gwendolen, the woman he's courting, has a penchant for the name.

> I hope you have not been leading a double life, pretending to be wicked and being really good all the time. That would be hypocrisy.
>
> *The Importance of Being Earnest*, Act 2

The film version (UK, 1952) is notable for Edith Evans's performance as Lady Bracknell (a name Wilde recklessly derived from the location of his lover Alfred Douglas's mother's country residence), particularly her delivery of the line 'A handbag?'

Impression: Sunrise (French title: *Impression, soleil levant*). A painting (1872) by Claude Monet (1840–1926), which gave rise to the term 'impressionism'. In 1873 the Salon rejected works by Monet, Pissarro, Renoir, Sisley and Cézanne, and the following year they mounted their own exhibition, calling themselves the Societé anonyme des artistes peintures, sculpteurs, graveurs. Reviewing the exhibition for the satirical magazine *Le Charivari*, Louis Leroy mockingly drew on Monet's title to dub the whole group 'impressionists'. The artists themselves took over the name, as their aim was indeed to record their impressions of what they saw. As Alfred Sisley wrote to a friend:

> The artist's impression is the life-giving factor, and only this impression can free that of the spectator.
>
> Monet is only an eye, but my God what an eye!
>
> PAUL CÉZANNE: remark to Vollard, quoted in Cooper, 'Claude Monet' (1957)

In Camera. *See* *HUIS CLOS*.

Index, The. The popular name for the *Index Librorum Prohibitorum* (Latin, 'index of prohibited books'), the Vatican's ever-changing list of proscribed publications, which Roman Catholics were forbidden to read except in special circumstances. The first Index was made by the Inquisition in 1557, although St Gelasius (pope 492–6) issued a list of prohibited writings in 494. In 1571 Pope Pius V set up a Congregation of the Index to supervise the list, and in 1917 its duties were transferred to the Holy Office. In addition to the Index there was the 'Codex Expurgatorius' of writings from which offensive doctrinal or moral passages were removed. The Index and Codex were abolished in 1966.

All books likely to be contrary to faith and morals, including translations of the Bible not authorized by the church, were formerly placed on the Index. Among authors wholly or partly prohibited were: Joseph Addison, Francis Bacon, Geoffrey Chaucer, Benedetto Croce, Gabriele D'Annunzio, René Descartes, Edward Gibbon, Oliver Goldsmith, Victor Hugo, John Locke, John Milton, Montaigne, Girolamo Savonarola, Voltaire and, for a long time, Copernicus, Dante and Galen.

Index Librorum Prohibitorum was also the title given to the first ever bibliography in English of erotic and pornographic writing. It was published in 1877 by Henry Spencer Ashbee (1834–1900), businessman, book collector and member of the Royal Academy of Madrid, who left his collections of erotic and Spanish literature to the British Museum. Some experts have suggested Ashbee as the pseudonymous 'Walter', author of the pornographic classic *My Secret Life* (1888–92).

Inextinguishable, The. The title of the symphony no 4 (1916) by the Danish composer Carl Nielsen (1865–1931), reflecting his belief that

> Music is life, and, like it, inextinguishable.
>
> CARL NIELSEN: motto of his symphony no 4

Infinite Divisibility. A painting (1942) by the French surrealist Yves Tanguy (1900–55), in which various agglomerations of biomorphic and man-made forms stand bleakly on a seemingly endless plain, casting long, sad shadows. Tanguy persisted in painting much the same thing for many years. The title indicates that the artist had not yet come to grips with quantum theory.

> Tanguy was the Watteau of surrealism.
>
> SARANE ALEXANDRIAN: *Surrealist Art* (1969)

INSECTS AND ARACHNIDS

The Wasps, a comedy (422 BC) by the Greek dramatist Aristophanes

The Bee's Wedding, the nickname of one of Mendelssohn's *SONGS WITHOUT WORDS* (1930–45) for piano

The CRICKET ON THE HEARTH, a Christmas book (1845) by Charles Dickens

'The Song of the Flea', Mussorgsky's setting (1879) of Mephistopheles's song in Gounod's *Faust* (*see* FAUST OR FAUSTUS, panel, pp.152–6)

The FLIGHT OF THE BUMBLE BEE, an orchestral interlude (1900) by Rimsky-Korsakov

MADAME BUTTERFLY, an opera (1904) by Puccini

'Metamorphosis', a short story (1915) by Franz Kafka, in which Gregor Samsa wakes up one morning to find that he has changed into a giant insect

The DAY OF THE LOCUST (1939) a novel by Nathanael West

LORD OF THE FLIES, a novel (1954) by William Golding

The Cricket in Times Square, a children's novel (1960) by the US writer George Selden

The Grasshopper, a film (1969) in which a woman flits from man to man

The Spirit of the Beehive, a film (1973) set in Spain in the 1940s

Papillon (French, 'butterfly'), a film (1973) based on the autobiography of the Devil's Island convict Henri Charrière, whose nickname was Papillon

Mosquito Coast, a novel (1981) by Paul Theroux

The WASP FACTORY, a novel (1984) by Iain Banks

Angels and Insects, novellas (1992) by A.S. Byatt (film version 1995)

Ladybird Ladybird, a film (1994) by Ken Loach about a mother whose children are taken into care (the title comes from the same nursery rhyme as *FLY AWAY HOME*)

Antz, a witty, computer-animated children's film (1998)

A Bug's Life, another computer-animated film for children (1998)

The Spider's Banquet, a ballet (1913) with music by Albert Roussel

The Day of the Scorpion, a novel (1968) by Paul Scott (*see* RAJ QUARTET, THE)

The Spider's Stratagem, a film (1970) by Bernardo Bertolucci about the mystery of a man apparently killed by the Fascists in 1936

The Scorpion God, three novellas (1971) by William Golding

The Childlike Life of the Black Tarantula, a novel (1975) by Kathy Acker

KISS OF THE SPIDER WOMAN, a novel (1976) by Manuel Puig (film version 1985)

Arachnophobia, a horror film (1990) about killer spiders

Inheritors, The. A novel by William Golding (1911–93), published in 1955 and described by Arthur Koestler as 'an earthquake in the petrified forests of the English novel'. The 'inheritors' of the title, which inverts Christ's dictum in St Matthew, are the first modern human beings, members of a warlike, weapon-using species who wipe out their peaceful Neanderthal predecessors.

> Blessed are the meek: for they shall inherit the earth.
>
> St Matthew 5:5

The Inheritors is also the title of a novel by Joseph Conrad (1857–1924) in collaboration with Ford Madox Ford, published in 1901.

In Memoriam A.H.H. A poem, or more accurately a series of poems, by Alfred, Lord Tennyson (1809–92), published in 1850. The 'A.H.H.' of the title was Arthur Henry Hallam (1811–33), a young man of great promise who had become a close friend of the poet at Cambridge. Hallam died while abroad, and Tennyson began *In Memoriam* the same year. As the poem progressed, it shifted from being simply an elegy to a more wide-ranging meditation on evolution ('nature red in tooth and claw'), mutability and religious belief.

Tennyson also memorialized his friend in another way – by naming his own son Hallam.

> [Of *In Memoriam*] It is beautiful; it is mournful; it is monotonous.
>
> CHARLOTTE BRONTË: letter to Mrs Gaskell, 27 August 1850

Inscape. An orchestral work by Aaron Copland (1900–90), first performed in 1967. The piece uses the twelve-note system of Arnold Schoenberg. The title borrows a word coined by the English poet Gerald Manley Hopkins (1844–89), who defined 'inscape' as 'the individual or essential quality of the thing'.

In the Night Kitchen. A picture book (1970) by the US illustrator Maurice Sendak (b. 1928). A boy called Michael is mixed into a batter by three identical fat bakers (drawn to resemble the comedian Oliver Hardy) after he falls from his bed into a Night Kitchen. He manages to escape on a flying-machine made of dough and returns to his bed. The inspiration for the book's title came from Sendak's childhood memory of a New York bakery that displayed the slogan 'We bake while you sleep!'

In the Realm of the Senses. *See* EMPIRE OF THE SENSES.

Intimate Letters. *See* DIARY OF ONE WHO DISAPPEARED.

Intolleranza 1960 (Italian, 'intolerance 1960'). An opera (or 'mural' as the composer called it) by the Italian communist Luigi Nono (1924–90), with a libretto by the composer, written in 1960. The work attacks contemporary evils such as fascism, nuclear weapons and racism, and at its first performance in Venice in 1961 there was a riot by neo-fascists. As a communist, Nono required special dispensation from the US State Department to attend the work's American premier in 1965. Nono later updated the work as *Intolleranza 1970.*

Into Thin Air. An acclaimed personal account (1997) by the US mountaineer and writer Jon Krakauer of the 1996 disaster on Mount Everest, in which, on a single day, eight climbers from a number of different expeditions died high on the mountain during a terrible storm. The title refers to the lack of oxygen at altitude, and to the frailty of human existence.

> Our revels now are ended. These our actors,
> As I foretold you, were all spirits and

Are melted into air, into thin air:

WILLIAM SHAKESPEARE: *The Tempest* (1611), IV.i

Invisible Man, The. The title of two very different novels. The first is a work of science fiction by H.G. Wells (1866–1946), published in 1897. In this story a scientist finds the secret of invisibility, which lures him into temptation. The first film version (1933), starring Claud Rains, was highly regarded, but its several sequels less so.

The second novel with this title was by the black US writer Ralph Ellison (1914–94). Published in 1952, it won the 1953 National Book Award for fiction. The novel tells the story of a Southern black who moves to New York, participates in the struggle against white oppression, and ends up ignored and living in a coal hole.

> I am an invisible man, I am a man of substance, of flesh and bone, fibre and liquids – and I might even be said to possess a mind. I am invisible, understand, simply because people refuse to see me.
>
> *The Invisible Man*, prologue

'Isabella, or The Pot of Basil'. A poem by John Keats (1795–1821), written in 1818 and published in 1820. The story of the poem comes from *The* DECAMERON. Isabella falls for a commoner, Lorenzo, rather than a nobleman as her brothers had planned. They kill him and bury him. Isabella digs him up, cuts his head off, and puts it in a pot and plants some basil on top. Then she –

> Hung over her sweet Basil evermore,
> And moistened it with tears unto the core.

The brothers steal the pot, find the head and are filled with remorse. Isabella goes into a decline and expires.

I Saw in Louisiana a Live-Oak Growing. An early painting, dating from 1963, by David Hockney (b.1937). Like *WE TWO BOYS TOGETHER CLINGING*, the title comes from Walt Whitman. Hockney explains:

> [The painting] is from the Whitman poem about the tree that's 'uttering joyous leaves of dark green' all its life without a friend or lover near. I thought, what marvellous lines about a man looking at a tree. The tree is painted upside down to make it look more alone; it was just as simple as that, really.
>
> *David Hockney by David Hockney* (1976)

I Sing the Body Electric. A collection of short stories (1969) by the US writer Ray Bradbury (b.1920). It is also the title of a novel (1993) by Adam Lively (b.1961), and was originally the title and first line of a poem (1855) by the US poet Walt Whitman (1819–92):

> I sing the Body electric;
> The armies of those I love engirth me, and I engirth them;
> They will not let me off till I go with them, respond to them,
> And discorrupt them, and charge them full with the charge of the Soul.

Island of Dr Moreau, The. A science-fiction novel by H.G. Wells (1866–1946), published in 1896 and anticipating modern genetic engineering. Prendrick, having survived a shipwreck, finds himself on Noble's Isle, where he comes across the Beast People. It turns out that these are the results of the surgical experiments of Dr Moreau, who is trying to make animals more human. It all turns out rather badly.

An early film version was entitled *The Island of Lost Souls* (1932). This was accompanied by the following publicity line:

> Out of the dark fantastic madness of his science he created her – the panther woman – throbbing to the hot flush of new-found love!

A more recent remake (1996) starred Marlon Brando.

Moreau's Other Island (1980) is an updating of the story by Brian Aldiss (b.1925). This time it is a US under-secretary of state, Calvert Roberts, who is stranded on an island inhabited by humans with animal-like deformities. It transpires that these creatures are the result of experiments by the thalidomide victim Mortimer Dart, and that Roberts has himself authorized the funding for Dart's research. Aldiss's title also echoes that of Shaw's play, *JOHN BULL'S OTHER ISLAND.*

> He's the Shakespeare of science fiction.
>
> BRIAN ALDISS: comment on H.G. Wells, on BBC TV's *Bookmark*, 24 August 1996

It Isn't This Time of Year At All. *See AS I WAS GOING DOWN SACKVILLE STREET.*

Ivory Tower, The. A novel by Henry James (1843–1916), posthumously published in 1917. To live in an ivory tower is to live in seclusion, divorced from everyday life, and wilfully or unwittingly excluding the harsh realities of the outside world. The phrase is first recorded in English in 1911 as a translation of French *tour d'ivoire*, a term used by the critic and poet

Charles Sainte-Beuve (1804–69) to refer to his fellow poet Alfred de Vigny (1797–1863).

> *Et Vigny plus secret,*
> *Comme en sa tour d'ivoire, avant midi rentrait.*
> ('And Vigny more discreet, as if in his ivory tower, retired before noon.')
>
> CHARLES SAINTE-BEUVE: *Les Pensées d'Août, à M. Villemain* (1837)

I WAS A ... and *I MARRIED A* ...

Both of these title formulas have proved popular for films, echoing sensational headlines in the tabloid press. Examples of *I Was a* ... include:

I Was a Spy (1933)
I Was an Adventuress (1940)
I Was a Prisoner on Devil's Island (1941)
I Was a Male War Bride (1949)
I Was a Communist for the FBI (1951)
I Was a Teenage Werewolf (1957)
I Was Monty's Double (1958)

Examples of *I Married a* ... include:

I Married a Nazi (1940)
I Married an Angel (1942)
I Married a Witch (1942)
I Married a Communist (1949)
I Married a Monster from Outer Space (1958)
I Married a Dead Man (1983)

J

Jamaica Inn. A historical adventure (1936) by Daphne du Maurier (1907–89). Jamaica Inn is a real inn on Bodmin Moor, Cornwall, and in the story it is the centre of the activities of a gang of smugglers, while divided loyalties inform the romantic aspects of the plot. A film version (1939) was directed by Alfred Hitchcock.

Jaws. A film (1975) directed by Steven Spielberg based on a novel of the same title by the US writer Peter Benchley (b.1940) – the grandson of the humorist Robert Benchley – about a man-eating great white shark that terrorizes a small seaside resort on the western seaboard of the United States. The title of Benchley's book was a last-minute inspiration that neither author nor publisher was immediately very happy with. Previous suggestions had included *Great White*, *The Shark*, *Leviathan Rising*, *The Jaws of Death*, *A Silence in the Water* and the rather less seriously intended *What's That Noshin' on My Laig?* Superfluous sequels were *Jaws 2* (1978), *Jaws 3-D* (1983) and *Jaws: The Revenge* (1987).

> Just when you thought it was safe to go back in the water.
>
> Publicity slogan for the sequel to *Jaws*

Benchley has subsequently devoted himself to the cause of shark conservation.

Jeffrey Bernard is Unwell. A play (1991) by Keith Waterhouse (b.1929) in which an alcoholic journalist recalls his past career in Fleet Street. Jeffrey Bernard (1932–97) was a real Fleet Street journalist famed for the ill-health often induced by his dissolute ways. The title refers to the announcement that regularly appeared in the place of his column in the *Spectator* when he was 'indisposed'.

Jekyll and Hyde. *See* DR JEKYLL AND MR HYDE, THE STRANGE CASE OF.

'Jena' Symphony. The nickname given to the symphony found by Fritz Stein in 1910 at Jena, a town in central Germany. For many years it was thought to be a juvenile work by Beethoven, although it has also been attributed to Friedrich Witt (1771–1837).

Jewel in the Crown, The. *See* RAJ QUARTET, THE.

John Bull, The History of. A collection of satirical pamphlets by John Arbuthnot (1667–1735), published in 1712. This collection included a reprint of Arbuthnot's *Law is a bottomless pit* (6 March 1712), an allegory of the War of the Spanish Succession, in which John Bull appears as a personification of England in the body of a successful trader (in later appearances he was often a farmer). Arbuthnot contrasts this figure with the bullying Lewis Baboon (the French) and the bamboozling Nicholas Frog (the Dutch).

> Bull, in the main, was an honest plain-dealing fellow, cholerick, bold, and of a very unconstant Temper; ... no man kept a better House than John, nor spent his Money more generously.
>
> JOHN ARBUTHNOT: *The History of John Bull* (1712), Part 1, chapter 5

Arbuthnot did not invent the character of John Bull, but firmly established him as an archetype.

John Bull was also the title of a jingoistic magazine established in 1906 by the arch-fraudster and politician Horatio Bottomley (1860–1932), largely with the intention of furthering his own dubious business ventures.

John Bull's Other Island. A play by George Bernard Shaw (1856–1950), first performed in 1904, and published in 1907. The play made Shaw's reputation as a dramatist in Britain. John Bull's 'other island' is Ireland, John Bull being the personification of England, popularized by John Arbuthnot in 1712 in his *History of* JOHN BULL.

> An Irishman's heart is nothing but his imagination.
>
> *John Bull's Other Island*, I

Johnny I Hardly Knew You. A novel (1977) by Edna O'Brien (b.1932) in which an older woman ends up killing her younger lover. The title comes from the traditional ballad 'Johnny, I hardly knew ye':

> Where are your eyes that looked so mild
> When my poor heart you first beguiled?
> Why did you run from me and the child?
> Och, Johnny, I hardly knew ye!

For the American market the title of O'Brien's novel was altered to *I Hardly Knew You*.

Jonathan Wild the Great, The Life of. A short novel by Henry Fielding (1707–54), published in 1743. Fielding's novel is a satire on the adulation of 'greatness', which he shows may simply consist of power over others. Fielding based his anti-hero on an actual criminal of the same name. The real Jonathan Wild (1683–1725) ended up dominating London's underworld and ran a number of highly organized rackets. Wild earned the name 'thief-taker general' from his practice of apprehending wanted villains (sometimes including members of his own gang) and claiming the reward. Eventually Wild was convicted of receiving stolen goods (his biggest business) and was hanged.

Journey into You Beaut Country. A painting (1961) by the Australian artist John Olsen (b.1928), combining abstract expressionist technique with a strong sense of the Australian landscape. 'You beaut' is an Australian term of approbation, here applied to 'Godzone country' itself.

Journey to the End of the Night (French title: *Voyage au bout de la nuit*). The first novel (1932) by the French writer Louis Ferdinand Céline (1894–1961). The central character, Ferdinand, wanders aimlessly and despairingly through the First World War and afterwards. The work was praised by some for its innovatory style, and excoriated by others for its savage pessimism and coarse language. Céline went on to become even more misanthropic, anti-French and anti-Semitic, and was suspected, and later exonerated, of collaboration with the Nazis in the Second World War.

Journey to the Surface of the Earth. A long-term art project, begun in 1969 by the Scottish 'artist-philosopher' Mark Boyle (b.1935), his wife Joan Hills and their children Georgia and Sebastian, collectively known as 'The Boyle Family'. The project involves producing meticulously detailed fibreglass replicas of very specific parts of the surface of the planet, which are selected by a member of the public throwing a dart into a map of the world. Examples include mud with tyre tracks by the River Rhine, a piece of Australian desert, and a section of pavement and street outside the Kelvin Hall in Glasgow. The title plays on that of the classic science fiction adventure *Journey to the Centre of the Earth* (1864) by Jules Verne (1828–1905).

Joy of ... . The beginning of various book titles alluding to a specific activity that presumably gave the writer pleasure and that he or she wishes to share with readers. The vogue was apparently launched with *The Joy of Cooking* (1931) by the American cookery expert Irma S. Rombauer. Forty years on Alex Comfort rejuvenated the formula with *The Joy of Sex* (1972), following it with a companion volume, *More Joy* (1974), and at the age of 70 finally updating it as *The New Joy of Sex* (1991). *The Joy of Sex: Pocket Edition* (1997) won THE ODDEST TITLE OF THE YEAR AWARD (*see* panel, pp.332–3).

Other *Joy of* ... titles have included *Joy of a Home Fruit Garden*, *Joy of Building*, *Joy of Flying*, *Joy of Hand-Weaving* and Leonard Bernstein's *Joy of Music*. In 1984 Nigel Rees published the ironically titled *Joy of Clichés*.

Jumpers. A play (1972) by Tom Stoppard (b.1937) in which a professor of ethics called George Moore – but sadly for him not *the* George Moore (1873–1958), the famous moral philosopher – struggles to cope with a variety of misfortunes, including the death of his pet hare. The jumpers of the title are the gymnasts of the play's opening scene, who are subsequently revealed to be professional philosophers, leaping under the direction of the distinguished Sir Archibald Jumper.

Juno and the Paycock. A play (1924) by the Irish dramatist Sean O'Casey (1880–1964), first performed at the Abbey Theatre, Dublin. It concerns the fate of a Dublin family, the Boyles, during the Civil War (1922–3). 'Juno' is Juno Boyle, the long-suffering but resilient wife of the work-shy 'Captain' Boyle, who spends his time 'strutting about the town like a paycock' (peacock).

The pairing of Juno and a peacock goes back to the ancient Greek fable in which Hera (the Greek version of Juno) sets the giant Argus, with his 100 eyes, to watch over Io, of whom she is jealous. Hermes, however, charms Argus to sleep with his lyre and slays him. Hera then sets the eyes of Argus in the tail of the peacock.

'Jupiter' Symphony. The nickname of the symphony no 41 in C, K551 (1788), by Mozart (1756–91), his last. The name first appears in British programme notes in the early 19th century, but its origin is unknown. It refers to the supreme god of the Romans, Jupiter, who is also a thunder god (the Greek equivalent is Zeus).

Jurassic Park. A film (1993) directed by Steven Spielberg, based on a novel of the same name (1990) by Michael Crichton (b.1942) about the chaos that overtakes an ambitious island theme park in which the main attractions are dinosaurs from the Jurassic period (205–135 million years ago). These have been recreated by scientists using the DNA in the dinosaur blood found in mosquitoes fossilized in amber.

Two sequels were entitled *The LOST WORLD* (1997) and *Jurassic Park III* (2001).

Justified Sinner, Confessions of a. *See CONFESSIONS OF A JUSTIFIED SINNER, THE PRIVATE MEMOIRS AND.*

Just What Is It that Makes Today's Homes So Different, So Appealing? A satirical and influential collage (1956) by Richard Hamilton (b.1922). A pioneering work of British Pop Art, the picture includes photographs of a muscleman, a woman with impossible breasts, a tape recorder and other consumer durables, various brand labels and so on. The title is in the style of an article heading from a home-interiors magazine. *See also $HE.*

K

Kandy-Kolored Tangerine-Flake Streamline Baby, The. The literary debut (1965) by the US journalist Tom Wolfe (b.1931). The book is a collection of essays in which the author introduced America to the 1960s – to the Twist, the Beatles, Bouffant Hairdos, Kar Kustomizers and much more. The provocative title catches the *Zeitgeist* by combining the hip and cool with crass commercialism.

Keep the Aspidistra Flying. A novel by George Orwell (1903–50), published in 1936. It tells the story of an assistant in a bookshop who has literary ambitions and a contempt for bourgeois materialism. In the end, however, he ends up being obliged to marry the girl he loves, and accepting the comforts of middle-class life.

The aspidistra is a resilient house plant with lace-shaped leaves. It was particularly popular from late Victorian times to the 1920s because of its ability to survive in gas-lit rooms, and it became a symbol of lower middle-class philistinism and dull respectability.

Orwell's title echoes a sentimental song popular during the First World War:

> Keep the Home-fires burning,
> While your hearts are yearning,
> Though your lads are far away
> They dream of Home.
>
> LEN GUIBERT FORD: 'Till the Boys Come Home!' (1914), with music by Ivor Novello

The song 'The Biggest Aspidistra in the World', by Jimmy Harper, Tommie Connor and Will E. Haines, and widely popularized by Gracie Fields (1898–1979), actually came out in 1938, two years after Orwell's novel.

'Kettledrum' Mass (German *Paukenmesse*). The nickname for the Mass in C (1796) by Haydn (1732–1809), which has prominent parts for kettledrums. Haydn himself called it *Missa in tempore belli* (Latin, 'Mass in time of war'), Austria then being at war with Revolutionary France; the kettledrums originated as martial instruments.

Killing Fields, The. A film (1984) based on the real-life relationship between US journalist Sidney Schanberg and his Cambodian translator Dith Pran following the withdrawal of US personnel from Phnom Penh, Cambodia, in 1975. The plot recounts Schanberg's attempts to locate Pran after the latter is seized for 're-education' by the communist Khmer Rouge. The 'killing fields' of the title were the paddy fields around Phnom Penh in which the Khmer Rouge executed their opponents. The part of Dith Pran was played by Haing S. Ngor, a doctor who had himself fled from the Khmer Rouge. In reality Dith Pran saw the killing fields himself for the first time only when he visited them as mayor of his home town, long after the Khmer Rouge had been thrown out. The phrase has since become a journalistic cliché.

Kill Your Darlings. A novel (2000) by Terence Blacker. The title refers to Sir Arthur Quiller-Couch's advice in his lecture, 'On Style', delivered in Cambridge on 28 January 1914:

> Whenever you feel an impulse to perpetuate a piece of exceptionally fine writing, obey it – wholeheartedly – and delete it before sending your manuscript to press. *Murder your darlings.*

'On Style' was the twelfth and last in a series of lectures, collectively published as *On the Art of Writing*. Quiller-Couch's advice recalls Dr Johnson:

> Read over your compositions, and where ever you meet with a passage which you think is particularly fine, strike it out.

This advice, given by Johnson on 30 April 1773, is quoted in Boswell's *Life* (1791). Johnson himself said he was quoting a college tutor.

Kim. A novel by Rudyard Kipling (1865–1936), published in 1901, and generally considered his finest work. Kim, the hero of the novel, is Kimball O'Hara, an orphan boy. Kim passes as a native Indian boy nicknamed

'Little Friend of All the World', takes up with a wise old Tibetan lama, and eventually becomes a secret agent on behalf of the British government. The British spy Kim Philby was nicknamed after him, his original forenames being Harold Adrian Russell. 'Kim's game' is a memory game introduced to the Boy Scouts by their founder, Robert Baden-Powell; it is a development of the 'Jewel Game' described in chapter ix of the novel.

Kind Hearts and Coronets. A British film comedy (1949), loosely based by Robert Hamer and John Dighton on the turn-of-the-century novel *Israel Rank* by Roy Horniman, about a lowly relation of the aristocratic D'Ascoyne family who murders his way to the dukedom he believes is rightfully his. Starring Dennis Price as Louis Mazzini, the amoral murderer, and Alec Guinness as eight of his blueblooded victims, the film owes its title to a poem by Alfred, Lord Tennyson (1809–92):

> Trust me, Clara Vere de Vere,
> From yon blue heavens above us bent
> The grand old gardener and his wife
> Smile at the claims of long descent.
> Howe'er it be, it seems to me,
> 'Tis only noble to be good.
> Kind hearts are more than coronets,
> And simple faith than Norman blood.
>
> 'Lady Clara Vere de Vere' (1842)

Kindly Ones, The. *See* EUMENIDES.

King and I, The. A musical play (1951) with a score by Richard Rodgers (1902–79) and book by Oscar Hammerstein II (1895–1960) about the experiences of an English governess who is engaged to care for the children of the King of Siam (Thailand). Filmed with Yul Brynner and Deborah Kerr in 1956, the play was based on the biographical book *Anna and the King of Siam* by Margaret Landon, in which she related the experiences of Anna Leonowens, the widow of a major in the Indian Army who in 1862 was invited by King Mongkut of Siam to teach his 67 children. Mrs Leonowens remained in Bangkok for five years, and later wrote about her experiences. The story was filmed for the first time in 1946, with the same title as Landon's book. It was actress Gertrude Lawrence, who played Anna in the first stage production, who first suggested the book would make a good musical. The story also provided the basis for the 1999 film *Anna and the King*.

King Solomon's Mines. A romantic adventure story (1885) by H. Rider Haggard (1856–1925). The original King Solomon's Mines (Mikhrot Shelomo ha-Melekh) are ancient copper mines at Timna', in the Negev Desert, Israel (King Solomon being the 10th-century BC king of Israel famous for his wealth and wisdom), but Haggard's story is set in southern Africa, and involves a lost diamond mine beyond the Solomon Mountains, sought by the Great White Hunter, Allan Quartermain, and his companions.

There have been three film versions: the 1935 film features Paul Robeson and Ecce Homo Toto as native Africans, while the visually stunning 1950 version stars Deborah Kerr and Stewart Granger; the 1985 version was poorly received. William Minter's 1986 study of 'Western interests and the burdened history of southern Africa' is entitled *King Solomon's Mines Revisited*.

King Solomon's Ring. A popular book (1949) on animal behaviour by the pioneering Austrian ethologist Konrad Lorenz (1903–89). In it he describes many of his discoveries and experiments, including that involving the imprinting of ducklings and goslings: it was Lorenz who found that at a certain stage after hatching, the young birds will adopt the nearest living creature as their mother, as long as it makes the appropriate quacks, and follow it around. Thus Lorenz himself became mother to many.

The original Solomon's ring enabled the ancient king of Israel (10th century BC) to understand and converse with the animal world. In addition, it helped him to overcome all opponents and to transpose himself to the celestial spheres, where he learned the secrets of the universe. The ring also sealed up the refractory jinn in jars and cast them into the Red Sea.

Kismet. A musical play (1953) based on a play (1911) by Edward Knoblock about a poet turned beggar who has a series of adventures reminiscent of *The* ARABIAN NIGHTS. The music of Alexander Borodin was arranged by Robert Wright and George Forrest. The title comes from the Turkish *qismet* ('portion' or 'lot') and is now commonly understood to mean 'fate'. Kismet is sometimes advanced as a more becoming alternative to 'Kiss me' in Horatio Nelson's putative last words, 'Kiss me, Hardy'.

Kiss, The. The title of a famous sculpture by Auguste Rodin (*see* FRANCESCA DA RIMINI, panel, pp.175–6). It is also the title of one of the most popular paintings (1908) of the Austrian painter Gustav Klimt (1862–1918), and of a well-known painting (1892) by the Norwegian artist Edvard Munch (1863–1944), of which he also made a woodcut version.

Kiss Me Kate. *See* TAMING OF THE SHREW, THE.

Kiss of the Spider Woman. A film (1985) based on a novel *El beso de la mujer araña* (1976) by the Argentinian writer Manuel Puig (1932–90). It is about the unlikely friendship that develops between a gay man and a political prisoner when they are thrown into the same cell in a South American prison. The title refers to a B-movie about the comic book superheroine 'Spider Woman' that the two discuss between sessions of torture at the hands of their captors.

Kleine Nachtmusik, Eine (German, 'a little night music' or 'a little serenade'). A serenade in four movements for either string orchestra or string quintet, K525 (1787), by Mozart (1756–91). *Nachtmusik* is an 18th-century synonym for serenade. *A Little Night Music* is a musical by Stephen Sondheim and Hugh Wheeler first produced in 1973.

Knot Garden, The. A semi-mystical opera by Michael Tippett (1905–98) with a libretto by the composer. It was first performed in 1974. A knot garden is an old-fashioned kind of formal garden (dating back to at least the 16th century) in which intricate, knot-like patterns around beds are delineated by low hedges, typically of box. The symbolic knot garden of Tippett's title is a revolving stage device, in which the various characters work out their relationships. The characters include a benevolent analyst, Mangus, who sets up an elaborate charade based on *The* TEMPEST to help the others work through their problems.

Kraken Wakes, The. A science-fiction novel (1953) by John Wyndham (pen-name of John Wyndham Parkes Lucas Beynon Harris; 1903–69). As a result of a global disaster, interstellar invaders settle on the seabed and flood Britain. The title was inspired by Tennyson's poem 'The Kraken' (1830):

> Below the thunders of the upper deep;
> Far, far beneath in the abysmal sea,
> His ancient, dreamless, uninvaded sleep
> The Kraken sleepeth.

In Norwegian folklore, the Kraken is a vast sea monster, possibly based on sightings of giant squid. It was first described by Pontoppidan in his

History of Norway (1752). It was said to be capable of dragging down the largest ships and when submerging to suck down vessels by the whirlpool it created. After he had finished MOBY-DICK, Hermann Melville wrote to Nathaniel Hawthorne:

> Leviathan is not the biggest fish; I have heard of Krakens.
>
> Letter, 17 November 1851

Krapp's Last Tape. A short one-man play (1958) by the Irish writer Samuel Beckett (1906–89). The scatologically named Krapp listens to monologues recorded by his younger self – who seems a stranger and a fool to the pessimistic old man. Almost the only action is the eating of a banana. The play was written for the Irish actor Patrick Magee.

> Perhaps my best years are gone ... but I wouldn't want them back.
>
> *Krapp's Last Tape*

Kreisleriana. A set of piano pieces, opus 16 (1838, revised 1850), by Robert Schumann (1810–56), dedicated to Chopin. The title comes from the character Johannes Kreisler created by E.T.A. Hoffmann (1770–1822) in his essays on music, collected in *Phantasiestücke in Callots Manier* (1814–15; 'fantasy pieces in the style of Callot'). These essays, originally contributed to the Leipzig *Allgemeine Musikalische Zeitung*, had a great influence on Romantic musical criticism. Kreisler also makes an appearance in Hoffmann's novel *Lebens-Ansichten des Katers Murr nebst fragmentarischer Biographie des Kapellmeisters Johannes Kreisler* (1820–2; 'the life and opinions of Kater Murr, with a fragmentary biography of Conductor Johannes Kreisler').

'Kreutzer' Sonata. The nickname of the sonata for violin and piano in A, opus 47 (1803), by Beethoven (1770–1827). It was composed for the Polish-born violinist George Bridgetower (1780–1860), the son of a European mother and an African father, and Bridgetower, with Beethoven on piano, gave the first performance in 1803. However, the two men quarrelled, and when the work was published in 1805 Beethoven dedicated it to the French violinist Rodolphe Kreutzer (1766–1831). Kreutzer was also a prolific composer, and his studies for solo violin are still used.

'The Kreutzer Sonata' (*Kreytserova Sonata*; 1891) is the title of a short story by Leo Tolstoy, in which the central character, Pozdynyshev, suspects his wife is having an affair with a neighbour with whom she plays the sonata. On the score of his string quartet no 1 (1924) the Czech composer Leoš Janáček (1854–1928) wrote 'Inspired by L.N. Tolstoy's *Kreutzer Sonata*', and the quartet is often given the subtitle *Kreutzer Sonata*.

'Kubla Khan'. A famously unfinished, opium-induced poem by Samuel Taylor Coleridge (1772–1834), who claimed to have written down as much as he could of what he had just been dreaming before being interrupted by the arrival of 'a person on business from Porlock'. Composed while Coleridge was living in Somerset in 1797–8, the poem was first published in *Christabel and Other Poems* (1816). It bears little relation to the historical Kublai Khan (1215–94), the grandson of Genghis Khan. Kublai led the Mongol conquest of China and made himself the first emperor of the Yuan dynasty in 1279. He was made famous in Europe by Marco Polo, who spent 20 years at Kublai's court.

See also XANADU.

L

Lachrimae, or Seaven Teares figured in seaven passionate Pavans. A collection of music for viols and lute by John Dowland (1563–1626), published in 1605. There are 21 pieces in all, but the seven pavans all begin with the theme of Dowland's song 'Flow my tears' (*lacrimae* is Latin for 'tears'). Dowland specialized in melancholy, the punning title of another pavan for lute being '*Semper Dowland Semper Dolens*' (Latin, 'always Dowland, always sad').

Lady Macbeth of the Mtsensk District. A formerly controversial opera by Dmitri Shostakovich (1906–75), with a libretto by the composer and A. Preiss, after an 1865 story by Nikolai Leskov (1831–95) about a woman who lives and dies by violence (as does Shakespeare's anti-heroine). It was first performed in 1934 and proved popular until the Soviet authorities started to show their disapproval of modernism in 1936. In that year *Pravda*, in a review rumoured to have been instigated by Stalin himself, sinisterly commented:

> It is a leftist bedlam instead of human music. The inspiring quality of good music is sacrificed in favour of petty-bourgeois clowning. This game may end badly.

The work was not revived in the Soviet Union until 1963, when it was staged under the title *Katerina Ismailova*. It was, however, performed in the United States in 1935; one American critic described the music as 'pornophony'.

'Lady of Shalott, The'. A poem by Alfred, Lord Tennyson (1809–92), published in 1832 and subsequently revised. The poem derives from the Arthurian romances, in which the Lady of Shalott is a maiden who falls in love with Sir Lancelot of the Lake, and dies because her love is unrequited. Shalott is the Astolat of Arthurian legend. Tennyson and other writers based the name on its French form, Ascolet or Escalot (this was the spelling in Malory's *Le Morte d'Arthur*). When Caxton printed this work in 1485, however, he misread the 'c' as a 't' – hence Astolat.

There is a well-known painting of the same title (1888) by John Waterhouse (1849–1917).

Lady of the Lake, The. A long narrative poem by Sir Walter Scott (1771–1832), published in 1810. The poem is set in 16th-century Scotland, in particular the Trossachs region of the southern Highlands. The lake of the title is Loch Katrine, first seen by a hunter pursuing a stag:

> And thus an airy point he won,
> Where, gleaming with the setting sun,
> One burnish'd sheet of living gold,
> Loch Katrine lay beneath him roll'd,
>
> canto 1, stanza 14

Soon afterwards, we are introduced to the Lady of the Lake herself, Ellen Douglas, who appears rowing a skiff. Ellen is the daughter of Lord James Douglas, who, like many other Douglases through Scottish history, was at odds with the king.

Schubert set three of Ellen's songs, including the 'Ave Maria', to music (1825), using Storck's translation. Rossini's opera *La Donna del lago* (1819) has a libretto by Leone Andrea Tottola based on Scott. Scott's poem helped to popularize the Trossachs as a tourist destination, and the tourist steamer that has for many years plied its trade on Loch Katrine is called SS *Sir Walter Scott*.

The 'Lady of the Lake' in Arthurian legend is entirely different – she is Vivien, the mistress of Merlin, and she lives in the middle of a lake surrounded by knights and damsels.

Lady's Not For Burning, The. A historical play (1948) by Christopher Fry (b.1907) about a beautiful alchemist who finds herself accused of witchcraft and is threatened with death by burning. The play is perhaps now best remembered for having furnished Margaret Thatcher, then prime minister, with her most famous quote, when at the 1980 Conservative Party Conference she asserted her determination not to perform a U-turn in her controversial economic policies:

> To those waiting with bated breath for that favourite media catchphrase, the U-turn, I have only one thing to say. You turn if you want to. The lady is not for turning.

The phrase was coined by speechwriter Sir Ronald Millar, and it is said that Mrs Thatcher was unaware of its source.

Lady Vanishes, The. A film thriller (1938) adapted by Sidney Gilliat from a novel *The Wheel Spins* by Ethel Lina White about the mystery surrounding the apparent disappearance of an elderly lady on board a trans-European train. Directed by Alfred Hitchcock, the film concentrates on the efforts of the hero and heroine to unravel the truth behind the woman's disappearance. The title of the film refers to a traditional magician's trick in which a woman is apparently made to disappear before the audience's very eyes. Anthony Page directed a remake (1979).

Lalla Rookh. An enormously popular and widely translated tale (1817) by Thomas Moore (1779–1852) about the daughter of the emperor of Delhi, Princess Lalla Rookh ('tulip cheek'), who travels to Kashmir to marry the king of Bucharia. This prose story frames four oriental tales in verse, told to the princess's party by a young Kashmiri poet called Feramorz with whom the princess falls in love and who turns out to be the king to whom she is engaged. (Lalla was the name of a real Kashmiri writer of the 14th century.) The four tales are 'The Veiled Prophet of Khorassan', 'PARADISE AND THE PERI', 'The Fire Worshippers' and 'The Light of the Harem'. The oriental setting was suggested to Moore by Byron. The great Scottish physicist Lord Kelvin (1824–1907) named his yacht *Lalla Rookh*, and the French composer Félicien-César David (1810–76) wrote an opera of the same name (1862).

'L'Allegro' and **'Il Penseroso'**. Two companion poems by John Milton (1608–74), written *c.*1631 and published in 1645. The Italian titles respectively mean 'the merry, cheerful man' and 'the thoughtful (i.e. melancholic) man'. 'Il Penseroso' begins:

> Hence, vain deluding joys,
> The brood of folly without father bred.

While in contrast 'L'Allegro''s first lines are:

Hence, loathèd Melancholy,
Of Cerberus, and blackest Midnight born ...

Choral settings include *L'allegro, Il penseroso, ed il moderato* (1740) by Handel (1685–1759) – the third section, 'the rational man', being added for balance by Handel's librettist Charles Jennens – and *L'allegro ed il penseroso* (1890) by Hubert Parry (1848–1918).

See also CRICKET ON THE HEARTH, THE.

'Lamentation' Symphony. The nickname of the symphony no 26 in D minor (*c.*1765) by Haydn (1732–1809). Some of its themes are similar to the plainsong settings of the biblical Lamentations of Jeremiah, sung in Catholic churches in the week leading up to Easter.

'Lament for the Makaris'. A poem by William Dunbar (?1456–?1513), the great poet of the Scottish Renaissance who may have died fighting the English at the battle of Flodden. *Makar* ('maker') is an old Scots word for a creative artist, particularly a poet, and Dunbar's poem is an elegy for a number of dead poets, including Chaucer, Gower, Barbour, Blind Harry and Henryson. After the title, Dunbar wrote a note indicating that he wrote the poem 'when he wes seik' ('when he was unwell'):

Sen he hes all my brether tane,
He will nocht let me live alane;
On forse I man his next prey be:
Timor mortis conturbat me.

('Since he has taken all my brothers, he will not let me live alone; perforce I must be his next prey: the fear of death confounds me.')

Lamia. A long narrative poem (1820) by John Keats (1795–1821) about a young man from ancient Corinth called Lycius, who falls in love with a beautiful woman who turns out to be Lamia, a sorceress who has been turned from a serpent into a human. When she is recognized by Lycius' mentor Apollonius of Tyana for what she is, she disappears. Keats took the idea from Robert Burton's *Anatomy of Melancholy* (1621), for which the source was Philostratus, *De Vita Apollonii*, book iv (3rd century AD).

Originally, for the Greeks and Romans, a lamia (Greek *lamuros*, 'voracious', 'gluttonous') was a female demon who devoured children and whose name was used to frighten them. She was a Libyan queen beloved by Zeus/Jupiter, but, robbed of her offspring by the jealous

Hera/Juno, she became insane and vowed vengeance on all children, whom she delighted to lure and consume. The race of lamiae, in Africa, were said to have the head and breasts of a woman and the body of a serpent. They enticed strangers into their embraces to devour them.

Land of Cockayne. *See* COCKAIGNE.

Land of the Mountain and the Flood. An overture by the Scottish composer Hamish MacCunn (1868–1916), written in 1887 when MacCunn was 19. The title, referring to Scotland, comes from Scott's *LAY OF THE LAST MINSTREL* (1805), canto 6, stanza 2:

> O Caledonia! stern and wild,
> Meet nurse for a poetic child!
> Land of brown heath and shaggy wood,
> Land of the mountain and the flood,
> Land of my sires! what mortal hand
> Can e'er untie the filial band
> That knits me to thy rugged strand!

Long popular in Scottish concert halls, MacCunn's overture became known to a wider audience as the theme music of the BBC TV series *Sutherland's Law*.

Landscape with a Man Killed by a Snake. A painting (*c.*1648) by the French artist Nicolas Poussin (?1594–1665). The dead man lies in a typically classical landscape, although there is no known Greek or Roman legend to which the painting might refer. It has been suggested that the scene somewhat resembles an area near Fondi in Italy, then regarded as dangerous because of its many snakes.

Landscape with the Fall of Icarus. A painting (*c.*1558) by Pieter Bruegel the Elder, in which the landscape and the ploughman in the foreground are, intriguingly, much more noticeable than the distant plunge into the sea of Icarus, only one of whose legs is visible. The painting is in Paris's Musée des Beaux Arts, and in the poem of that name (1940) by W.H. Auden (1907–73) we find:

> About suffering they were never wrong,
> The Old Masters …
> …
> In Brueghel's Icarus, for instance: how everything turns away
> Quite leisurely from the disaster; the ploughman may

Have heard the splash, the forsaken cry,
But for him it was not an important failure.

The painting also inspired 'Landscape with the Fall of Icarus' in *Pictures from Brueghel* (1963) by William Carlos Williams (1883–1963):

Unsignificantly
off the coast
there was
a splash quite unnoticed
this was
Icarus drowning.

Laocoön. One of the most famous of ancient Greek statues, attributed in Pliny's *Historia Naturalis* to the sculptors Hagesander, Polydorus and Athenodorus (2nd or 1st century BC). Laocoön, a priest of Apollo, was a son of King Priam of Troy, who, either because he offended Apollo or because he tried to prevent the entry of the Wooden Horse into Troy, was, along with his two sons, squeezed to death by serpents while sacrificing to Poseidon. The sculpture, made with astonishing skill from a single block of marble, depicts the three in their agonized death throes.

The piece, which is now in the Vatican, was rediscovered in a vineyard in Rome in 1506, and had a powerful impact on Michelangelo, among others – although Titian satirized the cult of the statue by making a woodcut of it in which the priest and his two sons are turned into monkeys. The adulation of the sculpture continued into the 18th century, when the German neoclassical theorist Johann J. Winckelmann (1717–68) famously praised its 'noble simplicity and calm grandeur':

The German philosopher and dramatist G.E. Lessing (1729–81) subsequently gave the title *Laokoon* to the book in which he attacked Winckelmann's aesthetic ideas.

Laodicean, A. A novel by Thomas Hardy (1840–1928), published in 1881. A laodicean is someone who is indifferent to religion, caring little or nothing about the matter, like the Christians of Laodicea in Asia Minor mentioned in Revelation 3:14–18:

> So then, because thou art lukewarm, and neither cold nor hot, I will spue thee out of my mouth.
>
> Revelation 3:16

Hardy's novel concerns a vacillating young woman, Paula Power, who cannot take the plunge when faced with the prospect of total immersion as a Baptist.

Large Glass, The. *See* BRIDE STRIPPED BARE BY HER BACHELORS, EVEN, THE.

'Lark' Quartet (German *Lerchenquartett*). The nickname of the string quartet in D, opus 64 no 5 (1789), by Haydn (1732–1809), one of the 'TOST' QUARTETS. The name derives from the high notes of the first violin at the start of the first movement.

Last Exit to Brooklyn. A grim and bleak novel (1964) by Hubert Selby Jr (b.1928), set in Brooklyn, New York, and consisting of a series of loosely connected episodes reflecting the seamy underside of urban life. There are some moments of tenderness among descriptions of violence and heterosexual and homosexual sex. The British publisher was found guilty of issuing an obscene publication in 1967, but a successful appeal against the judgment, led by John Mortimer QC, was made the following year. The title is a road sign on the expressway giving drivers a final chance to turn off for Brooklyn. A film version (1989) was directed by Uli Edel.

Last of the Mohicans, The. A romantic historical novel (1826) by the US writer James Fenimore Cooper (1789–1851), one of *The* LEATHER-STOCKING TALES. This tale is set in the hills and forests of northeastern North America at the time of the French and Indian Wars of the mid-18th century, and follows the adventures of Alice and Cora Munro, the frontiersman Natty Bumppo (also called Hawkeye), the unpleasant Huron leader Magua, and Chingachgook and his son Uncas, the last of the Mohicans – the rest of their tribe have been killed by the Hurons. At the end Uncas and Cora are forced to jump off a cliff to their deaths to escape their enemies.

Historically, Uncas was a 17th-century chief of the Mohegans, an Algonquian tribe of Connecticut. Cooper apparently confused the Mohegans with the Mahicans, an Algonquian confederacy that lived along the Hudson River.

There have been a number of film versions, the finest being those from 1936, with Randolph Scott as Hawkeye, and 1992, with Daniel Day-Lewis in the role.

Last Tango in Paris. A film (1972) co-written and directed by Italian director Bernardo Bertolucci (b.1940) about the sexual relationship that develops between Paul, a recently widowed American (played by Marlon Brando), and Jeanne, a young French woman (played by Maria Schneider), who is engaged to a New Wave film-maker, after they meet while flat-hunting in Paris. The affair ends with Paul's suicide. The title of the film, evoking the potent sexuality of the tango, underlines the physical passion of the couple's affair. The appearance of a pat of butter as an aid to sodomy was for many their abiding memory of the film.

Last Year in Marienbad (French title: *L'Année dernière à Marienbad*). A famously avant-garde film (1961) written by Alain Robbe-Grillet (b.1922) and directed by Alain Resnais (b.1922) in which a man apparently tries to persuade a woman that they know each other and may have had an affair. The truth of their relationship is left obscure: the suggestion is that they met 'last year in Marienbad' and planned to run away together.

Marienbad is the German name of Mariánské Lázne, a spa town in the western Czech Republic. It was once very fashionable, and visitors included Goethe, Chopin, Wagner, Ibsen, King Edward VII and Franz Kafka.

Laudon Symphony. The subtitle given by Haydn (1732–1809) to his symphony no 69 in C (before 1779), in honour of the Austrian field marshal Baron Gideon Ernest von Laudon (or Loudon; 1717–90). Laudon had distinguished himself in the Seven Years War (1756–63), defeating Frederick the Great of Prussia at Kunersdorf (1759) and Landshut (1760). A decade after Haydn's symphony Laudon was to capture Belgrade from the Turks (1789).

Laughing Cavalier, The. The popular name given to a well-known portrait (1624) of an unknown gallant by the Dutch painter Frans Hals (1581/5–1666). The painting, which is now in the Wallace Collection, London, is remarkable for the extraordinarily bold virtuosity of its brushwork. However, the popular title is something of a misnomer, as the subject is smiling rather than laughing.

Lavender and Old Lace. *See* ARSENIC AND OLD LACE.

Lavender Hill Mob, The. A sparkling film comedy (1951) from Ealing Studios, written by T.E.B. Clarke and directed by Charles Crichton, about a mild-mannered civil servant who decides to use his inside knowledge of bullion transport to steal a million pounds' worth of gold and then spirit it out of the country after melting it down into miniature Eiffel Towers.

The ludicrous notion that such a retiring, dull individual could pull off this breathtaking crime is underlined by the film's title, which cheekily conveys the unlikelihood of hardened criminals hailing from such a respectable part of London as Lavender Hill. The film stars Alec Guinness as the criminal mastermind, and Stanley Holloway as his right-hand man.

Lawrence of Arabia. *See* *SEVEN PILLARS OF WISDOM, THE*.

Lay of the Last Minstrel. A long narrative poem by Sir Walter Scott (1771–1832), published in 1805. The 'last minstrel' of the title is the narrator of the romantic and violent tale set in the Scottish Borders in the 16th century, in which Baron Henry of Cranstown woos 'the flower of Teviot', Lady Margaret of Bransome Hall. A 'lay' is an old word for a ballad.

Scott had previously mourned the passing of the art of the Border minstrels, and tried to preserve their heritage in the three volumes of his *Minstrelsy of the Scottish Border* (1802–3). Byron for one was not impressed:

> Thus Lays of Minstrels – may they be the last! –
> On half-strung harps whine mournful to the blast.
>
> BYRON: *English Bards and Scotch Reviewers* (1809)

See also *LAND OF THE MOUNTAIN AND THE FLOOD*.

Leatherstocking Tales, The. A series of five novels (1823–40) by the US writer James Fenimore Cooper (1789–1851), all featuring the frontiersman Natty Bumppo, a supremely capable woodsman, who is nicknamed Leatherstocking because of the long deerskin leggings he wears. The novels (not written in plot order) follow his career from youth till death. In plot order, with the names by which he is known in each, they are:

The Deerslayer (1841): Bumppo or Deerslayer

The LAST OF THE MOHICANS (1826): Hawkeye

The Pathfinder (1840): Pathfinder

The Pioneers (1823): Natty Bumppo or Leather-Stocking

The Prairie (1827): the trapper

There is a one-volume abridgement of the series by Allan Nevins, entitled *The Leatherstocking Saga* (1954). The name Hawkeye was adopted by one of the characters in the film *M*A*S*H*.

Leaves of Grass. The title given to successive editions of his ever-thicker collected poems by the US poet Walt Whitman (1819–92). The first edition (1855) was published anonymously, and only contained twelve poems. The last edition in which the author had a hand was the ninth, or 'deathbed' edition (1892). The title suggests the author's fervent celebrations of fecundity and multiplicity, the cycle of nature and of the universe.

> Walt's great poems are really huge fat tomb-plants, great rank graveyard growths.
>
> All that false exuberance. All those lists of things boiled in one pudding-cloth! No, no!
>
> D.H. LAWRENCE: *Studies in Classic American Literature* (1924), 'Whitman'

Lebewohl, Das (German, 'the farewell'). The title given to the piano sonata in E flat, opus 81a (1809), by Beethoven (1770–1827), from the name of the first of the three movements, which are '*Das Lebewohl*' ('the farewell'), '*Die Abwesenheit*' ('the absence') and '*Das Wiedersehen*' ('the return'). The work was dedicated to the Austrian Archduke Rudolf, who was forced to flee Vienna during the occupation of the city by Napoleon's troops. It is therefore somewhat ironic that the sonata is often given the French title *Les Adieux* ('the farewells').

Leningrad Symphony. The title given to the symphony no 7 by Dmitri Shostakovich (1906–75), which the composer wrote in 1941–2, during the German siege of Leningrad (St Petersburg). The Nazis were determined to obliterate Shostakovich's native city, as noted in a directive from General Walter Warlimont: 'The Führer has decided to raze the city of St Petersburg from the face of the earth. After the defeat of Soviet Russia there will be not the slightest reason for the future existence of this large city.' The German attack began in August 1941. As well as working on his symphony, Shostakovich joined the Leningrad fire brigade. At first the authorities requested that he leave the city, along with the rest of Leningrad's cultural elite, but Shostakovich refused until 29 September, when he was ordered to go. He left on 1 October, taking his unfinished score with him. Through that winter hundreds of thousands died in the besieged city, as Shostakovich worked to complete his symphony. The first performance took place on 5 March 1942 in Kuibyshev, but the first performance in Leningrad itself had to wait until 9 August 1942, when the starving remnants of the Leningrad Radio Orchestra, joined by Red Army musicians, gave a broadcast concert. Along the front line around the city, speakers were mounted to direct the defiant music towards the enemy positions.

> To the historic confrontation now taking place between reason and obscurantism, culture and barbarity, light and darkness. I dedicate my Seventh Symphony to our struggle against fascism, to our coming victory and to my native city of Leningrad.
>
> DMITRI SHOSTAKOVICH: dedication of the *Leningrad Symphony* (1942)

The siege of Leningrad was to continue until January 1944, resulting in over one million deaths from cold, famine and aerial bombardment.

Léonore. A play by Jean-Nicolas Bouilly (1763–1842), which provided the basis for a number of operas, most of which carry the subtitle 'married love': *Léonore, ou l'Amour conjugal* (1798) by Pierre Gaveaux (1761–1825); *Leonora ossia l'amore coniugale* (1804) by Ferdinando Paer (1771–1839); *L'Amor conjugale* (1805) by Johann Mayr (1763–1845); and, most famously, *Fidelio oder Die eheliche Liebe* (1805) by Beethoven (1770–1827). Leonore, the heroine, disguises herself as a young man, Fidelio (meaning 'the faithful one'), in order to rescue her husband, a political prisoner. The plot belongs to the genre of 'rescue opera', which became popular following the French Revolution (Bouilly himself wrote the libretto to the most popular rescue opera of its day, Cherubini's *Les Deux Journées*, first performed in 1800, and known in English-speaking countries as *The Water Carrier*). Beethoven notably struggled to get his opera right, going through three versions (1805, 1806, 1814); he referred to it as 'My crown of martyrdom'. Three rejected early overtures for the opera carry the title *Leonore*, and are often played as separate pieces. In 1952 the Swiss composer Rolf Liebermann (1910–99) updated the story in his opera *Leonore 40/45*, which has a libretto by Heinrich Strobel. It is set in France during the Second World War, and concerns the love of a French girl for a German soldier, who deserts, and with whom she is reunited at the end of the war. The English composer Elisabeth Lutyens (1906–84) wrote a chamber opera called *Infidelio* (1956).

Leopard, The. (Italian title: *Il Gattopardo*). A novel (1958; English translation 1960) by Giuseppe di Lampedusa (1896–1957), Duke of Palma and Prince of Lampedusa. It is set in Sicily, to which in May 1860 Giuseppe Garibaldi (1807–82) sailed with 1000 volunteers to win the island from the Bourbons. The narrative, in the form of a series of situations and character studies, describes the reactions to historical events of Fabrizio, Prince of Salina, and the Salina family between then and 1910, as the power of the aristocracy dwindles. The leopard is the family motif, which appears as the centrepiece of a vaulted ceiling in the family convent and, at the book's end, 'in red thread' on the border of a towel. The author died of cancer a week after the manuscript had been rejected by the house of Mondadori. He left instructions that his family should pursue publication, and the novel appeared under the imprint of Feltrinelli, becoming the best-selling and most widely translated 20th-century Italian novel.

> If we want things to stay as they are, things will have to change.
>
> *The Leopard*

A lavish film (1963) based on the book was directed by Luchino Visconti, himself a Marxist ex-aristocrat. The prince was played by Burt Lancaster, who said he based his character on that of the director.

Let's Talk Strine. A 'lexicon of modern Strine [Australian] usage' (1965) by Professor Afferbeck Lauder (Alistair Morrison), in which the clipped tones of Australian speech are spelled out phonetically, for example: 'Fried eye car nelpew' translates as 'I'm afraid I can't help you', 'Hacker chufa get?' as 'How could you forget?', and 'Nwotsa taller bat?' as 'Now what's that all about?' Afferbeck Lauder, the author, turns out to translate as 'alphabetical order'; he is 'Professor of Strine Studies, University of Sinny; Fellow of the Yarnurdov Foundation'. Another volume, *Nose Tone Unturned*, appeared in 1966. *See also* *FRAFFLY WELL SPOKEN*; *NO TURN UNSTONED*.

Leviathan. A seminal treatise (1651) on political theory by Thomas Hobbes (1588–1679), subtitled 'the Matter, Form, and Power of a Commonwealth, Ecclesiastical and Civil'. In it Hobbes justifies absolute monarchy as the guarantor of peace, without which man's life is 'nasty, brutish and short'. Hobbes characterizes the absolute state as Leviathan:

> By art is created that great Leviathan, called a commonwealth or state, (in Latin *civitas*) which is but an artificial man … and in which, the sovereignty is an artificial soul.
>
> *Leviathan*, Introduction

In the frontispiece of the book is an engraving of a crowned giant, representing the absolute power of the monarch, his body made up of lots of little figures, representing the individuals who make up the state.

> I have set forth the nature of man (whose pride and other passions have compelled him to submit himself to Government) together with the great power of his Governor, whom I compared to Leviathan, taking that comparison out of the two last verses of the one and fortieth of Job; where God having set forth the great power of Leviathan, called him King of the Proud.
>
> *Leviathan*, Part II, chapter xxviii

The giant creature Leviathan appears in the Bible not only in Job 41:1, but also Psalm 74:14, Psalm 104:26 and Isaiah 27:1. In addition, in rabbinical tradition Leviathan seduces Eve in its male incarnation of Samael, and Adam in its female incarnation of Lilith. The name itself is probably from Hebrew *lawo*, 'to twist', 'to writhe', with *tan* (only used in the plural, *tannīm*, from Arabic *tinīn*, 'dragon'), which may indicate either a whale or a sea serpent, or possibly even a crocodile, but in later phrase and fable it is generally treated as a great whale. He appears in *PARADISE LOST*, although Milton gives the giant marine mammal gills (and even Herman Melville, an expert on the whale, described Leviathan as a fish; *see KRAKEN WAKES, THE*):

> There Leviathan
> Hugest of living creatures, on the deep
> Stretched like a promontory sleeps or swims,
> And seems a moving land, and at his gills
> Draws in, and at his trunk spouts out a sea.
>
> JOHN MILTON: *Paradise Lost* (1667), Book VII

Milton had presumably heard that whales spout water, and mistakenly assumed that they did it through a trunk like the elephant.

Leviathan continues to cast his spell on the imagination:

> This is the end of running on the waves;
> We are poured out like water. Who will dance
> The mast-lashed master of Leviathans
> Up from this field of Quakers in their unstoned graves?
>
> ROBERT LOWELL: 'The Quaker Graveyard in Nantucket', *Poems 1938–1949* (1950). Nantucket in Massachusetts was formerly an important base for whalers.

> This is the black sea-brute bulling through wave-wrack,
> Ancient as ocean's shifting hills.
>
> W.S. MERWIN: 'Leviathan' (1956)

LETTERS, SYMBOLS AND INITIALS

See also LONG TITLES (panel, p.264); MONOSYLLABIC TITLES (panel, pp.305–6).

!!!, a book (1881) by George Hughes Hepworth

?, a book (1925) by Sir Walter Newman Flower

&, a collection of verse (1925) by the US poet e.e. cummings

AC/DC, a play (1970) by Heathcote Williams

'C', a novel (1924) by Maurice Baring

D.O.A., a thriller film (1950), the initials standing for 'dead on arrival'

E.T., a science-fiction film (1982)

G, a novel (1972) by John Berger

'G' Men, a film (1935) about a lawyer who becomes an FBI agent ('G' Man)

LHOOQ, Marcel Duchamp's title for his moustachioed *MONA LISA* (1920)

K2, an adventure film (1991) featuring the world's second highest mountain

L.627, a French police thriller film (1992)

M, a classic film (1931) by Fritz Lang

The Story of O, an anonymous pornographic classic

P.J., a private-eye film (1967)

Q, a horror film (1982)

Q&A, a crime film (1990) written and directed by Sidney Lumet (the letters stand for 'questions and answers')

Q.B. VII, a novel (1970) by Leon Uris

S.F.W., a satirical movie (1994) about the media (the initials stand for 'so fucking what')

S.O.B., a comedy film (1981) directed by Blake Edwards (the initials stand for 'son of a bitch')

U and I, a book (1991) by the US novelist Nicholson Baker about his obsession with the novelist John Updike

V, a novel (1963) by Thomas Pynchon and a long poem (1985) by Tony Harrison

W, a psychological suspense film (1973)

MADAME X, a portrait (1884) by Sargent, plus several melodramatic films

Z, a film (1968) written and directed by Costa-Gavras about a political assassination

A Zed and Two Noughts, a film (1985) by Peter Greenaway

There is also an alphabetically titled series of crime thrillers by the US novelist Sue Grafton, starting in 1982 with *'A' is for Alibi* (1982) and in 1999 reaching *'O' is for Outlaw*. She plans to call the last in the series *'Z' is for Zero*.

LHOOQ. The letters inscribed beneath a reproduction of the *MONA LISA*, on whose upper lip a moustache has been drawn, on the front cover of a 1920 Dada manifesto by Marcel Duchamp (1887–1968) and Francis Picabia (1879–1953). If the letters are read in French, they sound like '*elle a chaud au cul*', which means 'she's got a hot arse'. Compare *OH, CALCUTTA!*

Liebestod (German, 'love-death'). The title usually given to Isolde's swooningly romantic death scene at the end of the third act of the opera *Tristan und Isolde* (1865) by Richard Wagner (1813–83), although Wagner himself applied it to the love duet in the second act. Love and death are associated throughout the work, for example, in the substitution of the love potion for the poisonous draft at the end of the first act.

> To me *Tristan* is and remains a wonder! I shall never be able to understand how I could have written anything like it.
>
> RICHARD WAGNER: quoted in Headington, *The Bodley Head History of Western Music* (1974)

Lied von der Erde, Das (German, *The Song of the Earth*). A symphonic song cycle by Gustav Mahler (1860–1911), completed in 1908 and described by him as 'A Symphony for Contralto (or Baritone), Tenor and Orchestra'. The words to the songs are from six Chinese poems translated into German by Hans Bethge, with some alterations by Mahler. Although Mahler called the work a symphony he left it unnumbered; in 1907 his fatal heart disease had been diagnosed, and he was superstitiously aware that Beethoven, Schubert, Bruckner and Dvořák had all died after completing their ninth symphonies. Mahler did go on to write a symphony no 9 (asserting to the Fates that it was 'really the tenth'), and this was described by Alban Berg as

> The expression of exceptional love for this earth, the longing to live in peace in it, to enjoy nature to its depths before death comes, for he comes irresistibly.

Mahler was still working on his symphony no 10 at the time of his death. He did not live to hear the first performances of either *Das Lied von der Erde* or the ninth symphony.

Life and Death of Colonel Blimp, The. A film (1943) written and directed by Michael Powell (1905–90) and Emeric Pressburger (1902–88) about the life of a British colonel from his early army days in the Boer War through to 1943, in the midst of the Second World War. Starring Roger Livesey as Colonel Blimp, the film was controversial in sending up the pomposity of a certain type of elderly senior officer, and consequently incurred the wrath of Prime Minister Winston Churchill, who feared it would damage wartime morale: he had its exportation banned and only relented two years later, by which time the film had enjoyed huge success with British audiences.

The 'Colonel Blimp' character was not original to the film but was derived from the cartoons of David Low in the *London Evening Standard*. He was a plump, pompous ex-officer who was rigidly and blindly opposed to anything new. Hence 'Colonel Blimp' or 'blimp' came to be used of a military officer, or any person with stuffy or reactionary views.

The word 'blimp' was originally applied to an observation balloon in the First World War, the coinage apparently being based on *limp*, perhaps from the code name *Type B-limp*.

Life for the Tsar, A. An opera by the Russian composer Mikhail Ivanovich Glinka (1804–57), with a libretto by Baron Georgy Federovich Rosen, first performed in 1836. The story, set in 1612, tells how a Russian peasant, Ivan Susanin, is forced by invading Poles to act as a guide, but

Susanin leads them on a false trail, thus saving the first Romanov tsar, but at the cost of his own life. The opera was originally entitled *Ivan Susanin*, but the title was changed after Tsar Nicholas I (a Romanov) attended a rehearsal and gave permission for the opera to be dedicated to him. The piece established the Russian nationalist school of music, and opened every new opera season in both St Petersburg and Moscow until the 1917 Revolution. After the Revolution both title and text proved embarrassing to the Communist regime; the title reverted to *Ivan Susanin*, and in 1939 S.M. Gorodetsky revised the libretto, replacing the tsar with the nationalist hero Minin.

Light in August. A novel (1932) by William Faulkner (1898–1962), following the tragic career of the mixed-race central character, Joe Christmas. Faulkner's working title had been *Dark House*, but when he heard his wife comment on the unique quality of the light in August in the American South he was taken with the phrase, and used it as the final title.

Lilies of the Field. A film (1963) for which Sidney Poitier won an Oscar for his role as a black worker who helps some nuns to build a chapel.

> Consider the lilies of the field, how they grow; they toil not, neither do they spin:
> And yet I say unto you, That even Solomon in all his glory was not arrayed like one of these.
>
> St Matthew, 6:26–27

The same passage also inspired two novels, both entitled *Consider the Lilies* and both published in 1968, by Iain Crichton Smith (b.1928) and Auberon Waugh (1939–2001).

'Lilliburlero'. The refrain (and now the title) of a piece of political doggerel originally entitled 'A New Song', written by Lord Thomas Wharton (1648–1715) in 1687. It satirized Irish Catholics at the time of the appointment of General Talbot, the earl of Tyrconnel, as lord lieutenant of Ireland in 1687, and the rhyme influenced popular sentiment during the Glorious Revolution of 1688, by which the Catholic James II was replaced by the Protestant William of Orange. The orange lily was the symbol of William's Irish supporters, and the words '*Lilli burlero bullenala*' are said to be a corruption of the Irish *An lile ba léir é ba linn an lá* ('the lily was triumphant and we won the day').

> Ho, Brother Teague, dost hear de Decree?
> Lilli burlero bullena-la,
> Dat we shall have a new Debity [deputy],
> Lilli burlero bullena-la.
>
> THOMAS WHARTON: *Poems on Affairs of State* (1704), 'A New Song'

'Lilliburlero' was set to a 1686 tune called 'Quick Step', which itself has been traced to a book of psalm tunes published in Antwerp in 1540. When set by Purcell in 1689 it was referred to as 'A New Irish Tune', and now both tune and verse are referred to as 'Lilluburlero'. The tune is now used as the call sign of the BBC World Service.

> My uncle Toby would never offer to answer this by any other kind of argument, than that of whistling half a dozen bars of Lilliburlero.
>
> LAURENCE STERNE: *Tristram Shandy* (1759–67), book I, chapter 21

'Linz' Symphony. The nickname of the symphony no 36 in C, K425, by Mozart (1756–91). Mozart wrote the piece in 1783 while staying at the house of Count Thun in the city of Linz, Upper Austria, and the first performance also took place there.

Lion in Winter, The. A film (1968) adapted from his own play by James Goldman (b.1927). The 'lion' is the ageing Henry II (Peter O'Toole), king of England and ruler of the vast Angevin empire, stretching from the River Tweed to the Pyrenees, who at Christmas in 1183 holds a family reunion with his estranged sons (including the future kings Richard I and John) and his wife, Eleanor of Aquitaine (Katherine Hebpurn). Considerable fireworks result. The title should not be confused with a 1962 French film, *A Monkey in Winter*, a comedy starring Jean Gabin and Jean-Paul Belmondo.

Lion, the Witch and the Wardrobe, The. A fantasy (1950) for children by C.S. Lewis (1898–1963), the first of seven books about the mythical land of Narnia. The lion, known as Aslan, is a Christ-like figure. The witch has held Narnia in thrall for a hundred years. The wardrobe is the means through which four children from our world enter Narnia. A televised version was made in 1963, followed by a re-creation in the series *Chronicles of Narnia* (1988–90).

Little Foxes, The. A play (1939) by the US playwright Lillian Hellman (1907–84) about the machinations of the ambitious Regina Hubbard, who is prepared to sacrifice all those around her in the pursuit of material gain. The title comes from the Bible:

THE LITTLE BOOK OF ...

A title formula popularized in the later 1990s by Paul Wilson's *The Little Book of Calm* (1996), a pocket-sized guide to dealing with life's upsetting moments. It offers advice such as: 'Write down your worry', 'Breathe deeply', 'Avoid tense people' and 'Massage your forehead'. Other New-Age titles along these lines include *A Little Book of Eternal Wisdom*.

In 1998 Rohan Candappa published *The Little Book of Stress*, with the slogan 'Calm is for wimps. Get real. Get stressed.' It offers such advice as:

> Really tense up all your muscles
> Try to stay this way all day.
> If this proves impossible, you have yet
> again failed at a really simple task.

Other little books along these lines include *The Little Book of Bollocks* and *The Little Book of Farting*. In a somewhat larger, but still small, format are to be found such earthy offerings as *The Big Book of Filth* (1999), *The Big Book of Being Rude* (2000) and *The Big Book of Bodily Functions* (2001). *See also* PUPPETRY OF THE PENIS; VAGINA MONOLOGUES, THE.

Take us the foxes, the little foxes, that spoil the vines; for our vines have tender grapes.

Song of Solomon 2:15

'Little Gidding'. *See* FOUR QUARTETS.

Little Red Book, The. The popular name of *Quotations from Chairman Mao*, Lin Biao's simplified and dogmatized version of the thoughts of Mao Zedong. The book was a vade mecum of the young zealots of the Red Guard, who would wave it and quote it *en masse* during China's Cultural Revolution (1966–9). The popular name of the work simply described the book's physical form. Some 800 million copies of the booklet were said to have been sold or distributed from

1966 to 1971, and possession became virtually mandatory in China.

A rather different work appeared in Britain in 1971, under the title *The Little Red Schoolbook.* This gave frank advice to schoolchildren on sex and drugs as well as routine matters such as lessons and homework. At the time it was condemned as obscene or at best subversive. It was a translation of a Danish book, *Den lille røde bog for skoleelever* by Søren Hansen and Jesper Jensen, published in 1969.

'Little Russian' Symphony. The nickname of the symphony no 2, opus 17 (1873), by Tchaikovsky (1840–93), so named not because of its scale but because of its use of Ukrainian folk melodies – 'Little Russia' being an old Russian term for the Ukraine.

Little Shop of Horrors. A cult horror movie (1960) directed by Roger Corman (b.1926) about a carnivorous talking plant that quickly outgrows the flower shop of its dimwitted owner and becomes a voracious man-eating monster. The success of Corman's original inspired a stage musical with the same title in the 1980s and an inferior film remake in 1986.

Liver is the Cock's Comb, The. An immensely vibrant and colourful painting (1944) by the Armenian-American painter Arshile Gorky (1904–48). The canvas is crowded with the innovative biomorphic forms that constantly poured from Gorky's imagination, and among these one can certainly detect traces of poultry. Gorky's other intriguing titles include *The Diary of a Seducer* and *How My Mother's Embroidered Apron Unfolds in My Life.* One critic characterized Gorky's work as follows:

> Amid strange, soft organisms and insidious slits and smudges, petals hint of claws in a jungle of limp bodily parts, intestinal fists, pudenda, multiple limb folds.
>
> HAROLD ROSENBERG: in *Horizon*, 1962

'London' Symphony. The nickname of the symphony no 104 in D by Haydn (1732–1809), first performed in 1795 in London. It was the last of Haydn's twelve 'SALOMON' SYMPHONIES – all of which were in fact written for London, and hence are often collectively known as the 'London' Symphonies – and his last symphony altogether. Ralph Vaughan Williams (1872–1958) gave the title *London Symphony* to his symphony no 2 (1914, revised frequently thereafter), which includes various sounds of London, such as street cries, the chimes of Big Ben and the jingling of hansom cabs.

LONDON PLACES

See also STREETS (panel, pp.436–7).

A Chaste Maid in Cheapside, a comedy (1613) by Thomas Middleton

BARTHOLOMEW FAIR, a comedy (1614) by Ben Jonson

Old St Paul's, a historical novel (1841) by Harrison Ainsworth

COCKAIGNE, a concert overture (1901) by Edward Elgar, subtitled 'In London Town' (in this context 'Cockaigne' is related to 'Cockney')

The Westminster Alice (1902), a non-fiction work by Saki (H.H. Munro)

NAPOLEON OF NOTTING HILL, a novel (1904) by G.K. Chesterton

Handel in the Strand, an orchestral piece (1930) by Percy Grainger

Waterloo Bridge, a classic weepy film melodrama (1931, remake 1940)

HANGOVER SQUARE, a thriller (1941) by Patrick Hamilton, the title punning on Hanover Square in London

PASSPORT TO PIMLICO, a film comedy (1948)

The LAVENDER HILL MOB, a film comedy (1951)

The Ballad of Peckham Rye, a novel (1960) by Muriel Spark

84 CHARING CROSS ROAD, a correspondence between bibliophiles

METROLAND, a novel (1980) by Julian Barnes

London Fields, a novel (1989) by Martin Amis

The Wimbledon Poisoner, a novel (1990) by Nigel Williams

They Came From SW19, a novel (1992) by Nigel Williams

Dan Leno and the Limehouse Golem, a novel (1994) by Peter Ackroyd

Notting Hill, a romantic film comedy (1999)

Loneliness of the Long-Distance Runner, The. A novella (1959) by Alan Sillitoe (b.1928), published as the title piece of his first collection of stories. The long-distance runner is the protagonist and narrator, a lad in Borstal because of a 'bakery job', carrying on a running battle of wits with the governor, who sees him purely as a means to win the inter-institution cross-country race. Smith, as he is called, enters the sports ground for the final lap far ahead of his nearest rival, and then runs on the spot until he is overtaken. A compelling film version (1962) was directed by Tony Richardson and starred Tom Courtenay and Michael Redgrave.

Long Dark Tea-Time of the Soul, The. A humorous fantasy novel (1988) by Douglas Adams (1952–2001), in which 'holistic' private eye Dirk Gently attempts to solve the mysteries of the universe. An explosion at Heathrow Airport, London, is designated an Act of God – but, wonders, Dirk,

> What God would be hanging around Terminal Two of Heathrow Airport trying to catch the 15.37 to Oslo?

The title is an understated English swipe at the phrase 'the dark night of the soul', originally the title of a poem (Spanish: *Noche oscura del alma*) by St John of the Cross (1542–91), and subsequently associated with the experiences of other mystics. *The Oxford Dictionary of Quotations* (1999 edn) suggests that the phrase was actually introduced by David Lewis, the translator of St John of the Cross's *Complete Works* (1864).

Long Day's Journey into Night. A Pulitzer Prize-winning play (1956) by the US dramatist Eugene O'Neill (1888–1953). It depicts the four self-destructive members of the Tyrone family, who variously seek salvation in drugs and drink. The partly autobiographical work was written by O'Neill in the early 1940s but not produced until after his death. Its title reflects the time sequence within the play, which begins at 8.30 in the morning and ends around midnight on the same hot August day in 1912.

> A play of old sorrow, written in tears and blood.
>
> EUGENE O'NEILL: of *Long Day's Journey into Night*

Long Good Friday, The. A highly regarded film (1980), written by Barrie Keeffe, about a London gangster boss who embarks on a mission to find out who is murdering his henchmen. Starring Bob Hoskins as crime boss Harold and Helen Mirren as his wife Victoria, the film follows what happens in the course of a Good Friday in the early 1980s after Harold is given just 24 hours by his Mafia contacts to solve the mystery or risk a major deal with them falling through.

LONG TITLES

See also LETTERS, SYMBOLS AND INITIALS (panel, pp.255–6) MONOSYLLABIC TITLES (panel, pp.305–6).

Hepatopancreatoduodenectomy, a surgical handbook (1996) on the excision of liver, pancreas and duodenum, edited by F. Hanyu

The Tragedy of CHRONONHOTONTHOLOGOS, a burlesque (1734) by Henry Carey

The KANDY-KOLORED TANGERINE-FLAKE STREAMLINE BABY, a collection of journalism (1965) by Tom Wolfe

EVERYTHING YOU ALWAYS WANTED TO KNOW ABOUT SEX (BUT WERE AFRAID TO ASK), a Woody Allen film (1972)

The BLESSED VIRGIN CHASTISES THE INFANT JESUS BEFORE THREE WITNESSES: A.B., P.E. AND THE ARTIST, a painting (1926) by Max Ernst

Oh Dad, Poor Dad, Mamma's Hung You in the Closet and I'm Feelin' So Sad, a black comedy film (1966), based on a play by Arthur Kopit

NOURISHMENT: SLOW AND DIFFICULT ABSORPTION OF 600 GRAMMES OF MINCED MEAT WHICH DISTURB THE USUAL DIGESTIVE OPERATIONS, a piece of body art (1971) by Gina Pane

I Want to Spend The Rest of My Life Everywhere, With Everyone, One to One, Always, Forever, Now, a book (1997) by Britartist Damien Hurst

The Adventures of Philip on His Way Through the World, Showing Who Robbed Him, Who Helped Him, and Who Passed Him by, a novel (1861–2) by W.M. Thackeray

Joseph Stalin Gazing Enigmatically at the Body of V.I. Lenin as it Lies in State in Moscow in the Style of Jackson Pollock, a painting (1979) by Art and Language (Michael Baldwin and Mel Ramsden)

The TORTOISE RECALLING THE DRONE OF THE HOLY NUMBERS AS THEY WERE REVEALED IN THE DREAMS OF THE WHIRLWIND AND THE OBSIDIAN GONG, ILLUMINATED BY THE SAWMILL, THE GREEN SAWTOOTH OCELOT, AND THE HIGH-TENSION LINE STEPDOWN TRANSFORMER, a music work (1964) by LaMonte Young

Long Hot Summer, The. A film (1958) set in Mississippi, and based on the story *The Hamlet* (1928) by William Faulkner (1897–1962), in which one of the chapters is headed 'The Long Summer'. Subsequently, the phrase 'long hot summer' came to denote a period of civil unrest, such as that in the summer of 1967 in the United States, when riots erupted among underprivileged blacks in several cities.

Long Walk to Freedom. The autobiography (1994) of Nelson Mandela (b.1918), the first black president of South Africa, who, under the apartheid regime, had been jailed for three decades, largely on Robben Island. The title is said to have been inspired by the words in 'From Lucknow to Tripuri', an essay (1939) by Jawaharlal Nehru (1889–1964), who was to become the first prime minister of independent India:

> There is no easy walk-over to freedom anywhere, and many of us will have to pass through the valley of the shadow again and again before we reach the mountain-tops of our desire.

Look Back In Anger. A play (1956) by John Osborne (1929–94) about a young man's dissatisfaction with his marriage, his life and the world in general, in particular the hidebound conventions of the older generation. Jimmy Porter, the play's protagonist, represented the restless, frustrated youth of the immediate postwar generation, and the controversial play helped to establish Osborne as the archetypal 'Angry Young Man'. The title of the play enjoyed a new lease of life in the 1990s in the title, 'Don't Look Back In Anger', of a hit song by the British rock band Oasis.

> I doubt if I could love anyone who did not wish to see *Look Back in Anger*. It is the best play of its decade.
>
> KENNETH TYNAN

Look Homeward, Angel. A semi-autobiographical first novel (1929) by the US writer Thomas Wolfe about the childhood and youth of Eugene Gant. His publishers turned down earlier titles such as *O Lost* and *They Are Strange* and *They Are Lost*. Eventually his editor Maxwell Perkins, who famously knocked Wolfe's vast, messy manuscript into shape, came up with the final title, from a line of Milton's:

> Look homeward, angel now, and melt with ruth.
>
> JOHN MILTON: 'Lycidas' (1638)

Lord Jim. A novel (1900) by Joseph Conrad (1857–1924). Jim (we never know his second name) is a young ship's officer who leaps overboard in a crisis to save himself. In order to expiate his guilt, he wanders from place to place in the East, finally settling in a remote part of Malaya, where his integrity earns him the respect he has craved. A visitor asks:

> 'What's his name? Jim! Jim! That's not enough for a man's name.'
> 'They call him,' said Cornelius, scornfully, 'Tuan Jim here. As you may say Lord Jim.'

A film version (1964) was directed by Richard Brooks.

Lord of the Flies. A novel (1954) by William Golding (1911–93), illustrating how internal and external pressures can cause a society to disintegrate, exemplified in this case by a group of schoolboys marooned on a tropical island. The title represents one interpretation of the Hebrew term for Beelzebub, who appears in 2 Kings 1:2 as Baal-zebub, a Caananite god whose shrine is at Ekron, and in the New Testament as 'prince of the devils' (Matthew 12:24). In the story itself, the name 'Lord of the Flies' is applied to the fly-infested pig's head that the boys impale on a stick. There have been two film versions (1963 and 1990), the first directed by Peter Brook.

Lord of the Isles, The. A long narrative poem by Sir Walter Scott (1771–1832), published in 1815. The work is set at the time of the Scottish Wars of Independence in the early 14th century. Lord Ronald is the Lord of the Isles, beloved of the lovelorn Edith of Lorn. The title 'Lord of the Isles' is an ancient one. It was originally held by the Norse rulers of the Hebrides, and then passed to the Macdonalds, whose seat was in Islay. Although notionally vassals of the Scottish kings, the Lords of the Isles were in fact supreme in their fiefdom. James IV ended this situation in 1493, when he forfeited the title, which later become one of the titles borne by princes of Wales.

Lord of the Rings, The. The title of a trilogy of fantasy novels (1954–5) by J.R.R. Tolkien (1892–1973). The trilogy – comprising *The Fellowship of the Ring*, *The Two Towers* and *The Return of the King* – comprise a sequel to *The HOBBIT* (1937). 'The Lord of the Rings' is also the title of Sauron the Great, the ruler of Middle Earth, whose power depends on the possession of certain rings, especially the One Ring, the Ruling Ring and the Master Ring, which he has lost many years before and which he now seeks to regain to give him strength to cover the land in a second darkness.

The 1978 animated film of the trilogy was disappointing. A much more spectacular live-action film version of *The Fellowship of the Ring* was released in 2001, with sequels to come.

'Lost Leader, The'. A poem by Robert Browning (1812–89), published in 1845. The first line, 'Just for a handful of silver he left us', suggests Judas's betrayal of Christ. In fact the 'Lost Leader' of the title was Wordsworth, who had, over the years, shifted from republican radicalism to reactionary conservatism:

Shakespeare was of us, Milton was for us,
Burns, Shelley, were with us, – they watch from their graves!
He alone breaks from the van and the freemen,
– He alone sinks to the rear and the slaves!

Lost Weekend, The. A film (1945) adapted by director Billy Wilder and Charles Brackett from a 1944 novel by Charles R. Jackson about a struggling writer who surrenders to alcoholism one weekend after he falls victim to writer's block. Starring Ray Milland, the film caused a considerable stir: representatives of the liquor industry offered $5 million for the negative, so that it could be destroyed, fearing the effect it would have upon sales of alcohol, and members of the temperance movement also tried to have the film stopped, suspecting that it might actually encourage people to drink. The novel and film popularized the phrase 'lost weekend' for any period spent in dissolute living or drunkenness.

Lost World, The. An adventure novel (1912) by Sir Arthur Conan Doyle (1859–1930), in which the irascible and bearded Professor Challenger, accompanied by the explorer Lord John Roxton and the young newspaper reporter Edward Malone, goes in search of the 'Lost World' where he believes dinosaurs and ape-men still survive. The 'Lost World' is an imaginary volcanic plateau north of the Amazon in Brazil, but is based on the real cliff-girt plateaux, such as Mount Roraima, that stud the rainforests on the Venezuela–Brazil–Guyana border. In the novel the remote plateau has been given the name Maple White Land, after its discoverer, an artist and poet from Detroit, Michigan. The first, silent, film version (1925) deployed special effects that were remarkable for their time; the 1960 remake was derisory. The second of the *JURASSIC PARK* films, on a similar theme, was also entitled *The Lost World* (1997), as was a 2001 TV adaptation of Conan Doyle's story.

'Lotos-Eaters, The'. A poem by Alfred, Lord Tennyson (1809–92), published in 1832. In Homeric legend the lotus-eaters or *lotophagi* were people who 'ate of the lotus tree'. This was *Zizyphus lotus*, a shrub of the buckthorn family (*Rhamnaceae*) whose fruits were made into a wine thought to induce contentment. The lotus-eaters forgot their friends and homes and lost all desire of returning to their native country, their only wish being to live in idleness in Lotus-land (*ODYSSEY*, xi). Some of Odysseus's men fell prey to the lotus, and Tennyson has them sing:

> Surely, surely, slumber is more sweet than toil, the shore
> Than labour in the deep mid-ocean, wind and wave and oar;
> Oh rest ye, brother mariners, we will not wander more.
>
> Choric song, stanza 8

Tennyson's poem inspired a choral work of the same name (1892) by Hubert Parry (1848–1918).

Loudon Symphony. *See* *LAUDON SYMPHONY*.

Love for or ***of Three Oranges*** (Russian title: *Lyubov k tryom apelsinam*). A comic opera by Sergei Prokofiev (1891–1953) with a text by the composer, first performed in 1921. The story is based on a 1761 comedy by Carlo Gozzi (1720–1806). The oranges of the title are taken into the desert by a prince; each contains a princess, two of whom die of thirst, but the third survives and is united with the prince.

Love in a Cold Climate. A light novel (1949) by Nancy Mitford (1904–73). The environment is that of the eccentric, impoverished, aristocratic society in which she was brought up. The novel was originally to be called 'Diversion'. The final title recalls the remark made by the poet Robert Southey (1774–1843) in a letter to his brother about Mary Wollstonecraft's letters from Sweden and Norway:

> She has made me in love with a cold climate, and frost and snow, with a northern moonlight.
>
> 28 April 1797

Love Is a Many-Splendored Thing. A novel (1952) by the Chinese-Belgian woman doctor, Han Suyin, the pen name of Elisabeth Rosalie Matthilde Clare Chou (b.1917), now known as Dr Elisabeth Comber. The story, which became the basis of a film in 1955, depicts the doomed relationship between a US journalist (played in the film by William Holden) and a Eurasian doctor (Jennifer Jones). Han Suyin disliked the film, which is remembered mainly for the Oscar-winning theme song. The title came originally from a poem by Francis Thompson (1859–1907):

> The angels keep their ancient places;
> Turn but a stone and start a wing!
> 'Tis ye, 'tis your estrangèd faces,

That miss the many-splendoured thing.

FRANCIS THOMPSON: 'The Kingdom of God' (1913)

Love of Three Oranges. *See* LOVE FOR THREE ORANGES.

Love on the Dole. The first novel (1933) by Walter Greenwood (1903–74), set in the industrial town of Salford, where he was brought up. For one man, an apprenticeship leads only to the dole queue (*see below*) and a life of poverty when his girlfriend becomes pregnant. For another, marriage is on the cards when he is made redundant, and he dies after being beaten up while participating in a mass protest. His fiancée, who has to support an out-of-work brother and father, chooses to be the mistress of a local businessman rather than plumb the depths of poverty. A film version (1941) was directed by John Baxter.

Since the National Insurance Act of 1911, the dole has been used as the everyday term for unemployment benefit; to be 'on the dole' is to be receiving this benefit. The word dole (from Old English *dāl*, 'share') originally meant 'portion allotted', 'charitable gift', 'alms'. From Saxon times the strips of land, especially of common meadow, distributed annually were called doles.

Love's Labour's Lost. A comedy (*c.*1594) by William Shakespeare (1564–1616). The somewhat slight plot is thought to be Shakespeare's own invention. The king of Navarre and three of his courtiers have sworn to spend three years studying, away from the company of women, to defeat 'the huge army of the world's desires':

Our court shall be a little Academe,
Still and contemplative in living art.

I.i

However, the arrival of the princess of France and three of her ladies soon leads the would-be celibates to break their vows, and embark on some elaborate, disguised wooing. News of the death of the princess's father brings the fun to an end, the ladies leaving the gentlemen for a year, during which time the men must perform various penances. But perhaps the labour they have put into their love will not be entirely lost. The phrase 'labour of love' comes from the Bible:

Remembering without ceasing your work of faith, and labour of love,
and patience of hope in our Lord Jesus Christ, in the sight of God
and our Father.

Thessalonians 1:3

Kenneth Branagh's film version (2000) updates the setting to 1939, and incorporates a number of songs from Hollywood musicals.

In his *Palladis Tamia: Wits Treasury* (1598) Francis Meres (1565–1647) lists among Shakespeare's works a play called *Loue Labours Wonne*; this has not been identified; although it was formerly believed to be an alternative title for *ALL'S WELL THAT ENDS WELL*, the latter is now thought to have been written several years after the publication of Meres's work.

'Love Song of J. Alfred Prufrock, The'. A poem by T.S. Eliot (1888–1965), first published in 1915. It depicts the doubts and sexual inhibitions of a shy Bostonian by the name of J. Alfred Prufrock. Eliot took the name of his celebrated central character from that of a St Louis furniture company.

> I grow old ... I grow old ...
> I shall wear the bottoms of my trousers rolled ...
> I have heard the mermaids singing, each to each.
> I do not think that they will sing for me.
>
> T.S. ELIOT: 'The Love Song of J. Alfred Prufrock'

Lucia di Lammermoor. *See BRIDE OF LAMMERMOOR, THE.*

Lucky Jim. The first novel (1954) by Kingsley Amis (1922–95), recording the tribulations of Jim Dixon, a lecturer in history at a new university. 'Lucky' is in turn a justifiable and an ironic description of his fortunes. Although it was not the first of the wave of novels that gave their authors the sobriquet 'Angry Young Men', it was the one that did most to suggest the existence of such a movement. The title comes from a US song by Frederick Bowen and Charles Horwitz, which tells how a man waited for his childhood friend to die so that he could marry the girl they both wanted. Unhappily married, however, he wishes he were also dead: 'Oh, lucky Jim, how I envy him.' A film version (1957) was directed by John Boulting, with Ian Carmichael in the title role.

Lulu. The central character in a duet of plays, *The Earth Spirit*, originally *Erdgeist* (1895), and *Pandora's Box*, originally *Die Büchse der Pandora* (1903), by the German playwright Frank Wedekind (1864–1918). The plays are about the sexual career of Lulu, a dancer, and although her uninhibited enjoyment of sex is essentially innocent, her character has gone down as a symbol of feminine guile and eroticism, whose licentiousness proves fatal to the men who fall for her. At the close of the second play she is reduced to working as a prostitute in London and meets her end at the hands of Jack the Ripper. The character was suggested to Wedekind by the women he met while he was working on a ballet for the Folies Bergères in Paris around the turn of the century. Her name was probably intended to recall that of the biblical Lilith, Adam's rebellious first wife.

The opera, also named *Lulu*, by Alban Berg (1885–1935) was based on Wedekind's two plays, and it was first performed in Zurich in 1937 in the original two-act form in which the composer had left it at the time of his death. The missing third act was supplied by the Viennese composer Friedrich Cerha (b.1926), and the full work finally emerged in Paris in 1979 under the baton of the French composer and conductor Pierre Boulez.

Lusiads, The (Portuguese title: *Os Lusíadas*). The great Portuguese epic poem about Vasco da Gama, by Luis de Camões (*c.*1524–80). The title refers to the Latin name for Portugal, Lusitania, itself named after its legendary founder Lusus.

Luxe, calme et volupté. A hedonistic painting of nude bathers on a beach by Henri Matisse (1869–1954), executed with a free pointillist technique at St Tropez in 1904–5. The title comes from the refrain of *Invitation au Voyage* by Charles Baudelaire (1821–67):

> *Là, tout n'est qu'ordre et beauté,*
> *Luxe, calme et volupté*
>
> ('There all is order and beauty,
> Luxury, calm and delight')

The painting was bought in 1905 by the painter Paul Signac (1863–1935), one of the originators of the pointillist technique. Another painter, Raoul Dufy (1877–1953), wrote in 1925:

> On looking at that picture I grasped all the new reasons for painting; the realism of the impressionists lost its charm for me as I contemplated the miracle of the imagination introduced into draughtsmanship and colour.

Matisse returned to the theme in 1907–8; in contrast to the still painterly *Le Luxe*, *Le Luxe II* is characterized by flat planes of colour and hard outlines.

M

M. A classic film (1931) by Fritz Lang, his first exercise using sound. A child murderer (played by Peter Lorre) is terrorizing Berlin, driving the citizenry to hysteria. The police are getting nowhere, so the underworld decides to take on the job of catching the killer. He is eventually identified because a witness has managed to put on his back the mark 'M' (for *Mörder*, 'murderer'). In 1951 Joseph Losey directed a remake, transferring the story to Los Angeles.

Mac Flecknoe. A mock epic (1682) by John Dryden (1631–1700), subtitled 'A Satyr upon the True-Blew-Protestant Poet, T.S.' Dryden's satire is very much *ad hominem*, 'T.S.' being Dryden's rival dramatist Thomas Shadwell (?1642–92). In the poem Shadwell is depicted as Mac (son of) Flecknoe: Richard Flecknoe was a minor poet and dramatist, who had died around 1678, and in Dryden's satire 'Mac Flecknoe' succeeds him as king of the realm of dull poetry:

> The rest to some faint meaning make pretence,
> But Shadwell never deviates into sense.

Shadwell had his revenge during the Glorious Revolution, following the deposition of the Catholic James II: in 1689 Dryden, who had earlier converted to Catholicism, was dismissed from the poet laureateship, and, as a 'True-Blew-Protestant', Shadwell succeeded him.

Madame Butterfly. An opera by Giacomo Puccini (1858–1924), first performed at La Scala, Milan, in 1904, with a libretto by Giuseppe

Giacosa and Luigi Illica based on David Belasco's play *Madame Butterfly* (1900), in turn taken from John Luther Long's short story so titled (1898), itself inspired by an actual event. Many opera buffs perversely insist on using the Italian title, *Madama Butterfly*. The scene is set in Nagasaki in the early 20th century. The young and pretty geisha Cio-Cio-San (Madame Butterfly) marries Lieutenant Pinkerton of the US Navy, an arrangement that he treats lightly despite the warnings of the American consul, Sharpless. Deserted by her husband soon after the wedding, Butterfly awaits his return. She now has a son, 'Trouble'. She remains insistent that Pinkerton will return, and Sharpless hesitates to read her a letter from her husband saying that he now has an American wife. She refuses to listen, however, and undertakes an all-night vigil with her loyal servant, Suzuki. The next day, when Pinkerton returns with his new wife, Kate, Butterfly is obliged to face reality. Giving her young child an American flag to play with, she commits hara-kiri. The first performance at La Scala met with rejection by the audience, moving Puccini to exclaim:

> It is I who am right, I! You shall see!

Madame X. A portrait (1884) of the Parisian society beauty, Madame Gautreau, by the American painter John Singer Sargent (1856–1925). When he showed what he thought of as his masterpiece at the Salon, the critics reacted badly, regarding the picture as excessively erotic. Dismayed by this response, Sargent left Paris and settled in London, where he became a successful society portraitist, although he observed that

> Every time I paint a portrait I lose a friend.

Madame X is also the title of at least seven American films, based on *La Femme X* (1908), a play by the French dramatist Alexandre Bisson (1848–1912). It tells the story of a woman who after a scandal is forced by her jealous husband to leave her young son with him while she disappears from society. Her life thereafter goes downhill, until she finds herself being defended on a murder charge by the son she was forced to abandon all those years before. The title role has been played by Sarah Bernhardt (in the original stage production), Ruth Chatterton (1929), Gladys George (1937) and Lana Turner (1966), among others.

Madness of George III, The. A play (1991) by Alan Bennett (b.1934) depicting the political and personal turmoil arising from one of King George III's periodic bouts of insanity (believed by modern doctors to have been caused by porphyria). The play was subsequently filmed as

The Madness of King George; a possibly apocryphal anecdote ascribes the alteration of the title to the concern of the film's US backers that US audiences would assume the film was the third in a series of 'Mad George' movies.

Madonna of the Harpies. The informal name given to a painting (1517) by Andrea del Sarto (1486–1530), now in the Uffizi in Florence. The title comes from the fact that the Virgin is standing on a sculpted plinth bearing (not very prominent) harpies. The Madonna is actually a portrait of the painter's wife, Lucrezia.

> 'Rafael did this, Andrea painted that;
> The Roman's is the better when you pray,
> But still the other's Virgin was his wife –'
> Men will excuse me …
>
> ROBERT BROWNING: 'Andrea del Sarto' (1855)

Madonna of the Long Neck. The informal name given to a painting (*c.*1535) by the Italian Mannerist painter Parmigianino (1503–40), in which his usual manner of elongating the human form is taken to unusual lengths, with a strikingly elegant result. The composition inspired Max Ernst's subversive *BLESSED VIRGIN CHASTISES THE INFANT JESUS BEFORE THREE WITNESSES: A.B., P.E. AND THE ARTIST* (1926).

> The women of Parmegiano [sic] are coquettes.
>
> HENRY FUSELI: *Aphorisms on Art* (1789)

Mad World, My Masters, A. A comedy by Thomas Middleton (1580–1627), written between 1604 and 1607, and published in 1608. The plot is complicated and full of trickery, as befits the title, and features such characters as Follywit, Hairbrain, Penitent Brothel and Sir Bounteous Progress. The title has become something of a catchphrase, and was used by the BBC foreign correspondent John Simpson for the title of his memoirs (2001). A variation is found in the film *It's a Mad Mad Mad Mad World* (1963), a slapstick crime caper directed by Stanley Kramer.

maggot. A word that occurs in the titles of a number of instrumental pieces – usually country dances – by English composers from the 16th to the 18th century. For example, in *The Dancing Master* (1716) there are such titles as 'Barker's Maggots', 'Cary's Maggots' and 'Draper's Maggots'. The term was revived by Peter Maxwell Davies in his *Miss*

Donnithorne's Maggot (1974), a piece for mezzosoprano and chamber ensemble. A maggot was originally a fanciful idea or whimsy, from the notion that whimsical or fanciful or crotchety persons had maggots in their brains:

> Are you not mad, my friend? What time o' th' moon is't?
> Have not you maggots in your brain?
>
> JOHN FLETCHER: *Women Pleased* (1620), III.iv

In 1685 Samuel Welsey, father of the Methodists John and Charles, published a volume called *Maggots; or Poems on Several Subjects*. The word appears in the same sense in the titles of such modern novels as *Mr Fortune's Maggot* (1927) by Sylvia Townsend Warner and *A Maggot* (1985) by John Fowles.

Magic Flute, The (German title: *Die Zauberflöte*). An opera by Mozart (1756–91), with a libretto by Emanuel Schikaneder, first performed in 1791. In this mystical (and quasi-masonic) quest opera, the magic flute is bestowed on Tamino to protect him as he goes through various rites of passage, such as ordeal by fire and water. The story is based on one found in Christoph Wieland's collection of oriental folk tales (1786).

> The opera [*The Magic Flute*] ... is the only one in existence that might conceivably have been composed by God.
>
> NEVILLE CARDUS: in the *Manchester Guardian*, 1961

Magic Mountain, The (German title: *Der Zauberberg*). A novel (1924; English translation 1927) by Thomas Mann (1875–1955). The densely symbolic story is centred on a young man, Hans Castorp, who goes to visit his cousin at Haus Berghof, a high-altitude sanatorium for people with tuberculosis at Davos in the Swiss Alps. Castorp is fascinated by the place, and ends up staying there for years, searching for self-knowledge while prevaricating between the demands of reason and action on the one hand, and mysticism and decadence on the other. The novel is ultimately a symbolic study of the uneasy situation in Europe before the outbreak of the First World War, and explores the isolation of the world of art and philosophy (the mountain) from the crisis of contemporary existence below.

Magnetic Lady, The. A comedy by Ben Jonson (1572–1637), first performed in 1632, and published in 1641. Dryden described the play as one of Jonson's 'dotages'. The Magnetic Lady of the title is Lady Loadstone, a hostess who 'draws unto her guests of all sorts' – a loadstone being a piece of rock containing significant quantities of the magnetic mineral magnetite; such a stone can be used as a primitive compass. The magnetic/compass theme is rather wearily continued in the names of some of the other characters, for example, Compass (the hero), Needle (Lady Loadstone's steward), and Captain Ironside (brother to Compass).

Magnificent Seven, The. A Western film (1960) that was inspired by Akira Kurosawa's film *The Seven Samurai* (1954) and its story of a small band of rough-hewn heroes defending a village against hordes of bloodthirsty bandits. The success with which director John Sturges transposed the story to the Wild West inspired numerous imitations, not least four lesser sequels featuring survivors of the original seven. The title itself has since been aped not only by subsequent movies (*The Magnificent Seven Deadly Sins*, starring Spike Milligan and others, or *The Magnificent Two*, starring Eric Morecambe and Ernie Wise, for instance), but in many other spheres of human activity, including international espionage (the 'Magnificent Five' were, to the Soviets, the notorious British spies involved in the Burgess and Maclean spy scandal that erupted in the early 1960s).

Maidenhead of the first music that ever was printed for the Virginals, The. *See* PARTHENIA.

Maja Clothed, The and ***The Maja Nude.*** A pair of paintings (*c.*1800) by Francisco de Goya (1746–1828), depicting the same sturdy, big-busted, sensual young woman in the same pose – reclining on a chaise longue, staring frankly and challengingly at the viewer. In Spanish, a *maja* is a woman of the people (especially in Madrid), and Goya's is perhaps the first unidealized nude in Western art.

The paintings caused an immediate scandal, not only because painting any nude in Spain was deeply frowned upon (*see* ROKEBY VENUS, THE) – let alone a painting of such a provocative, real woman – but because it was popularly but mistakenly thought that the model for the two paintings was Maria Teresa, the feisty Duchess of Alba, Goya's one-time patron and occasional mistress, who immediately bought the two paintings. She was described by one art historian as 'the most vivacious, charming, impudent, generous and – when all is said and done – the greatest lady of the eighteenth century'. She certainly put many people's noses out of joint, including the king, the queen and their minister Godoy, and her sudden and unexpected death on 28 July 1802 was popularly imputed to poisoning.

The same historian as has been quoted above relates an anecdote regarding the controversial paintings:

> There is a story that when Alphonso XIII [abdicated 1931], the last reigning Bourbon, was being shown portraits by Velázquez and Goya of the most degenerate members of the royal family, the erstwhile Duke of Alba, who was conducting the tour of inspection, paused before each one and said emphatically: 'An ancestor of yours, Your Majesty.' Alphonso was extremely irritated by this, but his moment came when they passed *The Maja Nude*. Turning to his companion, he remarked: 'An ancestor of yours, Duke.' The Duke of Alba was so enraged that he promptly ordered the remains of his too-notorious ancestress to be exhumed in order to prove that she could not have been the original model – a fact which in any case emerges clearly from a comparison between Goya's numerous portraits or sketches of her and the object of scandal.
>
> JEAN-FRANÇOIS CHABRUN: *Goya* (1965), translated by J. Maxwell Brownjohn

Making Cocoa for Kingsley Amis. A poetry collection (1986) by Wendy Cope (b.1945), taking its title from that of one of the poems therein.

> It was a dream I had last week
> And some kind of record seemed vital.
> I knew it wouldn't be much of a poem
> But I love the title.
>
> 'Making Cocoa for Kingsley Amis'

The novelist Kingsley Amis (1922–95) made his name as one of the 'Angry Young Men' with *LUCKY JIM* (1954), but in later life was a notoriously hard-drinking misanthrope, for whom the alcohol-free beverage of Cope's title would have been anathema.

Maltese Falcon, The. A thriller (1930) by Dashiell Hammett (1894–1961), an early example of the 'hard-boiled' genre of US detective novels. A complex story of deception and self-deception, it features the private eye Sam Spade. The Maltese falcon is, or purports to be, an ancient artefact in the form of a jewel-encrusted falcon, emanating from Malta. The film of 1941, directed by John Huston as a remake of a 1931 version, was a triumph in every respect. It was Huston's first film as director, and it starred

Humphrey Bogart as Sam Spade and Peter Lorre as Joel Cairo. A 1936 film version of the story was entitled *Satan Met a Lady*.

Mamelles de Tirésias, Les (French, 'the breasts of Tiresias'). A surrealistic *opéra burlesque* by Francis Poulenc (1899–1963) with texts by the modernist poet Guillaume Apollinaire (1880–1918). It was first performed in 1947. The story tells of a couple who each change sex, the woman getting rid of her breasts while her husband gives birth to 40,000 children. In Greek mythology Tiresias was a Theban man who had spent seven years of his life as a woman. Zeus and Hera consulted him to resolve the argument as to whether men or women get more pleasure out of sex; Tiresias declared in favour of women and was struck blind by Hera. Tiresias became a seer and informed Oedipus of his true parentage. He also makes an appearance in Part III of T.S. Eliot's *The* WASTE LAND (1922):

> I Tiresias, though blind, throbbing between two lives,
> Old man with wrinkled female breasts, can see …

Man and Superman. A play by George Bernard Shaw (1856–1950), published in 1903 and first performed in 1905. It is subtitled *A Comedy and a Philosophy*. The hero, John Tanner, is intended as a Don Juan figure (his name echoes that of the original DON JUAN Tenorio), and in the third act, 'Don Juan in Hell', he dreams he is Don Juan. Tanner believes in the 'life force' behind a purposive, creative evolution towards ever higher forms of being. In order to pursue his own spiritual development he tries to escape from the attentions of Ann Whitefield, the woman pursuing him:

> Of all human struggles there is none so treacherous and remorseless as the struggle between the artist man and the mother woman.

In the end, however, Tanner realizes that women, as agents of reproduction, are also powerful agents of the life force. In Shavian terms, this represents the usual victory of instinctive woman over intellectual man. Don Juan may be the 'superman' of the title – the man who can identify the will of the universe, and carry it out – but it turns out that Tanner is not.

Shaw consciously borrowed the idea of the 'superman' from Nietzsche, who, in *Thus Spake Zarathustra*, held that 'Man is something to be surpassed', and that the new supermen (*Übermenschen*) would achieve an 'enhancement of life'.

Superman is also a popular hero of American comics. He was the creation of Jerry Siegel and Joe Schuster, who introduced him in *Action Comics* in 1938. He has lent his name to several films (starting with *Superman*, 1978) and to radio and TV series. There has even been a musical, *It's a Bird, It's a Plane, It's Superman* (an adaptation of a catchphrase from the radio series), turned into a television movie (1975).

Manchurian Candidate, The. A memorable film (1962) directed by John Frankenheimer, based on Richard Condon's novel of the same name (1959). It tells the story of a Korean War 'hero' (played by Laurence Harvey) who returns to the USA as a brainwashed zombie triggered to kill a liberal politician, his 'control' being his ambitious mother (played by Angela Lansbury). She goes on to order him to kill the presidential nominee, so that her husband, the vice-presidential candidate, can take over. Manchuria is the region of communist China to the north of North Korea. The expression 'Manchurian candidate' has subsequently been used to denote a person who has been brainwashed by some organization or foreign power and programmed to carry out its orders automatically.

Man for All Seasons, A. A play (1960), later a film (1967), by Robert Bolt (1924–95) about the Tudor statesman Sir Thomas More and his opposition to Henry VIII's divorce from Catherine of Aragon. The title was derived by Bolt from a description of More by his contemporary Robert Whittington (*c.*1480–*c.*1530), who wrote:

> More is a man of angel's wit and singular learning; I know not his fellow. For where is the man of that gentleness, lowliness and affability? And as time requireth, a man of marvellous mirth and pastimes; and sometimes of as sad a gravity: as who say: a man for all seasons.
>
> *Vulgaria* (1521)

Whittington in turn borrowed the tag from Erasmus, a friend of More's, who had described More in his preface to *In Praise of Folly* (1509) with the words *omnium horarum hominem* ('a man of all hours').

Manfred. A 'dramatic poem' by Lord Byron (1788–1824), published in 1817. Count Manfred is a gloomy, Faust-like Romantic hero (*see* FAUST OR FAUSTUS, panel, pp.152–6), who sells himself to the Devil and whose sin is his incestuous love for his sister (a not uncommon theme in Byron). He lives in splendid isolation in the Alps and longs for death.

Robert Schumann (1810–56) wrote incidental music for Byron's drama, opus 115 (composed 1848–9), some of it intended to accompany the spoken words on stage.

> What a masterpiece, but what despair! It's enough to make you long for death.
>
> GEORGES BIZET: on Schumann's *Manfred*, quoted in Dean, *Bizet* (1975)

The *Manfred Symphony*, opus 58 (1885), by Tchaikovsky (1840–93) portrays selected scenes from the drama. The symphony is unnumbered, but was composed between his 4th and 5th symphonies.

Man Who Came to Dinner, The. A film comedy (1941) adapted by Julius and Philip Epstein from a successful stage play by George S. Kaufman (1889–1961) and Moss Hart (1904–61) about an opinionated radio host, called Sheridan Whiteside, who is obliged by injury to outstay his welcome at the home of a suburban family. The original 'man who came to dinner' was the real-life US theatre critic Alexander Woollcott (1887–1943), who was renowned for his eccentric, domineering character. Far from being offended by his portrayal, Woollcott enjoyed the notoriety (he had long pleaded with Hart to be preserved for posterity in one of his plays) and ultimately played the part of Whiteside himself when the play went on tour.

> I'm perfect for the part. I'm the only man you know who can strut sitting down.
>
> ALEXANDER WOOLLCOTT: lobbying Hart for the role of Sheridan Whiteside

Man Who Mistook His Wife for a Hat, The. A collection of case studies (1985) by Oliver Sacks (b.1933), a clinical neurologist. The title piece concerns a musician suffering from visual agnosia:

> He reached out his hand, and took hold of his wife's head, tried to lift it off, to put it on. He had apparently mistaken his wife for a hat! His wife looked as if she was used to such things.

Man Who Never Was, The. A film (1955) based on the true Second World War story of one of the many disinformation efforts hatched by the Allies prior to D-Day. The aim was to mislead the Germans into thinking that the 'Second Front' would be opened somewhere other than Normandy. To this end British naval intelligence persuade a grieving father to part with the body of his son, who has died of pneumonia. They give the body the identity of a senior naval officer, and jettison him into the sea with false documents off neutral Portugal, where they know the currents will wash him ashore, and where they are confident that German spies will manage to see the documents. The plan works more or less perfectly, although in a fictional twist at the end, a German spy in London almost finds out the truth. The following words from an old ballad are spoken at the beginning and end of the film:

> But I hae dream'd a dreary dream,
> Beyond the Isle of Skye;
> I saw a dead man win a fight,
> And I think that man was I.
>
> ANONYMOUS: 'The Battle of Otterbourne'

'Man Who Was, The'. A short story (1891) by Rudyard Kipling (1865–1936) about a man who returns from imprisonment in Russia, many years after his capture during the Crimean War. His treatment had been so bad that he has lost his memory, and hence his identity, and has become 'the man who was'. Compare *MAN WHO NEVER WAS, THE*.

Man Who Was Thursday, The. A novel (1908), subtitled 'A Nightmare', by G.K. Chesterton (1874–1936). The book, much like Conrad's *Secret Agent*, is much concerned with anarchists, although the tone is lighter. Gabriel Syme is a detective posing as an anarchist poet in order to infiltrate an underground movement of real anarchists. He succeeds in penetrating a shady secret organization, whose various high office holders are known by days of the week; he himself is elected as Thursday. As the plot deepens, events become increasingly bizarre and dreamlike.

Man with the Golden Arm, The. A novel (1949) by Nelson Algren (born Nelson Algren Abraham; 1909–81), set in the Polish slums of Chicago. Francis Majcinek (known as Frankie Machine), a dealer in a gambling den, is said to have a 'golden arm', so sure is his handling of the cards, his cue when playing pool, the dice and his drumsticks. He is unable, however, to break out of his social environment, and this and his heroin addiction lead to his suicide. A rather muddled film version (1956) was directed by Otto Preminger, with Frank Sinatra in the title role.

'Maria Theresia' Symphony. The nickname of the symphony no 48 in C by Haydn (1732–1809), which was supposed to have been enjoyed by Maria Theresa on a visit in 1773 to the castle at Esterház, where Haydn worked as composer to Prince Nicolaus Esterházy. Maria Theresa

(1717–80) was the great archduchess of Austria and queen of Hungary and Bohemia (1740–80); 'Maria Theresia' is the German version of her name. The Haydn scholar H.C. Robbins Landon has suggested that the symphony that Maria Theresa actually heard on this occasion was no 50, also in C. The archduchess had not always been a fan of Haydn, having remarked when he was a mischievous pubescent chorister that 'That boy doesn't sing, he crows.' On the occasion of her visit to Esterház, Haydn reminded her that she had once beaten him for climbing the scaffolding at the Schönbrunn palace in Vienna. 'That thrashing,' responded the archduchess, 'yielded good fruit.'

Marino Faliero. A tragedy by Lord Byron (1788–1824), published in 1821. Marino Faliero (1274–1355) was doge of Venice (1354–5), but was executed after conspiring against the patricians of Venice. Byron adds a personal motivation to Faliero's involvement in the plot. His story also inspired a tragedy (1829) by Casimir Delavigne, an opera (1835) by Donizetti and a verse tragedy (1885) by Swinburne. Delacroix's painting *The Execution of the Doge Marino Faliero* (1826–7) is in the Wallace Collection, London.

Marriage-à-la-Mode. A tragicomedy by John Dryden (1631–1700), first performed in 1672 and published in 1673. The title means 'fashionable marriage', with perhaps a suggestion that the fashion is for 'open' marriages. However, in Dryden's play the would-be adulterers fail in their plans. *Marriage à la Mode* is also the title of a series of paintings by William Hogarth (1697–1764) attacking the follies and vices of the upper-class way of marriage. The paintings were completed in 1743 and then turned into a popular series of prints.

Marriage of Figaro, The (Italian title: *Le Nozze di Figaro*). An opera by Mozart (1756–91), with a libretto by Lorenzo da Ponte (1749–1838), first performed in 1786. The opera is based on the comedy *La Folle Journée* ['the mad day'] *ou le mariage de Figaro* (1784) by Pierre-Augustin Caron de Beaumarchais (1732–99). This was the sequel to Beaumarchais' previous comedy, *The* BARBER OF SEVILLE, the eponymous hero of which is Figaro. In the second play Figaro is valet to Count Almaviva, who has his eyes on Susanna, his wife's maid and Figaro's intended. After a number of complicated twists and turns, Figaro secures his bride and the Countess forgives her erring husband. Beaumarchais' critique of the behaviour of the aristocracy was regarded as dangerously revolutionary (indeed the French Revolution was to break out only a few years later), and in Mozart and Da Ponte's version – intended for Vienna, capital of one of the greatest autocracies in Europe – the political aspects are much toned down. The title of Jeremy Sams' sparkling translation of the libretto, *Figaro's Wedding*, renders the original Italian more immediately than the traditional form.

> I could not compose operas like *Don Giovanni* and *Figaro*. I hold them both in aversion. I could not have chosen such subjects; they are too frivolous for me.
>
> LUDWIG VAN BEETHOVEN: in *Beethoven: Impressions of Contemporaries* (1927)

Marriage of Heaven and Hell, The. An illustrated prose work by William Blake (1757–1827), who etched it in 1790–3. As the title suggests, Blake seeks to end and transcend moral and philosophical dualities by synthesizing opposites:

> Without contraries is no progression. Attraction and repulsion, reason and energy, love and hate, are necessary to human existence.
>
> 'The Argument'

The work was much admired by the would-be revolutionary libertarians of the 1960s, who often quoted the 'Proverbs of Hell' from the work, for example:

> The road of excess leads to the palace of wisdom.
> The tygers of wrath are wiser than the horses of instruction.

Horses of Instruction is the title of a work by the contemporary composer Steve Martland (b.1958).

'Marseillaise, La'. The hymn of the French Revolution and the national anthem of France. The words and music were written on the night of 24 April 1792 by Claude-Joseph Rouget de Lisle (1760–1835), an artillery officer in the garrison at Strasbourg, in response to a request by the mayor of Strasbourg for a military marching song following the outbreak of war with Austria on 20 April. Its original title was '*Chant de guerre pour l'armée du Rhin*' ('war song of the Rhine army'), but it became known as '*La Marseillaise*' after it was sung in Paris in July 1792 by troops from Marseilles. It has had a chequered career as the French national anthem, being dropped in non-republican phases. It was first adopted in 1795 but banned by Napoleon when he became emperor. The ban continued after the 1815 restoration, but was lifted after the 1830 revolution. It was banned again on the establishment in 1852 of the Second Empire of Napoleon III, and was not re-adopted until 1879, some years after the establishment of the Third Republic.

Allons, enfants de la patrie,
Le jour de gloire est arrivé.

('Come, children of the country, the day of glory has arrived.')

CLAUDE-JOSEPH ROUGET DE LISLE: '*La Marseillaise*' (1792), opening lines

Marteau sans maître, Le. (French, 'the hammer without a master'). A work by the one-time *enfant terrible* of the musical avant-garde, Pierre Boulez (b.1925). It was first performed in 1955 and established Boulez's reputation as a fiercely cerebral modernist. Scored for contralto and instruments, Boulez's piece is a setting of René Char's surrealist poems of the same title (1934). One critic described the work as 'Webern sounding like Debussy'.

Masaniello. *See* *MUETTE DE PORTICI, LA.*

M*A*S*H. A film (1970) directed by Robert Altman, and based on a novel by Richard Hooker. MASH is a US acronym for a mobile army surgical hospital, the word gruesomely evoking some of the casualties treated. The asterisks in the film's title suggest a swear word. The story is set in just such a unit, the 4077th mobile hospital, during the Korean War (1950–3), although at the time the film was made the USA was still fighting in Vietnam, and the film is a darkly comic anti-war satire. It gave rise to a somewhat lighter TV comedy series (1973–84), disowned by Richard Hooker because of its liberalism.

Masked Ball, A (Italian title: *Un Ballo in maschera*). An opera by Giuseppe Verdi (1813–1901), first performed in 1859. The libretto, by Antonio Somma, is based on the libretto written by Eugène Scribe for the opera *Gustave III ou Le Bal masqué* (1833) by the French composer Daniel Auber (1782–1871). Auber's opera was itself based on the actual assassination of King Gustav III of Sweden in 1792. Gustav's enlightened reforms had alienated the nobility, and the king became the victim of an aristocratic conspiracy: he was shot at the Stockholm opera house by Captain Jacob Johan Anckarström, and died two weeks later. Verdi had intended his opera for Naples, but the censor there refused to allow the assassination of a monarch to be shown on the stage. For the first performance in Rome Verdi transferred the action to 17th-century New

England, with Gustav rather absurdly becoming Riccardo, Earl of Warwick, the governor of Boston. It is at a masked ball that Riccardo's friend Renato (originally Count Anckerström) kills him, having joined an assassination conspiracy by Samuel (Count Ribbing) and Tom (Count Horn) in the mistaken belief that his wife has been having an affair with Riccardo. In some modern productions, the original Swedish setting is restored.

> I would be willing to set even a newspaper or a letter, etc. to music, but in the theatre the public will stand for anything except boredom.
>
> GIUSEPPE VERDI: letter to Antonio Somma (the librettist of *A Masked Ball*), 1853

Mask of Anarchy, The. A revolutionary and visionary ballad by Percy Bysshe Shelley (1792–1822), 'written on the occasion of the massacre at Manchester' – the Peterloo Massacre of 1819, inflicted by government troops on people attending a political meeting. The ballad was not published until 1832, long after the poet's death. The 'Mask' of the title is both a masque, in the sense of an allegorical pageant, and a disguise:

> I met Murder on the way –
> He had a mask like Castlereagh –
> Very smooth he looked, yet grim;
> Seven blood-hounds followed him.

Castlereagh was foreign secretary at the time of the massacre, and a hate-figure for radicals. Other reactionary politicians of the day – such as Eldon and Sidmouth – also appear.

> Last came Anarchy: he rode
> On a white horse, splashed with blood;
> He was pale even to the lips,
> Like Death in the Apocalypse.
>
> And he wore a kingly crown;
> And in his grasp a sceptre shone;
> On his brow this mark I saw –
> 'I AM GOD, AND KING, AND LAW'

At the end, after 'Anarchy, the ghastly birth,/Lay dead earth upon the earth', Shelley addresses the people of England:

> Rise like lions after slumber

In unvanquishable number –
Shake your chains to earth like dew
Which in sleep had fallen on you –
Ye are many – they are few.

Massacre at Chios, The. One of the best-known paintings (1823) by the French Romantic artist Eugène Delacroix (1798–1863). Chios is a Greek island a few miles off the west coast of Turkey, and was reputed to have been the home of Homer. In 1822, during the Greek War of Independence, the Turks massacred or sold into slavery many of its Christian inhabitants. The painter Jean-Antoine Gros described Delacroix's picture as 'the massacre of painting', while Stendhal remarked:

> This work always appears to me to be a picture that was originally intended to depict a plague, and whose author, after having read the newspapers, turned it into a massacre.
>
> STENDHAL: in *Le Journal de Paris*, 1824

Massacre at Paris, The. A play by Christopher Marlowe (1564–93), written *c.*1592. Only a fragmentary and corrupted text survives. The massacre in question was the St Bartholomew's Day Massacre (24 August 1572), the massacre of French Huguenots initiated by the queen mother, Catherine de' Medici. Some 3000 people were killed in Paris, and many more in the French provinces.

Master and Margarita, The (Russian title: *Master i Margarita*). A novel by Mikhail Bulgakov (1891–1940), combining dark humour, satire, fantasy and philosophy. It was completed in 1938, but not published in Russia until 1966–7 (in serial form); the English edition was published in 1967. In the 1930s the Devil visits Moscow, and, with the aid of a naked girl and a gun-toting, cigar-smoking man-sized cat, spreads chaos and mayhem and shows up the moral inadequacies of Soviet society. Standing apart from all this is the Master, a novelist of great integrity, and his beloved, Margarita. He is writing a book about the appearance of Jesus before Pontius Pilate in Jerusalem, long sections of which are included by Bulgakov. The book is prefaced by a quotation from Goethe's *Faust* (*see* FAUST OR FAUSTUS, panel, pp.152–6).

Mastersingers of Nuremberg, The. *See* MEISTERSINGER VON NÜRNBERG, DIE.

Mathis der Maler (German, 'Mathis the painter'). The title of an opera and a symphony by Paul Hindemith (1895–1963). The work is based on the life of the great German painter Matthias Grünewald (d.1528) and his startlingly expressionistic depiction of the Crucifixion on the *Isenheim Altarpiece* in Colmar, Alsace. In real life Grünewald was thought to be sympathetic to the Peasants' Revolt of 1524–5; in Hindemith's libretto he actually leads the peasants against the church, but then renounces worldly things and devotes himself to his art. The opera was due to be premiered in 1935, but, despite protests by (and ultimately the resignation of) the great conductor Wilhelm Furtwängler, the work was banned by the Nazis. Hindemith, who had to leave Germany, extracted music from the opera to make the symphony, which was performed that year. However, the première of the opera did not take place until 1938, in Zurich.

Matin, Le Midi, Le Soir, Le (French, 'morning, midday, evening'). The nicknames of three early symphonies by Haydn (1732–1809), respectively no 6 in D, no 7 in C and no 8 in G, all dating from 1761; the last is also known as *La Tempesta* or *Le Soir et la tempête* ('evening and storm'). The pieces are clearly evocative of their titles, but no more detailed descriptive programme has survived.

Má Vlast (Czech, 'my country'). A series of six symphonic poems by the Czech composer Bedřich Smetana (1824–84), written between 1874 and 1879. The six pieces are:

> *1 Vyšehrad.* This is the name of a fortress (*hrad* = 'castle') in Prague, dating back to the 9th century.
>
> *2 Vltava.* Known as the Moldau in German, this is the longest river in Bohemia, and joins the Labe (Elbe) some 30km north of Prague.
>
> *3 Šárka.* The name of the leader of the Bohemian Amazons, who, in Czech folklore, led a revolt against Přemysl after the death of his wife Libuše (the subject of an earlier opera by Smetana), the legendary founder of Prague. Smetana's fellow Czech Leoš Janáček (1854–1928) wrote an opera entitled *Šárka* (1887, frequently revised).
>
> *4 Z Českych Luhův a Hájův.* This is usually referred to by its English title, *From Bohemia's Fields and Groves.*
>
> *5 Tábor.* A town south of Prague, founded as a fortified settlement in 1420 by Jan Zizka and other followers of the Bohemian religious reformer (and Czech national hero) Jan Hus. It was named after the biblical Mount Tabor in northern Israel, site of the defeat of the Canaanites by the Israelites (*c.*11th century BC), and traditionally

the site of the Transfiguration of Jesus. The Czech town Tábor became the base of the radical Hussite group, the Taborites, who were eventually defeated, and the town captured, in 1452. Smetena's piece quotes the tune of the Hussite hymn 'Ye who are God's warriors'.

6 Blánik. A mountain in southern Bohemia associated with the Hussites.

Mazeppa. A historical character (1644–1709), who as a young man was page to John Casimir of Poland. The story for which he is celebrated is recounted in the *Histoire de Charles XII* by Voltaire (François-Marie Arouet; 1694–1778):

> The intrigue he had in his youth with the wife of a Polish gentleman having been discovered, the husband had him tied naked to the back of a wild horse, and then let it go. The horse, which was from the Ukraine, returned there carrying Mazeppa, who was half dead of exhaustion and hunger. Some peasants helped him; he stayed for a long time with them, and distinguished himself in many campaigns against the Tartars.

Mazeppa went on to become a Cossack hetman (chief), and Tsar Peter the Great made him prince of the Ukraine.

The passage from Voltaire is quoted (in French) in the 'Advertisement' to the poem *Mazeppa* (1819) by Byron (1788–1824), which has Mazeppa, now fighting for Charles XII of Sweden against Russia in the Great Northern War, recall the wild ride of his youth. There is also a poem by Victor Hugo (1802–85) on the subject, which was the inspiration of the painting *The Cossack Girl Finding the Body of Mazeppa* (1851) by Delacroix (1798–1863) and of the symphonic poem *Mazeppa* (1854) by Liszt (1811–86). In the poem *Poltava* (1829) by Pushkin (1799–1837) the emphasis is more on Mazeppa's alliance with the Swedes. The story of Mazeppa inspired a dozen or so operas in the 19th century, the only one of any note being that by Tchaikovsky (1840–93), first performed in 1884. There were also several plays on the subject, including one by the Polish dramatist Juliusz Slowacki (1809–49), first performed in 1840. In this, it became customary for the part of Mazeppa to be played by a woman; one of the most notable interpreters of the role was the American actress and poet Adah Isaacs Mencken (1835–68), who caused a stir when she appeared nearly naked, lashed to a galloping horse.

MEALS

The Harmonious Breakfast, a painting (1941) by Max Ernst

BREAKFAST AT TIFFANY'S, a novella (1958) by Truman Capote

Le DÉJEUNER SUR L'HERBE (French, 'lunch on the grass', 'the picnic'), a painting (1863) by Edouard Manet

The Naked Lunch, a novel (1959) by William Burroughs

Picnic at Hanging Rock, a mysterious film (1975) in which Australian schoolgirls disappear

TEA AND SYMPATHY, a play (1953) by Robert Anderson

The LONG DARK TEA-TIME OF THE SOUL, a humorous fantasy novel (1988) by Douglas Adams

Tea with Mussolini, a film (1999) set among the British ex-pats in Florence before and during the Second World War

Dinner at Eight, a film (1933) set during a society dinner, based on a play by George S. Kaufman and Edna Ferber

The MAN WHO CAME TO DINNER, a film comedy (1941)

Guess Who's Coming to Dinner, a film (1967) about racial prejudice

Babette's Feast, a film (1987) in which a French exile cooks for her Danish neighbours

La GRANDE BOUFFE, a film (1973) of gastronomic and sexual excess

Mean Streets. A film (1973) written and directed by Martin Scorsese (b.1942) about the violence of New York's criminal underworld. Starring Robert De Niro and Harvey Keitel, it took its title from a much-quoted line in 'The Simple Art of Murder' (1950) by US crime thriller writer Raymond Chandler (1888–1959):

> Down these mean streets a man must go who is not himself mean; who is neither tarnished not afraid.

Measure for Measure. One of the 'dark' comedies of William Shakespeare (1564–1616), written in around 1604. The story comes from George Whetstone's *Promos and Cassandra* (before 1578), itself based on the *Hecatommithi* (1565) of Giraldo Cinthio. The meaning of the title is as evasive as this difficult play, in which the duke of Vienna leaves the city in the hands of his deputy Angelo. Angelo revives old laws against sexual licence, and condemns Claudio for making Julietta, his betrothed, pregnant. Angelo is then shown up to be a villainous hypocrite when he promises to spare Claudio's life if his sister Isabella (a novice in a convent) consents to become his mistress – but she refuses. This is how Claudio puts it to Isabella:

> Which had you rather – that the most just law
> Now took your brother's life; or, to redeem him,
> Give up your body to such sweet uncleanness
> As she that he hath stain'd?
>
> II.iv

The title may suggest that crime will be met with punishment, but perhaps also that punishment should be in proportion to the crime. There is, however, a degree of irony involved, as, in addition to Angelo's casuistry, the play is full of moral compromise and relativism, and at the end the returning duke metes out some curious justice. The word 'measure' also suggests moderation, as in the proverb quoted elsewhere in Shakespeare:

> If the prince be too important, tell him there is measure in every thing.
>
> *Much Ado About Nothing* (1598–9)

Médecin malgré lui, Le (French 'the doctor in spite of himself'). A comedy by Molière (Jean-Baptiste Poquelin; 1622–73), first performed in 1666. The story, based on a medieval fable, tells how the woodcutter Sganarelle pretends he is a doctor to avoid being beaten, and ends up doing as well as a 'real' doctor. Gounod made an opera of the play in 1858, with only minor changes to Molière's text. The opera *Le Roi malgré lui* (1887; 'the king in spite of himself') by Emmanuel Chabrier (1841–94), based on a comedy by François Ancelot, uses the same title formula, and is also a tale of mistaken identity and disguises.

Mein Kampf (German, 'My Struggle'). The title adopted by Adolf Hitler (1889–1945) for the book embodying his political and racial theories and misreadings of history, which in due course became the Nazi 'bible'.

The first part was written when he was in prison after the abortive 'Beer Hall Putsch' of 1923. It was published in two parts (1925 and 1927).

> *Der breite Masse eines Volkes ... fällt einer grossen Lüge leichter zum Opfer als einer kleinen.*
>
> ('The broad mass of a nation ... will more easily fall victim to a big lie than to a small one.')
>
> ADOLF HITLER: *Mein Kampf*, I, x (1925)

Meistersinger von Nürnberg, Die (German, 'the mastersingers of Nuremberg'). An opera by Wagner (1813–83), with a libretto by the composer, first performed in 1868. Historically, the *Meistersinger* were literary and musical guilds found in a number of German cities in the 15th and 16th centuries. Most members were craftsmen or traders, in contrast to the earlier aristocratic *Minnesinger*. The rules and hierarchies of the guilds were very rigid. Wagner's opera includes a number of historical characters, including the *Meistersinger* Hans Sachs. In Wagner's story a rich goldsmith offers his daughter's hand to the winner of a singing competition. Her suitors are the hero, Walther von Stolzing (a knight), and the villain, Beckmesser, who pedantically criticizes his rival's song, but fails to prevent Stolzing from winning and becoming a member of the guild. Beckmesser is a malicious portrait of the Austrian music critic Eduard Hanslick (1825–1904), an ardent anti-Wagnerian. Wagner certainly had some scores to settle in the light of reviews like this:

> The Prelude to *Tristan and Isolde* reminds me of the old Italian painting of a martyr whose intestines are slowly unwound from his body.
>
> EDUARD HANSLICK: quoted in Norman Lebrecht, *Discord* (1982)

Die Meistersinger itself did not appeal to everybody. Nietzsche called it 'German beer music', while John Ruskin complained:

> Of all the affected, sapless, soulless, beginningless, endless, topless, bottomless, topsy-turviest, tongs-and-boniest doggerel of sounds I ever endured the deadliness of, that eternity of nothing was the deadliest – as far as the sound went.
>
> JOHN RUSKIN: letter, 1882

Men and Mountains. A piece for small orchestra by the modernist US composer Carl Ruggles (1876–1971), first performed in 1924, and revised for large orchestra in 1936. The three movements are 'Men', 'Lilacs' and 'Marching Mountains'.

> Great things are done when men and mountains meet;
> This is not done by jostling in the street.
>
> WILLIAM BLAKE: manuscript notebook

During a 1931 performance of the piece Charles Ives, the grand old man of modern American music, hissed at a restless member of the audience:

> You goddam sissy! – when you hear strong masculine music like this, get up and USE YOUR EARS LIKE A MAN!
>
> CHARLES IVES: quoted in Wooldridge, *Charles Ives* (1924)

Meninas, Las. A painting (1656) by Diego Velázquez (1599–1660) that is at the same time a court portrait of the young Infanta Margarita and her *meninas* (Spanish, 'maids of honour'), and a painting about painting, a tour de force of composition and the handling of space and atmosphere. The painter himself appears on the left of the infanta, looking past his canvas at the viewer – and presumably to his subject, King Philip IV and Queen Mariana, seen only faintly in a mirror in the back of the room, in the background of the picture. Luca Giordano called this picture 'the essence of painting', while Picasso (1881–1973) made many versions of it.

Men in Black. A hit comedy film (1997) starring Tommy Lee Jones and Will Smith as two of the 'Men in Black', black-suited, highly secretive government agents in dark glasses whose job it is to prevent the public learning that America is playing host to a variety of aliens of all shapes and sizes, from every corner of the cosmos. The agents' job is also to keep the more mischievous elements among the extra-terrestrials in order.

The existence of 'Men in Black' has long been asserted by US conspiracy theorists, convinced that their government has for decades covered up numerous sightings of flying saucers, alien abductions and so on. Anyone experiencing one of these 'CLOSE ENCOUNTERS' is likely to be paid a visit by gentlemen in dark suits, who sinisterly arrive in their big black cars, and as sinisterly depart. The existence of the 'Men in Black' was given additional credence as far as the more gullible were concerned by their appearance in the long-running TV series, *The X-Files*.

Mephisto Waltzes. *See* FAUST OR FAUSTUS (panel, pp.152–6).

'Mercury' Symphony (German *Merkursymphonie*). The nickname for the symphony no 43 in E flat (c.1771) by Haydn (1732–1809). The origin of the name is unknown.

METEOROLOGY

The Sunshine Boys, a film comedy (1975) with Walter Matthau and George Burns as a mutually antagonistic pair of old comics, billed as The Sunshine Boys

THREATENING WEATHER, a painting (1928) by René Magritte

'RAINDROP' PRELUDE, a piano piece (1839) by Chopin

'RAIN' SONATA, a sonata (1878–9) by Brahms for violin and piano in G, opus 78

Singin' in the Rain, a film musical (1952)

Finian's Rainbow, a musical comedy (1947) involving a crock of gold stolen from a leprechaun

Whistle down the Wind, a film (1961)

The WIND IN THE WILLOWS, a novel (1908) for children by Kenneth Grahame

A HIGH WIND IN JAMAICA, a novel (1929) by Richard Hughes

GONE WITH THE WIND, a romantic historical novel (1936) by Margaret Mitchell (film version 1939)

A POSTILLION STRUCK BY LIGHTNING, memoirs (1977) by Dirk Bogarde

Typhoon, a collection of short stories (1903) by Joseph Conrad

The TEMPEST, a play (1611) by William Shakespeare, and a painting (1914) by Oskar Kokoschka

The Perfect Storm, a film (2000) inspired by a real Atlantic storm in October 1991, and based on a book by Sebastian Junger (the title refers to the combination of meteorogical conditions that led to a particularly bad storm)

The Eye of the Hurricane, a poetry collection (1964) by Fleur Adcock

The Ice Storm, a bleak film (1997) about two dysfunctional families in America

Snow Falling on Cedars, a novel (1995) by David Guterson

Merz. A generic term (German for 'trash') applied by the German Dada poet and artist Kurt Schwitters (1887–1958) to his elaborate constructions of bits and pieces picked up from dustbins and gutters. 'I am a painter and I nail my pictures together,' he said. He also called the Dada journal that he founded in 1923 *Merz*. The term forms part of the title of many of Schwitters' works, for example, *Merzbild Einunddreisig* (1920), and his three *Merzbau* houses. He began the first of these houses in Hanover in 1923, and had not finished it when he went into exile in Britain in 1935; it was destroyed by Allied bombing in 1943. His last, again unfinished, *Merzbau* was in Ambleside, in the English Lake District, and is now in the Hatton Gallery in Newcastle.

Messiah. An oratorio, by far his most popular, by George Frideric Handel (1685–1759), first performed in 1742 in Dublin. The piece is frequently but inaccurately referred to as *The Messiah*. The word *Messiah* is from Hebrew *māshīach*, 'anointed one', and refers to the awaited leader of the Jews, who will deliver the nation from its enemies and reign in permanent triumph and peace. The word is the equivalent of the Greek word *Christ*, and it is applied by Christians to Jesus. Handel's oratorio is set to texts from the Bible, selected by the composer and Charles Jennens. The tradition among British audiences of standing during the 'Hallelujah Chorus' is said to originate from a performance at Covent Garden Theatre in 1743 attended by King George II, who stood as the music began, obliging the rest of the audience to do likewise. When Joseph Haydn heard the chorus, he remarked that Handel 'is the master of us all'.

Metroland. A novel (1980) by Julian Barnes (b.1946), drawing on the author's own London suburban childhood. Metroland is the region northwest of London served by the Metropolitan Railway, lovingly evoked in John Betjeman's poem 'The Metropolitan Railway' (1954) and further explored in his television programme *Metro-land* (1973). The name was adopted by the railway in 1915 as a term for the districts through which it ran, and *Metro-Land* was the title of its guidebook, issued annually from that year to 1932, the last full year of its existence as an independent company. Lady Metroland, née Margot Beste-Chetwynde, is the wife of Lord Metroland, né Sir Humphrey Maltravers, Minister of Transportation, in Evelyn Waugh's *DECLINE AND FALL* (1928).

> Metro-Land is a country with elastic borders which every visitor can draw for himself, as Stevenson drew his map of Treasure Island.
>
> *Metro-Land* (1932)

Midi, Le. *See MATIN, LE MIDI, LE SOIR, LE.*

Midnight Express. A film (1978) adapted by Oliver Stone from a book by Billy Hayes and William Hoffer based on Hayes's experiences in a Turkish prison after he was found guilty of trying to smuggle hashish out of the country. Directed by Alan Parker, the film owed its title to prison slang, 'taking the midnight express' meaning simply 'to escape'.

Midnight's Children. A novel (1981) by Salman Rushdie (b.1947), which won the Booker Prize for fiction. The midnight in question was on 15 August 1947, when India became independent. The children are the 581 born at that midnight, symbolic of Indian freedom and democracy. The narrator, who is one of them, is, like Rushdie himself, on the borderline between cultures. The book, which has been read as history and as fantasy, encompasses the story of India since independence. It is particularly critical of Prime Minister Indira Gandhi, who suspended democracy in India in 1975–7. She is presented by Rushdie as a witch, who symbolically orders the sterilization of midnight's children.

> At the stroke of the midnight hour, while the world sleeps, India will awake to life and freedom.
>
> JAWAHARLAL NEHRU: speech to the Indian Constituent Assembly, 14 August 1947

Midsummer Marriage, The. A mystical 'quest' opera by Michael Tippett (1905–98) with a libretto by the composer. The work, which was first performed in 1955, is consciously modelled on Mozart's *The MAGIC FLUTE*. The parts of Tamino and Pamina are taken by Mark and Jennifer, who quarrel on their wedding day and are obliged to undergo a series of trials, after which they are reunited. This also has echoes of the lovers' tiffs, transmutations and reconciliations in Shakespeare's *A MIDSUMMER NIGHT'S DREAM*. Another couple in Tippett's opera, Jack and Bella, take the parts of Mozart's Papageno and Papagena.

Midsummer Night's Dream, A. A comedy (*c.*1595–6) by William Shakespeare (1564–1616). On the eve of the marriage of Theseus, duke of Athens, to Hyppolyta, queen of the Amazons, Hermia is ordered by her father (with the sanction of the duke) to marry Demetrius, although she loves Lysander, while Demetrius is loved by Helena. All flee to the forest outside Athens. This forest is the realm of Oberon and Titania, the king and queen of the fairies, who have fallen out over the possession of a changeling child (*see* CHANGELING, THE). Oberon commands the mischievous Puck to fetch a plant that has been struck by Cupid's bolt. He explains:

The juice of it on sleeping eyelids laid
Will make or man or woman madly dote
Upon the next live creature that it sees.
II.i

His plan is for Puck to thus enchant Titania while she sleeps, and lay beside her Bottom the weaver, having first turned Bottom's head into the head of an ass. (Bottom and his companions are in the forest to rehearse a play for the forthcoming ducal nuptials.) Oberon also commands Puck to resolve the problems of the lovers in the forest by putting the magic love-juice on the eyelids of Demetrius, but Puck mistakes Lysander for his proper target, and considerable fallings-out and confusions among the various lovers follow throughout the night.

In the end Oberon and Titania and all four lovers are reconciled. Hermia and Lysander are forgiven by father and duke, and Bottom and his companions perform their play, an unintended burlesque of the story of Pyramus and Thisbe, for the duke and his bride. After the company retire to bed, Oberon and Titania 'and all their Train' appear to bless the house and marriage bed. At the end, alone on the stage, Puck craves the audience's indulgence:

If we shadows have offended,
Think but this, and all is mended,
That you have but slumb'red here
While these visions did appear.
And this weak and idle theme,
No more yielding than a dream …
V.i

Midsummer's Eve, the night of 23 June, comes shortly after the summer solstice (21 June), and since pagan times has been associated with magical happenings, particularly love-magic: one of many associated beliefs is that an infertile woman may conceive if she goes naked into her garden on Midsummer's Eve and picks a flower of the St John's wort. The time of year is also associated with madness, as Shakespeare was very much aware:

> Why, this is very midsummer madness.
>
> *Twelfth Night*, III.iv

In *A Midsummer Night's Dream*, he makes an explicit association between madness and love:

> The lunatic, the lover and the poet
> Are of imagination all compact.
>
> V.i

Before Puck rectifies the situation, the four lovers fall into a magically induced madness in which they love the wrong person. Titania and Bottom also suffer thus, but these errors are attributed to a dream:

> My Oberon! What visions have I seen!
> Methought I was enamour'd of an ass.
>
> Titania, in IV.i

> I have had a dream, past the wit of man to say what dream it was. ... I will get Peter Quince to write a ballad of this dream. It shall be called 'Bottom's Dream', because it hath no bottom ...
>
> Bottom, in IV.i

In 1826 the 17-year-old Felix Mendelssohn (1809–47) wrote his well-known overture, opus 21, to *A Midsummer Night's Dream*, and in 1842 added incidental music for the play, opus 61. The opera of the same name (1960) by Benjamin Britten (1913–76) uses a shortened version of Shakespeare's text, and casts Oberon as a countertenor. There is a performance of *A Midsummer Night's Dream* within the opera *Mignon* (1866) by Ambroise Thomas (1811–96), which is based on Goethe's *Wilhelm Meister*. *See also* MIDSUMMER MARRIAGE, THE.

The 1935 US film version of Shakespeare's play, directed by Max Reinhardt, is something of a classic of Hollywood-meets-the-Bard. Its stars include James Cagney as Bottom, Mickey Rooney as Puck, Olivia de Havilland as Hermia and Dick Powell as Lysander. Powell later said that he never did understand his lines. The 1996 film version is uneasily based on a Royal Shakespeare Company production.

Woody Allen adapted Shakespeare's title for his film *A Midsummer Night's Sex Comedy* (1982). Set at the beginning of the 20th century, it follows events during a weekend house party in upstate New York held by a Wall Street broker. The character played by Mia Farrow is called Ariel, a sprite from *The* TEMPEST.

Midwich Cuckoos, The. A science-fiction novel (1957) by John Wyndham (pen-name of John Wyndham Parkes Lucas Beynon Harris; 1903–69). All the women in the English village of Midwich are impregnated at the same time by an astral force, resulting in the births of a breed of children with frightening powers. They are 'cuckoos' in the sense that they are alien, like the chicks that hatch from eggs laid by cuckoos in the nests of other birds. A memorable film version appeared as *Village of the Damned* (1960); a remake (1995) was entirely forgettable.

'Military' Symphony. The nickname of the symphony no 100 in G (1794) by Haydn (1732–1809). It was one of the 'SALOMON' SYMPHONIES written for London. The second movement features a triangle, bass drum and cymbals, then instruments normally confined to a military band; there is also a martial-sounding trumpet call.

Mill on the Floss, The. A novel by George Eliot (1819–80), published in 1860. Eliot herself had proposed calling the book 'Sister Maggie' (Maggie Tulliver being the central character), and there were several other suggestions, but in the end Eliot's publisher, John Blackwood, came up with the current title. Eliot wrote:

> 'The Mill on the Floss' be it then! The only objections are that the mill is not strictly on the Floss, being on its small tributary, and that the title is of rather laborious utterance.

The mill is the home of Maggie and her brother Tom. Eliot intended the setting to be Lincolnshire, but her old neighbours in her childhood home in Warwickshire recognized local scenes in her descriptions – in particular the Round Pole, or Red Deeps, Maggie's attic retreat in the mill. The fictional River Floss itself plays an important symbolic role in the novel, as well as a more direct one in the tragic denouement.

Milton. A long poem by William Blake (1804–8). The work is Blake's response to *Paradise Lost*, and in it the spirit of Milton enters the poet's left foot.

> The reason Milton wrote in fetters when he wrote of Angels and God, and at liberty when of Devils and Hell, is because he was a true Poet, and of the Devil's party without knowing it.
>
> WILLIAM BLAKE: *The Marriage of Heaven and Hell* (1790–3)

The poet is also celebrated in Wordsworth's sonnet 'Milton! thou shouldst be living at this hour' (1807).

'Minute' Waltz. A nickname given to the waltz in D flat, opus 64 no 1 (1847), by Chopin (1810–49), although played properly it should last longer than a minute. It is the theme tune of BBC Radio 4's *Just A Minute*, in which contestants have to speak on a subject for 60 seconds without repetition, deviation or hesitation. An alternative nickname for Chopin's piece is the 'Dog' Waltz, as it was supposed to have been inspired by a dog chasing its own tail – the dog in question belonging to the novelist George Sand (Aurore Dudevant, Chopin's lover). *See also* 'CAT' WALTZ.

Miracle on 34th Street. A film (1947) adapted by George Seaton from a story by Valentine Davies about the extraordinary events that follow after a kindly old man calling himself 'Kris Kringle' is recruited as Macy's Santa Claus during New York's Christmas rush. His name plays on 'Christingle' (from German *Christkindl*, 'Christ child'), a lighted candle representing Christ as the light of the world, carried by children at Advent services, a tradition that originated in the Moravian Church. The 'miracle' that takes place in the film is the influence this latter-day Santa Claus (played by Edmund Gwenn) has in reminding busy shoppers of the true meaning of Christmas. There was an unnecessary remake in 1994.

'Miracle' Symphony. The nickname of the symphony no 96 in D (1791) by Haydn (1732–1809). It was one of the 'SALOMON' SYMPHONIES written for London. It was said that at the first performance a chandelier fell from the ceiling but miraculously missed the audience; however, the Haydn scholar H.C. Robbins Landon holds that this incident occurred during the first performance of symphony no 102 in B flat (1794).

Mirror Crack'd From Side to Side, The. A detective story by Agatha Christie (1890–1976), published in 1962. The US title is simply *The Mirror Crack'd*, and both versions are from the same passage by Alfred, Lord Tennyson:

Out flew the web and floated wide;
The mirror crack'd from side to side;
'The curse is come upon me,' cried
The Lady of the Shalott.

TENNYSON: 'The LADY OF SHALOTT', (1832)

Misérables, Les. (French, 'the destitute', 'the wretched', 'the outcasts'). A novel (1862) by Victor Hugo (1802–85), which paints a broad canvas of French society but centres on the life of Jean Valjean, a former convict who tries to help some of the oppressed. In French, *misérabilisme* has come to mean a preoccupation with the squalid side of life.

A musical (1980) based on the book has a score by Claude-Michel Schönberg (b.1944), lyrics by Herbert Kretzmer and libretto by Alain Boublil. The show became familiarly known as *Les Miz* after establishing itself as one of the longest running entertainments in London's West End.

Missa in tempore belli. *See* PAUKENMESSE.

Miss O'Murphy. The former title of one of the most famous nudes in art history, Francois Boucher's *Reclining Girl* (1751), sometimes also called *Nude on a Sofa*. The painting is innovative in the way that it focuses in on the naked girl, with no mythological setting, and in the uncomfortable but provocative pose the artist has obliged her to adopt, lying on her tummy with her legs apart. Despite the change of title, it is almost certain that this is a portrait of Louise O'Murphy (b.1734), the 15-year-old mistress of Louis XV and one of Boucher's favourite models.

Miss Smilla's Feeling for Snow (Danish title: *Frøken Smillas Fornemmelse for Sne*; US title: *Smilla's Sense of Snow*). A novel (1992; English translation 1993) by Peter Høeg (b.1957). Part mystery story on land and part adventure thriller at sea, it is told in the first person by a personable Inuit academic whose expertise in the subject of snow comes in useful in solving a murder.

Mit dem Hornsignal. *See* 'HORN SIGNAL' SYMPHONY.

Moab is My Washpot. The memoirs (1997) of the comic actor and novelist, Stephen Fry. The phrase comes from the Bible:

Moab is my washpot; over Edom will I cast out my shoe.

Psalms 60:8

Fry himself explained in the *Independent* (18 August 1999) that the real motive for choosing this title lay in the words that follow this quotation: 'Philistia, triumph thou because of me.' Fry saw this phrase as to do with 'vanquishing the Philistines':

> My adolescent self saw life as a war between the athlete and the aesthete, the inner life and the outer life. But then, I was something of a wanker.

Moby-Dick. A novel (1851) by the US writer Herman Melville (1819–91), a huge work in which a detailed account of the sperm whale and the whaling industry is intermixed with a wild and symbolic chase through time and space as the mad, hell-bent Ahab, captain of the *Pequod*, pursues Moby-Dick, the great white whale that had torn his leg off years before. In the end all but the narrator, Ishmael, perish, as the harpooned whale rams and sinks the ship.

> Now small fowls flew screaming over the yet yawning gulf; a sullen white surf beat against its steep sides; then all collapsed, and the great shroud of the sea rolled on as it rolled five thousand years ago.
>
> *Moby-Dick*, last words

The novel was first published in London on 18 October 1851 as *The Whale*, and then in New York on 14 November of that year as *Moby-Dick*. Between those two dates the astonishing news emerged of the sinking of the ship *Ann Alexander* by a whale in the Pacific. Melville – who had himself spent two years as a 'harpooneer' on a whaling ship – took the name of his whale from Mocha Dick, a notorious white whale that had killed many men and sunk two ships; an account of Mocha Dick's doings by J.N. Reynolds had appeared in *The Knickerbocker Magazine* in 1839. Another important source, telling of another whale-doomed ship, was Owen Chase's *Narrative of the Most Extraordinary and Distressing Shipwreck of the Whale-Ship Essex, of Nantucket* (1821).

While he was working on the book, Melville worried whether he was going to be able to make literature out of his raw material:

> Blubber is blubber you know, tho' you may get oil out of it, the poetry runs as hard as sap from a frozen maple tree …
>
> HERMAN MELVILLE: letter to Richard Henry Dana, Jnr, 1 May 1850

Even after he'd finished his masterwork, he warned a woman acquaintance:

> It is not a piece of fine feminine Spitalfields silk – but it is of the horrible texture of a fabric that should be woven of ships' cables and hausers. A Polar wind blows through it, & birds of prey hover over it. Warn all gentle fastidious people from so much as peeping into the book – on risk of a lumbago & sciatics.

Half a century later, the book still had not won over everybody in the literary (or maritime) world:

> Lately I had in my hand *Moby Dick*. It struck me as a rather strained rhapsody with whaling for a subject and not a single sincere line in the 3 vols of it.
>
> JOSEPH CONRAD: letter to Humphrey Milford, 15 January 1907

However, the book has had a profound impact on the American imagination and is often named as a candidate for the title of the GREAT AMERICAN NOVEL:

> Sailor, can you hear
> The Pequod's sea wings, beating landward, fall
> Headlong and break on our Atlantic wall
> Off 'Sconset ...
>
> ROBERT LOWELL: 'The Quaker Graveyard in Nantucket', *Poems 1938–1949* (1950)

Modern Love. A sequence of 50 connected poems by George Meredith (1828–1909), published in 1862. The title is bitterly ironic, in that the sequence follows the breakdown of a contemporary marriage (echoing the poet's own unhappy first marriage to Mary Ellen Nicolls).

Modest Proposal, A. A pamphlet issued by Jonathan Swift (1667–1745) in 1729. The full title is *A Modest Proposal for Preventing the Children of Ireland from being a Burden to their Parents or Country; and for Making them Beneficial to the Public.* Swift's viciously satirical proposal is indicated in the following passage:

> I have been assured by a very knowing American of my acquaintance in London, that a young healthy child well nursed is at a year old a most delicious, nourishing, and wholesome food, whether stewed, roasted, baked, or boiled, and I make no doubt that it will equally serve in a fricassee, or a ragout.

Mona Lisa. A portrait (1506) – perhaps the most famous painting in the world – by Leonardo da Vinci (1452–1519). The subject is an otherwise obscure Florentine lady named Lisa Gerhardini; *Mona* means 'Lady'. Some sixty years later Vasari recalled:

> Leonardo undertook for Francesco Zanobi del Giocondo the portrait of his wife Mona Lisa. She was very beautiful and while he was drawing her portrait he engaged people to play and sing, and jesters to keep her merry, and remove that melancholy which painting usually gives to portraits. This figure of Leonardo's has such a pleasant smile that it seems rather divine than human, and was considered marvellous, an exact copy of Nature.
>
> GIORGIO VASARI: *Lives of the Painters* (1568)

The name of the sitter's husband has given rise to the alternative title of the painting, *La Gioconda*, which by chance also translates as 'the merry one', but this is hardly appropriate for the enigmatically smiling lady. Many interpretations have been made of her slight, ambivalent smile; one of the most recent, put forward by the psychoanalyst Darian Leader in his *Stealing the Mona Lisa* (2002), is that it was brought about by Leonardo exposing himself. Here is a selection of other views:

> She is older than the rocks among which she sits; like the vampire, she has been dead many times, and learned the secrets of the grave.
>
> WALTER PATER: *Studies in the History of the Renaissance* (1873), 'Leonardo da Vinci'

> What voluptuousness … so like the seduction by the violins in the overture to *Tannhäuser*.
>
> MAURICE DENIS: 'Definition of Neotraditionism' (1890)

> The smile of *La Gioconda* was for too long, perhaps, the Sun of Art. The adoration of her is like a decadent Christianity – peculiarly depressing, utterly demoralizing. One might say, to paraphrase Arthur Rimbaud, that *La Gioconda*, the eternal *Gioconda*, has been a thief of the energies.
>
> ANDRÉ SALMON: *La jeune peinture française* (1912)

> Her hesitating smile which held my youth in a little tether has come to seem to me but a grimace …
>
> GEORGE MOORE: *Vale* (1914)

In contrast, all the Soviet leader Leonid Brezhnev could see in her was 'a plain, sensible-looking woman'. *See also* LHOOQ.

In 1911 the *Mona Lisa* was the subject of an astonishing theft. An Italian house painter called Vincenzo Peruggia entered the Louvre, managed to conceal the painting under his smock, and kept the canvas in a trunk in his lodgings for a couple of years before the police eventually caught up with him. Strangely enough, more people came to see the blank space on the wall where the picture had hung than had come to see the actual painting.

There is an opera (1915) entitled *Mona Lisa* by the German composer Max von Schillings (1868–1933), who had a great success with it. Amilcare Ponchielli's melodramatic opera *La Gioconda* (1876), with a libretto by Arrigo Boito, has nothing to do with Leonardo's painting, the eponymous heroine being a street singer. The same can be said of Gabriele D'Annunzio's tragedy *La Gioconda* (1898), in which she is a sculptor's model and *femme fatale*. D'Annunzio wrote the play for his mistress, the actress Eleanor Duse, who scored a great hit in the part. However, the painting did inspire *The Gioconda Smile* (1948), a play by Aldous Huxley (1894–1963). The more recent *Mona Lisa* (1986) is a film directed by Neil Jordan about an ex-con (played by Bob Hoskins) who works as a chauffeur for a call girl (Cathy Tyson), who is as enigmatic as the woman in Leonardo's portrait.

Monarch of the Glen, The. The best known painting (1850) by Sir Edwin Landseer (1802–73), depicting a red deer stag standing proud above the Highland heather. It was painted the same year as he was knighted (he was Queen Victoria's favourite painter). Compton Mackenzie (1883–1972) borrowed the title for his entertaining novel (1941) about a grand Highland laird down on his uppers – the basis for an anodyne TV series from the BBC (2000–1). Landseer's title may have been inspired by a line from Cowper:

> I am monarch of all I survey.
>
> WILLIAM COWPER: 'Verses Supposed to be Written by Alexander Selkirk' (1782)

In 'Transports of Delight', their song about London buses, Michael Flanders and Donald Swann refer to the world-famous red double-decker as 'that monarch of the road'.

MONOSYLLABIC TITLES

See also LETTERS, SYMBOLS AND INITIALS (panel, pp.255–6)

Antz, an animated children's film (1998)

Big, a comedy film (1988) in which a 13-year-old boy finds himself in the body of an adult (played by Tom Hanks)

Bird, a biopic (1988) of the jazz saxophonist Charlie Parker

Blam, a painting (1962) by Roy Lichtenstein (*see WHAAM!*)

Blast, a Vorticist journal (1914) edited by Wyndham Lewis

Bliss, a collection of short stories (1920) by Katherine Mansfield; also the title of a novel (1981) by Peter Carey

Blue, Derek Jarman's last film (1992), a meditation on Aids; also the title of a novel (1988) by Adam Lively

Box, a play (1968) by the US dramatist Edward Albee

Boy, a novel (1900) by Marie Corelli

BREATH, a very short play (1969) by Samuel Beckett

Cuts, a novel (1987) by Malcolm Bradbury

Da, a play (1973) by the Irish writer Hugh Leonard (film version 1988)

Drum, a film (1976) set in a New Orleans brothel in the slavery era

FILTH, a novel (1998) by Irvine Welsh

Flesh, a film (1968) produced by Andy Warhol

Fuck, a film (1969) directed by Andy Warhol

GREASE, a musical film (1978)

Head, a psychedelic film (1968) featuring The Monkees pop group

Heat, a film (1972) produced by Andy Warhol

Her, a novel (1973) by the US poet Lawrence Ferlinghetti

Hex, a film (1973) featuring magical powers in Nebraska

him, a play (1927) by the US poet e.e. cummings

'IF –', a poem (1910) by Rudyard Kipling

IF ..., a film (1968) directed by Lindsay Anderson

It, a silent film (1927) with Clara Bow as the original 'It girl'; also a novel for children (1977) by William Mayne, and a horror novel (1986) by Stephen King

King, a novel (1999) by John Berger

Luv, a comedy film (1967), based on a play by Murray Schisgal

North, a collection of poems (1975) by the Irish Nobel laureate Seamus Heaney

Oil!, a novel (1927) by the US writer Upton Sinclair about the Teapot Dome scandal under the administration of President Harding

Pi, a film (1998) about a mathematician on the edge of madness

Pulp, a comedy thriller film (1972) featuring a writer of pulp fiction

Quoof, a verse collection (1983) by the Northern Irish poet Paul Muldoon

Scum, a film drama (1979) about life in a young offenders' institution, commissioned then banned by the BBC

SHE, a romantic adventure story (1887) by H. Rider Haggard

Shock, a thriller film (1946)

Slag, a play (1970) by David Hare

Snatch, a London gangster film (2000) written and directed by Guy Ritchie

Sons, a novel (1932) by Pearl S. Buck

Sphinx, a novel (1986) by D.M. Thomas

Strife, a play (1909) by John Galsworthy

'Tis, a memoir (1999) by the Irish writer Frank McCourt

Trash, a film (1970) produced by Andy Warhol

Whaam! a painting (1963) by Roy Lichtenstein

MONTHS

The January Divan, a collection of verse (1980) by John Fuller

Crazy February, an ethnological study (1974) of the inhabitants of the Mayan Highlands of Mexico by Carter Wilson

The February Trouble, a private-eye novel (1994) by the US writer Neil Albert

A Full Moon in March, a collection of verse (1935) by W.B. Yeats

The April Fools, a romantic comedy film (1969)

The DARLING BUDS OF MAY, a comic novel (1958) by H.E. Bates

Milou in May, a French film (1989) written and directed by Louis Malle

June 30th, June 30th, a collection of verse (1978) by the US writer Richard Brautigan

May Week Was in June, a memoir (1990) by Clive James

5th of July, a play (1979) by the US writer Lanford Wilson

The Teahouse of the August Moon, a film comedy (1956) based on a play by John Patrick

August is a Wicked Month, a novel (1965) by Edna O'Brien

September, a novel (1919) by Frank Swinnerton; also the title of an introspective Woody Allen film (1987)

'September Song', a well-known song by the German composer Kurt Weill, from the musical *Knickerbocker Holiday* (1938)

The Hunt for Red October, a Cold War thriller film (1990), based on a Tom Clancy novel, in which the captain of a top-secret Soviet submarine attempts to defect to the West

November Boughs, a verse collection (1888) by the US poet Walt Whitman

The Dean's December, a novel (1982) by the US Nobel laureate Saul Bellow

December Bride, a film (1990) about a single mother defying conventions

Moon and Sixpence, The. A novel (1919) by W. Somerset Maugham (1874–1965) – inspired by the life of the artist Paul Gauguin (1848–1903) – about a London stockbroker who leaves behind wife, family and job to live and paint in Tahiti. Maugham explained the title to a friend:

> It means reaching for the moon and missing the sixpence at one's feet.

'Moonlight' Sonata. The nickname of the piano sonata in C sharp minor, opus 27 no 2 (1801), by Beethoven (1770–1827), which the composer himself entitled *Sonata quasi una fantasia* ('sonata, almost a fantasia'). The origin of the nickname lies in a review of the piece by Heinrich Rellstab (1799–1860), who aptly likened the famous opening movement to moonlight playing on the waters of Lake Lucerne in Switzerland. Franz Liszt described the middle movement as 'a flower between two abysses'. The sonata has also been nicknamed the 'Laube' Sonata, as it was supposedly composed in a bower (German *Laube*).

Moon Tiger. A Booker Prize-winning novel (1987) by Penelope Lively (b.1933). The novel presents the memories of Claudia Hampton, a dying historian, and centres on a love affair she had in Egypt during the Second World War, where she was working as a journalist. A 'moon tiger' (also called a 'tiger coil') is an anti-mosquito coil, which is lit at night and pervades the room – and scores one's throat – with a pungent scent.

More Pricks than Kicks. A collection of short stories (1934), comprising the first prose work by Samuel Beckett (1906–89). They all concern a student called Belacqua Shuah, whose first name is that of a Florentine musical instrument maker and friend of the Italian poet and philosopher Dante Alighieri (1265–1321), who used him in his *DIVINE COMEDY* as a symbol of indolence. This is reflected in the first line of the book:

> It was morning and Belacqua was stuck in the first of the canti in the moon.

The title reflects the answer given by Jesus to Paul:

> I am Jesus whom thou persecutest: it is hard for thee to kick against the pricks.
>
> Acts 9:5

Moronic Inferno, and Other Visits to America, The. A collection (1986) of essays and journalism on contemporary America by Martin Amis (b.1949). The title comes from a passage in Saul Bellow's novel *Humboldt's Gift* (1975):

> I knew what you needed in a big American city was a deep no-affect belt, a critical mass of indifference ... But now the moronic inferno has caught up with me.

Mother Courage and her Children (German title: *Mutter Courage und ihre Kinder*). A play (1941; English translation 1961) by the German dramatist Bertolt Brecht (1898–1956), first staged in Zurich. It is about an indomitable woman who fights to protect her family at the time of the Thirty Years War (1618–48). Mother Courage is the nickname of a canteen-woman called Anna Fierling: her courage avails her little, however, as she declines to become politically involved in the events that threaten her family and is thus doomed to lose them all. Brecht based his play loosely on *Die Landestörzerin Courasche* (1669), by the German author Hans Jacob Christoffel von Grimmelshausen (*c.*1622–76), who had served in the Thirty Years War before writing his account of the sufferings of the German peasants during the war.

Mother Goose. The origin of this character, who features in the titles of many collections of fairy stories and nursery rhymes, is somewhat obscure. The first collection of fairy tales in which she appears is *Contes de ma mère l'oye* (1697; 'tales of my Mother Goose') by Charles Perrault (1628–1703), but the French expression *conte de la mère l'oye* for a tale and its teller, or an old wives' tale, was already in existence; the phrase occurs, for example, in the issue of 12 June 1650 of Jean Loret's weekly gazette *La Mvze historique*. There is some more detailed discussion in the introduction to the *Oxford Dictionary of Nursery Rhymes*:

> *La Mère Oie* may well be a lineal descendant of *La Reine Pédauque*, otherwise *Berthe au grand pied*, and there may also be a relationship to *Fru Gode* or *Fru Gosen* of German folklore. Perrault's tales were first published in English by J. Pote and R. Montagu (London, 1729), with the title *Histories, or Tales of Past Times. By M. Perrault. Translated by Mr Samber.* The placard on the wall, in the frontispiece, reads 'Mother Goose's Tales', and despite a long-standing claim to the contrary, this is the earliest known use in the English language of the term 'Mother Goose'.
>
> IONA AND PETER OPIE: *The Oxford Dictionary of Nursery Rhymes* (1951, 1997)

The first English *title* to include Mother Goose was *Mother Goose's Melody; or Sonnets for the Cradle* (1781), compiled in the 1760s (possibly by Oliver Goldsmith; 1730–74) and published by the successors of John Newberry, the children's book publisher.

The Opies convincingly dismiss the long-accepted claim that the figure of Mother Goose is American in origin. According to this story, a certain Elizabeth Foster (b.1665), when she married Isaac Goose of Boston, Massachusetts, took over the care of his ten children by his first wife, and proceeded to produce six more herself. Her daughter Elizabeth went on to marry a printer, Thomas Fleet, who supposedly collected the tales his mother-in-law told and published them in 1719 as *Songs for the Nursery or Mother Goose's Melodies for Children.* This story is thought to have been launched by Fleet's great-grandson, John Fleet Eliot, in *The Boston Transcript* of 14 January 1860.

Mother Goose has made appearances in innumerable editions since then. Notable illustrators have included Kate Greenaway (1846–1901) and Arthur Rackham (1867–1939). An intriguing variant is *Father Goose* (1899) by L. Frank Baum (1856–1919), better known as the creator of the *Wizard of Oz.* Another variant, reported by the Opies, is the one issued by William Wrigley (1861–1932), the chewing-gum manufacturer, who 'thought it worth while distributing, over a two-year period, 14,000,000 "Mother Goose" books rewritten to tie chewing-gum into nursery jingles'. One might also mention *The Charles Addams Mother Goose* (1967), a cartoon collection by the US creator of the ghoulish Addams family, Charles Addams (1912–88).

Mother Goose has also appeared on the stage. One of the greatest successes of the English clown Joseph Grimaldi (1778–1837) was the pantomime *Harlequin and Mother Goose*, played at Covent Garden in 1806. Various versions of Mother Goose have continued to play an important part in the repertory of traditional British Christmas pantomimes. The French composer Maurice Ravel (1875–1937) created the music and scenario for a ballet *Ma mère l'Oye* in 1912, the origins of the music lying in a suite of children's pieces for piano duet, written by Ravel in 1908–10.

Mourning Becomes Electra. A trilogy of plays (1931) by the US dramatist Eugene O'Neill (1888–1953) set in New England during the US Civil War. The three parts are entitled 'Homecoming', 'The Hunted' and 'The Haunted'. The central character, Lavinia, wears mourning black in the first two plays, then in the third appears in bright colours until her lover Peter shoots himself and she dons black once again. The title deliberately evokes links with the ancient Greek legend of Electra, who urges her brother Orestes to avenge their mother's and her lover's murder of their father Agamemnon after he returns from the Trojan War. O'Neill's title did not initially find favour with his publishers, Harper and Brothers, who complained that it was 'meaningless', failing to understand that here O'Neill used the word 'becomes' in its rather old-fashioned sense of 'flatters'.

'Mourning' Symphony (German *Trauersinfonie*). The nickname of the symphony no 44 in E minor (*c.*1771) by Haydn (1732–1809), allegedly because the composer said he wanted the slow movement played at his funeral.

Mousetrap, The. A murder mystery by Agatha Christie that holds the record for the world's longest running play. It opened in London on 25 November 1952 at the Ambassador's Theatre and in 1974 moved next door to St Martin's. The evening of its 40th anniversary, in 1992, was the 16,648th performance. The audience, typically composed of tourists, is asked not to reveal the identity of the murderer, but a few have unsportingly divulged the secret. The title comes from the 'play-within-a-play' in *Hamlet*.

> *King*: What do you call the play?
> *Hamlet*: The Mouse-trap. Marry, how? Tropically. This play is the image of a murder done in Vienna.
>
> WILLIAM SHAKESPEARE: *Hamlet* (1601), III.ii

Moveable Feast, A. A memoir (1964) by the US writer Ernest Hemingway (1899–1961) of his life in Paris in the 1920s, along with other expatriate Americans such as F. Scott Fitzgerald, Gertrude Stein and Ezra Pound. The title was selected by his widow from a letter Hemingway wrote in 1950:

> If you are lucky enough to have lived in Paris as a young man, then wherever you go for the rest of your life, it stays with you, for Paris is a moveable feast.

A 'moveable feast' is a Christian festival, such as Easter, that falls on different dates in different years.

Moving Finger, The. A murder mystery (1942) by Agatha Christie, in which Miss Marple questions whether a suicide note ('I can't go on') is genuine, the supposed suicide having been the recipient of hate mail. The title comes from Edward Fitzgerald's *The Rubáiyát of Omar Khayyám* (1859), stanza 51:

> The moving finger writes; and, having writ,
> Moves on: nor all thy piety nor wit
> Shall lure it back to cancel half a line,
> Nor all thy tears wash out a word of it.

This in turn may allude to the unseen hand that writes a dire warning at BELSHAZZAR'S FEAST.

Mr Standfast. A thriller (1919) by John Buchan (1875–1940), the third in which Richard Hannay appears. German spies are still the problem, and the excitement ranges from London to Skye, from Switzerland to the South Tyrol, and from a French château to the battlefields of the First World War. One of the novel's themes is the significance of fortitude, loyalty and moral strength, represented in John Bunyan's *The Pilgrim's Progress* by Mr Standfast. The Mr Standfast character in Buchan's novel is Peter Pienaar, who is reading Bunyan's book, references to which recur throughout the novel. *See also* THIRTY-NINE STEPS, THE.

Mrs Warren's Profession. A play by George Bernard Shaw (1856–1950), written in 1893, published in 1898, but not performed – due to objections by the Lord Chamberlain (the theatre censor) – until 1902. The first production in New York was closed down owing to a storm of public protests. It transpires that Mrs Warren's profession is organized prostitution, and that she has worked her way up the ranks to a position where she has an interest in houses of ill repute all across Europe. The play is centred on the discovery of this fact by her well-educated but sheltered daughter, the 22-year-old Vivie. Vivie is initially sympathetic, but not when she finds out that her mother is still active at the peak of her profession.

> The only way for a woman to provide for herself decently is for her to be good to some man that can afford to be good to her.
>
> GEORGE BERNARD SHAW: *Mrs Warren's Profession*, act 4

Much Ado About Nothing. A comedy (*c.*1598) by William Shakespeare (1564–1616). Similar stories are found in a number of possible sources, such as Ariosto and Spenser. There are two plots. In one, the wittily sparring and apparently mutually hating Beatrice and Benedick are tricked into declaring their mutual love. In the other, the malcontent Don John seeks to wreck the proposed marriage of his nephew Claudio to Beatrice's cousin Hero by leading Claudio to believe he has seen Hero committing an act of unfaithfulness. Claudio falls for the trick, and at this point the play becomes more serious in tone. Claudio denounces Hero at the altar, and she collapses and is thought to be dead. Beatrice is distraught:

> *Benedick:* Come, bid me do anything for thee.
> *Beatrice:* Kill Claudio.
> *Benedick:* Ha! not for the wide world.
> IV.i

Although at this point things seem pretty bad for all concerned, everything is eventually resolved and it is all shown to have been 'much ado about nothing'. Yet because of the darkening of the tone before the final resolution, the title contains more than a little irony. The phrase 'much ado about nothing' has entered common usage, although it is not usually meant ironically. Kenneth Branagh's 1993 film version – with Branagh as Benedick and Emma Thompson as Beatrice – was visually and dramatically stunning.

Muette de Portici, La (French, 'the dumb girl of Portici'). An opera by Daniel François Esprit Auber (1782–1871), with a libretto by Eugène Scribe and Germain Delavigne, first performed in 1828. The opera, which is remarkable in that the heroine is a mute, is known as *Masaniello* in Britain and America. The story is based on a 1647 revolt in Naples against Spanish rule, and such was its revolutionary fervour that a performance in Brussels in 1830 sparked off the revolt that led to the independence of Belgium.

Murder in the Cathedral. A verse drama by T.S. Eliot (1888–1965), first performed and published in 1935. The title ironically echoes the titles of popular murder mysteries, such as Agatha Christie's *MURDER ON THE ORIENT EXPRESS* (1934), but the play more seriously deals with the murder of St Thomas à Becket in Canterbury Cathedral in 1170.

Murder on the Orient Express. A detective novel (1934; initially published as *Murder on the Calais Coach*) by Agatha Christie (1890–1976), involving her retired Belgian policeman Hercule Poirot. The original Orient Express ran from Paris via Vienna to Istanbul and other Balkan cities between 1883 and 1961. A film version (1974) directed by Sidney Lumet boasted a stellar cast, which included Albert Finney (as Poirot), Ingrid Bergman, Lauren Bacall, Sean Connery and Vanessa Redgrave.

MUSICAL INSTRUMENTS

Accordion Crimes, a novel (1996) by the US writer E. Annie Proulx

Bagpipe Muzak, a collection of verse (1991) by Liz Lochhead

Banjo on My Knee, a comedy film (1936) set on the Mississippi in the riverboat era

BELLS AND POMEGRANATES, a series of collections of poems and plays (1841–6) by Robert Browning

Bugles in the Afternoon, a Western film (1952)

'Peter Quince at the Clavier', a poem by the US poet Wallace Stevens, from *Harmonium* (1923)

RUM, BUM, AND CONCERTINA, the autobiography (1977) of George Melly

The TIN DRUM, a novel (1959) by Günter Grass

NO DRUMS, NO TRUMPETS, a war memoir (1983) by Alec Le Vernoy

The Fiddler's House, a play (1907) by the Irish writer Padraic Colum

The Violins of Saint-Jacques, a novel (1953) by Patrick Leigh Fermor

FIDDLER ON THE ROOF, a stage musical (1964) and film (1971)

The MAGIC FLUTE, an opera (1791) by Mozart

The Man with the Blue Guitar, a collection of verse (1937) by the US poet Wallace Stevens

Harmonium, a collection of verse (1923) by the US poet Wallace Stevens

A Harp of Fishbones, a collection of stories for children (1972) by Joan Aiken

The Travelling Hornplayer, a novel (1998) by Barbara Trapido

The Lyre of Orpheus, a novel (1988) by the Canadian writer Robertson Davies

CAPTAIN CORELLI'S MANDOLIN, a novel (1994) by Louis de Bernières

SHOOT THE PIANIST, a film (1960) by François Truffaut

The Piano, a film (1973) about a mute pianist settling in the wilds of New Zealand in the 19th century

The Trumpet-Major, a novel (1880) by Thomas Hardy

Musical Offering, The (German title: *Das musikalische Opfer*). A set of pieces, mostly for flute, violin and harpsichord, by J.S. Bach (1685–1750), composed in July 1747. In May 1747 Bach had visited Potsdam to see his son Carl Philipp Emanuel, and it was there that Frederick the Great (King Frederick II of Prussia) – himself a capable flautist – had given Bach a theme on which to improvise. Subsequently Bach used this theme as the basis of the pieces in *The Musical Offering*, which he then had lavishly printed and bound to present to the king (hence the 'offering' of the title). Bach's inscription on the score reads '*Regis Iussu Cantio Et Reliqua Canonica Arte Resoluta*' ('By order of the king, the theme and the rest resolved according to canonic art'); the initial letters of the inscription form the word *ricercar*, which is a complex contrapuntal fugue or canon – *The Musical Offering* mostly consists of canons and fugues. Various composers, including Anton Webern in 1935, have made orchestral arrangements from the set.

Music Makers, The. A musical ode for contralto, chorus and orchestra, op 69 (1912) by Edward Elgar (1857–1934), setting a poem called 'Music and Moonlight' (1874) by the minor English poet Arthur O'Shaughnessy (1844–81):

> We are the music-makers
> And we are the dreamers of dreams.
> Wandering by lone sea-breakers,
> And sitting by desolate streams;
> World-losers and world-forsakers,
> On whom the pale moon gleams:
> Yet we are the movers and shakers
> Of the world forever, it seems.

O'Shaughnessy is actually referring to poets as 'the movers and shakers' (a phrase that strangely only entered common usage in the 1970s, when it came to denote powerful people who initiate events and influence people). Elgar's piece includes many musical quotations, including several from his own earlier works.

My Egypt. A modernist painting (1927) of huge concrete grain elevators by the US painter Charles Demuth (1883–1935). The title draws a comparison (ironic or otherwise) with the monumental architecture of ancient Egypt, such as the pyramids or the massive round pillars of the temples.

My Fair Lady. A film musical (1964) based on a stage musical (1957) by Alan Lerner (1918–86) and Frederick Loewe (1901–88) depicting the transformation of roughly spoken cockney flower girl Eliza Doolittle into a well-groomed society lady through the efforts of the arrogant linguist Professor Henry Higgins. Starring Audrey Hepburn and Rex Harrison, the film was derived ultimately from the play *PYGMALION* (1913) by George Bernard Shaw (1856–1950). Shaw had reservations about the film and the musical was given a different title partly to differentiate it from the original play. The new title was extracted from a traditional rhyme:

> London Bridge is falling down, falling down, falling down,
> London Bridge is falling down, my fair lady.
>
> 'London Bridge is Falling Down'

> An Englishman's way of speaking absolutely classifies him.
> The moment he talks he makes some other Englishman despise him.
>
> ALAN JAY LERNER: lyric from *My Fair Lady* (1956), adapting Shaw's preface to *Pygmalion*: 'It is impossible for an Englishman to open his mouth without making some other Englishman hate him or despise him.'

My Family and Other Animals. An amusing memoir cum wildlife study (1956) by the zoologist Gerald Durrell (1925–95). It recalls his boyhood in Corfu in the 1930s, where his widowed mother set up an unorthodox household with his sister and brothers – one of whom was the poet and novelist Lawrence Durrell (1912–90). A sequel was entitled *Birds, Beasts and Relatives*.

My Sad Captains. *See* GAUDY NIGHT.

My Universities. An autobiographical novel (1923) by the Russian writer Maxim Gorky (1868–1936). Gorky was sent out to work at the age of eight by his impoverished grandfather, and proceeded to take on a number of menial jobs, as well as wandering the country as a tramp. His attempt to study at Kazan University came to nothing. The book tells of the 'school of hard knocks' that in his youth shaped him as an adult.

There was a brief fashion in the 1970s for college-style sweatshirts emblazoned with 'Ididntgoto University'.

N

Naked and the Dead, The. The first novel (1948) by Norman Mailer (b.1923). Mailer enlisted in the US Army in the Second World War with the idea of writing 'a short novel about a long patrol'. *The Naked and the Dead* is a long novel about a long patrol during the assault on a Pacific island, and the 14 members of the unit represent a microcosm of American society. The 'naked' of the title is referred to in the text: 'A shell sighed overhead, and unconsciously [Sergeant] Martinez drew back against a gunhousing. He felt naked.' The title phrase also recalls a phrase in the Apostle's Creed:

> He ascended into heaven, And sitteth on the right hand of God the Father Almighty; From thence he shall come to judge the quick and the dead.
>
> The Book of Common Prayer. In this context, 'the quick' means 'the living'.

A further possible influence on the title is the 1921 novel by F. Scott Fitzgerald, *The Beautiful and Damned*. The borrowing would be ironic, given that Fitzgerald's novel portrays a world in which the ultimate aim is 'the final polish of the shoe, the ultimate dab of the clothes brush, and a sort of intellectual There!' – whereas Mailer's gritty novel strips men down to their basic selves, facing them with their own weaknesses and with the reality of death.

A film version of Mailer's novel (1958), directed by Raoul Walsh, was shorn of the four-letter words that made the novel notorious.

Naked Ape, The. A popular study of human behaviour (1967) from the perspective of the discipline of ethology (animal behaviour) by Desmond Morris (b.1928). Morris coined the term himself:

> There are one hundred and ninety-three living species of monkeys and apes. One hundred and ninety-two of them are covered with hair. The exception is a naked ape self-named *Homo sapiens*.
>
> *The Naked Ape*, Introduction

Naked Lunch, The. A surrealistic novel by William Burroughs (1914–97), first published with this title in Paris in 1959. It was the last book to be censored by the US authorities, and when it was published in the United States in 1962 as *Naked Lunch* it had been shorn of its definite article. The novel was created by a form of linguistic collage from thousands of pages of notes Burroughs made during his long affair with the drug heroin. The Nobel Prize-winning author Samuel Beckett (1906–89) commented on the technique: 'That's not writing, it's plumbing.' The title was suggested to Burroughs by Beat Generation author Jack Kerouac (1922–69), who helped with the manuscript; according to Burroughs, it implies 'that frozen moment when everyone sees what is on the end of every fork'. David Cronenberg's film version (1991) explored the creation of the novel through the hallucinatory experiences of a writer.

> Writers live the sad truth just like everyone else. The only difference is, they file reports.
>
> *The Naked Lunch*

Name of the Rose, The (Italian title: *Il nome della rosa*). A historical novel (1980; English translation 1983) by Umberto Eco (b.1932). Eco is a professor of semiotics, and the novel is a metaphysical quest for truth and meaning in the form of a medieval thriller. The setting is a mountaintop Benedictine monastery, in which a learned Franciscan seeks the serial murderer of several monks. According to Eco, the cryptic Latin hexameter, with which the book closes, implies that 'departed things leave (only, or at least) pure names behind them'. Eco has said of the title:

> It came to me virtually by chance, and I liked it because the rose is a symbolic figure so rich in meanings that now it hardly has any meaning left.

A film version (1986) was directed by Jean-Jacques Annaud, with Sean Connery in the leading role.

Napoleon of Notting Hill. A novel (1904) by G.K. Chesterton (1874–1936), a fantasy of the future in which London is ruled by an elected king, who reintroduces medieval customs. The city falls into internecine warfare as the provost of Notting Hill (the 'Napoleon' of the title) objects to a road-building project.

Notting Hill also provided the setting and title of an immensely popular US film (1999) starring Hugh Grant and Julia Roberts as unlikely lovers.

National Velvet. A novel (1935) by Enid Bagnold (1889–1981). Velvet, a butcher's daughter, wins a piebald horse in a raffle. Disguised as a boy, she rides it in the Grand National, Britain's premier steeplechase. Although she is first past the winning post, she is disqualified for dismounting before the weighing-in. A popular film version (1945), directed by Clarence Brown, starred a 14-year-old Elizabeth Taylor.

Nausea (French title: *La Nausée*; alternative English title: *The Diary of Antoine Roquentin*). A novel (1938; English translation 1949) by the French existential philosopher Jean-Paul Sartre (1905–80). Roquentin, the protagonist, experiences nausea when he realizes that there is no reason for the existence of people or things:

> Things are entirely what they appear to be and *behind them* … there is nothing.

However, in the end he realizes that the very purposelessness of existence makes him absolutely free.

Ned Kelly. A hero of Australian folklore who became a favourite subject of the great Australian painter Sidney Nolan (1917–92). Kelly was a notorious bushranger, who wore home-made armour, including a trademark cylindrical tin helmet, for his armed escapades. He was hanged after being captured following a shoot-out in 1880. Nolan started his series of paintings of Kelly in 1946. In most of these paintings – such as *Kelly in Landscape* (1969), *Kelly (Dust Series)* (1971) – Kelly is part of what Nolan described as 'the great purity and implacability' of the Australian landscape.

> Truth comes from the barrel of a gun said
> he, truth resides in the rope said the
> judge. Both were right and both are
> dead, mixed in glory, shame and quicklime.
>
> SIDNEY NOLAN: 'notes for poems' (1971)

A film called *Ned Kelly* (1970), directed by Tony Richardson, starred the Rolling Stone lead singer Mick Jagger as the outlaw, while the Australian novelist Peter Carey (b.1943) won his second Booker Prize for fiction with *True History of the Kelly Gang* (2001).

'Nelson' Mass (German *Nelsonmesse*). The nickname of the Mass in D minor (1798) by Haydn (1732–1809), which he entitled *Missa in angustiis* ('Mass in time of need'). The work is said to celebrate Nelson's victory over the French fleet at the battle of the Nile (also called the battle of Aboukir Bay) in the same year; certainly the striking entry of timpani and trumpets in the *Benedictus* adds a martial touch to the work. Another story is that Nelson heard it in 1800 on his visit to Eisenstadt in eastern Austria, where Haydn was Kapellmeister to the Esterházy family. In English-speaking countries the work is sometimes referred to as the 'Imperial' Mass.

Never Give a Sucker an Even Break. A film comedy (1941) written by and starring the US comedian W.C. Fields (1879–1946).The story, which begins with Fields falling out of an aeroplane in pursuit of a bottle of whisky, was allegedly jotted down by Fields on the back of an envelope and sold to Universal Studios for $25,000. The film is now known chiefly for its title, which has long been quoted as a quintessentially Fieldsian bit of advice. Fields himself suggested shortening it to *Fields: Sucker*, thinking the longer version might be a trifle unwieldy. When first released in the UK it was less memorably titled *What a Man!*

Never Say Never Again. A film (1983) starring Sean Connery as secret agent James Bond, based on the spy novels of Ian Fleming (1908–64). The title – the first of a Bond film not to derive from Fleming – was an in-joke between the movie producers and Connery himself, who had sworn that his appearance in the earlier Bond movie, *DIAMONDS ARE FOREVER* (1971), would be his last.

'New World' Symphony. *See* 'FROM THE NEW WORLD'.

Nibelungenlied. *See RING, THE*

Nice Derangement of Epitaphs, A. A medieval whodunnit (1988) by Ellis Peters (b.1913), one of many featuring the detective monk Brother Cadfael. The malapropism of the title comes from Mrs Malaprop herself, in Sheridan's *The Rivals* (1775), III.iii:

> If I reprehend any thing in this world, it is the use of my oracular tongue, and a nice derangement of epitaphs!

Nigger of the 'Narcissus', The. A novel by Joseph Conrad (1857–1924), published in 1897. Conrad had originally intended calling the book *The Forecastle: A Tale of Ship and Men*, but found as he wrote it that the tale became increasingly dominated by the dying black man James Wait (the 'nigger' of the title):

> He seemed to hasten the retreat of departing light by his very presence … a black mist emanated from him; a subtle and dismal influence; a something cold and gloomy that floated out and settled on all the faces like a mourning veil.

Conrad had gathered material for his tale when he himself had sailed on a ship called the *Narcissus*, which he had joined at Bombay in 1883.

Nighthawks. A painting (1942) by the US artist Edward Hopper (1882–1967), showing people at an all-night coffee stand. A nighthawk is the same as a 'night owl', i.e. someone who likes to stay up all night. A nighthawk – also called a mosquito hawk or bulbat – is also the name for any of a group of American nightjars. *Nighthawks* has also been used as the title of two films, one (1978) about the night-time cruising of a gay British schoolteacher, and the other (1981) about American policemen pursuing a terrorist.

Night in Casablanca, A. A film comedy (1946) starring the Marx Brothers. Featuring Groucho Marx as the manager of a hotel in Casablanca much frequented by spies, it clearly owed a great deal to the Bogart classic CASABLANCA. Warner Brothers, which had released *Casablanca*, threatened to sue over the use of the word 'Casablanca' in the title, only for Groucho to retort that if they did then he would sue them in return over their use of the word 'Brothers'.

Nightmare, The. A painting (1782) by the Swiss-born British painter Henry Fuseli (1741–1825), in which a grotesque and demonic dwarf squats on the body of a sleeping woman, while a fiercely staring white horse bursts through the drapery behind her. The presence of this horse might suggest the etymology of the word 'nightmare', but this is not in fact the case. The word originally denoted a sensation in sleep as if something heavy were sitting on one's chest, formerly supposed to be caused by a monster who actually did this: the second part of the word is Old

English *mare* (Old Norse *mara*), an incubus, and the same idea appears in the French word for a nightmare, *cauchemar*, literally meaning 'the fiend that tramples'. It is this incubus creature that Fuseli is illustrating in the form of the dwarf.

Night on the Bare Mountain (Russian title: *Ivanova noch na Lysoy gore*). A symphonic poem by the Russian composer Modest Mussorgsky (1839–81), written in 1867 and subsequently revised. The most familiar version is actually an arrangement by Rimsky-Korsakov (1844–1908), who gave the work its first performance in 1908. The full title is *St John's Night on the Bare* [sometimes translated as 'bald'] *Mountain*, as the inspiration for the piece came from the story 'St John's Eve' by Gogol (1809–52), which features a witches' sabbath. Mussorgsky's piece is programmatic, describing the spirits of darkness and Chernobog (a pagan Slav god) gathering for a black sabbath. At the height of the orgiastic proceedings the bell of a little church is heard, dispersing the spirits with the onset of dawn. This is more or less the storyline used in the Walt Disney animation of the piece, in *Fantasia* (1940).

Night Watch, The. A huge group portrait (1642) by the Dutch painter Rembrandt van Rijn (1606–69), more properly entitled *The Militia Company of Captain Frans Banning Cocq* or *The Corporalship of Captain Banning Cocq's Civic Guards*. It was commissioned, along with several other group portraits, for a new hall of the Kloveniersdoelen, a branch of the civic militia of Amsterdam. The men are not in fact preparing for the night watch; the popular title derives from the fact that over the centuries the painting had been covered with varnish that darkened over time. When it was cleaned after the Second World War, it was suggested in some quarters that it be re-named 'The Day Watch'. It is not certain what ceremony the men are preparing for – perhaps the visit to the city in 1638 of the French queen mother, Marie de Médicis.

There is a romantic but apocryphal tale that Rembrandt's sitters were horrified by the portrait, in which the individuals (some of them with shaded faces) are subsumed to the overall demands of the composition. According to this myth, the sitters – who had all paid an equal share of the cost of the painting – demanded alterations, but Rembrandt refused to make any changes to his masterpiece. The painting was removed from the militia hall, Rembrandt's career as a successful society portraitist came to an end, and he died in penury. However, there is no evidence that the picture was not well received: Rembrandt was paid the handsome sum of 1600 guilders for it, and continued to receive important commissions for the rest of his life.

Nine Tailors, The. A detective novel (1934) by Dorothy L. Sayers (1893–1957). The Nine Tailors, perhaps standing for 'nine tellers', is a peal performed on the eight bells of the church of Fenchurch St Paul, where the amateur sleuth Lord Peter Wimsey is stranded, and where he investigates two deaths. Traditionally, bell-ringers ring 'nine tailors' (nine tolls on the funeral bell) for a man, six for a woman and three for a child. This may be linked to the proverb 'Nine tailors make a man' (15th–16th centuries), the meaning of which is disputed: the proverb may also suggest that a true gentleman purchases his clothes from a variety of suppliers, or that tailors are so enfeebled by their sedentary trade that they are only one-ninth man.

Nineteen Eighty-Four. A dystopian novel (1949) by George Orwell (1903–50). The book comprises a prophecy of the totalitarian future of mankind, portraying a society in which government propaganda and terrorism destroy human awareness of reality. It is generally thought that Orwell named the novel by reversing the last two figures of the year in which it was written, 1948, but an article by Sally Coniam in the *Times Literary Supplement* of 31 December 1999 proposed another theory. In 1934 Orwell's first wife, Eileen O'Shaughnessy, published a poem, 'End of the Century 1984', in *The Chronicle*, the school magazine of Sunderland Church High School, where she had been a pupil in the 1920s. The poem was written to mark the school's 50th anniversary, looking back then forward to the future and to the school's centenary in 1984. It seems likely that Orwell could have adopted the year accordingly, although for him it was a random date. Support for this lies in the poem's mention of 'telesalesmanship' and 'Telepathic Station 9', terms strangely modern for their time, which seem to prefigure Orwell's own 'Newspeak', 'teleprogrammes' and 'telescreen'.

Following the publication of Orwell's novel, the year 1984 – until it came and went – was long regarded as apocalyptic, and as such was even entered in the *Oxford English Dictionary*. Appropriately enough, a film version entitled *1984* starring John Hurt and Richard Burton was released in 1984.

Nixon in China. A 'post-minimalist' political opera by John Adams (b.1947), first performed in 1987. The opera concerns the visit that President Richard Nixon made to China in 1972 as part of his strategy of détente, and which led to the establishment of diplomatic relations between the United States and the People's Republic. One critic has commented of the opera that it 'proved to some listeners that there is more to minimalism than at first meets the ears'.

Nocturne in Black and Gold: The Falling Rocket. A painting (1874) by the American artist James McNeill Whistler (1834–1903), who mostly worked in England. Whistler gave musical or otherwise abstract titles such as 'Symphony', 'Harmony', 'Caprice', 'Arrangement' and 'Nocturne' to many of his paintings, in furtherance of his belief in aesthetic correspondences between the arts. The formalist titles preceded that part of the title concerned with the subject: for example, *Arrangement in Grey and Black, No 1: The Artist's Mother* (popularly known as *Whistler's Mother*; 1871–2) and *Arrangement in Grey and Black, No 2: Thomas Carlyle* (1873).

It was Whistler's *Nocturne in Black and Gold* that prompted a famously hostile review from Ruskin:

> I have seen, and heard, much of cockney impudence before now; but never expected to hear a coxcomb ask two hundred guineas for flinging a pot of paint in the public's face.
>
> JOHN RUSKIN: in *Fors Clavigera*, 1877

Whistler promptly sued for libel, and was awarded damages of one farthing. He had to pay his own costs, however, and was declared bankrupt in 1879, when he was obliged to sell his Chelsea house and move to Venice for a year.

No Drums, No Trumpets. The title of the English edition (1983) of a book by Alec Le Vernoy about his experiences in the Second World War. The publisher who titled it thus was alluding to the story in which the playwright J.M. Barrie counsels a young writer who cannot think of a title for his book: 'Are there any trumpets in it?', asks Barrie. 'No.' 'Are there any drums in it?' 'No.' 'Then why not call it *Without Drums or Trumpets*?'

No Exit. *See* HUIS CLOS.

Noli Me Tangere (Latin, 'touch me not'). A painting by Titian (1487/90–1576), of uncertain date, depicting the moment after the

Resurrection when Christ, withdrawing from her touch, spoke these words to Mary Magdalene, who had just recognized that he was not, after all, the gardener:

> Jesus saith unto her, Touch me not; for I am not yet ascended to my Father: but go to my brethren, and say unto them, I ascend unto my Father, and your Father; and to my God, and your God.
>
> John 20:17

There is a work with the same title, and the same subject, painted in 1520–6 by Correggio (1494–1534), in the Prado, Madrid.

Noli me tangere is the title of a novel in Tagalog (1886) by the Filipino writer José Rizal (1861–96). It recounts the evils and corruption of Spanish rule in the Philippines, and contributed to the growth of Filipino nationalism. It was translated into English in 1912 with the title *The Social Cancer*, noli-me-tangere being the name given to a kind of cancerous ulcer.

In botany, noli-me-tangere is an alternative name for touch-me-not, itself applied to various plants of the genus *Impatiens*, particularly *I. Noli-me-tangere*, in which the ripe seedpods explode when touched.

None but the Lonely Heart. A film (1944) adapted by the US playwright Clifford Odets from a novel of the same title by the Welsh writer Richard Llewellyn (pen-name of Dafydd Vivian Llewellyn Lloyd; 1906–83). It tells the story of a shiftless young Cockney who drifts into a life of crime. Starring Cary Grant and Ethel Barrymore, it took its title from a song written by the Russian composer Tchaikovsky (1840–93), which was itself based on 'Mignon's Song' in the Goethe novel *Wilhelm Meister* (*see also* MIDSUMMER NIGHT'S DREAM, A). In Tchaikovsky's song the relevant lyric is usually translated as:

> None but the weary heart can understand how I have suffered and how I am tormented.

North and South. A novel by Mrs Gaskell (1810–65), published in 1854–5 in Dickens's *Household Words*. The title refers to the industrial north of England and the rural south, and the book deals with the contrasts between the two, mainly in terms of poverty versus affluence. The 'North–South Divide' is still a political issue in Britain.

North by Northwest. A classic film thriller (1959) directed by Alfred Hitchcock and written by Ernest Lehman about an advertising executive who gets confused with another man and consequently finds himself pursued across the United States by people trying to kill him. Starring Cary Grant as the businessman driven to the point of madness by his experiences, the film derives its title from Shakespeare's *Hamlet*, specifically the passage in which the 'gloomy prince' denies the fact that he is actually mad:

> I am but mad north-northwest; when the wind is southerly I know a hawk from a handsaw.
>
> II.ii

Nostromo. A novel by Joseph Conrad (1857–1924), published in 1904. The story is set in an imaginary and unstable South American republic called Costaguana. (*Costa* is Spanish for 'coast'; *guano* is the excrement of seabirds, harvested off the cost of Chile and used as a fertilizer; in South American Spanish it is also a slang word for money.) Costaguana's wealth depends on its silver, and this silver ends up corrupting even the best of men – notably Nostromo himself, an Italian sailor who is now *capatez de cargadores* (head of the dockers). *Nostromo* is the Italian word for 'boatswain', from *nostro uomo*, 'our man'.

No Turn Unstoned. The memoirs (1982) of the actress Diana Rigg (b.1938). The saying 'A dramatic critic is a man who leaves no turn unstoned' is attributed to George Bernard Shaw, while the songwriter Arthur Wimperis (1874–1953) is said to have remarked of an evening at a music hall, 'My dear fellow, a unique evening! I wouldn't have left a turn unstoned.' The joke turns on 'to leave no stone unturned', a traditional expression meaning to carry out a thorough search.

'Not Waving but Drowning'. A poem by Stevie Smith (1902–71), written in 1953 when its author was suffering from clinical depression. Much of Smith's verse was characterized by an eccentric directness. In a poll conducted in 1995 'Not Waving but Drowning' emerged as Britain's fourth favourite poem.

> Nobody heard him, the dead man,
> But he still lay moaning:
> He was much further out than you thought
> And not waving but drowning.

'Not waving but drowning' has subsequently become a commonly used phrase describing a situation in which a gesture may be misinterpreted.

NUMBERS

Zéro de conduite (French, 'zero for conduct'), a film (1933) by Jean Vigo

0′ 00″, an experimental piece (1962) by the composer John Cage (*see 4′ 33″*)

ONE, TWO, BUCKLE MY SHOE, a detective story (1940) by Agatha Christie

ONE OF OUR AIRCRAFT IS MISSING, a film (1941) co-written and directed by Michael Powell and Emeric Pressburger

TWO ON A TOWER, a novel (1882) by Thomas Hardy

Two Cheers for Democracy, essays (1951) by E.M. Forster

The Two Cultures, a book (1959) by C.P. Snow on the disjuncture of the arts and sciences

The THIRD MAN, a film (1949) scripted by Graham Greene

The Three Faces of Eve, a classic film (1957) about a woman with a split personality

Three Colours: Blue (1993), *Three Colours: White* (1993) and *Three Colours: Red* (1994), a trilogy of Polish films, the colours referring to the French *tricoleur*

The Four Seasons (Vivaldi and others) (*see THE SEASONS* AND *THE FOUR SEASONS*, panel, pp.412–13)

FOUR SAINTS IN THREE ACTS, an opera (1934) by Virgil Thomson

The Fourth Protocol, a thriller (1984) by Frederick Forsyth

FOUR WEDDINGS AND A FUNERAL, a film comedy (1994)

Five Weeks in a Balloon, an adventure story (1863) by Jules Verne (film version 1962)

Five Children – and It, a novel for children (1902) by E. Nesbit

I Saw the Figure 5 in Gold, a 'poster-portrait' (1921) of the American poet William Carlos Williams by the US painter Charles Demuth. The title comes from a poem by Williams

SIX CHARACTERS IN SEARCH OF AN AUTHOR, a play (1921) by Luigi Pirandello

Six Degrees of Separation, a film (1993) about a conman, based on a play by John Guare. The title refers to the idea that everybody in the world is connected to everybody else via the acquaintances of their acquaintances, and so on to no more than the sixth degree

The SEVEN JOYS OF THE VIRGIN, a painting by Hans Memling

Seven Brides for Seven Brothers, a musical film (1954) set in the Wild West

SEVEN, a film (1995) about sins and a serial killer

8½, a semi-autobiographical film (1963) by the Italian director Federico Fellini, the title referring to the number of films he had made up to that point

Eight Mortal Ladies Possessed, a collection of short stories (1974) by the US dramatist Tennessee Williams

8 Heads in a Duffel Bag, a comedy gangster film (1997)

The NINE TAILORS, a detective novel (1934) by Dorothy Sayers

9½ Weeks, a famously steamy film (1986)

10, a comedy film (1979) starring Dudley Moore

A HISTORY OF THE WORLD IN 10½ CHAPTERS, a collection of linked short stories (1989) by Julian Barnes

10 Things I Hate About You, a film comedy (1999) based on *The* TAMING OF THE SHREW

Not Worth Reading. *See* STEAL THIS BOOK

Nourishment: slow and difficult absorption of 600 grammes of minced meat which disturb the usual digestive operations. A piece of body art, performed in Paris in 1971 by the Italian artist Gina Pane (b.1939). The performance was typical of her work, which often involves discomfort or pain; in this instance, the artist, having consumed the meat, made herself vomit it up again.

> As a dog returneth to his vomit, so a fool returneth to his folly.
>
> Proverbs 26:11

Novel on Yellow Paper. A novel (1936) by Stevie Smith (1902–71). After trying to get some of her poems published and being advised instead to 'go away and write a novel', she did just that, typing it in the firm's time (she worked for a publisher) on the firm's 'very yellow' carbon-copy paper. The book itself is an autobiographical exercise in the free association of ideas and experience.

Nozze di Figaro, Le. *See* MARRIAGE OF FIGARO, THE.

Nude Descending a Staircase. The title of two remarkably kinetic paintings (1911 and 1912) by the Dadaist Marcel Duchamp (1887–1968), subtitled respectively 'No 1' and 'No 2'. They have become as much an icon of early modernism as Picasso's *Les* DEMOISELLES D'AVIGNON. In a cubist style, the pictures evoke a sense of motion by repeating fragments of the same figure down a diagonal. Duchamp himself later remarked:

> When the vision of the *Nude* flashed upon me, I knew that it would break for ever the enslaving chains of Naturalism.

The poet X.J. Kennedy wrote of the paintings:

> One-woman waterfall, she wears
> Her slow descent like a long cape
> And pausing, on the final stair
> Collects her motions into shape.

Very similar in its approach is *Le Passage de la Vierge à la Mariée* (French, 'the transition from virgin to bride'), which Duchamp painted in 1912.

O

Odalisque. The title of a number of mostly sensual and luxurious paintings of reclining women, usually partially or completely nude, and usually in an Oriental setting. An 'odalisque' is a female slave or concubine, the word deriving via French from Turkish *ōdalik*, from *ōdah*, 'room'. The subject became popular in France in the early 19th century; a well-known example is *La Grande Odalisque* (1814) by Jean Auguste Dominique Ingres (1780–1867). There are other examples by Eugène Delacroix (1798–1863) and Pierre-Auguste Renoir (1841–1919), and several by Henri Matisse (1869–1954), including *Odalisque with Tambourine* (1926).

Odessa File, The. A thriller (1972) by Frederick Forsyth (b.1938) about a West German journalist's discovery of a nest of Nazi revivalists. A film of the same title was released in 1974. In real life Odessa or ODESSA was the acronym for Organisation der Ehemaligen SS-Angehörigen (German, 'organization of former SS members'), the best known of a number of secret organizations that sought to smuggle Nazis out of Germany to safety after the Second World War. It was founded in 1947, and among those it helped to escape was Adolf Eichmann. Favoured destinations were Franco's Spain, Arab countries of the Middle East, and South American countries such as Argentina and Paraguay. Odessa was wound up in 1952, and replaced by the Kameradenwerke ('comrade workshop').

THE ODDEST TITLE OF THE YEAR AWARD

Every year the Diagram Group offers a prize, via the column of the estimable Horace Bent in the *Bookseller* magazine, to the person in the trade who comes up with the oddest book title published that year. Many – but not all – of the winning titles are from professional, technical, academic and scientific publishers. Since the prize was established in 1978, winners have included:

- *Proceedings of the Second International Conference on Nude Mice* (1978)
- *The Madam as Entrepreneur: Career Management in House Prostitution* (1979)
- *Natural Bust Enlargement with Total Power: How to Use the Other 90% of Your Mind To Increase the Size of Your Breasts* (1985)
- *Lesbian Sadomasochism Safety Manual* (1990)
- *The Theory of Lengthwise Rolling* (1993)
- *Greek Rural Postmen and Their Cancellation Numbers* (1996)
- *The Joy of Sex: Pocket Edition* (1997)
- *High-Performance Stiffened Structures* (2000)
- *Butterworths Corporate Manslaughter Service* (2001)

Other submissions over the years have included:

- *Access to the Top of Petroleum Tankers*
- *Classic American Funeral Vehicles*
- *Cooking with Mud: The Idea of Mess in 19th-Century Art and Fiction*
- *Did Lewis Carroll Visit Llandudno?*
- *Diversity of Sulfate-reducing Bacteria Along a Vertical Oxygen Gradient in a Sediment of Schiermonnikoog*
- *Fancy Coffins To Make Yourself*
- *Guide to Eskimo Rolling*
- *John, I'm Only Dancing: Embarrassment as an Aesthetic Experience*

- *Lightweight Sandwich Construction*
- *New Caribbean Office Procedures*
- *Pet Packaging Technology*
- *Principles and Practices of Bioslurping*
- *Psoriasis at Your Fingertips*
- *Stink Bugs of Economic Importance in America North of Mexico*
- *Tea Bag Folding*
- *The Art and Craft of Pounding Flowers: No Pain, No Ink, Just a Hammer!*
- *The Complete Idiot's Guide to Near-Death Experiences*
- *The Flat-Footed Flies of Europe*
- *The Sexual Male: Problems and Solutions*
- *Twenty Beautiful Years of Bottom Physics*
- *What is a Cow?: And Other Questions That Might Occur to You When Walking the Thames Path*
- *Whose Bottom? A Lift-the-Flap Book*
- *Woodcarving with a Chainsaw*

'Ode to a Nightingale'. A poem by John Keats (1795–1821), written in 1819 and published in 1820. The nightingale is an unremarkable-looking brown bird, noted for its musical singing, usually heard at night – the name itself derives from the Old English *nihtegale*, literally 'night singer'. Keats heard the nightingale's song at his house at Hampstead, then a village north of London, and in the poem – one of the finest of Romantic lyric poems – the song of the 'immortal bird' is contrasted with the 'weariness, the fever, and the fret' of the world of mortals, 'Where youth grows pale, and spectre-thin, and dies.' These lines contain references to some of the symptoms of tuberculosis, from which Keats was suffering, and from which his brother Tom had recently died.

Among the titles Keats's poem has inspired are F. Scott Fitzgerald's *TENDER IS THE NIGHT* and Sidney Howard's play *ALIEN CORN*. *See also ENCHANTED CASTLE, THE.*

Odyssey. An epic poem attributed to the ancient Greek poet Homer (8th century BC). It records the adventures of Odysseus (whom the Romans called Ulysses), the king of the Greek island of Ithaca, on his decade-long homeward voyage from Troy (*see* ILIAD). The word 'odyssey' is now often used more generally for any great journey or undertaking, especially one that is pioneering. James Joyce (1882–1941) used the structure of the *Odyssey* as the basis of his modernist masterpiece *ULYSSES* (1922).

Of Human Bondage. A semi-autobiographical novel (1915) by W. Somerset Maugham (1874–1965). The title is that of one of the five parts of *Ethics* by the Dutch philosopher and theologian Benedict de Spinoza (1632–77), issued posthumously by his friends in 1677 in an anonymous volume.

Of Mice and Men. A novella (1937) by John Steinbeck (1902–68). It centres on two casual labourers, Lennie, a simple, sentimental giant who loves small animals but does not know his own strength, and his friend George. In a tragic ending, George's efforts are not enough to keep Lennie out of the trouble that he has unwittingly brought upon himself. The title is from 'To a Mouse' by Robert Burns (1759–96):

> The best-laid schemes o' mice an' men
>   Gang aft agley,
> And lea'e us nought but grief an' pain,
>   For promised joy.

A film version (1939) was directed by Lewis Milestone.

Oh, Calcutta! A stage revue (1969) devised by the British theatre critic Kenneth Tynan (1927), which caused a considerable furore for its sexual explicitness. The title was suggested to Tynan by his wife, Kathleen Tynan, who was writing an article about a painting of a nude by the French surrealist Clovis Trouille entitled *Oh! Calcutta! Calcutta!* Unbeknownst to the Tynans at the time, the French title was a pun on *oh, quel cul t'as* (meaning 'oh, what a lovely arse you've got'). Compare *LHOOQ*.

> The trouble with nude dancing is that not everything stops when the music stops.
>
> ROBERT HELPMANN: comment on *Oh, Calcutta!*

Oh, What a Lovely War! A musical (1963) created by Joan Littlewood's Theatre Workshop at the Theatre Royal, Stratford East, London, as a satirical commentary on the huge losses suffered in the First World War. The show featured lampoons of popular songs of the day, as sung by soldiers in the trenches.

> Oh, oh, oh, it's a lovely war,
> Who wouldn't be a soldier, eh?
> Oh, it's a shame to take the pay;
> As soon as reveille is gone,
> We feel just as heavy as lead,
> But we never get up till the sergeant
> Brings our breakfast up to bed …
>
> 'Oh, What a Lovely War!'

A film version – Richard Attenborough's directorial debut – was released in 1969.

Oldest Living Confederate Widow Tells All. A novel (1989) by Allan Gurganus (b.1947). The ancient widow of a Confederate veteran remembers the American South from the times of General Lee (1807–70) and Abraham Lincoln (1809–65) to Martin Luther King (1920–68) and the *Challenger* space shuttle disaster (1986). The inspiration was a story in the *New York Times* about widows of Confederate soldiers being still alive and receiving pensions from the government. It contained the phrase, 'oldest living Confederate widow', from which developed first a story, then a novella and finally a 736-page novel.

'Old Hundredth' or **'Old Hundred'.** A well-known and dignified hymn tune, to which 'All People That on Earth Do Dwell' is sung. The tune was so-called in the Tate and Brady Psalter of 1696. Its name there indicated the retention of the setting of W. Kethe's version of the 100th Psalm in the Psalter of 1563 by Sternhold and Hopkins. The tune is of older origin and is found as a setting of the 134th Psalm in Marot and Béza's Genevan Psalter of 1551. An even earlier version appears in the Antwerp collection *Souter Liederkins* of 1540.

'Old Man of the Sea, The'. One of the Sinbad the Sailor stories from *The* ARABIAN NIGHTS ENTERTAINMENT. In it the Old Man of the Sea hoists himself on Sinbad's shoulders and clings there for many days and nights, much to the discomfort of Sinbad, who finally gets rid of the Old Man by making him drunk. Hence, any burden, real or figurative, of which it is impossible to free oneself without the greatest exertions is called an 'old man of the sea'. Ernest Hemingway (1899–1961) adapted the title for that of his Pultizer Prize-winning novella *The Old Man and the Sea* (1952), about an old fisherman's struggle with a giant marlin.

Old Mortality. A novel by Sir Walter Scott (1771–1832), published in 1816. The story is set in the 17th century, when the Covenanters (Scots Presbyterians) fought Charles II's attempts to force episcopacy on Scotland. 'Old Mortality' was an actual historical character, who travelled round Scotland repairing the graves of Covenanting 'martyrs'. In the collected edition of the Waverley novels (1829–33), Scott wrote:

> This remarkable person, called by the title of Old Mortality, was well known in Scotland about the end of the last century. His real name was Robert Paterson. He was a native, it is said, of the parish of Closeburn, in Dumfries-shire, and probably a mason by profession – at least educated to the use of the chisel.

Scott himself had met him some thirty years before in Dunnotar churchyard in Kincardineshire. In Scott's framing narrative in the novel, Old Mortality visits Gandercleuch to repair gravestones, and there meets Peter Pattieson; their conversation forms the basis of *The Tale of Old Mortality* (as Scott called the novel in his manuscript).

Scott's novel (very indirectly) formed the basis – via the play *Têtes Rondes et Cavaliers* ('Roundheads and Cavaliers') by François Ancelot and Xavier Boniface Saintine – of the opera *I Puritani di Scozia* ('the Puritans of Scotland', 1835) by Vincenzo Bellini (1801–35), although somehow the action has shifted to Plymouth during the English Civil War, and the characters include Queen Henrietta Maria and Oliver Cromwell. The *Spectator* considered the opera 'a mass of drivelling imbecility'.

'Old Mortality' is also the title of a short story (1939) by the American writer Katherine Anne Porter (1890–1980).

Old Possum's Book of Practical Cats. *See* CATS.

Olympia. A painting (1863) by Edouard Manet (1832–83) of a reclining nude. Manet's nude shocked his audience when it was first exhibited in 1865 because of its realistic treatment of the subject (a conventional recumbent Venus), which is lit with a harsh white light. The frank and rather bored gaze with which the woman eyes the viewer, and her somewhat casual posture, suggested to Manet's contemporaries that she was a modern Parisian courtesan rather than a classical nude. The painter Gustave Courbet described her as 'the Queen of Spades after a bath'. However shocked they were, the public massed to see it:

> The crowd pressed forward as it does in the Morgue, to see Olympia, this slightly decomposed Olympia.
>
> PAUL DE SAINT-VICTOR: comment in *c.*1865

The scandal eventually subsided, and in 1907 *Olympia* was presented to the Louvre by the French statesman Georges Clemenceau. The painting is now in the Orsay Museum. Paul Cézanne (1839–1906) acknowledged Manet's title and subject in his painting *The Modern Olympia* (1872–3). A large, jagged bronze, almost abstract sculpture entitled *Olympia* (1960–2) by the US sculptor Reuben Nakian (1897–1986) just about suggests a female nude.

Manet's title has no apparent connection to Olympia, the valley in Elis in the western Peloponnese where the ancient Olympic Games were held. However, the name Olympia appears by his time to have become associated with prostitutes. For example, Emile Augier's popular French play *The Marriage of Olympia* (1855) concerns a prostitute who attaches herself to an otherwise respectable family. Earlier, the name was applied to an ideal or divine love, as in *Olympiados*, an epic by the Dutch Renaissance poet Jan Baptista van der Noot (*c.*1540–*c.*1595).

Once and Future King, The. A tetralogy of novels (1958) by T.H. White (1906–64), consisting of *The Sword in the Stone* (1938), *The Witch in the Wood* (1939), *The Ill-Made Knight* (1940) and *The Candle in the Wind* (1958) ('Candle in the Wind' is also the title of an Elton John song written initially in tribute to Marilyn Monroe and recycled, with enormous popular success, for Princess Diana following her death in 1997). *The Once and Future King* is a reworking of the Arthurian legend, beginning with Arthur's childhood, and offering with wit and pathos a parable for modern times. The title of *The Sword in the Stone* refers to the stone from which only the young Arthur can pull the magical sword Excalibur and so shows he is the rightful king; this first book in the tetralogy has become a classic of children's literature, but the subsequent volumes are more adult in tone. The overall title comes from *Le Morte D'Arthur* of Thomas Malory (*c.*1410–71), which has the following passage: 'And many men say that there is written on his tomb this verse:

Hic iacet Arthurus, rex quondam, rexque futurus.

('Here lies Arthur, once a king and a future king')

Book 21, chapter vii

The Sword in the Stone was turned into a Walt Disney cartoon film (1963).

One Day in the Life of Ivan Denisovich. (Russian title: *Odin den' Ivana Denisovicha*). A novella (1962; English translation 1963) by Alexander Solzhenitsyn (b.1918), first published outside the USSR. Life in one of Stalin's labour camps in 1950 is seen through the eyes of an inmate; the author was himself in such a camp from 1950 to 1953. A film version (1971), directed by Caspar Wrede and starring Tom Courtenay, was a fairly faithful adaptation of the original, with all its harrowing detail. *See also* GULAG ARCHIPELAGO, THE.

One Flew over the Cuckoo's Nest. A novel (1962) by Ken Kesey (b.1935). The narrator is the Chief, a Native American whose father was the last chief of his tribe. He is a patient in a mental hospital, in which authority is represented by 'Big Nurse'. The admission of McMurphy from prison precipitates a struggle between 'good' (the patients) and 'evil' (Big Nurse), with the 'liberation' of the patients from institutional restrictions as the stake. The film version (1975), directed by Milos Forman and starring Jack Nicholson as McMurphy, was an unexpected commercial success.

The term 'cuckoo' for an eccentric, fool or madman dates back to the late 16th century, deriving from the expression 'a cuckoo in the nest', denoting an oddity. 'Cuckoo's nest' (along with 'cuckoo academy' and 'cuckoo farm') arose as a term for a psychiatric institution in the USA in the 1960s; cuckoos notably don't make their own nests, but lay their eggs in those of other birds. The 'one flew over' in the title refers to the final escape of the Chief.

One Hundred Years of Solitude (Spanish title: *Cien años de soledad*). A novel (1967; English translation 1970) by the Colombian Nobel laureate Gabriel García Márquez (b.1928), generally regarded as the archetypal example of Latin American magic realism. The setting is the small, isolated Colombian village of Macondo, a fictional community that had previously appeared in García Márquez's *La hojarasca* (1955; *Leafstorm and Other Stories*) and in *La mala hora* (1962; *In Evil Hour*). The novel follows seven generations of the increasingly inbred Buendía family, the founders of the village, and their story parallels the history of Columbia itself.

One Million Years B.C. A film (1939) depicting the lives of a band of primitive cave-dwellers in prehistoric times. This version of human prehistory varied widely from scientific fact, with modern-looking humans pitting themselves against dinosaurs: the former did not emerge until around 100,000 years ago, while the latter had become extinct some 65 million years previously. This did not prevent a remake of the film, complete with dinosaurs, appearing in 1966 and starring Raquel Welch (in a fur bikini) and John Richardson in the roles originally taken by Carole Landis and Victor Mature. 'This is the way it was!' shrieked the posters. It wasn't.

One Thousand and One Nights, The. *See* ARABIAN NIGHTS ENTERTAINMENT.

One of Our Aircraft Is Missing. A film (1941) co-written and directed by Michael Powell (1905–90) and Emeric Pressburger (1902–88) about the crew of a Wellington bomber during the Second World War who are shot down but make their way back to England with the help of the Dutch underground. The title was inspired by a stock formula of wartime broadcasts about recent raids on enemy territory. The original title was *One of Our Aircraft Failed to Return*. In 1975 Walt Disney released a comedy adventure entitled *One of Our Dinosaurs is Missing*, apparently under the influence of the Powell Pressburger film.

One, Two, Buckle My Shoe. A detective story by Agatha Christie (1890–1976), published in 1940. The title comes from the nursery rhyme:

> One, two,
> Buckle my shoe;
> Three, four,
> Knock at the door;
> Five, six,
> Pick up sticks …

The rhyme goes back at least to the 18th century. The US title of the book is *The Patriotic Murders*.

On the Road. A novel (1957) by Jack Kerouac (1922–69), based on several wild trips across the United States with Neal Cassady (1926–68). In it he used the term Beat Generation 'to describe guys who run around the country in cars looking for odd jobs, girlfriends, and kicks'. The book became the prose manifesto of the culture it evokes. Crossing media, it also helped to define the genre of the 'road movie', in which the characters take to the road as an escape from something, and/or as a means of self-discovery. Male bonding between 'buddies' was a common element in such classics as *Easy Rider* (1969), at least until such feminist versions of the genre as *Thelma and Louise* (1991).

On Wenlock Edge. *See* SHROPSHIRE LAD, A.

Oranges Are Not the Only Fruit. A semi-autobiographical first novel (1985) by Jeanette Winterson (b.1959) about the childhood and growing up of a fictional Jeanette against the background of the religious fanaticism of her Pentecostal mother. The oranges of the title represent her mother's attitude to life, in which 'everything in the natural world was a symbol of the Great Struggle between good and evil'. The crunch comes when she abandons the forces of good, which she was destined to promote as a missionary, in favour of those of evil, having been discovered *in flagrante delicto* in bed with another girl. A televised version (1990) was adapted by Winterson from her own novel.

Origin of the Milky Way, The. A painting dating from around the 1570s by Jacopo Tintoretto (1518–94). The picture depicts an early episode in the career of Herakles (Hercules), the son of Zeus and the mortal Alcmene. According to one version of the legend, Alcmene, afraid of Hera's jealous anger, exposed her child, who was then swept up by Zeus and put to the breast of the sleeping Hera. When Hera awoke, Herakles was thrown from the breast and the milk that continued to spurt from the goddess's breast formed the Milky Way.

Our Lady of the Flowers. A novel (1943) by Jean Genet (1910–86), written with a pencil on brown paper while the author was in prison for theft. It portrays the underworld of Montmartre, inhabited by 'the girl-queens and boy-queens, the aunties, fags and nellies', among them 'Our Lady of the Flowers'. The 'dark and lovely flowers' are murders and treasons and executions that Genet hears about in his prison cell, from scraps of newspaper or prisoners' gossip; there is presumably an allusion to Baudelaire's *Les* FLEURS DU MAL ('flowers of evil'). 'Our Lady of the Flowers' is a creature called Divine, 'Lady of High Pansiness', 'Divine the Gaytime Girl', who 'died holy and murdered – by consumption' – and who was once a village youngster named Louis Culafroy. His/her title, and the manner of his/her death, is reminiscent of *La* DAME AUX CAMÉLIAS.

Genet's title, which recalls the formula used of many statues and paintings of the Madonna, is echoed in *Our Lady of the Potatoes*, a novel (1995) by Duncan Sprott.

Our Mutual Friend. A novel (1864–5) by Charles Dickens (1812–70). John Harmon is the son of a wealthy dealer in 'dust' (household waste), which becomes a prevailing symbol of money in the book. Harmon's harsh father has made a will by which he will only inherit if he marries Bella Wilfer. Harmon, who has been overseas for 14 years, is assumed to be dead (his papers are found on the body of a murdered man) and takes on a false identity to see what Bella is like. Harmon is the 'mutual friend' of Bella's father, the impoverished Reginald Wilfer, and the kindly Mr Boffin, who unknowingly employs Harmon as a secretary, inherits Harmon Senior's money and adopts Bella. Harmon falls in love with Bella, but she is initially spoilt by wealth, and rejects him, but in the end comes to see the worthlessness of money compared to love.

Ours, L'. *See* 'BEAR, THE'.

Out of Africa. An autobiographical memoir (1937) of her years in Kenya by Karen Blixen (1885–1962), who also wrote novels in her native Danish as Isak Dinesen, of her time running a farm near Nairobi in what is now Kenya. The title is based on a line from Pliny's *Historia Naturalis* (1st century AD):

> *Semper aliquid novi Africam adferre*
> ('Africa always brings [us] something new'),

often quoted as *Ex Africa semper aliquid novi* ('Always something new out of Africa'). Blixen's own title for her book was *Den afrikanske farm* ('The African Farm'). A critically acclaimed film version (1985) was directed by Sydney Pollack.

Over the Hills and Far Away. An orchestral piece by Frederick Delius (1862–1934), first performed in 1895. The title is the name of an old song or nursery rhyme dating from at least the early 18th century. It begins:

> Tom, he was a piper's son,
> He learnt to play when he was young,
> And all the tune that he could play
> Was, 'Over the hills and far away';
> Over the hills and a great way off,
> The wind shall blow my top-knot off.

Part of the song is quoted in Farquar's *The Recruiting Officer* (1706), and there is also a reference in Gay's *The BEGGAR'S OPERA* (1728):

> If with me you'd fondly stray
> Over the hills and far away.

The title of the song appears in 'A Song of the Road' in Robert Louis Stevenson's *UNDERWOODS* (1887):

> And what should Master Gauger play
> But 'Over the hills and far away'?

'Oxford' Symphony. The nickname of the symphony no 92 in G by Haydn (1732–1809). It was played when Haydn received an honorary doctorate from Oxford University in July 1791, but had actually been written in 1788.

'Ox Minuet' (German *Ochsenmenuett*). A minuet once attributed to Haydn, but actually written by his pupil Ignaz Xaver von Seyfried (1776–1841) and incorporated into his opera *Die Ochsenmenuett* (1823), which largely consists of arrangements of Haydn's music. The title comes from the story that Haydn had once written a minuet for a butcher in exchange for an ox.

P

***Pacific 231*.** A 'symphonic movement' (1923) by the Swiss composer Arthur Honegger (1892–1955) evoking the 'visual impression and physical enjoyment' produced by a steam locomotive (*Pacific 231* being the name of a US engine). Honegger seems to have felt a particular affinity with locomotives. In his book *I am a Composer* (1951) he wrote:

> I am like a steam engine: I need to be stoked up, it takes me a long time to get ready for genuine work.

***Paddy Clarke Ha Ha Ha*.** A novel (1993) by Roddy Doyle (b.1958), which won the Booker Prize for fiction. It records the day-to-day life in a Dublin suburb of a ten-year-old boy, with his reactions to the break-up of his parents' marriage, reflected in the chant of boys at his school:

> Paddy Clarke
> Has no da.
> Ha ha ha!

Pagliacci, I (Italian, 'the clowns'). A short opera by Ruggero Leoncavallo (1857–1919), with a libretto by the composer, first performed in 1892. The story of *crimes passionels* among travelling players is based on an actual incident in Calabria, related to Leoncavallo by his father, who had been the judge at the trial of the killer. In the opera, the actor Canio becomes so jealous of his wife Nedda that during their play, in which he plays Pagliaccio, a suspicious husband, and she Columbine, he stabs her and her lover. He turns to the audience and declares 'The comedy is over', echoing the words attributed to the dying Emperor Augustus ('*Plaudite, amici, comedia finita est*', 'Applaud, my friends, the comedy is over') – words that Beethoven also quoted on his deathbed. *I Pagliacci* – which the French composer Vincent d'Indy considered 'abominably commonplace' – traditionally forms part of a double bill with another piece of Italian *verismo*, *Cavalleria rusticana* (1889; 'rustic chivalry' – a tale of love and revenge in Sicily), by Pietro Mascagni (1863–1945), the programme being referred to as 'Cav and Pag'.

Painting. A painting (1951) by the US abstract expressionist Clyfford Still (1904–80). The picture is something of a bravura piece, displaying a variety of painterly possibilities.

Pale Fire. A novel (1962) by the Russian-born writer and lepidopterist Vladimir Nabokov (1899–1977). It is in the form of a 999-line poem (entitled 'Pale Fire'), purporting to be by a recently murdered academic, John Shade, with foreword, notes, commentary and index by an exiled European who was his neighbour. The title of both the novel and the poem comes from Shakespeare's *Timon of Athens* (*c*.1607):

> The moon's an arrant thief,
> And her pale fire she snatches from the sun.
> IV.iii

'Paradise and the Peri'. The second tale in Thomas Moore's LALLA ROOKH (1817). In Persian mythology, a peri (Persian, 'fairy', from Avestan *pairikā*, 'witch') was originally a beautiful but malevolent spirit. Later, peris were regarded as delicate, gentle, fairy-like beings, begotten by fallen spirits, who direct with a wand the pure in mind on the way to heaven. They are mentioned in the Koran. In Moore's tale, the Peri laments her expulsion from heaven, and is told she will be readmitted if she brings to the gate of heaven the 'gift most dear to the Almighty'. After a number of unsuccessful offerings, she brings to the gate of heaven a guilty old man, who weeps with repentance and kneels to pray. The Peri offers the 'Repentant Tear' and the gates fly open. Moore's tale inspired a cantata, opus 50 (1843), by Schumann (1810–56), a fantasy-overture, opus 42 (1862), by William Sterndale Bennett (1816–75) and a cantata (1870) by John Francis Barnett (1837–1916).

Paradise Lost. An epic poem in twelve books by John Milton (1608–74), one of the masterpieces of English literature. It was first published in

1667. The paradise that is lost is the Garden of Eden, and Milton's aim was 'to justify the ways of God to man' concerning the expulsion of Adam and Eve.

> Its perusal is a duty rather than a pleasure.
>
> SAMUEL JOHNSON: *Lives of the English Poets* (1779–81), 'Milton'

> Has any great poem ever let in so little light upon one's own joys and sorrows? I get no help in judging life; I scarcely feel that Milton lived or knew men or women.
>
> VIRGINIA WOOLF: diary entry, 1918

Milton's sequel, *Paradise Regained*, in four books, was published in 1671. According to this second epic, paradise was regained by Christ's resistance to the temptations of the Devil in the wilderness. These titles are recalled in *Paradise Postponed* (1985), a novel by John Mortimer (b.1923), which traces life in Britain from the Labour election victory of 1945 through to the Thatcherite 1980s.

Parental Admonition. The title given since the 18th century to a well-known painting (*c.*1655) by the Dutch genre and portrait painter Gerard Terborch (1617–81). It was mistakenly thought to represent a father giving advice to his daughter, although a partially erased coin that the 'father' is giving to the 'daughter' indicates that Terborch is actually illustrating a brothel scene.

'Paris' Symphonies. The name given to a set of symphonies, nos 82–7 (1785–6), by Haydn (1732–1809), commissioned by the Concert de la Loge Olympique, a Masonic concert society in Paris. The set includes the symphonies nicknamed 'The BEAR', the 'HEN' SYMPHONY and 'The QUEEN OF FRANCE'.

'Paris' Symphony. The nickname of the symphony no 31 in D, K297 (1778), by Mozart (1756–91). Mozart composed the piece on a visit to the city, and it had its first performance at the Concert Spirituel in Paris.

Parliament of Fowls, The. A long 'dream' poem by Geoffrey Chaucer (*c.*1343–1400), written some time between 1372 and 1386. It was first printed *c.*1477. The 'parliament' of the title is a conference of the birds, who meet to choose their mates on St Valentine's Day. The idea is based on an older tradition.

Parthenia. The title of a collection of 21 keyboard pieces by William Byrd, John Bull and Orlando Gibbons, published in 1611 or 1612 as a present for Princess Elizabeth (daughter of King James I) and her future husband, Frederick V, the Elector Palatine. Their wedding took place in February 1613. Parthenia is Greek for 'maidenhood', and the punning and frankly unashamed subtitle of the collection is *The Maidenhead of the first music that ever was printed for the Virginals* (the virginals being an early form of harpsichord, possibly so-named because the instrument was often played by young ladies). There is also a later sister volume, *Parthenia Inviolata*, containing anonymous pieces for virginals and bass viol (the title punning on 'inviolate' – i.e. virginal – and 'viol'). This second volume may have been produced for the marriage of King Charles I and Henrietta Maria in 1625.

Passage to India, A. A novel (1924) by E.M. Forster (1879–1970) whose three parts represent respectively the Muslim, Western and Hindu approaches to truth, rationality and spirituality. Forster visited India in 1912–13, and the Barabar Hills there became in his novel the Marabar Caves – the setting for the fateful encounter at the heart of the book. Forster returned to India for six months in 1921, to act as secretary to the Maharaja of Dewas, after which he went back to writing the novel, which he had begun in 1913. The title is from the poem of the same name by Walt Whitman (1819–92), of whom Forster wrote that there was 'no-one who can so suddenly ravish us into communion with all humanity or with death' (*Two Cheers for Democracy*). A film version (1984) of the novel was directed by David Lean.

Passionate Pilgrim, The. A collection of poems – largely on the subject of love (hence the title) – published in 1599 by the printer William Jaggard, who announced on the title page that they were 'By W. Shakespeare'. However, only a few have been identified as by him.

'The Passionate Pilgrim' is also the title of a short story (1875) by Henry James (1843–1916), about an American who (much like the author) has long harboured a passion for England, and eventually goes there.

'Passione, La' (Italian, 'the Passion'). The nickname of the symphony no 49 in F minor (1768) by Haydn (1732–1809). It is possible that it was intended for performance in Holy Week, and it is said that the sombre opening adagio is evocative of Christ's Passion.

Passport to Pimlico. A delightful film comedy (1948) about a district of London that declares itself to be an independent state after the discovery of an ancient charter identifying the area as part of Burgundy. Starring Stanley Holloway and Margaret Rutherford among the citizens of the breakaway republic, it was the first of the Ealing Comedies (so named because produced at the Ealing Studios, west London). *See also* *LAVENDER HILL MOB, THE.*

'Pastoral' Sonata. The name given by the Hamburg publisher August Cranz (1789–1870) to the piano sonata in D, opus 28 (1801) by Beethoven (1770–1827). Some say the title is appropriate to the first movement, while others detect a country-dance rhythm in the last movement.

Pastoral Symphony. The symphony no 6 in F, opus 68 (1808), by Beethoven, who gave it the title *Sinfonia pastorale*, and in the programme for the first performance it was described as 'more an expression of feeling than painting'. Beethoven described the movements as follows: 'Awakening of happy feelings on arriving in the country. Scene by the brook. Happy gathering of peasants. Thunderstorm. Shepherd's song. Happy and grateful feelings after the storm.'

> This is no question of gaily dressed shepherds ... it is a matter of nature in her simple truth.
>
> HECTOR BERLIOZ: Essay, on the *Pastoral Symphony*

> Is it not more profitable to see the sun rise than to listen to the Pastoral Symphony of Beethoven?
>
> MONSIEUR CROCHE (Claude Debussy)

Ralph Vaughan Williams (1872–1958) gave the title *Pastoral Symphony* to his symphony no 3 (1922, revised 1955). The title is also given to instrumental interludes in *siciliano* rhythm in Bach's *Christmas Oratorio* (1734) and in Handel's *MESSIAH* (1742), although in the latter case the composer called the piece 'Pifa' (i.e. representing music played on *pifferi*, shepherd's pipes).

There is a short story by the French writer André Gide (1869–1951) called 'The Pastoral Symphony' ('*La Symphonie pastorale*'; 1919), about a Swiss pastor who adopts, educates and seduces Gertrude, a blind orphan.

Patapoufs et Filifers. *See* *FATTYPUFFS AND THINIFERS.*

Pathétique Sonata. Beethoven's title for his piano sonata no 8 in C minor, opus 13, which was published in 1799 with the title *Grande sonate pathétique*. '*Pathétique*' here means not 'with pathos' but 'with emotion', 'moving'.

Pathétique Symphony. The subtitle of the symphony no 6, opus 74 (1893) by Tchaikovsky (1840–93). The description 'tragic' was initially suggested to Tchaikovsky by his brother Modest, but he preferred *pateti-chesky* (meaning 'with emotion' rather than 'with pathos'). Although Tchaikovsky did not use the French word *pathétique*, it is commonly used in English rather than 'pathetic', which has inappropriate connotations. Shortly after the first performance Tchaikovsky died.

Paukenmesse. *See* 'KETTLEDRUM' MASS.

Pavane pour une infante défunte (French, 'Pavan for a Dead Infanta'). A solo piano composition (1899) by Maurice Ravel (1875–1937), orchestrated by the composer in 1912. The title recalls the Spanish court custom of performing solemn dances at periods of royal mourning – the *infanta* being the eldest daughter of a ruling monarch of Spain who is not the heir to the throne. However, Ravel apparently had no particular princess in mind, and claimed that he opted for the title because he liked the sound of it.

A pavan or pavin is a stately dance that was popular in the 16th and 17th centuries, particularly with English composers. The origin of the name is uncertain. One theory has it originating in Spain, and attributes the name to the fact that the dancers stalk like peacocks (Latin *pavones*). Another theory traces its derivation to the Italian town of Padova (Padua).

'Peasant' Cantata. The name given to the secular cantata *Me hahn en neue Oberkeet* (1742; 'we have a new magistracy') by J.S. Bach (1685–1750). The name comes from the fact that the words are in Saxon dialect.

Pennies from Heaven. A multi-part TV drama (1978) by Dennis Potter (1935–94), starring Bob Hoskins and featuring, often ironically, a number of popular songs of the 1920s and 1930s. The title song was written in 1936 by the American Johnny Burke (1908–64):

> Every time it rains, it rains
> Pennies from heaven.
> Don't you know each cloud contains
> Pennies from heaven?

In November 1979 the new Conservative prime minister, Margaret Thatcher, sourly observed: 'Pennies don't fall from heaven. They have to be earned on earth.'

Persistence of Memory, The. The famous 'soft watches' painting (1931) by Salvador Dalí (1904–89). As Dalí helpfully explained in *Conquest of the Irrational* (1969):

> The famous soft watches are nothing else than the tender, extravagant, solitary, paranoic-critical camembert of time and space.

Peter Bell. A long poem by William Wordsworth (1770–1850), written in 1798 but not published until 1819. Peter Bell is a 'wild and woodland rover' who is reformed as he rides the donkey he steals from its drowned owner. The poem attracted much ridicule, J.H. Reynolds (1796–1852) publishing a parody with the same title in 1819. This explains the title of the better-known parody, *Peter Bell the Third*, by Percy Bysshe Shelley (1792–1822), also written in 1819. In this long poem Shelley attacks Wordsworth's shift from radical youth to conservative middle age (*see also* 'LOST LEADER, THE'). The work was too extreme politically to be published in Shelley's lifetime, but came out in 1839.

Peter Pan. A play (1904) by J.M. Barrie, in which the title character is the little boy who never grows up. The story begins when Peter enters the nursery window of the house of the Darling family to recover his shadow. He flies back to Never Never Land accompanied by the Darling children, to rejoin the Lost Boys. Eventually all are captured by Captain Hook's pirates, except Peter, who secures their release and the defeat of the pirates. The children, by now homesick, fly back to the nursery with their new friends, but Peter refuses to stay as he does not wish to grow up.

The name of Barrie's hero – which is now commonly applied to any man who appears reluctant to take on the responsibilities of adult life – combines that of the Greek god Pan and that of Peter Llewelyn Davies, one of the five young sons of Barrie's friends Arthur and Sylvia Llewelyn Davies (who became Mr and Mrs Darling in the play). Barrie explained to the boys that he made Peter Pan 'by rubbing the five of you violently together, as savages with two sticks produce a flame', but it was Peter Llewelyn Davies who came to be most closely associated with the character. He was named Peter after the title character in his grandfather George Du Maurier's novel *Peter Ibbetson* (1891). The five brothers generally met unhappy fates: one (George) died fighting in the First World War; another (Michael) drowned while at Oxford; and Peter himself (by then a publisher) committed suicide in 1960 by throwing himself under a train in the London Underground. Sir George Frampton's statue of Peter Pan in Kensington Gardens was not, incidentally, modelled on Peter Llewelyn Davies, but on his brother, Michael. The name of Wendy, the little girl who befriended Peter, was invented by Barrie and soon caught on as a new girl's name.

In 1929 Barrie donated the lucrative royalty rights to the play to the Great Ormond Street Hospital for Sick Children.

Walt Disney's animated version of *Peter Pan* appeared in 1953, and a sequel in 2002. In the disappointing live-action film *Hook* (1991), directed by Steven Spielberg, Peter Pan (Robin Williams) is a corporate lawyer who returns to Never Never Land to take on his old adversary (Dustin Hoffman). *The Lost Boys* is the title of an entirely unrelated film (1987) featuring vampire bikers.

Petrified Forest, The. A play (1935) by the US dramatist Robert E. Sherwood (1896–1955). An unsuccessful writer finds himself in a remote diner and persuades a gangster to kill him. His intention is that money from his life assurance will go to the impoverished daughter of the owner of the diner. When Sherwood started writing the play he had no idea of either title or setting, but found in his new office a road map, and placed his diner in the desert of eastern Arizona on the road to the Petrified Forest, an area (now a national park) noted for its fossilized tree trunks. The film version (1936) starred Leslie Howard, Bette Davis and Humphrey Bogart.

Petrushka. *See* PUNCH.

Phantom of the Opera, The (French title: *Le Fantôme de l'opéra*). A novel (published serially in 1910) by Gaston Leroux (1868–1927), in which the 'phantom' of the title is a composer called Erik who lives in seclusion under the Paris opera house and hides his hideously deformed face under a mask. He falls in love with a singer and commits a number of murders to achieve his desire, but in the end fails to get the girl. The unusual story was made into a film (1925) with Lon Chaney, 'the man of a thousand faces', in the name part, and following further cinematic versions in 1943 and 1962 was given a new lease of life in Andrew Lloyd Webber's identically titled hit musical (1986).

Philadelphia Story, The. A film (1940) based on a play by Philip Barry (1896–1949) about a spoiled Philadelphia heiress, Tracy Lord, who begins to have doubts about her forthcoming marriage to a dull company executive in the face of the taunts of her ex-husband and the growing interest of magazine reporter Mike Conner, who has been sent to Philadelphia by *Spy* magazine to cover the wedding. Directed by George Cukor, the film starred Katharine Hepburn (in a role specially written for her) alongside Cary Grant and James Stewart. It was remade as the musical *High Society* (1956), with Bing Crosby, Frank Sinatra and Grace Kelly.

'Philosopher, The' (German *Der Philosoph*). The nickname of the symphony no 22 in E flat (1764) by Haydn (1732–1809). The name comes from the solemn nature of the opening adagio.

Philosophy in the Boudoir. A disturbing painting (1947) by the Belgian surrealist René Magritte (1898–1967). The picture features a dress with breasts and a pair of high-heeled shoes with toes. The title presumably refers to the notorious *La Philosophie dans le boudoir* (1793) by the Marquis de Sade.

'Phoenix and the Turtle, The'. A poem attributed to William Shakespeare (1564–1616), which was included in Robert Chester's collection *Love's Martyr: or Rosalin's Complaint* (1601). It is based on the legendary love of the phoenix for the turtledove. The phoenix is a fabulous Arabian bird, the only one of its kind, which according to Greek legend lives a certain number of years, at the end of which it makes a nest of spices, sings a melodious dirge, flaps its wings to set fire to the pile, burns itself to ashes and comes forth with new life. The phoenix is a symbol of alchemy, and of the Resurrection. It was also adopted as a symbol by D.H. Lawrence (1885–1930), and appears on the covers of many of his books; his posthumous papers were published in 1936 under the title *Phoenix*.

The mythical bird features in some other titles. *The Phoenix* is an Old English poem, a beast allegory dating from the 9th century. *The Phoenix Nest* (1593) is a collection of poems by various authors (including Sir Walter Raleigh) edited by the unidentified 'R.S. of the Inner Temple'. The 'phoenix' of the title is Sir Philip Sidney (1554–86), the much mourned courtier, soldier and poet who had died at the battle of Zutphen, and the collection includes three elegies in his memory. Other phoenix titles include:

The Phoenix (1607), a play by Thomas Middleton

The Phoenix and the Carpet (1904), a children's story by E. Nesbit

Phoenix (1923), a play by Lascelles Abercrombie

The Phoenix and the Tortoise (1944), a verse collection by the US poet Kenneth Rexroth

A Phoenix Too Frequent (1946), a verse drama by Christopher Fry

The Phoenix Tree (1984), a novel by the Australian writer Jon Cleary

Physical Impossibility of Death in the Mind of Someone Living, The. The notorious shark in formaldehyde (1991) by Damien Hirst (b.1965). Hirst said of the work: 'I wanted the real thing, I wanted people to think "that could ... eat me".' The same could not be said of *Away From the Flock*, Hirst's 1994 sheep in formaldehyde. When exhibited at the Serpentine Gallery in London, someone poured ink into the sheep's tank; Hirst wasn't unduly upset.

Picture of Dorian Gray, The. The only novel of Oscar Wilde (1854–1900), published in 1890. Dorian Gray has his portrait painted as a young man, then keeps the picture in his attic. Gray stays young, while, in an echo of the FAUST legend (*see* FAUST OR FAUSTUS, panel, pp.152–6) the hidden portrait changes to show his advancing age and increasing depravity.

> The moral life of man forms part of the subject matter of the artist, but the morality of art consists in the perfect use of an imperfect medium.
>
> *The Picture of Dorian Gray*, preface

> Men represent the triumph of mind over morals.
>
> *The Picture of Dorian Gray*, chapter 4

There is a striking film version (1945), starring George Sanders and Hurd Hatfield. It is filmed in black and white, apart from when we see the portrait.

Pictures at an Exhibition (Russian title: *Kartinki s vystavki*). A set of piano pieces by Modest Mussorgsky (1839–81), composed in 1874. The exhibition was a memorial show for the Russian artist and architect Victor Hartmann, who had died the previous year. Mussorgsky evokes ten of Hartmann's pictures, linked by 'promenade' passages:

1. *The Gnome*
2. *The Old Castle*

3. *Tuileries* (children playing and fighting)
4. *Bydlo* (a Polish ox-drawn cart)
5. *Dance of the Unhatched Chickens*
6. *Samuel Goldenberg and Schmuyle*
7. *The Market at Limoges*
8. *Catacombs*
9. *Baba Yaga (the Hut on Fowl's Legs)* (Baba Yaga is a child-eating ogress of Russian folklore)
10. *The Great Gate of Kiev*

A number of composers have produced orchestrated versions, the most familiar of which is that by Maurice Ravel (1922).

'Pied Piper of Hamelin, The'. A poem by Robert Browning (1812–89), published in *BELLS AND POMEGRANATES*, vol. vii, *Dramatic Romances* (1845). The poem later became the basis of a cantata (1905) by Hubert Parry (1848–1918). The story had earlier appeared in English in James Howell's *Familiar Letters* (1645–55), and is set in 1284, when the town of Hameln in Westphalia was infested with rats. A mysterious stranger appears in the town and offers to rid it of the rats for a certain sum, which offer is accepted by the townspeople. The Pied Piper plays his pipe, and the rats follow him and drown in the River Weser. The Piper has fulfilled his contract, but payment is not forthcoming. On the following St John's Day he reappears and again plays his pipe. This time all the children of the town follow him and he leads them to a mountain cave, where all disappear save two: one blind, the other dumb or lame. Another version is that they were led to Transylvania, where they formed a German colony. The legend has its roots in the story of the Children's Crusade of 1212, in which thousands of German and French children disappeared.

Pilgrim's Progress, The. A prose allegory by John Bunyan (1628–88), the first part of which appeared in 1678 and the second in 1684. The pilgrim of the title is Christian, and his progress is explained in the subtitle: 'from This World to That Which Is to Come'. On his journey Christian is beset with trials and temptations, but he eventually reaches the Celestial City, where, in Part II, he is joined by his wife Christiana. The rustic simplicity and directness of the story have given it lasting appeal, and many expressions from it, such as 'the Slough of Despond', have entered the language. Other phrases and characters have provided titles: *MR STANDFAST*; *SHEPHERDS OF THE DELECTABLE MOUNTAINS*; *VANITY FAIR*. The work was formerly known to schoolchildren, to whom it was long recommended as a source of moral instruction, as 'Piggy's Poggy'.

Pincher Martin. A novel (1956) by William Golding (1911–93). Realistic flashbacks are combined with the tormented efforts of the guilt-ridden Martin, a naval officer – who has apparently survived his ship being torpedoed – to keep himself alive on a rock in the Atlantic. In the British armed forces and elsewhere, 'Pincher' has been a nickname for anyone surnamed Martin since the mid-19th century, when Admiral Sir William F. Martin was notorious for 'pinching' (arresting) sailors even for trivial offences. In the United States Golding's novel was published as *The Two Deaths of Christopher Martin*. It is possible that his choice of title was influenced by that of *Pincher Martin, O.D.* (1915), an early volume of stories and sketches of life in the Royal Navy by the naval officer and writer 'Taffrail' (Captain Henry Taprell Dorling; 1883–1968). Golding himself served in the Royal Navy in the Second World War.

Pippa Passes. A drama by Robert Browning (1812–89), not intended for performance. It was published in 1841 as the first volume of *BELLS AND POMEGRANATES*. Pippa is a poor Italian girl who 'passes' by four scenes involving different participants. We are shown both Pippa's innocent view of these characters, and the less uplifting reality. *Pippa Passes* is also the title of a novel (1994) by Rumer Godden (1907–98).

Pisan Cantos, The. Part of *The CANTOS* of Ezra Pound (1885–1972), the vast work-in-progress that occupied much of his later life. Pound wrote *The Pisan Cantos* in 1945, when he was held in a US army prison camp near Pisa for six months; his detention had resulted from his broadcasts on behalf of the Italian Fascists during the Second World War. *The Pisan Cantos* were published in 1948, while Pound was being held in St Elizabeth's Hospital for the criminally insane in Washington DC.

'Pit and the Pendulum, The'. A story (1843) by the US writer Edgar Allan Poe (1809–49). The narrator has been sentenced by the Spanish Inquisition to die by torture. In the dark of his prison cell he narrowly escapes falling down a pit, and later finds himself strapped down while a crescent-shaped blade on a giant pendulum slices closer and closer to his body. Luckily the prison rats gnaw through his bonds, but then the hot metal walls begin to close in on him, forcing him closer and closer to the pit … Roger Corman's 1961 classic film of the same title, starring Vincent Price, creates an intriguing plot as a prequel to the dungeon scene that comprises Poe's story.

Plague at Jaffa, The. One of the best known paintings (1804) by Antoine-Jean Gros (1771–1835), who accompanied Napoleon on many of his campaigns as a war artist. The subject of this painting comes from the beginning of Napoleon's Egyptian campaign, when his army was struck by plague in the city of Jaffa (now part of Tel Aviv-Jaffa in Israel). Gros shows Napoleon visiting his sick soldiers to restore morale, and even touching the sore of one infected man, as if working a miraculous cure. In fact, Napoleon is supposed to have issued orders for the sick to be poisoned, so as not to hinder the rest of his army.

Planets, The. A much-played orchestral suite by Gustav Holst (1874–1934), which had its first full public performance in 1920. The seven movements are: 'Mars, the Bringer of War', 'Venus, the Bringer of Peace', 'Mercury, the Winged Messenger', 'Jupiter, the Bringer of Jollity', 'Saturn, the Bringer of Old Age', 'Uranus, the Magician' and 'Neptune, the Mystic' (which also features a wordless female chorus). The theme from 'Jupiter' provided the music for the hymn 'I vow to thee, my country'. Astronomers will note the unastronomical order of the first three and the absence of Earth and Pluto (the latter was not discovered until 1930). However, the English composer Colin Matthews (b.1946) has written a piece for Pluto, which is now sometimes used to conclude performances of Holst's suite.

Playboy of the Western World, The. A play by the Irish playwright J.M. Synge (1871–1909), notable for its vigorous and poetic language. The play's supposed insults to 'Irish womanhood' provoked demonstrations when it was first staged at the Abbey Theatre, Dublin, in January 1907. It is about the disruption that follows when a feckless young man, Christy Mahon, arrives in a country pub in Mayo in the west of Ireland boasting that he is on the run after killing his own father. Although it is subsequently learned that he has done no such thing, he retains the spurious glamour he has acquired in the eyes of Pegeen Mike, the daughter of the landlord, and after he is driven out of the village she laments:

> Oh, my grief, I've lost him surely. I've lost the only Playboy of the Western World.

Playing the Moldovans at Tennis. *See* AROUND IRELAND WITH A FRIDGE.

Play It Again Sam. A film comedy (1972), based on a stage play (1969), written by and starring US comedian Woody Allen (b.1935). Allen plays a film critic who receives advice about his love life from the ghost of Humphrey Bogart, complete with trench coat. The title comes from a line in the classic Bogart movie *CASABLANCA* (1942), although it does not appear exactly in that form in the original film. The closest anyone gets to it is: 'Play it, Sam. Play "As Time Goes By",' as directed to the pianist Sam, played by Dooley Wilson. The song, incidentally, was nearly left out of the film at the request of its composer, Max Steiner, who begged Warner Brothers to drop it, fearing it would not work.

Plough and the Stars, The. A play by the Irish playwright Sean O'Casey (1880–1964), first produced at the Abbey Theatre, Dublin, in 1926, when its depiction of the sufferings of Dublin slum-dwellers during the Easter Rising of 1916 caused a riot. The title refers to the design on the flag of the Irish Citizen Army, the working-class organization that participated in the Rising, but was also intended by the author to suggest the contrast between the real and the ideal in life.

Plumed Serpent, The. A novel by D.H. Lawrence (1885–1930), published in 1926. In the novel Lawrence explores the possibilities of regenerating the spiritual traditions of particular places – in this case a fictionalized Mexico ruled by authoritarian leaders who are worshipped as gods, and who revive the rites of the Aztecs. The 'Plumed Serpent' is Quetzalcoatl, the feathered-serpent god of Mesoamerica, representations of whom go back more than 1000 years before the Aztecs. *See also* Q.

Pocketful of Rye, A. A detective story by Agatha Christie (1890–1976), published in 1953. The title comes from the nursery rhyme:

> Sing a song of sixpence,
> A pocketful of rye;
> Four and twenty blackbirds,
> Baked in a pie.

Poetaster, The. A comedy by Ben Jonson (1572–1637), first performed in 1601 and published in 1602. A 'poetaster' is a writer of inferior verse, *-aster* being a Latin suffix denoting a poor imitation of the real thing. In the play, set in the Rome of the Emperor Augustus, Jonson disguises his rivals Thomas Dekker (*c*.1572–1632) and John Marston (1576–1634) as the poetaster Crispinus and his friend Demetrius, while Jonson, with typical modesty, represents himself as the great Roman poet Horace.

Dekker responded with another comedy, *Satiromastix*, written, possibly in collaboration with Marston, in 1601, and published in 1602. The play uses the same characters as *The Poetaster*, although the tables are turned on Horace. The subtitle of *Satiromastix* is *The Untrussing of the Humorous Poet*, referring to Jonson's comedies of humours, *EVERY MAN IN HIS HUMOUR* and *Every Man out of His Humour*. The main title may mean 'satire-chewer' (from Latin *masticare*, to chew; playing on 'poet-taster'), although 'the satirist whipped' (from Latin *mastiga*, a whip) has also been suggested.

Point Counter Point. A satirical novel (1928) by Aldous Huxley (1894–1963). It is a roman à clef, featuring a large number of mostly unsympathetic characters drawn from the British upper classes and intelligentsia: there are thinly disguised portraits of, among others, D.H. and Frieda Lawrence, Augustus John, Sir Oswald Mosley, John Middleton Murry, Katherine Mansfield and Huxley himself. The title's reference to musical counterpoint (in which two or more melodic lines occur simultaneously, complementing one another) is reflected in some of the structural features of the novel; indeed, the overall structure of the book is said to be based on J.S. Bach's Suite No 2 in B minor.

Pomp and Circumstance. The collective title given by Edward Elgar (1857–1934) to five marches for orchestra, first performed separately between 1901 and 1930. The title comes from Shakespeare's *Othello*, III.iii:

> Farewell the neighing steed and the shrill trump,
> The spirit-stirring drum, th' ear-piercing fife,
> The royal banner, and all quality,
> Pride, pomp and circumstance of glorious war!

With slight alterations, the trio section of the first march became the finale of Elgar's *Coronation Ode* (1902), with words by A.C. Benson beginning 'Land of Hope and Glory'. This was later published as a separate song under that title. The song is traditionally performed with audience participation at the Last Night of the Proms (the annual London Promenade Concerts) and has also become associated with right-wing English nationalism.

Portnoy's Complaint. A novel (1969) by the US writer Philip Roth (b.1935). It is prefaced with a spoof definition of Portnoy's Complaint:

> A disorder in which strongly felt ethical and altruistic impulses are perpetually warring with extreme sexual longings, often of a perverse nature.

The main thrust of Alexander Portnoy's argument, retailed as a confession to his psychiatrist, concerns the repressive attitude of his mother, with whom he has carried on right into manhood a war of attrition (his main 'complaint'). His condition manifests itself in his compulsive masturbation as a boy (another 'complaint') and his subsequent obsession with having sex with Gentile women. A film version (1972) was directed by Ernest Lehman.

Portrait of a Lady, The. A novel by Henry James (1843–1916), published in 1881, and described by Graham Greene as 'a great leisurely built cathedral'. The title derives from that of many paintings by Old Masters, where the sitter has not been identified, for example the magnificent *Portrait of a Lady* in London's National Gallery by Lorenzo Lotto (*c.*1480–1556/7). The 'Lady' in James's novel is Isabel Archer, an American heiress in Europe, whose awful fate it is to marry the unfeeling wastrel and aesthete, Gilbert Osmond. The 1996 film version, directed by Jane Campion, starred Nicole Kidman as Isabel and John Malkovich as Osmond.

Portrait of Hugh Gaitskell as a Famous Monster of Filmland. A picture (1964) by the British Pop artist Richard Hamilton (b.1922), consisting of a blown-up newspaper photograph of Hugh Gaitskell (1906–63), the leader of the Labour Party from 1955 until his death in 1963, overlaid with an image of the actor Claude Rains as the Phantom from the 1943 film version of *The* PHANTOM OF THE OPERA. Hamilton was objecting to Gaitskell's opposition to unilateral nuclear disarmament, a policy that the Labour Party had voted for at the 1960 party conference; however, Gaitskell had successfully reversed this vote at the 1961 conference, following his famous 'Fight, and fight, and fight again' speech.

Portrait of the Artist as a Young Man, A. An autobiographical novel (1916) by James Joyce (1882–1941), extracted from a long work called *Stephen Hero*, a fragment of which was published in 1944. Stephen Dedalus, the protagonist, is not Joyce, but his consciousness is the means through which the author filters the relationship between imagination and reality. (Stephen later reappears in Joyce's *ULYSSES*.) The five chapters of *Portrait of the Artist* cover events from infancy to 1902, when Joyce made his first visit to Paris.

The title – one used often enough for paintings – suggested that of Dylan Thomas's *A Portrait of the Artist as a Young Dog* (1940), a collection of autobiographical short stories. Thomas might also have recalled the title of a famous painting by Gustave Courbet (1819–77): *Portrait of the Artist with a Black Dog* (1844).

Portrait of the Artist as an Old Man was the last work of the US novelist Joseph Heller (1923–99), published posthumously in 2000.

Portsmouth Point. A rumbustious concert overture by William Walton (1902–83), first performed in 1926. The work is based on a print by Thomas Rowlandson (1756–1827) depicting a crowded scene at the quayside.

Postillion Struck by Lightning, A. The title of the first volume of memoirs (1977) by the actor Dirk Bogarde (1921–99). Bogarde explains the title as coming from an old foreign-language phrasebook encountered during a childhood holiday, in which he found the useful expression, 'The postillion has been struck by lightning.' (A postillion is a person whose job it is to ride one of the horses drawing a coach.)

Postman Always Rings Twice, The. A film thriller (1946) based on the book (1934) by James M. Cain (1892–1977) about the liaison between a hobo and a bored waitress, which culminates in the murder of the latter's husband. Also made into a play and an opera, the film version starred Lana Turner and John Garfield. It was remade in 1981, with a screenplay by David Mamet and starring Jessica Lange and Jack Nicholson.

Cain offered two explanations for the title of this, his first novel. The first was that while he was writing the book the postman always rang his doorbell twice if he was bringing bills, but only once if he had personal mail. The second was that the postman would ring twice if he was delivering one of Cain's manuscripts after it had been rejected by a publisher: this happened so often that when the postman finally rang just once, to signify that the work had been accepted, the author gratefully altered the title to celebrate the fact.

Poule, La. *See* 'HEN' SYMPHONY.

'Prague' Symphony. The nickname of the symphony no 38 in D, K504 (1786), by Mozart (1756–91). It had its premiere in Prague in January 1787 when Mozart was visiting the city.

Pravda. A play (1985) by the British playwrights Howard Brenton (b.1942) and David Hare (b.1947) depicting the unprincipled behaviour of Lambert Leroux, a South African newspaper magnate, after he buys up two daily British newspapers. The play profited from the parallels that could be drawn with the media empires of Robert Maxwell and Rupert Murdoch, and it offered a bleak picture of how the truth can be manipulated by egocentric press barons. The title *Pravda* is an ironic reference to the Russian newspaper of the same name (meaning 'truth' in Russian), in which the propagandist influence over what was printed during the Soviet era was obvious even to the casual reader.

Precious Bane. A rural novel (1924) by Mary Webb (1881–1927), featuring a heroine, Prudence Sarn, who is disfigured by a hare-lip, as was the author herself. The plot abounds with romance and melodrama. The title, from *Paradise Lost* by John Milton (1608–74), has a rustic ring:

> Let none admire
> That riches grow in hell; that soil may best
> Deserve the precious bane.
> Book I

The book received posthumous publicity, when the prime minister, Stanley Baldwin, praised it at a Royal Literary Society dinner in 1928, and when Stella Gibbons wrote a parody, *COLD COMFORT FARM*.

Prelude, The. A long autobiographical poem by William Wordsworth (1770–1850), who started work on it in 1798–9, finished the first draft in 1805, but went on revising it throughout his life. The work was only published posthumously, in 1850, and Mary Wordsworth, his widow, supplied the title and subtitle, *Growth of a Poet's Mind*. The work covers the poet's boyhood, youth and young manhood, so the 'prelude' is to maturity, although the title may also reflect the poet's one-time intention to make *The Prelude* the introduction to a vast projected three-part work, entitled 'The Recluse', of which *The EXCURSION* forms the second part.

Prélude à l'Après-midi d'un faune. *See APRÈS-MIDI D'UN FAUNE, L'.*

Préludes, Les. A symphonic poem by Franz Liszt (1811–86), first performed in 1854. The title is that of a poem in *Nouvelles Méditations* *poétiques* (1822) by the French Romantic poet Alphonse de Lamartine (1790–1869), although the words inserted in the score by Liszt are not from Lamartine:

> What is our life but a series of preludes to that unknown song of which death sounds the first and solemn note?

Premonition of Civil War. A painting by the Spanish surrealist Salvador Dalí (1904–89), bearing the alternative title *Soft Construction with Boiled Beans*. It was painted in 1936, the year that the Spanish Civil War broke out. The composition largely consists of two humanoid constructions made of various limbs and other body parts. The lower figure is fiercely squeezing the breast of the grimacing upper figure, while various pieces of soft offal lie around, along with the eponymous beans. Dalí's support for Franco in the Civil War led to his expulsion from the surrealist movement in 1938.

Prester John. A novel (1910) by John Buchan (1875–1940) set in South Africa. The story concerns the involvement of the young Scottish hero in a complex plot, in which Prester John is an African preacher who returns to his country to lead a native uprising. 'Prester' means 'priest', and in medieval legend Prester John was a fabulous Christian emperor of Asia. He occurs in documents from the 12th century, and in Marco Polo's *Travels* he is lord of the Tartars. From the 14th century he becomes the emperor of Ethiopia (Abyssinia), where he was apparently still reigning in the time of Vasco da Gama (*c.*1469–1525).

Pricksongs and Descants. A collection of fictions (1969) by the US writer Robert Coover (b.1932). It contains ten of his earlier stories, tellings from new perspectives of traditional tales and pieces exploring the multiple possibilities of fiction. A pricksong is an archaic term for a piece of music written down or 'pricked', while a descant is an often ornate treble part sung above the main tune of a piece.

Pride and Prejudice. A novel by Jane Austen (1775–1817), published in 1813. As in SENSE AND SENSIBILITY, the title refers to two of the main characters: the aloof and wealthy Fitzwilliam Darcy, and the spirited but impoverished Elizabeth Bennet, who, through a variety of circumstances, is long prejudiced against him. In the end both overcome their respective failings and marry each other. Austen may have borrowed her title from Fanny Burney's *Cecilia* (1782):

> 'The whole of this unfortunate business,' said Dr Lyster, 'has been the result of PRIDE AND PREJUDICE.'

There was a successful film adaptation in 1940 (Aldous Huxley had a hand in the screenplay), and there have also been a number of TV serializations.

Primary Colors. An anonymously published novel (1996), about a Southern governor running for US president; the subtitle is 'A Novel of Politics'. The fact that the governor was a philanderer and his wife fiercely ambitious left readers in no doubt that the book was based on Bill Clinton's first presidential campaign, in 1992. Publication caused much speculation among the American chattering classes as to the identity of the author, which later turned out to be Joe Klein of the *New Yorker*.

The 'primary' in the title refers to a US preliminary election in which voters in a state select which candidate of their party they would like to run for president; while in painting, 'primary colours' are the three pigments, red, yellow and blue, from which all other pigments may be mixed. The novel was turned into a film (1998) starring John Travolta and Emma Thompson.

Prisoner of Chillon, The. A poetic monologue by Lord Byron (1788–1824), published in 1816. Byron wrote the poem shortly after visiting the castle of Chillon, which juts into the waters of Lake Geneva. The 'prisoner' of the poem is the Genevan François de Bonnivard (1493–1570), whose patriotic resistance on behalf of his city to the duke of Savoy and the bishop of Geneva resulted in his imprisonment underground in the castle of Chillon from 1532 to 1536. Byron departs somewhat from the historical record; for example, he makes his prisoner the last of six brothers, all of whom, together with their father, have died 'For the God their foes denied'. Byron later wrote in the 'Advertisement' for the poem:

> When this poem was composed, I was not sufficiently aware of the history of Bonnivard, or I should have endeavoured to dignify the subject by an attempt to celebrate his courage and his virtues.

Prisoner of Zenda, The. A romantic novel (1894) by Anthony Hope (Sir Anthony Hope Hawkins, 1863–1933), in which an English gentleman, Rudolf Rassendyl, finds himself impersonating the king of Ruritania, who is a prisoner in the castle of Zenda. He falls in love with Flavia, the king's betrothed, but gallantly surrenders her when the king is released. The castle of Zenda is as imaginary as the *Mitteleuropische* kingdom of

Ruritania, the name of which is derived from Latin *rus, ruris* 'the countryside', while '-ania' comes from the standard ending of the names of Roman provinces, such as Lusitania. The name Ruritania has since been applied to any small state where politics and romantic intrigue are the natural order of the day. Hope wrote a sequel, *Rupert of Hentzau* (1898). The 1937 film version of *The Prisoner of Zenda*, with Ronald Coleman as Rudolf and the king, has become a classic of its kind, while the two remakes (1952 and 1979) have not.

Private Memoirs and Confessions of a Justified Sinner, The. *See* CONFESSIONS OF A JUSTIFIED SINNER, THE PRIVATE MEMOIRS AND.

Professor, The. A novel by Charlotte Brontë (1816–55), written in 1846, but not published until 1857, after Charlotte's death. Like *Villette* (1853), the novel draws on Charlotte's experiences in 1843 as a pupil-teacher in Brussels ('Villette' is Charlotte's name for the city). There she fell in love with a brilliant teacher, Constantin Héger, although he was married and encouraged her to discipline her feelings. The 'professor' of the novel's title refers to the character William Crimsworth, who, like M. Paul Emmanuel in *Villette*, has a powerful impact on a young female pupil-teacher. Both characters are thought to be strongly based on Héger.

Prothalamion. *See* EPITHALAMION.

'Prussian' Quartets. The nickname for a set of string quartets by Mozart (1756–91), commissioned by Friedrich Wilhelm II, king of Prussia (1786–97), and written in 1789–90. Six were requested but only three delivered: no 21 in D, K575; no 22 in B flat, K589; and no 23 in F, K590. As the king was an amateur cellist, each of the quartets has a prominent part for the cello. The set is also referred to as 'The King of Prussia' Quartets.

Psmith in the City. A comic novel (1910) by P.G. Wodehouse (1881–1975), the first featuring an eccentric young snob who had earlier appeared in a boys' paper, the *Captain*, in 1908. The subsequent Psmith books are *Psmith Journalist* (1910) and *Leave it to Psmith* (1923). Psmith's full name is Rupert (or Ronald) Eustace Smith, and the initial P is an affectation, as is the monocle he sports. Although educated at Eton, he claims to be a socialist and calls everyone 'Comrade'. Wodehouse based Psmith on Rupert D'Oyly Carte (1876–1948), son of Richard D'Oyly Carte, the producer of Gilbert and Sullivan operas.

PROMETHEUS

Prometheus (Greek for 'forethought') was one of the Titans of Greek myth, and his sacrifice on behalf of humanity has inspired many works of art. He was the son of Iapetus and the ocean nymph Clymene (or Themis). It is said that Zeus, having been tricked by Prometheus over his share of a sacrificial ox, denied humanity the use of fire. Prometheus then stole fire from Hephaestus (the smith god) to save the human race. For this he was chained by Zeus to Mount Caucasus, where an eagle preyed on his liver all day, the liver being renewed at night. He was eventually released by Hercules, who slew the eagle. It was to counterbalance the gift of fire to humanity that Zeus sent Pandora to earth with her box of evils. In some versions of the myth, Prometheus was the actual creator of the first humans, whom he modelled out of clay.

The story of Prometheus is told in the *Theogeny* of Hesiod (8th century BC), and was the subject of a trilogy of plays by Aeschylus (*c*.525–456 BC). Only one of these plays, *Prometheus Bound*, survives; in it Zeus is portrayed as a tyrant, and Prometheus not only helps humans to survive, but also gives them the arts and sciences.

In the late 18th and early 19th centuries, Prometheus became a great hero to Romantic humanists and revolutionaries; Karl Marx, in his doctoral dissertation (1841), declared that 'Prometheus is the noblest saint and martyr in the calendar of philosophy.' The verse drama *Prometheus Unbound* (1820) by Percy Bysshe Shelley (1792–1822) takes the Greek story as its starting point, but creates its own mythic world to construct an allegory of liberation.

> The author of the *Prometheus Unbound* has a fire in his eye, a fever in his blood, a maggot in his brain, a hectic flutter in his speech, which mark out the philosophic fanatic.
>
> WILLIAM HAZLITT: *Table Talk* (1821–2), 'On Paradox and Common-Place'

The work inspired *Scenes from Prometheus Unbound* (1880), a large-scale choral piece by the English composer Hubert Parry (1848–1918), and *Music for a Scene from Shelley* (1935) by the US composer Samuel Barber (1910–81).

Shelley's wife, Mary Shelley (1797–1851), picked up the theme in her novel *Frankenstein, or The Modern Prometheus* (1818):

> ... a book about what happens when a man tries to have a baby without a woman.
>
> ANNE K. MELLOR: in the *Sunday Correspondent*, 8 April 1990

In this Gothic tale Dr Frankenstein's creation of 'the creature', and the tragic consequences that follow, suggest a critique of the Promethean hubris of modern science. The association of Prometheus with the industrial and scientific revolutions is reflected in the historical work *The Unbound Prometheus: Technological Change and Industrial Development in Western Europe from 1750 to the Present* (1969) by David S. Landes. The British science-fiction writer Brian Aldiss (b.1925) neatly melded the titles of the two Shelleys in his novel *Frankenstein Unbound* (1974), in which a scientist is transported back in time and encounters the Shelleys, Byron, and Dr Frankenstein – and his creature. Mary Shelley's tale of terror has inspired numerous films, one of the earliest and best of which is *Frankenstein* (1931), starring Boris Karloff as the monster.

Many other writers, composers and artists have created works based on the story of Prometheus, including Calderón de la Barca, Goethe, Byron, André Gide, Beethoven, Liszt, Fauré, Scriabin, Carl Orff, Brancusi, José Orozco and Kokoschka.

P'Tang Yang Kipperbang. A bitter-sweet TV play (1982) by Jack Rosenthal (b.1931). The title is a schoolboy chant, and the play, set in 1950s London, tells the tale of a cricket-obsessed schoolboy suffering from first love. Real bits of John Arlott's radio cricket commentary are heard during the course of the play.

Pulcinella. *See* PUNCH.

Pulp Fiction. A violent but entertaining film thriller (1994), written and directed by Quentin Tarantino (b.1963), in which four tales about the criminal underworld are cleverly interwoven in circular fashion. The title deliberately evokes the kind of trashy, violent crime fiction published in pulp magazines, a genre of lowbrow American literature at its most popular in the 1920s and 1930s. The magazines – originally printed on rough paper made of cheap wood pulp – contained sensationalist crime writing, often highly erotic in nature, and helped to create the character of the laconic 'tough guy'

PUNCH

The character of Mr Punch (Punchinello in full; Italian Pulcinella; French Polichinelle), familiar from Punch and Judy puppet shows, owes its origin to the *commedia dell'arte* character Pulcinella, a clownishly eccentric curmudgeon probably first played by the Italian comedian Silvio Fiorillo in the early 17th century (the name is a diminutive of *pulcino*, a young chicken). Some trace the origin of the character to southern Italy:

> And on the other side of the mountains ... [were the peasants] of Acera, who were incurably facetious and produced the archetype of clowns, Pulcinella.
>
> NORMAN LEWIS: *Within the Labyrinth* (1950)

In the English version Mr Punch is nasty, violent and dishonest, with a hooked nose and a hunched back. In a fit of jealousy he strangles his infant child, whereupon his wife Judy (originally Joan) belabours him with a bludgeon until he retaliates and beats her to death. He flings both bodies into the street, but is arrested and shut in prison whence he escapes by means of a golden key. The rest is an allegory showing how the light-hearted Punch triumphs over Ennui, in the shape of a dog; Disease, in the disguise of a doctor; Death, who is beaten to death; and the Devil himself, who is outwitted. In subsequent

English versions Jack Ketch (the name of a real 17th-century executioner), instead of hanging Punch, gets hanged himself.

> That's the way to do it!
>
> MR PUNCH: catchphrase

The character appears in various guises in music. *Pulcinella* is a ballet (later an orchestral suite) by Igor Stravinsky (1882–1971), first performed in 1920 with choreography by Massine and décor by Picasso. The music is derived from works attributed to the 18th-century Italian composer Giovanni Batista Pergolesi (1710–36), and was likened by Constant Lambert in his book *Music Ho!* (1934) to scrawling moustaches on the faces in an old engraving. The Russian puppet Petrushka also derives from the Italian figure Pulcinella, and is the central character in another Stravinsky ballet of that name. The opera *Punch and Judy* by Harrison Birtwistle (b.1934), with a libretto by Stephen Pruslin, was first performed in 1968 and has been described as Britain's first truly modern opera. Literary and dramatic appearances include *A Punch for Judy* (1920), a play by the US dramatist Barry Philip (1896–1949), and *Punch: The Immortal Liar* (1921), a collection of poetry by the US writer Conrad Aiken (1889–1973).

The humorous weekly magazine, *Punch, or the London Charivari*, was named after Mr Punch, who featured in the cover design for many decades. The magazine first appeared in July 1841, closed in 1992, and was relaunched in 1996. The subtitle of the magazine comes from the *Charivari*, a French satirical magazine launched in 1832, *charivari* being a French word for an uproar caused by banging pans and kettles, accompanied by hissing and booing, to express disapproval, especially at an unpopular wedding. The word derives from Late Latin *caribaria*, 'headache', from Greek *karē*, 'head', and *barus*, 'heavy'. An early contributor to *Punch* was the dramatist and humorist Douglas Jerrold (1803–57), who in 1843 published *Punch's Letters to His Son*.

Puppetry of the Penis. A cabaret show conceived by Simon Morley and David Friend, and first performed by them in Australia in 1998. The two men, who claim the show is a revival of 'the ancient art of genital origami', manipulate their penises, scrotums and testicles into a variety of objects, such as a hamburger, a windsurfer and a mollusc. The official publicity describes the show as 'an over-18 non-sexual show'. *See also* VAGINA MONOLOGUES, THE.

Puritani di Scozia, I. *See* OLD MORTALITY.

Pygmalion. One of the best known plays of George Bernard Shaw (1856–1950), first performed in 1913 and published in 1916. For a bet, Henry Higgins, a professor of phonetics, trains Eliza Doolittle, a Cockney flower girl, to pass herself off as a grand lady. The title refers to the Greek legend of Pygmalion, a sculptor and king of Cyprus. According to the version in Ovid's *Metamorphoses* (1st century AD), Pygmalion falls in love with the ivory statue he has made of his ideal woman. At his earnest prayer the goddess Aphrodite gives life to the statue, and he marries it.

The relationship of Higgins and Eliza is romanticized in the musical version, *MY FAIR LADY.*

Q

Q. A horror film (1982) written and directed by Larry Cohen. Q is the Aztec god Quetzalcoatl, the PLUMED SERPENT, who reappears in present-day Manhattan to feed on its inhabitants. *Q* was also the title of an anarchically innovative 1970s TV series by the comedian Spike Milligan (1918–2002).

Q.B. VII. A novel (1970) by the US writer Leon Uris (b.1924). The title stands for the name of the court, Queen's Bench number seven, in which a libel trial is played out between an American novelist and a Polish surgeon who he has suggested performed experimental sterilizations on Jews in a concentration camp.

Quartet for the End of Time. A chamber work for violin, clarinet, cello and piano by the French composer Olivier Messiaen (1908–92). The work was written in 1941 while Messiaen was a prisoner of war of the Germans in Silesia, which explains the unusual combination of instruments, and perhaps also the eschatological title.

Quatre cent coups, Les (English title: *The 400 Blows*). A semi-autobiographical film (1959) by François Truffaut, the first in a series starring Jean-Pierre Léaud as Antoine Doinel, Truffaut's alter ego. In this film Léaud plays the twelve-year-old Antoine, who runs away from home and ends up in a juvenile detention centre. *Faire les quatre cent coups* is a French idiom meaning 'to sow one's wild oats', 'to get into big trouble'.

Queen Mab. A long poem by Percy Bysshe Shelley (1792–1822), published in 1813. The poem mixes blank verse and lyrics, visions of the future with polemics against commerce, war, the church, meat, monarchy and marriage. Queen Mab appears near the beginning in her chariot, and sums up her role:

> ... it is yet permitted me, to rend
> The veil of mortal frailty, that the spirit,
> Clothed in its changeless purity, may know
> How soonest to accomplish the great end
> For which it hath its being, and may taste
> That peace, which in the end all life will share.
>
> canto 1, line 180

Mab is a figure derived from ancient British folklore, the name perhaps deriving from Welsh *maban*, 'baby'. Mab is the 'fairies' midwife', employed by the fairies to deliver mortals' brains of dreams:

> *Romeo:* I dreamed a dream tonight.
> *Mercutio:* Oh, then, I see Queen Mab hath been with you.
>
> WILLIAM SHAKESPEARE: *Romeo and Juliet* (1594), I.iv. Mercutio goes on to give a long description of Mab. In Berlioz's *Romeo and Juliet* symphony (1839) there is a 'Queen Mab Scherzo'

When Mab is called 'queen' it does not mean sovereign (although Shelley takes it thus, hailing her as 'Fairy Queen!' when she first appears); it is Titania, as wife of Oberon, who is queen of the fairies. 'Queen' when applied to Mab simply means 'female' (Old English *cwēn*, modern dialect *quean*). Some believe the name may be related to the Irish Medb or Maeve, the goddess-queen of Connacht.

'Queen of France, The' or ***'La Reine'*** (French, 'the queen'). The nickname of the symphony no 85 in B flat (1785) by Haydn (1732–1809), one of the 'PARIS' SYMPHONIES. It was said to be a favourite of the ill-fated Queen Marie Antoinette.

Queen of Spades, The (Russian title: *Pikovaya dama*). An opera by Tchaikovsky (1840–93), with a libretto by his brother Modest, first performed in 1890. The story is adapted from a novel by Alexandr Pushkin (1799–1837), published in 1834. Hermann loves Lisa, whose grandmother is an elderly countess known as the Queen of Spades, because of her reputed success at cards. Wishing to win enough money to marry Lisa, Hermann tries to get the secret out of the countess, but she dies of fright. He is later visited by her ghost, who gives him her secret.

Hermann becomes more obsessed with cards than with Lisa, and she, feeling abandoned, drowns herself. When he follows the ghost's instructions and places his all on the ace, the card is revealed as the Queen of Spades. The ghost reappears and Hermann goes mad and kills himself. In 1888, before he embarked on the composition of the opera, Tchaikovsky wrote:

> I am not going to write *The Queen of Spades* ... it does not appeal to me and it would end up very ordinary.

However, once the work was done he wrote to Modest:

> Unless I'm entirely mistaken, this opera is a masterpiece.

Novosti thought it was 'interesting in parts'.

Quiet Flows the Don. *See* AND QUIET FLOWS THE DON.

Quo Vadis? A novel by the Polish Nobel laureate Henryk Sienkiewicz (1846–1916), published in 1896 and translated into many languages. The story concerns the persecution of Christians in Rome under Nero, and was turned into a spectacular film (without the question mark) by Mervyn Le Roy (1951). The title comes from the Acts of Peter in the biblical Apocrypha, in which Peter asks '*Domine, quo vadis?*' ('Lord, where are you going?) when he encounters the risen Christ on the Appian Way during his flight from Nero's Rome. Christ replies that he is on his way to Rome 'to be crucified again', upon which the shamefaced Peter turns around and goes back to Rome to meet his death. According to tradition he asked to be crucified head downwards and related his meeting with Christ as he was nailed to the cross. *Domine, Quo Vadis?* is the title of a late painting (*c.*1602) by Annibale Carracci (1560–1609).

R

Rabbit. The nickname of Harry Angstrom, the hero of a series of four novels by John Updike: *Rabbit, Run* (1960), *Rabbit, Redux* (1971; *redux* is Latin for 'brought back', 'restored'), *Rabbit Is Rich* (1981) and *Rabbit at Rest* (1990). His byname comes from his former glory days as a high school basketball champion. He subsequently becomes the owner of a car sales agency, but is generally limited and complacent in his attitudes, as a sort of latter-day Babbitt, the eponymous hero of the novel (1922) by Sinclair Lewis (1885–1951) (though the resemblance between the names is presumably coincidental). He finally dies of a heart attack during a playground game of basketball.

Radetzky March. A march by Johann Strauss the elder (1804–49), written in 1848, the year that the Austrian field marshal Count Joseph Radetzky (1766–1858) crushed the Italian revolutionaries at the battle of Custozza.

Radical Chic and Mau-Mauing the Flak Catchers. A collection of essays (1970) by the US journalist Tom Wolfe (b.1931). The term 'radical chic' was coined by Wolfe to denote high society's adoption of radicals and radical issues as fashion accessories. The term subsequently came to apply to anything left-wing that seemed to be embraced on grounds of being fashionable rather than through personal conviction.

> Radical Chic ... is only radical in Style; in its heart it is part of Society and its tradition – Politics, like Rock, Pop, and Camp, has its uses.
>
> TOM WOLFE in *New York* (8 June 1970)

The other parts of the title are more obscure. The Mau Mau were an African secret society which in the 1950s used violence and terror in an attempt to end British rule in Kenya. By 1957 the movement had been crushed by the British, but Kenya gained its independence in 1963. The origin of the name Mau Mau is uncertain. To 'catch flak' is to be the object of criticism and recrimination, 'flak' being Second World War slang for anti-aircraft fire (from German *Fl(ieger)a(bwehr)k(anone)*, 'aircraft defence gun').

Raft of the Medusa, The. One of the best known works (1819) by the French Romantic painter Théodore Géricault (1791–1824). It hangs in the Louvre, Paris. The painting depicts a shocking episode in French naval history, when in 1816 the officers of the shipwrecked *Medusa* abandoned their men to float on a raft, leading to the deaths of 139 of the 154 originally set adrift. The painting, which unflinchingly shows the dead and the dying in a lurid light, caused a political scandal.

The story inspired an opera, *Le Naufrage de la Méduse* (1839), by the German-born French composer Friedrich von Flotow (1812–83), with a libretto by Albert Grisar and Auguste Pilati. It is also commemorated in *Das Floss der Medusa*, a controversial oratorio by the German composer Hans Werner Henze (b.1926), described by the composer as an *oratorio volgare e militare*. It was commissioned by Hamburg Radio, and dedicated to Che Guevara, the revolutionary guerrilla leader. Its first performance in 1968 was disrupted by demonstrators and police intervention.

'Rage over a Lost Penny'. The fanciful nickname given to an early, uncompleted piano piece by Beethoven (1770–1827), published posthumously as opus 129.

Ragged-Trousered Philanthropists, The. A novel by Robert Tressell (pen-name of Robert Noonan; 1870–1911). Subtitled *Being the story of twelve months in Hell, told by one of the damned, and written down by Robert Tressell*, it was written between 1907 and 1910, in the hope that money from the book might give his only daughter some financial security. It was first published, posthumously, in 1914 in an abridged form; a full edition was published in 1955. The book takes the form of an account of the lives of a band of men who work for an unscrupulous decorating firm (as Noonan had himself); the author ironically refers to these workers as 'philanthropists' as they slave away for low wages at the 'noble and unselfish task' of making money for their bosses. The novel became a classic of the British Labour movement.

'Raindrop' Prelude. The nickname for the prelude in D flat for piano, opus 28 no 15 (1839), by Chopin (1810–49). The repeated A flat is said to represent the sound of raindrops falling from the roof of the villa in Majorca he shared with his new lover, the novelist George Sand (Aurore Dudevant), in the autumn of 1838, until the weather broke and he became ill.

'Rain' Sonata. A nickname given to the sonata for violin and piano in G, opus 78, by Brahms (1833–97) because it uses the theme of the composer's own *Regenlied* ('rain song'), from opus 59.

Rain, Steam, and Speed – the Great Western Railway. One of the later paintings of J.M.W. Turner (1775–1851), in which the subject matter – a steam train crossing a bridge – is rendered almost abstract, as part of the interplay of the natural elements. The work was first exhibited at the Royal Academy, London, in 1844, and now hangs in the National Gallery, London. The location of the scene is said to be a railway bridge over the Thames near Maidenhead, and apparently Turner prepared for the painting by sticking his head out of the window of either a train or a coach in a rainstorm.

> He [Turner] seems to paint with tinted steam, so evanescent, and so airy.
>
> JOHN CONSTABLE: letter to George Constable, 1836

Raj Quartet, The. A tetralogy of novels by Paul Scott (1920–78), following the lives of a wide range of characters during the last five years of the British Raj (the period of British rule in India), ending with the independence of India and Pakistan in 1947. The four novels are:

The Jewel in the Crown (1966)
The Day of the Scorpion (1968)
The Towers of Silence (1971)
A Division of the Spoils (1975)

The Jewel in Her Crown is a painting of Queen Victoria, Empress of India, with some of her Indian subjects (India being the jewel in Victoria's crown). It is used for instructional purposes by Edwina Crane, an elderly mission schools' supervisor in Mayapore, who commits suicide by self-immolation after her house is ransacked by a mob. Events in Mayapore are a microcosm of what will happen nationally during the next few years. The title of *The Day of the Scorpion* refers to the old belief that if a scorpion is surrounded by a ring of flame it will sting itself to death (whereas it is actually curling up in the intense heat). *The Towers of Silence* refers to the towers on top of which the Parsees of India expose their dead. *A Division of the Spoils* takes the story up to the violence surrounding the partition of the subcontinent into India and Pakistan at independence. The title *The Jewel in the Crown* was given to a much admired television version of all four novels (1984). Scott's last novel, *Staying On* (1977), which won the Booker Prize, follows the lives of two minor British characters from *The Raj Quartet*, who opt to stay on in India after independence.

Rake's Progress, The. A 'moral narrative' by William Hogarth (1697–1764), painted in 1733–5 and subsequently made into popular engravings. The series followed the success of Hogarth's *The Harlot's Progress* (engraved 1732), in which a country girl meets her downfall at the hands of immoral Londoners. The story of *The Rake's Progress* concerns the decline and fall of one Tom Rakewell, who deserts Anne Trulove for the delights of London in the company of Nick Shadow, who turns out to be the Devil. Tom ends up in Bedlam, and the moral of the tale is: 'For idle hearts and hands and minds the Devil finds a work to do.'

The Rake's Progress, a 'neoclassical' opera by Igor Stravinsky (1882–1971), has a libretto by W.H. Auden (1907–73) and Chester Kallman (1921–75), and is loosely based on Hogarth. The opera was first performed in 1951; for the 1975 Glyndbourne revival, striking sets and costumes were designed by David Hockney (b.1937). A comedy film of the same title (UK, 1945) follows the career of a 1930s playboy, who somewhat surprisingly ends up as a war hero.

Rákóczi March. A patriotic Hungarian march tune, written around 1809 by an unknown composer, possibly the gypsy violinist János Bihari (1764–1827). It was arranged for military band by Nicolas Scholl, who published it under his own name. The *March* is in honour of Ferenc

Rákóczi II (1676–1735), prince of Transylvania, who in 1703 became the leader of the 'Kuruc', a Hungarian peasant revolt against the country's Austrian Habsburg rulers. Fighting continued until 1711, when the Hungarians were finally defeated and Rákóczi left his country for ever. The music of the *Rákóczi March* has been arranged by a number of composers, including Berlioz (1803–69) in his *Hungarian March*, which became part of his *Damnation of Faust* (*see* FAUST OR FAUSTUS, panel, pp.152–6). Berlioz frankly admitted in his preface to the latter:

> People have asked why the author made his hero go into Hungary. He did so because he wishes to compose a piece of instrumental music whose theme is Hungarian.

Liszt (1811–86) used the tune in his orchestral *Rákóczi March* and in one of his *Hungarian Rhapsodies* for piano, and it is also heard in the operetta *The Gypsy Baron* (1885) by Johann Strauss the younger (1825–99).

Rape of the Lock, The. A mock-heroic epic by Alexander Pope (1688–1744), published in 1712. Unlike the rape (or abduction) of Helen that started the Trojan War, the only assault in Pope's work is upon a lock of hair belonging to the heroine Belinda:

> The Peer now spreads the glitt'ring *Forfex* wide,
> T'enclose the Lock; now joins it, to divide.
> ...
> The meeting Points the sacred Hair dissever
> From the fair Head, for ever and for ever!
> Then flashed the living Lightning from her Eyes,
> And Screams of Horror rend th'affrighted Skies.
> Not louder Shrieks to pitying Heav'n are cast,
> When Husbands or when Lap-dogs breathe their last.

Pope's story is based on a real event, when a certain Lord Petre snipped a tress from the unwilling head of Miss Arabella Fermor, causing a ruction between their respective families.

'Rasumovsky' Quartets (or '**Razumovsky**' or '**Rasoumovsky**'). A set of three string quartets (nos 7–9), opus 59 (1806), by Beethoven (1770–1827). They were dedicated to his friend Count Andreas Kyrillovich Rasumovsky (1752–1836), then Russian ambassador to Vienna, who was a keen amateur violinist and played second violin in his own quartet. Beethoven also dedicated his fifth and sixth symphonies to Count

Rasumovsky (alongside Prince Lobkowitz, another of Beethoven's patrons). In the quartets Beethoven makes some musical nods towards Russia – for example he marks two passages as *thème russe*; that in the third movement of no 8 was later used by Mussorgsky in his opera *Boris Godunov*.

Rayogram. The name that the American Dadaist (and later surrealist) Man Ray (1890–1976) gave to many of his pictures made using a technique he had invented in 1917. This involved placing objects on photographic film and then exposing it to light, so making a kind of photograph without using a camera. In 1922 he published a collection of Rayograms under the title *Les Champs délicieux* (French, 'the delightful fields').

'Razor' Quartet (German *Rasiermessequartett*). The nickname given to the string quartet in F minor, opus 55 no 2, by Haydn (1732–1809). The story is that when the London music publisher John Bland visited Haydn he found the composer disconsolately shaving. 'I'd give my best quartet for a good razor,' complained Haydn. Bland, seeing an opportunity, gave Haydn a new set of razors, and in return Haydn presented Bland with this quartet. Unfortunately for the story, the 'Razor' Quartet was actually first published (in 1789) by another London publisher, Longman and Broderip.

Rebel without a Cause. A film (1955) adapted by Stewart Stern and Irving Shulman from the story 'Blind Run' by Robert M. Lindner. The rebel of the title is a rebellious teenager whose unruly behaviour culminates in a death-defying challenge in which he and a rival drive their cars full speed towards the edge of a cliff. Starring James Dean, Natalie Wood and Sal Mineo, the film acquired iconic status among the restless young of the 1950s, Dean in particular often being referred to as the 'rebel without a cause'.

Red and the Black, The (French title: *Le Rouge et le noir*). A novel (1830) by Stendhal (Marie Henri Beyle; 1783–1842). The novel is set during the period after the fall of Napoleon in 1815, and the central character, Julien Sorel, an ambitious young son of a carpenter, seeing no future in the army (symbolized by the colour red), looks for a career in the church (symbolized by the colour black). As it transpires, he attempts to make his way via seduction and attempted murder – activities that may also be symbolized by the colours of the title.

RED AND SCARLET

The RED AND THE BLACK, a novel (1830) by Stendhal

The SCARLET LETTER, a novel (1850) by Nathaniel Hawthorne

Red Cotton Night-cap Country, a long poem (1873) by Robert Browning

A Study in Scarlet, a Sherlock Holmes mystery (1888) by Sir Arthur Conan Doyle

The RED BADGE OF COURAGE, a novel (1895) by Stephen Crane

The SCARLET PIMPERNEL, a historical novel (1905) by Baroness Orczy

The Red Shoes, a ballet film (1948) written and directed by Michael Powell and Emeric Pressburger

The Red Balloon, a French fantasy film (1955)

The THIN RED LINE, a war novel (1963) by James Jones

The Red and the Green, a novel (1965) by Iris Murdoch

Three Colours: Red (1994), a Polish film (*see* NUMBERS, panel, pp.328–9)

Red Badge of Courage, The. A novel (1895) by Stephen Crane (1871–1900) about the experiences of a naive young recruit in the Union forces during the US Civil War. It was adapted as a film (1951) by director John Huston and Albert Band. Although Crane had no personal experience of war, the star of the film, Audie Murphy, was the most decorated US soldier of the Second World War. The 'red badge' of the title refers to the bloody wounds of soldiers hurt in battle.

Reformation Symphony. The title of the symphony no 5 in D minor, opus 107, by Felix Mendelssohn (1819–47). Mendelssohn wrote the work in 1830 to celebrate the 300th anniversary of the Augsburg Confession, the historic confession of the Protestant faith compiled by Melanchthon (Philipp Schwartzerd; 1497–1560) in consultation with Luther and presented to Emperor Charles V at the imperial diet at Augsburg in 1530.

However, Catholic objections prevented Mendelssohn's symphony from being performed in Augsburg, and the first performance, in Berlin, had to wait until 1832. Mendelssohn tried to make the work interdenominational: in the first movement he quotes the 'Dresden Amen', composed for the Catholic royal chapel at Dresden by Johann Gottlieb Naumann (1741–1801), while in the last movement he quotes Luther's chorale '*Ein' feste Burg*' ('A Safe Stronghold').

'Reine, La'. *See* 'QUEEN OF FRANCE, THE'.

Relâche. The word used in French theatres to indicate that there are no performances that day was adopted as the title of a surrealist ballet (1924) with music by Erik Satie (1866–1925), choreography by Jean Börlin, text by Francis Picabia (1879–1953) and a film episode directed by René Clair (1898–1981). When the audience turned up at the theatre in Paris for the first night, they found the theatre closed; the real first night took place three days later.

Remembrance of Things Past. The title given to the first English translation (1922–31) of the seven-novel sequence *À la recherche du temps perdu* (1913–27) by the French writer Marcel Proust (1871–1922). Proust's *roman-fleuve* constitutes a meditation on the nature of time, the self, memory and experience, and is also a quasi-autobiographical study of people and the society in which they move, in the course of which the protagonist, Marcel, assumes a variety of roles before ultimately regaining his lost vocation as a writer.

When C.K. Scott-Moncrieff started publishing his translation of the work in 1922, the year of Proust's death, he gave it an evocative but not entirely accurate title taken from Shakespeare:

> When to the sessions of sweet silent thought
> I summon up remembrance of things past.
>
> Sonnet 30

The title was well in keeping with the florid tone of his translation (completed by Stephen Hudson), and its poetic resonance doubtless helped to sell the work. Proust, however, was not writing about idle remembrance but about arduous research (*recherche*), as he himself exemplified in the twelve years of illness and solitude that he spent writing the sequence. When, therefore, a freshly revised translation of the work was published in 1992, it was given a title much closer to the intention of the original: *In Search of Lost Time*.

The novels that make up the sequence – with Proust's title followed by Scott-Moncrieff's – are:

Du côté de chez Swann (1913; *Swann's Way*)

À l'ombre des jeunes filles en fleurs (1919; *Within a Budding Grove*)

Le Côté de Guermantes (1920–1; *The Guermantes Way*)

Sodome et Gomorrhe (1921–2; *Cities of the Plain*)

La Prisonnière (1923; *The Captive*)

Albertine disparue (1925; *The Sweet Cheat Gone*)

Le Temps retrouvé (1927; *Time Regained*)

Attempts to adapt elements of Proust's great work for stage or screen seem inevitably doomed to failure, however well they capture his social milieu. Examples include the film *Swann in Love* (1983), with Jeremy Irons in the title role, and the perceptively titled *A Waste of Time* by Robert David Macdonald, written for the Glasgow Citizens' Theatre in the early 1980s.

Repo Man. A blackly comic film (1984), directed by Alex Cox, set in a bleak Los Angeles about a young punk who becomes a 'repo man' – a repossession man, employed by finance companies to repossess goods (usually cars, as in the film) whose buyer has defaulted on payments.

Resistible Rise of Arturo Ui, The (German title: *Der aufhaltsame Aufstieg des Arturo Ui*). A play (1958) by the German dramatist Bertolt Brecht (1898–1956) about the career of a small-time Chicago gangster as he seeks to establish a stranglehold over the city's cauliflower business. Arturo Ui himself is a thinly disguised portrait of the Nazi dictator Adolf Hitler, although the character was first suggested to Brecht when he read newspaper reports in New York about the killing of a real-life gangster called Dutch Schulz. These he combined with details culled from his reading of a biography of Al Capone and his viewing of numerous American gangster movies.

Resurrection Symphony. The subtitle of the symphony no 2 (1894) by Gustav Mahler (1860–1911), the last movement containing a setting for soprano, contralto, chorus and orchestra of the poem *Aufersteh'n* ('resurrection') by the German poet Friedrich Gottlieb Klopstock (1724–1803). When the conductor Hans von Bülow heard the symphony he exclaimed:

> If that was music, I no longer understand anything about the subject.

Reverend Robert Walker Skating on Duddingston Loch, The. A delightfully unusual portrait (*c.*1784) by the Scottish painter Sir Henry Raeburn (1756–1823). Walker was minister at Duddingston village, below the craggy hill of Arthur's Seat (all now within the City of Edinburgh).

> Iron and ice release a sweeter music than yesterday's psalms, and the effortless inscription of these rings round and round the centre of the loch is more persuasive than any sermon.
>
> JAMES AITCHISON: 'Uncertain Grace'

Revolt of Islam, The. A poem in twelve cantos by Percy Bysshe Shelley (1792–1822), published in 1818. Shelley wrote of the work in his preface:

> It is an experiment on the temper of the public mind, as to how far a thirst for a happier condition of moral and political society survives, among the enlightened and refined, the tempests which have shaken the age in which we live.

Shelley refers, of course, to the French Revolution, and the original title of *The Revolt of Islam* was to have been 'Laon and Cynthia: or The Revolution in the Golden City, A Vision of the Nineteenth Century'. However, in the reactionary temper of the times, both Shelley's publisher and printer feared prosecution, so Shelley made some revisions, changed the title and moved the action to the Orient.

'Revolutionary' Étude. The nickname of the étude (study) in C minor, opus 10 no 12 (1831), by Chopin (1810–49). The piece is said to reflect Chopin's fervent patriotic feelings at the time of the Polish revolt against Russian rule in 1830–1. The so-called November Insurrection broke out on 29 November 1830, and in January 1831 the Polish Sejm (parliament) declared that Tsar Nicholas I was no longer king of Poland. Fighting continued until September, when Russian forces finally crushed the revolt, after which thousands of Polish revolutionaries went into exile in France. Chopin himself was visiting Vienna at the time the revolt started; he never returned, settling in Paris in the summer of 1831.

> I'm a revolutionary, money means nothing to me.
>
> FRÉDÉRIC CHOPIN: remark in 1833, quoted in Hedley, *Chopin* (1947)

Rhapsody in Blue. A work for piano and orchestra by George Gerswhin (1898–1937), orchestrated by Ferde Grofé (1892–1972) and first performed in New York in 1924 by Paul Whiteman's jazz orchestra, with Gershwin on piano. As the title suggests, the work successfully fuses jazz and classical music. The title plays with the convention of naming a classical composition 'sonata in F', 'symphony in G minor', and so on. 'The Blues' is a melancholy musical form originating among the blacks of the US South, and became a key influence on jazz. The word 'rhapsody' (from the Greek *rhapsōidia*, 'epic poem', from *rhaptein*, 'to sew together', and *ōidē*, 'song') began to be adopted by composers in the 19th century for a highly rhetorical, emotional and loosely structured piece of music. The opening sequence of Gershwin's *Rhapsody*, beginning with a wailing call on the clarinet, accompanies the start of the film *Manhattan* (1979), written, directed and starring Woody Allen, himself a jazz clarinettist.

> The *Rhapsody* is not a composition at all. It's a string of separate paragraphs stuck together – with a thin paste of flour and water.
>
> LEONARD BERNSTEIN: in the *Atlantic Monthly*, 1955

'Rhenish' Symphony (German *Rheinische Sinfonie*). The name given to the symphony no 3 in E flat, opus 97 (1850), by Schumann (1810–56). The symphony was written shortly after Schumann had taken up the post of municipal director of music at Düsseldorf, a city on the River Rhine. With his wife Clara, Schumann subsequently took a cruise down the Rhine to Cologne, where he had the idea of writing a symphony that 'perhaps here and there reflects a bit of local colour' (as he wrote to his publisher). In particular, the fourth movement is said to have been inspired by the installation of Cardinal Archbishop Geissel at Cologne Cathedral.

Rhinoceros. A play (1959) by the Romanian-born French playwright of the Absurd, Eugène Ionesco (1912–94), depicting how an ordinary man in a small French town discovers that everyone he knows is gradually turning into a rhinoceros. In Ionesco's hands the disease 'rhinoceritis' became an allegory for the spread of fascism through the populations of Europe in the years before the Second World War.

Riddle of the Sands, The. A thriller (1903) by Erskine Childers (1870–1922), set against the background of the Anglo-German naval arms race prior to the First World War. The 'sands' are the mudflats and sandbanks of the Friesian Islands, and the 'riddle' is to resolve the mystery that lies there. Ultimately two Englishmen thwart the traitorous aim of a former British naval officer who is preparing for a German invasion of Britain. This, Childers's only novel, is memorable as much for its descriptive passages on sailing as for its gripping story line. A rather tame film version (1978) was directed by Tony Maylam.

At the time he wrote the novel, Childers was a clerk in the House of Commons, but he was also an ardent devotee of the cause of Irish nationalism, and resigned his Commons position in 1910. In July 1914, just before the outbreak of the First World War, he used his own yacht to smuggle German guns to Irish nationalist volunteers. Although he worked as a British intelligence officer during the war, he became a minister in the self-constituted Irish parliament (Dáil Eireann) in 1921. He joined the Republican side in the civil war that followed the Anglo-Irish treaty of December 1921, and was captured, court-martialled and shot on the orders of the Irish Free State government for the illegal possession of a revolver.

'Rider' Quartet. *See* 'HORSEMAN' QUARTET.

Rienzi. The title of a number of works inspired by the story of the Italian popular leader Cola di Rienzo (1313–54). The son of an inn-keeper, Rienzo initiated a revolution against the nobility in Rome on 20 May 1347 and declared himself tribune of the people, with the intention of restoring the glory of ancient Rome. The pope issued a bull against him, and in December he was overthrown by the Roman nobles and the disappointed populace. He was later reconciled with the pope and in August 1354 was sent by him to restore papal authority in Rome. However, his harsh rule was resented and he was killed by a mob in October. Among the works inspired by his story are a blank-verse tragedy (1828) by Mary Russell Mitford (1787–1855), a novel (1835) by Edward Bulwer-Lytton (1803–73) and an opera (*Rienzi, the Last of the Tribunes*, 1842) by Wagner (1813–83).

Rime of the Ancient Mariner, The. *See ANCIENT MARINER, THE RIME OF THE.*

Ring, The (in full *The Ring of the Nibelung*; German title: *Der Ring des Nibelungen*; also called *The Ring Cycle*). A cycle of four operas by Richard Wagner (1813–83), with text by the composer. The four are *Das Rheingold* ('the Rhine gold', 1869), *Die Walküre* ('the Valkyrie', 1870), *Siegfried* (1876) and *GÖTTERDÄMMERUNG* ('twilight of the gods', 1876). The story is based on the great medieval German epic poem the *Nibelungenlied* ('song of the Nibelung'), written down around 1200 by an unknown Austrian living on the Danube. The *Nibelungenlied* itself was derived from old Scandinavian legends contained in the *Volsung Saga* and the *Edda*. Possible historical roots of the stories lie even further back, with the destruction of the Burgundian kingdom by the Huns in the 5th century and subsequent stories of the Frankish Merovingian dynasty around the 6th and 7th centuries.

The Nibelung are a race of dwarves, and in Wagner's version of the story, one of the Nibelung, Alberich (the German version of Oberon), steals the golden horde of the Rhine maidens. Out of this gold he makes a ring that renders the wearer supremely powerful, yet at the cost of the loss of love. The ring is stolen by the god Wotan, and is then guarded by the dragon Fafner. The warrior-hero Siegfried kills Fafner, takes the ring and wins the Valkyrie (warrior-maiden) Brünnhilde. Alberich's son Hagen wants to recover the ring, and eventually kills Siegfried. Brünnhilde builds a funeral pyre for Siegfried, and rides into the flames wearing the ring. The waters of the Rhine cover the earth, and the ring returns to the Rhine maidens. The British composer Sir Arthur Sullivan described Wagner's characters as 'thieves, liars and blackguards', while Claude Debussy described *The Ring* as 'irresistible as the sea'.

Wagner dedicated the work to his patron, Ludwig II ('mad King Ludwig') of Bavaria. He described his cycle as 'a festival drama for three days and a preliminary evening', and the first complete performance of the cycle was at the Bayreuth festival theatre on 13–17 August 1876. The cycle has since been staged there annually, and Bayreuth rapidly became a pilgrimage destination for all serious Wagnerians. The difficulties of staging *The Ring* without absurdity have often been remarked upon. Writing in 1877, Otto Henne am Rhyn observed of *Das Rheingold*:

> This idea would be quite a good one, were it not that the nixies resembled bathing ladies of the demi-monde more than figures of popular legend.

The opera cycle as a whole has been the subject of extensive critical and scholarly scrutiny. One of the more unfortunately titled works in this field is *Penetrating Wagner's Ring* (1978), by John L. Di Gaetanao.

Other interpretations of the legend include:

Der Held des Nordens (1808–10, 'the hero of the north'), a dramatic trilogy by the German writer Friedrich Heinrich Karl de La Motte, Baron Fouqué (1777–1843), the author of UNDINE (*see* panel, p.484).

Die Niebelungen Trilogie (1862) of the German dramatist Friedrich Hebbel (1813–63), comprising *Der Gehörnte Siegfried* ('the invulnerable Siegfried'), *Siegfrieds Tod* ('Siegfried's death') and *Kriemhilds Rache* ('Kriemhild's revenge').

The Story of Sigurd the Volsung and the Fall of the Nibelungs (1876), an epic poem by William Morris (1834–96) based on the Scandinavian sagas; Sigurd is the Norse version of Siegfried, while the Volsungs are the family he belongs to. Morris didn't think much of Wagner's project, which was to be completed in the same year as his own:

> I look upon it as nothing short of desecration to bring such a tremendous and world-wide subject under the gaslights of an opera: the most rococo and degraded of all forms of art – the idea of a sandy-haired German tenor tweedledeeing over the unspeakable woes of Sigurd, which even the simplest words are not typical enough to express!
>
> WILLIAM MORRIS: letter, 1873

The line of fortifications along the western frontier of Germany built in the 1930s was named the Siegfried Line after the Wagnerian hero; this inspired the British song from the Second World War, 'We'll Hang out Our Washing on the Siegfried Line'.

Ring and the Book, The. A poem of over 20,000 lines by Robert Browning (1812–89), published in four parts in 1868–9. The work consists of a series of dramatic monologues, each character providing a different perspective on a murder trial in 17th-century Rome. The story is based on a collection of old documents (the 'Book' of the title) that Browning had picked up at a market in Florence, concerning the trial of Count Guido Franceschini on a charge of murdering his wife Pompilia. The 'Ring' of the title is Browning's metaphor for the creative process by which the poem itself has come to be written. As the goldsmith uses alloy to make a gold ring, so the poet adds the alloy of his art to the gold of the historical record in the 'Book'.

Ring of Bright Water. A moving account (1960) by the naturalist Gavin Maxwell (1914–69) of his life with two otters on the west coast of Scotland. The book became the basis of the 1969 film of the same name. The title is from Kathleen Raine's 1952 poem 'The Marriage of Psyche':

> He has married me with a ring, a ring of bright water
> Whose ripples spread from the heart of the sea,
> He has married me with a ring of light, the glitter
> Broadcast on the swift river.

Rise and Fall of the City of Mahagonny. (German title: *Aufstieg und Fall der Stadt Mahagonny*). A ferocious political satire of an opera by Kurt

Weill (1900–50), with a libretto by Bertolt Brecht (1898–1956). It was first produced in 1930, following an earlier, simpler version of 1927. Mahagonny is an imaginary city of material pleasure, with a capitalist morality: when the hero, Jimmy Mahoney, is arrested and brought to trial, he is sentenced to two days' imprisonment for indirect murder, four years for seduction by means of money and is condemned to die for failing to pay his whisky bill.

Rite of Spring, The. A ballet with music by Igor Stravinsky (1882–1971) and choreography by Vaslav Nijinksy (1890–1950). It was first performed by Diaghilev's Ballets Russes in 1913 at the Théâtre des Champs-Elysées, Paris. It is often referred to by its French title, *Le Sacre du printemps*. The subtitle of the work is 'pictures from pagan Russia', and its two parts are titled 'The Adoration of the Earth' and 'The Sacrifice'. The hitherto unknown ferocity of the music's grinding discords and rhythms caused a riot at the first performance. One contemporary critic commented that it was 'rather a *Massacre du printemps*'; Diaghilev himself called it 'the 20th century's Ninth Symphony'.

Rites of Passage. A Booker Prize-winning novel (1980) by William Golding (1911–93), the first volume of *To the Ends of the Earth: A Sea Trilogy*. The other volumes are *Close Quarters* (1987) and *Fire Down Below* (1989). In ethnography, a rite of passage is a ceremony or event marking an important stage in someone's life, such as birth, initiation, marriage or death. The term translates French *rite de passage*, coined by the French ethnographer Arnold van Gennep (1873–1957) in his major work *Les Rites de passage* (1909), in which he considered such ceremonies. In his title Golding puns on 'passage' in the sense of sea journey, all three books being set in the 18th century on a ship travelling to Australia.

Road to Wigan Pier, The. An investigation (1937) by George Orwell (1903–50) into the conditions of the unemployed in the towns of Wigan, Sheffield and Barnsley in the north of England. The book was commissioned by the Left Book Club, and the title is somewhat ironic. There are fine piers in several British seaside resorts, notably Eastbourne, Brighton, Blackpool, Weston-super-Mare and Southend. Wigan, however, is an inland town and does not have a pier as such. What passes for a pier is the remains of a gantry, now little more than a few iron girders, protruding from a wall by the Liverpool–Leeds canal. As such, it is a curiosity and a tourist attraction in its own right. The story goes that the name arose when a trainload of miners was delayed in Wigan next to a coal-wagon gantry. The area was flooded at the time, and when a miner asked a local where they were, the facetious reply came: 'Wigan pier'. The tale spread and was soon picked up by music-hall performers who used it to mock the middle classes and their holidays at resorts that had proper piers.

Roaratorio. A piece of electronic music by John Cage (1912–92), written in 1979. The work, whose title puns on 'roar' and 'oratorio', uses thousands of words from James Joyce's *FINNEGANS WAKE*.

Robert le Diable. (*see* panel, pp.388–9)

Rob Roy. A novel by Sir Walter Scott (1771–1832), published in 1817. As in several of Scott's other novels, the title character is not in fact the central hero. The real Robert MacGregor (1671–1734), who often signed his name 'Rob Roy' ('Red Rob'), was obliged to take the name Campbell after the MacGregor clan was proscribed in 1693. Having lost his lands to the conniving Duke of Montrose, he became a notorious outlaw, and played an ambivalent role in the 1715 Jacobite Rising. He was eventually arrested and sentenced to transportation, but was pardoned in 1727. He is buried in the churchyard at Balquhidder, Perthshire. One of Rob Roy's sons, Robin Oig, appears briefly in *Kidnapped* (1886) by Robert Louis Stevenson (1850–94). There is an overture by Berlioz (1803–69) entitled *Rob Roy* (1832). There have been two film versions very loosely inspired by the historical character: *Rob Roy the Highland Rogue* (1953) and *Rob Roy* (1995).

Rock Drill, The. An aggressively mechanistic sculpture of a robot-like figure by Jacob Epstein (1880–1959). One of the most famous works of early British modernism (sculpted in 1913–14), the figure has certain drill-like qualities, and was originally displayed on a real drill. Epstein himself commented:

> Here is the armed, sinister figure of today and tomorrow. No humanity, only the terrible Frankenstein's monster we have made ourselves into.

One of the volumes of Ezra Pound's *The CANTOS* is entitled *Section: Rock-Drill* (1955).

ROBERT LE DIABLE

Robert le Diable (French, 'Robert the Devil') was the byname of Robert I, 6th Duke of Normandy (*c.*1010–35), the father of William the Conqueror. He acquired his name (which appears in the titles of a number of literary works and operas) from his daring and cruelty; however, he was also called Robert le Magnifique ('the Magnificent'). After his death he began to appear in distorted form in legend and romance. Although in reality he supported monastic reform and died on his way back from making the pilgrimage to Jerusalem, there is a Norman tradition that his wandering ghost will not be allowed to rest until the Last Judgment.

In the 12th-century French romance, *Robert le Diable*, he is the son of a duke of Normandy, born in answer to prayers to the Devil. At first he uses his great strength only for evil, until he is relieved from his curse by undergoing certain ordeals, including eating his food from the mouth of a dog. He becomes the court fool of the Holy Roman Emperor, saves Rome from the Saracens, turns down the emperor's daughter and leaves the court to become a hermit.

Other verse versions appeared in the 14th century, and in 1496 Wynken de Worde, who had taken over Caxton's printing business, published an English translation of one of these under the title *The Life of Robert the Devil*. A century later Thomas Lodge (*c.*1557–1625) brought out his prose romance *Robert Second Duke of Normandy, Surnamed Robin the Divell* (1591).

In the 19th century there were a number of operas about Robert, the most memorable being *Robert le Diable* (1831) by Giacomo Meyerbeer (1791–1864), with a libretto by Eugène Scribe. In this very different version of the story, Robert, Duke of Normandy, is the son of a mortal woman and the Devil. The action is set in Palermo in the 13th century; historically, the Norman Robert Guiscard had conquered Sicily in 1091, but Norman rule ended there before the end of the 12th century. In the opera, Robert is tempted by the Devil to use demonic means to win his beloved Isabella, and receives the necessary magic branch at an orgy involving ghostly nuns. However, Isabella brings him back to the straight and narrow, making him break the branch, denounce the Devil and marry her.

The man who attempted to assassinate Louis XV, Robert François Damiens (1715–57), was also called Robert le Diable.

Rocky Horror Show, The. A successful stage rock musical (1973), written by Richard O'Brien. It was adapted for the big screen as *The Rocky Horror Picture Show* (1975). The title reflects the show's anarchic mixture of rock and roll music and horror-film clichés, all delivered in a high camp style. The show quickly attracted a cult following and both live performances and showings of the film (often at midnight) were commonly attended by audiences wearing the outlandish costumes of such favourite characters as Dr Frank N. Furter and Riff Raff the hunchbacked butler.

Rocky Mountains and Tired Indians. One of the most frequently reproduced earlier paintings of David Hockney (b.1937). It dates from 1965, when Hockney was teaching at Boulder, Colorado. Hockney recalls:

> I was given a studio that had ... no windows to view the Rocky Mountains ... So ... the whole picture is an invention from geological magazines and romantic ideas (the nearest Indians are at least three hundred miles from Boulder). The chair was put in just for compositional purposes, and to explain its being there I called the Indians tired.
>
> *David Hockney by David Hockney* (1976)

Rokeby Venus, The. The popular name for *The Toilet of Venus* (otherwise known as *Venus and Cupid*) by Velázquez (1599–1660), a rear view of a reclining nude painted *c.*1651 and now in the National Gallery in London. The popular name derives from the fact that until 1905 it hung in Rokeby Hall, Yorkshire, as part of the collection of the Morritt family.

Roman de Fauvel ('romance of Fauvel'). A medieval French poem by Gervais du Bus, written *c.*1310–14. A manuscript of the poem dated 1316 is of particular interest to musicologists, as it includes a large number of musical works, going back over the previous century. The hero of the poem – which attacks abuses in the Church – is Fauvel, a fawn-coloured stallion (*fauve* = fawn), the letters of whose name spell out a variety of sins: *Flatterie*, *Avarice*, *Vilenie* (v written as u), *Variété*, *Envie* and *Lâcheté*.

Ronde, La. A play (1903) by the Austrian playwright Arthur Schnitzler (1862–1931) in which the action traces a series of ten interlinked sexual liaisons. The title reflects the play's circular structure: it begins with a prostitute having sex with a soldier and ends with a count picking up the same prostitute. A highly regarded French film version (1950), set in Vienna in 1900, was directed by Max Ophuls, while the 1964 remake directed by Roger Vadim, despite a screenplay by Jean Anouilh, was less well received.

Room at the Top. The first novel (1957) by John Braine (1922–86). It is an iconoclastic story of an opportunist, amoral, working-class young man, Joe Lampton, who achieves social acceptance and material prosperity. Braine returned to this formula and to his original characters in *Life at the Top* (1962). The words 'There is always room at the top' are attributed to the US politician Daniel Webster (1782–1852), said when he was advised against joining the overcrowded legal profession. Simone Signoret won an Oscar for her part in the film (1958), when she played the married woman with whom Lambton has a brief affair.

Room of One's Own, A. A long essay by Virginia Woolf (1882–1941), published in 1929. The essay grew out of two lectures that Woolf had delivered to women students at Cambridge University the previous year, in which she addressed the difficulties that women writers had faced, and would continue to face, until they had the freedom and security of 'a room of one's own' and 'five hundred a year'. For Woolf herself, the 'room of one's own' was the attic room of J.M. Keynes's house at 46 Gordon Square in London.

> A room of one's own can be a womb, but it can also be an ivory tower, a prison and a grave. Its dangers and promise are inherent in all Virginia Woolf's work.
>
> STEPHEN COOTE: *The Penguin Short History of English Literature* (1993)

Room with a View, A. A largely comic novel (1908) by E.M. Forster (1879–1970), set in Florence and England, which explores the differences between Italian and English temperaments. It opens with a contretemps in a pension largely occupied by English visitors to Italy about the rooms with a view that had been promised, instead of which they have 'north rooms, looking into a courtyard, and a long way apart'. The novel was the subject of a popular and successful film (1985) from the team of Ismail Merchant (producer), James Ivory (director) and Ruth Prawer Jhabvala (screenplay). 'A Room with a View' is also the title of a song (1927) by Noël Coward.

Roots. A sociological study (1976), with fictional interpolations, by the African-American writer Alex Haley (1921–92). It purports to be a chronicle of his family through seven generations, beginning with the African, Kunte Kinte, who was brought as a slave from Gambia to Annapolis in 1767. The bestseller won a Pulitzer Prize and had an even greater impact when it was made into a gripping television mini-series (1977).

Roots is also the title to the sequel (1959) to the play *CHICKEN SOUP WITH BARLEY* by Arnold Wesker (b.1932).

Rosencrantz and Guildenstern are Dead. A play (1966) by Tom Stoppard (b.1937) focusing on the fate of two minor characters from William Shakespeare's *Hamlet* (*c.*1601). Rosencrantz and Guildenstern are the two 'attendant lords' who accompany Hamlet to England; they are secretly carrying letters asking the English king to execute their master, but end up being executed themselves after Hamlet inserts their own names in the fatal document. The names Rosencrantz and Guildenstern were fairly common in Denmark in Shakespeare's time and the full title is a straight quotation from the last scene of the original play, in which news of their demise is perfunctorily reported by the First Ambassador in the aftermath of Hamlet's own death and that of the king, Claudius:

> The sight is dismal;
> And our affairs from England come too late:
> The ears are senseless that should give us hearing,
> To tell him his commandment is fulfill'd,
> That Rosencrantz and Guildenstern are dead.

Rose Tattoo, The. A play (1951) by the US playwright Tennessee Williams (1911–83) about a Sicilian widow's quest for love. The title of the play refers most obviously to the rose tattoo that is described as adorning the chest of the widow's dead husband, but it also relates to the name of the widow, Serafina Delle Rose, and that of her spouse, Rosario. The prevalence of rose imagery in the play reflected the author's preoccupation with his sister Rose, who was troubled by mental illness throughout her life. Other 'rose' titles that he considered included *Novena to a Rose, A Candle to a Rose, A Rose for Our Lady, A Rose from the Hand of Our Lady* and *Perpetual Novena to a Rose*. However, the play began life under the alternative titles *The Eclipse of May 29, 1919* and *Stornella*.

Rosie the Riveter. A comedy film (1944), largely only of historical interest. The character of Rosie the Riveter had already been established during the Second World War by government propagandists as a rousing archetype of all the American women engaged in jobs that in peacetime were regarded as a male preserve. Rosie was depicted as a young woman wearing slacks and armed with a rivet gun. She was commemorated in song and depicted by Norman Rockwell on the cover of the *Saturday Evening Post*, where she rolled up her sleeves beneath the words, 'We Can Do It!' At the end of the war Rosie's skills were quickly forgotten, and government propagandists encouraged her to return to the role of homemaker and breeder.

'Roxolane, La'. The nickname of the symphony no 63 in C (*c*.1777–80) by Haydn (1732–1809). Some authorities suggest that Haydn named the slow movement 'La Roxolane' after the heroine of a recently successful play, while others suggest that the series of variations in the allegretto are based on a French song called 'Roxelane'. An opera entitled *Le couronnement de Roxolane*, by 'Gaetano' (Kajetan Majer; 1750–92), was first performed in Warsaw in 1783.

Rubbing Piece. A masochistic performance work (1970) by the US body artist Vito Acconci (b.1940). During the performance Acconci rubbed his arm until he produced a sore. He was photographed every five minutes, so that posterity might appreciate his genius. In 1972 he developed his oeuvre with *Seedbed*, which featured a daily display of masturbatory activity.

'Rule, Britannia'. A patriotic song with words by James Thomson (1700–48) and music by Thomas Arne (1710–78). It first appeared in a masque entitled *Alfred*, produced in August 1740 at Cliveden House, near Maidenhead, Berkshire. It was written at the command of the Prince of Wales and performed before him. The original opening was:

> When Britain first, at Heaven's command,
> Arose from out the azure main,
> This was the charter of the land,
> And guardian angels sung this strain:
> 'Rule, Britannia, rule the waves;
> Britons never will be slaves.'

In the rising of 1745 'Rule, Britannia' was sung by the Jacobites with modifications appropriate to their cause.

In the later 1990s the phrase 'Cool Britannia' – punning on the song title – was coined to signify the revitalized and youthful Britain that many saw emerging in 1997 on the election of Tony Blair's 'New' Labour government.

Britannia, as a personification of Britain, first appears as a female figure reclining on a shield on a coin of Antoninus Pius, the Roman emperor who died in AD 161. She reappeared on English copper coins in 1665, in the reign of Charles II. The model was Frances Stewart, afterwards Duchess of Richmond. The engraver was Philip Roetier.

> The king's new medall, where, in little, there is Mrs Stewart's face ... and a pretty thing it is, that he should choose her face to represent Britannia by.
>
> SAMUEL PEPYS: *Diary*, 25 February 1667

The figure of Britannia continued to grace one face of the old penny until decimalization in 1971.

Rum, Bum, and Concertina. The autobiography (1977) of the British jazz musician and writer George Melly. The title phrase – suggesting the joy of drink, sex and music – derives from the phrase 'rum, sodomy and the lash', Winston Churchill's characterization of the Royal Navy. He used it in response to an argumentative naval officer:

> Don't talk to me about naval tradition. It's nothing but rum, sodomy and the lash.

The remark has been reported as dating from 1911 and from the Second World War. The version quoted above comes from Peter Gretton, *Former Naval Person* (1968), while Harold Nicolson in his diary entry for 17 August 1950 has:

> Naval tradition? Monstrous! Nothing but rum, sodomy, prayers and the lash.

The version, 'rum, buggery and the lash', may predate Churchill altogether.

Rum, Sodomy and the Lash was the title of an album by the Irish punk-folk band The Pogues in the 1980s.

R.U.R. A play (1920) by the Czech playwright Karel Čapek (1890–1938) about a rebellion by robots against their human masters. Standing for

'Rossum's Universal Robots', *R.U.R.* inaugurated a new genre in science fiction, and incidentally introduced a new word to the English language: 'robot' (derived by Karel's brother Josef from the Czech *robota*, meaning 'drudgery').

'Russian' Quartets. The nickname for the six string quartets, opus 33 (1781), by Haydn (1732–1809) dedicated to Grand Duke Paul of Russia. They are also called *Gli Scherzi* (Italian, 'the jokes'), as the minuets are all marked 'scherzo' or 'scherzando' (i.e. faster and more playful than normal). On the title page of an old edition the set is called *Jungfernquartette* ('maiden quartets'). The set includes the 'BIRD' QUARTET and what is sometimes known in English-speaking countries as the 'How Do You Do?' quartet (because the phrase fits the first theme).

S

Sacred and Profane Love. An early work of the Venetian Renaissance painter, Titian (*c.*1488–1576), painted in 1512–15, and now in the Borghese Gallery, Rome. The title was actually given to the painting about a century later. The work depicts the twin Venuses of Neoplatonic theory, the clothed one representing the creative forces of the natural world and the naked one eternal and divine love.

The Sacred and Profane Love Machine is a novel by Iris Murdoch (1919–99), published in 1974. It deals with the two families of Blaise Gavender, one consisting of his wife and son and the other of his mistress and his son by her.

Sacre du printemps, Le. *See* RITE OF SPRING, THE.

Sad Pavan for these Distracted Times, A. A keyboard piece by the English composer Thomas Tomkins (1572–1656). The 'distracted times' are those of the English Civil War. *See also* PAVANE POUR UNE INFANTE DÉFUNTE.

Sailor Who Fell from Grace with the Sea, The (Japanese title: *Gogo no eiko*). A novel (1963; English translation 1965) by Yukio Mishima (1925–70), about a group of boys who reject the adult world. When the mother of one of them begins an affair with a naval officer, the boy initially worships the man as a hero. Subsequently, after spying on them in bed, he turns vindictive and castrates his former hero. In 1970 Mishima mounted a doomed coup attempt in favour of the emperor against the prevailing administration; when the coup failed, he disembowelled himself with his sword.

A film version (1976) of the novel, directed by Lewis John Carlino, was set in Dartmouth and described by the critic Benny Green in *Punch* as an 'everyday tale of torture, scropophilia, copulation, masturbation, dismemberment and antique dealing'.

'St Anne's' Fugue. The nickname in English-speaking countries of the organ fugue in E flat by J.S. Bach (1685–1750), published in part III of the *Clavierübung* (1739). It is so called because it begins with the same notes as the English hymn tune known as 'St Anne', which in turn acquired this name because it was composed by William Croft (1678–1727), organist at St Anne's Church, Soho, London. 'St Anne' was first published in 1708 and is usually sung to the words 'Oh God, our help in ages past'.

St Anthony Variations. A set of variations, opus 56 (1873), by Johannes Brahms (1833–97). Brahms created two versions, one for orchestra and one for two pianos, and called them *Variations on a Theme by Haydn*, Haydn having used the theme in a divertimento for wind ensemble. The theme, known as the 'St Anthony Chorale', has since been shown to be not original to Haydn, hence the change of title.

Saint Paul's Suite. A suite for string orchestra, opus 29 no 2 by Gustav Holst (1874–1934). It was written in 1912–13 for the orchestra of St Paul's Girls' School, London, where Holst taught music.

Salad Days. A whimsical musical comedy by Julian Slade and Dorothy Reynolds, first performed at the Bristol Old Vic in 1954. Set in London, the story features the young graduates Timothy and Jane, a magic piano called Minnie, a night-club called Cleopatra and a flying saucer. The title comes from Cleopatra's lines in Shakespeare's *Antony and Cleopatra* (*c.*1607):

> My salad days,
> When I was green in judgement, cold in blood ...
>
> I.v

'Salad days' has subsequently become a common expression denoting one's 'green' youth, and has also inspired a number of other titles, including *The Salad Days* (1988), Douglas Fairbanks Jnr's first volume of memoirs, and numerous cookery books and magazine articles. Salad Days is also the name of a Swansea-based 'post-punk' band.

ST CECILIA

St Cecilia, the patron saint of the blind and of music (especially church music) features in a number of titles. She was a noble Roman lady who lived in the 2nd and 3rd centuries, and was martyred for giving her goods away to the poor. At first the authorities tried to burn her, but the flames did not harm her, so they cut off her head instead. The date of her death is traditionally given as AD 230, but is uncertain. She was not associated with music until the 15th or 16th century, probably through a misreading of a Latin text. Subsequently the legend emerged that she was the inventor of the organ, and that an angel visited her because of her musical skill. Her husband Valerian saw the heavenly visitor, who gave to both of them a crown of martyrdom, which he had brought from Paradise.

St Cecilia's Day is 22 November, and from 1683 the Worshipful Company of Musicians of the City of London processed on this day to St Paul's Cathedral for a special service. Many composers and poets were called upon to provide odes and hymns for this occasion. Henry Purcell (1659–95) produced four choral works entitled *Ode for St Cecilia's Day* (1683, 1692), with English and Latin texts. John Dryden (1613–1700) wrote more than one work in her honour. One of these, *A Song for St Cecilia's Day* (1687), begins:

> From harmony, from heavenly harmony
> This universal frame began:
> From harmony to harmony
> Through all the compass of the notes it ran,
> The diapason closing full in Man.

Dryden's *Alexander's Feast; or the Power of Musique. An Ode In Honour of St Cecilia's Day* (1697) was accompanied by music by Jeremiah Clarke (*c.*1670–1707). In 1736 Handel (1685–1759) made another choral setting of *Alexander's Feast*, with some alterations to the text.

At length divine Cecilia came,
Inventress of the vocal frame.

JOHN DRYDEN: *Alexander's Feast* (1697)

Handel's oratorio *Ode to St Cecilia* (1739) also uses Dryden's text. Other writers who provided poems for the occasion included John Oldham (1653–83), William Congreve (1670–1729) and Joseph Addison (1672–1719).

Music alone with sudden charms can bind
The wand'ring sense, and calm the troubled mind.

WILLIAM CONGREVE: 'Hymn to Harmony'

Music, the greatest good that mortals know,
And all of heaven we have below.

JOSEPH ADDISON: 'A Song for St Cecilia's Day' (1694)

Ode for Musick, on St Cecilia's Day (*c.*1708) by Alexander Pope (1688–1744) was probably not set to music, nor performed on St Cecilia's Day. The poem concludes:

Of *Orpheus* now no more let Poets tell,
To bright *Cecilia* greater Pow'r is giv'n;
His Numbers rais'd a Shade from Hell,
Hers lifts the Soul to Heav'n.

Other musical works on the subject include the *Mass for St Cecilia* (1882) by Charles Gounod (1818–93) and the *Hymn to St Cecilia* (1942) by Benjamin Britten (1913–76) to words by W.H. Auden (1907–73). Notable visual representations of the saint include *St Cecilia and the Angel* (*c.*1610) by Orazio Gentileschi (1563–1639); *Scenes from the Life of St Cecilia* (1611–14) for the church of San Luigi dei Francesi, Rome, by Domenichino (1581–1641); and *The Crowning of St Cecilia* (1725) in Santa Cecilia, Trastevere, by Sebastiano Conca (1680–1784).

A characteristically Gothic take on the St Cecilia legend is provided by Heinrich von Kleist (1777–1811) in the short story 'St Cecilia or The Power of Music' (in *Erzählungen*; 'stories', 1810–11).

SALOME

The story of the 1st-century biblical anti-heroine – with its hothouse combination of sex, potential blasphemy and terminal violence – has had an enduring fascination for creative artists (mostly male) through the ages.

The events in which Salome is involved are mentioned in Matthew 14:2–12 and Mark 6:16–28, although she herself is only named in the account of Flavius Josephus, the 1st-century Jewish historian. Salome was the daughter of Herodias and step-daughter of Herod Antipas, tetrarch of Galilee, puppet ruler in Palestine under the Romans. St John the Baptist criticized the marriage of Herodias and Herod, on the grounds that Herodias was the divorced wife of Herod's half brother. This infuriated Herodias. Herod put John in prison, but, either because 'he feared the multitude, because they counted him as a prophet' (Matthew 14:5) or because he 'feared John, knowing that he was a just man and an holy' (Mark 6:20), he did not want him killed. Herodias did. When her daughter danced before Herod on his birthday, he was so pleased that he said to her, 'Ask of me whatsoever thou wilt, and I will give it thee'. Salome consulted her mother, who persuaded her to ask for the head of John the Baptist. Herod was obliged to grant the request, and the head of the prophet was brought to Salome on a platter.

In later tradition, Herod makes the promise to Salome in order to persuade her to dance before him, and the dance she dances is the dance of the seven veils.

Visual depictions of Salome begin in the early Renaissance with Masolino da Panicale (*c.*1383–1447). There are also Salomes by Sebastiano del Piombo (*c.*1485–1547), Titian (*c.*1487/90–1576) and Alonso Berruguete (*c.*1488–1561).

The violent eroticism of the Salome story struck a chord with the 'decadent' artists of the later 19th century. The French symbolist painter Gustav Moreau (1826–98) produced more than one version: *The Apparition (Dance of Salome)* (*c.*1876), and *Dance of Salome* (*c.*1876). There is also a polychromatic sculpture of Salome by the German artist Max Klinger (1857–1920). Aubrey Beardsley's illustrations for Oscar Wilde's play (1894; *see below*) are particularly well known, and made their creator notorious. In symbolist literature, Salome appears in the work of the Portuguese decadent, Eugénio de Castro (1869–1944), whose *Salomé e Outros Poemas* ('Salome and other poems') was published in 1896.

From the same period comes the opera *Hérodiade* (1881) by Jules Massenet (1842–1912), with a libretto by Paul Milliet and Henri Grémont, based on the Flaubert story 'Hérodias', in *Trois Contes* (1877). In this version of the story John the Baptist reciprocates the love of Herodias's daughter, who kills herself after her jealous stepfather has John executed.

In the play *Salome* (1892) by Oscar Wilde (1854–1900) – originally written in French – Salome is sexually obsessed with John. She begs for a kiss from his lips, is disgustedly refused, dances the dance of the seven veils and wins the decapitated head – to which she pours out her passionate feelings and kisses its lips. Wilde intended to make his audience 'shudder', but before he could do so the censor stepped in and banned it on he grounds that it depicted biblical characters. The French version was published in 1893, and the following year an English translation appeared, illustrated by Aubrey Beardsley (1872–98).

The opera *Salome* by Richard Strauss (1864–1949) used Hedwig Lachmann's German translation of Wilde's play. It was first performed in 1905 in Dresden, with the soprano Marie Wittich (1868–1931) creating the title role. On the first night a ballerina performed the infamous dance, but at subsequent performances the heroically built Wittich insisted on performing it herself. In cities around the world audiences flocked to be shocked – although those in Vienna were disappointed when Gustav Mahler's planned staging at the Vienna Opera House was aborted by the censor. In Berlin the Kaiser tried (but failed) to stop the opera being performed, while in New York the 1907 premiere was greeted by the newspaper headline:

> 4000 SURVIVE THE MOST APPALLING TRAGEDY
> EVER SHOWN ON THE MIMIC STAGE

Shortly afterwards an outraged public demanded the Met drop it from their repertoire. As for the music, the distinguished French composer Saint-Saëns, revealing the breadth of his reading, commented:

> From time to time the cruellest discords are succeeded by exquisite suavities that caress the ear with delight. While listening to it all I thought of those lovely princesses in Sacher Masoch who lavished upon young men the most voluptuous kisses while drawing red-hot irons over their lovers' ribs.
>
> CAMILLE SAINT-SAËNS: quoted in Harding, *Saint-Saëns* (1965)

All this notoriety was only good for business. From the royalties Strauss built a splendid villa in Garmisch, Bavaria, which became his home.

Strauss's *succès de scandale* seems to have encouraged a number of others to attempt the story on stage. However, the opera *Salomé* (1908), by the French composer Antoine Marriotte (1875–1944), and also based on Wilde's play, failed to find a permanent place in the repertoire. The equally neglected 'mimodrama' (drama without words) *La Tragédie de Salomé* (1907) had music by the French composer Florent Schmitt (1870–1958). In contrast, in the same prewar period, world renown came to the Canadian-born dancer Maud Allan (1883–1956) – regarded as one of the founders of modern dance – who, with bare feet, see-through skirt and a skimpy bead halter, realized her *Vision of Salomé* on the stage. A later dance version, the ballet *Salome* (1978) choreographed by Flemming Flindt, had music by Peter Maxwell Davies (b.1934).

Salome was a natural choice of subject for film-makers from the earliest days. Theda Bara – the original screen 'vamp' – starred in the 1918 version, while Nazimova (Alla Nazimova, Russian *actrice fatale*; 1879–1945) took the role in the 1923 recreation of Wilde and Beardsley. In the 1953 Rita Hayworth vehicle ('the supreme screen achievement of our time', said the posters), Salome dances to *save* the life of John the Baptist. Ken Russell's 1987 film, *Salome's Last Dance*, depicts Wilde watching his play performed by the whores in a brothel. The very curious *Salome Where She Danced* (US, 1945) features a dancer suspected of being a spy during the 1866 Austro-Prussian War, who ends up in Arizona.

Finally, picking up the head-on-a-plate motif, the winning entry in a 1960s *New Statesman* competition, which also provided the title of a book of such winners, read:

> Salome dear, not in the fridge.

See also SUNSET BOULEVARD.

'Salomon' Symphonies. The collective name given to the last twelve symphonies, nos 93–104, by Haydn (1732–1809). These include the symphonies nicknamed the 'SURPRISE' (no 94), the 'MIRACLE' (no 96), the 'MILITARY' (no 100), the 'CLOCK' (no 101), the 'DRUM ROLL' (no 103) and the 'LONDON' (no 104). The reason they are collectively known as the 'Salomon' Symphonies (or alternatively the 'London' Symphonies) is because Haydn wrote them for his visits to London in 1791–2 and 1794–5, which were arranged by the German-born concert promoter Johann Peter Salomon (1745–1815), who had settled in London in the 1780s. It was Salomon who gave Haydn the idea for an oratorio based on Milton's *Paradise Lost* – an idea that was to bear fruit in *The* CREATION (*see* panel, p.91). Salomon was also a friend of Beethoven, helped to found the Philharmonic Society of London, and is buried in Westminster Abbey.

Samson Agonistes. A tragic drama by John Milton (1608–74), apparently never intended for performance. There is some debate as to the date of its composition, but it was first published in 1671. *Agonistes* is Greek for 'champion' or 'wrestler', and the work deals with the biblical hero when he is a prisoner of the Philistines, 'EYELESS IN GAZA at the mill with slaves'.

T.S. Eliot (1888–1965) adapted Milton's title for *Sweeney Agonistes* (1932), his unfinished 'Fragments of an Aristophanic melodrama'. Sweeney, Eliot's anti-hero of proletarian physicality, had already featured in two earlier poems (1920), 'Sweeney Erect' (in which Sweeney is likened to an orang-utan) and 'Sweeney Among the Nightingales', and also makes an appearance in 'Mr Eliot's Sunday Morning Service', during which:

> Sweeney shifts from ham to ham
> Stirring the water in his bath.

In *Sweeney Agonistes*, Sweeney wishes to carry Doris off to a desert island, where he will be the cannibal and she the devoured missionary:

> That's all the facts when you come to brass tacks:
> Birth, and copulation, and death.

The character's name may have been inspired by that of the murderous barber, *SWEENEY TODD*.

Sardanapalus. A legendary king of ancient Assyria, possibly a conflation of three actual rulers. His story is told by the Greek historian Diodorus Siculus (*fl.* 1st century BC). Sardanapalus was renowned for his luxurious lifestyle, which in the end led to the downfall of his kingdom. The king then ordered that all his favourite possessions, together with his concubines, servants and himself, should be burnt in a great pyre. The story inspired the tragedy *Sardanapalus* (1821) by Byron (1788–1824), and the painting *The Death of Sardanapalus* (1827) by Delacroix (1798–1863), now in the Louvre, Paris.

Sartor Resartus: The Life and Opinions of Herr Teufelsdröckh. A partly humorous philosophical satire (1833–4) – initially inspired by Swift's *A TALE OF A TUB* – by the Scottish writer Thomas Carlyle (1795–1881). *Sartor resartus* is Latin for 'the tailor re-tailored' or 're-patched', and the first part is a philosophical inquiry (in the manner of the German Romantics) into the metaphysical nature of clothes, and how clothes may stand as symbols of the transience of most human constructs:

> Language is called the garment of thought: however, it should rather be, language is the flesh-garment, the body of thought.
>
> Book I, chapter 11

Such speculations are supposedly based on the thinking of the eccentric Diogenes Teufelsdröckh, Professor of Things in General at the University of Weissnichtwo (German, 'know not where'). The second part of the book consists of a biography of Teufelsdröckh, in which many aspects of Carlyle's own life may be detected.

Satanic Verses, The. A novel (1988) by Salman Rushdie (b.1947). Questions of faith and doubt underlie this panoramic vision of the clash of cultures between East and West, which encompasses Britain during the

Thatcherite era, India, and the mystical landscape in which the Prophet Mahound does battle. The 'satanic verses' are whispered by Shaitan in the ear of Mahound, who then repudiates them:

> The Devil came to him in the guise of the archangel, so that the verses he memorized ... were not the real thing but its diabolical opposite, not godly, but satanic.

The novel gave offence to Muslims for certain remarks put into the mouths of its characters. As a result, a Muslim *fatwa* (legal ruling) was issued by the Ayatollah Khomeini, the religious leader of Iran, declaring Rushdie an apostate who should be killed for insulting the Prophet Muhammad. On 24 September 1998, after Rushdie had spent the intervening period in hiding, the government of the Islamic Republic of Iran announced that it had no intention, nor would it take any action, to threaten Rushdie's life or anybody associated with his work, or encourage or assist anybody to do so.

Satiromastix. *See* POETASTER, THE.

Saudades. A set of three songs (1917) by the English composer Peter Warlock (Philip Heseltine; 1894–1930), with texts by Li Po, Shakespeare and Callimachus. *Saudades do Brasil* is the title of two volumes of piano pieces (composed 1920–1 and later orchestrated) by the French diplomat and composer Darius Milhaud (1892–1974), who in 1917–19 had been an attaché with the French legation in Rio de Janeiro.

The Portuguese word *saudade* evokes a complex of emotions: poignant nostalgia, yearning, melancholy and loneliness; as a state of mind it has been described as 'anxiety tempered by fatalism'. A *saudade* is also a poem of longing, and the mood (which may embrace a reverence for nature) is regarded as a key ingredient of much Portuguese poetry; indeed, *saudosismo* became something of a cult towards the end of the 19th century.

Savoy Operas. The collective name often given to the operettas of Gilbert and Sullivan (W.S. Gilbert, 1836–1911; and Arthur Sullivan, 1842–1900), most of which were first staged at the Savoy Theatre, London. The theatre, built by Richard D'Oyly Carte, opened in 1881 with a performance of *Patience*. The members of the D'Oyly Carte Company who played in the operettas were referred to as 'Savoyards'.

Scapegoat, The. A painting (1855) by the Pre-Raphaelite William Holman Hunt (1827–1910). Hunt, who painted the work in Palestine, has gone back to the original, literal meaning of his title, and depicts an abandoned goat apparently mired in quicksand at the edge of the Dead Sea. Among the ancient Hebrews, the scapegoat played a part in a ritual for the Day of Atonement laid down by the Law of Moses (Leviticus 16). Two goats were brought to the altar of the Tabernacle and the high priest cast lots, one for the Lord, and the other for Azazel (a demonic being); the Lord's goat was sacrificed and the other was the scapegoat, and the high priest having, by confession, transferred his own sins and the sins of the people to it, it was taken to the wilderness and allowed to escape.

Hunt himself described the subject of his painting as

> The Church on Earth, subject to all the hatred of the unconverted world.
>
> WILLIAM HOLMAN HUNT: exhibition catalogue (1856)

In the same year a critic described Hunt's subject as

> A mere goat, with no more interest for us than the sheep which furnished yesterday's dinner.
>
> UNNAMED CRITIC: quoted in Ironside, *Pre-Raphaelite Painters* (1948)

> Hunt laughed over the wicked libel that he had starved a goat for his picture, though certainly four died in his service, probably feeling dull when separated from the flock.
>
> CAROLINE FOX: Journal, 1860

Scapino. The cowardly and unreliable servant in the Italian *commedia dell'arte*, with a bearded mask and a hooked nose, usually dressed in baggy tunic and trousers and a feathered hat, and carrying a wooden sword. He is the hero of the comedy *Les Fourberies de Scapin* (1671) by Molière (1622–73), of which Thomas Otway (1652–85) made an English version, *The Cheats of Scapin* (1677). William Walton (1902–83) composed a comedy overture called *Scapino* in 1940, with the subtitle 'after an etching from Jacques Callot's *Balli di Sfessania*, 1622'.

Scaramouche. The title of a ballet (1913) with music by Jean Sibelius (1865–1957), and also of a suite for two pianos (1939) by Darius Milhaud (1892–1974), later arranged for saxophone or clarinet and orchestra. Milhaud's suite was adapted from his incidental music to *The Flying*

Doctor, a play staged in 1937 at the Théâtre Scaramouche in Paris, hence the title. Scaramouche is the French version of the Italian *commedia dell'arte* character Scarramuccia, a braggart and a fool, very valiant in words, but a poltroon (coward). He is usually dressed in a black Spanish costume. The name may derive from Italian *schermire*, 'to fence', the character originally being a vainglorious soldier before evolving into an unreliable servant. One of the most famous exponents of the role was Tiberio Fiorilli (*c.*1608–94), who became known as Scaramuccia Fiorilli. He came to England in 1673, and astonished audiences with his feats of agility.

Scarface. A gangster film (1932) directed by Howard Hawks, with a screenplay by Ben Hecht and others. The 1983 remake was directed by Brian de Palma and had a screenplay by Oliver Stone. The name of the eponymous anti-hero is Tony Camonte (played by Paul Muni) in the 1932 version; in the 1983 version he is called Tony Montana (played by Al Pacino). The character is based on the real-life gangster Al Capone (1899–1947), who acquired the nickname Scarface from the scar on his left cheek caused by a razor slash in a Brooklyn gang fight in his younger days.

Scarlet Letter, The. A novel (1850) by the US writer Nathaniel Hawthorne (1804–64), set in 17th-century Puritan New England, when a scarlet A for 'adulteress' was branded or sewn on a guilty woman's dress. Hawthorne's heroine, Hester Prynne, is condemned to wear such a letter after the birth of her illegitimate child Pearl. Hester refuses to name the father, the young minister Arthur Dimmesdale. He refuses to own up until the end, when he climbs onto the pillory with Hester and Pearl, and bears his chest, where guilt has burnt a scarlet letter on his flesh. He then dies in Hester's arms. There have been at least a dozen film versions, none of them memorable.

The association of the colour scarlet with moral laxity probably originates with the scarlet woman or scarlet whore of Revelation, where she is the woman seen by St John in his vision 'arrayed in purple and scarlet colour', sitting 'upon a scarlet coloured beast, full of names of blasphemy, having seven heads and ten horns', 'drunken with the blood of the saints, and with the blood of the martyrs', upon whose forehead is written 'Mystery, Babylon the Great, The Mother of Harlots and Abominations of the Earth' (Revelation 17:1–6).

SCATOLOGY

An Essay Upon Wind; with Curious Anecdotes of Eminent Peteurs, an anonymous work (1787), possibly by Charles James Fox, and dedicated to the Lord Chancellor

Constipation and Our Civilization, a polemic (1943) by James Charles Thomson

The Great Piss-up, a painting (1962–3) by Georg Baselitz

Piss Flowers, a sculpture by Helen Chadwick (1953–96), consisting of casts of cavities she formed by urinating in the snow

Trickle Treat, a guide to 'diaperless toilet training' (1991) by Laurie Boucke

FLYING SHIT, a work (1994) by Gilbert and George

The Gas We Pass: The Story of Farts, a monograph (1994) by Shinta Cho

Wind Breaks: Coming to Terms with Flatulence, a self-help book (1995) by Terry Dorcen Bolin and Rosemary Stanton

The Zen of Bowel Movements, 'a spiritual approach to constipation' (1995) by Kathy A. Price

The ADORATION OF CAPTAIN SHIT AND THE LEGEND OF THE BLACK STAR PART TWO, a painting (1998) by Chris Ofili, incorporating elephant dung

Shitting Pretty: How To Stay Clean and Healthy While Travelling, a handy little guide (2000) issued by the US publisher Traveler's Tales

Scarlet Pimpernel, The. A bestselling novel (1905) by the Hungarian-born British novelist Baroness Orczy (Mrs Montague Barstow; 1865–1947). 'The Scarlet Pimpernel' (a plant of the primrose family, *Anagallis arvensis*) is the byname of the spy hero, Sir Percy Blakeney, who is the head of the League of the Scarlet Pimpernel, a band of young Englishmen pledged to rescue the aristocratic victims of the Reign of Terror that followed the French Revolution. He outwits his French opponents through his courage and ingenious disguises, identifying himself in his secret rescue missions by a signet ring with the image of a scarlet pimpernel flower. The verse with which Blakeney mocks his chief enemy, Citizen Chauvelin, one of Robespierre's most cunning agents, is well known:

> We seek him here, we seek him there,
> Those Frenchies seek him everywhere.
> Is he in heaven? – Is he in hell?
> That demmed, elusive Pimpernel?
>
> chapter xii

A period film version (1934), starring Leslie Howard, Merle Oberon and Raymond Massey, was directed by Harold Young.

Scheherazade. *See* ARABIAN NIGHTS ENTERTAINMENT.

Schindler's Ark (US title: *Schindler's List*). A novel with historical interpolations (1982) by the Australian novelist Thomas Keneally (b.1935), which won the Booker Prize for fiction. It describes the life and times of Oskar Schindler (1908–74), an ethnic German born into a Catholic family living in Moravia (incorporated into the new republic of Czechoslovakia in 1918 and now part of the Czech Republic). During the Second World War Schindler, playboy industrialist and 'discoverer of unprocurables', saved some 1100 Polish Jews by setting up at his own expense a personal 'labour camp' within the concentration camp in Cracow and passing the men and women off as 'skilled workers'. The highly regarded film version (1993), entitled *Schindler's List*, was directed by Steven Spielberg.

Schindler's List. *See* SCHINDLER'S ARK.

Schlagobers. A 'gay Viennese' ballet with music by Richard Strauss (1864–1949) and choreography by Kröller, first performed in 1924. The story is a fantasy set in a sweet shop in which the sweets come to life. *Schlagobers* is the Austrian name for fresh whipped cream, as served in Viennese coffee houses. 'Too much air and not enough cream' was the verdict from the critic George Bulanda on Strauss's orchestral suite adapted from the ballet.

School for Scandal, The. A comedy by Richard Brinsley Sheridan (1751–1816), first produced in 1777. The title refers to a set of fashionable but malicious gossips who 'strike a character dead at every word'. The 'school' is held at the house of Lady Teazle, and includes such figures as Sir Benjamin Backbite, Lady Sneerwell and Mrs Candour.

'Schoolmaster, The' (German *Der Schulmeister*). The nickname of the symphony no 55 in E flat (1774) by Haydn (1732–1809), thought to derive from the somewhat serious mood of the second movement, in which some have detected in the dotted rhythm the admonitory wagging of a pedagogic finger.

School of Athens, The. One of four frescoes by Raphael (1483–20) painted *c.*1509 in the Stanza della Segnatura, a room in the papal apartments in the Vatican. The work was commissioned by Pope Julius II, who also commissioned Donato Bramante to design the new St Peter's and Michelangelo to design his tomb and (against his will) to paint the Sistine Chapel ceiling. The frescoes in the Stanza della Segnatura are intended to demonstrate how neoplatonist philosophy justifies the power of the Roman Catholic Church. The School of Athens depicts Plato and Aristotle and a host of other philosophers, both ancient and modern, in a calm and balanced composition. The classical architectural setting – reminiscent of the new St Peter's – was painted from designs by Bramante, who himself acted as the model for the mathematician Euclid in the painting. Raphael's portrait of his patron, Pope Julius, is in the National Gallery, London.

> It took a soul as beautiful as his, in a body as beautiful as his, to experience and rediscover the true character of the ancients in modern times.
>
> JOHANN J. WINCKELMANN: on Raphael, in *Thoughts on the Imitation of Greek Art in Painting and Sculpture* (1755)

School of Love, The. The popular, although misleading, title of *Mercury Instructing Cupid before Venus* (*c.*1532), a painting by Correggio (1494–1534) in the National Gallery, London. Mercury is actually teaching the infant Cupid, the god of love, how to read, but the popular name probably derives from the domestic tenderness of the scene, all three figures appearing unusually human for immortals.

Schöpfung, Die. *See* CREATION (panel, p.91).

Schweigsame Frau, Die. *See EPICENE, OR THE SILENT WOMAN.*

Scoop. A novel by Evelyn Waugh (1903–66), published in 1938. The novel draws on Waugh's own experiences as a war correspondent for the *Daily Mail* during the Italian campaign in Abyssinia (Ethiopia) in

1936. In the novel, the *Daily Beast* intends to send out the novelist John Boot as its man in the war-torn African state of Ishmaelia. In error, the job goes to the *Beast*'s retiring writer of nature notes, William Boot. This Boot is more accustomed to penning lines such as –

> Feather-footed through the plashy fen passes the questing vole …

Waugh based some aspects of William Boot on W.F. (Bill) Deedes, then reporting for the *Morning Post*. Deedes, like Boot, arrived in Abyssinia with an extraordinary quantity of luggage (his paper didn't expect him to return, or at least not for a long time), causing Waugh much mirth. Deedes himself, in a BBC Radio interview in 2001, said that he indeed shared Boot's naivety (and his volume of luggage), but that he was much less 'shambolic'. Deedes went on to become one of Britain's most distinguished journalists, and was for many years editor of the *Daily Telegraph*.

William Boot lives on in another guise – as the pseudonymous author of 'Unauthorised Returns', a humorous column in the *Bookseller* magazine.

Scotch (or ***Scottish***) ***Symphony.*** The symphony no 3 in A minor, opus 56, by Felix Mendelssohn (1809–47). He began work on it during a visit to Scotland in 1829, but did not complete it until 1842. The symphony is not programmatic, although Mendelssohn used part of a Scottish folk song in the scherzo. The work was dedicated to Queen Victoria, whose favourite composer Mendelssohn became.

Scotland for Ever! A painting (1881) by the celebrated military artist Lady Elizabeth Butler (1846–1933), depicting a pell-mell cavalry charge. The cavalry in question are the Royal Scots Greys, who in the early afternoon of 18 June 1815 took part in a massive and successful attack against French forces near a village called Waterloo.

'Scots wha hae wi' Wallace bled'. A poem (1794) by Robert Burns (1759–96), in which King Robert the Bruce rouses his men before the great Scottish victory over the English at Bannockburn (1314). The title is Scots for 'Scots who have bled with Wallace', referring to the national hero Sir William Wallace, who had been executed by the English in 1305.

Scouting for Boys. A book, published in fortnightly parts in 1908, by Robert Baden-Powell (1857–1941), the founder of the Scout Movement. It includes advice on healthy living (particularly camping in the wild and the avoidance of self-abuse), and a number of 'camp fire yarns'. Other interesting Scouting titles include *Scouts in Bondage* (1930), an adventure story by Geoffrey Prout (possibly a relative of Samuel Gillespie Prout, author of the 1881 classic, *'Hurrah!' A Bit of Loving Talk with Soldiers*). Not to be outdone, The Girl Guides Association issued a little volume in 1977 entitled *Whippings and Lashings*, which includes such advice as 'Do not fumble or use fancy methods.'

Scream, The. A painting (1893) by the Norwegian artist Edvard Munch (1863–1944) depicting a distorted, skeletal figure with gaping rictus and hands over its ears, as if in agony as shockwaves of colour press in on him from the sky and the fjord below. The painting was part of Munch's *Frieze of Life* series, and in 1895 he made a woodcut version. The image has become an icon of the angst of the individual in the modern world, and is frequently used as an image of mental illness.

> One evening I was walking along a path, the city was on one side and the fjord below. I felt tired and ill. I stopped and looked out over the fjord – the sun was setting, and the clouds turning blood red. I sensed a scream passing through nature; it seemed to me that I heard the scream. I painted this picture, painted the clouds as actual blood. The colour shrieked. This became *The Scream*.
>
> EDVARD MUNCH: Diary, 1889

Screaming Popes, The. A series of paintings executed between 1949 and the mid-1950s by Francis Bacon (1909–92). They were inspired by the portrait of Pope Innocent X by Velázquez (1599–1660), a painting described by Sir Joshua Reynolds in the 18th century as 'the most beautiful picture in Rome'. Sir Joshua would not have appreciated Bacon's reworkings, which are nightmarish depictions of hysterical terror, sometimes accompanied by hunks of meat. As one critic put it: 'The major influence on Bacon has been his own surname.'

Sea Drift. *See* SEA SYMPHONY, A.

Seagull, The. A play (1896) by the Russian dramatist Anton Chekhov (1860–94). It tells of the unrequited love of Trepliov, a young writer, for Nina, an actress, who favours an older, more successful writer, Trigorin. Trepliov kills a seagull and lays it at Nina's feet as a symbol of his despair, and then unsuccessfully attempts suicide. Two years later Nina, abandoned by Trigorin, compares herself to the dead seagull, and Trepliov, despite having achieved some success as a writer, kills himself.

THE SEASONS and *THE FOUR SEASONS*

The Seasons or *The Four Seasons* have provided titles for many works.

One of the best known is the sequence of four violin concertos, *The Four Seasons* (*Le quattro Stagioni*) by the Italian composer Antonio Vivaldi (1678–1741), published in 1725 as part of a sequence of twelve violin concertos entitled *Il cimento dell'armonia e dell' inventione* ('the contest between harmony and invention'), opus 8.

The Seasons (1726–30) by the Scottish poet James Thomson (1700–48) is a long poem in blank verse consisting of a book per season plus a final 'Hymn' to Nature. Thomson's treatment of landscape in the poem constitutes a notable step towards the Romantic sensibility, although his language is still predominantly Augustan.

Thomson's work provided the inspiration for the secular oratorio *The Seasons* (*Die Jahreszeiten*) by Haydn (1732–1809), first performed in 1801. Thomson's words, translated and adapted by Baron van Swieten, provided the libretto; the English text usually used in British performances is actually a translation back into English from van Swieten's German. '*The Seasons* nearly broke my back,' Haydn is reported to have said.

There is a set of piano pieces by Tchaikovsky (1840–93) called *The Seasons* (1876), and a one-act ballet *The Seasons* (1900), with music (an orchestral suite written in the 1890s) by Alexander Glazunov (1865–1936) and choreography by Marius Petipa (1819–1910).

The 1981 US film *The Four Seasons*, written and directed by and starring Alan Alda, observes the tensions and resolutions among three married couples over the course of four seasonal holidays together. By the time of the film, Vivaldi's *Four Seasons* was universally familiar, being heard as 'wallpaper music' in every possible circumstance; the work had also given its name to a type of pizza.

Other works with the title *The Four Seasons* include:

- Four landscape scrolls by the Japanese artist Sesshu (1420–1506); incidentally, 'pictures of the four seasons' (*shiki-e*) was a Japanese genre of painting of the late Heian period (10th–12th centuries)
- A series of paintings (1563) by the Italian painter Giuseppe Arcimboldo (1527–93), in which – in Arcimboldo's usual manner – each season is represented by a head made up of vegetable matter (for example, summer is composed of ripe fruit, winter by a withered old tree trunk)
- A series of paintings (1660–4) by the French classical painter Nicolas Poussin (1593/4–1665)
- A long poem (published 1818) by the Lithuanian writer Kristijonas Donelaitis (1714–80), depicting village life through the year

The Fifth Season (1973) is a piece of music theatre about the Vietnam War by the Dutch composer Piet Schat (b. 1935).

See also MAN FOR ALL SEASONS, A.

Sea Symphony, A. The symphony no 1 by Ralph Vaughan Williams (1872–1958), first performed in 1910. The piece is scored for soprano, baritone, chorus and orchestra, and consists of settings of poems by Walt Whitman about the sea. Frederick Delius (1862–1934) drew on the same poet for the text of his *Sea Drift* for baritone, chorus and orchestra, completed in 1903 and first performed in 1906.

Sea, the Sea, The. A novel by Iris Murdoch (1919–99), published in 1978 and winner of that year's Booker Prize.

> The sea, which lies before me as I write, glows rather than sparkles in the bland May sunshine.
>
> opening words

The book centres on Charles Arrowby, a theatre director who retires from the glamour of London to an isolated seaside home, where his plans come awry and his large ego comes under assault. The title is from the Greek historian Xenophon (431–*c*.350 BC), who in his *Anabasis* recounts from personal experience the story of the 'Ten Thousand', the band of Greek mercenaries in the service of Cyrus of Persia who fought their way across Kurdistan and Armenia back to the Greek colony of Trapezus (Trabzon) on the Black Sea – hence the famous exclamation at this climactic moment of the march, '*Thalassa, thalassa*' ('The sea! the sea!').

Second of May 1808, The. *See* THIRD OF MAY 1808, THE.

Selfish Gene, The. A book (1976) by the biologist Richard Dawkins (b.1941) that popularized the evolutionary theory that living organisms are primarily the means by which genes perpetuate themselves. This helped to explain the continuing existence of characteristics that do not necessarily benefit an individual organism. The book did much to popularize the field of sociobiology.

> They are in you and in me; they created us, body and mind; and their preservation is the ultimate rationale for our existence ... they go by the name of genes, and we are their survival machines.
>
> chapter 2

Self-portrait with Bandaged Ear. A self-portrait (1889) by Vincent van Gogh (1853–90). Already mentally unstable, in October 1888 van Gogh had been joined in Arles, Provence, by Paul Gauguin, and the two began to work together. However, they had very different ideas about art, and very different temperaments. After a fierce quarrel with Gauguin, on Christmas Eve van Gogh cut off part of his left ear. He spent two weeks in hospital, and then made this self-portrait. In April 1889 he committed himself to the insane asylum at Saint-Rémy-de-Provence. He released himself in May 1890, and shot himself in July, dying two days later.

> Misery will never end.
>
> VINCENT VAN GOGH: dying remark to his brother Theo, quoted in Udhe, *Vincent van Gogh* (1947)

> No one knew him. He lived alone, like a dog. People were afraid of him ... He ran around the fields with these huge canvases. Boys used to throw stones at him.
>
> UNNAMED OLD MAN: quoted in Herbert, *Barbarian in the Garden* (1985)

Semper Dowland Semper Dolens. *See* LACHRIMAE, OR SEAVEN TEARES FIGURED IN SEAVEN PASSIONATE PAVANS.

Sense and Sensibility. A novel by Jane Austen (1775–1817), published in 1811. As in *PRIDE AND PREJUDICE*, the title refers to two of the main characters: the sensible, quiet and dignified Elinor Dashwood, and her highly emotional and demonstrative sister, Marianne. 'Sensibility' is an 18th-century usage for 'feeling' or 'sentiment'.

> Miss Austen being, as you say, without 'sentiment', without *poetry*, maybe *is* sensible, real (more *real* than *true*), but she cannot be great.
>
> CHARLOTTE BRONTË: letter to George Henry Lewes, 18 January 1848

The film version (1995), directed by Ang Lee and with a screenplay by Emma Thompson (who also plays Elinor), was a surprise commercial hit.

Sentimental Journey through France and Italy by Mr Yorick, A. A novel by Laurence Sterne (1713–68), written after his own two journeys to the Continent. Despite the title, the narrator, Parson Yorick (on holiday here from his part in the author's *Tristram Shandy*), never reaches Italy. The name Yorick is derived from that of the court jester whose skull Hamlet apostrophizes in Shakespeare's play (V.i). The 'sentimental' aspect of the journey derives from the narrator's desire not to sightsee as in the conventional Grand Tour, but to meet with the natives of the places he visits. Yorick himself is an emotional man, being often reduced to tears: 'Dear sensibility! source inexhausted of all that's precious in our joys, or costly in our sorrows!' The parson also has a weakness for the opposite sex:

> So that when I stretch'd out my hand, I caught hold of the Fille de Chambre's —
>
> *A Sentimental Journey*, closing words

Serjeant Musgrave's Dance. A play (1959) by John Arden (b.1930) about a group of soldiers who arrive in a mining town in northern England apparently on a recruiting drive, but who are subsequently revealed to be deserters traumatized by their involvement in an atrocity while on service overseas. Serjeant Musgrave, the leader of the soldiers, dances a wild dance in front of the skeleton of a former comrade before threatening to kill 25 people of the town when they fail to rally to his cause. Following Musgrave's arrest, the miners join in their own celebratory circle dance.

Set in a Silver Sea. The first volume (1984) in his *History of Britain and the British People* by Sir Arthur Bryant (1899–1985), subtitled 'The Island

Peoples from Earliest Times to the Fifteenth Century'. The title is from Shakespeare:

> This royal throne of kings, this scepter'd isle …
> This fortress built by Nature for herself
> Against infection and the hand of war …
> This precious stone set in the silver sea …
> This blessed plot, this earth, this realm, this England …
>
> *Richard II* (1595), II.i

Another phrase from this speech was borrowed for *This Sceptered Isle*, BBC Radio 4's series by Christopher Lee on the history of Britain, published in two volumes (1997, 1999).

In his *Eminent Churchillians* (1994) the historian Andrew Roberts described Bryant as the 'Uriah Heep of historical writing'.

Seven. A somewhat bleak film (1995) starring Brad Pitt and Morgan Freeman as detectives on the track of a serial killer, each of whose victims is supposedly a perpetrator of one of the seven deadly sins: pride, covetousness, lust, envy, gluttony, anger and sloth. In promotional material for the film it was often referred to as *Se7en*. *The Seven Deadly Sins* is the title of a youthful work by the Flemish painter Hieronymus Bosch (*c.*1450–1516), a series of prints by the Netherlandish artist Pieter Bruegel (*c.*1525–1629), a ballet-drama (1933) by Kurt Weill (1900–50) and Bertolt Brecht (1898–1956), a collection of verse (1941) by the Swedish poet Karin Boye (1900–41) and a 1952 French film, comprising seven sinful episodes, each with a different scriptwriter and director. The film *The Magnificent Seven Deadly Sins* (1971) is a series of comedy sketches starring Bruce Forsyth, Joan Sims, Roy Hudd, Spike Milligan and others.

Seven Days in May. A political thriller (1962) by Charles Waldo Bailey II and Fletcher Knebel, turned into a gripping film (1964) directed by John Frankenheimer. The signing of a nuclear disarmament treaty with the Soviets prompts reactionary elements in the US military establishment to plan a coup to overthrow the president. The seven days in question are those between the time that the US president is informed of a possible plot and when the coup is due to take place. President John F. Kennedy had agreed the Nuclear Test Ban Treaty with the USSR in 1963, and the film-makers received considerable cooperation from the White House.

Seven Deadly Sins, The. *See* SEVEN.

Seven Joys of the Virgin, The. A panoramic painting by the German-born Netherlandish painter Hans Memling (*c.*1433–94), commissioned for the tanners' chapel in the Frauenkirche in Bruges. The title is somewhat misleading, as many more than seven scenes are depicted (although some of these involve no joy for the Virgin): the Annunciation, the Nativity, the annunciation to the shepherds, the appearance of the star to the three kings, the visit of the kings to Herod, their journey to Bethlehem, the adoration of the kings, the massacre of the innocents, the flight into Egypt, the temptation of Christ, the Resurrection, the NOLI ME TANGERE, Christ at Emmaus, Peter on the water, the appearance of Christ to his mother, the Ascension, Pentecost, the death of the Virgin and the Assumption. The traditional 'seven joys' are: the Annunciation, the Visitation, the Nativity, the Epiphany, the Finding in the Temple, the Resurrection and the Ascension.

The Seven Sorrows of the Virgin is a work attributed to the Netherlandish painter Adriaen Isenbrandt (d.1551), a pupil of Gerard David. The traditional 'seven sorrows' are: Simeon's prophecy, the flight into Egypt, the loss of the Holy Child, meeting Christ on the way to Calvary, the Crucifixion, the taking down from the Cross and the entombment.

seven last words from the Cross, the. Christ's final utterances in his mortal life, which have formed the texts for various examples of Passion music. As recorded in the different Gospels the seven last words are:

1. 'Father, forgive them; for they know not what they do.' Luke 23:34
2. 'Today shalt thou be with me in paradise.' Luke 23:43
3. 'Woman, behold thy son! … Behold thy mother!' John 19:26–27
4. 'Eli, Eli, lama sabachthani? [that is to say,] My God, my God, why hast thou forsaken me?' Matthew 27:46
5. 'I thirst.' John 19:28
6. 'It is finished.' John 19:30
7. 'Father, into thy hands I commend my spirit.' Luke 23:46

The German composer Heinrich Schütz (1585–1672) used these texts for his short oratorio *The Seven Words of Our Beloved Redeemer and Saviour Jesus Christ* (1645; German title: *Die sieben Worte unsers lieben Erlösers und Seligmachers Jesu Christi*). There are three versions of the *Seven*

Last Words of the Saviour on the Cross (German title: *Die sieben letzen worte des Erlösers am Kreuz*) by Haydn (1732–1809). The original is an orchestral work commissioned in 1785 by Cadiz Cathedral in Portugal for performance on Good Friday; the seven slow movements were designed to separate the bishop's sermons on each of the seven last words. The work was published the following year in Vienna as *7 sonate, con un' introduzione, ed al fine un terremoto* (Italian, 'seven sonatas, with an introduction, and at the end an earthquake'). The 'earthquake' of the title is mentioned in Matthew 27:50–54.

In 1787 Haydn arranged the work for string quartet, opus 51, and this set formed his quartets nos 50–6. Around 1796 Haydn again returned to the music, arranging it as a cantata.

Seven Pillars of Wisdom, The. An autobiographical account by the British soldier, archaeologist, Arabist, classical scholar and writer T(homas) E(dward) Lawrence (1888–1935) of his adventures in Arabia during the First World War. Lawrence took his title from the Bible:

> Wisdom hath builded her house, she hath hewn out her seven pillars.
>
> Proverbs 9:1

It is not clear why *seven*, although seven is commonly a mystical or sacred number and crops up frequently in the Bible. Lawrence famously mislaid the first draft of his manuscript in 1919 while changing trains at Reading.

The book formed the basis for the Oscar-winning epic film *Lawrence of Arabia* (1962) directed by David Lean (1908–91) with a screenplay by Robert Bolt (1924–95), starring Peter O'Toole in the title role.

Seven Samurai, The. *See* MAGNIFICENT SEVEN, THE.

Seventh Seal, The. A highly regarded film (1957) directed by the Swedish director Ingmar Bergman (b.1918). A vision of a medieval land ravaged by the Black Death, the film impressed and mystified audiences around the world. The title refers to a verse in the Bible:

> And when he had opened the seventh seal, there was a silence in heaven about the space of half an hour.
>
> Revelation 8:1

Seven-Year Itch, The. A stage comedy (1952) by George Axelrod, in which a married man has a fling with the girl upstairs. The title refers to the theory that marriages are most in danger from adulterous disruption after a period of seven years. The film version (1955) starring Marilyn Monroe did much to popularize the phrase.

Severed Head, A. A novel (1961) by Iris Murdoch (1919–99). In spite of its macabre title and solemn themes, which include adultery, incest, castration, violence and suicide, this is also a comedy about valuing relationships. The narrator is told by Honor Klein, with whom he is in love:

> I am a severed head such as primitive tribes and old alchemists used to use, anointing it with oil and putting a morsel of gold upon its tongue to make it utter prophecies.

A stage version of the novel was written by J.B. Priestley in collaboration with Murdoch, and was published in 1963. A film version, written by Frederic Raphael and directed by Dick Clement, followed in 1970.

sex, lies, and videotape. A film (1989) written and directed by Steven Soderbergh about an impotent film-maker who gets emotionally involved in the marital discord that has developed between an old college friend and his wife. The catalyst for trouble is the collection of videotapes he has made interviewing women about their sex lives. The title may also echo the late 1970s punk anthem by Ian Drury, 'Sex 'n' Drugs 'n' Rock 'n' Roll'.

Shaker Loops. The title of a string septet (1978) by the US minimalist composer John Adams (b.1947). The work re-uses some material from an earlier string quartet, *Wavemaker*, and in 1983 Adams arranged *Shaker Loops* for string orchestra. The title refers to 'shake', an alternative term for a trill, and also the ecstatic religious sect, the Shakers; while 'loop' refers to tape loops of the kind used by Adams's fellow minimalist Steve Reich, which helped to inspire the ceaseless motion of Adams's work. The four movements are entitled 'Shaking and Trembling', 'Hymning Slews', 'Loops and Verses' and 'A Final Shaking'.

Shamela. A parody of Samuel Richardson's novel *Pamela, or Virtue Rewarded* (1740), published pseudonymously in 1741 by Henry Fielding (1707–54). The full title is *An Apology for the Life of Mrs Shamela Andrews*. The pun on 'sham' and 'Pamela' sums up Fielding's annoyance at the pious moralizing of Richardson's work, which he cynically subverts in his own version of the story.

> How charming, how wholesome, Fielding always is! To take him up

after Richardson is like emerging from a sick room heated by stoves into an open lawn, on a breezy day in May.

SAMUEL TAYLOR COLERIDGE: *Table Talk* (1836)

***Shape of Things to Come, The*.** A novel by H.G. Wells (1866–1946), published in 1933. The title has given rise to a common expression. Wells's novel chillingly predicts war in 1939 followed by plague, rebellion, a new glass-based society, the first rocketship to the moon and the establishment of a world government in 2059. The work formed the basis of Alexander Korda's acclaimed film *Things to Come* (1935), with music by Arthur Bliss.

shark in formaldehyde, Damien Hirst's. *See* PHYSICAL IMPOSSIBILITY OF DEATH IN THE MIND OF SOMEONE LIVING, THE.

***Shaving of Shagpat, The*.** 'An Arabian Entertainment' by George Meredith (1828–1909), published in 1856. Shagpat is a sorcerer who has put the city under enchantment via the medium of a single hair on his head. After many adventures, the hero, Shibli Bagarag, succeeds in shaving Shagpat and so breaks the spell.

***She*.** A romantic adventure story (1887) by H. Rider Haggard (1856–1925). 'She' is Ayesha, an apparently immortal African queen, and the story concerns the efforts of the hero to avenge the murder of an ancestor who was a priest of Isis. Ayesha is frequently referred to as 'She who must be obeyed'; the mischievous Conservative backbencher Julian Critchley applied the same name to Margaret Thatcher, while the barrister Rumpole in the stories by John Mortimer (b.1923) also refers to his wife in this way. There have been two film versions (1935, 1965) of Haggard's novel, the first transposed from Africa to the Arctic. The African queen reappears in Haggard's *Ayesha* (1905).

She is also the title of a vast sculpture by the French artist and film-maker Nikie de Saint-Phalle (b.1930), exhibited in Sweden in 1963 under the title *Hon*, the Swedish word for 'she'. It consists of a hollow recumbent woman, measuring 25m × 6m × 9m, into which viewers enter via the vagina.

Finally, 'She' is the title of a romantic song by Charles Aznavour, revitalized by Elvis Costello for the soundtrack of the film *Notting Hill* (*see* NAPOLEON OF NOTTING HILL).

***$he*.** A picture of a toaster and a fridge with a woman styled to match by Richard Hamilton (b.1922). Executed in 1958–61 the work had a major influence on Pop Art in Britain. The punning title presumably refers to the commodification of human beings in the consumer society.

sheep in formaldehyde, Damien Hirst's. *See* PHYSICAL IMPOSSIBILITY OF DEATH IN THE MIND OF SOMEONE LIVING, THE.

Sheep May Safely Graze (German *Schafe Können Sicher Weiden*). A much arranged aria (originally for soprano, two recorders and figured bass) from the secular cantata *Was mir behagt* ('what I enjoy') by J.S.Bach (1685–1750). The cantata is also called the *Hunt Cantata*, as the words by Salomo Franck celebrate the joys of hunting. The cantata was written for the birthday festivities of the duke of Saxe-Weissenfels in February 1713, and the aria likens a secure people ruled by a good prince to safely grazing sheep in the care of a good shepherd.

Sheherazade. *See* ARABIAN NIGHTS ENTERTAINMENT.

'Shepherd-Boy' Étude. The nickname of the piano étude in A flat, opus 25 no 1, by Chopin (1810–49). Chopin apparently told a pupil that as he wrote the piece he had imagined a shepherd boy sheltering in a cave from a storm and playing his pipe.

Shepherds of the Delectable Mountains. A short opera ('pastoral episode') by Ralph Vaughan Williams (1872–1958), with a libretto by the composer drawn from *The Pilgrim's Progress*. It was first performed in 1922.

> They came to the Delectable Mountains.
>
> JOHN BUNYAN: *The Pilgrim's Progress*, part 1 (1678)

It is from the Delectable Mountains that the Celestial City (i.e. heaven) can be seen. Vaughan Williams absorbed much of *Shepherds* into his longer opera *The Pilgrim's Progress* (1951).

Shoot the Pianist (French title: *Tirez sur le pianiste*). A film (1960) by François Truffaut, intended as a homage to the American B-feature *film noir*. The story, based on a novel by David Goodis, follows the adventures of a café pianist (played by Charles Aznavour) who becomes involved with a bunch of criminals. The title recalls the notice seen by Oscar Wilde in a dancing saloon in America:

> Please do not shoot the pianist. He is doing his best.
>
> Quoted in OSCAR WILDE, *Impressions of America* (*c.*1882–3), 'Leadville'

Shrimp and the Anemone, The. The first novel (1944) in the Eustace and Hilda trilogy by L.P. Hartley (1895–1972). The trilogy follows the course of the relationship between the sickly Eustace and his elder sister, symbolically represented in the first book when Hilda tears a shrimp from the grip of an anemone, killing the shrimp and disabling the anemone. The second volume, *The Sixth Heaven* (1946), continues their story, and at the end of the third novel, *Eustace and Hilda* (1947), Eustace dies in his sleep, and Hilda, whom he has cured from psychosomatic paralysis after a disastrous affair, retires into a nunnery.

Shropshire Lad, A. A series of 63 poems by A.E. Housman (1859–1936), published in 1896. Ignored on first publication, the poems became enormously popular during the First World War, evoking as they did the traditional English rural landscape:

That is the land of lost content,
I see it shining plain,
The happy highways where I went
And cannot come again.

Housman began the poems before he had actually visited Shropshire, which in his vision is as much a countryside of the mind as a real place, although scattered with actual landmarks such as Bredon, the Wrekin and Wenlock Edge. In many of the poems Housman – in his professional life a distinguished classicist – adopts the voice of a rural labourer, the 'Lad' of the title. The tone is nostalgic, often pessimistic, with the army or the hangman waiting:

And naked to the hangman's noose
The morning clocks will ring
A neck God made for other use
Than strangling in a string.

A Shropshire Lad, IX

This wilful gloominess has proved prone to parody:

What still alive at twenty-two,
A clean upstanding chap like you?
Sure, if your throat 'tis hard to slit,
Slit your girl's, and swing for it.

HUGH KINGSMILL: 'Two Poems, after A.E. Housman' (1933), no 1

George Butterworth (1885–1916), who was killed in action on the

Somme, composed a song cycle and an orchestral rhapsody, both with the title *A Shropshire Lad*. Several other English composers, including Vaughan Williams, John Ireland and Ivor Gurney, made settings of some of the poems. Vaughan Williams's effort, the song cycle *On Wenlock Edge* (1909), was loathed by the poet.

See also BLUE REMEMBERED HILLS.

Sicilian Vespers, The (French title: *Les Vêpres siciliennes*). An opera by Giuseppe Verdi (1812–1901), with a libretto in French by Eugène Scribe and Charles Duveyrier. It was first performed in Paris in 1855 on the occasion of the Great Exhibition, for which the work was commissioned.

Historically, the Sicilian Vespers is the name given to the massacre of the French in Sicily in 1282. The massacre was occasioned by the brutality and tyranny of the rule of Charles of Anjou (1227–85), and more immediately by the insulting behaviour of some French soldiers at vespers (early evening service) in the church of Santo Spirito outside Palermo on Easter Monday (30 March). Some 2000 French inhabitants of Palermo were killed that night, which was followed by a general revolt in the island. The Aragonese intervened to support the rebels, and ended up (in 1302) as the new rulers of Sicily.

In Verdi's story – balancing French and Italian sensitivities – the loyalties of the Sicilian patriot Arrigo are tested when the French governor, Guy de Montfort, reveals that he is Arrigo's father. After various further complications Arrigo is to marry another patriot, Elena, with Montfort's blessing. Elena, however, knows that the ringing of the wedding bell is the signal for the massacre to begin, and says she cannot marry. However, Montfort forces the hands of the two lovers together. The bell rings out, and Montfort and the rest of the French are slaughtered.

Silence of the Lambs, The. A horror novel (1989) by Thomas Harris (b.1940) about a homicidal genius, psychiatrist and cannibal, Hannibal Lecter. The title refers to a traumatic childhood experience of his potential victim, Clarice Starling, a female trainee investigator, who recalls the lambs on the farm where she was brought up being rounded up and taken away for slaughter, and the relief she experienced when their cries could no longer be heard. At the book's enigmatic ending, 'she sleeps deeply, sweetly in the silence of the lambs'. A film version (1990), starring Anthony Hopkins and Jodie Foster, was directed by Jonathan Demme.

Harris published a sequel, *Hannibal*, in 2000; a film version was released in 2001.

Silex Scintillans. A collection of religious poetry (1650) by the metaphysical poet Henry Vaughan (1621–95). The title is Latin for 'glittering flint' or 'striking flint'.

Silken Ladder, The (Italian title: *La Scala di seta*). An opera by Rossini (1792–1868), now principally known for its overture. The libretto is by Giuseppe Foppa, and it was first performed in 1812. The story is based on a French comedy, *L'Échelle de soie*, by François de Planard, and concerns a man who uses a silken ladder to reach the bedroom of his wife, to whom he is secretly married, but who lives in the house of her jealous father.

Silver Darlings, The. A novel (1941) by the Scottish writer Neil Gunn (1891–1973), set in Caithness in the far northeast of Scotland in the early 19th century. The 'silver darlings' is a traditional name for herring, for centuries the staple food of many coastal communities in Scotland.

Silver Tassie, The. A play (1928) by the Irish playwright Sean O'Casey (1880–1964) in which the author laments the loss of life in the First World War. The 'silver tassie' of the title is a silver cup brought home in victory by Dublin footballer Harry Hegan in the first act. The play formed the basis for an opera (2000) of the same title by the English composer Mark-Anthony Turnage (b.1960).

Sinfonia Antarctica. The atmospheric seventh symphony of Ralph Vaughan Williams (1872–1958). The title is Italian for 'Antarctic symphony'. The piece was adapted from Vaughan William's music for the film *Scott of the Antarctic* (1948), starring John Mills, James Robertson Justice and Kenneth More. The symphony, which was first performed in Manchester in 1953, includes parts for wind machine, vibraphone, wordless soprano solo and women's chorus. At a rehearsal of the piece the conductor Sir John Barbirolli instructed the chorus: 'I want you to sound like twenty-two women having babies *without* chloroform.'

Sir Gawain and the Green Knight. *See* GREEN KNIGHT, THE.

Six Characters in Search of an Author (Italian title: *Sei personaggi in cerca d'autore*). A play by the Italian dramatist Luigi Pirandello (1867–1936), first performed in 1921. In the play the actors in a theatre act out the destiny of a family of six strangers who have interrupted their rehearsal. When they first appear the family believe they are merely characters in a play and are in search of the author to find out what is to become of them; after the actors show them their fate they are appalled, despite the actors' insistence that their fate is not real.

Skin of Our Teeth, The. A play (1942) by the US playwright Thornton Wilder (1897–1975) in which the characters jump about almost at whim through the whole range of human history. The title appears in the text when one of the characters describes how they came through the Napoleonic Wars 'by the skin of our teeth' (in other words, very narrowly indeed). The saying is an old one, appearing in the Bible:

> My bone cleaveth to my skin and to my flesh, and I am escaped with the skin of my teeth.
>
> Job 19:20

Skull beneath the Skin, The. A detective novel (1982) by P.D. James (b.1920). The title is a quotation from T.S. Eliot on the Jacobean playwright John Webster, author of *The* WHITE DEVIL and *The Duchess of Malfi*:

> Webster was much possessed by death
> And saw the skull beneath the skin.
>
> T.S.ELIOT: 'Whispers of Immortality' (1919)

Slaughterhouse-Five. A novel (1969) by the US writer Kurt Vonnegut Jr (b.1922), drawing on his experience of witnessing, as a prisoner of war, the Allied destruction of Dresden by fire bombs during the Second World War. The framework of the book concerns Billy Pilgrim, who is transported by aliens through a time warp, enabling him to witness events in the past of which he has foreknowledge. So it is that, with other US prisoners, he finds himself shut up in a slaughterhouse (Slaughterhouse-Five) in Dresden when the city is bombed. An interesting film version (1972) was directed by George Roy Hill.

Slavers Throwing Overboard the Dead and Dying – Typhon Coming On. A painting by J.M.W. Turner (1775–1851), 'the most tremendous piece of colour that was ever seen', according to W.M. Thackeray. The painting is based on a real incident in 1783, when 132 seriously ill slaves were thrown overboard from the slaveship *Zong*. This enabled the ship's owners to claim the insurance, which covered drownings but not deaths from disease. The painting was first exhibited in 1840 at the Royal Academy, London. It was owned for many years by John Ruskin, who sold it to America, and it now hangs in the Museum of Fine Arts, Boston, Massachusetts. When Mark Twain saw the painting he described it as

> A tortoiseshell cat having a fit in a platter of tomatoes.

Sleep of Reason Brings Forth Monsters, The. The title of one of the etchings (*c.*1798) in the series *Los Caprichos* (*The Caprices*) by the Spanish painter Francisco de Goya (1746–1828). The picture depicts a seated figure – apparently an artist with paper and pen next to him – slumped across a desk, while bats, owls and a lynx cluster and hover about him. The Spanish title 'El sueño de la razón produce monstruos' appears on the side of the desk. Goya initially explained the title and picture thus:

> The artist dreaming. His only purpose is to banish harmful, vulgar beliefs and to perpetuate in this work of caprices the solid testimony of truth.

He subsequently replaced this with the subtitle:

> Imagination abandoned by reason produces impossible monsters; united with her, she is the mother of the arts.

The creatures depicted are not in fact 'impossible monsters', and it has been suggested that the owl who appears to be trying to awaken the artist is symbolic of Athene, Greek goddess of wisdom and the arts.

The Sleep of Reason (1968) is the title of one of the novels in C.P Snow's roman-fleuve, *Strangers and Brothers.*

Small Back Room, The. A suspense novel (1943) by Nigel Balchin (1908–70) about a disabled bomb-disposal expert in the Second World War whose efficiency and nerve are eroded by drink, emotional problems and bureaucracy. It draws on Balchin's experience as a psychologist in the War Office, and as deputy scientific adviser to the Army Council, with the rank of brigadier. An interesting film version (1949) was directed by Michael Powell and Emeric Pressburger.

The title echoes the term 'backroom boys', applied to the unpublicized scientists and technicians in the Second World War who contributed much to the development of scientific warfare and war production. The ultimate source of the phrase was the song 'See What the Boys in the Back Room Will Have', sung by Marlene Dietrich in the film *Destry Rides*

Again (1939). Her spirited rendering of this inspired Lord Beaverbrook to use the words in a speech on war production (24 March 1941):

> Now who is responsible for this work of development on which so much depends? To whom must the praise be given? To the boys in the back rooms. They do not sit in the limelight. But they are the men who do all the work.

Small is Beautiful. An influential book (1973) by the German-born British economist E.F. Schumacher (1911–77), subtitled 'A Study of Economics as if People Mattered'. Schumacher argues in favour of small-scale institutions and sustainable development, and against capital-intensive, high-tech solutions, especially in the Third World. The title phrase has entered popular usage.

Soir, Le. *See* MATIN, LE MIDI, LE SOIR, LE.

Some Like It Hot. A sparkling film comedy (1959), written by Billy Wilder (1906–2002) – who also directed – and I.A.L. Diamond (1920–88). Jack Lemmon and Tony Curtis star as two jazz musicians who disguise themselves as women and join an all-girl band in Miami in order to escape the murderous attentions of some gangsters after they accidentally witness the St Valentine's Day Massacre. The title of the film evokes not only the heat of the situation in which the two heroes find themselves and the 'hot' jazz they play, but also the highly charged eroticism of Marilyn Monroe's performance as the band member hotly pursued by Lemmon and Curtis. There is also a link with the 18th-century nursery rhyme about 'pease porridge':

> Some like it hot,
> Some like it cold,
> Some like it in the pot
> Nine days old.

Some Tame Gazelle. The first novel (1950) by Barbara Pym (1913–80). It is a *roman-à-clef* in that Harriet and Belinda, two spinster sisters, are based on Pym's sister and herself, and other characters on people Pym knew as an undergraduate at Oxford, represented now in middle age. Both sisters turn down offers of marriage, preferring their known routine to the uncertainties of the married state:

> Some tame gazelle or some gentle dove or even a poodle dog – something to love, that was the point.

The title and the reference are from a song by Thomas Haynes Bayly (1797–1839):

> Some tame gazelle, or some gentle dove:
> Something to love, oh, something to love!

They also recall the parody by Charles Dickens (1812–70) of lines of Thomas Moore (1779–1852), put into the mouth of Dick Swiveller:

> I never loved a tree or flower, but 'twas the first to fade away; I never nursed a dear Gazelle, to glad me with its soft black eye, but when it came to know me well, and love me, it was sure to marry a market-gardener.
>
> *The Old Curiosity Shop*, chapter lvi

Something Wicked This Way Comes. A science fiction-fantasy (1962) by Ray Bradbury (b.1920). When a circus comes to town, two boys watch an old woman becoming young again and a man's severed leg being reconnected. The transformations are a deep mystery to them. The title quotes the words of the Second Witch about Macbeth in Shakespeare's *Macbeth* (1606):

> By the pricking of my thumbs
> Something wicked this way comes.
>
> IV.i

A film version (1983) directed by Jack Clayton presented the original as a grim fairy tale.

See also BY THE PRICKING OF MY THUMBS.

Song of the Earth, The. *See* LIED VON DER ERDE, DAS.

Song of the Shirt, The. A poem by Thomas Hood (1799–1845), first published in PUNCH in 1843. The song is sung by an impoverished seamstress obliged to do piece work.

> With fingers weary and worn,
> With eyelids heavy and red,
> A woman sat, in unwomanly rags,
> Plying her needle and thread –
> Stitch! stitch! stitch!
> In poverty, hunger and dirt.
> And still with a voice of dolorous pitch
> She sang the 'Song of the Shirt'.

Hood's own epitaph reads 'He sang the Song of the Shirt'.

Songs without Words (German title: *Lieder ohne Worte*). The title Felix Mendelssohn (1809–47) gave to eight books of his piano pieces, each book containing six pieces, written between 1830 and 1845. Some of them were actually composed by Mendelssohn's sister, Fanny (1805–47). Mendelssohn coined the term 'song without words' for a piano piece in which there is a clear melodic line, with an accompaniment; he also wrote one *Lied ohne Worte* for cello and piano (1845). Various of the pieces have acquired titles not given to them to the composer, such as 'The Bee's Wedding', 'Spinning Song', 'Spring Song', etc.; the only pieces named by Mendelssohn are 'Venetian Gondola Song' (three pieces so named), 'Duetto' and 'Folk Song'.

Sonnets from the Portuguese. A sequence of sonnets by Elizabeth Barrett Browning (1806–61), published in 1850. They recount the course of her courtship and marriage to the poet Robert Browning (1812–89), but she disguised this by pretending that they were translations of Portuguese poems. This itself had a personal significance, in that Robert Browning had expressed his admiration for her poem 'Catarina to Camoens' – Luis de Camões (*c.*1524–80) being the author of *The* LUSIADS (1572), the great Portuguese epic poem about Vasco da Gama.

Soon to Be a Major Motion Picture. *See* STEAL THIS BOOK.

Sorcerer's Apprentice, The (French name: *L'Apprenti Sorcier*). A 'scherzo based on a ballad of Goethe' for orchestra by Paul Dukas (1865–1935), first performed in 1897. The apprentice sorcerer tries out some spells while his master is away, with chaotic consequences. The origin of the story is a dialogue by Lucian (*fl.* 2nd century AD). In Walt Disney's *Fantasia*, the apprentice is played by Mickey Mouse.

Sordello. A long poem by Robert Browning (1812–89), published in 1840. Sordello (*c.*1200–before 1269) was an Italian-born troubadour poet, whose patrons included Raymond Berengar IV of Provence and Charles of Anjou (later Charles I of Naples and Sicily). He was admired by Dante, and he appears in the *Purgatorio* as a guide. Browning uses him to explore the spiritual development of an individual, and the choices that must be made between art and action. The poem is challenging and complex, and was greeted with general derision and incomprehension on first publication.

> When it was written, God and Robert Browning knew what it meant; now only God knows.
>
> ROBERT BROWNING: attributed comment on *Sordello*

Tennyson said that he only understood the first line of the poem ('Who will, may hear Sordello's story told') and the last line ('Who would has heard Sordello's story told') – but that both were untrue.

'Sosban Fach' (Welsh, 'Little Saucepan'). The Welsh rugby song of this name is usually associated with the town of Llanelli, whose civic emblem is a saucepan. The first verse was originally written in 1873 as part of a poem by Richard Davies (1833–77), known by the bardic name of Mynyddog ('Man of the Mountain'). It was later altered by Talog Williams, an accountant from Dowlais, who added four verses and the chorus, the whole forming a sort of parody of a nursery rhyme or even a nonsense song. Characters mentioned include Meri Ann, Dafydd the servant, Joni Bach and Dai Bach the soldier, although it is not clear what relevance they have, if any, to the story, which involves a boiling saucepan and a crying baby. The tune to which the song is sung, reminiscent of a Welsh hymn, is one of those most frequently heard at rugby matches.

Sot-Weed Factor, The. A novel (1960; revised edition 1967) by John Barth (b.1930). Barth took as his starting point an actual satirical poem published in 1708, *The Sot-Weed Factor: or, A Voyage to Maryland. A Satyr. In which Is Described, The Laws, Government, Courts, and Constitutions of the Country; and also the Buildings, Feasts, Frolics, Entertainments and Drunken Humours of the Inhabitants of that Part of America. In Burlesque Verse.* The author of the poem was one Ebenezer Cook, a writer of whom nothing else is known. In the poem Cook is an Englishman who comes to America to look after a sot-weed (tobacco) plantation, but it is now thought that Cook was an American. Barth's novel, which is written in an 18th-century style, is a fictional reconstruction of Cook's exploits and a commentary on aspects of the poem, with historical and critical digressions. Cook is also thought to have been the author of *Sot-Weed Redivivus: or the Planter's Looking-Glass ... by E.C., Gent.* (1730), a poem about the over-production of tobacco.

Sound and the Fury, The. A novel (1929) by the US writer William Faulkner (1897–1962). A tragic family situation, stemming originally from a brother's obsession with his sister, is told from four different points of view, employing stream-of-consciousness techniques. The brother's own account suggests:

a tale
Told by an idiot, full of sound and fury,

Signifying nothing.

SHAKESPEARE: *Macbeth*, V.v (1606)

An unimaginative film version (1959) was directed by Martin Ritt.

South Riding. A regional novel (1936) by Winifred Holtby (1898–1935), in which the author reveals the complexities and conflicts of local government, and explores the characters of those involved in the decision-making revealed. South Riding is a fictional creation; in local-government terms, Yorkshire was until 1974 divided into the North, West and East Ridings (the last named was restored in 1996). There could never be more than three Ridings, as the word derives from *thriding*, from Old Norse *thrithjung*, 'a third part'. South Riding does, however, have affinities with the East Riding of Yorkshire, where Holtby was born and brought up. A film version (1937) was directed by Victor Saville.

Spectre de la Rose, Le (French, 'the ghost of the rose'). A poem by Théophile Gautier (1811–72), which has inspired a number of other works with the same title. Gautier's poem opens:

Soulève ta paupière close
Qu'effleure un songe virginal!
Je suis le spectre d'une rose
Que tu portais hier au bal.

('Lift your closed eyelid, lightly touched by a virginal dream. I am the ghost of a rose that you wore at yesterday's ball.')

Berlioz set the poem (along with other poems by Gautier) in his song cycle for soprano and orchestra, *Nuits d'Été* ('summer nights'), completed in 1856. The ballet *Le Spectre de la Rose* (1911), inspired by Gautier, was choreographed by Fokine, designed by Léon Bakst and danced by Nijinsky, using the music of Weber's *Invitation to the Dance*, opus 65 (1819). The film *Spectre of the Rose* (1946), written and directed by Ben Hecht, is about a ballet dancer who is almost murdered by her mad husband. Finally, the fantasy novel *Spectre of the Black Rose* (1998), volume 2 in the series 'Ravenloft Terror of Lord Soth', by James Lowder and Veronica Whitney-Robinson, may be indebted to Gautier for its title, if for nothing else.

Splendor in the Grass. A film (1961) directed by Elia Kazan with Natalie Wood and Warren Beatty as sexually frustrated high-school kids in 1920s Kansas. The title comes from Wordsworth:

Though nothing can bring back the hour
Of splendour in the grass, of glory in the flower;
We will grieve not, rather find
Strength in what remains behind ...

WILLIAM WORDSWORTH: 'Ode. Intimations of Immortality' (1807)

Spring Symphony. The title of works by Schumann and Benjamin Britten. Schumann gave the title (German *Frühlingssymphonie*) to his symphony no 1 in B flat, which he wrote in early 1841. It was conducted by Mendelssohn at its first performance in Leipzig shortly afterwards. Originally Schumann also gave names to each of the four movements – 'The Advent of Spring', 'Evening', 'Happy Playmates' and 'Full Spring' – but subsequently abandoned these. Writing to Ludwig Spohr, Schumann said the work was inspired by 'the spirit of spring', rather than being 'intended to describe or paint anything definite'.

Benjamin Britten's *Spring Symphony*, opus 44 (1949), is scored for vocal soloists, mixed chorus, boys' choir and orchestra, and is perhaps more of a cantata than a symphony. The texts are from a number of English poets, including Spenser, Herrick, Milton, Blake and Clare, and the finale incorporates the medieval 'Cuckoo Song':

Sumer is icumen in,
Lhude sing cuccu!
Groweth sed, and bloweth med
And springeth the wude nu.

ANONYMOUS: 'Cuckoo Song' (*c*.1250); med = meadow

The sonata for violin and piano in F, opus 24 (1801), by Beethoven (1770–1827) is known as the 'Spring' Sonata, for reasons unknown but presumably associated with the open-air freshness of its framing movements.

Stalky & Co. A collection of short stories by Rudyard Kipling (1865–1936), published in 1899. 'Stalky' is the leader of a gang of schoolboys. His real name is Arthur Corkran, and his nickname represents a school slang word meaning 'clever', 'wily'. The gang have a healthy contempt for school discipline, organized sports and most of their teachers, and they indulge in ritual 'gloats' or vocalizations of victory on scoring a point over any of their enemies. Kipling based the stories on contemporaries of his at the United Services College at Westward Ho! in Devon.

Stalky himself was modelled on Lionel Charles Dunsterville

(1865–1946), who in adult life became an army major-general. In the First World War Dunsterville led a 1000-strong British and Commonwealth force, nicknamed Dunsterforce, which in January 1918 marched north from Persia to support the establishment of an independent Transcaucasia. The region was subsequently absorbed by the Soviet Union.

'Star-Spangled Banner, The'. The national anthem of the United States of America. The words were written in 1814 during the War of 1812 by Francis Scott Key (1779–1843). Shortly after the British burned Washington DC, Key witnessed the intensive – but unavailing – British bombardment of Fort McHenry, Baltimore, on 13–14 September 1814. On the morning of 14 September Key, on board a ship in Chesapeake Bay, saw the Union flag still flying above the fort:

> Oh, say can you see by the dawn's early light
> What so proudly we hail'd at the twilight's last gleaming,
> Whose broad stripes and bright stars through the perilous fight
> O'er the ramparts we watch'd were so gallantly streaming?
> And the rockets' red glare, the bombs bursting in air,
> Gave proof through the night that our flag was still there.
> Oh, say does that star-spangled banner yet wave
> O'er the land of the free and the home of the brave?
>
> FRANCIS SCOTT KEY: 'The Star-Spangled Banner' (1814)

Key's poem was first published under the title 'Defence of Fort M'Henry'. In 1939 Fort McHenry – originally named after James McHenry, a signatory of the Constitution and US secretary of war (1796–1800) – was designated a 'national monument and historic shrine'. Key himself became something of a national monument; his name is preserved, for example, in the name of the American novelist F(rancis) Scott Fitzgerald.

Ironically, the tune of 'The Star-Spangled Banner' is by a British composer, John Stafford Smith (1750–1836), who called it 'Anacreon in Heaven'; it was written for the Anacreontic Society of London, and subsequently became a popular drinking song.

'The Star-Spangled Banner' became the American national anthem by an act passed by Congress on 3 March 1931. The banner is, of course, the Stars and Stripes – the white stars on a blue ground representing each of the states (now numbering 50), and the red and white stripes representing the 13 original states at the time of the Declaration of

Independence in 1776. The basic flag design, then with 13 stars in a circle, was adopted by Congress on 14 June 1777.

Steal This Book. A work of political philosophy (1971) by the US radical Abbie Hoffman (1936–89). In 1968 Hoffman, with Jerry Rubin, Paul Krassner and Ed Saunders, founded the Youth International Party (YIP) – the Yippies. They were more politicized than the 'peace and love' Hippies, and were vehement in their opposition to American capitalism and the Vietnam War. In the same year, Hoffman published *Revolution for the Hell of It*. Hoffman's autobiography (1980) was entitled *Soon to Be a Major Motion Picture*, a claim made by publishers on the covers of innumerable books (none ever omitting the word 'major').

In 1914 Sir George Compton Archibald Arthur published a book entitled *Not Worth Reading*.

Steel Magnolias. A popular play by the US writer Robert Harling, set in a Southern beauty salon. It was first performed in 1987 and turned into a film in 1989. The nickname 'the Steel Magnolia' was originally applied to Rosalynn Carter, wife of Jimmy Carter, Democratic president of the USA (1977–81), on account of her 'steely' temperament and Southern origins (magnolia being associated with the South). The Steel Magnolias are also a rock group.

Sting, The. A film (1973) written by David S. Ward about an elaborate 'numbers racket' set up by two conmen to cheat a gangster out of a fortune. Starring Paul Newman and Robert Redford as the conmen and featuring the ragtime music of Scott Joplin, the film was a huge success and revived the word 'sting' (in disuse since the 1930s) as slang for a con trick or robbery.

Stir Crazy. A film (1980) about two New Yorkers (played by Gene Wilder and Richard Pryor) who plan their escape from prison when wrongly convicted of a bank robbery. 'Stir crazy' is a slang term for mentally disturbed, especially as a result of being imprisoned. The expression is of US origin, although 'stir' is British 19th-century jargon for a prison, perhaps from Romany *sturbin*.

Stone Guest, The. *See* DON JUAN (panel, pp.120–2).

Stop in the Name of Love. A guide to 'ejaculation control for life' (1994) by Michael Riskin, taking its title from the famous song (1969) by the Supremes.

Story of a Real Man, The. An opera by Prokofiev (1891–1953), with a libretto by Mira Mendelssohn, the composer's second wife, based on a novel of 1946 by Boris Polevoy. Although Prokofiev had been rapturously received during his 1927 tour of the Soviet Union – which encouraged him to return there to settle in 1933 – he sometimes got into trouble with the Stalinist cultural commissars over his 'formalism' (short-hand for elitist, cosmopolitan modernism). He himself held that 'Formalism is music that people don't understand at first hearing'. After the Second World War cultural restrictions were tightened even further, under the direction of Politburo member Andrei Zhdanov, who in a 1947 speech declaimed: 'The people do not need music which they cannot understand.' Prokofiev's response to the so-called *Zhdanovshchina* (anti-Western cultural campaign) was *The Story of a Real Man*. The 'real man' is a Soviet pilot who has lost both legs, and yet is determined to return to action. Even this heroically patriotic theme did not satisfy Prokofiev's critics, who after its first, private performance in Leningrad (St Petersburg) in 1948, denounced its 'infatuation with modernist trickery'. The opera did not get its first public performance until 1960, in Moscow, seven years after the death of both Prokofiev and Stalin.

Strange Case of Dr Jekyll and Mr Hyde, The. *See* DR JEKYLL AND MR HYDE, THE STRANGE CASE OF.

Strange Meeting. A novel (1971) by Susan Hill (b.1942) about a young officer returning to the Front in the First World War. The title is that of a poem by Wilfred Owen (1893–1918), the soldier-poet who was killed just before the war ended.

> I am the enemy you killed, my friend.
> I knew you in this dark: for you so frowned
> Yesterday through me as you jabbed and killed …
> Let us sleep now.
>
> WILFRED OWEN: 'Strange Meeting' (written 1918)

Streetcar Named Desire, A. An intense drama (1947) by the US playwright Tennessee Williams (1911–83) about the relationship between faded Southern belle, Blanche DuBois, and her brother-in-law, Stanley Kowalski. It was subsequently turned into a successful film (1951), directed by Elia Kazan, starring Marlon Brando and Vivien Leigh. The play had several titles before the final one, including *The Moth*, *Blanche's Chair in the Moon* and *The Poker Night*. The eventual title was inspired by a streetcar labelled 'Desire' (for its destination, Desire Street), which, together with another called 'Cemeteries', plied the main street in the district of New Orleans where Williams lived. In the play the names are taken symbolically, Blanche contending that her sister Stella's marriage is a product of lust, as aimless as the 'streetcar named Desire' that shuttles through the narrow streets. The name of the street does not denote a place of pleasure but derives from the French girl's name Désirée. A monument, the 'Streetcar Named Desire', now stands on the site near the French Market. The play is a leitmotif in Pedro Almodóvar's film *Todo Sobre Mi Madre* (*All About My Mother*, 1999).

> They told me to take a streetcar named Desire, then transfer to one called Cemeteries.
>
> TENNESSEE WILLIAMS: *A Streetcar Named Desire* (Blanche's first line)

STREETS

See also LONDON PLACES (panel, p.262).

Fleet Street Eclogues, two collections of verse (1893, 1896) by John Davidson

Quality Street, a play (1901) by J.M. Barrie

Sinister Street, a novel (1913–14) by Compton Mackenzie

Broadway Melody, the first film musical (1929), followed by the sequels *Broadway Melody of 1936*, *Broadway Melody of 1938* and *Broadway Melody of 1940*

Angel Pavement, a novel (1930) by J.B. Priestley

Handel in the Strand, an orchestral piece (1930) by Percy Grainger

Tobacco Road, a novel (1932) by the US writer Erskine Caldwell

42ND STREET, a classic film musical (1933)

Broadway, an abstract painting (1935) by the US artist Mark Tobey

Laburnum Grove, a comedy film (1936) in which a suburban father shows criminal interests

AS I WAS GOING DOWN SACKVILLE STREET, a memoir (1937) by Oliver St John Gogarty

The Family from One End Street, a children's novel (1937) by Eve Garnett

La CHEMINÉE DU ROI RENÉ, a wind quartet (1939) by Darius Milhaud (La Cheminée du roi René is the name of an old street in Aix-en-Provence)

BROADWAY BOOGIE-WOOGIE, a painting (1942–3) by Mondrian

Miracle on 34th Street, a Christmas film (1947)

Green Dolphin Street, a romantic adventure film (1947) starring Lana Turner

SUNSET BOULEVARD, a film melodrama (1950)

The Cricket in Times Square, a children's novel (1960) by George Selden

MEAN STREETS, a film (1973) written and directed by Martin Scorsese

84 CHARING CROSS ROAD, a correspondence between bibliophiles

Bleecker Street, a collection of verse (1980) by Jeremy Reed

Union Street, a novel (1982) by Pat Barker

A Nightmare on Elm Street, a horror movie (1984)

White Woman Street, a play (1992) by Sebastian Barry

On Green Dolphin Street, a novel (2001) by Sebastian Faulks

Mulholland Drive, a film (2002) by David Lynch

Stuffed Owl, The. 'An anthology of bad verse' published by Percy Wyndham Lewis (1882–1957) in 1930 and taking its title from Wordsworth:

> The presence even of a stuffed Owl for her
> Can cheat the time; sending her out
> To ivied castles and to moonlight skies,
> Though he can neither stir a plume, nor shout;
> Nor veil, with restless film, his staring eyes.
>
> WILLIAM WORDSWORTH: *Miscellaneous Sonnets*, III, xiii (1827)

The expression 'stuffed owl' is still sometimes applied to poetry that treats trivial or inconsequential subjects in a grandiose manner.

Sturm und Drang (German, 'storm and stress'). The subtitle of a play, *Der Wirrwarr, oder Sturm und Drang* (1776; 'confusion, or storm and stress'), by the German dramatist Friedrich Maximilian von Klinger (1752–1831). This subtitle gave a name to the *Sturm und Drang* movement of the later 18th century in Germany and Austria, marked by extravagant passion and powerful expressions of emotion, and so anticipating the full-blown Romantic movement that was to follow. Goethe (1749–1832), Schiller (1759–1805) and Johann Gottfried von Herder (1744–1803) are particularly associated with *Sturm und Drang* in literature and drama, while Haydn's symphonies of the 1760s and 1770s exemplify *Sturm und Drang* in music. Klinger himself, after a youth of white-hot creativity dashing off numerous dramas in a similar angry, emotional vein as *Der Wirrwarr*, ended up as a general in the Russian army, married to a natural daughter of the Empress Catherine the Great.

'Such a Parcel of Rogues in a Nation'. A poem by Robert Burns (1759–96), beginning:

> Fareweel to a' our Scottish fame,
> Fareweel our ancient glory.

The 'rogues' were those members of the Scottish Parliament who voted in 1707 for the abolition of their own Parliament and for the union of Scotland with England, in return for 'English gold'. Although bribery was involved in some cases, historians have not found evidence that the entire vote was corrupt.

Burns's words were set to music in the 1960s by Ewan McColl. After an interval of nearly 300 years, the Scottish Parliament was reconvened in 1999.

Such Sweet Thunder. A Shakespearian suite (1957) by the US jazz composer Duke Ellington (1899–1974). The title comes from Shakespeare's *A MIDSUMMER NIGHT'S DREAM* (*c*.1595–6):

> I was with Hercules and Cadmus once
> When in a wood of Crete they bay'd the bear
> With hounds of Sparta; never did I hear
> Such gallant chiding, for, besides the groves,
> The skies, the fountains, every region near,
> Seem'd all one mutual cry. I never heard
> So musical a discord, such sweet thunder.
>
> IV.i

In the series of vignettes Ellington matches Shakespearian characters to the individual style of his soloists: for example, Johnny Hodges on saxophone is a fervent Cleopatra and Jimmy Hamilton on clarinet a haughty Caesar, while Cat Anderson on trumpet reaches wildly high notes as Hamlet in 'Madness in Great Ones' – it was said that only a dog could hear his highest notes.

Summer of a Dormouse, The. A volume of memoirs (2000) by the novelist and libertarian barrister John Mortimer (b. 1923). The title is from Byron's journal for 7 December 1813:

> When one subtracts from life infancy (which is vegetation), – sleep, eating, and swilling – buttoning and unbuttoning – how much remains of downright existence? The summer of a dormouse.

In a letter dated 17 November 1972 the critic Kenneth Tynan had written of the same phrase: 'If I ever write an autobiography, Byron has found me the title.'

Summer's Lease. A novel (1988), part social comedy, part mystery story, by John Mortimer (b.1923). The plot centres on a villa in Tuscany on temporary lease for the summer holidays to an accident-prone, articulate family. The title is from Shakespeare:

> Shall I compare thee to a summer's day?
> Thou art more lovely and more temperate:
> Rough winds do shake the darling buds of May,
> And summer's lease hath all too short a date.
>
> Sonnet 18

See also DARLING BUDS OF MAY, THE.

Sunday Afternoon on the Island of the Grande Jatte. A painting (1884–5) by the French neo-impressionist Georges Seurat (1859–91). Executed with an innovative 'pointillist' (or 'divisionist') technique, the painting shows Parisian promenaders and picnickers enjoying their day off in the shade of the trees or on the sunlit grass by the edge of the water, where others sail or row their boats. The composition is crowded, yet balanced and classically calm – although contemporary critics greeted it with such words as 'bedlam' and 'scandal'. Seurat spent much of the winter of 1884/5 on the Grand Jatte, an island in the River Seine, making dozens of studies for his monumental (2m × 3m) canvas. The painting inspired the musical *Sunday in the Park with George* (1984) by the US composer and lyricist Stephen Sondheim (b.1930). Seurat returned to the location in 1888 when he painted the deserted and rather gloomy *Grey Weather, Grande Jatte.*

> He is a saint of Sunday in the open air, a fanatic disciplined
> By passion, courage, passion, skill, compassion, love: the love of life
> and the love of light as one, under the sun, with the love of life.
>
> DELMORE SCHWARZ: 'Seurat's Sunday Afternoon along the Seine'

Sunday, Bloody Sunday. A film (1971), directed by John Schlesinger and with a screenplay be Penelope Gilliatt, about a weekend in the life of a triangle consisting of a homosexual older man (Peter Finch), a bisexual younger man (Murray Head), and a heterosexual woman (Glenda Jackson). The title reflects the awful ennui of the old-fashioned British Sunday; it has nothing to do with more notable Bloody Sundays: the massacre of more than 100 demonstrators in St Petersburg in 1905; the assassination of 14 British agents in Dublin in 1920, and the killing of 12 spectators at a Gaelic football match on the same afternoon; or with the shooting dead of 13 unarmed civil rights demonstrators by British paratroopers in Londonderry in 1972.

> Didn't I know there was a famous Irish Bloody Sunday ... Didn't I know about the Russian Bloody Sunday? Yes, I said. But it still wasn't the English bloody Sunday.
>
> PENELOPE GILLIATT: *Making Sunday Bloody Sunday*, Introduction (1986)

The title is also that of a song (1983) about the 1972 incident by the Irish rock band U2.

'Sun' Quartets (German *Sonnenquartetten*). The nickname of the set of six string quartets, opus 20, by Haydn (1732–1809), written in 1772. The firm that first published the set had a colophon depicting the sun. They are also called *Die Grossenquartetten* ('the great quartets'). The music critic Sir Donald Tovey said of them: 'There is perhaps no single ... opus in the history of instrumental music which has achieved so much.'

Sunset Boulevard. A classic film melodrama (1950) written and directed by Billy Wilder. The film is a fairly savage dissection of the vanities of Hollywood, and features Gloria Swanson as Norma Desmond, a fading star of the silent screen (which Swanson herself then was) who grabs hold of William Holden, playing Joe Gillis, a young screenwriter down on his luck. Her plan is that he should write a SALOME (*see* panel, pp.399–402) for her that will revive her fortunes. Sunset Boulevard, one of the main streets of Hollywood and Beverly Hills, was the site of Hollywood's first film studio, built in 1911.

Sun-Treader, The. A large-scale orchestral piece by the modernist US composer Carl Ruggles (1876–1971), completed in 1931. The title comes from Browning's apostrophe to Shelley:

> Sun-treader, life and light be thine for ever!
>
> ROBERT BROWNING: *Pauline* (1833)

Suppose They Gave a War and Nobody Came? A would-be satirical US film (1969) starring Tony Curtis and Ernest Borgnine. The title refers to a phrase common at the time of the anti-Vietnam War demonstrations and was the title of an article by Charlotte Keyes in *McCall's* magazine (October 1966). The origin of the saying is in the epic poem *The People, Yes* (1936) by Carl Sandburg (1878–1967):

> Little girl ... Sometime they'll give a war and nobody will come.

After the film, Allen Ginsberg (1926–97) worked the question into his poem 'Graffiti' (1972):

> What if someone gave a war & Nobody came?
> Life would ring the bells of Ecstasy and Forever be Itself again.

Surfeit of Lampreys, A. A detective novel (1941; originally published in the USA as *Death of a Peer*, 1940) by Ngaio Marsh (1899–1982). The charming but cash-strapped Lamprey family is notorious for its party games. When Uncle Gabriel Lamprey dies, Chief Detective Roderick Alleyn is called in.

The lamprey (family *Petromyzonidae*) is a parasitical and primitive (indeed jawless) fish resembling (although taxonomically far removed from) the eel. According to the chronicler Robert Fabyan (d.1513), King Henry I of England died in 1135 following an encounter with such a beast:

> King Henry being in Normandy, after some writers, fell from or with his horse, whereof he took his death; but Ranulphe says he took a surfeit by eating of a lamprey, and thereof died.
>
> *The New Chronicles of England and France* (1516)

A surfeit is not necessarily an excess, however; it can be a nausea or vomiting fit resultant upon the consumption of something disagreeable to one's constitution.

'Surprise' Symphony. The nickname given to the symphony no 94 in G (1791) by Haydn (1732–1809) because the peaceful slow movement is suddenly interrupted by a fortissimo chord.

> That will make the ladies scream.
>
> JOSEPH HAYDN: quoted in Gyrowetz, *Memoirs* (1848)

In Germany and Austria the symphony is called *Der Symphonie mit der Paukenschlag* ('the symphony with the drum stroke').

Surrender of Breda, The. A painting (1634–5) by Velázquez (1599–1660). It is beautifully composed, unrhetorical and unusual in the calm way it depicts a near-contemporary event – with the participants dressed in contemporary (rather than classical) costume. Velázquez painted it for the throne room of the new Buen Retiro palace, outside Madrid. The event depicted took place on 5 June 1625, when the Dutch – who had been revolting against Spanish rule for decades – were obliged to surrender the town of Breda, in the southwestern Netherlands, to the Spanish. The painting shows Justin of Nassau handing over the keys of the town to General Ambrogio Spinola. In 1637 Prince Frederick Henry of Orange recaptured the town, and the 1648 treaty of Westphalia brought Spanish recognition of Dutch independence, the ceding of Breda to the Netherlands and the end of the Thirty Years War that had devastated so much of northern Europe. *See also* *SWEARING OF THE OATH OF RATIFICATION OF THE TREATY OF MÜNSTER, THE*; *TRIUMPH OF DEATH, THE.*

Surrounded Islands. An environmental art project (1983) by the Bulgarian-born US artist Christo (Christo Javacheff, b.1935), in which he temporarily surrounded eleven small islands in Biscayne Bay, Florida, with skirts of pink plastic floating on the sea. Christo has also wrapped several famous buildings and other structures in various materials, including the Reichstag in Berlin and the Pont Neuf in Paris.

Susanna's Secret (Italian title: *Il Segreto di Susanna*). A comic opera by Ermanno Wolf-Ferrari (1876–1948), with a libretto by Enrico Golisciani, first performed in 1909. The smell of tobacco smoke in the house makes Susanna's husband suspect that she has a secret lover – whereas, in fact, she is a secret smoker. At the time of the opera's composition, only very 'liberated' women would allow themselves to be seen with a cigarette.

Swallows and Amazons. The first of a series of twelve children's novels by Arthur Ransome (1884–1967), the English writer, journalist and, briefly, husband of Evgenia Schelepin, Leon Trotsky's secretary. *Swallows and Amazons* (1930) is set in the English Lake District and, like the novels that followed it, deals with the adventures of children on holiday and reflects Ransome's love of sailing and other outdoor pursuits. The Swallows are the four children of the Walker family, John, Susan, Titty and Roger, and they are named after their boat, *Swallow*; the Amazons are Nancy and Peggy Blackett, who are named after their boat, *Amazon*. The eleven novels that followed were, in order of publication: *Swallowdale* (1931), *Peter Duck* (1932), *Winter Holiday* (1933), *Coot Club* (1934), *Pigeon Post* (1936), *We Didn't Mean to Go to Sea* (1937), *Secret Water* (1939), *The Big Six* (1940), *Missee Lee* (1941), *The Picts and the Martyrs* (1943) and *Great Northern?* (1947). These later novels introduce new characters and settings as diverse as the Norfolk Broads, the North Sea, the South China Sea and the Outer Hebrides. A rather tame film version (1974) was directed by Claude Whatham.

Swearing of the Oath of Ratification of the Treaty of Münster, The. A group portrait (1648) by the Dutch genre and portrait painter Gerard Terborch (1617–81). The treaty of Münster is what the Dutch call the treaty of Westphalia of 1648, which ended the Thirty Years War (or the Eighty Years War, as the Dutch call it, having embarked on their bid for freedom from Spanish rule in 1568). By this treaty the Spanish recognized the independence of the United Provinces of the Netherlands. Terborch had been in Münster, a city in Westphalia, for a couple of years before the peace negotiations came to a conclusion, and then spent two years in Madrid. For earlier pictures related to the Dutch Revolt, *see* TRIUMPH OF DEATH, THE; SURRENDER OF BREDA, THE.

Sweeney Agonistes. *See* SAMSON AGONISTES.

Sweeney Todd, the Demon Barber of Fleet Street. A play (1847) by George Dibdin, originally entitled *A String of Pearls, or the Fiend of Fleet Street*. The fictitious barber murders his customers, who are then used as ingredients in the meat pies sold by Todd's neighbour. The US composer and lyricist Stephen Sondheim (b.1930) used the story as the basis of a musical (1979). In Cockney rhyming slang, Sweeney denotes the Flying Squad (Sweeney Todd), Scotland Yard's elite crime-busting unit. The term dates from the 1930s, but became known to a wider audience via the television crime drama series *The Sweeney* (1975–82).

Sweet Smell of Success. A much admired film melodrama (1957) set in the world of New York journalism, written by Clifford Odets and Ernest Lehman, directed by Alexander Mackendrick and starring Burt Lancaster and Tony Curtis. *The Oxford Dictionary of Quotations* (1999 edn) appears to suggest the film's title as the origin of the well-known phrase. Pauline Kael described the film as 'A sweet smell of perversity, a study of dollar and power worship'.

Swiss Family Robinson, The. A novel concerning a family shipwrecked on a desert island, by a Swiss pastor, Johann David Wyss (1743–1818). It was first published in German in 1812–13 as *Der schweizerische Robinson*. The 'Robinson' in the title is not the name of the family but rather recalls the classic of the genre, Daniel Defoe's *Robinson Crusoe* (1719). There have been two film versions (US, 1940 and UK, 1960).

Symphonia Domestica ('domestic symphony'). A symphonic poem by Richard Strauss (1864–1949), first performed in 1904. The piece is autobiographical, representing a day at home with the Strausses, with themes for the composer, his wife and their baby.

> My wife's a bit rough, but that's what I need.
>
> RICHARD STRAUSS: remark to Mahler, quoted in Norman Lebrecht, *Discord* (1982)

Symphonie cévenole. *See* SYMPHONY ON A FRENCH MOUNTAIN SONG.

Symphonie fantastique. A large-scale orchestral work, opus 14 (1830), by Hector Berlioz (1803–69). *Fantastique* in French means 'fantastic' in the sense of 'uncanny, eerie, weird'. Berlioz subtitled the work *Épisode de la vie d'un artiste* ('episode in the life of an artist'), and provided a detailed programme for the music – an innovation that paved the way for a mass of Romantic symphonic poems, tone poems and other pieces of programmatic and/or pictorial music throughout the rest of the 19th century.

The 'artist' of the subtitle is a thinly veiled self-portrait of the composer, who was only 26 at the time of composition and lovesick for the Irish actress Harriet Smithson – represented in the work by a musical *idée fixe* (another innovation, anticipating the Wagnerian leitmotif). Berlioz's programme may be summarized thus: hopelessly obsessed with his beloved, the artist takes opium, dreams he has killed her and that he is subsequently executed, after which he is subjected to torments at a witches' sabbath (hence the subtitle of Berlioz's 1832 sequel, *Lélio, ou La Retour à la vie*). The movements are entitled:

Reveries – Passions
A Ball
Scene in the Country
March to the Scaffold
Dream of a Witches' Sabbath

In this last movement the theme of the *idée fixe* is bound up with the terror of the DIES IRAE plainchant melody.

The music of the symphony can be appreciated without any knowledge of the programme – although Rossini was provoked by the wildness and novelty of the whole experience to remark 'What a good thing it isn't music.' Others were similarly baffled:

> I believe that Berlioz, when a young student of medicine, never dissected the head of a handsome murderer with greater unwillingness than I feel in analysing the first movement.
>
> ROBERT SCHUMANN: in *Neue Zeitschrift*, 1835

Berlioz did in fact end up marrying his *idée fixe*, Harriet Smithson, on 3 October 1833. The London *Court Journal* cattily observed:

> Miss Smithson was married last week, in Paris, to Derlioz [sic], the musical composer. We trust this marriage will insure the happiness of an amiable young woman, as well as secure us against her reappearance on the English boards.

Unfortunately, the marriage did not 'insure the happiness' of either Harriet or Hector. It was a miserable affair, Berlioz soon finding that his earlier image of Harriet as Shakespearian heroine was very different from the reality of Harriet at home. The couple did live together for a few years in Montmartre – in a house that was later a frequent subject of Maurice Utrillo, the Parisian postcard painter – but later separated, although Berlioz maintained a certain devotion to Harriet until her death in 1854.

> My life is to me a deeply interesting romance.
>
> HECTOR BERLIOZ: letter to Humbert Ferrand, 1833

Symphonie funèbre et triomphale (French, 'triumphal funeral symphony'). A symphony for military band, chorus and strings, opus 15, by Hector Berlioz (1803–69). It was commissioned by the French government in 1840 for the tenth-anniversary celebrations of the July Revolution of 1830, in which the autocratic and reactionary Charles X was replaced by the 'Citizen King' Louis Philippe (who himself became autocratic and reactionary and was overthrown in the 1848 revolution). The first performance – in the open air, at the inauguration of the Bastille column – was a shambles, with the music being drowned out by the drummers.

Symphonie pathétique. *See* PATHÉTIQUE SYMPHONY.

'Symphony of a Thousand'. The nickname of the symphony no 8 (1906) by Gustav Mahler (1860–1911). Large numbers of performers – but not as many as 1000 – are required, although there were in excess of this number at the first performance in 1910. The work is in two parts: the first part, for two choruses and orchestra, is based on the medieval hymn to the Holy Ghost, *Veni, creator spiritus*, attributed to Rhabanus Maurus (d.856), archbishop of Mainz; the second part, for eight solo singers, chorus and orchestra, is entitled 'Concluding Scene from Faust', the text being drawn from the scene of Faust's final redemption in Goethe's *Faust* (*see* FAUST OR FAUSTUS, panel, pp.152–6). When Mahler wished to convey the experience of his symphony to a correspondent, he wrote:

> Imagine the whole universe beginning to sing and resound.
>
> GUSTAV MAHLER: letter, 1906

Symphony on a French Mountain Song (French title: *Symphonie sur un chant montagnard français*). A symphony with solo piano, opus 25 (1886) by Vincent d'Indy (1851–1931). The subtitle is *Symphonie cévenole* as the work is based on a folk song d'Indy collected in the Cévennes mountains of southern France (*see* *TRAVELS WITH A DONKEY*).

T

Taken at the Flood. A detective story (1948) by Agatha Christie (1890–1976). The US title is *There is a Tide*. Both titles come from the same passage in Shakespeare:

> There is a tide in the affairs of men,
> Which, taken at the flood, leads on to fortune;
> Omitted, all the voyage of their life
> Is bound in shallows and in miseries.
>
> SHAKESPEARE: *Julius Caesar* (1599), IV.iii

This was later parodied by Byron:

> There is a tide in the affairs of women,
> Which, taken at the flood, leads – God knows where.
>
> BYRON: *Don Juan* (1819–24), canto 6, stanza 2

Tale of a Tub, A. The title of a comedy (1633) by Ben Jonson (1572–1637), and also of a satire (1704) by Jonathan Swift (1667–1745). The phrase – meaning a cock-and-bull story, a rigmarole, a nonsensical romance – was well established before Jonson wrote his play. For example, in John Webster's *The White Devil* (1612), II.i, is found the line:

> A mere tale of a tub, my words are idle.

Jonson's comedy follows the attempts of various suitors to win the hand of Audrey, and the name of one of the key characters is Squire Tub.

Swift's satire portrays allegorically the failings of the Anglican, Roman Catholic and Nonconformist churches, respectively personified by three brothers, Martin, Peter and Jack. In his preface, Swift explains how sailors, when threatened by a whale, throw a tub overboard to distract it; Swift's whale was Hobbes's *LEVIATHAN*.

Tamburlaine the Great. A blank-verse drama by Christopher Marlowe (1564–93), written *c.*1587–8 and published in 1590. Marlowe drew on the *Life of Timur* by the Spanish writer Pedro Mexia (published in English in 1571), an account of the brutal Turkish-Mongol conqueror Timur (1336–1405). Timur was known in Turkish as Timur Lenk ('Timur the lame'), hence the anglicized versions Tamburlaine or Tamerlane. The latter forms the title of a 1701 tragedy by Nicholas Rowe (1674–1718), in which Tamerlane represents King William III (this was intended as a compliment).

Taming of the Shrew, The. A comedy (*c.*1592) by William Shakespeare (1564–1616). The subplot is based on a tale by Ariosto (1474–1533), while there is some dispute as to the relationship between Shakespeare's play and an anonymous play with the same title from around the same time. The 'shrew' of the title is the fiery-tempered Katharina, whose father will not let her younger sister Bianca wed until Katharina is off his hands. Enter Petruchio, a gentleman from Verona, who, to gain Katharina's dowry, and to help his friend woo Bianca, sets about courting Kate.

> Thou must be married to no man but me;
> For I am he am born to tame you, Kate,
> And bring you from a wild Kate to a Kate
> Conformable as other household Kates.
>
> II.i

He succeeds in his suit, marries her and proceeds to 'tame' her with a succession of humiliations and discomforts. In the end he wins a bet with two other men as to who has the most submissive wife.

The story is the basis of the exuberant and witty 1948 musical comedy *Kiss Me Kate* (film version 1953) with a score by Cole Porter (1892–1964), in which rehearsals of a musical version of Shakespeare's play are enlivened by the fact that the actor playing Petruchio is cast alongside his ex-wife as Katharina, while his current girlfriend plays her younger sister. The title comes from a phrase that Petruchio uses more than once in the original play, for example:

> Kiss me, Kate, we will be married o'Sunday.
>
> II.i

Katharina: Husband, let's follow, to see the end of this ado.
Petruchio: First kiss me, Kate, and we will.
Katharina: What! in the midst of the street?

V i

The film *10 Things I Hate About You* (1999) uses Shakespeare's story as the basis of an American teenage comedy, with mixed success.

'Tam-o'-Shanter'. A narrative poem by Robert Burns (1759–96), published in 1791. Tam-o'-Shanter, the hero, comes across a witches' sabbath on his way home, a little the worse for drink. The witches pursue him, but he rides his horse hard. Just as he is about to cross a bridge (the witches not being able to follow him over water), a young witch, Cutty Sark ('short shift'), grabs the horse's tail and it comes off in her hand. Tam's name means 'Tom of Shanter', the latter being a farm near Kirkoswald, Ayrshire, with Tam himself based on its tenant, Douglas Graham. Burns regarded the poem as his finest, a judgment shared by Sir Walter Scott.

Burns's poem has inspired a number of pieces of music with the same title: the orchestral *Scottish Rhapsody* no 3 (1911) by the Scottish composer Alexander Mackenzie (1847–1935); a 'symphonic ballad' (1911) by the New England composer George Chadwick (1854–1931); and a concert overture by the English composer Malcolm Arnold (b.1921), opus 51 (1955).

The floppy Scots beret sometimes worn with the kilt is called a tam-o'-shanter in Tam's honour, while *Cutty Sark* was adopted as the name of a famous clipper (now docked at Greenwich), and subsequently as the name of a brand of whisky.

Taras Bulba. A 17th-century Ukrainian Cossack leader. His two sons Andrea and Ostap were killed in 1628 at the battle of Dubno, fighting the Poles, and he himself was captured and executed. *Taras Bulba* is the title of a short story by Nikolai Gogol (1809–52), an opera (1890) by the Ukrainian composer Mykola Lysenko (1842–1912), and, most famously, an orchestral rhapsody by the Czech composer Leoš Janáček (1854–1928).

Tarzan. The famous foundling reared by apes in the African jungle was created in 1912 by Edgar Rice Burroughs (1875–1950). Tarzan has had countless adventures in novels and films, in which he communes with animals, rescues damsels in distress and discovers long-lost civilizations. The first novel of 24 in which he appears is *Tarzan of the Apes* (1914). In the 'monkey language' that Burroughs invented for him, his name means 'white skin', from *tar*, 'white', and *zan*, 'skin'. He is given this name by his foster-mother, Kala the ape. The name came to be adopted for any apparent 'he-man' and was bestowed by the media on the Conservative politician Michael Heseltine (b.1933), not only for his height and blond hair but also with reference to an incident of 1976 when he brandished the House of Commons mace to protect it. Tarzana, now a suburban residential section of Los Angeles, was named in honour of Tarzan.

Taste of Honey, A. A play (1958) by Shelagh Delaney (b.1939) about the experiences of a young working-class girl, Jo, who finds herself pregnant after a brief affair with a black naval rating. The film (1961), directed by Tony Richardson and starring Rita Tushingham as Jo, was admired as a fine example of 'kitchen sink' drama. The title echoes a line in the Bible:

> I did but taste a little honey with the end of the rod that was in mine hand, and, lo, I must die.
>
> 1 Samuel 14:43

Tate bricks, the. The name by which the installation entitled *Equivalent VIII*, by the American sculptor and poet Carl Andre (b.1935), has become popularly known. The installation, consisting of 120 firebricks arranged in a rectangle two bricks deep, was first created in 1966 and purchased by the Tate Gallery, London, in 1972. The great public outcry did not erupt for another four years, however, when it was prompted by a person throwing dye over the work in protest at what they considered to be a waste of public money.

Tea and Sympathy. A play (1953) by the US writer Robert Anderson about the problems faced by a sensitive teenage boy at an elite New England boarding school who is accused of homosexuality. The 'tea and sympathy' in question is provided by the housemaster's wife. A bowdlerized film version followed in 1956.

> All you're supposed to do is every once in a while give the boys a little tea and sympathy.
>
> ROBERT ANDERSON: *Tea and Sympathy* (1953), I

The phrase 'tea and sympathy' has come into more general usage to denote caring and hospitable behaviour towards a troubled person.

Telephone, The. A one-act comic opera by Gian Carlo Menotti (b.1911), with a libretto by the composer, first performed in 1947. The heroine,

Lucy, is more attached to her telephone than to her suitor, Ben. He is trying to tell her something but is constantly interrupted by the phone ringing and her insistence on answering it. Eventually he leaves the apartment and calls her from a phone box – to propose. She accepts as long as he never forgets her number. A revived production in 2001, sponsored by Nokia, featured prominent product placement and a ring-tone from the aria 'La donna é mobile' in Verdi's *Rigoletto* (1850–1).

Tempest, The. A play (1611) by William Shakespeare (1564–1616). The play starts with the tempest of the title, a storm conjured by Prospero and his spirit Ariel. Prospero, who now lives with his daughter Miranda on an enchanted isle, was once the duke of Milan, but became too immersed in his books of magic and was ousted by his brother. The tempest is designed to wreck the ship carrying Prospero's enemies – the usurping brother together with his ally, the king of Naples, and his son Ferdinand – and bring them to his shore. Prospero's aim is to lead those who have wronged him to repentance, and to marry Ferdinand to Miranda as a symbol of reconciliation and forgiveness. At the end, having succeeded, he surrenders his superhuman powers:

> But this rough magic
> I here abjure …
> … I'll break my staff,
> Bury it certain fathoms in the earth,
> And deeper than did ever plummet sound
> I'll drown my book.
> V.i

As this was Shakespeare's last play as sole author (he subsequently collaborated with John Fletcher on *Henry VIII* and *The Two Noble Kinsmen*), this speech is sometimes taken as the playwright's farewell to the theatre. The play has given rise to a number of titles, including:

BRAVE NEW WORLD, a dystopian novel (1932) by Aldous Huxley

'CALIBAN UPON SETEBOS', a dramatic monologue (1864) by Robert Browning

COME UNTO THESE YELLOW SANDS, a painting (1842) by Richard Dadd

FULL FATHOM FIVE, a painting (1947) by Jackson Pollock

INTO THIN AIR (1997), a book about the 1996 Everest disaster by Jon Krakauer

THIS MUSIC CREPT BY ME UPON THE WATERS, a verse drama (1953) by Archibald MacLeish

The Tempest is also the title of a vividly expressionist painting (1914) by Oskar Kokoschka (1886–1980). Subtitled *The Bride of the Wind*, the work, painted in a broad painterly style somewhat reminiscent of El Greco, depicts a man and a woman swirling together in space. The painting reflects the stormy relationship between Kokoshka and his mistress, Alma Mahler, the widow of the composer.

There are also several pictures dating from 1926–7 by the German surrealist Max Ernst (1891–1976) entitled *The Bride of the Wind*. These feature two or more wild horses storming through the air.

The piano sonata in D minor, opus 31 no 2 (1801–2), by Beethoven (1770–1827) is nicknamed 'The Tempest', because when he was asked to explain the meaning of the piece the composer responded 'Read Shakepeare's *Tempest*.' Among other musical works inspired by the play and sharing its title are the incidental music, opus 109 (1925), by Sibelius (1865–1957) and the symphonic fantasy, opus 18 (1873), by Tchaikovsky (1840–93).

Tempesta, La. *See MATIN, LE MIDI, LE SOIR, LE.*

10. A comedy film (1979) directed by Blake Edwards and starring Dudley Moore as a sexually obsessed middle-aged composer who marks his girls 1 to 10 depending on their performance. His co-star, Bo Derek, scores 11, provoking Moore into embarrassing pursuit.

Ten Days that Shook the World. A book (1919) by the US journalist John Reed (1887–1920), an eyewitness account of the Bolshevik Revolution in Russia in November 1917. Reed, who came from a wealthy background, was one of the leading radical figures in the USA, became a friend of Lenin and helped to found the US Communist Party. Accused of treason in the USA, he fled to Soviet Russia, where he died of typhus. After his death the US Communist Party established many 'John Reed' clubs for writers and artists in US cities. His life is the subject of the film *Reds* (1981), directed by and starring Warren Beatty.

Tender Is the Night. A novel (1934) by F. Scott Fitzgerald (1896–1940) charting the deterioration of a symbolically named psychiatrist, Dick

Diver, who marries one of his patients, a schizophrenic. In some respects the story complements the autobiographical novel, *Save Me the Waltz* (1932), by Fitzgerald's wife Zelda (1900–48), whom he married in 1920 and who was from 1937 almost permanently in a home for the mentally ill. Fitzgerald wrote and rewrote the work under various titles several times. The final title comes from 'ODE TO A NIGHTINGALE' by John Keats (1795–1821):

> Already with thee! Tender is the night,
> And haply the Queen-Moon is on her throne.

A patchy film version (1961) was directed by Henry King.

> For a while after you quit Keats all other poetry seems to be only whistling or humming.
>
> F. SCOTT FITZGERALD: letter to his daughter, 3 August 1940

Ten Little Niggers. A detective novel (1939; as *And Then There Were None*, 1940; also published as *Ten Little Indians* and *The Nursery Rhyme Murders*) by Agatha Christie (1890–1976). The changes of title were largely due to political correctness. The references are to the familiar nursery rhyme, written as a song by Frank Green in 1868 or 1869:

> Ten little nigger boys went out to dine;
> One choked his little self, and then there were nine [etc] ...
> One little nigger boy living all alone;
> He got married, and then there were none.

This was undoubtedly inspired by Septimus Winner's 'Ten Little Injuns', published in England a short while earlier, and still remembered in American nurseries. A classic film version (1945) was meticulously directed by René Clair as an enjoyable black comedy.

1066 and All That. A classic humorous survey of British history (1930) by W.C. Sellar (1898–1951) and R.J. Yeatman (1898–1968), comprising 'a subtle mixture of schoolboy howlers, witty distortions and artful puns'. The book was designed to satirize the smugness of the English and the teaching of history by rote, but ironically itself became a historical icon. A typical definition is 'The Cavaliers (Wrong but Wromantic) and the Roundheads (Right but Repulsive)'. 1066, as the date of the Norman Conquest, probably still remains the best known date in British history, 'all that' being the blur of dates and events that occurred before and after it.

Ten for 66 and All That is the title of the autobiography of the

Australian leg-spin bowler Arthur Mailey (1886–1967), punning on the title of Sellar and Yeatman's book and celebrating his feat of taking ten wickets for 66 runs for the Australians against Gloucestershire in 1921. In 2001 England's World Cup hat-trick hero, Sir Geoff Hurst, published an autobiography with the punning title *1966 and All That.*

tent, Tracey Emin's. *See* EVERYONE I'VE EVER SLEPT WITH.

10 Things I Hate About You. *See* TAMING OF THE SHREW, THE.

Texas Chainsaw Massacre. A notorious horror movie (1974), written by Kim Henkel and Tobe Hooper, in which a family of chainsaw-wielding unemployed slaughterhouse workers terrorize a Texas community, desecrating the local cemetery and decorating their house with human and animal remains. The title proclaimed the film's horror credentials, although it contains few scenes with much gore. It was loosely based upon the atrocities committed in real life by deranged Wisconsin farmer Ed Gein, whose bloodthirsty activities also influenced Alfred Hitchcock's *Psycho*.

That Obscure Object of Desire (French title: *Cet Obscur Objet du Désir*). A film (1977), written and directed by the Spanish film director Luis Buñuel (1900–83), about an upright French businessman's obsessive love for a beautiful young Spanish woman called Conchita, the object of his desire. The obscurity of Conchita's character and of her feelings for her admirer was emphasized by Buñuel's device of casting two actresses, Carole Bouquet and Angela Molina, in the role.

That Which I Should Have Done I Did Not Do. A typically detailed and almost hallucinatory painting (1931–41) by the US artist Ivan Albright (1897–1983), showing an ancient, heavily panelled closed door, bleakly evoking the tomb (a wreath appears to be attached). The title is adapted from the Book of Common Prayer:

> We have left undone those things which we ought to have done;
> And we have done those things which we ought not to have done;
> And there is no health in us.
>
> Morning Prayer, General Confession

There is a Tide. *See* TAKEN AT THE FLOOD.

Theresienmesse (German, 'Theresa Mass'). The nickname for the Mass in B flat (1799) by Haydn. Unlike Haydn's 'MARIA THERESIA' SYMPHONY, the title does not refer to Maria Theresa (1717–80), the archduchess of Austria – who had been dead for nine years at the time Haydn wrote this

Mass. It may, however, refer to the wife of the Holy Roman emperor Francis II (their daughter Marie-Louise married Napoleon in 1810).

They Shoot Horses, Don't They? A film (1969) adapted by James Poe and Robert E. Thompson from a novel of the same title (1935) by the US writer Horace McCoy (1897–1955). The film depicts the hardships suffered during the era of the Great Depression, and the action revolves around a Chicago dance marathon where the prize is three meals a day and $1500 in cash. The title crops up in the script as the reply given when the drifter Robert, one of the dancers, is asked why he has murdered another participant. It encapsulates the prevailing belief that when times are so hard there is little room for losers, who like horses with broken legs should be put out of their misery.

Thief of Baghdad, The. *See* ARABIAN NIGHTS ENTERTAINMENT.

Thieving Magpie, The (Italian title: *La Gazza ladra*). An opera by Gioacchino Rossini (1792–1868), with a libretto by Giovanni Gherardini, first performed in 1817. The piece is based on the comedy *La Pie voleuse* (1815) by Jean Marie Théodore Baudouin d'Aubigny and Louis Charles Caigniez. In European folklore, the magpie (*Pica pica*, a black-and-white – 'pied' – member of the crow family) is widely held to be dishonest, vain and associated with ill fortune (hence the rhyme 'One for sorrow' etc.). Magpies are said to take little decorative man-made objects to decorate their nests, hence 'magpie' has become a term for a person who hoards small objects. Jackdaws have a similar reputation – as celebrated in J.H. Barham's poem, 'The Jackdaw of Rheims' (1840), in which a jackdaw steals the cardinal's ring and is cursed, resulting in its present scruffy appearance. In Rossini's opera, a maidservant, Ninetta, is accused of stealing a silver spoon but is saved from execution when it is revealed that a magpie is the thief. The overture, with its solo for snare drum, is often performed as a separate concert piece.

> The point is … a person feels *good* listening to Rossini. All you feel like listening to Beethoven is going out and invading Poland. Ode to Joy indeed. The man didn't even have a sense of humour. I tell you … there is more of the Sublime in the snare-drum part of *La Gazza Ladra* than in the whole Ninth Symphony.
>
> THOMAS PYNCHON: *Gravity's Rainbow* (1973)

Things Fall Apart. The first novel (1958) by the Nigerian writer Chinua Achebe (born Albert Chinualumogo, 1930). Its theme is the mutual incomprehension between Ibo tribal communities and white officials in the 1890s. The title comes from the poem 'The Second Coming' (1921) by W.B. Yeats (1865–1939):

> Things fall apart; the centre cannot hold;
> Mere anarchy is loosed upon the world,
> The blood-dimmed tide is loosed, and everywhere
> The ceremony of innocence is drowned.

Thinker, The. *See* FRANCESCA DA RIMINI (panel, pp.175–6).

Thin Man, The. A comedy mystery film (1934), starring William Powell and Myrna Loy as the ever-bantering and happily tippling husband-and-wife sleuth team Nick and Nora Charles, who, with the aid of their wire-haired terrier Asta, investigate the disappearance of the tall, eccentric inventor Clyde Wynant (Edward Ellis), who is the 'Thin Man' of the title. The screenwriters Albert Hackett and Frances Goodrich based their sparkling script on the novel *The Thin Man* (1932) by Dashiell Hammet (1894–1961), who is said to have based the wisecracking and mutual teasing of Nick and Nora on his own relationship with the playwright Lillian Hellman (1905–84). There were several more *Thin Man* films, generally less successful than the first.

Thin Red Line, The. A Second World War novel (1963) by the US writer James Jones (1921–77) – author of the more admired *FROM HERE TO ETERNITY* – about US troops fighting the Japanese on Guadalcanal in the Solomon Islands. The novel has inspired two films (1964 and 1998). The latter version was written and directed by Terrence Malick. The meaning of the title is somewhat obscure, although it may suggest blood and gore, of which there is plenty. It is not clear that there is any relation, apart from a vague military one, to the original 'thin red line'. This was the description given by W.H. Russell, *The Times*' Crimean War correspondent, of the red-coated 93rd Highlanders at the battle of Balaclava (1854), who, standing two-ranks deep rather than in a traditional square, halted a Russian attack.

The Thin Blue Line was the title of a 1990s television comedy series about the British police by Ben Elton (b.1959).

Third Man, The. A thriller (1950) by Graham Greene (1904–91) from his own script for the stylish film (1949) directed by Carol Reed. Set in postwar Vienna, it concerns a US writer who arrives to stay with his friend, Harry Lime, only to discover that Lime has apparently been murdered. His chauffeur was driving the car that ran him down, and his doctor was on the scene. According to a witness, however, a third man was there when the body was moved. In the film Lime was memorably played by Orson Welles, who also contributed some of the dialogue. The title 'the third man' was aped by the British press in the early 1960s during the Burgess and Maclean spy scandal, in the course of which Kim Philby was thus identified; Anthony Blunt was later unmasked as 'the fourth man'.

Third of May 1808, The. A huge, dramatic, fiercely realistic painting (1814), also called *The Execution of the Defenders of Madrid*, by Francisco de Goya (1746–1828). The painting depicts a firing squad shooting their brightly lit victims under a louring sky. The event recorded by Goya was one of hundreds of executions of Spanish insurgents in Madrid, who mounted a brief rebellion against Napoleon's occupying forces. Goya also painted a companion piece, *The Second of May 1808* (1814), otherwise known as *The Charge of the Mamelukes*, which shows the Madrid rebels being attacked by Napoleon's Egyptian cavalry. The paintings had a profound influence on Edouard Manet, who described Goya as 'the most curious master'; Manet's *The* EXECUTION OF THE EMPEROR MAXIMILIAN (1867) takes a similar approach to a similar subject as Goya's *Third of May*.

After the exile of the Spanish king, Napoleon's brother Joseph Bonaparte had, earlier in 1808, become king of Spain. Goya, like many liberal Spaniards, welcomed the change, and remained as court painter. However, he became sickened by the repressiveness and brutality of the French (*see* DISASTERS OF WAR, THE). After Napoleon's forces were expelled from Spain in 1814 Goya painted these two pictures, and was reinstated as court painter to the restored Spanish king, Ferdinand VII.

> He painted with his fists and elbows, flourished
> The stained cape of his heart as history charged.
>
> SEAMUS HEANEY: on Goya, in 'Summer 1969'

Thirty-Nine Steps, The. A thriller (1915) by John Buchan (1875–1940). Defined by Buchan himself as a 'shocker' and written while recovering from illness, it was originally to be called 'The Black Stone'. It is a picaresque story of a chase and marks the introduction of the character Richard Hannay, who reappears in other novels. Against a background of German spy scares, Hannay has to prove his innocence when charged with murder as he is pursued by both the police and foreign spies the length and breadth of Britain. The resolution of the plot turns on Hannay's recognizing that a cryptic message about 'the thirty-nine steps' must refer to a set of steps down to the sea at a coastal town. Richard Hannay has been played by three different actors in film versions of the novel: Robert Donat in 1935, Kenneth More in 1959 and Robert Powell in 1978. The site of the 'thirty-nine steps' themselves is a genuine one in Kent, on the low cliffs not far from Broadstairs (whose own name means 'broad steps'). *See* MR STANDFAST.

This is Spinal Tap. A spoof documentary (1984) written by Christopher Guest, Michael McKean, Harry Shearer and Rob Reiner about an ageing British heavy metal band on a disastrous tour of the United States. The accuracy of this satire about the rock business fooled many people into thinking that Spinal Tap was a real rock group. The wheel turned full circle when the band actually conducted a US tour with their second album *Break Like the Wind* in the early 1990s.

This Music Crept by Me upon the Waters. A verse drama (1953) by the American poet and dramatist Archibald MacLeish (1892–1982). The title is from Shakespeare's *The* TEMPEST (1611), and refers to the song *COME UNTO THESE YELLOW SANDS*, sung by the unseen Ariel and heard by the shipwrecked Ferdinand on the shore, who believes his father drowned:

> Where should this music be? I' th' air or th' earth?
> It sounds no more; and sure it waits upon
> Some god o' th' island. Sitting on a bank,
> Weeping against the King my father's wreck,
> This music crept by me upon the waters,
> Allaying both their fury and my passion
> With its sweet air; thence I have follow'd it,
>
> *The Tempest*, I.ii

Ariel goes on to sing *FULL FATHOM FIVE*.

This Sceptered Isle. *See SET IN A SILVER SEA*.

Threatening Weather. A haunting painting (1928) by the Belgian surrealist René Magritte (1898–1967). In a clear blue sky over a calm bay appear three giant objects – a woman's torso, a tuba and a chair – all painted to look like clouds.

Three-Cornered Hat, The. A popular ballet by the Spanish composer Manuel de Falla (1876–1946), based on a short novel, *El sombrero de tres picos* (1874), by Pedro de Alarcón (1873–91). Alarcón's story satirizes the *corregidores*, Spanish government officials or magistrates, often regarded as overbearing and prone to intrigue. Falla's first version of the music was in the form of a pantomime entitled *El corregidor y la molinera* ('the magistrate and the miller's wife'), which was first performed in 1917. The ballet version with the present title was first staged by Diaghilev's Ballets Russes in 1919, with choreography by Léonide Massine and costume designs by Pablo Picasso. Alarcón's story also forms the basis of the 1895 opera *Der Corregidor* by Hugo Wolf (1860–1903).

Three Men in a Boat. A novel (1889) by Jerome K. Jerome (1859–1927), regarded by many as a comic classic. The story concerns three young men who go on a boating holiday on the Thames, with a dog. Jerome followed this success with *Three Men on the Bummel* (1900). There have been two film versions (1933 and 1956) and a one-man stage adaptation by Rodney Bewes.

Threepenny Opera, The. (German title: *Der Dreigroschenoper*). The best known of the collaborations of the playwright Bertolt Brecht (1898–1956) and the composer Kurt Weill (1900–50). It was first performed in 1928. The work is a modern version of John Gay's *The* BEGGAR'S OPERA (1728), the biggest hit of 18th-century London, and is set in the criminal underworld of Soho at the beginning of the 20th century. Brecht's title – like Gay's – suggests that this, unlike other operas, is not going to be a refined or extravagant affair for the moneyed classes. The German text of *The Threepenny Opera* is based on a translation of Gay by Gerhart Hauptmann, and some of the lyrics are drawn from Rudyard Kipling and from François Villon (the 15th-century criminal-poet). One of the best known songs is 'Mack the Knife', the name given by Brecht to Gay's original character, Macheath.

Three Studies for Figures at the Base of a Crucifixion. The unsettling painting (1944) with which Francis Bacon (1909–92) first came to prominence. The canvas displays disturbingly contorted grey figures against a harsh orange background. 'I deform and dislocate people into appearance; or hope to … I don't think of it as horror. I think of it as life,' said Bacon.

Thus Spake Zarathustra. *See* ALSO SPRACH ZARATHUSTRA.

TILL EULENSPIEGEL

Till Eulenspiegel, the peasant hero of many popular tales of mischievous pranks and crude jests (usually at the expense of 'respectable' society), is thought to be based on an actual 14th-century German villager living in Brunswick. The name Eulenspiegel (Dylulenspegel in Low German) literally means 'owlglass'. The earliest surviving collection of stories is *Ein kurtzweilig Lesen von Dyl Vlenspiegel* ('a funny book about Till Eulenspiegel'), printed in Antwerp in 1515. This attained widespread popularity and was translated into many languages, the 1560 English edition being entitled *Here beginneth a merye Jest of a man that was called Howleglas*.

Interest in Till revived in the 19th century, with the picaresque novel *La Légende et les aventures héroïques, joyeuses, et glorieuses d'Ulenspiegel et de Lamme Goedzak au pays de Flandres et ailleurs* (1866; 'the legend and heroic, joyful and glorious adventures of Eulenspiegel and of Lamme Goedzak in the land of Flanders and elsewhere') by the Belgian writer Charles de Coster (1827–79); Coster's version is set in the 16th century, and Till sets out to avenge his father, burnt as a heretic by the Inquisition. The Belgian symbolist artist Félicien Rops (1833–98) gave the title *Uylenspiegel* to his satirical and subversive magazine, in which he published much of his erotic graphic work. There is an epic poem *Till Eulenspiegel* (1928) by the Nobel laureate Gerhart Hauptmann (1862–1946).

Among the many musical works inspired by Till, the only one that has established a firm place in the repertoire is the symphonic poem *Till Eulenspiegels lustige Streiche, nach alte Schelmenweise* (1895; 'Till Eulenspiegel's Merry Pranks, after an Old Rogue's Tune') by Richard Strauss (1864–1949), which ends with Till being hanged, although his playful spirit lives on.

Timber. *See* UNDERWOODS.

Time's Arrow. A novel (1991) by Martin Amis (b.1949) about a Nazi war criminal, in which the normal chronological order of events is reversed. The phrase 'time's arrow' to denote the concept of time travelling from past to future as if in a physical dimension was coined by the astronomer Arthur Eddington (1882–1944):

> Let us draw an arrow arbitrarily. If as we follow the arrow we find more and more of the random element in the world, then the arrow is pointing towards the future; if the random element decreases the arrow points towards the past ... I shall use the phrase 'time's arrow' to express this one-way property of time which has no analogue in space.
>
> ARTHUR EDDINGTON: *The Nature of the Physical World* (1928)

TIMES OF DAY

See also MEALS (panel, p.289).

Each Dawn I Die, a prison film (1939) starring James Cagney and George Raft

Le MATIN, LE MIDI, LE SOIR (French, 'morning, midday, evening'), the nicknames of three early Haydn symphonies

AS I WALKED OUT ONE MIDSUMMER MORNING, a memoir (1969) by Laurie Lee

9 to 5, a film comedy (1980) with Jane Fonda and Dolly Parton as fellow office workers

High Noon, a Western film (1952)

Love in the Afternoon, a romantic comedy film (1957) written and directed by Billy Wilder

AT FIVE IN THE AFTERNOON, an abstract painting (1949) by Robert Motherwell

The LONG DARK TEA-TIME OF THE SOUL, a comic novel (1988) by Douglas Adams

An Evening's Love, a play (1668) by John Dryden

The CELTIC TWILIGHT, Irish tales (1893) by *W.B. Yeats*

A Hard Day's Night, a Beatles film (1964)

TENDER IS THE NIGHT, a novel (1934) by F. Scott Fitzgerald

23:58, a French film (1993) in which the takings of the 24-hour Le Mans motorbike race are stolen

Midnight Cowboy, a film (1969) about a Texan gigolo in New York

MIDNIGHT EXPRESS, a film (1978) set in a Turkish prison

MIDNIGHT'S CHILDREN, a novel (1981) by Salman Rushdie

JOURNEY TO THE END OF THE NIGHT, a novel (1932) by Louis Ferdinand Céline

---

Tin Drum, The (German title: *Die Blechtrommel*). The first novel (1959; English translation 1962) by the German Nobel laureate Günter Grass (b.1927). *The Tin Drum* traces German history from the coming of the Nazis to the complacency of the postwar West German 'economic miracle' through the experiences of Oskar Matzerath, who at the age of three decides he will not grow any more, but rather express himself by beating on his tin drum. A film version (1979) was directed by Volker Schlöndorff.

Tinker, Tailor, Soldier, Spy. A spy thriller (1974) by John Le Carré (pen-name of David Cornwell; b.1931). It is the first of a trilogy in which the enigmatic British spymaster George Smiley closes in on his adversary, the Soviet Karla. The title reflects the children's fortune-telling rhyme when counting cherry stones or other small objects:

> Tinker, Tailor,
> Soldier, Sailor,
> Rich man, Poor man,
> Beggarman, Thief.

A television adaptation (1979) memorably starred Alec Guinness as Smiley.

To Be or Not to Be. A satirical film (1942), combining romance, comedy and stylish propaganda, directed (from a story of his own) by Ernst Lubitsch. It stars Jack Benny and Carol Lombard as the Polish actors

Joseph and Maria Tura, who help to thwart a Nazi attempt to destroy the Polish Resistance. Prior to the German invasion, the actors are obliged by the censors to take off their anti-Nazi play and put on *Hamlet*, from where the title comes:

> To be, or not to be – that is the question:
> Whether 'tis nobler in the mind to suffer
> The slings and arrows of outrageous fortune,
> Or to take arms against a sea of troubles,
> And by opposing end them?
> III. i

At one point the Nazi Ehrhardt is talking to Tura, whom he does not recognize, and comments on Tura's acting:

> What he did to Shakespeare, we are now doing to Poland.

In the context of the brutal German occupation, and the threat of annihilation hanging over the entire Polish people, the significance of Hamlet's question takes on additional poignancy.

In 1983 Mel Brooks released a remake, starring himself and Anne Bancroft.

'Toccata of Galuppi's, A'. A dramatic lyric by Robert Browning (1812–89), published in *Men and Women* (1855). A toccata was a type of keyboard display piece, *toccare* meaning 'to touch' in Italian. Baldassare Galuppi (1706–85) was an Italian composer who produced several operas in London between 1741 and 1743. However, the toccata of Browning's title is entirely imaginary.

To Circumjack Cencrastus. A poem sequence (1930) by the Scottish poet Hugh MacDiarmid (C.M. Grieve; 1892–1978). Cencrastus is a serpent, 'a beist of filthy breath', whom MacDiarmid pulled from James Watson's *Choice Collection* (1709), and whom he associated with a winding path called the Curly Snake near his boyhood home at Langholm, in the Scottish Borders. He also associated it with the Gaelic saying 'It's a big beast there's no room for outside'. *Circumjack* is an old Scots word (from the Latin *circumjacere*) meaning 'to lie around', so the poet's intention is to encompass the serpent, rather than the other way round. Although the serpent makes appearances throughout the poem sequence, it never quite manages to unify the whole. The language of the sequence is MacDiarmid's 'synthetic' Scots (*see* DRUNK MAN LOOKS AT THE THISTLE, A).

A TIME TO ...

This fairly common title formula is based on a famous passage from the Bible:

> To every thing there is a season, and a time to every purpose under the heaven:
> A time to be born, and a time to die; a time to plant, and a time to pluck up that which is planted;
> A time to kill, and a time to heal; a time to break down, and a time to build up;
> A time to weep, and a time to laugh; a time to mourn and a time to dance;
> A time to cast away stones, and a time to gather stones together; a time to embrace, and a time to refrain from embracing;
> A time to get, and a time to lose; a time to keep, and a time to cast away;
> A time to rend, and a time to sew; a time to keep silence, and a time to speak;
> A time to love, and a time to hate; a time of war, and a time of peace.
>
> Ecclesiastes 3:1–8

Titles inspired by this passage include:

- *A Time to Dance*, the title of three works: a verse collection (1935) by C. Day Lewis; a short-story collection (1982) by the Northern Irish writer Bernard MacLaverty; and a novel (1990) by Melvyn Bragg. There is also *A Time to Dance, No Time to Weep*, a non-fiction work (1987) by the novelist Rumer Godden
- *A Time to Speak* (1941) and *A Time to Act* (1943), wartime addresses in defence of liberal democracy by the American poet and dramatist Archibald MacLeish
- *A Time to Change*, a verse collection (1951) by the Indian poet Nissim Ezekiel
- *A Time to Kill*, the title of two works: an espionage thriller (1951)

by Geoffrey Household; and a novel (1989) by the US writer John Grisham about a southern US lawyer defending a black man who has killed the two white men who brutally raped his young daughter. A film version of the latter came out in 1996

- *A Time to Love and a Time to Die*, a novel (1954) by the German writer Erich Maria Remarque, in which a German officer in the Second World War resolves problems at home but is then killed in action. An American film version was released in 1958
- *A Time to Keep*, a collection of short stories (1969) by the Orkney poet and novelist George Mackay Brown.

Today is the Tomorrow You Were Promised Yesterday. A work (1976) by the British artist Victor Burgin (b.1941). It comprises a monochrome photograph of a bleak English housing estate with a poem about an idyllic Pacific shore. The title – and the Pacific reference – recall Gauguin's *WHERE DO WE COME FROM? WHAT ARE WE? WHERE ARE WE GOING?*

Tod und das Mädchen. *See* DEATH AND THE MAIDEN (panel, p.105).

To Infinity and Beyond. 'A Cultural History of the Infinite' (1987) by Eli Maor, who explains in his preface:

> I took the title *To Infinity and Beyond*, from a telescope manual that listed among the many virtues of the instrument the following: 'The range of focus of your telescope is from fifteen feet to infinity and beyond.'

In the *Toy Story* films (1995, 2000), 'To infinity and beyond' is the catch-phrase of the astronaut doll, Buzz Lightyear.

To Kill a Mockingbird. The only novel (1960) by the US writer Harper Lee (b.1926), which won the Pulitzer Prize for fiction. The trial of a black man accused of raping a white woman and its aftermath are seen through the eyes of Scout, the six-year-old daughter of the white defence lawyer, Atticus Finch. Although clearly innocent, the man is found guilty and is subsequently shot 17 times by prison guards while, it is claimed, he was trying to escape. The editor of the local paper writes a courageous leader comparing the death to 'the senseless slaughter of songbirds by hunters and children'. The common, or northern, mockingbird (*Mimus polyglottos*) is a noted songbird and mimic, and its range extends from the northern USA to Mexico. It particularly favours suburban habitats, and sometimes sings at night. A film version (1962) was directed by Robert Mulligan, with an Oscar-winning performance by Gregory Peck as Finch.

Tombeau de Couperin, Le. A piano suite by Maurice Ravel (1875–1937), written in 1917, in which each of the six movements is dedicated to a friend killed in the First World War. The title means 'the tomb (or tombstone) of Couperin', referring to the great French composer and harpsichordist François Couperin (1668–1733). A number of 17th-century French composers used *tombeau* in the titles of works lamenting the death of some notable person; for example, Denis Gaultier's *Tombeau* for lute in memory of the lutenist de Lenclos. Ravel later orchestrated four of the six movements, which have provided music for two ballets. The homage of one composer to another using a similar formula is found in the orchestral work *At the Tomb of Charles Ives* by the US composer Lou Harrison (b.1917).

Tom Thumb, a Tragedy. Actually a farce by Henry Fielding (1707–54), sending up contemporary bombastic tragedies. It was first performed in 1730, and published the following year as *The Tragedy of Tragedies, or, The Life and Death of Tom Thumb the Great*. The name 'Tom Thumb' for any dwarfish of insignificant person derives from the hero of the old nursery tale, popular from the 16th century. In 1830 *Tom Thumb* was the name given by the American inventor Peter Cooper (1791–1883) to his small but powerful locomotive for the Baltimore and Ohio Railroad. Shortly afterwards, the American dwarf Charles Sherwood Stratton (1838–83) was called 'General Tom Thumb' when he was first exhibited by the showman Phineas T. Barnum.

Tono-Bungay. A novel (1909) by H.G. Wells (1866–1946), in which ideas about society are blended with scientific projections of the future. Wells himself described it as a 'social panorama in the vein of Balzac'. Tono-Bungay is a patent medicine, by means of which George Ponderevo's uncle Edward, having lost everything on the stock exchange, builds up a business empire, before going bankrupt again and being charged with forgery. In the meantime George has been designing aeroplanes and airships, in one of which he takes Edward to France to escape justice.

Tora! Tora! Tora! A film about the Japanese attack on Pearl Harbor on 7 December 1941, made in 1970 by a joint US–Japanese production team. Reconstructing events on both the American and Japanese sides, the film concentrates on the attack itself and the reasons why it was not prevented by the American military, rather than looking at the wider political context. 'Tora, Tora, Tora' was the code name used by the Japanese to indicate the success of their mission. *Tora* is Japanese for 'tiger'.

Tortoise Recalling the Drone of the Holy Numbers as They Were Revealed in the Dreams of the Whirlwind and the Obsidian Gong, Illuminated by the Sawmill, the Green Sawtooth Ocelot, and the High-tension Line Stepdown Transformer, The. An avant-garde musical work (1964) by the American composer LaMonte Young (b.1935), a pupil of Karlheinz Stockhausen. The piece, which is governed by the principles of indeterminacy, is part of the ongoing performance for voices and electronic devices entitled *The Tortoise, His Dreams and Journeys*. Another piece from the main work is entitled *The Tortoise Droning Selected Pitches from the Holy Numbers for the Two Black Tigers, the Green Tiger and the Hermit* (1964).

'Tost' Quartets. The name for three sets of string quartets by Haydn (1732–1809), composed in 1789–90 and all dedicated to the violinist Johann Tost. The quartets comprise: opus 54, nos 1–3; opus 55, nos 1–3; and opus 64, nos 1–6. Opus 55 no 2 is known as the 'RAZOR' QUARTET and opus 64 no 5 as the 'LARK' QUARTET. Haydn's symphonies nos 88 and 89 (1787) are also known as the 'Tost' symphonies, because the composer entrusted Tost with negotiating the sale of them in Paris.

Totes Meer. One of several paintings by Paul Nash (1889–1946) depicting aerial conflict in the Second World War, during which he was an official war artist – as he had been in the First World War. The title is German for 'dead sea', and the picture shows a sea of shot-down German aeroplanes in which the wings become waves. Painted in 1940–1, the work was reproduced on a Royal Mail stamp in 1965 to commemorate the Battle of Britain (1940). Anna Adams wrote in her poem 'Totes Meer – by Paul Nash 1940–1':

> … we are shown
> no scars, no mutilations, no burnt boys
> but, bleached by moonlight, aircraft wreckage thrown
> into an open grave for broken toys.

To the Lighthouse. A novel (1927) by Virginia Woolf (1882–1941). The novel explores, via stream-of-consciousness narration, the ambiguities of time and the contrast between the sexes, as embodied in Mrs and Mr Ramsay – said to be based on Woolf's mother and her father, Sir Leslie Stephen. Although the book is set on the west coast of Scotland, the lighthouse in question is modelled on the lighthouse on a little rocky island off Godrevy Point, across the bay from St Ives, Cornwall – where Woolf had spent childhood holidays. In the first part of the book the Ramsays' youngest son, James, is eager to visit the lighthouse, but this is not achieved until years later, by which time his brother and mother are dead.

Touch Not the Cat. A romantic thriller by the Scottish author Mary Stewart (b. 1916), published in 1976. The title comes from the motto of the Mackintosh clan, in full 'Touch not the cat but a glove', where 'but' means 'without'. The motto is a punning one. The crest of the Mackintosh clan is a 'cat-a-mountain salient guardant proper', with 'two cats proper' for supporters. Their clan was the clan Cattan or Chattan, thus 'touch not the clan Cattan'. The saying is quoted in Sir Walter Scott's *The Fair Maid of Perth* (1828).

Tower, The. A collection of poems by W.B. Yeats (1865–1939), published in 1928. The title poem refers to the ruined Norman castle near Gort in County Galway that Yeats had bought and made his summer home, calling it Thoor Ballylee. In the poem Yeats climbs the Tower to survey the landscape of a traditional, heroic way of life, now gone:

> I pace the battlements and stare
> On the foundations of a house …
> …
> And send imagination forth
> Under the day's declining beam …

The Tower becomes an important symbol in several of Yeats's later poems, for example in part II of 'Meditations in Time of Civil War':

An ancient bridge, and a more ancient tower,
...
A winding stair, a chamber arched with stone,
A grey stone fireplace with an open hearth,
A candle and written page.

The winding stair appears again in *The Winding Stair and Other Poems* (1933), and, metaphorically, as a gyre (the spiral flight of a falcon), in various poems, including 'The Gyres'. The final appearance of the Tower is in 'The Black Tower', written a week before Yeats's death in January 1939.

Towers of Silence, The. *See* RAJ QUARTET, THE.

Town Like Alice, A. A novel (1949) by Nevil Shute (1899–1960). A young Englishwoman, who has, with her group, suffered incredible privations in Malaya during the Second World War at the hands of the Japanese, uses an inheritance to transform Midhurst, a depressed settlement in the north of Australia, into 'a town like Alice [Springs]'. A film version (1956), directed by Jack Lee, was freely adapted from the first part of the novel. 'Town Called Malice' is the title of a song by the English punk band the Jam.

Toy Symphony (German title: *Kindersymphonie*, 'children's symphony'). A simple three-movement orchestral work with additional parts for toy instruments such as cuckoo, quail-pipe, rattle, etc. The work was once attributed to Haydn, but is now thought to be by Mozart's father Leopold (1719–87), with the parts for toy instruments inserted by Haydn's brother Michael (1737–1836). Other toy symphonies have been written by Andreas Romberg (1767–1821) and Malcolm Arnold (b. 1921).

Tragic Comedians, The. A novel (1880) by George Meredith (1828–1909). The novel is based on the true story of Ferdinand Lassalle (1825–64), the German socialist who founded the General German Workers' Association in 1863, Germany's first social democratic party. In 1864 Lassalle went to Switzerland, where he met and fell in love with Helene von Dönniges. Her family opposed the match, and Lassalle was killed in a duel with her former fiancé, Yanko von Racowitza. In Meredith's novel, Helene is Clotilde, Lassalle is Alvan and Racowitza is Marko. James Hall (b.1917) borrowed the title for his 1963 study of seven modern British novelists.

TOWNS AND CITIES

See also LONDON PLACES (panel, p.262); STREETS (panel, pp.436–7).

The Alexandria Quartet, a tetralogy (1957–60) of novels by Lawrence Durrell

The Battle of Algiers, a film (1954) about the Algerian war of independence

The AMITYVILLE HORROR, a horror film (1979)

Timon of Athens, a play (*c.*1607) by William Shakespeare

Funeral in Berlin, a spy thriller (1964) by Len Deighton

The SURRENDER OF BREDA, a painting (1634–5) by Velázquez

BRIGHTON ROCK, a novel (1938) by Graham Greene

OH, CALCUTTA!, a stage revue (1969) devised by Kenneth Tynan

CASABLANCA, a romantic film melodrama (1942)

Les Parapluies de Cherbourg, a French film musical (1964)

CONCORD SONATA, a piece (1909–15) by Charles Ives (referring to Concord, Massachusetts)

'HOW THEY BROUGHT THE GOOD NEWS FROM GHENT TO AIX', a poem (1845) by Robert Browning

GUERNICA, a painting (1937) by Pablo Picasso

'The PIED PIPER OF HAMELIN', a poem (1845) by Robert Browning

Our Man in Havana, a comic spy novel (1958) by Graham Greene

HIROSHIMA MON AMOUR, a feature film (1959) by Alain Resnais

The PLAGUE AT JAFFA, a painting (1804) by Antoine-Jean Gros

'JENA' SYMPHONY, a symphony attributed to Friedrich Witt (1771–1837)

LENINGRAD SYMPHONY, Shostakovich's symphony no 7 (1941–2)

'LINZ' SYMPHONY, Mozart's symphony no 36 (1783)

London Lickpenny, a verse collection (1973) by Peter Ackroyd

LAST YEAR IN MARIENBAD, a film (1961) by Alain Resnais

'*La MARSEILLAISE*', the French national anthem (1792)

Mexico City Blues, a collection of verse (1959) by the US writer Jack Kerouac

Miss V from Moscow, a spy film (1942)

New York, New York, a hard-edged musical film (1977) starring Lisa Minelli and Robert de Niro, directed by Martin Scorsese

A Yank at Oxford, a film (1937) starring Robert Taylor

LAST TANGO IN PARIS, a film (1972) co-written and directed by Bernardo Bertolucci

The PHILADELPHIA STORY, a romantic comedy film (1940)

The PISAN CANTOS, a sequence of poems (1945) by Ezra Pound

PORTSMOUTH POINT, a concert overture (1926) by William Walton

'PRAGUE' SYMPHONY, Mozart's symphony no 38 (1786)

Road to Rio, a comedy film (1947) with Bob Hope, Bing Crosby and Dorothy Lamour

The Roman Spring of Mrs Stone, a novel (1950) by Tennessee Williams (film version 1961)

Welcome to Sarajevo, a film drama (1997) set in 1992 at the start of the Bosnian war

DEATH IN VENICE, a novella (1912) by Thomas Mann (film version 1971)

The Two Gentlemen of Verona, a comedy (1592–3) by William Shakespeare

The Maid of Warsaw, a novel (1854) by Ernest Charles Jones

The ROAD TO WIGAN PIER, a sociological investigation (1937) by George Orwell

Tragic Symphony (German title: *Tragische Symphonie*). Schubert's name for his symphony no 4 in C minor, D417 (1816). At one time Mahler intended to use this title for his symphony no 6 in A minor (1904), the finale of which originally included three terrible blows with a hammer, to represent 'the three blows of fate that fall on a hero, the last one cutting him down as a tree is felled'. Mahler subsequently removed the final hammer blow, and the title, from the score, and later looked back on the hammer blows as a premonition of the three terrible blows that befell him in 1907, his *annus horribilis*: his dismissal from the directorship of the Vienna State Opera; the diagnosis of his fatal heart condition; and the death of his eldest daughter Maria at the age of four.

The *Tragic Overture* (German title: *Tragische-ouvertüre*), opus 81 (1880), by Brahms (1833–97) is an orchestral work intended for the concert hall rather than as an overture to any particular tragedy. The title reflects the mood of the piece.

Trainspotting. A novel (1993) by Irvine Welsh (b.1957), filmed to much acclaim in 1996. Written largely in a phonetic Scottish patois, Welsh's book consists of a series of loosely connected episodes illustrative of the lives of Edinburgh junkies, wideboys and psychopaths. On the long-disused Leith Central Station

> an auld drunkard … lurched up tae us, wine boatil in his hand. … 'What yis up tae, lads? Trainspottin, eh?' he sais, laughing uncontrollably at his ain fucking wit.

'Trainspotting' is also a term for the junkie's attempt to find 'tracks' (veins) in which to inject heroin, reflecting the obsessional nature of the original recreational activity – collecting railway locomotive numbers.

Transfigured Night. *See* VERKLÄRTE NACHT.

Trauersymphonie. *See* 'MOURNING' SYMPHONY.

Travels with a Donkey. A travel book by Robert Louis Stevenson (1850–94), published in 1879. In full the title is *Travels with a Donkey in the Cévennes*, the Cévennes being the chestnut-cloaked hills in the southern part of France's Massif Central, where today there is a long-distance footpath designated 'Le Grande Randonnée "Stevenson"'. The donkey was called Modestine.

> For my part, I travel not to go anywhere, but to go. I travel for travel's sake. The great affair is to move.
>
> *Travels with a Donkey*, 'Cheylard and Luc'

Traviata, La. *See* DAME AUX CAMÉLIAS, LA.

'Tread Softly For You Tread on My Jokes'. An essay by Malcolm Muggeridge (1903–90), in *The Most of Malcolm Muggeridge* (1966). The title parodies W.B. Yeats's early poem, 'He Wishes for the Cloths of Heaven' (1899):

> I have spread my dreams under your feet;
> Tread softly because you tread on my dreams.

Très Riches Heures du duc de Berri, Les (French, 'the very rich hours of the duke of Berri'). An ornately illuminated book of hours (a devotional book including prayers to be said at specific times) made by the Limbourg brothers for their patron, Jean de Berri, brother of the powerful Philip the Bold of Burgundy. The work, in the International Gothic style, was incomplete at the time of the death of the three brothers – Herman, Jean and Pol – in 1416, presumably in an epidemic. Each month is accompanied by a beautifully detailed painting showing peasants engaged in seasonal agricultural work, as well as courtly activities, and several of the paintings include one of the duke's castles.

Trial, The (German title: *Der Prozess*). A posthumously published novel (1925; English translation 1937) by Franz Kafka (1883–1924). Set in a nightmarish, proto-totalitarian world, it concerns the tribulations of Josef K., who is arrested and brought before a court, but the charges against him are never stated. He is driven to find out what he is supposed to have done wrong, and to seek acquittal – which he never succeeds in doing, but is taken to the edge of the city and killed 'like a dog'.

Orson Welles directed a haunting film version (1963). In the opera *The Visitation* (1966), the US composer Gunther Schuller (b.1925) transfers Kafka's *The Trial* to the Southern states of the USA, and Josef K. becomes a black student called Carter Jones.

Trilby. A novel (1894; dramatized 1895) by George du Maurier (1834–96), that was enormously popular for many years. The eponymous heroine is Trilby O'Ferrall, an artist's model who cannot sing unless she is hypnotized by Svengali. She becomes a famous performer under his influence but loses her voice when he dies. The trilby (a wide-brimmed soft felt hat) is so named from its being worn by one of Trilby's student friends, Little Billee, in one of du Maurier's illustrations for the book. The term 'Svengali' has also entered more general usage to denote anyone with a sinister, mesmerizing mental power over others.

Triumph of Death, The. A painting (*c.*1560–9) by the Netherlandish painter Pieter Bruegel the Elder (*c.*1525–69). The painting is a panoramic and horrifying vision in which the skeletal legions of Death round up and destroy the living. The dark landscape is littered with battles, corpses, skulls, executions and despair. Fires burn in the distance, while bodies hang from gibbets, trees and wheels. The vision derives from the Apocalypse and Ecclesiastes, but Bruegel had a singularly political purpose – to show the horrors of the massacres of the Protestant Dutch by their Catholic Spanish rulers. But he also shows how kings, cardinals and emperors (i.e. the might of Rome and the Habsburgs, the oppressors of his countrymen) are brought low by Death.

Triumphs of Oriana, The. A collection of madrigals by various composers compiled by Thomas Morley (1557–1602) and published in 1601. The name 'Oriana' was frequently applied by poets to Queen Elizabeth I (as in 'the peerless Oriana'), although originally, in the medieval Spanish romance *Amadis of Gaul*, Oriana, the beloved of Amadis, was the daughter of the British king Lisuarte.

In Morley's collection each madrigal has the refrain:

Then sang the shepherds and nymphs of Diana:
Long live fair Oriana.

This refrain originated in Nicholas Yonge's second volume (1597) of *Musica Transalpina* (his collection of Italian madrigals), as the English version of the conclusion of 'Ove tra l'herb e i fiori' by Giovanni Croce (*c.*1557–1609):

Poi concordi seguir Ninfe e Pastori,
Viva la bella Dori.

This refrain is common to all the madrigals in the Italian collection *Il Trionfo di Dori* (1592; 'the triumph of Doris'), on which *The Triumphs of Oriana* is modelled.

Tropic of Cancer. A semi-autobiographical novel (1934) in experimental form by the US writer Henry Miller (1891–1980). Unashamedly exhibitionistic, the book reflects Miller's bohemian life and sexual activities in Paris during the 1920s and 1930s. *Tropic of Capricorn* (1939) is a companion volume, recalling his childhood and earlier life in the United States. Both books were banned in the United States until the 1960s. Of *Tropic of Cancer*, the poet and critic Ezra Pound (1885–1972) commented:

'At last an unprintable book which is readable.' The Tropics of Cancer and Capricorn are two parallel lines of latitude either side of the Equator between which the sun can be directly overhead at noon. Miller commented that

> Cancer is separated from Capricorn only by an imaginary line …
> You live like a rock in the midst of the ocean; you are fixed while everything about you is in turbulent motion.

A film version (1970) was directed by Joseph Strick.

Trout Fishing in America. An experimental novel (1967) by Richard Brautigan (1935–84). It represents a quest for an alternative lifestyle, free from the constraints of modern living, in the form of a search for the perfect trout stream.

'Trout' Quintet (German *Forellenquintett*). The nickname for the piano quintet, D667, by Schubert (1797–1828), composed in 1819. The fourth of the five moments, written at the request of a friend, consists of variations on Schubert's own song *Die Forelle* ('The Trout'), D550 (1817).

True-Born Englishman, The. A satirical poem (1701) by Daniel Defoe (1660–1731), attacking those who were hostile to King William III because he was Dutch. In the poem Defoe points out that there is no such thing as a 'true-born Englishman':

> The Romans first with Julius Caesar came,
> Including all the nations of that name,
> Gauls, Greeks, and Lombards; and by computation,
> Auxiliaries or slaves of every nation.
> With Hengist, Saxons; Danes with Sueno came,
> In search of plunder, not in search of fame.
> Scots, Picts, and Irish from th' Hibernian shore:
> And conqu'ring William brought the Normans o'er.
> All these their barb'rous offspring left behind,
> The dregs of armies, they of all mankind;
> Blended with Britains who before were here,
> Of whom the Welsh ha' blessed the character.
> From this amphibious ill-born mob began
> That vain, ill-natured thing, an Englishman.
>
> …

> A True-Born Englishman's a contradiction,
> In speech an irony, in fact a fiction.

True Grit. A film Western (1969) based on a novel (1968) of the same title by Charles Portis (b.1933). The film starred John Wayne as an indomitable one-eyed marshal, 'Rooster' Cogburn, who is eventually persuaded to help a determined teenage girl avenge herself upon her father's murderers. According to Portis, he picked up the phrase while researching memoirs about the old West, in which all manner of heroes were praised for their 'grit' (meaning their determination or courage):

> I had never seen it in such profusion as in these books. There was grit, plain grit, plain old grit, clear grit, pure grit, pure dee grit (a euphemism for damned) and true grit. Thus the hard little word was in my head when I began the story.

He jotted the phrase down on the title page of his script for use within the text when it became appropriate, and then realized it would make a good title itself. Portis was not, as he admitted himself, the first writer to make use of the phrase: as early as 1897 Bram Stoker quoted it in his novel *Dracula*.

Trumpet Voluntary. The title given by Henry Wood (1869–1944), the founding conductor of the London Promenade Concerts ('the Proms'), to his arrangement for organ, brass and kettledrums of a harpsichord piece once thought to be by Purcell, but now known to be 'The Prince of Denmark's March' by Jeremiah Clarke (*c.*1673–1707). The piece is now most often heard played on the trumpet stop of the organ. A 'voluntary' is an organ solo (sometimes improvised) played before or after a church service, especially in the Church of England.

Turandot. An unfinished opera by Giacomo Puccini (1858–1924), with a libretto by Giuseppe Adami and Renato Simoni, first performed posthumously in 1926. The libretto was based on a play (1762) by the Italian dramatist Carlo Gozzi (1720–1806), but the story can be traced back to a tale given by Antoine Galland as part of his translation of *The Arabian Nights* (1704–8). The central character of the title is a Chinese princess called Turandot, who vows vengeance on all men for some past grievance but offers to marry any nobleman who can solve three riddles. If he cannot, she will kill him. A prince does solve them, but she initially refuses to marry him, before changing her mind. The princess's name is of Persian origin and means 'daughter of the Turanians', i.e. of the northern people (to the Arabians) who inhabited ancient Turkestan. The final '-dot' is related to English 'daughter'. Ferruccio Busoni (1866–1924) also wrote an opera (1917) with this title, which was similarly based on Gozzi's play. The aria 'Nessun dorma' ('nobody is sleeping') from Puccini's opera, sung by Luciano Pavarotti, achieved an unlikely new lease of life as the anthem of the 1990 World Cup in Italy.

Turangalîla Symphony. A massive and mystical symphony by Olivier Messiaen (1908–92), composed between 1946 and 1948 and first performed in 1949. *Turangalîla* is Sanskrit, the composer translating it as 'a love song, a hymn to joy, time, movement, rhythm, life and death'. Apparently the word should be pronounced with the accent and a prolonged sound on the last two syllables. The music includes Indian influences and features parts for piano and ondes martenot, an early form of electronic keyboard. The Beatles claimed the symphony influenced the ending of their song 'A Day in the Life', which inspired the disc jockey John Peel to play it on his radio programme.

Turkey: Yesterday, Today and Tomorrow. A serious work by Sir Telford Waugh, which famously prompted the unserious remark from his cousin, Arthur Waugh (1866–1943), father of the novelist Evelyn: 'Sounds like Boxing Day.'

'Turn of the Screw, The'. A long short story by Henry James (1843–1916), published in 1898. The tale may or may not be a ghost story. A governess believes she sees the wicked spirits of her predecessor and her illicit lover, Peter Quint (an echo of Peter Quince, the carpenter in *A MIDSUMMER NIGHT'S DREAM*). She also believes her charges, Miles and Flora, are in touch with these spirits and in danger of demonic possession; in the end Miles dies in her arms:

> We were alone with the quiet day, and his little heart, dispossessed, had stopped.

The title refers to the tightening of a thumbscrew, an old form of torture, reflecting the governess's mental torment. The phrase has now become a common expression.

James's story inspired a two-act chamber opera by Benjamin Britten (1913–76), with a libretto by Myfanwy Piper, first performed in 1954.

Britten compared the process of composing it to 'squeezing toothpaste out of a tube that's nearly finished'.

James's story also formed the basis of the atmospheric film *The Innocents* (1961), directed by Jack Clayton and with a screenplay by Truman Capote and William Archibald. The 1992 film version, reverting to the original title but not the original subtlety, attracted this comment from *Variety* magazine: 'This is one screw that needed no further turning.' Another even less subtle film, a bizarre 'prequel' to the James story, was given the title *The Nightcomers* (1971). Directed by Michael Winner, it stars Marlon Brando and Stephanie Beacham as, respectively, Peter Quint and the previous governess, who indulge in some highly charged sexual activities, and the story purports to 'explain' why the children in James's story become 'evil'.

Twelfth Night; or, What You Will. A comedy (*c.*1601) by William Shakespeare (1564–1616). The main plot proceeds from the shipwreck on the shores of Illyria of Viola and her twin brother (and close likeness) Sebastian. Both believe the other dead. Viola disguises herself as a youth, adopts the name Cesario, and becomes a page and friend to Orsino, the duke of Illyria. She falls in love with him, but he is besotted with Olivia, and sends Cesario to further his suit. Olivia, however, is in mourning for her late brother, and is disinclined to reciprocate – and in the end starts to fall in love with Cesario, such is 'his' skill in furthering Orsino's suit. In the end all is resolved, as Cesario look-alike Sebastian turns up to be swept off his feet by Olivia, while Viola reveals her sex to Orsino, who is naturally delighted.

It is presumed that Shakespeare wrote the play for performance at the annual Twelfth Night revels. These were held on the eve of the twelfth day after Christmas, the Feast of the Epiphany, celebrating the visit of the Three Wise Men to the infant Jesus. The Epiphany marked the Last Day of Christmas, the end of the winter festivities overseen in medieval and Tudor times by the Lord of Misrule (an echo of the ancient Roman Saturnalia), who might reverse the normal order of rank and precedence. So Twelfth Night marked the last spurt of merriment before the sober business of the rest of the year returned.

> Dost thou think, because thou art virtuous, there shall be no more cakes and ale?
>
> II.iii

So says the ever-festive Sir Toby Belch to Olivia's puritanical steward Malvolio, the key characters in the broadly comic subplot. Just as Orsino's suit to Olivia emanates from his being in love with the idea of love, and just as Olivia's mourning for her brother is excessively prolonged, so both Belch's endless roistering and Malvolio's perpetual gloom are presented as immoderate. The festive season is the season to be jolly, but cannot be prolonged after Twelfth Night. The play ends with the Clown singing a melancholy song, alone on stage:

> When that I was and a little tiny boy,
> With hey, ho, the wind and the rain,
> A foolish thing was but a toy,
> For the rain it raineth every day.
> V.i

Twilight of the Gods. *See* GÖTTERDÄMMERUNG.

Twilight of the Idols. *See* GÖTTERDÄMMERUNG.

Two Foscari, The. A tragedy by Lord Byron (1788–1824), published in 1821. Byron's story is based on that of Francesco Foscari (1373–1457), doge of Venice (1423–57). After his son Jacopo was banished on suspicion of treason, Foscari was forced to abdicate, and died soon thereafter. The story also inspired the opera *I due Foscari* (1844) by Verdi (1813–1901).

2 Minutes, 3.3 Seconds. A sculpture (1962) by the British Pop artist Billy Apple. Three apples (from which the artist took his name) stand in a line: one is whole, one is about a quarter gnawed, and the third is eaten to the core. It is likely that the title refers to the time taken to eat this much fruit. Billy Apple later moved on from his interest in apples to concentrate on making neon rainbows. Compare John Cage's *4′ 33″*.

Two on a Tower. A novel by Thomas Hardy (1840–1928), published in 1882. The story concerns the love of Lady Viviette Constantine for a young astronomer, Swithin St Cleeve, who works at the top of a tower. The novel proceeds from melodrama to tragedy (of a sort), as the heroine drops dead from joy when the hero returns to the tower from a long absence in South Africa.

2001: a Space Odyssey. A science-fiction novel (1968, from his own screenplay) by Arthur C. Clarke (b.1917). While the novel demonstrates Clarke's ability to extrapolate from known data, it also represents a philosophical quest for the meaning of life and an investigation into the evolutionary process. *2010: Odyssey Two* (1982) is a sequel; it was followed by *3001: the Final Odyssey* (1997). The film version (1968), directed by Stanley Kubrick, was a masterly blend of technical wizardry and obscure symbolism, criticized by some for its tedium but praised by others for its moments of striking imagery. The music was by various composers but most memorable of all was the 'Sunrise' opening of Richard Strauss's *ALSO SPRACH ZARATHUSTRA* (1896). The film acquired cult status as a vision of the technological future, even if space exploration had not advanced nearly as far in reality by 2001. It inspired a sequel (1984) directed by Peter Hyams under the title *2010*, but fans of the original movie were not impressed and gave it the alternative title *Ten Past Eight*.

David Bowie's song 'A Space Oddity' plays none too subtly on Clarke's title.

See also ODYSSEY.

U

Ulysses. A novel (1922) by James Joyce (1882–1941), regarded by many as the 20th century's most important work of fiction in the English language. The novel is famous for its innovative use of language and its experimental use of stream-of-consciousness techniques. T.S. Eliot commented: 'James Joyce has no style but is the vacuum into which all styles rush.' The book was published by a small press in Paris in 1922, after three US judges had banned further publication of chapters in the United States, and it was immediately acclaimed as a work of genius.

The narrative centres on a single day, 16 June 1904, the day on which Joyce had his first formal date with Nora Barnacle (1884–1951), a barmaid with whom he shared the rest of his life. The book tells of the day in the life of its Jewish-Irish hero, Leopold Bloom, his wife Molly, and Stephen Dedalus, the protagonist of the author's *A PORTRAIT OF THE ARTIST AS A YOUNG MAN* (1916). The structure of the book is intended to parallel that of Homer's *ODYSSEY*, with Odysseus's decade of wandering compared to Bloom's single day of roaming in Dublin. Bloom thus represents Odysseus (whom the Romans called Ulysses), Molly answers approximately to Odysseus's wife Penelope and Dedalus corresponds to his son Telemachus. Joyce described his Homeric parallel – which he worked out in considerable detail – as a bridge across which he could march his 18 episodes, after which the bridge could be 'blown skyhigh'. 16 June is now often known (and celebrated), especially in Ireland, as 'Bloomsday'.

Ulysses was eventually cleared for publication in the USA, the judge concluding:

> Whilst in many places the effect of *Ulysses* on the reader undoubtedly is somewhat emetic, nowhere does it tend to be aphrodisiac.

It was published in the USA in 1934, and in Britain in 1936.

In 2001 *The Bookseller* magazine reported that a bookshop assistant had been asked for a copy of *James Joyce Is Useless*.

See also FINNEGANS WAKE.

Unanswered Question, The. A short 'philosophical' orchestral work (1906) by the US composer Charles Ives (1874–1954). The subtitle of the work is 'A Contemplation of a Serious Matter'. The two instrumental groups in the piece represent the Real and the Transcendental, and are obliged to deploy an element of improvisation.

Unbearable Lightness of Being, The (Czech title: *Nesmesitná lehkost bytí*). A novel (1984) of the magic realism school by Milan Kundera (b.1929). The fates of two couples are played out against a background of communist rule in Czechoslovakia. In such circumstances, there is an unbearable foreboding even when the 'sweet lightness of being' rises 'out of the depths of the future'. A film version (1987) was directed by Philip Kaufman.

Under Milk Wood. A radio play by Dylan Thomas (1914–53), first broadcast by the BBC on 25 January 1954. The original title of the first part was *Llareggub* ('bugger all' spelt backwards), the name of the Welsh seaside town in which the author introduces such characters as Myfanwy Price the dressmaker, her lover Mog Edwards the draper, the Rev. Eli Jenkins and Captain Cat. Friends persuaded the poet to opt for *Under Milk Wood* as the title, having convinced him that US readers would not understand his joke. Milk Wood is the wood above the town where Polly Garter has illicit meetings with the 'gandering hubbies' of other women. Laugharne, the town in Dyfed where Thomas is buried, is often identified as the model for his Llareggub.

Under the Greenwood Tree. A lightly humorous bucolic novel (1872) by Thomas Hardy (1840–1928). The greenwood tree is a traditional landmark in English Arcadias. It appears, for example, in the song in Act II scene v of Shakespeare's *As You Like It*:

Under the greenwood tree
Who loves to lie with me,
And turn his merry note
Unto the sweet bird's throat,
Come hither, come hither, come hither.
Here shall he see
No enemy
But winter and rough weather.

An earlier (15th-century) appearance is in the anonymous 'May in the Green-Wood':

To se the dere draw to the dale
And leve the hilles hee,
And shadow him in the leves grene
Under the green-wode tree.

Under the Volcano. A novel (1947) by Malcolm Lowry (1909–57), intended to be one part of a Dante-esque novel sequence to be called 'The Voyage that Never Ends'. Lowry wrote the first draft in Mexico in sight of the volcano Popocatapetl, after a spell in hospital in the United States, which failed to cure his alcoholism. The presence of the volcano looms over the account of a disillusioned British consul, destroyed by drink and drugs, during the Mexican Day of the Dead in 1939. The film version (1984) was directed by John Huston.

Underwoods or ***The Underwood.*** A collection of poems by Ben Jonson (1572–1637), published in 1640. 'Underwood' is an old word for 'undergrowth'. The title reflects the double meaning of the Latin word *silva*, which can mean both a wood and a collection. Jonson used the pun in two other publications, *Timber* (1640), a miscellany of notes and observations, and the poetry collection *The Forest* (1616).

Robert Louis Stevenson (1850–94) consciously borrowed the title for his volume of poetry, *Underwoods* (1887):

Of all my verse, like not a single line;
But like my title, for it is not mine.
That title from a better man I stole;
Ah, how much better, had I stol'n the whole!

Underwoods, foreword

UNDINE

Undine was a water nymph in the folklore of central Europe. According to the legend, she was created without a soul, but if she marries a mortal and bears his child, she will acquire a soul, along with all the pains and penalties of the human condition. She falls in love and marries the knight Huldbrand, but his affections later turn to the mortal Bertalda. In the end she draws her husband back down with her into her watery realm. As the spirit of the waters, Undine became one of the elemental spirits of the Swiss alchemist and physician Paracelsus (1493–1541).

The story of Undine was popularized in the Romantic era by Friedrich Heinrich Karl de La Motte, Baron Fouqué (1777–1843), a German writer of French descent. In his fairy tale *Undine* (1811), the heroine marries a knight called Hildebrand, but is later betrayed by her uncle Kuhleborn and the lady Berthulda. Fouqué's story inspired several operas, including those by E.T.A. Hoffmann (1816) and Albert Lortzing (1845), and a ballet (1958) by Hans Werner Henze, with choreography by Frederick Ashton. One of the piano pieces in Ravel's *Gaspard de la nuit* (1908) is entitled *Ondine*. The South African writer Olive Schreiner (1855–1920) evoked the sprite in the title of her posthumously published feminist novel *Undine* (1929). Variants of the story are found in the opera *Das Donauweibchen* (1798; 'the Danube sprite') by Ferdinand Kauer, with a libretto by K.F. Hensler, and in the Slav story of the water spirit Rusalka, the eponymous heroine of an opera (1901) by Antonín Dvorák, which also draws on the Hans Christian Andersen story, 'The Little Mermaid'.

'Unfinished' Symphony. The popular name of the symphony no 8 in B minor, D579, by Franz Schubert (1791–1828). Two movements are complete, and sketches exist for a third (a scherzo). Schubert composed these in October–November 1822, and sent the score to the Graz Music Society when he was made an honorary member, but the music was forgotten and not rediscovered until 1865, when it received its first performance. Some have suggested that Schubert may actually have completed the symphony, but most scholars believe that this was just another of Schubert's several unfinished projects.

Unknown Political Prisoner, The. A sculpture (1951–2) by Reg Butler (1913–81), which in 1953 won an international competition for a piece with such a title, against competition from established figures like Alexander Calder, Naum Gabo and Barbara Hepworth. Actually, the piece only exists as a maquette in the Tate; it proved impractical to build the full-sized version, which would have been gigantic, so what we are left with is more properly entitled *Project for Monument to the Unknown Political Prisoner*. Butler, whose name the piece made, described it as 'an iron cage, a transmuted gallows or guillotine on an outcrop of rock'. The title echoes the Tomb of the Unknown Warrior, the burial place in Westminster Abbey, London, of the remains of an unknown British soldier killed in the First World War; this tomb – and others like it in other capitals of the world – is a focus of commemoration of the dead of the world wars of the 20th century.

Unofficial Rose, An. A novel by Iris Murdoch (1919–99), published in 1962. Randall, a rose grower (like the author), leaves his wife for a young woman with whom he is smitten. The title comes from:

> Unkempt about those hedges blows
> An English unofficial rose;
> And there the unregulated sun
> Slopes down to rest when day is done …
>
> RUPERT BROOKE: *The Old Vicarage, Grantchester* (1912)

Untitled. A 'title' given to many works of art. Some examples follow:

Untitled (1938–9) by Giorgio Cavallon

Untitled (1937) by Willem de Kooning

Untitled (1959) by Raymond Parker

Untitled (1963) by R.B. Kitaj

Untitled (1965) by James Rosenquist

Untitled (1968) by Cy Twombly

Some artists paradoxically call their works *Untitled*, and then add a title in parentheses. Examples include:

Untitled (Kiss), a vast photographic print (1995) of an osculatory event by Sonia Boyce

Untitled (Ostend), an assemblage in a box (*c.*1954) by Joseph Cornell

Untitled (USA Today), a big heap of sweets wrapped in red, silver and blue shiny paper (1990) by Felix Gonzalez-Torres

Untitled (Joke), a non-joke silkscreened onto a red background (1987) by Richard Prince

Untitled is also the title of the novel written by Richard Tull, the central character of Martin Amis's novel *The Information* (1995).

Urn Burial. *See* HYDRIOTAPHIA.

U.S.A. A trilogy of novels (1930–6) by the US writer John Dos Passos (1896–1970), presenting from a left-wing perspective a sprawling and somewhat embittered panorama of America in the first three decades of the 20th century. As a background to the fictional stories of a wide range of characters there is a documentary assemblage of biographies of real people such as Henry Ford, Woodrow Wilson, Eugene Debs, J.P. Morgan and Joe Hill, plus the 'newsreel' – news clippings, popular songs, advertisements and headlines. A third form of narrative, the 'camera eye', presents the author's own stream-of-consciousness impressions of his subject. The trilogy comprises: *The 42nd Parallel* (1930), covering the period up to the First World War; *1919* (1932), covering the war and the Paris Peace Conference; and *The Big Money* (1936), covering the 1920s Jazz Age boom and the Depression of the 1930s. The 42nd parallel marked the southern border of the Oregon Territory acquired by the USA from Britain in a treaty of 1846.

Usual Suspects, The. A crime thriller (1995) starring Gabriel Byrne and Kevin Spacey, with a clever and complex Oscar-winning screenplay by Christopher McQuarrie. The title was already a commonly used phrase, originating in the 1942 film CASABLANCA. When Major Strasser, a German, is shot, the local Vichy police chief, Louis Renault (who is by this stage clearly sympathetic to the Allied cause, and who has seen who killed Strasser) issues the famous order:

> Round up the usual suspects.
>
> JULIUS AND PHILIP EPSTEIN: screenplay for *Casablanca* (1942)

US STATES

ALABAMA, a painting (1965) by Robert Indiana (whose surname is also the name of a state)

Alaska, a novel (1988) by the US writer James A. Michener

Raising Arizona, a comedy film (1987) by the Coen brothers

The Arkansas Traveller, a fantasy film (1938)

California Suite, a film (1978) based on a play by Neil Simon

Bastard out of Carolina, a novel (1992) by the US writer Dorothy Allison

Colorado Territory, a Western film (1949)

A CONNECTICUT YANKEE IN KING ARTHUR'S COURT, a novel (1889) by Mark Twain

Dakota, a Western film (1945)

Florida Poems, a collection (1989) by the US poet and dramatist Richard Eberhart

Georgia, a film drama (1995)

Hawaii, a novel (1959) by the US writer James A. Michener

My Own Private Idaho, a film (1991) about a male prostitute written and directed by Gus Van Sant

Illinois Poems, a collection (1941) by the US writer Edgar Lee Masters

Indiana, a novel (1832) by the French writer George Sand

Kansas Raiders, a film (1951) about Jesse James and Quantrill's Raiders during the American Civil War

The Kentucky Fried Movie, a film compilation of comedy sketches (1977)

I SAW IN LOUISIANA A LIVE-OAK GROWING, a painting (1963) by David Hockney

The Maine Woods, an autobiographical work (posthumously published 1864) by Henry David Thoreau

Maryland, a film drama (1940)

The Michigan Kid, a Western film (1947)

Mississippi Burning, a film (1988) about the murder of Civil Rights activists in the early 1960s

The Missouri Breaks, a Western film (1976)

Montana, a Western film (1950) starring Errol Flynn

The Nebraskan, a Western film (1953)

The Nevadan, a Western film (1950)

The Hotel New Hampshire, a novel (1981) by John Irving

New Jersey Drive, a film (1995) about the rough side of urban life

New Mexico, a Western film (1952)

New York, New York, a musical film (1977)

Oklahoma!, a musical (1943) by Richard Rodgers and Oscar Hammerstein

The Oregon Trail, a Western film (1959)

Rhode Island Blues, a novel (2000) by Fay Weldon

Tennessee Johnson, a film (1943) about President Andrew Johnson

TEXAS CHAINSAW MASSACRE, a notorious horror movie (1974)

The Virginians, a novel (1857–9) by W.M. Thackeray

'I Was Born in West Virginia', a traditional song

Wyoming, the title of two Western films (1940, 1947)

Utopia. A political romance (1516) by Sir Thomas More (?1477–1535), in which he gives the name Utopia ('Nowhere', from Greek *ou*, 'not', and *topos*, 'place') to an imaginary island where everything, including laws, morals and politics, is perfect, and in which the evils of existing laws and the like are shown by contrast. Hence the word 'Utopia' is applied to any idealistic but impractical scheme. The opposite of a Utopia is a dystopia, an imaginary world that is much worse than our own. More recent books in the utopian or dystopian genre include *EREWHON* (an anagram of 'nowhere'), *HERLAND*, *BRAVE NEW WORLD* and *NINETEEN EIGHTY-FOUR*.

Utopia Limited, or The Flowers of Progress (1893) is a comic opera with music by Arthur Sullivan (1842–1900) and words by W.S. Gilbert (1836–1911), in which Utopia is run as a limited liability company. Among the many *Road to* … comic films with Bob Hope and Bing Crosby is *Road to Utopia* (1945), set during the 1896 Klondike Gold Rush.

V

V. The first novel (1963) by Thomas Pynchon (b.1937), an author of such reclusive habits that the only known photograph of him was taken in 1955. The title initial is the name under which a mysterious woman manifests herself at key moments of disaster that have contributed to the formation of modern Europe and America. V appears in various guises, including Victoria Wren, Vera Meroving, Venus, Virgin and Void. (The shape of the letter V may also symbolize the collision course of two otherwise unrelated chains of events.) The two protagonists, among 200 named characters, are Herbert Stencil, obsessed with finding V, which he never does, and Benny Profane, an accident-prone realist. As Stencil's father notes in his journal: 'There is more behind and inside V than any of us had suspected. Not who, but what: what is she.'

V is also the title of a long poem (1985) by Tony Harrison (b.1937), representing a kind of updating to the miners' strike of *GRAY'S ELEGY*. The V of the title is a symbol of conflict ('versus'). Harrison's television broadcast of the poem in 1987 was controversial for its unflinching use of 'four-letter words'.

Vagina Monologues, The. A stage show (1998) by the US feminist Eve Ensler, based on a large number of interviews she conducted in various parts of the world with women, asking them about their relationships with their vaginas. Topics covered include masturbation, rape, periods, birth, the names given to vaginas, what vaginas might wear if they dressed up, what they might say, and so on.

Celebrities have queued up to speak the monologues on stage, memorably on 'V-day' (St Valentine's Day) 2001, before 18,000 people in Madison Square Gardens, New York, when the many speakers included the likes of Glenn Close, Brooke Shields, Isabella Rossellini, Gloria Steinem, Calista Flockhart, Oprah Winfrey, Phoebe Snow and Jane Fonda. Other women criticized the show for equating sex with violence rather than pleasure, while Camille Paglia lambasted the 'psychological poison of Ensler's archaic creed of victimization'. *See also* *PUPPETRY OF THE PENIS*.

Valley of the Dolls. A cult film (1967) based on a book of the same title (1968) by Jacqueline Susann (*c.*1926–74) about drug-taking among aspiring Hollywood film stars. The 'dolls' of the title are the pills on which the three main characters, all struggling actresses, are dependent; it is thought that Susann may well have coined this usage, and the expression 'valley of the dolls', a mainly US term for drug dependence, certainly comes from the title of the book. The similarly titled film *Beyond the Valley of the Dolls* (1970), directed by Russ Meyer, had little in common with the first film other than a theme of drug and alcohol addiction in show business. It became an even bigger cult success.

Valse triste (French, 'sad waltz') or ***Trauerwalzer*** (German, 'mourning waltz'). The publisher's names for a waltz for piano by Schubert (1797–1828), composed in 1816 and published in 1821. Schubert was not best pleased, remarking:

> What kind of a jackass ever wrote a Valse triste?

(Sibelius was one such: he gave the title to part of his incidental music, opus 44 (1903), for Arvid Järnefelt's play *Kuolema*.) Another version of Schubert's piece, with the title *Le Désir*, was for long attributed to Beethoven.

Vanity Fair. The best known novel (1847–8) by W.M. Thackeray (1811–63), which has a notable heroine in the form of Becky Sharp. Set during the Napoleonic Wars, the work satirizes the weaknesses and follies of human nature.

Vanity Fair is also the title of a fashionable magazine, founded by Captain Tommy Bowles (1842–1922), grandfather of the Mitford sisters and a holder of strong views on the correct way to bathe; one of the early editors was Frank Harris (1856–1931), better known for his sexually frank memoirs, *My Life and Loves* (1923–7).

The original Vanity Fair occurs in part 1 of John Bunyan's *PILGRIM'S PROGRESS* (1678). Bunyan's Vanity Fair was established by the demonic trio of Beelzebub, Apollyon and Legion in the town of Vanity:

> It beareth the name of Vanity-Fair, because the town where 'tis kept, is lighter than vanity.

This last phrase closely echoes Psalm 62 in the Book of Common Prayer:

> The children of men are deceitful upon the weights, they are altogether lighter than vanity itself.

Bunyan's Vanity Fair lasts all year round as a market for houses, lands, trades, places, honours, preferments, titles, countries, kingdoms, lusts, pleasures and delights of all sorts.

The vanity tradition goes back to Ecclesiastes 1:2:

> Vanity of vanities, saith the Preacher, vanity of vanities; all is vanity.

Thackeray picks up the Latin version of 'Vanity of vanities' at the end of his novel:

> Ah! *Vanitas Vanitatum!* Which of us is happy in this world? Which one of us has his desire? or, having it, is satisfied? – Come, children, let us shut up the box and the puppets, for our play is played out.

Venus de Medici. A statue thought to date from the 4th century BC. It was dug up in the 17th century in the villa of Hadrian at Tivoli, near Rome, in eleven pieces. It was kept in the Medici Palace at Rome until its removal to Florence by Cosimo III de' Medici (1642–1723). Since 1860 it has been in the Uffizi Gallery, Florence. Byron described his reaction to the statue in *Childe Harold*:

> We gaze and turn away, and know not where,
> Dazzled and drunk with Beauty, till the heart
> Reels with its fullness …
>
> LORD BYRON: *Childe Harold's Pilgrimage*, IV (1818)

Venus de Milo (French, 'the Venus of Melos'). One of the world's most famous statues, depicting Aphrodite (the Greek version of Venus, goddess of love) nude from the hips up. Her arms have been broken off. Dating from the 2nd century BC, it was unearthed on the Greek island of Melos in 1820 and acquired for the French government by the French admiral

Jules Sébastien César Dumont d'Urville (1790–1842). It is now in the Louvre, Paris (hence the French title). It was probably carved at Antioch, and based on an earlier (4th-century), Corinthian original. The Romans made many copies.

Venus of Cnidus. An apparently exquisite statue by the ancient Greek sculptor Praxiteles (4th century BC) purchased by the inhabitants of Cnidus, an ancient Greek city in Asia Minor. The Cnidians refused to part with it, although Nicomedes, king of Bythnia, offered to pay off their national debt as its price. It was subsequently removed to Constantinople, and was destroyed in the great fire during the reign of Justinian (AD 532). It was the first lifesize statue to show Venus completely nude.

Verklärte Nacht (German, 'transfigured night'). A string sextet for two violins, two violas and two cellos, opus 4, by Arnold Schoenberg (1874–1951), composed in 1899, and adapted for string orchestra by him in 1917. The piece was inspired by a poem of the same name by Richard Dehmel (1863–1920) about a man and a woman walking in the moonlight. Many have noted how the music picks up and develops the erotic chromaticism of Wagner's *Tristan und Isolde*, one contemporary commenting:

> It sounds as if someone had smeared the score of *Tristan* while it was still wet.

Vertigo. A suspense film (1958) directed by Alfred Hitchcock and starring James Stewart and Kim Novak, based on a novel *D'Entre les morts* by Pierre Boileau and Thomas Narcejac (the book was written specifically for Hitchcock to adapt). It concerns a detective with a fear of heights who falls in love with a woman who falls to her death. The detective is then startled to see what is apparently her double. The film includes innovative camera techniques to suggest the experience of vertigo.

View from the Bridge, A. A play (1955) by the US playwright Arthur Miller (b.1915) about a Brooklyn longshoreman who takes two illegal immigrants into his home but subsequently informs the authorities of their presence after one of them falls in love with his wife's niece, for whom he has a liking himself. The title reflects both the immediate environment of the play (the Brooklyn waterfront) and the detached observation of events as delivered by the local lawyer, Alfieri, who narrates the story.

View to a Kill, A. A film (1985) in the long-running series of James Bond secret agent movies based on the novels of Ian Fleming (1906–64). Roger Moore played Bond. Fleming's original story was published in 1960 with the rather more meaningful title 'From a View to a Kill'. This may have been suggested by Anthony Powell's novel *From a View to a Death* (1933), which in turn took the idea from the traditional foxhunting ballad 'D'ye ken John Peel', written in 1832 by John Woodcock Graves:

> Yes, I ken John Peel, and Ruby too,
> Ranter and Ringwood, Bellman and True,
> From a find to a check, from a check to a view,
> From a view to a death in the morning.

A 'check' in foxhunting language signifies a loss of scent, while a 'view' is the cry that signals the actual sighting of a fox.

Vile Bodies. A novel (1930) by Evelyn Waugh (1903–66), satirizing the manners of the 'bright young things' of the period in a recognizable but fantasized political and social setting. The 'vile bodies' are those of the characters who spend their time going from party to party, to the fury and puzzlement of their elders. The words have a biblical echo:

> Who shall change our vile body, that it may be fashioned unto his glorious body.
>
> Philippians 3:21

Village of the Damned. *See MIDWICH CUCKOOS, THE.*

Villette. *See* PROFESSOR, THE.

Virgin Soldiers, The. A novel (1966) by Leslie Thomas (b.1931). Set in Malaya during the years 1948–52, it reflects the experiences of British soldiers garrisoned there to combat the threat of communist guerrillas: 'Some of this army were good soldiers; others were not.' A significant strand of the story concerns the sexual initiation of a 19-year-old private by a Chinese prostitute, with whom he falls in love. A sharply observed film version (1969) was directed by John Dexter.

Vision of Judgement, A. The title of two related works, the first (1821) by Robert Southey (1774–1843), and the second (1822), in response, by Lord Byron (1788–1824). Southey was by then poet laureate and an arch-reactionary, and his loyal poem involves the resurrection of the dead George III and his entry into heaven. In his preface, Southey attacked

Byron's poetry, referring to Byron and some of his contemporaries as the 'Satanic School'. Byron responded in *his* preface:

> In this [Southey's] preface it hath pleased the magnanimous Laureate to draw the picture of a supposed 'Satanic School', the which he doth recommend to the notice of the legislature; thereby adding to his other laurels the ambition of those of an informer.

In his parody Byron goes on to hold George III up to ridicule and contempt:

> And when the gorgeous coffin was laid low,
> It seemed the mockery of hell to fold
> The rottenness of eighty years in gold.

The woes and follies of his reign are then rehearsed. Southey himself is portrayed as a mercenary hack, a former radical who 'Had turn'd his coat – and would have turned his skin'. He even offers to write Satan's life and to 'add you [i.e. the Devil] to my other saints'. In the end, 'King George slipp'd into heaven':

> And when the tumult dwindled to a calm,
> I left him practising the hundredth psalm.

Vivisector, The. A novel (1970) by the Australian Nobel laureate Patrick White (1912–90). It is a rags-to-riches study of an eminent artist who as a child is bought from his parents by a wealthy couple. The course of his many relationships, some intense, some fleeting, is marred by the fact that he uses people dispassionately in the interests of his art, in the same way as a vivisector exploits animals.

Vogelquartett. *See* 'BIRD' QUARTET.

Voice of the Turtle, The. A play (1943) by the Anglo-American playwright John Van Druten (1901–57) about a wartime romance between a young actress and a serviceman. The title is biblical in origin (and 'turtle' here is a turtle dove):

> Rise up, my love, my fair one, and come away.
> For, lo, the winter is past, the rain is over and gone;
> The flowers appear on the earth; the time of the singing of birds is come, and the voice of the turtle is heard in our land.
>
> Song of Solomon 2:10–12

Volpone, or The Fox. One of the greatest comedies of Ben Jonson (1572–1637), first performed in 1605–6, and published in 1607. The main character, Volpone, is a cunning and wealthy Venetian; *volpone* is Italian for an old fox or a crafty dog. The names of other characters also reflect their dispositions: for example, Mosca is a parasite (Italian *mosca*, 'fly'), while Corvino greedily awaits Volpone's death in expectation of an inheritance (*corvo*, 'raven').

Vox clamans in deserto (Latin, 'a voice crying in the wilderness'). A song cycle (1923) for soprano and small orchestra by the US modernist composer Carl Ruggles (1876–1971). The text comes from three poems: 'Parting at Morning' by Robert Browning; 'Son of Mine' by Charles Henry Meltzer; and 'A Clear Midnight' by Walt Whitman.

> The voice of him that crieth in the wilderness, Prepare ye the way of the Lord, make straight in the desert a highway for our God.
>
> Isaiah 40:3

W

Waiting for Godot. A play, originally written in French with the title *En attendant Godot*, by Samuel Beckett (1906–89). It was first performed in Paris in 1953 and opened to acclaim in Britain, in a translation by the author. The play is ostensibly about a pair of tramps, Estragon and Vladimir, who wait interminably for the arrival of the mysterious Godot. The only other characters are Lucky, Pozzo and a Boy. Beckett cast doubt upon suggestions that Godot was in fact God ('If Godot were God, I would have called him that'), and there has been much debate over Godot's identity and significance. Because the play was written originally in French, other theories have suggested a link with the French *godillot* or *godasse* (slang words for 'boot'), as boots are discussed in the text, and with a tale that the author once came across a crowd watching the Tour de France cycle race and, on asking what they were doing, was informed, 'We are waiting for Godot' (that being the name of the slowest rider in the field). Alternatively, it was claimed, Beckett was once accosted by a prostitute while loitering in the Rue Godot de Mauroy in Paris and, on declining her advances, was asked impatiently what he was hanging about there for – was he perhaps 'waiting for Godot?' (as in the name of the street).

Walden, or Life in the Woods. An account (1854) by the US writer Henry David Thoreau (1817–62) of the two years (1845–7) he spent living on his own as an experiment in self-sufficiency. He built a hut in the woods by

Walden Pond, near the town of Concord, Massachusetts, grew his own food and contemplated his surroundings.

> Our life is frittered away by detail ... Simplify, simplify.
>
> *Walden*, 'Where I lived, and what I lived for'

Some years later, among the remains of his hut, were found many bent nails, suggesting that Thoreau's practical skills were not all they might have been.

'Waldstein' Sonata. The nickname of the piano sonata no 21 in C, opus 53 (1804), by Beethoven (1770–1827), dedicated to his friend and patron, Count Ferdinand von Waldstein (1762–1853). A Viennese aristocrat, Waldstein had arrived in Bonn in 1788, and soon became a fervent admirer of Beethoven. In 1792, as the French Revolutionary armies marched into the Rhineland and Beethoven left Bonn for Vienna, Waldstein wrote in the composer's album:

> With the help of unremitting labour you shall receive Mozart's spirit from Haydn's hands.

Waldstein was also the patron of another well-known figure: Giovanni Giacomo Casanova (1725–98) saw out his final years as the count's librarian at his castle of Dux in Bohemia.

Walkabout. A film (1971), directed by Nicolas Roeg and with a screenplay by Edward Bond, based on a novel by James Vance Marshall. A schoolgirl and her younger brother are left in the Australian desert when their father kills himself. They are rescued by a young Aboriginal man, and they accompany him on his journey through the wilderness. 'To go walkabout' is an expression that arose among Australian Aborigines, meaning to withdraw from modern society for a while to make a journey in the bush, living in a traditional manner. The term has since been appropriated by the British royal family's PR machine for a royal visit which involves meeting and greeting the general public.

Walk on the Wild Side, A. A novel (1956) by the US writer Nelson Algren (1909–81), set in New Orleans during the Great Depression. It reflects the author's preoccupation with the criminal underworld and poverty-stricken vagrants, whose experiences he investigated and shared as a journalist. There is an emphasis on alternative sexual lifestyles. A film version was directed by Edward Dmytryk in 1962. Lou Reed's hit song 'Walk on the Wild Side' (1972) was an ode to the denizens of Andy

Warhol's films of the 1960s. The 'girlie' backing singers were in fact Mick Jagger and David Bowie.

Wally, La. An opera by Alfredo Catalani (1854–93), with a libretto by Luigi Illica, first performed in 1892. It was Catalani's last and most successful opera, inspiring Toscanini to name his own daughter Wally after the heroine of the piece. The absurd (to English ears) title, and the story, derive from the novel *Die Geyer-Wally* (1875) by Wilhelmine von Hillern. La Wally and her lover end up dying in an avalanche.

'Wanderer' Fantasia. The nickname for the *Fantaisie* for piano in C, D760 (1822), by Schubert (1791–1828). In the adagio there are variations on Schubert's song '*Der Wanderer*', D493 (1816).

War and Peace. An epic novel (published serially, 1864–9) by the Russian writer Leo Tolstoy (1828–1910). He originally planned to call it *1825*, then, as he realized the core of his story lay during the Napoleonic Wars, he called it *1805*, and this was the title used in the initial published episodes. At one point he re-titled it *ALL'S WELL THAT ENDS WELL*, conceiving at that point that all would end happily. But as Tolstoy became more and more immersed in developing his philosophy of history, and his theories on the nature of war, he settled on the final sweeping title.

There have been two film versions. The first (1956) is a Hollywood production, directed by King Vidor, and lasts nearly three and a half hours. The second (1967) is a much-admired Soviet production directed by Sergei Bondarchuk; it was originally in four parts, totalling nearly nine hours, and was shown in the UK in two parts totalling over seven hours, reduced to something over six hours for the USA. The BBC TV serial of the novel, adapted by Jack Pulman and with Anthony Hopkins as Pierre, was broadcast in 1972–3. Tolstoy's novel also formed the basis of the opera, opus 91 (1941–53), by Prokofiev (1891–1953) to a libretto by the composer and Mira Mendelson.

War of the Worlds, The. A science-fiction novel by H.G. Wells (1866–1946), published in 1898. The worlds in question are Mars and Earth: the Martians land in Woking, Surrey, and begin to destroy humanity, before succumbing to a bacterial disease.

Wells's near-namesake, the US writer, director and actor Orson Welles (1915–85), first made a name for himself when he broadcast a radio version of *The War of the Worlds* as if the events were currently taking place live in New Jersey. The broadcast, which went out on 30

October 1938 and which was intended as a Halloween prank, caused widespread panic among listeners.

War Requiem. A sombre, anti-war choral work by Benjamin Britten (1913–76), which combines nine poems by the First World War poet Wilfred Owen (1893–1918) with the words of the Latin requiem mass. The work was performed in the new Coventry Cathedral in 1962, which replaced the medieval cathedral destroyed in a German bombing raid in 1940. Britten, a lifelong pacifist, saw it as a work of reconciliation, and at the first performance the soloists were Galina Vishnevskaya (a Russian), Dietrich Fischer-Dieskau (a German) and Peter Pears (a Briton). Stravinsky described the requiem as 'Kleenex music'.

Warsaw Concerto. A stirringly romantic musical score written by Richard Addinsell (1904–77) for the film *Dangerous Moonlight* (1941). The film centres on a Polish pianist who escapes from the Nazis, flies with the Polish Air Force in the Battle of Britain and loses his memory. This romantic melodrama was a huge hit with wartime audiences.

War That Will End War, The. A non-fiction work by H.G. Wells (1866–1946), published in 1914. Wells predicts such a war as the prelude to a 'World State'. It was not long before people optimistically and naively started referring to the First World War as 'the war to end wars'.

> At eleven o'clock this morning came to an end the cruellest and most terrible war that has ever scourged mankind. I hope we may say that thus, this fateful morning, came to an end all wars.
>
> DAVID LLOYD GEORGE: speech to the House of Commons, 11 November 1918

Wasp Factory, The. The first novel (1984) by the Scottish writer Iain Banks (b.1954). It is a study of insanity that veers between psychological acuity and grotesque fantasy. The central character, 16-year-old Frank, has already been responsible for three violent murders. He lives with his father on a remote Scottish island, where he constructs a 'wasp factory' out of an old clock face to which he has added various tunnels and compartments, each with a special significance. From time to time he introduces a live wasp into this, using the route it takes and the fate it suffers as a prediction of the future. If it enters the fire compartments, for example, this means there will be a fire; if it enters the water compartments, there will be a drowning.

Waste Land, The. A densely allusive poem (1922) by T.S. Eliot (1888–1965) that is now recognized as one of the landmarks of modernist literature. The title, like the poem itself, expresses the sense of futility and disillusion that followed in the wake of the First World War. More specifically, it refers to an incident in the second book of Malory's *Le Morte Darthur*, in which the knight Balyn deals King Pellam the 'Dolorous Stroke' that causes the 'Waste Land', a disaster that devastates three kingdoms and whose effects can only be alleviated by the quest for the Holy Grail. The poem has furnished titles for several subsequent literary works, including Evelyn Waugh's *A HANDFUL OF DUST* (1934), Iain M. Banks's *CONSIDER PHLEBAS* (1987) and Edna O'Brien's novel *August is a Wicked Month* (1985), this last playing with the poem's famous opening lines:

> April is the cruellest month, breeding
> Lilacs out of the dead land.

In the years following its publication, the poem attracted numerous admirers, including university undergraduates, who allegedly chanted it from college windows as an act of artistic rebellion:

> After luncheon he stood on the balcony with a megaphone which had appeared surprisingly among the bric-a-brac of Sebastian's room, and in languishing tones recited passages from The Waste Land to the sweatered and muffled throng that was on its way to the river.
>
> EVELYN WAUGH: *Brideshead Revisited* (1945)

> Queen Elizabeth the Queen Mother once described T.S. Eliot as 'a rather lugubrious man in a suit' who 'looked like a bank manager and read us a poem called "The Dessert"'.
>
> PENDENNIS: in the *Observer*, 15 July 2001

> [*The Waste Land*] was only the relief of a personal and wholly insignificant grouse against life; it is just a piece of rhythmical grumbling.
>
> T.S. ELIOT: *The Waste Land* (ed. Valerie Eliot, 1971), epigraph

Water Music. An orchestral suite by George Frideric Handel (1685–1759). A number of different early editions, with notable variations, exist, and the date and occasion of the music's composition is not known for certain. In 1712 Handel had gone to London on leave of absence from the employ of the Elector of Hanover, but had never returned. Instead, in 1714, the Elector succeeded to the British throne as George I, and it was long said that Handel wrote the *Water Music* for a royal party on the Thames in 1715 to make his peace with his former employer. All this is undocumented, although it is known that Handel wrote music for a royal procession on the Thames in 1717.

The title was re-used by two avant-garde composers of the 20th century. *Water Music* by Tory Takemitsu (1930–96) is for Noh dancer and tape, while in John Cage's *Water Music* (1952) the pianist also uses containers of water, a radio, whistles and playing cards.

Waverley. The first novel of Sir Walter Scott (1771–1832), published in 1814. The title is the name of the hero, Edward Waverley, a name derived from the ruined Waverley Abbey, near Farnham, Surrey. Scott published all his subsequent novels as 'by the author of Waverley', remaining anonymous as the 'Great Unknown' until 1827. Thus the novels became known as the 'Waverley novels'. The title also gave its name to Edinburgh's principal railway station, and to a kind of biscuit. There is an overture by Berlioz (1803–69) entitled *Waverley* (opus 1, 1827–8).

Waves, The. A novel by Virginia Woolf (1882–1941), published in 1931. The novel is highly experimental, dissolving the world into the streams of consciousness of six characters, followed from childhood to old age. Nothing is fixed, all is flux, like the waves of the recurring seascapes that give some shape to the novel. Waves can also be seen as a figure for the human experience, an analogy of consciousness moving through time and space.

Way of All Flesh, The. A novel by Samuel Butler (1835–1902), posthumously published in 1903. The work, which is semi-autobiographical, follows the fortunes of a family through four generations. In particular it reflects Butler's rejection, as a young man, of the values – church, home and conventional Christianity – of his own father, the Rev. Thomas Butler. The book, one of the works which marked the beginning of the anti-Victorian reaction, became very popular, especially in the 1920s.

The phrase 'the way of all flesh' – suggesting mortal frailty (both physical and moral) – seems to have been current since the 17th century:

> 'Tis the way of all flesh.
>
> THOMAS SHADWELL: *The Sullen Lovers* (1668), V

> Alack, he's gone the way of all flesh.
>
> WILLIAM CONGREVE (attributed): *Squire Bickerstaff Detected*

We Are Making a New World. A stark painting (1918) by Paul Nash (1889–1946), which has become as iconic of the wastefulness of war as the poems of Wilfred Owen or Siegfried Sassoon. After being injured in the First World War, Nash became an official war artist (a role he took on again in the Second World War). The title of this painting is heavily ironic: a low pale sun radiates tenuous beams of light over a shattered landscape of craters and splintered trees. The work hangs in the Imperial War Museum, London. *See also* TOTES MEER.

We Are the People Our Parents Warned Us Against. A book (1968) about the hippie phenomenon by Nicholas Von Hoffman. The title is based on the remark that the bohemian painter Augustus John made to his fellow bohemian painter Nina Hamnett:

> We have become, Nina, the sort of people our parents warned us about.

'Wedge' Fugue. The nickname of the organ fugue in E minor, BWV 548, by J.S. Bach (1685–1750) so called because the subject proceeds by gradually widening intervals (E, D sharp–F sharp, D–G sharp, C sharp–A, C–A sharp, B–B).

Weir of Hermiston. An unfinished novel by Robert Louis Stevenson (1850–94), published posthumously in 1896. 'Weir' here is not a hydrological feature, but rather the name of the hero, Archie Weir, whose tyrannical father is Adam Weir, Lord Hermiston, a hanging judge based on the historical Lord Braxfield (1722–99). Braxfield was a notorious hounder of Scottish radicals, and his pithy remarks from the bench were gleefully recorded by his contemporaries:

> [To an eloquent prisoner in the dock] Ye're a vera clever chiel, man, but ye wad be nane the waur o' a hanging.
>
> Quoted in John Gibson Lockhart, *Life of Scott* (1837–8)

> [To a political prisoner who claimed that Christ had been a reformer] Muckle he made o' that; he was hanget.
>
> Quoted in Lord Cockburn, *Memorials of His Times* (1856)

Critics (including Henry James, a great admirer) have generally agreed that *Weir of Hermiston* shows that at the time of his final illness Stevenson was heading away from juvenile adventures towards something truly great in fiction.

Wellington's Victory or ***Battle Symphony*** or ***Battle of Victoria*** or ***Battle of Vitoria***. The various alternative English titles for Beethoven's occasional piece, *Wellingtons Sieg, oder die Schlacht bei Vittoria* (the misspelling was Beethoven's), opus 91, composed in 1813 to celebrate Wellington's decisive victory over Napoleon's forces at Vitoria in northeastern Spain on 21 June of that year. The crudely programmatic music includes quotations from 'GOD SAVE THE KING' and 'RULE, BRITANNIA'. The work was originally designed to be played on the panharmonicon, the mechanical instrument invented by J.N. Maelzel (also the inventor of the metronome), but Beethoven rescored it for orchestra, in which form it was first performed in December 1813. Beethoven sent a copy of the score to the Prince Regent (the future George IV), but was irritated to receive no response.

Well of Loneliness, The. A novel (1928) by Radclyffe Hall (pseudonym of Marguerite Radclyffe-Hall; 1880–1943). This study of lesbian love, written by a lesbian partly to demonstrate the isolation of those of similar inclinations, was banned in Britain for many years and finally published in a small, high-priced edition in a plain cover. Its heroine is the 'invert', Stephen Gordon, who is obliged to release her lovers to a conventional world while she herself remains trapped inside a 'well of loneliness'.

Well-Tempered Clavier, The (German title: *Das Wohltemperierte Clavier*). The title given by J.S. Bach (1685–1750) to his two sets of preludes and fugues for keyboard (1722 and 1744), each set containing 24 pieces in each of the major and minor keys – hence they are sometimes referred to as 'The Forty-eight'. 'Clavier' is a generic term for any keyboard instrument, such as a harpsichord or clavichord, and 'well-tempered' refers to the system of tuning known as 'equal temperament'. In the equal-temperament system the instrument is tuned so that all the semitones are equal, as opposed to the earlier system whereby each key is tuned with mathematical precision. The disadvantage of this latter system is that while some keys will be exactly in tune, others will be wildly out, whereas with equal temperament the notes in all the keys are very slightly out of tune. Bach's purpose in writing a piece in every key was to show the flexibility of the equal-temperament system – the system employed to this day.

West Side Story. A much performed American musical by Leonard Bernstein (1918–90), with lyrics by Stephen Sondheim (b.1930). It was first staged in 1957. The story is an updated version of *Romeo and Juliet* set in New York's West Side dockland area, with the Montagues and Capulets being replaced by rival teenage gangs, the Sharks and the Jets. The rivalry erupts into violence as a result of the love between Tony, one of the Jets, and Maria, the sister of the leader of the Sharks. The 1961 film version won an Oscar for best picture.

Westward Ho! A tub-thumping historical novel (1855) by Charles Kingsley (1819–75) about Elizabethan seadogs thrashing the Spaniards. Perhaps uniquely, the title gave its name to a place: Westward Ho! is a resort on the north Devon coast, the area where much of Kingsley's story took place.

'Westward Ho' is the name commonly given to a large-scale painting of the settlement of the American West by the German-born painter Emanuel Leutze (1816–68). The correct title of the work, commissioned in 1860 to decorate a stairway in the Capitol in Washington, DC, is *Westward the Course of Empire Takes Its Way,* itself a quote from the poem 'On the Prospect of Planting Arts and Learning in America' by George Berkeley (1685–1753). The popular name probably derives from the cry 'Westward Ho!', frequently heard in old Western films as the settlers get their wagons rolling across the Prairies.

Kingsley's title, in the form *Westward Hoe*, was first used in 1607 for a comedy by the Jacobean playwrights John Webster (*c.*1578–*c.*1626) and Thomas Dekker (?1572–1632), which involves an escapade to Brentford, in Essex. The same year Webster and Dekker also produced a *Northward Hoe.* The title formula had previously been used by George Chapman (?1559–1634), Ben Jonson (1572–1637) and John Marston (1576–1634) in another comedy, *Eastward Hoe* (1605), in which the less deserving characters are shipwrecked on the Isle of Dogs, in east London, a once despised area (but now the site of the Canary Wharf development). Chapman and Jonson were briefly imprisoned for including some rude comments about James I's Scots courtiers in the play.

Westward Ha! is the title of a miscellaneous collection (1948) by the US humorist S.J. Perelman (1904–79).

> Olivia: There lies your way, due west.
> Viola (as Cesario): Then westward-ho!
>
> WILLIAM SHAKESPEARE: *Twelfth Night* (1601), III. i

We Two Boys Together Clinging. A painting (1961) by David Hockney (b.1937) in which the homoerotic subject is executed in Hockney's distinctive early Pop art style. Hockney himself has written about the painting in *David Hockney by David Hockney* (1976):

> We Two Boys Together Clinging is from Walt Whitman:
>
> We two boys together clinging,
> One the other never leaving …
> Arm'd and fearless, eating, drinking, sleeping, loving.
>
> … At the time of the painting I had a newspaper clipping on the wall with the headline 'TWO BOYS CLING TO CLIFF ALL NIGHT'. There were also a few pictures of Cliff Richard pinned up nearby, although the headline was actually referring to a Bank Holiday mountaineering accident.

Whaam! One of several paintings of jet fighters in action executed in enlarged comic-book style by the Pop artist Roy Lichtenstein (1923–97). *Whaam!*, which dates from 1963, includes the words 'I pressed the fire control … and ahead of me rockets blazed through the sky … ' This results in the 'Whaam!' of the title as the enemy fighter explodes in flames. Similar works by Lichtenstein include *Blam* (1962), in which a Soviet or Red Chinese Mig fighter suffers a direct hit. He also had a gentler side: in such works as *Good Morning, Darling* (1964) he drew on teen romances for his inspiration.

What Maisie Knew. A novel by Henry James (1843–1916), published in 1897. Maisie Farange is the twelve-year-old child of divorced parents, and the picture of their corrupt lives (and the infidelities of their new spouses) is largely told through her, although she maintains her innocence in the face of this knowledge. In the end she chooses to live with her old governess. The title may be an ironic homage to that of the popular children's book *What Katie Did* (1872) by the US writer Susan Coolidge (Saray Chauncey Woolsey, 1845–1905), and its successors, *What Katie Did at School* (1873) and *What Katie Did Next* (1886).

What's Bred in the Bone. A novel (1985) by the Canadian writer Robertson Davies (1913–95), the second in his Cornish Trilogy, each of which deals with a different art. The first, *The Rebel Angels* (1981), concerns literature, the third, *The Lyre of Orpheus* (1988), has music as its theme, while *What's Bred in the Bone* concerns the forgery of Old Master paintings.

> What's bred in the bone will come out in the flesh.
>
> Proverb, late 15th century

For the error bred in the bone
Of each woman and each man
Craves what it cannot have,
Not universal love
But to be loved alone.

W.H. AUDEN: 'September 1st 1939'

When Did You Last See Your Father? *See AND WHEN DID YOU LAST SEE YOUR FATHER?*

'When Lilacs Last in the Dooryard Bloomed'. An elegy on the death of President Abraham Lincoln (1809–65) by the US poet Walt Whitman (1819–92), published in 1865–6 and incorporated into *LEAVES OF GRASS* in 1867. Lincoln was assassinated on the evening of 14 April 1865, and died the following morning. It was lilac time.

When lilacs last in the dooryard bloomed,
And the great star early drooped in the western sky in the night,
I mourned, and yet shall mourn with ever-returning spring.

There is a musical setting for soloists, chorus and orchestra (1970) by the US composer Roger Sessions (1896–1985). The US writer Ray Bradbury (b.1920) entitled one of his collections of poetry *When Elephants Last in the Dooryard Bloomed* (1973).

Where Angels Fear to Tread. A novel (1905) by E.M. Forster (1879–1970), the inspiration for which was a piece of gossip, overheard while he was in Italy, about an English tourist who formed a *mésalliance* with an Italian. The plot centres on the efforts of the members of an English family to 'rescue', from his Italian father, the baby whose mother, related to them by a former marriage, has died in childbirth. The title is from Alexander Pope (1688–1744):

For Fools rush in where Angels fear to tread.

An Essay on Criticism

A film version (1991) was directed by Charles Sturridge.

Where Do We Come From? What Are We? Where Are We Going? A painting (1897–8) by the French symbolist Paul Gauguin (1848–1903), made during his sojourn in Tahiti. The wide, mural-like painting, typical of Gauguin's willed 'primitivism', is replete with semi-naked Polynesian women, idols and brightly coloured foliage. The content and atmosphere are as mysterious as the title, although both broadly suggest an allegory of life. Gauguin attempted suicide shortly after finishing the painting.

In 2001 the US poet Dennis Finnell published a collection called *The Gauguin Answer Sheet: After Paul Gauguin's Where Do We Come From? What Are We? Where Are We Going?*

See also TODAY IS THE TOMORROW YOU WERE PROMISED YESTERDAY.

Whisky Galore. A novel (1947) by Compton Mackenzie (born Edward Montague Compton; 1883–1972). Said by him to be based loosely on the wreck of the SS *Politician* (which became the fictional SS *Cabinet Minister*) off Eriskay with a cargo of whisky, it is a satire on Scottish life, manners, religion and superstitions, whose starting point is a wreck in similar circumstances during a grave shortage during the Second World War of *uisge beatha* (Gaelic, 'water of life'). A fast-paced film version (1948) was directed by Alexander Mackendrick. Fourteen bottles of whisky from the real-life wreck fetched a total of over £12,000 at auction in Glasgow in 1993.

Whistler's Mother. *See* NOCTURNE IN BLACK AND GOLD: THE FALLING ROCKET.

White Devil, The. A multi-corpse tragedy by John Webster (*c.*1578–*c.*1626), first published in 1612. Webster drew on a recent notorious scandal in Italy, in which the duke of Bracciano had fallen for Vittoria Accoramboni. In 1581 Bracciano had Vittoria's husband murdered and married her; Bracciano had already murdered his first wife Isabella. After Bracciano's death Isabella's relatives had Vittoria murdered. Webster broadly follows this story, although he implicates Vittoria in the murder of her husband, and not only she, but her brother Flamineo and Bracciano himself are killed at the end (in reality Bracciano died a non-violent death). When Vittoria is tried in Act III, her hypocritical accusers sentence her to 'a house of penitent whores'; in the 16th and 17th centuries 'white devil' was a slang term for a prostitute.

White Noise. A comic novel (1985) by the US writer Don DeLillo (b.1936), centring on an 'airborne toxic event' and the manufacture of an experimental drug to cure the fear of death. White noise is the term for either electronic signals or sound in which all frequencies are present at equal intensity, and thus have no meaning. It is also popularly used to mean a background noise of which one is generally unaware until it changes or stops.

Who's Afraid of Virginia Woolf? A play (1962) by the US playwright Edward Albee (b.1928) depicting the tense relationship between a sharp-tongued college professor and his embittered wife. Filmed in 1966 with Richard Burton and Elizabeth Taylor in the two main roles, the play owed its memorable title to a line of graffiti scribbled in soap on a mirror in a bar in New York's Greenwich Village that the author happened to visit in the 1950s. The quip, evidently derived from the song title 'Who's Afraid of the Big Bad Wolf' from the Disney cartoon *The Three Little Pigs* (1933), was later redefined by Albee as meaning 'who's afraid of living without false illusions'.

Why Bring That Up? A guide to coping with seasickness (1936) by Joseph Franklin Montague, author of *Troubles We Don't Talk About* (1927), a book on diseases of the rectum.

Wild Duck, The. A tragicomedy (1884) by the Norwegian dramatist Henrik Ibsen (1828–1906). Hjalmar Ekdal is a happy but self-deluded man, until an old friend, Gregers Werle – an egotistical idealist thoughtlessly committed to absolute truth, whatever the cost – exposes certain secrets that persuade Ekdal that his daughter Hedvig is not his own. Ekdal rejects Hedvig, but Werle persuades her that she can win back her father's love if she kills her beloved pet duck. In the end, she kills herself.

Wilderness of Mirrors. A book (1980) by David C. Martin about James J. Angleton (1917–87), the leading counter-intelligence specialist of the CIA, who is said to have used the phrase 'a wilderness of mirrors' to characterize the world of espionage. The term originally comes from T.S. Eliot's poem 'Gerontion' (1920):

> These with a thousand small deliberations
> Protract the profit of their chilled delirium,
> Excite the membrane, when the sense has cooled,
> With pungent sauces, multiply variety
> In a wilderness of mirrors.

Wild Geese, The. An adventure film (1978) about mercenaries in Africa, starring Richard Burton, Roger Moore and Richard Harris. The original 'Wild Geese' were those Irishmen who went into exile after the defeat of Catholic resistance to William of Orange in the late 17th century, and took up military service in the armies of various Catholic monarchs in Europe.

Was it for this the wild geese spread
The grey wing upon every tide ...

W.B. YEATS: 'September 1913'

Willy Wonka and the Chocolate Factory. *See* *CHARLIE AND THE CHOCOLATE FACTORY.*

Wind in the Willows, The. A novel (1908) for children by Kenneth Grahame (1859–1932), in which the main (satisfyingly anthropomorphized) characters are a mole, a water rat and a toad. The book was developed from stories told by Grahame to his son Alastair, born in 1900, and inspired by the river and wood at Cookham Dean, Berkshire, where Grahame was brought up by his grandmother. On its publication the anonymous reviewer in the *Times Literary Supplement* reported: 'As a contribution to natural history the work is negligible.'

The story was originally called *The Mole and the Water-Rat*. It was then retitled *The Wind in the Willows*, itself the original title of the chapter called 'The Piper at the Gates of Dawn', in which Mole and Rat have a vision of Pan. Grahame finally decided in favour of the alliterative title.

What was he doing, the great god Pan,
Down in the reeds by the river?

ELIZABETH BARRETT BROWNING: 'A Musical Instrument' (1862)

A pantomimic film version (1996) was directed by Terry Jones.

Wings of the Dove, The. A novel by Henry James (1843–1916), published in 1902. Two lovers conspire to ensure their future by agreeing that one should marry a dying heiress, but in the process their love dies too. The title comes from the Old Testament:

My heart is sore pained within me: and the terrors of death are fallen upon me.
Fearfulness and trembling are come upon me, and horror hath overwhelmed me.
And I said, Oh that I had wings, like a dove! for then would I fly away, and be at rest.

Psalms 55:4–6

The film version (1997) starred Helena Bonham Carter.

Winter's Tale, The. A play (*c.*1610–11) by William Shakespeare (1564–1616), variously described as a comedy, a tragi-comedy and a romance. The story comes from *Pandosto, or the Triumph of Time* (1588) by Robert

Greene (*c.*1559–92). The play formed part of the wedding celebrations in the winter of 1612–13 of James I's daughter Elizabeth Stuart to Frederick V, the Elector Palatine (the marriage that 100 years later resulted in the Hanoverian succession).

Somewhat jarringly perhaps for such an occasion, the main plot of the play turns on the irrational jealousy of Leontes, king of Sicilia, who believes his pregnant wife Hermione, has cuckolded him with his friend Polixenes, king of Bohemia. Just prior to the moment when Leontes accuses his wife face-to-face, she and their first child, the boy Mamillius, are talking:

> *Hermione:* Pray you sit by us
> And tell's a tale.
> *Mamillius:* Merry or sad shall't be?
> *Hermione:* As merry as you will.
> *Mamillius:* A sad tale's best for winter. I have one
> Of sprites and goblins.
>
> II.i

We never actually hear this 'winter's tale', as Mamillius whispers it in his mother's ear, until Leontes has him dragged away from her. He orders her to be put in prison, Perdita ('the lost one') – the infant daughter she gives birth to – to be abandoned on some deserted shore, and Polixenes to be killed. However, the courtier sent to poison Polixenes flees with him to Bohemia, while the courtier who abandons Perdita on a remote shore of Bohemia is presumed dead after the famous stage direction 'Exit, pursued by a bear'. Mamillius dies of grief at his mother's treatment, Hermione herself is reported dead, and Leontes is filled with sorrow and remorse.

Meanwhile, back in Bohemia, Perdita is brought up in Arcadian manner by shepherds, and many years later is wooed by Polixenes' son, Florizel. Such an unsuitable match angers Polixenes, and Florizel and Perdita flee to the court of Leontes. There Perdita's true identity is revealed, and the two old friends, Leontes and Polixenes, now reconciled, approve the marriage of their children. When Leontes, still grief-struck, is taken to see a statue of Hermione, it comes alive, and it transpires that Hermione's death was faked to save her life.

The dynastic match between Sicilia and Bohemia echoes that of Princess Elizabeth and the Protestant Elector. Ironically, Elizabeth was to become queen of the real (land-locked) Bohemia, when in 1619 the Protestant Bohemians offered the throne to Frederick. He was crowned in

November 1619, but deposed a year later by the Catholic forces of the Habsburg emperor, as the Thirty Years War got underway. Elizabeth spent most of the rest of her life in exile, becoming known as 'the Winter Queen'.

'Witch Minuet'. *See* 'FIFTHS' QUARTET.

Woman in White, The. A mystery novel (1860) by Wilkie Collins (1824–89). The mysterious woman who dresses entirely in white is Anne Catherick. She is held in a lunatic asylum, and bears an uncanny resemblance to a young heiress, Laura Fairlie. The complex plot involves the attempt by Laura's villainous husband, Sir Percival Glyde, to persuade the authorities that his wife is Anne Catherick and should be locked up – so that he can get his hands on her inheritance.

Collins's title is deliberately echoed in *The Woman in Black*, a sinister Victorian-style ghost story (1983) by Susan Hill (b.1942) in which a ghost takes revenge for the death of her child by taking the lives of other children. *See also MEN IN BLACK.*

Women Beware Women. A tragedy by Thomas Middleton (1580–1627). It has not been established when he wrote it (some time before 1622), but the work was published posthumously in 1657. The admonitory title primarily refers to the character Livia (although none of the other characters is particularly savoury). In the main plot Livia distracts Leontio's mother with a game of chess while the duke seduces Leontio's wife, Bianca. In the subplot Livia persuades her niece Isabella that she is not related to Uncle Hippolito, Livia's brother, so that mutual lust may be consummated. The corpse count by the end of the play is high. Apparently T.S. Eliot was alluding to the scene featuring the game of chess in the title of Part II of *The WASTE LAND* (1922), 'A Game of Chess', although the only reference to chess is in the lines:

> And we shall play a game of chess,
> Pressing lidless eyes and waiting for a knock upon the door.

Middleton's political satire, *A GAME AT CHESS*, which he wrote in 1624, was also admired by Eliot.

World According to Garp, The. A novel (1978) by the US writer John Irving (b.1942). T.S. Garp is the son of Jenny Fields, who is generally physically repelled by men but who as a nurse in the Second World War decides she wants a child. She chooses as father of her child a terminally brain-injured airman, whose only utterance is the meaningless syllable

'Garp'; the 'T.S.' of the son's name stands for 'Technical Sergeant'. When Garp grows up he becomes the author of a novel called *The World According to Bensenhaver*, while his mother, retaining her nurse's uniform, becomes a charismatic feminist leader. Both are eventually assassinated. A film version (1982), directed by George Roy Hill, starred Robin Williams in the title role and Glenn Close as his mother.

World, the Flesh and the Devil, The. *See* FLESH AND THE DEVIL.

Wreckers, The. An opera by the English composer and suffragette Ethel Smyth (1858–1944), with a libretto by Henry Brewster, first performed (in German, in Leipzig) in 1906. 'Wreckers' were Cornish villagers who deliberately lit fires on rocky shores to lure ships to destruction so that their cargoes could be plundered. In Smyth's opera, set in 18th-century Cornwall, the heroine and her lover try to prevent such a wreck, and die by drowning.

WRITERS, ARTISTS AND COMPOSERS

MAKING COCOA FOR KINGSLEY AMIS, a poetry collection (1986) by Wendy Cope

'Andrea del Sarto', a dramatic monologue (1855) by Robert Browning

Homage to Mistress Bradstreet, a biographical ode (1956) to the colonial American poetess, Anne Bradstreet (*c.*1612–72), by the US poet John Berryman

The BROWNING VERSION, a play (1949) by Terence Rattigan

Benvenuto Cellini, an opera (1838) by Hector Berlioz

Le TOMBEAU DE COUPERIN, a piano suite (1917) by Maurice Ravel

'Mr Eliot's Sunday Morning Service', a poem (1920) by T.S. Eliot

FLAUBERT'S PARROT, a novel (1984) by Julian Barnes

'A TOCCATA OF GALUPPI'S', a poem (1855) by Robert Browning

MATHIS DER MALER, an opera (1938) by Paul Hindemith about Matthias Grünewald

Handel in the Strand, an orchestral piece (1930) by Percy Grainger

Wrestling Ernest Hemingway, a film (1993) starring Robert Duvall and Richard Harris as an odd couple

In Memoriam James Joyce, a long poem (1955) by Hugh MacDiarmid

'How Pleasant to Know Mr Lear', the preface to *Nonsense Songs* (1871) by Edward Lear

'Fra Lippo Lippi', a dramatic monologue (1855) by Robert Browning

Homage to Manet, a painting (1910) by Sir William Orpen, featuring portraits of his artist friends and Manet's painting of Eva Gonzalès

Homage to Matisse, a verse collection (1971) by the New Zealand poet Ian Wedde

Milton in America, a novel (1996) by Peter Ackroyd in which the poet escapes to America before the Restoration

Here I Give Thanks to Mondrian, a painting (1961) by the New Zealand artist Colin McCahon

'Homage to Sextus Propertius', a poem (1919) by Ezra Pound

Shakespeare in Love, a romantic comedy film (1998)

Shakespeare Wallah, a film (1965) in which English actors tour India

Taverner, an opera (1971) by Peter Maxwell Davies about the Tudor composer John Taverner (*c.*1490–1545)

'Abt Vogler', a dramatic monologue (1864) by Robert Browning; Abbé Georg Joseph Vogler (1749–1814) was a German composer, organist and teacher

I Shot Andy Warhol, a biopic (1996) of the founder of SCUM (the Society for Cutting Up Men)

The Apotheosis of Winckelmann, a painting (1768) by Joseph-Marie Vien, referring to the Neoclassical theorist (*see* LAOCOÖN)

'In Memory of W.B. Yeats', a poem (1939) by W.H. Auden

WR – Mysteries of the Organism. A film (1971) by the Yugoslav writer and director Dusan Makavajev (b.1932). WR is Wilhelm Reich (1897–1957), the Austrian psychoanalyst who, in *The Function of Orgasm* (1927), argued that frequent orgasms were necessary for the avoidance of neurosis. He advocated both sexual and political liberation, left Germany in 1933 and settled in the USA in 1939, where his ideas became increasingly unusual. He built (and rented out) special 'orgone' boxes to concentrate 'orgones', units of cosmic energy he believed were necessary for health. This led to his prosecution by the US Food and Drugs Administration, and he died in prison. Sympathizers believed the prosecution was politically motivated. Makavajev's film intersperses an account of Reich's career with a satirical look at contemporary politics, sexual and otherwise, in both the Eastern and Western Blocs. It was the first film featuring an erect penis to be passed by the British Board of Film Censors, although when shown later on television the penis (which is being wrapped in plaster of paris to make a mould for a sculpture) was heavily pixillated.

Wuthering Heights. The ultimate novel of doomed romantic passion (albeit with many a socially and psychologically realistic twist), written by Emily Brontë (1818–48) between October 1845 and June 1846, and published in 1847. Wuthering Heights is the name of the moorland manor house that features centrally in the book; there are some ruins called High or Top Withins near the Brontës' home at Haworth, West Yorkshire, associated with the fictional house. The adjective of the title is explained at the beginning of the novel by the narrator Lockwood:

> Wuthering Heights is the name of Mr Heathcliff's dwelling. 'Wuthering' being a significant provincial adjective, descriptive of the atmospheric tumult to which its station is exposed in stormy weather.

When Mrs Gaskell visited High Withins in 1853, she commented on the contrast between the house's bleak exterior and the 'snugness and comfort' inside.

Xanadu. The exotic Xanadu of the poem 'KUBLA KHAN' by Samuel Taylor Coleridge (1772–1834) has given rise to a number of titles.

In Xanadu did Kubla Khan
A stately pleasure dome decree ...

'Kublai Khan', opening lines

The Road to Xanadu: A Study in the Ways of the Imagination (1927) by the US scholar John Livingston Lowes (1867–1945) traces the sources of Coleridge's inspiration, and is regarded as a classic of its type. *Xanadu* is also the title of a poem/film (1992) by Simon Armitage (b.1963), and of a film musical (1980) with Gene Kelly and Olivia Newton-John, in which the classical Greek muse of dance and choral song, Terpsichore, comes down to earth and becomes involved in a roller disco.

Coleridge's Xanadu was Shang-tu, the summer capital of the Mongol emperors of China, founded by Kublai Khan in 1256 and subsequently visited by Marco Polo. Shang-tu was known as the 'city of 108 temples', and its walls enclosed a large park. The site of Shang-tu – the city itself was destroyed in the Red Turban Muslim Rebellion of 1358 – is at the Inner Mongolian town of Dolon Nor (Chinese Duolun).

Y

'Yankee Doodle'. A song that was possibly first introduced by British troops in America during the Seven Years War (1756–63). It was certainly sung by British troops during the American Revolution (1775–83) to deride the revolting colonists, who later adopted it as their own. It is now a quasi-national air of the United States. There are several suggested origins of the tune, which was first printed in Britain in 1778 and in America in 1794, but none is conclusive.

> Yankee Doodle came to town
> Riding on a pony;
> Stuck a feather in his cap
> And called it Macaroni.

The term 'Yank' or 'Yankee' for a New Englander (and subsequently any citizen of the USA) is of uncertain origin. It is perhaps derived from the Dutch *Jan Kees*, 'John Cheese', a nickname used derisively by Dutch settlers in New York (then called New Amsterdam) for English colonists in Connecticut. 'Macaroni' is an 18th-century term meaning a dandy, derived from the dandy's imitation of Continental European fashions.

Young Adolf. A blackly comic novel (1978) by Beryl Bainbridge (b.1934) in which the 23-year-old Adolf Hitler (1889–1945) – a moody, difficult and quite useless wastrel – visits his half-brother Alois in Bainbridge's native city of Liverpool in 1912. Some historians believe it possible that

Hitler spent a year visiting relatives in Liverpool prior to the First World War. Bainbridge suggests he was so embarrassed by his experiences there that he never subsequently mentioned the visit.

You Only Live Twice. The fifth film (1967) in the long-running series of James Bond films based on the secret agent novels of Ian Fleming (1906–64). Scripted by Roald Dahl and starring Sean Connery as Bond, the film derived its title from the proverbial 'you only live once' tag, as used in a Fritz Lang crime thriller as early as 1937. It is justified within the script by Bond faking his own death and then reappearing to thwart the plans of arch-villain Donald Pleasence.

Z

Z. *See* LETTERS, SYMBOLS AND INITIALS (panel, pp.255–6).

Zauberflöte, Die. *See MAGIC FLUTE, THE.*

Zoo Story, The. A one-act play (1959) by the US playwright Edward Albee (b.1928) about a chance meeting between two men on a public bench that culminates in one of them being knifed to death after they clash over possession of the bench. The title refers to the visit one of the men has just made to a zoo, although it is the 'human zoo' that is really under discussion:

> You have everything in the world you want; you've told me about your home, and your family, and your own little zoo. You have everything, and now you want this bench. Are these the things men fight for?

Index by Author, Composer or Artist

'Harp' Quartet
'Kreutzer' Sonata
Lebewohl, Das
'Moonlight' Sonata
'Pastoral' Sonata
Pastoral Symphony
Pathétique Sonata
'Rage over a Lost Penny'
'Rasumovsky' Quartets
'Waldstein' Sonata
Wellington's Victory

Bellow, Saul
Henderson the Rain King

Bennett, Alan
Madness of George III, The

Bennett, Arnold
Anna of the Five Towns

Berlin, Irving
Annie Get Your Gun

Berlioz, Hector
Harold in Italy
Symphonie fantastique
Symphonie funèbre et triomphale

Bernstein, Leonard
West Side Story

Beuys, Joseph
How to Explain Pictures to a Dead Hare

Biao, Lin
Little Red Book, The

Bierce, Ambrose
Devil's Dictionary, The

Bihari, János
Rákóczi March

Blacker, Terence
Kill Your Darlings

Blake, William
Marriage of Heaven and Hell, The
Milton

Bliss, Arthur
Colour Symphony, A

Blixen, Karen
Out of Africa

Boccaccio, Giovanni
Decameron, The

Bogarde, Dirk
Postillion Struck by Lightning, A

Bolt, Robert
Man for All Seasons, A

Bosch, Hieronymus
Garden of Earthly Delights, The

Boucher, François
Miss O'Murphy

Bouilly, Jean-Nicolas
Léonore

Boulez, Pierre
Marteau sans maître, Le

Boyce, William
'Heart of Oak'

Boyle Family, The
Journey to the Surface of the Earth

Bradbury, Malcolm
Eating People is Wrong

Bradbury, Ray
Fahrenheit 451
Golden Apples of the Sun, The
I Sing the Body Electric
Something Wicked This Way Comes

Brahms, Johannes
German Requiem, A
'Rain' Sonata
St Anthony Variations

Braine, John
Room at the Top

Brautigan, Richard
Trout Fishing in America

Brecht, Bertolt
Caucasian Chalk Circle, The
Mother Courage and her Children
Resistible Rise of Arturo Ui, The
Rise and Fall of the City of Mahagonny
Threepenny Opera, The

Brenton, Howard and **Hare, David**
Pravda

Brighouse, Harold
Hobson's Choice

Brink, André
Dry White Season, A

Britten, Benjamin
Burning Fiery Furnace, The
Gloriana
Spring Symphony
War Requiem

Brontë, Charlotte
Professor, The

Brontë, Emily
Wuthering Heights

Brown, Dee
Bury My Heart at Wounded Knee

Browne, Thomas
Hydriotaphia, Urn Burial, or, A Discourse of the Sepulchral Urns lately found in Norfolk

Browning, Elizabeth Barrett
Sonnets from the Portuguese

Browning, Robert
Bells and Pomegranates
Blot in the 'Scutcheon, A
'Caliban upon Setebos'
'Childe Roland to the Dark Tower Came'
'How They Brought the Good News from Ghent to Aix'
'Lost Leader, The'
'Pied Piper of Hamelin, The'
Pippa Passes
Ring and the Book, The
Sordello
'Toccata of Galuppi's, A'

Bruegel, Pieter (the Elder)
Blind Leading the Blind, The
Hunters in the Snow
Landscape with the Fall of Icarus
Triumph of Death, The

Bryant, Arthur
Set in a Silver Sea

Buchan, John
Mr Standfast
Prester John
Thirty-Nine Steps, The

Bulgakov, Mikhail
Master and Margarita, The

Bull, John
'God Save the King' (attrib.)

Bunyan, John
Pilgrim's Progress, The

Burgess, Anthony
Clockwork Orange, A
Homage to QWERTYUIOP

Burgin, Victor
Today is the Tomorrow You Were Promised Yesterday

Burns, Robert
'Auld Lang Syne'
'Comin' thro' the Rye'
'Scots wha hae wi' Wallace bled'
'Such a Parcel of Rogues in a Nation'
'Tam-o'-Shanter'

Burroughs, William
Naked Lunch, The

Butler, Elizabeth
Scotland for Ever!

Butler, Reg
Unknown Political Prisoner, The

Delaney, Shelagh
Taste of Honey, A

DeLillo, Don
White Noise

De Lisle, Claude-Joseph Rouget
'*Marseillaise, La*'

Delius, Frederick
Over the Hills and Far Away

Demuth, Charles
My Egypt

De Quincey, Thomas
Confessions of an English Opium Eater

Dibdin, George
Sweeney Todd, the Demon Barber of Fleet Street

Dickens, Charles
Bleak House
Cricket on the Hearth, The
Great Expectations
Our Mutual Friend

D'Indy, Vincent
Symphony on a French Mountain Song

Dos Passos, John
U.S.A.

Douglas, George
House with the Green Shutters, The

Dowland, John
Lachrimae, or Seaven Teares figured in seaven passionate Pavans

Doyle, Roddy
Paddy Clarke Ha Ha Ha

Dryden, John
Absalom and Achitophel
All for Love
Annus Mirabilis
Aureng-Zebe
Hind and the Panther, The
Mac Flecknoe
Marriage-à-la-Mode

Du Bus, Gervais
Roman de Fauvel

Duchamp, Marcel
Bride stripped bare by her Bachelors, even, The
Fountain
LHOOQ
Nude Descending a Staircase

Dukas, Paul
Sorcerer's Apprentice, The

Dumas, Alexandre (*fils*)
Dame aux camélias, La

Du Maurier, Daphne
Jamaica Inn

Du Maurier, George
Trilby

Dunbar, William
'Lament for the Makaris'

Durrell, Gerald
My Family and Other Animals

Dvořák, Antonín
'American' Quartet
'*Dumky*' Trio
From the New World

Eco, Umberto
Foucault's Pendulum
Name of the Rose, The

Edgeworth, Maria
Castle Rackrent

Elgar, Edward
Cockaigne
Dream of Gerontius, The
Enigma Variations
Music Makers, The
Pomp and Circumstance

El Greco
Burial of Count Orgaz, The

Eliot, George
Mill on the Floss, The

Housman, A.E.
Shropshire Lad, A

Howard, Sidney
Alien Corn

Hughes, Richard
High Wind in Jamaica, A

Hugo, Victor
Misérables, Les

Hunter, Evan
Blackboard Jungle, The

Huxley, Aldous
Antic Hay
Brave New World
Eyeless in Gaza
Point Counter Point

Ibsen, Henryk
Wild Duck, The

Indiana, Robert
Alabama
God is a Lily of the Valley

Ingres, Jean Auguste Dominique
Odalisque

Ionesco, Eugène
Bald Prima Donna, The
Rhinoceros

Irving, John
World According to Garp, The

Isherwood, Christopher
Ascent of F6, The
Goodbye to Berlin

Ishiguro, Kazuo
Artist of the Floating World, An

Ives, Charles
Concord Sonata
Unanswered Question, The

James, Henry
Ambassadors, The
Awkward Age, The
Golden Bowl, The
Ivory Tower, The
Portrait of a Lady, The
'Turn of the Screw, The'
What Maisie Knew
Wings of the Dove, The

James, P.D.
Skull beneath the Skin, The

Janáček, Leoš
Cunning Little Vixen, The
Diary of One Who Disappeared
From the House of the Dead
Glagolitic Mass

Jerome, Jerome K.
Three Men in a Boat

Johns, Jasper
Flag

Jones, James
From Here to Eternity
Thin Red Line, The

Jonson, Ben
Bartholomew Fair
Epicene, or The Silent Woman
Every Man in His Humour
Magnetic Lady, The
Poetaster, The
Underwoods
Volpone, or The Fox

Joyce, James
Finnegans Wake
Portrait of the Artist as a Young Man, A
Ulysses

Kafka, Franz
Trial, The

Keats, John
'Belle Dame sans Merci, La'
'Eve of St Agnes, The'
Hyperion
'Isabella, or The Pot of Basil'
Lamia

Lively, Adam
I Sing the Body Electric

Lively, Penelope
Moon Tiger

Lloyd Webber, Andrew
Beautiful Game, The
Cats

Longhi, Pietro
Exhibition of a Rhinoceros at Venice

Lorenz, Konrad
King Solomon's Ring

Lowry, Malcolm
Under the Volcano

McCullers, Carson
Heart is a Lonely Hunter, The

MacCunn, Hamish
Land of the Mountain and the Flood

MacDiarmid, Hugh
Drunk Man Looks at the Thistle, A
To Circumjack Cencrastus

McEwan, Ian
Cement Garden, The

Mackenzie, Compton
Whisky Galore

MacLeish, Archibald
This Music Crept by Me upon the Waters

Magritte, René
Philosophy in the Boudoir
Threatening Weather
Treachery (or Perfidy) of Images, The

Mahler, Gustav
Lied von der Erde, Das
Resurrection Symphony
'Symphony of a Thousand'

Mailer, Norman
Naked and the Dead, The

Mallarmé, Stéphane
Après-midi d'un faune, L'

'Malley, Ern'
Darkening Ecliptic, The

Mamet, David
American Buffalo

Mandela, Nelson
Long Walk to Freedom

Manet, Édouard
Absinthe Drinker, The
Déjeuner sur l'herbe, Le
Execution of the Emperor Maximilian, The
Olympia

Mann, Thomas
Death in Venice
Dr Faustus (*see* FAUST OR FAUSTUS, panel, pp.152–6)
Magic Mountain, The

Maor, Eli
To Infinity and Beyond

Marlowe, Christopher
Massacre at Paris, The
Tamburlaine the Great
Tragical History of Dr Faustus, (*see* FAUST OR FAUSTUS, panel, pp.152–6)

Márquez, Gabriel García
One Hundred Years of Solitude

Marsh, Ngaio
Surfeit of Lampreys, A

Martin, David C.
Wilderness of Mirrors

Mason, A.E.W.
Four Feathers, The

Matisse, Henri
Luxe, calme et volupté

Maurois, André
Fattypuffs and Thinifers

Maxwell, Gavin
Ring of Bright Water

Mortimer, John
Summer of a Dormouse, The
Summer's Lease
Voyage round My Father, A

Morton, John Maddison
Box and Cox

Motherwell, Robert
At Five in the Afternoon
Elegies to the Spanish Republic

Mozart, Leopold
Toy Symphony (attrib.)

Mozart, Wolfgang Amadeus
Così fan tutte
'Dissonance' Quartet
'Haffner' Serenade
'Haydn' Quartets
'Jupiter' Symphony
Kleine Nachtmusik, Eine
'Linz' Symphony
Magic Flute, The
Marriage of Figaro, The
'Paris' Symphony
'Prague' Symphony
'Prussian' Quartets

Muggeridge, Malcolm
'Tread Softly For You Tread on My Jokes'

Munch, Edvard
Scream, The

Murdoch, Iris
Green Knight, The
Sea, the Sea, The
Severed Head, A
Unofficial Rose, An

Mussorgsky, Modest
Night on the Bare Mountain
Pictures at an Exhibition

Nabokov, Vladimir
Pale Fire

Nash, Paul
Totes Meer
We Are Making a New World

Newman, Barnet
Euclidian Abyss, The

Nichols, Peter
Day in the Death of Joe Egg, A

Nielsen, Carl
Four Temperaments, The
Inextinguishable, The

Nietzsche, Friedrich
Also sprach Zarathustra

Nin, Anaïs
Delta of Venus

Niven, David
Bring on the Empty Horses

Nono, Luigi
Intolleranza 1960

O'Brien, Edna
Fanatic Heart, A
Johnny I Hardly Knew You

O'Brien, Flann
At Swim-Two-Birds

O'Brien, Richard
Rocky Horror Show, The

O'Casey, Sean
Juno and the Paycock
Plough and the Stars, The
Silver Tassie, The

Ofili, Chris
Adoration of Captain Shit and the Legend of the Black Star Part Two, The

Oldenburg, Claes
Hamburger with Pickle and Tomato Attached

Olsen, John
Journey into You Beaut Country

Ondaatje, Michael
English Patient, The

O'Neill, Eugene
Iceman Cometh, The
Long Day's Journey into Night
Mourning Becomes Electra

Orczy, Baroness
Scarlet Pimpernel, The

Orff, Carl
Carmina Burana

Orwell, George
Animal Farm
Down and Out in Paris and London
Keep the Aspidistra Flying
Nineteen Eighty-Four
Road to Wigan Pier, The

Osborne, John
Look Back In Anger

Osborne, Nigel
Electrification of the Soviet Union, The

Owen, Wilfred
'Dulce et Decorum Est'
Strange Meeting

Pane, Gina
Nourishment: slow and difficult absorption of 600 grammes of minced meat which disturb the usual digestive operations.

Parmigianino
Madonna of the Long Neck

Parry, Hubert
Glories of Our Blood and State, The

Pasternak, Boris
Doctor Zhivago

Patmore, Coventry
Angel in the House, The

Peale, Charles Wilson
Exhumation of the Mastodon

Peters, Ellis
Nice Derangement of Epitaphs, A

Phillips, Peter
For Men Only, MM and BB Starring

Picasso, Pablo
Demoiselles d'Avignon, Les
Guernica

Pirandello, Luigi
Six Characters in Search of an Author

Poe, Edgar Allan
'Pit and the Pendulum, The'

Pollock, Jackson
Full Fathom Five

Pope, Alexander
Dunciad, The
Rape of the Lock, The

Potter, Dennis
Pennies from Heaven

Poulenc, Francis
Mamelles de Tirésias, Les

Pound, Ezra
Cantos, The
Pisan Cantos, The

Poussin, Nicolas
Et in Arcadia Ego
Landscape with a Man killed by a Snake

Powell, Anthony
Dance to the Music of Time, A

Praxiteles
Venus of Cnidus

Prokofiev, Sergei
Love for or *of Three Oranges*
Story of a Real Man, The

Proust, Marcel
Remembrance of Things Past

Puccini, Giacomo
Bohème, La
Girl of the Golden West, The

Madame Butterfly
Turandot.

Pullman, Philip
His Dark Materials

Pushkin, Aleksandr
Bronze Horseman, The

Pym, Barbara
Some Tame Gazelle

Pynchon, Thomas
Gravity's Rainbow

Raeburn, Henry
Reverend Robert Walker Skating on Duddingston Loch, The

Ransome, Arthur
Swallows and Amazons

Raphael
Belle Jardinière, La
School of Athens, The

Raphael, Frederic
Glittering Prizes, The

Rattigan, Terence
Browning Version, The

Ravel, Maurice
Boléro
Pavane pour une infante défunte
Tombeau de Couperin, Le

Ray, Man
Rayogram

Reed, John
Ten Days that Shook the World

Remarque, Erich Maria
All Quiet on the Western Front

Rembrandt van Rijn
Anatomy Lesson of Dr Tulp, The
Night Watch, The

Rider Haggard, H.
King Solomon's Mines
She

Rigg, Diana
No Turn Unstoned

Rimsky-Korsakov, Nikolai
Flight of the Bumble Bee, The

Riskin, Michael
Stop in the Name of Love

Robbins, Harold
Carpetbaggers, The

Rodgers, Richard and **Hammerstein, Oscar**
King and I, The

Rodin, Auguste
Kiss, The

Rosenquist, James
F-111

Rossetti, Dante Gabriel
Beata Beatrix

Rossini, Gioacchino
Barber of Seville, The
Silken Ladder, The
Thieving Magpie, The

Roth, Philip
Great American Novel, The
Portnoy's Complaint

Ruggles, Carl
Men and Mountains
Sun-Treader, The
Vox clamans in deserto

Runyon, Damon
Guys and Dolls

Rushdie, Salman
Midnight's Children
Satanic Verses, The

Sacks, Oliver
Man Who Mistook His Wife for a Hat, The

Sackville-West, Vita
All Passion Spent

Tempest, The
Twelfth Night; or, What You Will
Winter's Tale, The

Shange, Ntozake
for colored girls who have considered suicide when the rainbow is enuf

Shaw, George Bernard
Androcles and the Lion
Arms and the Man
Back to Methuselah
John Bull's Other Island
Man and Superman
Mrs Warren's Profession
Pygmalion

Shelley, Percy Bysshe
Adonais
Alastor, or The Spirit of Solitude
Cenci, The
Epipsychidion
Mask of Anarchy, The
Queen Mab
Revolt of Islam, The

Sheridan, Richard Brinsley
School for Scandal, The

Sherwood, Robert E.
Petrified Forest, The

Sholokhov, Mikhail
And Quiet Flows the Don

Shostakovich, Dmitri
Lady Macbeth of the Mtsensk District
Leningrad Symphony

Shute, Nevil
Town Like Alice, A

Sibelius, Jean
Scaramouche

Sienkiewicz, Henryk
Quo Vadis?

Sillitoe, Alan
Loneliness of the Long-Distance Runner, The

Simon, Neil
Barefoot in the Park

Slade, Julian and **Reynolds, Dorothy**
Salad Days

Smart, Elizabeth
By Grand Central Station I Sat Down and Wept

Smetana, Bedřich
From My Life
Má Vlast

Smith, Stevie
'Not Waving but Drowning'
Novel on Yellow Paper

Smollett, Tobias
Atom, The History and Adventures of an (attrib.)

Smyth, Ethel
Wreckers, The

Snow, C.P.
Corridors of Power

Solzhenitsyn, Alexander
Gulag Archipelago, The
One Day in the Life of Ivan Denisovich

Somerset Maugham, W.
Cakes and Ale
Moon and Sixpence, The
Of Human Bondage

Southey, Robert
Vision of Judgement, A

Spenser, Edmund
Amoretti
Colin Clouts Come Home Again
Epithalamion
Faerie Queene, The

Spring, Howard
Fame is the Spur

Stein, Gertrude
Autobiography of Alice B. Toklas, The

Thomson, Virgil
Four Saints in Three Acts

Thoreau, Henry David
Walden, or Life in the Woods

Tinguely, Jean
Homage to New York

Tintoretto, Jacopo
Origin of the Milky Way, The

Tippett, Michael
Child of Our Time, A
Knot Garden, The
Midsummer Marriage, The

Titian
Noli Me Tangere
Sacred and Profane Love

Tolkein, J.R.R.
Hobbit, The
Lord of the Rings, The

Tolstoy, Leo
War and Peace

Tompkins, Thomas
Sad Pavan for these Distracted Times, A

Toole, John Kennedy
Confederacy of Dunces, A

Tressell, Robert
Ragged-Trousered Philanthropists, The

Turner, J.M.W.
Fighting 'Temeraire', The
Rain, Steam, and Speed – the Great Western Railway
Slavers Throwing Overboard the Dead and Dying – Typhon Coming On

Twain, Mark
Connecticut Yankee in King Arthur's Court, A

Tynan, Kenneth
Oh, Calcutta!

Uris, Leon
Q.B. VII

Van Druten John
Voice of the Turtle, The

Van Eyck, Jan
Arnolfini Marriage, The

Van Gogh, Vincent
Self-portrait with Bandaged Ear

Varèse, Edgard
Density 21.5

Vaughan, Henry
Silex Scintillans

Vaughan Williams, Ralph
Sea Symphony, A
Shepherds of the Delectable Mountains
Sinfonia Antarctica

Velázquez, Diego
Meninas, Las
Rokeby Venus, The
Surrender of Breda, The

Verdi, Giuseppe
'Anvil Chorus, The'
Masked Ball, A
Sicilian Vespers, The

Vonnegut, Kurt
Slaughterhouse-Five

Wagner, Richard
Flying Dutchman, The
Götterdämmerung
Liebestod
Meistersinger von Nürnberg, Die
Ring, The

Waller, Robert James
Bridges of Madison County, The

Walton, William
Belshazzar's Feast
Portsmouth Point

Warlock, Peter
Capriol Suite
Saudades

Index of Sources

This index lists, under source work or author name, those titles appearing in this book that are derived from the words of other writers.